The Ethnographer's Magic

The Ethnographer's Magic and Other Essays in the History of Anthropology

George W. Stocking, Jr.

The University of Wisconsin Press

The University of Wisconsin Press
2537 Daniels Street
Madison, Wisconsin 53718

3 Henrietta Street
London WC2E 8LU, England

4 6 8 7 5

Printed in the United States of America

Library of Congress Cataloging in Publication Data
Stocking, George W., 1928–
The ethnographer's magic and other essays in the history of anthropology / George W. Stocking, Jr.
448 pp. cm
Includes bibliographical references and index.
ISBN 0-299-13410-5 ISBN 0-299-13414-8 (pbk.)
1. Ethnology—History. 2. Anthropology—History. I. Title.
GN308.S76 1992
305.8—dc20 92-25829

"The Ethnographer's Magic: Fieldwork in British Anthropology from Tylor to Malinowski" was originally published in *Observers Observed: Essays on Ethnographic Fieldwork* (*History of Anthropology* Vol. 1), pp. 70–120. Madison: The University of Wisconsin Press, 1983.

"The Boas Plan for the Study of American Indian Languages" was originally published in *Studies in the History of Linguistics: Traditions and Paradigms*, edited by Dell Hymes, pp. 454–84. Bloomington: Indiana University Press, 1974. Reprinted by permission of the editor.

"Anthropology as *Kulturkampf*: Science and Politics in the Career of Franz Boas" was originally published in *The Uses of Anthropology* (a special publication of the American Anthropological Association, Number 11), edited by Walter Goldschmidt, pp. 33–50. Washington, D.C., 1979. Reprinted by permission of the Association.

"Ideas and Institutions in American Anthropology: Thoughts Toward a History of the Interwar Years" was originally published in *Selected Papers from the American Anthropologist, 1921–45*, edited by George W. Stocking, Jr., pp. 1–53. Washington, D.C.: American Anthropological Association, 1976.

"Philanthropoids and Vanishing Cultures: Rockefeller Funding and the End of the Museum Era in Anglo-American Anthropology" was originally published in *Objects and Others: Essays on Museums and Material Culture* (*History of Anthropology*, Vol. 3), pp. 112–45. Madison: The University of Wisconsin Press, 1985.

"Maclay, Kubary, Malinowski: Archetypes from the Dreamtime of Anthropology" was originally published in *Colonial Situations: Essays on the Contextualization of Ethnographic Knowledge* (*History of Anthropology*, Vol. 7), pp. 9–74. Madison: The University of Wisconsin Press, 1991.

"The Ethnographic Sensibility of the 1920s and the Dualism of the Anthropological Tradition" was originally published in *Romantic Motives: Essays on Anthropological Sensibility* (*History of Anthropology*, Vol. 6), pp. 208–76. Madison: The University of Wisconsin Press, 1989.

"Paradigmatic Traditions in the History of Anthropology" was originally published in *Companion to the History of Modern Science*, edited by R. C. Olby, G. N. Cantor, J. R. R. Christie and M. J. S. Hodge, pp. 712–27. London: Routledge, 1990. Reprinted by permission of the publishers.

For my students and colleagues

Contents

The Ethnographer's Magic

Retrospective Prescriptive Reflections

Taken together, the introductory sections in this volume may be read as a kind of historiographical equivalent of the self-reflective essays on the ethnographic process that since the 1960s have become widespread in anthropology. Frankly egocentric and guardedly self-revelatory—though one hopes not solipsistic—they are intended to provide a background for the essays and to broach issues that may be implicated in them.

When I came to the University of Chicago in 1968 at the initiative of the Department of Anthropology, I was also given an appointment in the Department of History. In 1974, when a majority of the historians refused to join in the anthropologists' recommendation that I be promoted to full professor, the impasse was resolved by my resignation from the Department of History—although I have since retained the somewhat marginal status of "associate member." At the time, I heard informally that one reason for the historians' reluctance was the feeling that while I could do vignettes, I could not "paint the big picture." The remark was galling, but it was not without basis. Books have come hard for me. There have been several that were never finished (1991c), and the two published ones are neither of them conventional historical narratives, though they do treat fairly large topics. As its subtitle suggests, the first, *Race, Culture, and Evolution,* was frankly a series of *Essays in the History of Anthropology* (1968a); the second, *Victorian Anthropology* (1987a), can be read as such, although its "multiple contextualizations" are perhaps more integrated structurally than some readers have appreciated.

During the two decades between those books there were quite a few essays, which taken together had the substance of more than one book. Their impact, however, was dispersed among various journals and edited volumes (e.g., 1973a). Because a number of them appeared in the *History of Anthropology* series which I have edited since 1983 for the University of Wisconsin Press, it seemed a likely project to bring together in a single volume some of these, along with others published elsewhere. Such a book might be useful both to those who had encountered only one or two of the essays and to a wider audience previously unaware of their existence.

Although they treat diverse episodes in two national anthropological traditions, the essays I have chosen fall within several overlapping circles of coherence. They range over a century in the history of anthropology, during which an institutionally and intellectually diffused discourse based on traveller's accounts became an academic discipline grounded in systematic ethnographic research. Within that temporal span, they focus primarily on two figures who were highly influential in the development of modern ethnographic fieldwork and the academic institutionalization of anthropology, as well as in the more general formation of their respective national traditions: Franz Boas and Bronislaw Malinowski. Since neither has yet been the subject of a full-scale biography, the present essays, which draw on extensive research in unpublished manuscript materials, may perhaps serve for a time as orientations to their works and lives (see also 1968a, 1984b, 1986b). They also treat, albeit in a somewhat recursively microcosmic fashion, various major themes in the history of anthropology besides the development of an academically based fieldwork tradition: anthropology's powerfully mythic aspect and its persisting strain of romantic primitivism; the ambiguities, ironies, and contradictions of its implication in a larger sociopolitical sphere; its problematic integration of a variety of natural scientific and humanistic inquiries; and the pervasive tension between its generalizing scientific aspirations and its subjectively constituted "data." To provide a kind of background or overview for the episodically focused essays, I have included my one attempt so far to cover the whole history of anthropology; although the commentary surrounding it dictated its placement at the end of the volume, some readers may care to read the essay first, as orientation rather than synthesis.

There is, however, another set of themes, less visible in the essays themselves than in the brief introductory passages prefacing each one. These have to do with my own marginal relation to the discipline of anthropology and my role for several decades as its chief historian. Although I came to Chicago at the initiative of the anthropologists, my previous appointment at Berkeley was in a history department, and I have always regarded myself as essentially an historian. I went to Berkeley in 1960 to teach American social history, and the move toward the history of anthropology, though foreshadowed in a doctoral dissertation on American social scientists and race theory, was in some respects fortuitous. Shortly after my arrival there, I was invited to participate in a conference on the history of anthropology sponsored by the Social Science Research Council (Hymes 1962). The invitation came from A. I. Hallowell, whose seminar on the history of anthropology I had attended at the University of Pennsylvania, who had served as one of my dissertation supervisors, and who was a leading spirit behind the conference. In retrospect, it seems clear that this meeting—at which I was one of four historians among a group of leading anthropologists—gave me both a platform and an audience.

During the same period, the founding of the *Journal of the History of the Behavioral Sciences* provided a larger context for my historiographical enterprise. Although I do not recall so regarding it at the time, and do not now, the essay-editorial I wrote in 1965 "On the limits of presentism and historicism in the historiography of the behavioral sciences" could be seen as an attempt, through methodological prescription, to stake out a territory for the disinterested professional historian, by arguing that present disciplinary commitments could seriously distort an understanding of the past of a discipline (cf. 1966, 1967). Since then, my work has been situated within the history of the inquiries variously called moral, social, behavioral, or human sciences, and by extension the history of science generally. But if at times my professional identity has been oriented in this direction, my major scholarly concerns have been defined primarily by residence in what has been widely regarded as the country's premier anthropology department.

If not unique, this situation has been unusual enough to set me off from most historiographers of human scientific disciplines. Many maintain their fundamental identity as intellectual or cultural historians, writing for others of their kind (Stanton 1960); likely as not to move on to topics in other fields, they have no overriding commitment to defending or changing the discipline whose history they recount, though the relativizing tendency of historicism, especially in certain recent modes, may have a generally subversive effect. Others are historians only by intellectual avocation, writing primarily for members of their own human scientific discipline, often for the quite explicit purpose of legitimating a particular present standpoint and criticizing others (Harris 1968). These two types do not exhaust the range of disciplinary historiographers, who since the 1960s have substantially increased in numbers. But they may serve to define the intellectual arena into which I entered (GS 1967).

In contrast to the first group, I am by departmental affiliation an anthropologist; although I envision my work as part of a broader history of the human sciences, anthropology has long been my primary subject matter and anthropologists my primary audience. But in contrast to the second group, I regard my historiography as a full-time professional craft —relatively disinterested, broadly contextualized, oriented more toward the past than the present. My major anthropological reference points are still located in the late-nineteenth and early-twentieth-century period of my doctoral dissertation—as opposed to those of my colleagues, which were established during the period of their own graduate education, reshaped perhaps by the issues of the intervening years. On the other hand, while my reading remains largely in the past of anthropology, at the day-to-day level of student advising, proposal hearings, dissertation defenses, department meetings, and hallway conversations, I have long been involved in the on-going life of the anthropological discipline, and if only by a kind of intellectual osmosis have developed some sensitivity to its present concerns. If over the years this position has been in some respects uniquely privileged, it has also been inherently problematic—not least in being somewhat Chicago-centric.

One measure of its difficulty is in fact my failed attempt to write a history of the University of Chicago Department of Anthropology. I had thought to use my own department as a microcosm for the development of anthropology in the twentieth century, placing the rich detail of its intellectual and institutional life in broader sociocultural context. But although I had access to a large body of manuscript materials, could interview living informants, and received several hundred responses, sometimes quite intimately detailed, to an alumni questionnaire, I found it impossible to get beyond the third chapter—roughly the point at which some present colleagues began to be major actors. The issues and the personalities of the past began to be involved with those of the present; no longer an historian writing from the documents of the deafened dead, I began to feel my disciplinary marginality more acutely. I might imagine myself a disinterested observer, inclined at department meetings to see both sides of potentially divisive issues and often to abstain when matters came to a vote. But in fact I was also a committed participant, concerned for the department's well-being in the present and for my place within it, both of which were implicated in the study of its past. In the end, all I produced was a library exhibit catalogue; although it sought to deal seriously in a noncelebratory way with the history of the department, it was in fact published as part of its semicentennial celebration (1979a).

My difficulty with the departmental history is echoed at a more general disciplinary level. Having entered anthropology through the back door of its history, rather than the front door of its present concerns, and envisioning myself ultimately as historian observer rather than as anthropologist participant, I am not entirely comfortable with the recent history of the discipline, and am very hesitant to try to define its future—reassuring myself that were it somehow to end tomorrow, my own historical enterprise would not want for subject matter. But it is clear nonetheless that anthropology has changed a great deal since I entered it in the late 1960s. Those years were the onset of what has been called the "crisis of anthropology": an interrelated series of observational, methodological, epistemological, theoretical, ethical, and demographic problems which, articulating with similar concerns in other social sciences, followed hard upon the end of the European colonialism, in the context of postcolonial warfare abroad and radical social upheavals at home (cf. 1982b, 1983b). Whether the changes since then amount to the "reinvention of anthropology" called for at the time by some is perhaps still a moot point (Hymes 1973). But there can be no doubt that anthropology today is in many ways different from *Anthropology Today*—the title of a symposium in 1952 which remained a primary reference point at the time of my first contact with the field (Kroeber 1953).

Although as a graduate student I took only two anthropology courses from Hallowell, I have recently (in conducting seminars on anthropology "before the crisis" and since its "reinvention") become aware of the extent to which my own intellectual orientation was defined by the positivistic social science of the 1950s, which was a major influence on the program in American Civilization at the University of Pennsylvania. In reworking my dissertation while teaching historiography at Berkeley, I abandoned the notion that history could become systematically social scientific, and since then have been a member of an anthropology department that played an important role in the intellectual critique of 1950s positivism. But there is enough positivistic residue in my own thinking to leave me with a certain intellectual sympathy for the scientizing strain in anthropology, and to leaven with scepticism my intellectual sympathy for what might be called the literizing relativisms of the recent period. Echoing the reduplicative ambivalence of a more influential scion of the fifties (Geertz 1984), I am at times inclined to think of myself as "anti-anti-anti-relativist"; and at others, to drop one or more of the antithetic prefixes.

My ambivalent relation to certain contemporary trends in anthropology is evident also in regard to "postmodernism." Acknowledging it somewhat reluctantly as a condition of contemporary cultural life, I am considerably more reluctant to accept it as a standpoint for understanding the past. Before my year at the Getty Center for the History of Art and the Humanities in 1988–89, I do not recall being more than vaguely aware of the phenomenon (if indeed it may be spoken of in the singular). But living in Los Angeles, spending my days among art historians, enjoying the intellectual companionship of George Marcus (an influential spokesperson of the newer tendencies in anthropology), I could not fail to attend to it, and since then I have become more directly cognizant (cf. Stephens 1990). Pressed for a definition, however, I am inclined to fall back on one offered by a friend at a meeting of the American Anthropological Association several years ago, in recounting the cocktail-party witticism of a distinguished postmodern architect. According to this unquestionably horse's mouth authority, the defining criteria of POMO were twofold: "the random use of historical motifs for purely decorative purposes"; and "it's got to be a little goofy." Assimilating these to the crotchets of my own craft, I later somewhat caustically recast them as "anachronism" and "*non sequitur.*" But when I subsequently passed these pairings on to an historian of postmodern persuasion, he gave back a more sympathetic translation as "pastiche" and "decentering" (cf. Megill 1989).

While there is no doubt much of postmodernism that is lost in this sequential anecdotal translation, it seems to me to capture, from several distinct points of view, essential aspects of the phenomenon. And while, to my taste, the move from goofiness and *non sequitur* to decentering is somewhat recuperative, that from decorative historical randomness to anachronism to pastiche leaves the first criterion still in a presentist ahistorical limbo. As sympathetic as I am to the project of historical *de*familiarization, experience with recent cohorts of students precociously socialized to the deconstructive discourses of race, class, and gender has made me feel that the historian's task must sometimes also be construed as one of *re*familiarization. In this context, historicism, which once presented itself to me in terms of the differentness and disjunction of the past, seems now also to require an insistence on coherence and continuity.

At the same time, I have recently come to appreciate that my own history, rather than being decentered, has largely been what might today be called canonical. Despite the fact that my doctoral dissertation began as a quasi-quantitative study of the writings of several hundred social scientists (as opposed to a few "representative men") my work since then has, for the most part, focussed on major figures in the succession of dominant paradigmatic viewpoints in hegemonic anthropological traditions (cf. 1983b). It has not sought to rescue neglected precursors of paradigmatic alternatives once lost and now to be regained (Vincent 1990), nor to examine anthropology historically from the perspective of those who have been its subject "others" (Fabian 1983). These, and other alternative histories, can be fruitful and indeed necessary historiographical or critical enterprises. But my own work has dealt primarily with well-known anthropologists in what, for better or worse, have been the main lines of disciplinary development. To recapture their understanding historically still seems to me a useful and a necessary enterprise. One of the most satisfying compliments I ever received came when one of his late students said to me, "You gave us back Boas"—returned him, as it were, to the canon, after those early posthumous years in which his work was dismissed by some, as indeed it still sometimes is, as having little positive theoretical interest (e.g., Wax 1956).

Of late, however, the matter of canonicity has arisen in another sense, having to do with the status as well as the substance of my history. Coming to anthropology as an outsider, I won a certain position as house historiographer, and my work was for a time perhaps more appreciated than criticized. Recently, however, critical voices have been raised against the "dean" or "doyen" of the field; my work has been attacked as atheoretical or inductivist (Jarvie 1989), as lacking relevance to current anthropological debates (Kuper 1991), and as excluding anthropologists from the history of anthropology (Winkin 1986).

Without attempting here to respond systematically, and granting that I do not defend a general theoretical orientation or attempt directly to elucidate historically the theoretical issues of the present, I would suggest that the programmatic "historicism" I advocated in 1965 has long since been qualified by my residence among anthropologists and by further historiographical reflection. These have made me more appreciative of the role of present interest in the definition of a field for historical inquiry, of the various modes by which historical understanding may be cultivated, and of the different standards by which it may be evaluated (cf. 1982c). This has been reflected in my own writing, and in the various editorial roles in which I have been involved.

In choosing foci for the *History of Anthropology* volumes, a major consideration has been their resonance to present disciplinary concerns (1983a). If some of these concerns (the problematic character of fieldwork, the reevaluation of structural-functionalism, the colonial context of ethnographic research) might in the 1980s be regarded as yesterday's news, insofar as they have been issues since the 1960s, at least one of them (the role of museums and material culture [1985]) caught a wave of rising interest. Moreover, the series was deliberately conceived as a cooperative venture of anthropologists and historians; both are substantially represented on the editorial board, and every volume has included contributions by both groups.

The goals of resonance and representation have been constrained somewhat by the availability of material in a sparsely populated field. *HOA* does not commission articles, but tries to gather in what is "out there" that is relevant to the topic, ready for publication, not otherwise committed, during the period that a volume is in process. Rather than being able to select from a large number of candidates a group of suitably resonant and representative essays treating systematically all the aspects of a volume theme, we are usually in the position of trying to give a kind of *ex post facto* unity to a series of essays dispersed intermittently over a general topic area.

But aside from these external constraints, it is also true that the attempt to achieve resonance and representation within a field of scarce resources has been constrained by an editorial vision of "the historian's craft" that tends to privilege an approach to general issues through the historically specific, and a presentation in a literary mode. Although critiquers of anthropology, Foucaultians, deconstructionists, and new historicists have not for the most part seen *HOA* as a likely venue, it has been more open to the "literizing" than the "scientizing" tendency in anthropology, to such an extent that it has been seen by one French reviewer as a mouthpiece for the former within contemporary American anthropology (Jorion 1985). Similarly, while it has not been systematically devoted to the critique of anthropology, its historicization of dominant paradigms has contributed indirectly to that venture. All of this, despite my own ambivalence on some of these issues.

This brief excursus on *HOA* editorial policy is included here simply to suggest by implication how my own historiography relates to various tendencies that have emerged since my entry to the field—tendencies which I would be inclined to call "neopresentist" (in contrast to the rubric "new historicist," which is in fact applied to some of them). At the very least, this incipiently auto-deconstructive process may have provided some leads for reviewers of more presentist persuasions. But I hope that it may also have suggested something of the spirit in which I have undertaken the history of anthropology—and, being now past the age of easy reformation, will probably continue to pursue it for a few more years. If asked *cui bono?*, I would appeal to a body of work that scholars of quite different persuasions than my own have apparently found useful.

In addition to these more general historiographical reflections, several comments on the volume itself may be in order. The prefaces I have provided for each essay offer a more specific contextualization, remarking on its genesis and, briefly, on some of the particular issues, historiographical and substantive, that it suggests. I have not attempted to revise or update the essays themselves, except for a few deletions, a few improvements in my sometimes rather dense and parenthetic style, and occasional references to relevant recent work in the history of anthropology. It should perhaps be explicitly stated, however, that I have not attempted a systematic bibliographical updating; for more extensive references to the later literature, readers may wish to consult the numbers of the *History of Anthropology Newsletter*, the bibliographies compiled by Paul Erickson (1984–88), or the annual critical bibliographies of *Isis*. I have tried by deletion and cross-reference to eliminate or reduce redundancies where essays refer to the same historical material; but where this would have created a break in the flow of narrative or argument, I have let the repetition stand.

One of the adaptations I long ago made to writing for anthropologists was to adopt (and in *HOA* slightly to adapt) their documentary style, with short parenthetical citations, a limited number of substantive footnotes, and a single list of references cited. Although there are advantages (other than sheer authorial convenience) to the anthropological mode, the differences between it and traditional historical documentation are not without implications for anyone interested in the differentiation of disciplinary discourses by what I have called below "methodological values" (p. 279). Without exploring these implications here, I simply note that aside from disrupting (in an inherently anachronistic manner) the flow of narrative or argument, parenthetical citations are particularly ill-suited to the identification of manuscript sources. However, since the restructuring of documentation would have been a major project, I have maintained the style to which I became acculturated—trying only to keep the interruptive parentheses as short as possible, and apologizing in advance for the burden of deduction this may occasionally place on scholars interested in pursuing particular issues further.

In their original form each of the essays contained acknowledgments to various individuals and institutions who offered advice and assistance in my research, or gave me permission to quote from manuscript material. Without attempting to repeat all of these acknowledgments here, I reaffirm them all collectively, and refer the reader to the original versions for specific details. For their contributions to the present volume, I would like to thank colleagues at Chicago and elsewhere who helped in ways too particular or too diffuse for adequate acknowledgment; Anthony Picarello, who helped me to prepare the index; and Betty Steinberg, who was, as usual, a wonderfully (and constructively) supportive editor. Finally, there is my wife Carol, who for more than two decades has given me great freedom to follow my muse even when it seemed to go astray, and has admirably suffered my irritability when I lost its track.

1

The Ethnographer's Magic

Fieldwork in British Anthropology from Tylor to Malinowski

During the early years of my membership in the Chicago Department of Anthropology, colleagues on several occasions urged me to undertake ethnographic fieldwork. I took this both as compliment and critique: on the one hand, as an encouragement to legitimate my membership in the community by participation in its initiation ritual; on the other hand, as a suggestion that without such initiation, I could never really understand what anthropology was all about. At other times, some of my colleagues were inclined to think of my participation in the life of the department as itself a kind of fieldwork—joshing me about notes I occasionally took during department meetings. And sometimes I, too, have glossed my departmental membership, and other sorts of personal and professional experiences, as in some respect analogues of the fieldwork experience.

The personal experiences include several visits to my wife's paternal relatives in Yugoslavia, peasants from the Voyvodina, one of them a woman who had moved to Belgrade and married a Montenegrin lawyer. I recall especially attempting, with the assistance of my fully bilingual Serbian father-in-law, to administer Morgan's kinship questions to her husband when they visited us during a year in Palo Alto. The continuing redefinition of categories by an informant for whom many of them were no longer functional, the assertive editing role of the translator, who, though he had left Serbia in 1907, enjoyed (in more than one sense) the status of a *starats* (or respected elder) and was perfectly willing to impose his version as authoritative, or to shut off discussion of a particular topic if he decided it was irrelevant—these and other aspects of the experience gave me a vivid sense of the difficulties of translating categories across cultural and linguistic barriers.

When I was in England doing archival research on the history of British anthropology, I tended to think of my informal contacts and several extended conversations with leading elder anthropologists as work with informants and of the notes I recorded afterwards as field notes. Archival research itself has occasionally suggested analogies, especially when I have delved into dusty files not yet fully sorted and catalogued: on one hand, the exhilarating, even joyful, immediacy of intimate contact with aspects of a past life now hidden from general view; on the other, the blooming, buzzing confusion of materials that seem at times like a jumble of jigsaw puzzles, passing by on a conveyor belt, which one scans for pieces that might turn out later to be parts of particular puzzles for which there are no pictures on the box. But the historian's archive is not the ethnographer's field. You cannot directly question dead informants; nor need you worry about their reactions, or how your inquiry might affect their lives. Written records are very different from oral testimony, as my anthropological colleagues, who privilege the latter, have on many occasions made a point of telling me. Other types of experience may have been in one or another respect like fieldwork (and may have helped me to understand it), but they were not the same.

Never having experienced the incorporative ritual itself, and sensing that my inquiry was in various ways a very different one from theirs, I have always felt myself ultimately an outsider to the anthropological tribe. Adopting a customary anthropological usage, I tended sometimes to think of them as "my people." But in fact my relationship to them differed from that of anthropologists to their peoples in that, although never properly initiated, I was nevertheless a permanently tenured member of the group, and enjoyed all the privileges thereof, which at Chicago have included the freedom to follow my teaching interests wherever they may lead. Despite a few sardonic comments from my colleagues, I have for some years taught occasional courses on the history of fieldwork.

The paradox of the noninitiate teaching about the central tribal rite may be mitigated, to some extent, by a further paradox: although ethnographic fieldwork is virtually a *sine qua non* for full status as an anthropologist, the same cannot be said of formal fieldwork training. This, despite the fact that since 1960 fieldwork has become in many respects problematic—practically, epistemologically, and ideologically—and the "self-reflexive" autobiographical account of fieldwork experiences has emerged as a distinct ethnographic genre (Rabinow 1977).

The history of fieldwork training remains to be explored; until it is, any generalization is likely to be impressionistic. Practice has clearly varied with different mentors on different matters at different institutions in different subfields and different national traditions during different periods. Malinowski made much more of fieldwork method than did Boas, whose courses on method were devoted to technical linguistics and statistics, and whose half-hour pre-field briefings have since been the subject of anecdotal comment (e.g., Mead 1959b). There have of course long been questionnaires and manuals, and such specific techniques as the genealogical method, the village census, or psychological tests of various sorts (Urry 1984). Summer field schools or long-term team research at a particular site have sometimes provided a kind of apprentice-training (Foster et al. 1979; GS 1980b). There have been moments (like the 1950s) and places (e.g., Manchester) of more widespread methodological self-consciousness (cf. Epstein 1967) and occasional attempts at systematization (Werner et al. 1987). My general sense, however, is that training has most often been informal and unsystematic, and frequently lacking almost entirely (cf. R. Trotter [1988], which indicates that only 20 percent of "prestigious departments" require training in ethnographic research methods). Certainly there is a pervasive belief that there is something ultimately ineffable about fieldwork; an epistemological ideology of cultural immersion justifies a methodological practice that at some point becomes a matter of sink or swim.

At Chicago, "pre-field" seminars have characteristically focussed on the theoretical or conceptual problems of a research project; fieldwork training as such has not been a regular part of the formal course curriculum. My own role in that curriculum has been somewhat ambiguous. Almost all the courses I teach relate to my research interests in the history of anthropology, with at best an occasional or indirect relationship to anthropology as it is currently practiced. In each cohort, some students have taken a course or a seminar in the history of anthropology, and several have written masters' theses (cf. Bashkow 1991; Hanc 1981; Schrempp 1983). However, in the few instances where the question arose, I have advised students that to get a job in anthropology they would do better to write a doctoral dissertation based on fieldwork. Technically, a "library dissertation" has been acceptable to the department, and there have been a small number of these on topics in historical anthropology. What is at issue, however, is not a formal rule, but a cultural definition of what it is to be an anthropologist. Of the handful of students I recall who undertook library dissertations on historical topics only one obtained employment in a department of anthropology. It may well be that this situation is now changing, as fieldwork becomes in many respects more problematic, and anthropology becomes more historically oriented. At a recent meeting of students and faculty, one of our more promising "pre-field" students remarked that he was not interested in studying "people in far-away places." Coming from an informant in a student category informally marked for fieldwork, this (how representative?) piece of ethnographic data (heresy?) was more than a bit disconcerting. For even today, when some senior anthropologists who began as field ethnographers are themselves turning to historical topics or textual reanalyses, the traditional cultural norms of the discipline remain very strong. Recently, when I did suggest the possibility of a library dissertation to a student whose published work seemed a more than adequate basis for an historically grounded ethnographic account, he was strongly urged into the field by other advisors.

In this context, it has seemed perhaps a useful contribution to teach a course occasionally in which students could work on the history of ethnographic practice in the area in which they intended to do fieldwork and I could learn something about fieldwork in different historical situations. In most of the several incarnations of this course, some attention has been given to the New Guinea diaries of Bronislaw Malinowski, the publication of which in 1967 helped to precipitate the "crisis of anthropology," and the interpretation of which has since been a central thread in a continuing discussion of the ethnographic process by anthropologists and interested outsiders. Over the years, the focus of the course has roughly paralleled the development of that discussion, as it moved from problems of ethics and reflexivity (Rabinow 1977) to those of "ethnographic authority" (Clifford 1983) and the creation of ethnographic texts (Marcus & Cushman 1982; Geertz 1988), to the "poetics and politics" of ethnography (Clifford & Marcus 1986), and more recently to the consideration of specific regional traditions in relation to general theoretical developments in the discipline (Fardon 1990). Originally devoted to fieldwork *per se*, the course has broadened to encompass ethnographic practice, including not only the means by which information was gathered, but its subsequent entextualization. Lately, by focussing on a single national tradition and ethnographic area, I have tried to relate ethnographic practice to the history of anthropological theory.

Given my outsider's status, and my failure actually to have done fieldwork, one might suspect in all of this a certain sublimation: lacking, even rejecting, the real experience, I sought instead to experience it vicariously. It is possible that I have tended somewhat to romanticize it, to cast in mythic terms a reality I have never known. It is also possible that, focussed on the past rather than the present of anthropology, I have been more interested in what it has been than in what it is becoming. I have tried, however, to approach fieldwork in a wide-ranging historical fashion, augmented by the efforts of students with more specific ethnographic interests. At the very least, I have perhaps read more about fieldwork, in more different times and places, than many anthropologists, and have also examined manuscript materials of a number of different ethnographers. If the specifics of their field notes are usually beyond my ethnographic or linguistic competence, such materials nevertheless give at least indirect insight into the ethnographic process (cf. Sanjek 1990).

In the event that I should write a more general history of anthropology, I hope to do it through a series of case studies focussing on particular ethnographic episodes. For oddly enough, though fieldwork has become the distinctive feature of anthropological inquiry, the history of anthropology has not heretofore been written from this standpoint. As a step in this direction, *Observers Observed* became the first volume in the *History of Anthropology* series, with "The Ethnographer's Magic" serving as a partially synthetic introduction to the more specifically focussed essays in the rest of the volume.

In the informal give-and-take of everyday disciplinary life, anthropologists occasionally speak of themselves in terms traditionally applied to tribal groups or folk societies. Since both are entities a more rigorously professional discourse has come to regard as problematic, one hesitates to suggest that an investigative community has taken on some of the characteristics of its subject matter. But there are similarities nonetheless, especially in relation to what has come to be regarded as the constitutive experience of social/cultural anthropology—and this in a multiple sense, since it at once distinguishes the discipline, qualifies its investigators, and creates the primary body of its empirical data. Even in an age when it is becoming increasingly difficult to carry on in traditional terms, fieldwork by participant observation, preferably in a face-to-face social group quite different from that of the investigator, is the hallmark of social/cultural anthropology (Epstein 1967; Jarvie 1966; GS 1982b).

As the central ritual of the tribe, fieldwork is the subject of a considerable mythic elaboration. Although there are variant versions of the charter myth in different national anthropological traditions (Urry 1984), there is one so widely known as to require no recounting, even among nonanthropologists. Its hero is of course the Polish-born scientist Bronislaw Malinowski, who, while interned as an enemy alien in Australia during World War I, spent two years living in a tent among the Trobriand Islanders, and brought back to Britain the secret of successful social anthropological research (Kaberry 1957; Leach 1965; Powdermaker 1970). Although Malinowski had by the 1960s lost his status as shaper of anthropological theory (R. Firth 1957, 1981; Gluckman 1963), his place as mythic culture hero of anthropological method was at once confirmed and irrevocably compromised by the publication of his field diaries (Malinowski 1967), which revealed to a far-flung progeny of horrified Marlows that their Mistah Kurtz had secretly harbored passionately aggressive feelings toward the "niggers" among whom he lived and labored—when he was not withdrawing from the heart of darkness to share the white-skinned civilized brotherhood of local pearlfishers and traders (e.g., Geertz 1967; cf. Conrad 1902).

Disillusion has elicited a small body of literature either further scrabbling at the hero's feet of clay (Hsu 1979) or attempting to refurbish his image (including some strained attempts to suggest he may never have actually said the damning word [Leach 1980]). But it has so far led no one to probe historically the mythic origins of the Malinowskian fieldwork tradition. Seeking neither to debunk nor to defend, the present essay (cf. GS 1968b, 1980b) attempts to place Malinowski's Trobriand adventure in the context of earlier British fieldwork, and to show how his achievement—and its self-mythicization—helped to establish the special cognitive authority claimed by the modern ethnographic tradition (cf. Clifford 1983).

From the Armchair to the Field in the British Association

Let us begin with the state of anthropological method before the culture hero came upon the scene—for this, too, is part of the myth we seek to historicize. A good place to start is the year before Malinowski's birth, a moment which in mythic time is still part of the pre-promethian period when evolutionary titans, seated in their armchairs, culled ethnographic data from travel accounts to document their vision of the stages of creation of human cultural forms. While the major early statements of evolutionary anthropology (e.g., McLennan 1865; Tylor 1871) were based on essentially this sort of information, it is also the case that the evolutionary anthropologists were very seriously concerned with improving the quantity and quality of their empirical data. Their initial approach to the problem in the early 1870s had been through the preparation of *Notes and Queries* "to promote accurate anthropological observation on the part of travellers, and to enable those who are not anthropologists themselves to supply the information which is wanted for the scientific study of anthropology at home" (BAAS 1874:iv). In assuming that empirical data collected by gentleman amateurs abroad could provide the basis for the more systematic inquiries of metropolitan scholar-scientists, anthropologists were in fact following in the footsteps of other mid-Victorian scientists (cf. Urry 1972). But by 1883, events were already in process that were to draw more closely together the empirical and the theoretical components of anthropological inquiry.

By this time, E. B. Tylor, who had just come to Oxford as Keeper of the University Museum and Reader in anthropology, was in regular correspondence with people overseas who were in a position to collect first-hand ethnographic data—notably the missionary ethnographer Lorimer Fison (TP:LF/ET 1879–96). And while Tylor's position did not involve regular graduate training of students as fieldworkers in anthropology, his lectures were attended by several whose careers in the colonies were to provide significant ethnographic data, including the Melanesian missionary Robert Henry Codrington and the explorer of Guiana (and later colonial official) Everard Im Thurn (TP: lecture registers; Codrington 1891; Im Thurn 1883). Furthermore, when anthropology achieved full section status in the British Association in 1884, Tylor was instrumental in establishing a Committee "for the purpose of investigating and publishing reports on the physical characters, languages, and industrial and social condition of the North-western Tribes of the Dominion of Canada" (BAAS 1884:lxxii; cf. Tylor 1884). Founded with an eye toward the United States Bureau of Ethnology, which was already "sending out qualified agents to reside among the western tribes for purposes of philological and anthropological study," the Committee began by preparing a "Circular of Inquiry" for the use of government officers, missionaries, travellers, and others "likely to possess or obtain trustworthy information." The data thus obtained were to be edited and synthesized by Horatio Hale, whose "experience and skill in such research" were attested by his role in the U.S. Exploring Expedition some fifty years before (BAAS 1887:173–74; Stanton 1975).

Occasioned by the earlier British Association questionnaire's having gone out of print, the Committee's new circular was largely stripped of theoretical orienting remarks—with which Tylor, especially, had embellished his sections of *Notes and Queries* (BAAS 1874:50, 64, 66). Although Tylor (apparently the principal author) still directed the inquirer toward many of its presumed empirical manifestations, the circular contains no explicit mention of "animism." More strikingly, in trying to reach "the theological stratum in the savage mind" inquirers were cautioned against asking "uncalled for questions," but urged rather to watch "religious rites actually performed, and then to ascertain what they mean." Similarly, the collection of myth-texts "written down in the native languages" and "translated by a skilled interpreter" was "the most natural way" to get at "ideas and beliefs that no inquisitorial cross-questioning" would induce the Indian story-teller to disclose (BAAS 1887:181–82). Tylor was throughout his career concerned with issues of method, and one assumes that a decade of further reflection in the context of his correspondence with such observers-on-the-spot as Lorimer Fison had contributed to a heightened ethnographic sophistication. By this time, he was no longer willing to rest satisfied with research by questionnaire. From the beginning of the Northwest Coast project, it was assumed that, based on the results of such inquiry, some of the "more promising districts" would be the subjects of "personal survey" by Hale, or (when it became evident that his age would make this impossible) by an agent who "would act under his directions" (BAAS 1887:174; cf. J. Gruber 1967).

From Missionaries to Academic Natural Scientists

The Committee on the North-western Tribes of Canada was only one of a number established by the British Association in the 1880s and 1890s for empirical anthropological research both in the colonial empire and within the United Kingdom.[1] In the present context, however, it is particularly noteworthy for the personnel who were to serve as Hale's agents in the field. The first man chosen was a missionary who had worked for nineteen years among the Ojibwa and who travelled summers farther west to recruit Indian children for his mission school (Wilson 1887:183–84). The Reverend E. F. Wilson, however, was soon to be replaced by a young man better known in the history of ethnographic methodology: the German-born physicist-turned-ethnologist Franz Boas, whose work on Vancouver Island in the fall of 1886 brought him to the attention of Hale and the Committee. Although the details of Boas' decade-long relationship with the British Association Committee are for the most part beyond the scope of the present inquiry (Rohner 1969; GS 1974c:83–107), it is worth noting

1. Aside from several committees specifically concerned with physical anthropological or archeological data, BAAS committees with an ethnographic focus included: one on "the tribes of Asia Minor" (BAAS 1888:lxxxiii); one on "the natives of India" (BAAS 1889:lxxxi); one on "the transformation of native tribes in Mashonaland" (BAAS 1891:lxxx); one for an "ethnographical survey of the United Kingdom" (BAAS 1892:lxxxix); one for an "ethnological survey of Canada" (BAAS 1896:xciii). There were also several committees appointed to support or supervise expeditions initiated outside the Association: one for Haddon's Torres Straits Expedition (BAAS 1897:xcix); one for W. W. Skeat's Cambridge Expedition to Malaya (BAAS 1898:xcix); one for W. H. R. Rivers' work among the Todas (BAAS 1902:xcii).

that his employment marks the beginning of an important phase in the development of British ethnographic method: the collection of data by academically trained natural scientists defining themselves as anthropologists and involved also in the formulation and evaluation of anthropological theory.

The shift from Wilson to Boas symbolizes also a more deeply rooted, longer-run and somewhat complex shift in the anthropological attitude toward missionary ethnographers. In the pre-evolutionary era, James Cowles Prichard—another armchair speculator who, from a somewhat different theoretical viewpoint, was also concerned with the quality of his data—had preferred information collected by missionaries to that of "naturalists" because the latter made only brief visits and never learned the native language (1848:283; cf. GS 1973a). The centrality of religious belief in the evolutionary paradigm tended, however, to compromise data collected by those whose primary commitment was to the extirpation of "heathen superstition," and Tylor's orienting commentary in *Notes and Queries* had clearly been intended to facilitate the careful observation of savage religion by people whose prejudices might predispose them to distort it (BAAS 1874:50). It was not until two anthropological generations later, after a corps of researchers actually trained academically in anthropology had entered the ethnographic arena, that the modern opposition between missionary and ethnographer was established in the ateliers of Boas and of Malinowski (Stipe 1980). Most of the earlier British natural scientists-cum-anthropologists still maintained a working ethnographic relationship with missionaries (GS 1988a). Nevertheless, this intermediate generation contributed significantly to the emergence of an ethnographic method that (whatever its underlying analogies to the missionary experience) was perceived by its practitioners as characteristically "anthropological."

Although the key figure in the early phase of this process was Alfred Cort Haddon, his career line was followed, up to a point, by another naturalist/ethnographer: Walter Baldwin Spencer. Both were part of that post-Darwinian generation for whom it first became a marginally realistic option as an undergraduate to decide "I want to become a scientist" (cf. Mendelsohn 1963). Spencer was a protégé of the zoologist Henry Moseley at Oxford (Marett & Penniman 1931:10–46); Haddon, of the physiologist Michael Foster at Cambridge (Quiggin 1942; Geison 1978). Both began their careers as zoologists in universities at the imperial periphery—although it was a good deal easier for Haddon to return to the academic center from Dublin than it was for Spencer off in Melbourne. Both became interested in ethnographic data while carrying on zoological fieldwork; capitalizing permanently on their newfound interest, both ended their careers as anthropologists.

Haddon in the Torres Straits: 1888–1899

Haddon first went out to the Torres Straits in 1888 in the hope that an important scientific expedition might help him escape what seemed after seven years the dead end of a provincial professorship. His scientific goals were archetypically Darwinian: to study the fauna, the structure, and the mode of formation of coral reefs. Having been told "that a good deal was already known" about the natives of the area, he "had previously determined not to study them" (1901:vii) — although he did take along the *Questions on the Customs, Beliefs and Languages of Savages* James Frazer had privately printed in 1887 to facilitate research on *The Golden Bough.* Haddon had barely arrived, however, before he began collecting "curios" he apparently hoped to sell to museums to recoup some of the expenses of the trip. On the island of Mabuaig, where he settled for a longer stay, he would join the already missionized natives round their campfire for evening prayers, and as they talked on into the night in pidgin, he asked them what life had been like before the white men came. As the older men "yarned," Haddon became convinced that if he neglected this ethnographic opportunity, it was likely to be lost forever (Quiggin 1942:81–86). Although he continued his zoological research, he filled every spare moment with ethnography, and before his departure his primary interest had clearly shifted to anthropology. Because he was a biologist concerned with the geographical distribution of forms over a continuous area (in the manner of Darwin in the Galapagos), his most systematic ethnological concern was with material culture — the provenience and distribution of those "curios" he had been collecting. But he also recorded a considerable amount of general ethnographic data, which upon his return was published in the *Journal of the Anthropological Institute,* organized in terms of the categories of "that invaluable little book," *Notes and Queries on Anthropology* (1890:297–300).

In the context of the ethnographic reorientation already evidenced in the British Association, it is not surprising that Haddon's data were of interest to leading anthropologists (Quiggin 1942:90–95). As an academic man with field experience in ethnography, he was a rarity in British anthropology, and soon made his way to its front ranks by the same process through which he trained himself in the research orientations then dominating it: physical anthropology and folklore. Taking over as the principal investigator in Ireland for the British Association's Ethnographic

Survey of the British Isles, which the anthropologists and folklorists co-sponsored in the 1890s (Haddon 1895b), he soon won an appointment as lecturer in physical anthropology at Cambridge, a position that for some years he held jointly with his Dublin chair. Although he drew on his Torres Straits material for a volume on *Evolution in Art* (1895a), he felt that his data were inadequate for an ethnographic monograph he had outlined in the early 1890s (HP [1894]). To complete them, and to expand his Cambridge foothold into a "School of Anthropology," he began to plan for a second and strictly anthropological expedition (HP: AH/P. Geddes 1/4/97).

For Haddon, "anthropology" still had the embracive meaning it had gained in the nineteenth-century Anglo-American evolutionary tradition, and which it might also be expected to have for a field naturalist, to whom the behavior, cries, and physical characteristics of animals were all part of a single observational syndrome. Aware, however, that some areas of anthropological inquiry had developed a technical elaboration beyond the limitations of his own competence, and anxious to introduce the methods of experimental psychology to accurately "gauge the mental and sensory capacities of primitive peoples," Haddon took as his model the great nineteenth-century multidisciplinary maritime exploring expeditions – on the basis of one of which Moseley had made his reputation and won his position at Oxford (Moseley 1879). He therefore sought "the co-operation of a staff of colleagues, each of whom had some special qualification," so that they could divide the labor of anthropological inquiry, one doing physical measurement, another psychological testing, another linguistic analysis, another sociology, and so forth (Haddon 1901:viii).

As it happened, Haddon ended up with three experimental psychologists. His first choice had been his Cambridge colleague W. H. R. Rivers, who after early training in medicine had come under the influence of the neurologist Hughlings Jackson and gone on to study experimental psychology in Germany. Upon his return, Rivers was asked by Foster to lecture on the physiology of the sense organs at Cambridge, and there introduced the first course of instruction in experimental psychology in Britain (Langham 1981; Slobodin 1978). Unwilling at first to leave England, Rivers proposed his student Charles Myers to take his place; another student, William McDougall, volunteered himself before Rivers decided after all to come along (HP: WR/AH 11/25/97; WM/AH 5/26/97). At Codrington's suggestion, Haddon had been working since 1890 on his linguistic data with Sydney Ray, a specialist in Melanesian languages who made his living as a London schoolteacher, but who managed now to get an unpaid leave (RC/AH 4/9/90; SR/AH 6/6/97). Haddon's own student Anthony Wilkin – still an undergraduate – was recruited to handle the photography and assist with physical anthropology (AW/AH 1/27/98). Charles Selig-

Alfred Haddon (seated) and other members of the Torres Straits Expedition (standing, left to right): William Rivers, Charles Seligman, Sidney Ray, and Anthony Wilkin. (Courtesy of the University Museum of Archaeology and Anthropology, Cambridge)

man, a doctor friend of Myers and McDougall who also volunteered his services, rounded out the group as specialist in native medicine (CS/AH 10/28/97).

Supported by money from the university, various scientific societies, and the British and Queensland governments, the members of the expedition arrived by commercial steamer in the Torres Straits late in April 1898. They all began work on Murray (Mer) Island in the eastern straits, where the three psychologists continued testing the natives until late August, when Myers and McDougall went off as advance guard for research in Sarawak, to which the expedition had been invited by Rajah Brooke (at the instigation of district officer Charles Hose). Within three weeks of their arrival on Mer, however, Haddon, Ray, Wilkin, and Seligman were off for a two-month trip to Port Moresby and several nearby districts on the Papuan coast. Leaving Seligman to work northwest along the mainland, the other three rejoined Rivers on Mer late in July. Early in September all four sailed from Mer to meet Seligman in the Kiwai district, where they left Ray to work on linguistics, while the others went southwest for a month's work on Mabuaig. Late in October, Rivers and Wilkin left for England, while Haddon, Ray, and Seligman took a three-week jaunt to Saibai and several smaller islands, and then back to the Cape York Peninsula, whence they departed in late November for four months' work in Sarawak and Borneo (Haddon 1901:xiii–xiv).

Detailing the itinerary is to the point, since it was on the basis of this rather hurried research, carried on entirely in pidgin English, that there were to be produced eventually six large volumes of ethnographic data—not to mention Haddon's popular narrative account (1901), materials incorporated into later books by Seligman on *The Melanesians of British New Guinea* (1910) and by Hose and McDougall on *The Pagan Tribes of Borneo* (1912), as well as numerous journal articles. Of course, Haddon drew also on materials he had collected in 1888, but much of his ethnography was frankly carried on at second hand: he culled extensively from missionary and travel accounts, and relied heavily on material provided by traders, missionaries, and government employees, either on the spot, or in his extensive subsequent ethnography-by-mail (HP:passim). His most important ethnographic intermediary, a government schoolmaster named John Bruce who had lived for a decade on Mer, was the acknowledged source of perhaps half of the information recorded in the volume on Mer sociology and religion (Haddon 1908:xx). This is not to minimize the labors of Haddon and his colleagues, who surely produced a large amount of data in relatively short ethnographic episodes (including, one may note, some of the very earliest ethnographic cinematography [Brigard 1975]), and who at many points evidenced a considerable thoughtfulness and sensitivity about problems of ethnographic method. It is simply to emphasize that there was still some distance from Torres Straits to fieldwork in what was to become the classic anthropological mode.

Observing the Stone Age at First Hand in Australia

Spencer's ethnography is much closer in style to that of later social anthropology. Like Haddon's, however, it developed as a deviation from zoological research. While still at Oxford, Spencer had attended Tylor's lectures, watched him demonstrate the making of stone tools, and helped Moseley and Tylor begin the installation of the Pitt Rivers collection of material culture in a new annex to the University Museum (SP: WS/H. Govitz 2/18/84, 6/21/85). During his early years at Melbourne, Spencer was too preoccupied with teaching biology for research of any sort, and when he joined the Horn Expedition to the Central Australian desert in 1894, it was as zoologist—the anthropological work being delegated to E. C. Stirling, a lecturer in physiology at Adelaide. Stirling, however, was more interested in physical anthropology and material culture than in Australian marriage classes, and he seems not to have risen to the opportunity when at Alice Springs the expedition came upon the local equivalent of Haddon's Murray schoolmaster (Stirling 1896). Frank Gillen was an outgoing Irish republican who for twenty years had served as station master of the transcontinental telegraph and "sub-protector" of the local aborigines. Although he habitually referred to them as "niggers," and to fieldwork as "niggering," Gillen got on very well with the Arunta, and had already been collecting information on their customs, a portion of which was published in the report of the expedition (Gillen 1896). He did not get along so well with Stirling, but he took to Spencer, and the two became fast friends – despite Gillen's occasional irritation when Spencer reproved his racial epithets (Gillen once berated Spencer for his own "arrogant assumption of superiority so characteristic of your Nigger-assimilating race" [SP: FG/WS 1/31/96; cf. Mulvaney & Calaby 1985]).

On returning from central Australia, Spencer put Gillen in touch with Fison, the leading authority on Australian marriage classes, who by this time had retired to Melbourne (SP: FG/WS 8/30/95). Soon, Spencer and Gillen had joined forces for further research – Spencer writing from Melbourne to pose evolutionary questions about marriage classes; Gillen writing back with the ethnographic data he obtained. Gillen, however, soon became dissatisfied with what he felt was "only a splendid verification" of work previously done by Fison and Howitt (1880). Complaining that "getting at the 'why' of things is utterly hopeless" because "when driven into a corner they always take refuge in the alcheringa," Gillen reported to Spencer that he was "on the track of a big ceremony called Engwura" (7/14/96). By offering the rations necessary to support a gathering of far-flung clansmen, he was able, "after much palaver," to convince the Arunta elders to hold the great periodic initiation ceremony one more time (8/n.d./96).

When Spencer arrived in November 1896, Gillen introduced him as his younger classificatory brother, thereby entitling Spencer to membership in the same Witchity Grub totem to which Gillen himself belonged. Fison and Howitt, as great Oknirabata (men of influence) in southeastern Australian tribes, and ultimate recipients and judges of the information to be collected, were assigned to the lizard and wildcat totems, on the basis of sketch portraits drawn by the two ethnographers (SP: FG/WS 2/23/97). Although Gillen had expected the ceremonies to last only a week, they went on for three months, during which he and Spencer lived at or near the Arunta camp, observing the ceremonies, discussing with the natives (in pidgin and Gillen's somewhat limited Arunta) the associated myths and religious beliefs (Spencer & Gillen 1899). Their racial attitudes and evolutionary theoretical assumptions seem not to have inhibited a considerable degree of empathetic identification: finally discovering the profound religious significance of the churingas, and assimilating aboriginal belief to his own lost Roman Catholicism, Gillen expressed bitter regret for his previous casual treatment of these sacred objects (7/30/97).

When the ceremonies ended, Spencer and Gillen had a wealth of ethnographic detail about native ritual life of a sort that armchair anthropologists had never previously experienced. Frazer, who soon became Spencer's own mentor-by-correspondence, had never felt himself so close to the Stone Age (1931:3; Marett & Penniman 1932). But despite the evolutionary framework in which it had been conceived and into which it was received, the monograph that appeared in 1899 was recognizably "modern" in its ethnographic style. Rather than running through the categories of *Notes and Queries* or some other armchair questionnaire, *The Native Tribes of Central Australia* was given focus by a totalizing cultural performance. Coming at a point when evolutionary theory was already somewhat in disarray, and offering data on totemism that conflicted with received assumption, it had tremendous impact. Malinowski suggested in 1913 that half of the anthropological theory written since had been based upon it, and all but a tenth heavily influenced by it (1913c).

Malinowski no doubt also recognized an ethnographic style that was closer to his own than Haddon's—whose expedition had not yet returned from the Torres Straits when *Native Tribes* was published. Its status as an ethnographic innovation was compromised, however, by Spencer's failure to leave significant academic progeny. Rather than creating an anthropological school, he was incorporated into an already established line of Australian ethnologists (Mulvaney 1958, 1967). As Fison had been to Tylor, so he became one of Frazer's "men-on-the-spot." Although Frazer never left the armchair, he was a great encourager of anthropological fieldwork. For several decades he worked hard to sustain the researches of John Roscoe, a missionary among the Baganda who had responded to his questionnaire. In 1913 he even tried to get the Colonial Office to appoint Roscoe government anthropologist in East Africa (FP: JF/JR 11/27/13; cf. Thornton 1983). Frazer often said that the efforts of fieldworkers would long outlast his own theoretical musings. But his insistence on a sharp separation of ethnography and theory (which should "regularly and rightly be left to the comparative ethnologist" [1931:9]) ran counter to the emerging tradition of fieldworker academics, and his hermetic style prevented him from leaving academic anthropological offspring. Accepting a role as Frazer's ethnographic agent in Australia, Spencer also died heirless. Left hanging on a collateral branch off in the colonies, he was effectively removed from the myth-making process in British anthropology, where lineage relations have played a powerful role (Kuper 1983).

The "Intensive Study of Limited Areas" before the Great War

In the meantime, Haddon and his colleagues were becoming recognized as the "Cambridge School" (Quiggin 1942:110–30). Although the early Torres Straits volumes contained data on physiological psychology, social organization, and totemism that were significant for contemporary theoretical discussions, it was less the empirical data it collected than the expedition itself as a symbol of ethnographic enterprise that established the group's reputation. And it took several years to achieve a solid institutional base in the university. Frazer's effort, shortly after the expedition's return, to memorialize the Board of General Studies for the establishment of regular instruction in ethnology produced for Haddon only a poorly paid lectureship to replace the one in physical anthropology to which W. L. Duckworth had been appointed in his absence (HP: JF/AH 10/17/99, 10/28/99). It was not until 1904 that a Board of Anthropological Studies was set up, and not until five years later that a diploma course was established and Haddon given a readership (Fortes 1953).

From the time of his return, however, Haddon busily propagandized for more anthropological "field-work" (a term, apparently derived from the discourse of field naturalists, which Haddon seems to have introduced into that of British anthropology). In his presidential addresses to the Anthropological Institute and in popular articles, he spoke of the pressing need of "our Cinderella Science" for "fresh investigations in the field" carried on by men trained as "field-anthropologists" (1903b:22). Warning against the "rapid collector," he emphasized the urgent necessity not simply to gather "specimens" but to take the time to "coax out of the native by patient sympathy" the deeper meaning of the material collected. Always inclined to view scientific work in the same spirit of rationalized cooperative endeavor that characterized his mildly socialist politics, Haddon suggested that "two or three good men should be always in the field" supported by an international council that would set research priorities (1903a:228–29). His own conception of these priorities was captured in the slogan "the intensive study of limited areas."

It is not clear, however, that Haddon meant by this the sort of intensive study that was shortly to emerge. Coming from zoology, he was oriented toward the study of "biological provinces." His proposal for a steamer expedition to Melanesia that would drop off investigators on different islands, returning to pick them up several months later, was intended to clarify the distribution and variation of forms in a region, with emphasis particularly on transitional forms and areas. His ultimate ethnological goal was still the elucidation of the "nature, origin and distribution of the races and peoples" of a particular region, and the clarification of their position in evolutionary development (1906:187). Even so, the movement was clearly toward a more focussed, extended, and intensive ethnography—and toward a distinction between "survey" and "intensive" work.

Haddon was not the only Torres Straits alumnus to contribute to the reputation of the Cambridge School. For a number of them the expedition was either the beginning or a significant turning point in a quite distinguished career. Ray's reputation as a brilliant Melanesian linguistic scholar never managed to provide a paying alternative to his London schoolteacher's job (Haddon 1939), and within two years of his return Wilkin died of dysentery contracted while doing archeological research in Egypt. But McDougall and Myers went on to become leaders in psychology—authoring influential early textbook introductions to social and experimental psychology, respectively (Drever 1968; Bartlett 1959). Before leaving anthropology, Myers did further fieldwork in Egypt, and Seligman and Rivers were of course the leading field anthropologists of their generation in Britain. After Torres Straits, Seligman (teaming later with his wife Brenda) worked successively in New Guinea and Ceylon (1910, 1911; R. Firth 1975) before beginning a long series of investigations in the Anglo-Egyptian Sudan in 1910 (1932; Fortes 1941). Rivers went on to do research in Egypt, then among the Todas in India, and came back twice for further work in Melanesia before returning to psychology during World War I (Slobodin 1978). Though much of their own work was of what came to be called the "survey" variety, both men played a role in training a rising generation of field researchers whose work was in an increasingly more "intensive" mode—Rivers at Cambridge in cooperation with Haddon; Seligman at the London School of Economics, where he joined the Anglo-Finnish sociologist Edward Westermarck, who himself did extensive fieldwork in Morocco (1927:158–96). At Oxford, all three Torres Straits alumni served occasionally as informal extramural ethnographic mentors to the several fieldworkers recruited into anthropology by Marett and his colleagues in the Committee on Anthropology established there in 1905 (Marett 1941).

Bronislaw Malinowski was a member of this pre–World War I group, and in fact the last of them actually to get into the field. A. R. Radcliffe-Brown (not yet, however, hyphenated) was the first; in his case the Torres Straits model was still in evidence, with all the functions of its divided scientific labor to be carried on by one lone investigator. Brown was actually in the field less than the two years normally listed for his Andaman expedition (1906–8), and much of his research was apparently carried on among the "hangers-on" around the prison camp at Fort Blair (cf. Tomas 1991). His attempt to study unacculturated Little Andamanese was frus-

Seligman at work, Hula. "The anthropologist must relinquish his comfortable position . . . on the verandah . . . where he has been accustomed to collect statements from informants . . . [and] go out into the villages" (Malinowski 1926a:147). (Courtesy of the University Museum of Archaeology and Anthropology, Cambridge)

trated by his difficulties with their language ("I ask for the word 'arm' and I get the Onge for 'you are pinching me'" [HP: AB/AH n.d., 8/10/06]). But if his Andaman work is less notable ethnographically than for its later recasting in the mold of Durkheimian theory, it was nonetheless clearly a further step toward a more intensive fieldwork style (Radcliffe-Brown 1922; GS 1984b).

The year of Brown's return saw two other young academic ethnographers off with Rivers to the southwestern Pacific on the Percy Sladen Trust Expedition. While Rivers' own work seems mostly to have been done on board the mission ship *Southern Cross* as it sailed from island to island, Gerald C. Wheeler (from the London School of Economics) and A. M.

Hocart (from Oxford) undertook much more intensive study. Wheeler spent ten months among the Mono-Alu in the Western Solomons (1926:vii); Hocart, after working for ten weeks with Wheeler and Rivers on Eddystone Island (1922), settled in Fiji for four years, where as schoolmaster he collected a very rich body of ethnographic data (RiP: AH/WR 4/16/09; cf. HoP).

In the remaining years before the war, more than half a dozen young anthropologists left English universities for the field. Brown was back in 1910 for a year's work in Western Australia (White 1981). That same year saw Diamond Jenness, an Oxonian from New Zealand whose sister had married a missionary in the D'Entrecasteaux, off to Goodenough Island (Jenness & Ballantyne 1920). Two young Finns followed Edward Westermarck to England to work under Haddon's tutelage in "the intensive study of limited areas" (GS 1979b): Gunnar Landtman went to New Guinea for two years to explore in depth the Kiwai area Haddon and his colleagues had surveyed in 1898 (Landtman 1927); Rafael Karsten worked among three tribes of the Bolivian Gran Chaco in 1911 and 1912 (Karsten 1932). The group included also two Oxford-trained women: Barbara Freire-Marreco, who worked among the Pueblo in the American Southwest (Freire-Marreco 1916), and Marie Czaplička (another Polish emigre) who spent a strenuous year on the Arctic Circle in Siberia working among the Tungus (Czaplička 1916). And when Malinowski went to the southeastern Papuan coast to follow up another Torres Straits survey in the fall of 1914, yet another offspring of the Cambridge School, John Layard, was settling in for two years' work in Atchin off the coast of Malekula (Layard 1942).

Thus by the outbreak of the Great War it could already be said that fieldwork was to anthropology "as the blood of martyrs is to the Roman Catholic Church" (Seligman, as quoted in R. Firth 1963:2). The failure of these other early "intensive studies" to figure more prominently in the myth-history of British anthropology (Richards 1939) is perhaps in part a reflection of biographical accident and institutional circumstance. Both Karsten and Jenness were soon caught up in further "intensive" (and extended) studies in quite different (and difficult) areas—among the Peruvian Jibaro and the Canadian Eskimo, respectively (Karsten 1935; Jenness 1922–23). Landtman's field notes were actually lost in shipwreck; it was only by hiring a diver that he was able to salvage the trunk that contained them (Landtman 1927:ix). Layard returned from Malekula to suffer an extended incapacitation from mental distress (Langham 1981:204). Hocart came back from Fiji to serve four years as captain on active duty in France and spent the 1920s as government archeologist in Ceylon (Needham 1967). Czaplička died young in 1921 (Marett 1921). Although several of them had successful careers, none of them (save, belatedly, Radcliffe-Brown) established himself in *British* academic life. Jenness emigrated to Canada, where he eventually succeeded Edward Sapir as director of the anthropological division of the Canadian Geological Survey (Swayze 1960). Karsten and Landtman returned to take up professorial positions in Finland (NRC 1938:157). Hocart, an unsuccessful competitor of Radcliffe-Brown's for the chair in anthropology at Sydney (MPL: Seligman/BM 3/18/24), came no closer to a major academic position than the chair in sociology at Cairo (Needham 1967). Layard became involved in Jungian psychology (McClancy 1986); Wheeler, the co-author with Hobhouse and Ginsberg of the *Material Culture of the Simpler Peoples* (Hobhouse et al. 1915), seems to have left anthropology for the translation of travel accounts from the Danish (HP: CW/AH 12/23/39). Even Malinowski had trouble finding a place in academic life; as late as 1921 he was considering returning to Poland (MPL: Seligman/BM 8/30/21), and it was only with Seligman's help (including a quiet subvention of his salary) that he was able to establish himself at the London School of Economics (CS/BM 1921–24).

Something more than delayed or institutionally marginal careers, however, would seem to be involved in the lapsed remembrance of these other academic ethnographers of Malinowski's generation. Although some of them (notably Hocart) are revealed in their field notes as extremely sensitive and reflective practical methodologists (HoP: reel 9, passim), their early monographs did not present them as self-conscious ethnographic innovators. The closest approximation to Malinowski's *Argonauts* is Landtman's flat-footedly descriptive (and rather cumbrously titled) *Kiwai Papuans of British New Guinea: A Nature-Born Instance of Rousseau's Ideal Community* (1927). Insofar as one can infer from its photographic representation, and from his long letters to Haddon from the field, Landtman's ethnographic situation seems roughly analogous to that of Malinowski in the Trobriands. But although he recorded observational data, Landtman conceived his method primarily in terms of working closely with individual (and paid) informants (or, more aptly in one letter to Haddon, "teachers" [HP: GL/AH 8/28/10]). Although he did learn some Kiwai, and wrote a perceptive little essay on the nature of pidgin as a language in its own right (1927:453–61), the many quoted passages in his ethnography make it clear that he worked primarily in the latter tongue. His efforts, nonetheless, were favorably viewed by the Kiwai ("this white man he another kind, all same me fellow" [HP: GL/AH 4/4/11]), and ultimately received Malinowski's imprimatur as well. If Malinowski failed to mention in his review (1929d) that this "master of the modern sociological method in fieldwork" had entered the field five years before his own arrival in the Trobriands, his neglect was perhaps understandable. By this time professor of anthropology at the London School of Economics, Malinowski had

succeeded to Haddon and Rivers as the leading exponent of the "intensive study of limited areas." With *Argonauts* by then five years in print, the transformation of a research strategy into a methodological myth had already been accomplished.

Rivers and the "Concrete" Method

To place Malinowski's achievement in context, however, it is necessary to look more closely at the evolution of "intensive study." If the actual ethnographic practice of the initiates of the Cambridge School is only indirectly accessible, we can say with some certainty what "intensive study" was intended to be, because the man who did the most to define it published, on the eve of Malinowski's departure for the field, several fairly explicit statements of what such work involved. That man was not Haddon, of course, but Rivers. Coming to ethnology from experimental psychology—one of the more methodologically explicit areas of the human sciences—Rivers brought with him a high degree of self-consciousness about problems of method; but he also possessed an uninhibited (Mauss said "intrepid") explanatory imagination (Mauss 1923), and was quite capable of pursuing a pet hypothesis well beyond the limits to which rigorous method could carry him. As manifested in the far-fetched migration-theories of his *History of Melanesian Society* (1914a), and in his subsequent association with the hyperdiffusionism of William Perry and Grafton Elliot Smith, the latter tendency was seriously to compromise his historical reputation (Langham 1981:118–99). But during the decade or so before his death in 1922, Rivers was the single most influential British anthropologist. Haddon described him in 1914 as "the greatest field investigator of primitive sociology there has ever been" (HP: AH Rept. Sladen Trustees), and his "concrete method" provided for Malinowski, as for many others, the exemplar of sound ethnographic methodology.

Rivers' methodological contributions tend in disciplinary memory to be subsumed within a rather narrow conception of the "genealogical method" he developed in Torres Straits, as if all he provided was a convenient (and some would now say questionable [Schneider 1968:13–14]) means for gathering kinship data. For Rivers, however, the study of kinship was a derived advantage, and by no means marked the limits of the usefulness of genealogies. Although he was not the first ethnographer to collect them, Rivers' interest seems to have stemmed from his psychological work, rather than from any ethnographic precursors. His model was apparently the research into human heredity carried on by the polymathic psychologist/statistician/eugenicist Sir Francis Galton, who as anthropometrist was also one of the leading figures in British anthropology (Pearson 1924:334–425).

Before departing for the Torres Straits, Rivers had consulted with Galton (GP: WR/FG 1/4/97), and his original goal in collecting genealogies was much the same as that which had previously motivated Galton's *Inquiries into Human Faculty* (1883): "to discover whether those who were closely related resembled one another in their reactions to the various psychological and physiological tests" (Rivers 1908:65). Upon realizing, however, that the genealogical memories of the islanders went back as far as three or even five generations, Rivers "with the stimulus of Dr. Haddon's encouragement" began to collect the data for its potential sociological utility as well (1900:74–75).

Using only a few basic English categories ("father," "mother," "child," "husband," "wife"), Rivers tried in pidgin English, sometimes clarified (or further complicated) by a native interpreter, to get from each informant the personal names and marital connections of his parents, siblings, children, and grand-relatives: "what name wife belong him?", "what piccaninny he got?"; making sure that the terms were used in their "real" or "proper" English (i.e., biological) sense, and did not elicit some classificatory or adoptive relative—"he proper father?", "he proper mother?" (Haddon 1901:124–25). In the context of a later sophistication as to the ambiguities of social and biological kinship, and the problematic character of all such ethnographic elicitation, the image of Rivers' ethnography-in-process given to us by Haddon is likely to elicit a smile. Who knows just what meaning "proper" conveyed in the semantics of pidgin English as applied to the categories of Mabuaig kinship? (C. Howard 1981). To Rivers, however, the method seemed self-correcting against error or even deliberate deception, because the same set of relationships could be elicited on separate occasions (and even by different observers) from different informants in the same (or overlapping) genealogies (1899). Thus even after Rivers had returned to England, the "chief" of Mabuaig, anxious to draw up his own record "for the use and guidance of his descendants," created another version (recorded and sent along by the local trader) which save for "minor discrepancies" confirmed information previously collected by Rivers (1904:126). At the very least, there would seem to have been some agreement among informants as to what "proper" meant.

Rivers, however, felt no need for such benefit of doubt. Despite occasional acknowledgments of the difficulties of "exact" translation, he managed to convince himself that he was dealing with "bodies of dry fact . . . as incapable of being influenced by bias, conscious or unconscious, as any subject that can be imagined" (1914a:I, 3–4). Furthermore, they provided the basis for a "scientific" approach to the reconstruction of the history of human social forms. Although in principle the genealogical method required the exclusion of native kinship categories, which tended to obscure the "real" biological relationships, Rivers' attention was inevitably focussed on the systematic aspect of the native terms he was excluding. Thus when it came to summarizing the various personal-name genealogies for all the Mabuaig Islanders, he used native kin terms to draw up "the genealogy of an ideal family" which illustrated a kinship system "of the kind known as classificatory" (1904:129). In this context he was quickly led to the "rediscovery" (Fortes 1969:3) of Lewis H. Morgan's *Systems of Consanguinity* (1871; cf. Rivers 1907) – if such a term is appropriate for assumptions that had been the common currency of Australian ethnography from the time of Fison and Howitt. Rivers became committed to the idea that the elemental social structure of any group would be systematically revealed in its kinship terminology. While later writers have emphasized the utility of paradigmatic models of such systems for comparative purposes (Fortes 1969:24), Rivers himself was more impressed that he had found an area of human behavior where "the principle of determinism applies with a rigor and definiteness equal to that of any of the exact sciences" – since "every detail" of systems of relationship could be traced back to some prior "social condition arising out of the regulation of marriage and sexual relations" (1914b:95). Even after he had abandoned his early "crude evolutionary point of view" for the "ethnological [historical] analysis of culture" (1911:131- 32), he continued to feel that his methods provided the basis for reliable reconstructions of major historical sequences of human social development (1914a).

Our concern here, however, is less with how Rivers' "invention" of the genealogical method led to a set of theoretical concerns which, subsequently dehistoricized by Radcliffe-Brown, were to be central to later British social anthropology (GS 1984b). It is rather, insofar as it can be kept separate, with his somewhat paradoxical contribution to the development of ethnographic method. On the one hand, Rivers' elaboration of the genealogical method offered a staunchly positivistic approach, a kind of "quick methodological fix," by which scientifically trained observers, "with no knowledge of the languages and with very inferior interpreters," could "in comparatively short time" collect information that had remained hidden from the most observant long-term European residents, even to the point of laying bare the basic structure of the indigenous society (1910:10). The model here is Rivers on the deck of the *Southern Cross* interrogating an informant through an interpreter, during one of the brief stops of its mission circuit. But there were other aspects of his ethnographic experience that led toward a more sophisticated longer-term "intensive study," one that might enable the scientific observer to achieve something analogous to the more empathetic, extensively detailed, and broadly penetrating knowledge that had previously characterized the very best missionary ethnographers.

In his more confidently positivistic moments, Rivers tended to see the genealogical (generalized as the "concrete") method as the solution to almost every ethnographic problem. It provided a framework in which all members of a local group could be located, and to which could be attached a broad range of ethnographic information on "the social condition of each person included in the pedigrees"—data on residence, totems, and clan membership, as well as miscellaneous behavioral and biographical information (1910:2). In addition to its utility in collecting sociological data, however, it could be used in the study of migrations, of magic and religion, of demography, of physical anthropology, and even of linguistics. Most important, it enabled the observer "to study abstract problems, on which the savage's ideas are vague, by means of concrete facts, of which he is a master" (1900:82). It even made it possible "to formulate laws regulating the lives of people which they have probably never formulated themselves, certainly not with the clearness and definiteness which they have to the mind trained by a more complex civilization" (1910:9). Not only could the observing scientist delineate the actual social laws of a particular group, he could detect also how far its ostensible social laws "were being actually followed in practice" (1910:6). The power of the genealogical method was attested by independent observers—"men on the spot" such as G. Orde Brown, who after telling Rivers that kinship data were unobtainable among a particular Kenyan group, was urged to try Rivers' method: "and now I find that he was right, and that I was completely wrong, in spite of my then three years experience of these people" (HP: GB/AH 2/8/13). It was also evident in Rivers' fieldwork, which although for the most part frankly of the survey variety, did indeed provide a large amount of data in a relatively short time.

No doubt Rivers' insouciant assurance of the power of positivistic thinking was buttressed both by traditional ethnocentric assumptions about the evolution of the capacity for abstract thought and by the experimental psychological studies he carried on in these terms (Langham 1981:56–64). But it is worth noting that at some points he interpreted savage concreteness as due to lexical rather than cognitive deficiency, and suggested that "he certainly cannot be expected to appreciate properly the abstract terms of the language of his visitor" (1910:9). At such moments, one feels the pull of Rivers' actual experience toward a somewhat different ethnographic style, which while ultimately perhaps no less scientistic, implied a greater sensitivity to the difficulties of cultural translation and the necessity for long-term intensive study to overcome them.

Rivers did attempt one piece of fieldwork that verged on such "intensive study." In 1902, he went to the Nilgiri Hills of southern India to study the Todas, whose polyandry had long made them an important ethnographic case for the evolutionary paradigm (Rooksby 1971). Although his difficulties in fitting Toda data within an evolutionary framework seem to have been a factor in his subsequent "conversion" to diffusionism, Rivers presented his results merely as a "demonstration of anthropological method" in the "collecting" and "recording" of ethnographic material (1906:v). He planned only a six-month stay, and worked through interpreters, but his brief methodological introduction suggests that he intended his work as an "intensive study." His many interpolated comments on how he obtained particular bits of information indicate that most of his accounts of Toda ceremony were narratives obtained through informants in "public" morning and "private" afternoon sessions. But he made it a point to obtain as many independently corroborating accounts as he could and to pay only for an informant's time rather than for particular items of information (7–17). He also moved about observing for himself, and in at least one instance was allowed to witness one of the most sacred Toda ceremonies. Within days, however, the wife of the man who arranged this died. This and similar misfortunes befalling two other Toda "guides" were ascribed by their diviners to "the anger of the gods because their secrets had been revealed to the stranger." Rivers' sources of information ran dry, and he came away from India "knowing that there were subjects of which [he] had barely touched the fringe," and suspecting that there were "far more numerous deficiencies" of which he was not even aware (2–3; cf. Langham 1981:134–35, where Rivers' increasing "ethnographic empathy" is linked to the experience of his 1908 expedition).

The 1912 Revision of *Notes and Queries*

When the British Association established a committee to prepare a revised edition of *Notes and Queries* the year after *The Todas* was published, Rivers, Haddon, and Myers (joined later by Seligman) were all members. The publication that eventuated in 1912, apparently after some conflict between the young turks and the old guard (Urry 1972:51), was in many respects a new departure. The book was ostensibly still directed to "travellers" and nonanthropologists who might "supply the information which is wanted for the scientific study of anthropology at home" (BAAS 1912:iii–iv). Despite the urging of "friendly critics" who had argued the virtues of a "narrative form," many sections still reflected the "old lists of 'leading questions'" that had characterized the three Tylorian editions. Nevertheless, the "friendly critics" had clearly had a major impact. J. L. Myres, the Oxford archeologist who was the only contributor to author more pages, described Rivers' contribution as "a revelation" that set a new "standard for workmanship in the field" (Urry 1972:51). It is quite evident that the "workers in the field" for whom Rivers wrote, although lacking perhaps an "advanced knowledge in anthropology," were not casual travellers but people in a position to undertake "intensive study."

The centerpiece of the whole volume, Rivers' "General Account of Method," may be regarded as a programmatic systematization of the ethnographic experience of the Cambridge School. The distinction between "intensive study" and "survey" was here recast in linguistic terms. Because (as it was suggested elsewhere in the volume) "language is our only key to the correct and complete understanding of the life and thought of a people" (BAAS 1912:186), the investigator's first duty was "to acquire as completely as possible" a knowledge of their language (109). To that end the volume incorporated "Notes on Learning a New Language" by the American linguistic anthropologist J. P. Harrington—although Rivers still felt it was better to rely on an interpreter, supplemented by native words, than on "an inadequate knowledge of the language" (124). While Rivers gave special prominence to the genealogical method, its justification was now cast in rather different terms: by enabling the inquirer "to use the very instrument which the people themselves use in dealing with their social problems," it made it possible to study "the formation and nature of their social classifications," excluding "entirely the influence of civilised categories" (119).

Although the nature of "the thought of people of the lower culture" was still used to justify Rivers' first rule of method ("the abstract should always be approached through the concrete"), he now placed great emphasis on the problem of category differences: "native terms must be used wherever there is the slightest chance of a difference of category," and "the greatest caution must be used in obtaining information by means of direct questions, since it is probable that such questions will inevitably suggest some civilised category" (BAAS 1912:110–11). Similarly, special attention must be paid to volunteered information, even if it interrupted one's train of thought: instead of complaining of the difficulty of keeping an informant to the point, the investigator should recognize that "the native also has a point, probably of far more interest than his own" (112).

Rivers' "investigator" was still more an "inquirer" than an "observer," but he was strongly encouraged to get the corroboration of "two or more independent witnesses," and cautioned also that disagreements among them were "one of the most fruitful sources of knowledge"—"a man who will tell you nothing spontaneously often cannot refrain from correcting false information" (BAAS 1912:113). Wherever possible the investigator was to supplement verbal accounts with the actual witnessing of ceremonies, and "to take advantage of any events of social importance which occur during your stay," since "the thorough study of a concrete case in which social regulations have been broken may give more insight . . . than a month of questioning" (116). Last but not least, the inquirer was to develop "sympathy and tact," without which "it is certain that the best kind of work will never be done." Although urged on grounds of expedience ("people of rude culture are so unaccustomed to any such evidence of sympathy with their ways of thinking and acting" that it would "go far to break down their reticence"), Rivers cautioned that natives would be "quick to recognize whether this sympathy was real and not feigned" (125).

To suggest that the new ethnographic orientation embodied in the 1912 *Notes and Queries* clearly reflected the field experience of a new breed of academician-cum-ethnographer is not to say that it was unrelated to developments in anthropological theory. A sense of crisis in evolutionary theory had been evident in Great Britain as early as the mid-1890s, when Tylor, responding to Boas' critique of "The Comparative Method of Anthropology," had suggested the need for "tightening the logical screw" (GS 1968a:211). The malaise was particularly evident in relation to the study of religion, where Andrew Lang's defection from the Tylorian camp (1901), R. R. Marett's interpretation of Codrington's Melanesian "mana" as a pre-animistic religious phenomenon (Marett 1900), and the debates precipitated by Spencer and Gillen's Arunta data (Frazer 1910) all contributed to a strong feeling that something was wrong with both the categories and the data in terms of which armchair anthropologists were interpreting primitive religion. This discomfort was reflected in the revised *Notes and Queries* in an essay by Marett (never himself a field ethnographer) on "the study of magico-religious facts" (BAAS 1912:251–60). The hyphenation was both a reflection of the fact that "framers of general theory" were "in dispute" and an exhortation to the ethnographer to collect data from the "point of view" of primitive folk, "uncoloured by his own" (251). Eschewing questionnaires, Marett argued that "the real scheme of topics . . . must be framed by the observer himself to suit the social conditions of a given tribe" (255). The observer must not ask "why" but "what," focussing on the rite in all its complex concrete detail—"at the same time keeping at arm's length our own theological concepts, as well as our anthropological concepts, which are just as bad, since they have been framed by us to make us understand savagery, not by savagery to enable it to understand itself" (259). In this context, then, the "concrete method" was not simply a means of getting at abstractions that the savage could not himself articulate, but a way of collecting "concrete facts" uncontaminated by European evolutionary abstractions that had come to seem more than a bit problematic.

As a kind of footnote to the new edition of *Notes and Queries,* Rivers in 1913 published a statement on the needs of ethnography in which he further elaborated certain aspects of "intensive study" that may have seemed inappropriate to argue in the earlier collaborative effort. In specifying just what type of anthropological research was most pressingly urgent, Rivers narrowed and refined the conception of intensive study that had emerged in the work of the Cambridge School. On the one hand, he explicitly subordinated certain traditional concerns of a general anthropology, either because their data were less immediately endangered (in the case of archeology) or because pursuing them risked destroying the rapport necessary for intensive sociological study (in the case of material culture and physical anthropology [Rivers 1913:5–6, 13]). Similarly, because of the "disturbance and excitement produced among natives by the various activities of the different members of an expedition," he now urged that ethnographic work should be carried on by single investigators "working alone" (10–11). As further justification, he argued that the labor of ethnography should be undivided because its subject matter was indivisible. In a "rude" culture (and there are several indications that he now thought of culture in the plural), the domains civilized men designated as politics, religion, education, art, and technology were interdependent and inseparable, and it followed that "specialism in the collection of ethnographic details must be avoided at all costs" (11). Rivers did insist, however, on the specialization of the ethnographer's role itself: because government officials and missionaries had little time after the performance of their regular duties, because they lacked appropriate training, and because their occupations brought them into conflict with native ideas and customs (even, in the case of missionaries, to the point of embracing the "duty to destroy" them), Rivers now felt that ethnography was best carried on by "private workers," preferably with special training or experience "in exact methods in other sciences" (9–10). Such were the preconditions of "intensive work," which Rivers defined as that "in which the worker lives for a year or more among a community of perhaps four or five hundred people and studies every detail of their life and culture; in which he comes to know every member of the community personally; in which he is not content with generalized information, but studies every feature of life and custom in concrete detail and by means of the vernacular language" (7).

That, one might suggest, was just what Malinowski did in the Trobriands. Malinowski's enactment of Rivers' program was, however, more than a matter of taking the new *Notes and Queries* into the field and following instructions. It involved a shift in the primary locus of investigation, from the deck of the mission ship or the verandah of the mission station to the teeming center of the village, and a corresponding shift in the conception of the ethnographer's role, from that of inquirer to that of participant "in a way" in village life. It also required a shift in theoretical orientation, since as long as "the aim of anthropology [was] to teach us the history of mankind" (Rivers 1913:5) the bustle of village activity could have only mediate rather than intrinsic interest. And finally, it required not only enactment but embodiment—or precisely the sort of mythic transformation Malinowski provided.

Malinowski from the British Museum to Mailu

Before his mythopoeic ethnographic experience in the Trobriands, Malinowski himself had served an apprenticeship as armchair anthropologist. His introduction to anthropology had in fact come when, during a period of medically enforced withdrawal from chemical and physical research, he read (or had read to him by his mother [FP: BM/JF 5/25/23]) the second edition of Frazer's *Golden Bough* (1900). Complicated as it is by a complexly motivated rhetorical inflation, Malinowski's debt to Frazer has been a matter of debate (Jarvie 1964; Leach 1966; cf. Malinowski 1923, 1944). Malinowski later spoke of having been immediately "bound to the service of Frazerian anthropology"—"a great science, worthy of as much devotion as any of her elder and more exact sister studies" (1926a:94). There is no doubt a link between the epistemological concerns of Malinowski's doctoral dissertation at the University of Cracow (Paluch 1981; Ellen et al. 1988) and the warp threads of magic, religion, and science on which Frazer wove his rich tapestry of transfigured ethnographic detail. But Malinowski had chosen Frazer as a "masterpiece" of English literary style, and his more convincing acknowledgments reflect his appreciation of Frazer's compelling representation of exotic but generically human experience within a vividly recreated landscape (FP: BM/JF 10/25/17)—the "scene/act ratio" which, according to the literary critic Stanley Hyman (1959:201, 225, 254), provided the "imaginative core" of Frazer's work, and was later strikingly evident in Malinowski's *Argonauts.*

From a literary viewpoint Malinowski's anthropology may be regarded as a seedling of the *Golden Bough.* And there are no doubt also substantive and even theoretical concerns in which the bond to Frazerian anthropology is evident (Malinowski 1944). But from a more general methodological and theoretical viewpoint, the differences are clear enough. Carrying forward the tradition of armchair speculation from within the very precincts of the Cambridge School, Frazer defended his questionnaire in the face of Rivers' "concrete method" (FP: JF/J. Roscoe 5/12/07). During the decade after 1900 when his (somewhat disapproving) master Tylor had begun to withdraw into senescence, theoretical debate in British anthropology swirled around the issues Frazer used to give thematic focus to his literary efforts: the nature of primitive religion, and particularly the problem of totemism—on which Frazer by 1910 had offered three different "theories," all of which were incorporated into his four-volume compendium on *Totemism and Exogamy* (cf. Hyman 1959:214–15). By that time, the theoretical malaise in British anthropology was becoming acute. One consequence was a generally heightened sense of ethnographic urgency—the previously noted feeling that received ethnographic categories were somehow inadequate, and that what was needed was a new body of data unencumbered by theoretical assumption. But evolutionary theory itself had by now been called into question. Rivers was shortly to announce his "conversion" to an "historical" diffusionary point of view (1911), and Radcliffe-Brown had already begun the Durkheimian reworking of his Andaman data which, in the context of subsequent debates with Rivers, led him to turn away from diachronic problems almost entirely (GS 1984b).

At this point Malinowski, after a year at Leipzig where he studied with the psychologist Wilhelm Wundt and the economic historian Karl Bücher, came to England to study anthropology (Symmons 1958–60). Introduced by Haddon to Seligman, he entered the more cosmopolitan (and sociological) London School of Economics, where he became a student of both Seligman and Westermarck. Carrying on extensive library research in the British Museum, Malinowski entered actively into the on-going discussion of totemism, starting with a critique of Frazer's interpretation of the *intichiuma* ceremony (1912), continuing with a brief review of Durkheim's *Elementary Forms* (1913b), and culminating with his as yet untranslated Polish publication on *Primitive Beliefs and Forms of Social Organization: A View of the Genesis of Religion with Special Respect to Totemism* (1915b). While these efforts are all still contained within the general framework of evolutionary assumption, there is another one that reflects a shift from ultimate origins and long-term diachronic development toward more specifically historical or purely synchronic problems.

Regarded from a substantive point of view, Malinowski's *Family among the Australian Aborigines* (1913a) is an attempt, following the line pioneered by his teacher Westermarck (1891), to attack such evolutionary warhorses as "primitive promiscuity" and "marriage by capture," as well as the whole Morganian notion of the "classificatory system of kinship," on the basis of a systematic analysis of all the available literature from the ethnographic realm that provided evolutionists like Frazer with their type case of *truly* "primitive man." Constructively, the book is Malinowski's most Durkheimian work: his primary concern is to demonstrate the interrelation both of the idea of kinship and of the family as a social institution with "the general structure of society" (1913a:300). At the same time, it may also be regarded as a methodological exercise—another attempt to tighten Tylor's "logical screw." Malinowski shows a notable concern with the definition of analytic categories not "directly borrowed from our own society" (168). And he is even more systematically concerned with developing rigorous method in the evaluation of ethnographic evidence. In doing so, he turns to history in a quite technical and professional sense, using Langlois and Seignobos' historiographical text (1898) as a model for the treatment of the major Australian ethnographic sources by "the strict rules of historical criticism," and analyzing conflicting testimony so that future fieldwork might be focussed on key issues of fact (1913a:19). That same orientation toward the field is evident in his already somewhat critical view of Durkheimian sociology, which he tended to regard as a closet philosophy hypostatizing a metaphysical "collective mind" to the neglect of the activities of real human individuals (1913b). Malinowski felt that Durkheimian interpretation was constrained by the "complete absence in our ethnographic information of any attempt to connect the data of folk-lore and the facts of sociology" (1913a:233), or as he sometimes was inclined to pose it, "social belief" and "social function"—a term which in Malinowski's often rather *un*Durkheimian usage tended to mean "actual behavior." From this point of view, the Australian monograph was not so much an armchair exercise as the prolegomenon to Malinowski's future fieldwork.

His entry into the field, however, was delayed by exigencies of funding. From 1911 on Seligman, along with Haddon and Rivers (from both of whom Malinowski also received guidance), pursued various possible fieldwork sites, including the Sudan, to which Seligman's own interests had shifted (MPL: BM/CS 2/22/12), and *faute de mieux,* back in Poland "among our peasants" (HP: BM/AH 11/12/11). However, it was not until 1914, when the British Association met in Australia, that Seligman got Malinowski a travelling fellowship, and he received his fare to the antipodes as secretary of the Association's anthropological section. His introduction to the field after the August meetings was clearly designed by Seligman to focus more intensively on the boundary region between two major ethnic groups his own earlier survey work had distinguished (Seligman 1910:2, 24–25; R. Firth 1975). Malinowski began by working in Port Moresby with Ahuia Ova, a village constable who had served as Seligman's primary informant in conversations "held on the verandah of the house where he lived with his uncle Taubada, the old chief of Hododai" (Seligman 1910:ix; BPL: BM/CS 9/10/14; F. Williams 1939).

Malinowski quickly became dissatisfied, however, with these "ethnographic explorations," on grounds that foreshadow his later ethnographic mode: "(1) I have rather little to do with the savages on the spot, do not observe them enough and (2) I do not speak their language" (1967:13). The latter defect he seems to have remedied when he settled down for more intensive research on the island of Mailu. By the time he left in late January he was quite fluent in the lingua franca of the area (Motu)—an accomplishment sufficiently remarkable that, lest it be disbelieved, he felt it necessary in his published account "to explicitly boast of my facility for acquiring a conversational command of foreign languages" (1915a:109). The problem of observation "on the spot" was not so easily solved: throughout the Mailu diary, Malinowski's days begin with the phrase "went to the village." There are momentary glimpses, however, of a more intimate ethnographic style. On a trip he made in early December surveying groups along the far southeastern coast, in several villages he stayed in the *dubu* or men's house—on one occasion for three successive nights during a native feast. Although "the stench, smoke, noise of people, dogs and pigs" left him exhausted, Malinowski clearly had a sense of the ethnographic potential of a more direct involvement and returned to Mailu resolved that he "must begin a new existence" (1967:49, 54–55).

Malinowski later suggested that the next few weeks on Mailu, when the absence of the local missionary left him "quite alone with the natives," were his most productive period on Mailu (1915a:109). One would hardly guess this from his diary, where he recounts being left with "*absolutely* nobody" for more than a week because he foolishly refused to pay the £2 the Mailu demanded to allow him to accompany them on a trading expedition (1967:62). But against such private records of frustration one must pose some of the material from the published Mailu ethnography. Recounting how he overcame difficulties in getting at "magico-religious" beliefs, Malinowski tells how at a certain point the Mailu became convinced that the deserted mission house in which he stayed was ghost-ridden. His "cook boy" and some village men who used to sleep there stopped doing so. Later, when one evening the conversation turned to ghosts, Malinowski, professing his ignorance of such matters, asked their advice, and got a great deal of information about topics previously closed to him. Generalizing in the published account, he commented: "My experience is that direct questioning of the native about a custom or belief never discloses their attitude of mind as thoroughly as the discussion of facts connected with the direct observation of a custom, or with a concrete occurence, in which both parties are materially concerned" (1915a:275). Implicit in that last phrase was the essence of a fieldwork style significantly different from that formalized by Rivers in *Notes and Queries.*

Malinowski was by no means entirely satisfied with his Mailu research (HP: BM/AH 10/15/15). Analyzing his data in Melbourne in the spring of 1915, he decided that work done alone with the natives was "incomparably more intensive than work done from white men's settlements, or even in any white man's company; the nearer one lives to a village and the more he sees actually of the natives the better" (1915a:109). The obvious conclusion was that he should live in the village. But as those nights in the *dubu* testify, total immersion was not easy for him. It has been argued that a solution was suggested to him during his brief stay on Woodlark Island early in 1915 (Wax 1972:7), where he lived "in a tent of palm leaves" only sixty meters from the village—"happy to be alone again with N. G. boys[,] particularly when I sat alone . . . gazing at the village . . ." (1967:92). The ethnographer's tent—fragile canvas artifact of civilized Europe—embodied a similar ambivalence. Pulling its flaps behind him, Malinowski could to some extent shut out the native world and retire to his novels when the strain of the very intensive study of a very limited area became too great.

The Trobriands: From Rider Haggard to Conrad

With financial support from the Australian government that had nominally interned him (Laracy 1976), Malinowski was off to the field again in June 1915. Although Seligman wanted him to go to Rossel Island to examine another of the "three points of the Massim triangle" (MPL: CS/BM n.d.), Malinowski set off for the Mambare district on the northern coast of New Guinea (BM/CS 5/6/15). He decided, however, to stop on the way on Kiriwina in the Trobriands, where Seligman had once worked briefly, because they were "the leaders of the whole material and artistic culture" of the area (BM/CS 6/13/15). Although totally "pacified" for more than a decade, the Trobriands were, compared to many island and coastal areas of New Guinea, relatively unacculturated. Malinowski arrived during the season of the *mila-mala* festival, the ceremonial high point of the annual cycle, and his attention was immediately engaged by the phenomena that were to be the subjects of his later monographs: the "ceremonial gardening," the "beliefs and ceremonies about the spirits," and their "peculiar and interesting" system of trading (BM/CS 7/30/15). In the Trobriands—in contrast to the islands of the Torres Straits—these did not have to be *recaptured* from the memories of elders, or *reconstructed* from fragmentary data surviving into the present, or *recreated* by people cajoled into performing defunct ceremonies. Here they could be directly observed. More than that, this was apparently one of those cases where there was a close "fit" between ethnographer and subject—Malinowski later contrasted the relative ease of his work in Kiriwina with difficulties he encountered elsewhere (1967:227). At the time, he was clearly captivated. When he received news of the unexpected departure of the Mambare missionary from whom he had hoped to get an ethnographic orientation, he extended his Trobriand stay, apologizing to Seligman for remaining in an area he had already covered. By mid-October, when he fired his interpreter, Malinowski already had enough Kiriwinian so that for three weeks he had only used pidgin English "a sentence or so per diem." Having moved inland from the government station to the village of Omarakana, he wrote to Seligman that he was "absolutely alone amongst niggers [*sic*]." Denying himself both whiskey and women ("the other 'white man's solace'"), he was getting "such damned good stuff" that he had decided not to go to Mambare after all (9/24/15, 10/19/15). Save for fortnightly "Capuan days" he enjoyed back on the coast in Gusaweta (1967:259), he apparently remained in Omarakana for almost six months.

This is not the place to attempt to answer all the questions raised about Malinowski's fieldwork by the "revelations" of his diaries—Joycean documents whose adequate interpretation awaits a detailed indexing and contextualization with other materials (cf. GS 1986b, 1990). Perhaps because they are not primarily "about" his fieldwork, they do not in any case treat his first Trobriand expedition (1967:99). We know from later reflections that despite dispensing with an interpreter, Malinowski was not yet able to "follow easily conversations among the natives themselves" (1935:I, 453). We know also that he was still very much under Rivers' methodological influence: "it was my ambition to develop the principle of the 'genealogical method' into a wider and more ambitious scheme to be entitled the 'method of objective documentation'" (1935:I, 326; RiP: BM/WR 10/15/15). For contemporary evidence of his methodological concerns, the best source is "Baloma: The Spirits of the Dead in the Trobriands" (1916), which he wrote during the interval between his first and second Trobriand trips.

Despite the suggestion of one critic that Malinowski's (actually, Marett's) slogan was "study the ritual and not the belief" (Jarvie 1964:44), and despite his characterization as an "obsessional empiricist" (Leach 1957:120), what is striking in "Baloma" is precisely the attempt to penetrate native belief, and his insistence on the inadequacy of any uninterpreted "pure facts"—and by implication Rivers' "concrete method"—to the task (cf. Panoff 1972:43–45). "Baloma" reveals Malinowski as an aggressively interactive fieldworker. In contrast to *Notes and Queries,* he defends the use of leading questions under certain circumstances (1916:264); he questions beliefs the natives take for granted (208); he suggests alternative possibilities (227–28); he forces them on apparent contradictions (167); he pushes them, as he says, "to the metaphysical wall" (236)—and is upon occasion pushed toward it himself. Rejecting the notion that it was "possible to wrap up in a blanket a certain number of 'facts as you find them' and bring them all back for the home student to generalize upon," he insists that "field work consists only and exclusively in the interpretation of the chaotic social reality, in subordinating it to general rules" (238). In at least one critical instance, this approach seems to have led Malinowski astray: his trader friend

Billy Hancock later wrote to him indicating that the natives had never corrected an early interpretation of the reincarnation of the *baloma* because they were afraid to "contradict the doctor" (GS 1977a). But Malinowski's ethnographic style seems also to have generated a large and variegated body of data. In marked contrast to the ethnographic notes of Haddon, which contain a disproportionate amount of second-hand material, derived either from printed sources or correspondence with "men on the spot" (HP:passim), and with those of Rivers, which tend to have the schematic character one might expect of the "concrete method" (RiP:passim), Malinowski's field notes are richly documented in the materials of his own observation, recorded to a considerable extent in the native language (MPL:passim).

From a substantive point of view "Baloma" is a treatise on the relation of individual to collective belief; viewed methodologically, it is an attempt to deal in a general way with the problems posed by this mass of information, and particularly with the problem of informant variation. How was one to synthesize as one "belief" the "always fragmentary" and "at times hopelessly inadequate and contradictory" answers to the question "How do the natives imagine the return of the *baloma?*" (1916:241). Perhaps because he was temperamentally disinclined to allow them to contradict him rather than each other, Malinowski's solution—arrived at *ex post facto* in the analysis of his field data—was to distinguish between "social ideas or dogmas" (beliefs embodied in institutions, customs, rites, and myths, which, "believed and acted upon by all," were absolutely standardized), "the general behavior of the natives towards the object of a belief," and opinions or interpretations that might be offered by individuals, groups of specialists, or even the majority of the members of a community (245, 252–53). Some such distinction between cultural idea and individual opinion, often overlaid with one between "rules and regularities" and actual behavior, was characteristic of all Malinowski's later methodological prescriptions, as well as his more theoretically oriented ethnographic writings (cf. 1922b:24). Often seen as anti-Durkheimian, it was anti-Riversian as well. Though it apparently privileged a customary or institutional realm where native belief was homogeneous, it gave tremendous weight to the conflict of cultural rule and individual impulse which made savage society "not a consistent logical scheme, but rather a seething mixture of conflicting principles" (1926c:121).

After a year and a half in Australia, Malinowski left for the Trobriands again late in October 1917. The fact that he returned is itself methodologically significant. Shortly after arriving back in Sydney in 1916, Malinowski was still thinking in terms of pursuing Seligman's Rossel Island project as soon as he "worked out the Trobriand material" (HP: BM/AH 5/25/16). But it is clear that his understanding of the demands of "intensive study" evolved in the interim, and when official permission to visit Rossel was denied, he was free to return to Kiriwina (Laracy 1976). Writing to Frazer en route back, he noted how "whilst in the field, . . . the more elementary aspects" of many subjects "become soon so familiar they escape notice"; at the same time, "once away from the natives," memory could not take the place of "direct observation." He had therefore spent much of the Australian interim going through all his material to create a "condensed outline," which had opened "a whole series of new questions" he now needed to pursue (FP: BM/JF 10/25/17).

Although Malinowski did not settle this time in Omarakana, his return to the same area, after having left it for an extended period, may also (if the experience of many other anthropologists applies) have helped to cement more closely his relationships with Trobriand informants. These were scarcely the relationships of "social parity" that one retrospective (and distinctly American democratic) commentator has suggested are a condition of participant observation (Wax 1972:8). Malinowski's retinue of two or three New Guinean "boys" (one of whom on at least one occasion he seems to have struck [1967:250]) does indeed call up images of the colonial "petty lordship" manifest also in some of his diary fantasies (140, 167, 235). But in a stratified society like the Trobriands (where the chief sat upon a platform so commoners need not crawl upon the ground in passing [Wax 1972:5; cf. Malinowski 1929a:32–33]), social parity—which bears a problematic relationship to understanding—is itself a rather problematic notion. That Malinowski, in return for half a tobacco stick a day, was allowed to pitch his tent in the restricted central area of Omarakana (1935:I, 41), that he was apparently addressed in terms connoting high rank (1929a: 61), and doubtless did not walk bent-backed in front of his next-door neighbor, the village chief To'uluwa, may have opened up more areas of Trobriand life to him than any other readily available status—even as it also may have in some respects distorted his perspective (cf. Weiner 1976).

The critical issues would seem to be the mode of interaction and the quality of relationships he was able to establish. Insofar as the activity of the fieldworker may be divided into different modes (participation, observation, and interrogation [Wax 1972:12]—or perhaps more neutrally, doing, seeing, and talking), it is certainly true that Malinowski (like every other fieldworker since?) gathered more information by the last two than by the first. But one might argue that from the point of view of gathering information, participation is to some extent a contextual phenomenon—as the often very brief references to his actual fieldwork in the diary of the second Trobriand trip suggest: "I went to a garden and talked with the Teyava people of gardening and garden magic" (1967:276). In the case of frequently sparer references such as "*buritila'ulo* in Wakayse-Kabwaku"

Malinowski at work, Omarakana. "Feeling of ownership: it is I who will describe them or create them. . . . This island, though not 'discovered' by me, is for the first time experienced artistically and mastered intellectually" (Malinowski 1967:140 [December 1, 1917], 236 [March 26, 1918]). (Courtesy of Helena Wayne Malinowska and the London School of Economics)

(291), it is even harder to say just what went on. That is the sole reference in the diary to a major event in his fieldwork, a competitive food-display recounted in some detail in *Coral Gardens and Their Magic* (1935:I, 181–87). Although the diary indicates that a good bit of Malinowski's "talking" was in one-to-one sessions with informants compensated by tobacco, it is evident throughout his ethnographies that much of it was in the context of events he observed and ceremonies at which he "assisted"—a vague team, perhaps reflecting the meaning of the French *assister,* but appropriately chosen by Malinowski to imply a certain degree of participation. There were many situations in which his participation was severely limited indeed. His diary reveals him as always left on the beach when the natives left on a Kula expedition (1967:234, 245) – and *Argonauts* suggests why: when an expedition Malinowski had been allowed to join late in 1915 was forced back by adverse winds, To'uluwa attributed this bad luck to his presence (1922b:479). But if he was sometimes forced to rely on simple question-and-answer, Malinowski clearly regarded this as a distinctly inferior style of work. Although he felt that concrete documentation and the collection of texts were essential components of a correct style, his methodological ideal – frequently realized in practice – remained that established in Mailu: discussion with one or more informants of a mutually (if differentially) experienced activity or event. Only thus could one "integrate native behavior into native significance" (1935:I, 86).

As far as the quality of his relationships with the Trobrianders is concerned, it is a serious mistake to judge these simply on the basis of a selective reading of the more negative sections of the diary (Hsu 1979). Without minimizing the pervasive tone of loneliness, frustration, and aggression or the evolutionary racial terms in which these feelings were often expressed, without denying the explicit racial epithets,[2] one must keep in mind that the diary functioned as a safety valve for feelings Malinowski was unable or unwilling to express in his daily relations. At the level of methodological principle, Malinowski insisted on the critical importance of "personal friendships [to] encourage spontaneous confidences and the

2. On the basis of the facsimile page of the Polish original reproduced as frontispiece of the published translation of Malinowski's diaries (1967), it has been argued (Leach 1980) that "nigger" is an inappropriate translation of the actual term Malinowski used: *nigrami.* I was assured by my one-time student Edward Martinek, who did research on Malinowski in a number of archives in Cracow, Poland, that *nigrami* is not properly a Polish word. What Malinowski seems to have done is to render the English racial epithet phonetically ("nigr") and add the Polish ending "-ami," which I am told by Norbert Guterman, the translator of the diaries, indicates the instrumental case (cf. Symmons 1982). That Malinowski knew and used the English epithet at the time of the Trobriand diary is evident in several sources quoted in this paper. The significance of his usage is a complex matter (cf. GS 1968b). It is certainly not to be taken casually as "proof" of thoroughgoing racism. But neither will it do to argue that the word did not then have derogatory racial meaning. Spencer's reaction to Gillen's usage suggests otherwise. An unpublished fragment of Haddon's from the 1890s speaks of "niggers" as "a term of reproach which implies a hatred and superciliousness similar to that with which the Jews regard the Gentiles, the Greeks the Barbarians, and which the Chinese still hold for 'foreign devils'" (HP:[1894]). Indeed, as early as 1858 Sir Henry Maine reproved those who "contemned the idiosyncracies of their dark-skinned fellow-creatures: If an Englishman thinks and talks of a Hindoo as a Nigger, what will be his ideas of a Bheel or a Khond?" (Maine 1858:129). These examples suggest that the key to usage lies in the geography of race relations. *Nigrami* does not appear in Malinowski's first New Guinea diary, nor does "niggers" in the letters of this period, but only after he had spent several years on the colonial periphery.

repetition of intimate gossip" (1929a:282–83). How "real" these friendships were is too complex an issue to venture on here. One may assume that they shared the inherent ambiguity and asymmetry of almost all ethnographic relations (cf. the suggestive remarks of Forge 1967). But it is surely presuming a great deal to characterize Malinowski as "an anthropologist who hates the natives" (Hsu 1979:521).

As for the Trobrianders' reaction to him, we can be sure that when they were wearied by his questions or hurt by his occasional angry outbursts, they rebuffed him. But any number of details in both the diary and the ethnographies—particularly *The Sexual Life of Savages,* which is the most revealing of the imponderabilia of his daily ethnographic behavior—testify that he was usually on fairly good terms with them. Clearly, it would be a mistake to take at face value the ironic passage in *Argonauts* where he suggests that he was accepted as a necessary nuisance "mitigated by donations of tobacco" (1922b:6; cf. Young 1979:14–15). The number of his informants (who frequently appear, one may note, as identifiable individuals in the ethnographies), the *kayaku* or congregations in his tent (1967:103), the magic offered for him during illness (1922b:244), the numerous sexual confidences (1929a:passim), suggest something more than a necessary nuisance. No doubt he remained in Trobriand minds a European, set apart from them by many things—some of them rather subtle and even paradoxical, like his encyclopedic collection of private magic, of which no Trobriander commanded more than a small fragment (1929a:373; cf. below, p. 252). But he was clearly a European of a special sort—as was evident in their surprise that he, so unmissionary in other respects, should have argued the "missionary view" of physiological paternity (1929a:187). It was evident even after his death, when he was still remembered as "the man of songs" (Hogbin 1946)—doubtless from the time when in order to frighten away *mulukwausi,* or flying witches, he sang "kiss my ass" to melodies from Wagner (1967:157).

Distracted by all that venting of negative affect, one may neglect the insights his diaries offer into Malinowski's ultimate ethnographic purpose. In the Mailu diary, Malinowski was still greatly under the influence of Rivers, whom he described to Haddon in 1916 as his "patron sain[t] in fieldwork" (HP: BM/AH 5/25/16). In contrast, the second Trobriand diary reveals Malinowski frequently in debate with Rivers, not only in his "concrete" methodological but also in his "historical" interpretive mode (1967: 114, 161, 229, 254, 280). If the *History of Melanesian Society* was to be the outcome of the turn from evolution to history, then the place of diachronic approaches in ethnological inquiry seemed problematic indeed. Unlike Rivers, who was (at this point in his career) willing to put aside psychological problems (1916), Malinowski both by temperament and ethnographic experience was impelled toward them. He did not reject history entirely—as late as 1922 he was still talking about doing a migration study in the Riversian mode (1922b:232). But it is clear already in "Baloma," and quite explicit in the early pages of the Trobriand diary, that psychological problems were "the deepest essence of [his] investigations": "to discover what are [the native's] main passions, the motives for his conduct, his aims, . . . his essential deepest way of thinking" (1967:119). At this point, he saw himself "back to Bastian"—or, in an English context, perhaps to Frazer. But in contrast to that of the evolutionists, Malinowski's social psychology was grounded not in some hypothetical diachronic sequence, but in the on-going events of a contemporary ethnographic situation, closely observed by a method that sought to probe more deeply than Rivers ever had. The contrast was suggested in ideas he recorded for the preface to his planned ethnography: "[Jan] Kubary as a concrete [i.e., Riversian] methodologist; Mikluho-Maclay as a new type. Marett's comparison: *early ethnographers as prospectors*" (1967:155; cf. below, p. 219). It is in the context of this implied contrast between the surveying of an ethnographic surface and the mining of its deeper psychological meaning—as well as that of transforming national identity—that one must gloss Malinowski's reported proclamation of his ultimate anthropological ambition: "Rivers is the Rider Haggard of anthropology; I shall be the Conrad" (R. Firth 1957:6; cf. MPY: BM/B. Seligman 6/21/18; cf. Kirschner 1968; Langham 1981:171–77).

Argonauts as Euhemerist Myth

That self-proclaiming epigram is of course multiply-meaningful, and one may find in it also perhaps a clue to the method of Malinowski's ethnography—taking that word now not in the sense of recording ethnographic data in the field, but in the sense of its subsequent representation in a published monograph (cf. Marcus & Cushman 1982). Malinowski (whose choice of adjectives can scarcely have been accidental) was himself acutely conscious of the chasm between "the *brute* material of information . . . and the final *authoritative* presentation of the results" (1922b:3)—or, as he elsewhere equally revealingly phrased it, between "the slight dust of little bits of information—here and there, chaotic, unequal even in their credibility" and the "final ideals of knowledge": "the essential nigger [*sic*] as an illustration and document to our Conception of Man" (MPL: "Method" n.d.). The problem was how "to convince my readers" that the ethnographic information offered them was "objectively acquired knowledge" and not simply "a subjectively formed notion" (ibid.). At the level of explicit formulation, Malinowski usually tended to discuss the issue in terms one might expect of a physicist-turned-ethnographer under the methodological shadow of Rivers. Just as in "an experimental contribution to physical or chemical science," the critical thing was to be "absolutely candid" about one's method (1922b:2). But although Malinowski devoted detailed (if not fully revealing) attention to certain aspects of his method, his consciousness of other aspects is only infrequently and implicitly evident. We may assume from his epigrammatic proclamation an awareness that the ethnographer was ultimately a literary artificer. Nevertheless, his explicit models are all from Science, and we are left to our own literary critical devices to explicate the method of his artifice (cf. Payne 1981)—and thereby to appreciate fully the manner in which he constituted his authority, which may be regarded as the prototype for the authority of all of modern ethnography, in both the senses I have suggested (cf. Clifford 1983).

The most explicit attempt to validate that authority is in the introductory chapter of *Argonauts* (1922b:1–25). There Malinowski groups the "principles of method" under three main headings: "proper conditions for ethnographic work" (6); knowledge of the "principles," "aims," and "results" of modern "scientific study" (8); and the application of "special methods" of "collecting, manipulating, and fixing" evidence (6). The latter are also grouped under three rubrics: "statistic documentation by concrete evidence" of the "rules and regularities of tribal life" (17, 11); collecting "the imponderabilia of actual life and of typical behavior" in order to put "flesh and blood" on the "skeleton" of the tribal constitution (20, 17); and the creation of a *corpus inscriptionum* of native opinion and utterance to illustrate "typical ways of thinking and feeling" (23–24). Viewed in terms of specific methodological canons, Malinowski's introduction offers little Rivers had not proposed in *Notes and Queries.* His method is less a matter of disembodied rules, however, than of total personal style. His apparently more innovative methodological injunctions—the keeping of an "ethnographic diary," the making of "synoptic charts," and the preliminary sketching of results—all emphasize the constructive problem-generating role of the ethnographer. But what is really critical is to place this "active huntsman" in a certain situation. Cut off from "the company of white men," he will "naturally" seek the society of natives not his "natural companions," engaging in "natural intercourse" with them rather than relying on "paid, and often bored, informants." Waking up "every morning to a day presenting itself more or less as it does to the native," he finds that his life "soon adopts quite a natural course very much in harmony with his surroundings." Corrected for repeated "breaches of etiquete," he has "to learn how to behave." Taking part "in a way" in village life, he ceases "to be a disturbing element in the tribal life" (7–8). Loneliness thus becomes the *sine qua non* of ethnographic knowledge, the means by which one becomes able in a *natural* way to observe a culture from the inside, and thereby "grasp the native's point of view, his relation to life, and realize *his* vision of *his* world" (25).

Although Malinowski tried to formulate the "ethnographer's magic" as a prosaic "application of a number of rules of common sense and well-known scientific principles" (6), his real problem was not so much to tell his readers how to accomplish the ultimate divinatory task, as to convince them that it could be done, and that he had done it. If "empty programme" were to be translated into "the result of personal experience" (13), then his own experience of the native's experience must become the reader's experience as well—a task that scientific analysis yielded up to literary art.

In this context, Malinowski's Frazerian apprenticeship (and perhaps also those tent-bound bouts of novel reading in the Trobriands) served his ethnography very well indeed. As early as 1917, he confided in Frazer that it was "through the study of your works that I have come to realize the paramount importance of vividness and colour in descriptions of life" (JF: BM/JF 10/25/17). Throughout his book Frazer's "scene/act ratio" is employed to place the reader imaginatively within the actual physical setting of the events Malinowski reconstructs: "When, on a hot day, we enter the deep shadow of fruit trees and palms, and find ourselves in the midst of the wonderfully designed and ornamented houses hiding here and there in irregular groups among the green . . ." (1922b:35). More important still, perhaps, is a device one might call the "author/reader equation": "Imagine yourself suddenly set down surrounded by all your gear, alone on a tropical beach close to a native village while the launch . . . which has brought you sails away out of sight . . ." (4). Introduced to Malinowski's opening methodological excursus in this ambiguously autobiographical fashion, we are encouraged not only to share his ethnographic "tribulations," but—partaking of the authority his experience legitimated—to come along with him as he follows the Trobrianders on their "perilous and difficult enterprises." As Malinowski's original title (*Kula: A Tale of Native Enterprise and Adventure in Eastern New Guinea* [HP: BM/AH 11/25/21]) suggested, his ethnography has essentially a narrative structure. Beginning with the construction of the *waga* or canoe, through its launching and departure, we are taken on an ambitious overseas expedition across the sea arm of Pilolu (with a pause for the account of a mythical shipwreck), on to the Amphletts, Tewara, and Sanaroa, stopping for magical ceremonies on the beach of Sarubwoyna, to the climactic Kula exchanges in Dobu and the journey home—where we witness a return visit from the Dobuans, and tie up the loose ends of the "inland Kula" and its "remaining branches and offshoots." With Malinowski at our side intervening when necessary to explain particular ethnographic details or to provide more extended disquisitions on the sociology, mythology, magic, and languages of the Kula, we have followed the Trobrianders through the epic event that periodically focusses all the energies of their existence. At the end we are prepared to believe that we have glimpsed their "vision of the world," and "the reality which [they] breathe and by which [they] live" (517).

This is by no means all that Malinowski's narrative style has accomplished. Characteristically, chapters open with references to a present action or situation: "the canoe, painted and decorated, stands now ready to be launched" (1922b:146); "our party, sailing from the north, reach first the main island of Gumasila" (267). True, there are occasional contrasts between "nowadays" and "olden days," and several chapters in fact end with speculations of an historical diffusionist character (289). Characteristically, however, Malinowski writes in the active voice and present tense, employing what one critic has called a "syntax of agency" (Payne 1981:427). By bringing the reader along as eyewitness to the on-going Kula events, he establishes the conviction that they exemplify life in the Trobriands to this very day. Previous ethnographies had described reconstructed behavior as if it were present practice, and subsequent ethnographies (including his own) did not emulate the event-narrative form of *Argonauts.* But it was Malinowski's *Argonauts* that validated the temporal context in which modern ethnography is normally situated: the vague and essentially atemporal moment we call "the ethnographic present" (Burton 1988).

As the Homeric (and Frazerian) resonances of its actually published title suggest, something was going on in this primal ethnographic scene besides the narrative re-creation of actual experience. At one point in his discussion of the Trobriand shipwreck myth, Malinowski suggests that it is not always easy "to make a distinction between what is mere mythopoetic fiction and what is . . . drawn from actual experience" (1922b:236); and despite his professed methodological candor, it is clear that Malinowski himself sometimes blurred that distinction. It takes an attentive reader to realize from the printed narrative that he never actually sailed with a Kula expedition after that ill-fated venture toward Kitava in 1915. At one point he does in fact explicitly tell us that most of his narrative is "reconstructed," arguing that for one who has "seen much of the native's tribal life and has a good grip over intelligent informants," such reconstruction is neither "fanciful" nor "very difficult" (376). But along the way we have been encouraged by ambiguous phrases ("I have seen, indeed followed") to believe that he had done something more than catch up in a cutter (1967: 242). Similarly, while attentive readers may note that he did sometimes pay informants (1922b:409), without the benefit of his diary one would scarcely guess just how often he retreated to Billy Hancock's compound at Gusaweta for refuge from "sickness and surfeit of native" (6). From that same diary we know that his time reckoning was somewhat unreliable—

in general, he was not actually in the field for quite so long as *Argonauts* suggests (cf. 1922b:16, 1967:216).

A certain vagueness as to the situation of events in time is of course one aspect of the myth-making process. Another is the peopling of the mythopoeic moment with characters of archetypical significance. In this context it is interesting to consider the cast of characters of *Argonauts* (cf. Payne 1981). Most numerous, and manifestly central to the account, are the "natives": distinguished often by tribal group or status, frequently named, occasionally subsumed within the category "savage" (and in the privacy of his diary, by the epithet "nigger"), but most explicitly denied the archetypifying capitalization of Primitive Economic Man—a rubric Malinowski was at some pains to destroy (1922b:60). Brushed at times with the exotic colors of noble savagery, they are more often painted in rather prosaic tones. Although it is organized around their adventure, and they are on one occasion referred to as "homeric heroes" (295), they are not in fact the heroes of Malinowski's romance. His attitude toward them is often that of "gentle irony"—a literary mode which was to characterize much of modern ethnography (Payne 1981:421; cf. Clifford 1988; Thornton 1983). The ethnographer not only is capable of sharing their vision of their world, but he knows things about it that they will never know, and brings to light phenomena which "had remained hidden even from those in whom they happened" (1922b:397).

Such phenomena were also hidden from the second group of characters: "the minor cast of cramped minds" who had "gotten the natives all wrong" in the past—administrators, missionaries, traders, all "full of the biassed and pre-judged opinions inevitable in the average practical man" who had "lived for years in the place . . . and who yet hardly knew one thing about them really well" (Payne 1981:421). Some of them were clearly archetypifications of painful experiences Malinowski had with very real people—notably the Mailu missionary Saville, who had in fact provided him with valuable information, but whose "underhanded dealings" had first provoked his professed "hatred of missionaries" (1967:31, 42). In the methodological introduction to *Argonauts* they all appear briefly as a "stock of strawmen" who by stark contrast highlight the virtues of Malinowski's method. Even previous ethnographers of the concrete Riversian sort are by implication chided for their failure to come down off the verandah.

In contrast to these two sets of characters is a third, who stands apart, capitalized, in heroic singularity: the Ethnographer. Appositional equation to the first person singular leaves no doubt as to his actual identity (1922b:34), and the equation is confirmed iconographically in photographs of "the Ethnographer's tent" placed strategically at the beginning and end of the book, before and after the expedition it recounts (16, 481). Marking him off from all other Europeans, the methodological introduction has affirmed his divinatory powers. At its end we know full well that only he, who ventured there alone and made his loneliness the instrument of divining knowledge, can now lead us also into the heart of darkness.

Considered in this light, *Argonauts* is itself a kind of euhemerist myth—divinizing, however, not its ostensible Trobriand heroes, but the European Jason who brings back the Golden Fleece of ethnographic knowledge. Long before Susan Sontag used Lévi-Strauss as the model of the "Anthropologist as Hero" (1966), Malinowski had created the role for himself. But that his purpose was not simply self-serving is evident in unpublished notes toward his introduction, in which he was concerned not only with the problem of auctorial authority (how to "convince my readers"), but also with the situation of the ethnographic beginner, who enters the field "paralyzed with fear of all sorts of traps and barriers" (MPL: "Method" n.d.). In this context, it seems clear that the introduction to *Argonauts* was never intended really to be a "true" description of Malinowski's fieldwork experience. Description was only the device by which he made prescription compelling. Even if the self-advancing striving of his vigorous ego had allowed, it would not have served his confidence-inspiring prescriptive purposes to dwell there upon his own frustrations and failures (cf. the later relatively innocuous "Confessions of Ignorance and Failure" [1935:I, 452–82]). He wanted to make the apprentice ethnographer "aware beforehand that we had a method of attacking" all those "initial difficulties which are so very hard to surmount" ("Method," n.d.). More than that, he wanted to legitimate the style of fieldwork upon which that novice was to embark. For novice ethnographers as much as general readers, the problem was not so much to enumerate principles of method, but to convince them that the task could be done. In this context, every aspect of *Argonauts*—structure as well as argument, style as well as content, anecdote as well as precept, implication as well as statement, omission as well as inclusion—all contributed to the euhemerist validating myth.

Several years later, in writing on the role of "Myth in Primitive Psychology," Malinowski emphasized the intermingling of its pragmatic and legitimating functions: myth was at once "a warrant, a charter, and often even a practical guide to the activities with which it is connected" (1926a: 108). It was "not an explanation in satisfaction of a scientific interest, but a narrative resurrection of a primeval reality, told in satisfaction of deep religious wants, moral cravings, social submissions, assertions, even practical requirements" (101). Expressing, enhancing, and codifying belief, vouching for "the efficiency of ritual," it came "into play when rite, ceremony, or a social or moral rule demands justification, warrant of antiquity, reality, and sanctity" (107). Malinowski had spoken explicitly in his diary of "the revolution" he wanted to "effect in social anthropology" (1967:289), and it is hard to read his later essay, with its final spirited plea for an "open-air anthropology" (1926a:147), without feeling that he had sought more or less consciously in *Argonauts* to provide a mythic charter for its central ritual.

Malinowski's Mythic Charter and Modern Ethnography

Whether or not he went about it in consciously mythopoeic fashion, Malinowski succeeded in validating the authority of his method to both readers and apprentice ethnographers alike. The world's premier reader of ethnographies, Sir James G. Frazer, gave the work his imprimatur: living "as a native among the natives for many months," Malinowski had portrayed them "in the round and not in the flat"—not like Molière's "dummies dressed up to look very like human beings," but like the "solid" characters of Cervantes and Shakespeare, "drawn not from one side only but from many" (Malinowski 1922b:vii, ix). Seligman, whose ethnographic taste was as prosaic as his fieldwork style (R. Firth 1975), was less impressed. Despite the fact that *Argonauts* was dedicated to him, he continued to regard *Baloma* as Malinowski's best work, tending to view his later writings as compromised by popularizing purpose (MPL: CS/BM 8/5/31). With Rivers recently dead, it was Haddon who spoke in public for the Cambridge School, lauding the book as "the high-water mark of ethnological investigation and interpretation," which would "prove of great value for the guidance of future fieldworkers" (Haddon 1922).

That it served as such reflects the fact that no other early published work of the prewar cohort paid such explicit and extended attention to ethnographic (as opposed to interpretive) method (cf. Radcliffe-Brown 1922). Their initial ethnographic reports were drably institutional monographic publications (Hocart 1922; Karsten 1923; Landtman 1917) whose manifest level of methodological self-consciousness in one case lent itself to Marett's revealing prefatory comment: "Touring, indeed, proves the ideal method of anthropological research" (Jenness & Ballantyne 1920:7). In this context, the first chapter of *Argonauts* (published, with Haddon's assistance, by a leading commercial publisher [HP: BM/AH 12/20/21]) was the single most accessible statement of the "modern sociological method of fieldwork"—especially for nonanthropologists, who would be unlikely to read Rivers' chapters in *Notes and Queries.* Effectively appropriating to himself experience that had in fact been shared by others (including "The Ethnographer's Tent," which Westermarck, for instance, had taken to Morocco [1927:158]), at once archetypifying it and rendering it in concrete narrative form, Malinowski validated not only his own fieldwork but that of "modern anthropology" (cf. Panoff 1972:54). A man of great ambition and no mean entrepreneurial talent, he was able to make himself the spokesman of a methodological revolution, both within anthropology, and in some ways more important, to the nonanthropological academic and intellectual community.

By 1926, when he was the "star" of the Hanover Conference of the [American] Social Science Research Council, Malinowski had won over a critically important sector of that community: the "philanthropoids" of the Rockefeller Foundation. In the late 1920s he served as their chief informal anthropological advisor, much to the dismay of Grafton Elliot Smith, who could not understand why "the sole method of studying mankind is to sit on a Melanesian island for a couple of years and listen to the gossip of the villagers" (RA: ES/Herrick 2/13/27). For a time, the seminars of Elliot Smith's diffusionist protégé William Perry at University College rivaled Malinowski's in attracting students to anthropology. But reinforced by the requirement that the Rockefeller-funded fieldworkers of the International African Institute should spend a year in his seminar, Malinowski's methodological charisma soon won out (see below, pp. 193–95). Most of those who were to claim the status of social anthropologist in the British sphere served an apprenticeship with Malinowski; and while a number of them were later to turn away from him to find their theoretical inspiration in Radcliffe-Brown, they continued to regard Malinowski as the archetypical fieldworker (Gluckman 1963, 1967). Even in America, which had its own Boasian variant of the mythic fieldwork charter, Malinowski's influence was asserted, both from a distance and in person on periodic visits after 1926. Despite the fact that the railroad and the Model T facilitated a more transient fieldwork, young ethnographers seem to have measured themselves against a Malinowskian model. Thus Sol Tax, emulating Malinowski's "ideal method of ethnography" (and having no knowledge of those "cook boys" mentioned only in the diary), started out his work among the Fox in the summer of 1932 by living "in a camp of my own in the midst of native camps," only to discover that the Indians thought him silly to "stay out there and cook for myself like a squaw when I could get to town in five minutes" (Blanchard 1979:423).

That the central mythic symbol of the tent could have such potency from afar suggests some final observations. Malinowski seems to have devoted more attention in his seminars to discussing details of fieldwork method than is often now the case, and the correspondence of his students from the field indicates that those synoptic charts were taken very seriously (Richards 1957:25; cf. MPL: AR/BM 7/8/30). But the fieldwork style he validated was less a matter of concrete prescription than of placing oneself in a situation where one might have a certain type of experience. Like the situations that elicited Trobriand magic, it was one that was initially threatening and could be dangerous, and in which "the elements of chance and accident" often determined success or failure. As Malinowski (echoing Marett) had suggested in "Myth in Primitive Psychology," the function of magic consisted in "the bridging over of gaps and inadequacies in highly important activities not yet completely mastered by man" (1926a:139–40). The gap between the specific methodological prescriptions of fieldwork and the vaguely defined goals of ethnographic knowledge had thus to be filled by what Malinowski himself had called "the ethnographer's magic" (1922b:6). And just as in primitive psychology myth functioned "especially where there is a sociological strain" (1926a:126), in anthropological psychology it functioned especially where there was an epistemological strain.

Despite his breezy public confidence that all would be well once anthropologists stepped outside the "closed study of the theorist" and came down from "the verandah of the missionary compound" into the "open air of the anthropological field" (1926a:99, 146–47), it is clear that at times Malinowski felt that strain, and we may assume that so also did those who followed in his footsteps. In retrospect, however, one is struck with the relative dearth of discussion of certain underlying assumptions of fieldwork method (cf. Nash & Wintrob 1972). It is tempting to suggest that Malinowski's ethnographic bravura made it seem unnecessary. Even those whose own research did not live up to (or even model itself upon) his prescriptions were nevertheless sustained by his preemptive archetypification. Thus it was that the problem of instant linguistic competence has rarely been raised either as a general issue (cf. Lowie 1940) or in regard to particular ethnographic monographs—despite the fact that few apprentice ethnographers may be presumed to share Malinowski's remarkable linguistic facility. For almost four decades Malinowski's mythic charter functioned to sustain the ethnographic enterprise, helping several generations of aspiring ethnographers to "get on with the work." By the time his diaries were published, however, changing colonial circumstances had fundamentally altered the ethnographer's situation; and in the context of a protracted epistemological malaise (heightened no doubt by their publication), it has seemed necessary to many anthropologists to examine more systematically all that was so casually subsumed by that deceptively innocent charm phrase: "the ethnographer's magic."

2

The Boas Plan for the Study of American Indian Languages

Although not published until 1974, this essay was written for a conference on the history of linguistics held at the Newberry Library in Chicago in February 1968, during what was for me a critical transition year. In recounting the genesis of the conference, Dell Hymes indicated that the "germ of the idea" had emerged from the Social Science Research Council's 1962 conference on the history of anthropology—which had been, as it were, my official debut as an historian of anthropology (Hymes 1974:vii; cf. Hymes 1962). During the fall preceding the Newberry conference, I was at the University of Pennsylvania, where I sat in on Hymes's course in anthropological linguistics during the first leg of a two-stage fellowship for postdoctoral training in anthropology—the second leg of which concluded with my appointment in the Department of Anthropology at the University of Chicago. By this time, I had published several articles in the history of anthropology (1960, 1968a), as well as the programmatic manifesto on historicism and presentism in the historiography of the human sciences (1965). That essay was originally planned as a joint venture with Hymes, and incorporated a long passage by him arguing the need for a history of linguistic anthropology, which I cited as an instance of "enlightened presentism." The essay was circulated to the participants before the linguistics conference, and my charge was to speak generally about "transcending 'textbook' chronicles and apologetics." However, my recent brief (and impermanent) initiation into one of the more technically demanding areas of anthropological inquiry made so general an exhortation seem somehow presumptuous. So I chose instead to try to contribute substantively to the historiography of linguistic anthropology.

As it turned out, that project was not without presumption. My review of the early linguistic correspondence and publications of Franz Boas suggested that a previous account (Voegelin 1952) based solely on published materials had been subject to a certain presentist distortion. I offered my recontextualization of the "Boas plan" somewhat hesitantly, however, since some of the issues were at or beyond the margins of my technical competence. Emboldened by a generally favorable reception, even by the author whose work mine qualified, I belatedly acquiesced in the organizers' request to write a brief historiographical piece as well. In it, I argued, along loosely Kuhnian lines, against the notion that "at a certain point scientific linguistics 'begins'—and henceforth everything is part of the same unbroken universe of discourse" (1974e:511). Suggesting that even in the case of figures as close to us as Boas, "we must reject the notion that our perception of the linguistic past is immediate or direct" (514), I insisted that history was more a moral than a technical discipline, requiring above all a certain attitude, analogous to that of the anthropological fieldworker: a self-conscious awareness and suspension not only of disbelief, as in the theatre, but also of beliefs "about the true nature of linguistic method and theory" (517).

Paradoxically, however, the overall effect of this brief venture into the history of linguistics was to convince me that there were limitations to the kind of history a nonlinguist could write. Not only did I have trouble following certain interpretations that seemed clearly presentist; I had difficulty also "reading the *Handbook of American Indian Languages*, or interpreting the field notes of Boas, or the field reports of Sapir" (1974e:518). As an historian, I could more easily treat "broad questions concerning the relation of race and language, or of linguistic and evolutionary theory, or the origins and philosophy of language." But there was also "a real need for a kind of micro-historical study which can only be carried on by people with technical linguistic competence" (ibid.).

I did not attempt to resolve all the issues implicated in this acknowledgment, which echoes, but does not replicate, the traditional (and no doubt oversimple) distinction between "internalist" and "externalist" histories of science. In practice my own history (and that of the *History of Anthropology* series), although privileging the specific and the microcosmic, has been directed toward more general and broadly contextualized issues, rather than toward the technical or conceptual development of the discipline. So much so that there have been complaints that its interest is effectively antiquarian, with no clear relevance to the issues confronting anthropologists today. But among the many forms that historical inquiry in the human sciences may appropriately take, I would still acknowledge the legitimacy of a more technically oriented history, in which, discontinuity to the contrary notwithstanding, there may be an accumulative methodological, substantive, and conceptual development over longer periods of time. From this point of view, the Newberry conference was for me a step (taken as I accepted a problematic self-definition as "anthropologist") toward acknowledging a more interactive relationship between historical understanding and present disciplinary concerns.

From the point of view of the history of ethnographic method, what has been called the "Boas plan" should be seen in relation to a more general anthropological agenda that had emerged around 1900. While Boas did not, like Malinowski, offer a methodological manifesto, the aims of his ethnography may be extrapolated from testimony he gave in 1904 to a committee investigating alleged improprieties in the distribution of material he had gathered while working simultaneously for the Bureau of American Ethnology and the American Museum of Natural History. The issue was the ownership and location of ethnographic materials collected with government money, and in order to defend their distribution between the two institutions, Boas offered a succinct statement of the field ethnographer's task. "I have instructed my students," he said,

> to collect certain things and to collect with everything they get information in the native language and to obtain grammatical information that is necessary to explain their texts. Consequently the results of their journeys are the following: they get specimens; they get explanations of the specimens; they get connected texts that partly refer to the specimens and partly simply to abstract things concerning the people; and they get grammatical information. The line of division is clear: the grammatical material and the texts go to the Bureau, and the specimens go to the New York Museum. (Quoted in GS 1977b; cf. Hinsley 1981)

Although Boas' training was in the natural sciences, the aims of his ethnography were those of traditional humanistic scholarship: to create for a preliterate people with no historical records a body of primary materials analogous to those by which European scholars studied the earlier phases of their own cultural history. These would include physical remains of their art and industry; literary materials in which their history and cultural life were described in their own words; and grammatical material derived from the latter—all of them more or less direct expressions of the "genius" of the people, as free as possible from the "alternating sounds" imposed by the cultural categories of an outside observer (cf. GS 1974d; M. Smith 1959). It is as part of this broader ethnographic strategy that the "Boas plan" should be appreciated.

That Franz Boas played a central role in the definition of twentieth-century American Indian linguistics, and that the *Handbook of American Indian Languages* (1911a) represents in some respects a charter for that study, are of course commonplaces (Emeneau 1943:35; Hymes 1964:7–9). But the specific character of what Carl Voegelin called "The Boas Plan for the Presentation of American Indian Languages" (Voegelin 1952), and the intellectual, institutional, and interpersonal context in which the *Handbook* was produced are matters that bear some further investigation. Voegelin's own treatment of these issues was quite frankly a bit speculative and hypothetical, and based solely on the internal evidence of the *Handbook* itself. On this basis, he suggested the possibility that Boas himself "wrote the grammars which are editorially attributed to another anthropologist or anthropologists." Perhaps somewhat more seriously, he argued that

> if Boas were writing today, we might feel that it was no more natural and fitting to have him appear as the author of Tsimshian, Kwakiutl, and Chinook (based on his own field work), and as co-author of Dakota, than it was to have him appear as the author of *Structural Restatements of Maidu, Fox, Hupa, Tlingit and Haida* (based on the field notes gathered by Dixon, Jones, Michelson, Goddard, and Swanton)—in short, to regard Boas as the author of nine out of the ten sketches of Part I of the *Handbook.* (440–41)

Voegelin went on to extrapolate from the twenty grammars ultimately published in the four volumes of the *Handbook* a rather detailed model of the "general plan of presentation" to which Boas referred in his Introduction (1911a:vi). As will be evident in what follows, Voegelin's version of the Boas "master plan" seems to me to have a somewhat different and more highly structured character than Boas himself had in mind. Fortunately, however, these matters need not be approached solely in terms of internal analysis of published materials. Perhaps scholars with more linguistic sophistication than I possess will also take advantage of the manuscript materials in the American Philosophical Society and the Smithsonian Archives of Anthropology to complete the historical examination which this essay presumes only to initiate.[1]

The Genesis of the *Handbook*

The *Handbook* was the major fruit of a linguistic connection with the Bureau of American Ethnology that can be traced almost to the beginning of Boas' career as anthropologist. In the fall of 1885 he wrote to the Bureau asking for a copy of John Wesley Powell's *Introduction to the Study of Indian Languages* (1880) as a guide to the analysis of Eskimo linguistic materials which were originally to have been included in the report subsequently published by the Bureau on his ethnographic work among the Eskimo of Baffinland (BE: FB 10/3/85). The request itself suggests that at this point Boas was somewhat unsure of himself in linguistics, and other evidence indicates that he had no formal linguistic training and little systematic contact with the European tradition of comparative linguistics. True, sometime in this period he apparently met and subsequently did exchange at least one communication with Heymann Steinthal. But if Boas' later work gives this contact a special retrospective significance, it seems nonetheless to have been quite fleeting: Boas later "regretted never having attended" Steinthal's lectures (Jakobson 1944:188; Harrington 1945:98; BP: HS/FB 9/15/88). When it came to analyzing the Eskimo linguistic materials, Boas seems to have relied a good bit on the help of H. J. Rink, a Dane who had lived among them for some years, and who in fact was responsible for preparing the translations of Boas' Eskimo texts (BE: FB 9/15/85, 10/3/85, 10/30/85, 5/13/87).

Starting then as an untrained novice, Boas achieved his linguistic competence during his first decade of general ethnographic work on the Northwest Coast, and there is every indication that he was largely self-taught. There is evidence that he may have referred to such works as Friedrich Müller's *Grundriss der Sprachtwissenschaft* (BP: H. Hale/FB 4/30/88), and that he had a rather generalized familiarity with European philological traditions. He clearly read other European and American work on the languages that concerned him. Through his close relationship with Horatio Hale in his work for the British Association for the Advancement of Science he had fairly direct access to an American philological tradition going back to Gallatin. But the rather antagonistic tenor of his relationship to Hale

1. Quite aside from limitations imposed by my lack of training in linguistics (cf. GS 1974e), I should note that this study is based largely on correspondence before the end of 1909—a period which includes the genesis and completion of the ten grammars in Volume I, as well as of Sapir's Takelma grammar in Volume II (although the latter was not published until 1922).

Franz Boas in the years of "the Boas plan"—from the *Festschrift* published in 1906 on the occasion of the twenty-fifth anniversary of his doctorate. (Courtesy of the American Philosophical Society)

suggests what other sources confirm: the major context of his "self-professionalization" was that of his own fieldwork. It was in the process of recording myths and traditions from various Indian informants that he worked out his problems of orthography and developed his characteristic approach to the analysis of language (Jakobson 1944:188; Lowie 1943:183–84; Dell Hymes, personal communication; cf. J. Gruber 1967).[2]

Within a relatively short time, however, Boas had already drawn on this experience to offer a general critique of the traditional approach to "Alternating Sounds" which foreshadowed many of the characteristically relativist assumptions of his mature linguistic work (1889; cf. GS 1968b: 157–60). And from an early point he was confident enough of his own competence to offer Powell unsolicited reports on his research and discussions of linguistic problems in the Northwest area, as well as a proposal for a five-year program of research on the Salish languages (BE: FB/Powell 8/8/88; FB/H. Henshaw 12/3/88). However, Boas was in fact able to get from the Bureau only piecemeal support for linguistic research supplementary to the general ethnographic work he was carrying on for the British Association (FB/Powell 12/22/88; FB/Henshaw 3/8/90). Furthermore, his letters in this period suggest that despite his interest in more intensive study of Salish, he was still working largely in terms of regional surveys, vocabulary lists, grammatical "notes," and problems of the classification of stocks (FB/Henshaw 1/24/89, 10/20/89, 3/8/90)—that is, that he operated largely within a Powellian framework, and was not yet in practice primarily concerned with the systematic and intensive study of grammatical structures.

This pattern seems to have begun to change with Boas' encounter in 1890

2. Since this essay was written in 1968, I have come across an article of Hale's treating the same problem Boas treated in his essay "On Alternating Sounds" (Hale 1884; cf. Boas 1889). In it, Hale recounts an experiment he performed by accident in 1882. He and Professor Alexander Melville Bell were simultaneously recording the words of an Iroquois informant, and in a number of instances, Hale recorded as "r" a sound Bell recorded as "l." On this basis, as well as that of evidence from missionary vocabularies, Hale concluded that the general phenomenon of "intermediate articulation" lay not "in the speaker's utterance, but in the ear of the listener"—that "the sound as spoken was an indistinct articulation, . . . and that the hearer, unaccustomed to sounds of this peculiar character, involuntarily made distinctions where none really existed." The argument is somewhat Boasian, and one might use it to support Jacob Gruber's suggestion that Hale was an important source of the major ingredients of Boas' anthropology—although Gruber himself did not (1967). Although it is certainly possible that Boas was familiar with Hale's article, I can find no reference to it in Hale's letters to Boas, and there is no overlap whatsoever between the data offered by Hale and that used by Boas. Furthermore, the differences between the articles are quite striking: in Hale's piece there is not the slightest trace of Boas' argument in psycho-physical terms, and in the end, Hale used alternating sounds as the basis of a rather strained argument about the process of differentiation within linguistic stocks. On the whole, I am still inclined to minimize Hale's influence on Boas, in this as in other matters.

with Chinook. Although at first the problem was simply to determine its relation to Salish, Boas quickly became fascinated by the intricacies of the language for their own sake (BE: FB/Henshaw 5/16/90, 7/14/90), and much of his linguistic effort of the 1890s was devoted to a study of the several branches of the Chinookan stock with a view to the "elucidation" of its structure (FB/Powell 1/18/93).

Unfortunately, however, Boas' relation to the Bureau was considerably attenuated (under rather acrimonious circumstances) in 1894, when he was pushed out of his job at the Field Museum as a result of a reorganization of Bureau personnel which sent William Holmes to Chicago. A year and a half later—apparently in part as compensation for this maltreatment—Boas was offered a permanent job in charge of the editorial work of the Bureau. Although he came close to taking it, he instead accepted the appointment which was to settle him permanently in New York City (BP: retrospective account by Boas, 1911; BE: FB/Powell 6/19/95; FB/W. J. McGee 6/27/95, 1/26/96).

From 1896 on, however, Boas' relations with the Bureau were close (although not always amicable) throughout the period until the *Handbook* was published. Furthermore, it seems clear they were resumed in a somewhat different context from that in which they had been disrupted. Later retrospective comments on his own early linguistic work suggest that it was from about this time that Boas regarded his largely autodidactic linguistic competence as having achieved an adequately professional level (1900:708). And the Bureau, which in the late 1880s had thought him a bit of a pushy novice, now clearly recognized him as a, if not the, leading student of Indian languages. It is also from this time that one finds evidence of a continuous systematic attempt by Boas to train students who would carry on linguistic work at a thoroughly professional level. After 1899, when John Swanton went to South Dakota in an attempt to revise Sioux texts which had been collected for the Bureau by the Reverend J. Owen Dorsey, students trained in Boas' linguistic seminar at Columbia were annually engaged in linguistic fieldwork under Bureau auspices.

Finally, as far as Boas' linguistic orientation itself is concerned, one may regard his paper on the "Classification of the Languages of the North Pacific Coast" at the World's Fair Congress of Anthropology late in 1893 as marking the culmination of his early interest in classificatory problems. In its concluding paragraph he suggested the need for more intensive study of linguistic structures (1894:346). And in fact his own work for the Bureau in the late 1890s focussed largely on a continuing analysis of the material he had previously collected in Chinook and Tsimshian.

Exactly when the *Handbook* was conceived is not clear. At later points Boas mentioned the years 1895, 1897, and 1898, and suggested that it "had its inception in an attempt to prepare a revised edition of John Wesley Powell's *Introduction to the Study of Indian Languages,*" which had gone out of print, and had also begun "to prove inadequate" (1911a:v). In fact, however, as late as 1898 Boas asked for and received two copies of Powell's *Introduction* to give to his own fieldworkers (BE: FB/McGee 4/15/98, 4/21/98). On the other hand, a letter of the preceding year indicates that Powell had in mind some major linguistic project which Boas was to undertake (FB/McGee 4/12/97).

The first specific mention of the *Handbook,* however, occurs in the spring of 1901, when Boas wrote a letter to W. J. McGee, acting head of the Bureau, recalling that they had "been discussing now and again the desirability of publishing a handbook of North American Languages," and suggesting that his recently published sketch of Kwakiutl grammar in the *American Anthropologist* (1900) was prepared as a kind of model for the sort of treatments he had in mind. Boas felt that he had "trained now a sufficient number of young men to make it possible to take up work of this kind systematically," and that with the cooperation of the American Museum, Columbia, Harvard, and the University of California, it would be possible to do the necessary fieldwork and bring the *Handbook* to completion within five or six years (BP: FB/McGee 4/4/01, 4/20/01; cf. 6/18/02). McGee and Powell responded favorably, and the following month Boas received an appointment as Honorary Philologist in the Bureau (McGee/FB 4/5/01, 5/22/01; S. P. Langley/FB 5/23/01).

Although fieldwork was carried out in the summers of 1901 and 1902, planning was still clearly in preliminary stages, and the whole proposal had to be renegotiated when McGee was forced out of the Bureau after Powell's death in 1902 (Hinsley 1981). Boas' personal relations with William Holmes, the new Bureau chief, were poor; and Boas' previous relations with McGee and the Bureau became something of an issue in the uproar surrounding McGee's departure. For a time, financial support for linguistic work was seriously curtailed (BP: Holmes/FB 1/6/03). By the end of 1903, however, revised and more detailed plans for the *Handbook* were finally approved, and Boas sent out invitations to the proposed collaborators (FB/Holmes 3/5/03, 5/9/03, 11/2/03; Holmes/FB 11/25/03, 12/8/03).

Creating a Corps of Collaborators

In order to consider the problem of the *Handbook*'s authorship, it will be helpful to examine its personnel in a more systematic way—and not only those whose names appeared in print as collaborators, but also those whose names might have and did not. In the first place, one notes the exclusion of both missionaries and old-line Bureau members. (For present purposes, the partial exceptions of Swanton, who *became* a member of the Bureau, and Goddard, who *had been* a missionary, are not really to the point.) These omissions are hardly accidental, and have a good deal to do with defining both the intellectual context of the *Handbook* and the interaction patterns which define its authorship.

The historical significance of the *Handbook* tends to be distorted by our image of Powell and the Bureau as systematically involved in linguistic research. Although it is generally known that Powell's classification of American languages was lexical rather than morphological, the degree to which Boas' *Handbook* represented a radical departure in the study of Indian languages still tends perhaps to be obscured by the mountainous bibliographies, with numerous entries by missionary linguists, which went into the production of the Bureau's *Indian Linguistic Families of America North of Mexico* in 1891 (Darnell 1971a). Bureau members did collect considerable bodies of linguistic material, but before Boas' time they published relatively little in the way of extended grammatical analysis. And despite all this material, despite decades of speculation on the "incorporating" or "polysynthetic" character of American Indian languages, the amount of detailed and systematic study of specific Indian languages which would stand professional scrutiny—at least as far as Franz Boas and Edward Sapir were concerned—was virtually nil, and Boas' attitude toward these two important groups of nineteenth-century linguistic students reflected this estimate.[3] From 1896 on, a recurring part of Boas' activity for the Bureau was in effect to exercise a veto power on the entry of missionaries (and others) into what might be loosely called the "American Indian linguistics establishment." When missionaries wrote to the Bureau asking to consult unpublished manuscript materials or offering their own manuscripts for publication, the issue was as a matter of routine referred to Boas. Characteristically, Boas would suggest that the missionary had no knowledge of scientific philology, or that he should be restricted to the published works of the Bureau, or—on one occasion—that while the missionary's work was better than some, it need not be published, since Boas' own investigators were about to undertake work on the same tribe (BE: FB/McGee 4/11/98; FB/Holmes 12/7/03, 11/23/04, 1/31/06, 7/14/06, 1/8/08; Holmes/FB 3/25/07, 1/15/08; BP: Holmes/FB 12/8/03; Holmes/Verwyst 5/9/07; cf. FB/A. Huntington 1/30/06).

3. Sapir 1917a; cf., however, the comments of Carl Voegelin: "Boas' predecessors did their best work on constituents within a grammar rather than on comprehensive grammars, though some of the best examples, as Dorsey's on Iowa-Oto person markers, remain in manuscript in the BAE archives" (personal communication). On the relation between Boas and the work of the Bureau, cf. Darnell 1969.

As far as the men of the Bureau are concerned, the most likely candidate was Albert Gatschet, an older scholar for whose abilities Boas had a fairly high regard. Gatschet's health was poor, and in fact he died before the *Handbook* was completed. Nevertheless, Boas proposed to McGee in 1900 that Gatschet should write a thirty-page sketch for each of the languages he had studied but not published so that the large body of material he had collected in the course of a long career would be usable by other investigators after his death (BP: FP/McGee 2/4/00; McGee/FB 3/1/00; cf. FB/J. Dunn 11/7/07; BE: FB/Holmes 11/26/07, 12/5/07). The task was analogous to – although quantitatively much more difficult than – the job of preparing a sketch for the *Handbook* according to Boas' original conception, which envisioned a total of about fifty pages on each language, including texts (BP: FB/Holmes 3/5/03). Thus Boas' failure at any point even to mention the possibility of Gatschet's working on the *Handbook* may still signify something of a general attitude toward Bureau linguists, especially in the context of his derogatory remarks elsewhere on the competence of the older generation of American anthropologists, and the markedly evolutionary assumptions that pervade the grammar of the Klamath Gatschet published in 1890 (FB/Z. Nuttall 5/16/01).

The fate of the one Bureau man whom Boas did include in his plans is even more illuminating. Boas hoped to have J. N. B. Hewitt, a slightly eccentric long-time Bureau employee of Tuscarora descent, do a sketch of Iroquois grammar. After several years of fruitless attempts through Holmes' mediation to get Hewitt to produce, Boas finally succeeded – after he himself had begun the study of Iroquois – in conferring directly with Hewitt on the project. He was soon to discover that although Hewitt spoke two Iroquois dialects fluently, had a good knowledge of the details of the language, and could "analyse each word," he had no "clear idea regarding the grammar of the whole language." Although Boas hoped that he might get Hewitt to stay long enough in New York so that he himself could "systematize Hewitt's knowledge by questioning him," it was never possible to arrange this, and the proposed Iroquois sketch had to be abandoned (BP: FB/Holmes 5/9/03; FB/Hewitt 8/30/07; BE: FB/Holmes 10/30/07, 1/27/08, 3/8/09, 8/1/09).[4]

Hewitt was not the only potential contributor who "washed out." Even among Boas' own students there was a fairly rigorous selection. As if to symbolize the growth of his own linguistic competence, Boas felt that his

4. The Hewitt episode has interesting implications for Boas' methodological assumptions (cf. below, the idea that languages should be described as if a native were to define the categories of his own language). Apparently the critical variable was in fact formal training with Boas. William Jones, whose attenuated heritage still included fluent Fox, became one of the collaborators on the *Handbook* after graduate study under Boas.

first doctoral student at Clark University, Alexander Francis Chamberlain, would prove inadequate to do a study of Kootenay, since he tended to get lost in detail, and "the essential points are liable to be obscured" (BE: FB/Holmes 6/5/05, 6/3/08). Even after he was established at Columbia, Boas had several failures before he began to develop the group of promising young men whom he referred to in connection with his early plans for the *Handbook*. One, a Dr. Emil Seytler, seemed talented, but was rejected as irresponsible; a man named Henning proved to be a clerk and not a scientist (FB/McGee 1/26/96, 11/4/97, 11/25/97, 3/5/98). And even among the young men he later spoke of so favorably to McGee, there was one notable washout. Boas' earliest enumeration of the languages he planned to cover included two to be studied by one H. H. St. Clair (BP: FB/Holmes 3/5/03). St. Clair in fact did fieldwork during several summers, and two of the sketches in the second volume of the *Handbook* (Takelma and Coos) note a debt to field notes he collected. St. Clair's main work, however, was on the Shoshone, and at least in the beginning, Boas thought rather highly of his linguistic abilities (it was in fact St. Clair who carried out Boas' first attempt to use a phonograph as a field technique) (FB/Holmes 5/9/03, 6/2/03). Unfortunately, however, St. Clair did not "feel the necessity of reporting regularly on the progress of his work," and Boas found this "failure to communicate with the home office . . . intolerable" (BE: FB/Holmes 1/19/03, 2/13/03). Apparently over St. Clair's rather angry opposition, he was eliminated from the group of collaborators, and from American Indian linguistics as well (BP: FB/St. Clair 2/8/05).

In addition to those whom Boas eliminated, there was one who eliminated himself, and this, too, casts light on the nature of the group who finally collaborated. When the invitations to participate were sent out, Boas asked his first Columbia Ph.D., A. L. Kroeber, who had become professor of anthropology at the University of California, to write a sketch on the Yurok language (BP: FB/ALK 12/11/03). From the beginning, Kroeber was reluctant. He was not sure he had the time, he preferred to do Yuki, and he was concerned with what Boas would "do with the contributions" after he received them (ALK/FB 12/27/03, 2/21/04, 3/27/04). When he did agree to participate, it was in a rather short, curt note which made painfully clear that it was an act of submission by a man whose assertion of his own scholarly individuality had not reached the point of permitting him to refuse his *guru* outright (3/27/04). After he sent in the Yuki manuscript, Kroeber balked at making additions Boas requested (5/21/06). When the publication of the *Handbook* was delayed for several years more, Kroeber suggested early in 1908 that he withdraw the Yuki on the grounds that he now felt that he had made mistakes in the phonetics, but could not spend the time required to do further fieldwork. Instead, he offered

Boas material he had already published on Yokuts, with the comment that he understood that Boas was "thoroughly editing all the contributions," and could "probably best get just what you want" by editing this (2/1/08). Boas returned the Yuki manuscript and rather curtly indicated that he preferred not to use the Yokuts (2/11/08).

None of the six early participants whose sketches saw publication showed any such recalcitrance as Kroeber. Four of them had been — or still were — doctoral students under Boas. Of these, three were still clearly in a dependent relation to him. Unlike St. Clair, they reported regularly from the field to the home office, and their letters make it clear that the psychic tone of the relationship was that of disciple and master. Edward Sapir was indeed for a time wont to close his letters "yours very respectfully" (BP: ES/FB 7/4/05). John Swanton on several occasions explicitly gave Boas permission to rework his manuscripts any way Boas wished (JS/FB 2/2/05, 5/31/05, 11/27/07). William Jones's death in the Philippines before the final revision of his Fox manuscript gave Boas complete freedom to do the same.

Thalbitzer

In addition to these three, William Thalbitzer, a Danish scholar trained in the classical tradition of Indo-European philology, had published a volume on Eskimo phonetics which, in attitude if not in genesis, was at several points strikingly Boasian (Thalbitzer 1904:xii). Boas clearly chose him with this in mind, and Thalbitzer — still a bit unsure of his English — was more than anxious to have Boas' help and to give him what he wanted (BP: WT/FB 2/13/07, 12/20/07, 6/1/08). Pliny Goddard, although in fact a onetime lay missionary, was even then taking his Ph.D. in linguistics at the University of California under Benjamin Ide Wheeler and in close association with Kroeber, who despite his recalcitrance was clearly Boasian in his basic approach to American Indian linguistics. Goddard was also anxious to please, and ended by formally thanking Boas for what he had done to improve his Hupa sketch (PG/FB 10/20/08). Roland Dixon, who had first studied Maidu grammar as a doctoral student under Boas before he joined the Harvard faculty, was his own man in a way the other collaborators were not, but there was no fundamental difference in linguistic point of view. Paradoxically, Sapir, even though his Takelma sketch was in fact his doctoral dissertation, was by virtue of sheer linguistic brilliance the most independent of all. His is the one case where there is clear evidence of a partial reversal in the current of intellectual influence. Indeed, Boas asked Sapir to contribute a short essay on certain semantically significant phonetic peculiarities of Chinook to his own sketch of that language (FB/ES 3/29/09, 3/31/09, 4/5/09).

Sapir gave info to Boas

Clearly then, the conditions of interaction were very favorable to Voegelin's interpretation of the authorship of the *Handbook*. Boas had rigorously winnowed and for the most part himself trained a group of still quite dependent young scholars whom he saw as "contributors" to a single, on-going enterprise he had single-handedly initiated: the establishment of American Indian linguistics on a scientific basis whose assumptions he was at no small pains to define. And one can indeed find passages in his correspondence that might be used to bolster Voegelin's interpretation. During the period of his most intense editorial work, in January 1908, Boas complained to William Holmes that "perhaps you do not appreciate the amount of labor involved in the final editing of all the sketches, some of which I have practically to rewrite entirely" (BE: FB/WH 1/20/08; cf. 8/30/07, 3/8/09). However, others letters in the same period would seem to indicate that Boas was referring to St. Clair's Shoshone, which was never published; to his own Tsimshian; to the sketch of Sioux, on which his name appeared as co-author with Swanton; as well as perhaps Swanton's Tlingit, on which it did not (BP: FB/Swanton 1/13/08; FB/Laufer 3/11/08; BE: FB/Holmes 1/27/08, 5/6/08, 6/3/08). As far as the rest are concerned, the correspondence would indicate that, however extensive Boas' editorial role, it was hardly that of author. He in effect specifically rejected the opportunity to do a "structural restatement" of Kroeber's Yokuts. The relatively minor additions to Jones's Fox manuscript he explicitly relegated to Truman Michelson, on the grounds that he himself had no time for them (BE: FB/Holmes 8/9/09). Thalbitzer's Eskimo, despite the acknowledgment to Boas' "assistance in the revision and finishing," was the last sketch commissioned and arrived well along toward the completion of Boas' editorial work (BP: WT/FB 6/1/08, 7/18/08), and its somewhat divergent character suggests that he did little to remodel it.[5] Dixon seems to have been quite willing to resist Boas' suggestions when he felt the evidence did not support them, as well as on his own initiative to add new material in the galley proofs (Dixon/FB 3/2/09, 3/8/09). And with Goddard's Hupa, the suggestions Boas made for changes were offered as such, and were generally of a fairly specific character (FB/PG 11/23/07, 12/28/07; PG/FB 12/18/07, 10/20/08).

Indeed, it is the character of Boas' editorial work that provides the most important evidence on the problem of authorship. A good portion of his attention seems in fact to have been directed to such problems as the uniformity of systems of headings and indentation (BE: FB/collaborators 7/16/04; FB/Holmes 1/8/08), and there is evidence to suggest that his plan of presentation was conditioned by aesthetic as well as strictly linguistic

5. Thalbitzer's sketch is suggestive as a kind of test case for the character of Boas' influence on the *Handbook*. Thalbitzer, who had been trained with Vilhelm Thomsen and Otto Jespersen, tried hard, out of a European tradition, to follow Boas' approach. The divergences of his presentation suggest that the others (who had all, save Goddard, studied with Boas) took for granted much that Thalbitzer labored with.

criteria. In only one instance did he feel that a sketch had "not conformed to the general plan of the book." The issue was not linguistic, however—Boas thought Sapir's Takelma was excellent. It was simply that it was too detailed and too long in its planned position, and would have either to be placed at the end or else published in a second volume (as in fact it was) (FB/Holmes 6/24/09; cf. Darnell 1990:16–24).

As far as the substance of the various sketches was concerned, Boas' editing seems largely to have had to do with the addition of new material rather than with reworking the analyses themselves. The first manuscripts were turned in toward the end of 1904, but the project dragged on so long that the results of further research had often to be incorporated. Boas himself made a trip to the Carlisle Indian school and worked with Indian informants in New York in 1908, which apparently had a good deal to do with the reworking of the Sioux and Tsimshian (BE: FB/Holmes 1/27/08, 2/12/08, 4/15/08). Even when the Kwakiutl was in galley proofs, he felt that he had to add considerable material in the light of his more recent deeper understanding of the language (FB/Holmes 6/24/09, 6/28/09, 8/1/09). In the same manner, he frequently asked collaborators to add examples to illustrate particular grammatical points, or to expand a portion of their argument. As far as one can judge from the correspondence, such restructuring as he proposed was of a fairly specific character: he suggested to Goddard a reanalysis of the Hupa verb and to Swanton a reclassification of Tlingit prefixes, and to both of them a tabular presentation of verbal forms, in order to point up a morphological relationship he felt existed between the two languages (BP: FB/PG 11/23/07, 12/28/07; FB/JS 11/25/07, 12/26/07; cf. Boas 1911a:133, 190). On the whole, there seems to me no evidence (with perhaps the exception of Swanton's Tlingit) to sustain any attribution of authorship other than that indicated in the *Handbook*'s table of contents.

The Critique of Evolutionary Linguistics

This conclusion of course depends in part on the answer to the second problem posed in the beginning of this essay: the purpose and nature of the Boas model itself. Voegelin suggested that Boas' "unflagging interest in linguistic structures" and his "masterful insistence on having linguistic structures so stated that they could be readily compared" was related to his tendency to explain language similarities in diffusional rather than genetic terms, and that the "Boas plan" was devised "in order to obtain the kind of cross-genetic comparability essential" to such explanation (1952:439). Perhaps reflecting his own continuing interest in issues of typology and structure,[6] Voegelin's analysis of the "Boas plan" (under the headings of "sounds," "processes," and "meanings") seems to me to have given it a great deal more structural coherence than Boas intended. Thus Voegelin suggested in regard to "sounds" that one could make the various treatments of consonant sounds systematically "comparable" by rearranging them so that they read from left to right in the order of contact points in the mouth from front to back: b-d-g; p-t-k; p'-t'-k'. In this form Voegelin offered a "Generalized Model of Stops in American Indian Languages" as an example of how one could make Boas' "general plan explicit." Voegelin did note that Boas in fact accepted any arrangement a collaborator offered (443). What he did not note is that even Boas' own grammars differ in the order of arrangement of consonants (1911a:289, 429, 565). The point may seem trivial, but what is involved is in fact a rather important historical issue: was Boas a modern structuralist in historical disguise, or was he rather concerned with quite different issues, for which the arrangement of consonant sounds might not be at all critical, or in terms of which a less systematic arrangement might even seem more appropriate?

Turning to "processes," Voegelin suggested that what Boas usually called "grammatical processes" could be arranged in a continuum according to their association with problems of meaning. According to the resulting alphabetical typology, A to E stood for "non-semantic processes," and F to K for "grammatical processes" proper, the whole series reflecting the continuum of actual speech, with "sound replacement" at one end and "word order" at the other (1952:445–50). There is undoubtedly a sense in which Boas was profoundly concerned with the continuum of actual speech; and for reasons which I shall discuss below, he did in fact subordinate and place at the end of each sketch the discussion of syntactical problems. Nevertheless, to my layman's eye Voegelin's typology bears only a tenuous derivative relationship to what actually appears on the printed pages of the *Handbook*. Most of what Voegelin called the first half of the continuum was simply the material treated in the separate sections called "phonetics." As for the "grammatical processes" proper, Voegelin seems to me to have obscured the issue by defining them rather vaguely in terms of the "representation" of the speech continuum. Boas himself defined grammatical processes in terms of their function of expressing the "relations" of the ideas

6. Apart from its relation to Voegelin's long-run scholarly interests (cf. 1955; Voegelin & Voegelin 1963), the Boas plan paper seems to have been written in the specific context of his work on two other key articles in which problems of descriptive models, structural restatements, typology, etc., were foremost in his mind—as evidenced by the fact that each of the three articles refers in footnotes to each of the other two (cf. 1954; Voegelin & Harris 1952).

expressed by "single" or "definite" "phonetic groups," and suggested that there were in fact only two such processes: "composition in a definite order, which may be combined with a mutual phonetic influence of the component elements upon one another, and inner modification of the phonetic groups themselves" (1911a:27). In fact the phenomena that were listed as grammatical processes in the various grammars are, at least terminologically, somewhat more differentiated. They include "affixation," "suffixation," "reduplication," "vocalic changes," "stem modification," "position," and "juxtaposition," and on one occasion, "incorporation." Taken as a whole, Boas' "grammatical processes" represent less a "continuum" than alternative ways for relating the elementary ideas of each single phonetic group, each present to varying degrees in the different languages of the world.

As "the next task in the Boas plan of presentation" Voegelin listed "meanings"—the determination of the "ideas expressed by grammatical processes," or synonymously, "grammatical categories." According to Voegelin, Boas' discussion of these was "a kind of promissory note" (reissued later by Sapir and Whorf) that "we would at last obtain reliable data on the various Weltanschauungen as reflected in the various native languages of primitive man in the New World, and thus attain an attested contrast to the Weltanschauung derived from European languages." It is in this context that Voegelin suggested that Boas' later collaborators became "relatively cool toward the idea of separate essays on grammatical categories, while Boas became more devoted" (1952:450–51). Actually, even in Volume I the essays on "ideas expressed by grammatical categories" were very unevenly developed; nor were Boas' own treatments uniformly elaborate. For the most part these essays were simply brief summary statements of the most general themes of the grammatical analyses which followed them, and attenuation or absence is perhaps not so crucial as Voegelin suggested. But the important point is that they were less a promissory note than the embodiment of an analytic premise, and that it is this analytic premise, rather than any specific presentational structure, that underlies the Boas plan for American Indian linguistics. Quite diverse presentations could be and were found equally consistent with this premise. Indeed, it in effect required such diversity.

To understand why this should have been the case, it is necessary to consider in a bit more detail the context in which the *Handbook* was conceived. In the first place, it may help to look briefly at several American Indian grammars of the late nineteenth century. Matthews' Hidatsa (1877) and the Riggs-Dorsey Dakota (1893) were each structured in terms of the eight parts of speech we still learn today: Noun, Pronoun, Verb, Adverb, Adjective, Preposition, Conjunction, and Interjection. These were the basic categories; and while Gatschet's Klamath was from Boas' point of view much more satisfactory, it nevertheless contained statements that cast considerable light on what was implied in such categorization. In discussing inflection, Gatschet suggested that what was from an evolutionary point of view first the product of physical (i.e., phonetic) law and psychological principle was "finally subjected to rational logic . . . by which grammatical categories are established." Prior to this, what one found were merely *conventional* as opposed to *logical* principles. The existence of logical principles had to do with the degree of definition of the parts of speech, and from this point of view the Aryan languages were clearly at the top of the evolutionary scale (1890:I, 399).

Other late-nineteenth-century sources suggest that "grammatical processes," too, could be viewed in evolutionary terms. Powell's *Introduction* (which Boas' *Handbook* was intended to replace) distinguished a series of "grammatical processes" not dissimilar from Boas'. But Powell saw them in evolutionary terms as solutions to the evolutionary problem created by the fact that ideas increased at a more rapid rate than the words that represented them. Grammatical processes were methods of expressing a large number of ideas with a small number of words. Under the general process of "combination," Powell listed four of these methods: juxtaposition, compounding, agglutination, and inflection. But these methods were also called "stages," and though Powell tended to regard even inflection as an inheritance from barbarism, he had no doubt that English was the highest language in the world because its grammatical processes were highly specialized (i.e., word derivation was accomplished by combination; syntax, by placement) and because the parts of speech were highly differentiated (1880:55–58, 69–74).

It would be a mistake to imply that all nineteenth-century American thought on Indian languages was systematically structured along the lines I have suggested. What is involved is rather a matter of recurring themes and unstated assumptions. Furthermore, these could be integrated in various frameworks. Powell had insisted earlier that American Indian languages differed in degree but not in kind from Indo-European languages (1877:104; cf. Brinton 1890:319). This was not, however, an argument against evolutionary ethnocentrism, but rather an implicit argument against another widely held nineteenth-century view of American languages: the suggestion, deriving from such men as Peter Duponceau, Wilhelm von Humboldt, Francis Lieber, and Heymann von Steinthal, that Indian languages differed fundamentally in type from other languages of the world—that they were "incorporative," or "polysynthetic," or "holophrastic" in character. Daniel Garrison Brinton, whose classification of American languages on morphological grounds appeared almost simultaneously with Powell's lexical classification in 1891, insisted on a distinction between these three processes (1890:320–22). Brinton argued that American languages were polysynthetic in their method of word building, incorporative as regards the structure of their verbal forms (with the nominal and pronominal elements subordinated by incorporation into the verb stem), and holophrastic from the point of view of the psychic impulse which underlay the processes of polysynthesis and incorporation, the impulse "to express the whole proposition in one word" (359). Incorporation, however, was their distinguishing species characteristic, and Brinton was at great pains to explain away any apparent exceptions, and to argue that *all* American Indian languages were incorporative (307, 366–388). Powell was much more willing to allow for diversity of process, and in fact left "incorporation" out of his list—for which Brinton later rebuked him (358; cf. Darnell 1988).

The issue here is not the differences between various individual exemplars of nineteenth-century linguistic thought. Some of them saw the origin of speech in the sentence, others in the word, some in the noun, some in the verb; some of them were highly ethnocentric, others relatively relativistic. The issue is rather the sort of assumptions that tend to run through them all, whether in a systematic, a random, or even a self-contradictory way. Thus Brinton at times waxed ecstatic on the beauty of Indian tongues, and was inclined to argue on occasion that Aryan inflection was no nearer linguistic perfection than Algonkin incorporation (1890:323). But he was equally capable of viewing his morphological types in evolutionary terms, of arguing that the higher languages separated the "material" from the "formal" elements; that incorporation was "vastly below the level of inflected speech"; that outside of incorporation, American languages had "no syntax, no inflections, nor declension of nouns and adjectives" (336, 342–43, 353). He even wrote an article hypothesizing the characteristics of paleolithic speech on the basis of American Indian languages. In it he argued that their present character suggested that paleolithic speech had neither tense, mode, nor person; that "what are called 'grammatical categories' were wholly absent in the primitive speech of man"; and that the process of incorporation was evidence of the "gradual" or evolutionary "development of grammar." In the course of his argument, Brinton made a large number of categorical statements about the empirical reality of American Indian languages: that "abstract general terms" were "absent" or "rare"; that their only distinction of gender was between animate and inanimate; and that "a grammatical sex distinction, which is the prevailing one in the grammars of the Aryan tongues, does not exist in any American dialect known to me" (405, 406, 407).

Boas' profound concern with certain of the issues posed by evolutionary linguists is evident as early as November 1888, when he wrote his essay "On Alternating Sounds." It is not certain whether he was already familiar with Brinton's ideas on paleolithic speech, which were presented to the American Philosophical Society during the same year. However, his argument would suggest that he was: what Brinton had interpreted as traces of the "vague," "fluctuating," and still tentative language of paleolithic man, Boas saw as "alternating perceptions of one and the same sound" by an observer whose own language had no equivalent (1889:52; Brinton 1890: 397–99; cf. GS 1968a:158–59). Indeed, the argument in Boas' discussion of "Grammatical Categories" in the Introduction to the *Handbook* is clearly built on the logic of his interpretation of alternating sounds twenty-three years before. "Since the total range of personal experience which language serves to express is infinitely varied, and its whole scope must be expressed by a limited number of phonetic groups, it is obvious that an extended classification of experiences must underlie all articulate speech"—not as Powell had seemed to imply, evolved human speech, but human speech in general. These classifications would be "in wider or narrower groups the limits of which may be determined from a variety of points of view," which "show very material differences in different languages, and do not conform by any means to the same principles of classification." English offered a wide variety of terms for water; Eskimo a wide variety of terms for snow. The principle of "selection of such simple terms must to a certain extent depend upon the chief interests of a people," and for this reason, "each language, from the point of view of another language, may be arbitrary in its classification." Every language "may be holophrastic from the point of view of another," and "holophrasis can hardly be taken as a fundamental characteristic of primitive languages" (1911a:24–27).

It was in this context that Boas offered the definition of grammatical processes I have referred to already. He then went on to argue that the "natural unit of expression was the sentence" and to suggest that our concept of the word was entirely artificial, evident only as the outcome of analysis, and that "the same element may appear at one time as an independent noun, then again as part of a word, . . . which for this reason we are not inclined to consider as a complex of independent elements." After illustrating the point with references to the grammar of the Reverends Riggs and Dorsey, Boas offered one of his characteristically indirect punch lines:

> It seemed important to discuss somewhat fully the concept of the word in its relation to the whole sentence, because in the morphological treatment of American languages this question plays an important role. (1911a:27–33)

Turning then to the problem of "Stem and Affix," Boas went on to argue that the "separation of the ideas contained in a sentence into material contents and formal modifications is an arbitrary one, brought about, presumably, first of all, by the great variety of ideas which may be expressed in the same formal manner by the same pronominal and tense elements"—not, as Brinton and others would have had it, as the result of evolutionary progress. The method of treating material contents as the "subject-matter of lexicography" and formal elements as "the subject-matter of grammar" was simply the result of an ethnocentric Indo-European point of view. In American languages the distinction was often quite obscure and arbitrary, "owing to the fact that the number of elements which enter into formal compositions becomes very large" (33–35).

Boas then went on to discuss "grammatical categories" and to reject the notion that the Indo-European "system of categories" was present in every language. Indo-European languages classified nouns according to gender, plurality, and case, verbs according to person, tense, mood, and voice. Boas argued, on the one hand, that similar distinctions could be achieved by quite different means than we were accustomed to; on the other, that entirely different distinctions were possible, based on the tendency of each language "to select this or that aspect of the mental image" involved in a given idea as *necessary* to be expressed. If it was true, as Brinton had argued, that "true gender was on the whole rare" in American languages, this was because "the sex principle" was "merely one of a great many possible classifications" of nominal forms. Similarly, we said "the man is sick," whereas a Kwakiutl was in effect required to say "that invisible man lies sick on his back on the floor of the absent house," because the categories of visibility and nearness were obligatory in Kwakiutl (1911a:35–43).

Involved in all of this was of course the idea that there were underlying (although culturally conditioned) psychological differences between languages which were expressed in their vocabulary and their morphology. That these psychological differences might eventually be catalogued comparatively was indeed a promissory note. But the method of analysis that was predicated on their existence was not.

The Analytical Treatment of Languages

The unifying leitmotif of Boas' correspondence relating to the *Handbook* is the word "analytical." The very first proposal to McGee suggests that the guiding idea embodied in the 1900 paper on Kwakiutl grammar was "to describe the language in an analytical way, giving the fundaments of the phonetics, grammatical processes, and grammatical categories" (BP: FP/McGee 4/4/01). Two years later, in restating the plan more elaborately to Holmes, Boas wrote that "my plan is to make the sketches strictly analytical, and it will be necessary to lay down definitely the fundamental points of view of analysis to be followed by all the collaborators" (FB/

WH 5/9/03). At a number of points, Boas offered qualifying or appositive statements that suggest what he meant by "purely analytical." Most important an analytic treatment involved "a presentation of the essential traits of the grammar as they would naturally develop if an Eskimo, without any knowledge of any other language, should present the essential notions of his own grammar" (FB/Thalbitzer 1/30/07). In other words, "grammatical categories" were to be derived internally from an analysis of the language itself rather than imposed from without. One must strive therefore "to keep out the point of view of Indo-European languages as thoroughly as possible," to formulate grammatical categories "without reference to the current classifications [of categories] of Indo-European languages, which have helped to obscure the fundamental traits of American languages for so long a time" (FB/J. Dunn 11/7/07).

It is in this context that one must understand Boas' detailed instructions to collaborators in July 1904. True, he enclosed a draft of his Kwakiutl sketch (and apparently of his general introduction as well), with the request that collaborators "adhere to a division into sections and paragraphs similar to the one here adopted." True, he offered his recent article on Chinook vocabulary (1904a) as a model for the treatment of that section (BE: FB/collaborators 7/16/04). But both the correspondence and the resulting grammars make it clear that the Kwakiutl headings were illustrative rather than obligatory. The crucial principle governing the sequence of topics was expressed in later letters to Hewitt and Thalbitzer:

> I have found it convenient in practically all the sketches to divide the subject-matter of morphology in such a way, that I have first treated what might perhaps be called the etymological processes, or the elements which enter into composition in a word or sentence-word, without giving the syntactic relations involved in the subject-predicate of the sentence; that is to say, I have practically taken every morphological part that has nothing to do with syntax first, and all the syntactic elements (for instance, pronomial parts, etc.) after this portion has been settled. (BP: FB/JH 8/30/07; cf. FB/WT 1/30/07)

Brinton and other evolutionists had treated syntax as an evolutionary development and minimized its role in American languages. By arguing that the problem of relating the phonetic groupings which expressed various ideas could be and in fact was handled by various alternative processes which, given the character of American languages, were better regarded as matters of "etymology" (or word formation), and by relegating the treatment of traditional syntactical issues to a secondary position, Boas did two things. On the one hand, he emphasized the amount of "syntax" in Indian languages; on the other he in effect suggested that the traditional notion of syntax was in itself an ethnocentric concept.

Turning to the grammars themselves to see how Boas' instructions were carried out, one notes that the emphasis in each grammar was indeed on the etymological processes by which phonetic groups were related to each other and on the different sorts of ideas conveyed by classes of phonetic groups. Insofar as the traditional "parts of speech" were systematically treated, they appeared usually as subheadings within a framework constructed on this basis—although in Goddard's Hupa one can still detect the old structure in terms of parts of speech. References to syntax were usually relegated to rather brief discussions at the end under the headings "syntactical particles," "syntactical relations," or "character of sentence." Beyond this, one is struck by the occasions in which the presentation or interpretation of the data seems implicitly to have been directed at undercutting particular generalizations about Indian languages or about primitive languages in general that I have suggested were current in nineteenth-century evolutionary linguistic thought: if Brinton argued that Indian languages had few conjunctions, then Boas noted the numerous conjunctions in Chinook (1911a:636; Brinton 1890:344–45). On the other hand, one notes the infrequency of reference to "incorporation" as a grammatical process. It is almost as if the underlying theme of the book were the attempt to discuss American Indian languages without reference to the specific process that many nineteenth-century linguists had argued was their central structural principle.

Beyond these evident similarities of analytic approach, the striking thing about the grammars is their apparent diversity. Within the general framework I have suggested, the headings of analysis and the order of their presentation seem quite varied. But the present argument would in fact call for precisely this sort of diversity. If the goal was to describe each language in terms of its "inner form" and to derive its categories by a purely internal analysis, and if as Boas suggested to Kroeber the choice of languages had been guided by the desire to have "as many psychologically distinct types as possible" (BP: FB/AK 4/4/04), then diversity of presentation was the logical result of consensus on the method of analysis. (It is perhaps in this context that we should understand the "interspersing" of "non-semantic processes among grammatical processes" that Voegelin suggested filled the sketches with "complex statements which crowd out simple patterns" [1952:445].) Boas in fact made the basis of this general diversity quite explicit in his Introduction:

> Owing to the fundamental differences between different linguistic families, it has seemed advisable to develop the terminology of each independently of the others, and to seek for uniformity only in cases where it can be obtained without artificially stretching the definition of terms. (1911a:82)

In the context of a critique of nineteenth-century assumptions, the insistence on the diversity and variety of Indian linguistic forms and processes was simply the obverse of the prevailing failure to mention incorporation.

In the light of the discussion to this point we may perhaps better understand certain "peculiarities of technical terminology" that Voegelin alleged appeared in "grammar after grammar of the first volume of the Handbook." Voegelin referred specifically to "composition" and to "coalescence." He suggested that "composition" was used "in a wide sense to summarize all linear morphemes which may appear in a word (as prefixes before stems, infixes within stems, and suffixes after stems) instead of in the usual narrow-sense use of 'composition' for compounding—for sequences of (generally) two stems serving as a base for affixation" (1952:440). There is a passage in an article by Kroeber published at about this time that perhaps suggests why the *Handbook* should have used the term in the broad sense Voegelin described:

> It is thoroughly misleading to designate the same process respectively "composition" and "incorporation" according as one has in mind his own or other forms of speech. Some day philologists will approach their profession not with the assumption that language must differ in kind or in being relatively better or worse, but with the assumption that the same fundamental processes run through them all, and with the realization that it is only by starting from the conception of their essential unity of type and method that their interesting and important diversities can be understood. (1911:583–84)

Kroeber was in fact inclined to define "incorporation" out of existence (1911: 583–84; cf. 1909a, 1910). His attempt to do so got him into a bit of a controversy with Edward Sapir (Sapir 1911). But Sapir's agreement on the underlying issue is quite evident, particularly in his own comments on the notion of "coalescence."

Voegelin suggested that "coalescence" was used in the *Handbook* as a "sort of chemical metaphor for alterations and contractions occuring when an affix is juxtaposed to a stem," and that Sapir, "evidently amused at this metaphor," "poked gentle fun" at it in his Takelma grammar (1952:440). The quality of their relationship in this period makes it unlikely that Sapir would even indirectly poke fun at Boas in a doctoral dissertation Boas supervised. More to the point, however, is the fact that "coalescence" appears only incidentally in the *Handbook,* and then as rather more a common-sense than a technical term. What Sapir was talking about was an entirely different matter, and bears directly on the more general issue I am discussing. The passage quoted by Voegelin occurs in a general discussion of Takelma morphology, in which Sapir attacks the use of the terms "incorporation," "polysynthesis," and "agglutination" as "catch-words" to describe the general structure of American Indian languages, and of Takelma in particular.

> If we study the manner in which the stem unites in Takelma with derivative and grammatical elements to form the word, and the vocalic and consonantic changes that the stem itself undergoes from grammatical purposes, we shall hardly be able to find a tangible difference in general method, however much the details may vary, between Takelma and languages that have been dignified by the name "inflectional." It is generally said, in defining inflection, that languages of the inflectional as contrasted with those of the agglutinative type make use of words of indivisible psychic value, in which the stem and the various grammatical elements have entirely lost their single individualities, but have "chemically" (!) coalesced into a single form-unit; in other words, the word is not a mere mosaic of phonetic materials, of which each is the necessary symbol of some special concept (stem) or logical category (grammatical element). (1922b:52–53)

Although Sapir does not indicate this in so many words, the idea that inflected words coalesced chemically whereas agglutinated words were merely stuck together was simply a variant of the sort of thinking I have been discussing—in slightly different form, the notion goes back to Wilhelm von Humboldt (1836; cf. GS 1973b). It was not at Boas, but at certain pervasive assumptions in nineteenth-century linguistics, that Sapir was poking fun.

Indeed, Sapir went on to argue in a manner quite consistent with Boas' general discussion of the "Characteristics of American Languages" (Boas 1911a:74–76) that from one point of view Takelma might be regarded as polysynthetic, from another, incorporative, from another, inflective, and that a "more objective, unhampered study of languages"—Boas would have said "analytic"—would "undoubtedly reveal a far wider prevalence than has been generally admitted of the inflectional type." The problem was that investigation had been sidetracked by taking "trivial characteristics" like sex gender and the presence of cases as "criteria of inflection," when in fact "inflection has reference to method, not to subject-matter" (Sapir 1922b:54). It requires only a slight extension of Sapir's comment to get at the whole point of the Boas plan: grammatical categories had reference to method (or better process) and to cultural focus—not to any *a priori* ethnocentric or evolutionary notion of subject matter.

Boas and the Comparison of Linguistic Structures

If the discussion so far has perhaps clarified the central point of the Boas plan, there are still several matters relating to its genesis and significance which merit brief discussion: Boas' attitude toward the problem of the classification of American languages; his relation to the tradition of thinking on language and world view that is customarily traced back from Whorf and Sapir through Boas and sometimes Brinton to Wilhelm von Humboldt; and his relation to the subsequent tradition of structural linguistics in America.

In regard to the first of these, I have already noted Voegelin's suggestion that the purpose of the *Handbook* was to facilitate the "cross-genetic comparability" that was essential to "diffusional linguistics." While there is some basis for this interpretation, there are complexities that bear some comment. In the first decade or so of his linguistic work, Boas was by no means uninterested in genetic approaches to linguistic classification, and his early interest in the systematic study of structures in fact reflected his concern with genetic rather than diffusionary problems. After returning from the Northwest in 1888, he wrote Powell a letter in which he argued that, despite the number of borrowed words in Tlingit and Haida, their "grammatical structure" was "so much alike that they must be considered remote branches of the same stock" (BE: FB/JP 8/8/88). The same interest was still evident in his 1893 paper, where his advocacy of deeper study of structures was offered as a solution "in the present state of linguistic science" to the problem of defining the "generic connection" within each of the four groups of languages on the Northwest Coast (1894:346). Various letters indicate that Boas thought of the *Handbook*, at least in its early stages, as a "morphological classification" of American languages, and that the languages were chosen in order to facilitate comparison of differing psychological types in a single broad geographical region (BE: FB/Holmes 2/13/04: BP: FB/Kroeber 4/4/04). I have already noted his insistence that Goddard and Swanton point up a relationship he found between Tlingit and Athapaskan, which, along with his earlier suggestion of the kinship of Haida and Tlingit, in effect tied together the three major components of Sapir's Na-dene—a fact that is all the more interesting in the light of Boas' later attitude towards Sapir's genetic reconstructions (1911a:46; Sapir 1915; Boas 1920a; Darnell 1971b).

On the other hand, there is no doubt that there was a development in Boas' thought on these problems that reflects a tendency toward increasing skepticism also evident in other areas of his anthropological thought (GS 1974d). From the beginning of his career, Boas had resisted "premature classification." When Kroeber and others were laboring in 1905 over a reformulation of Powell's scheme of American languages, Boas' response (although the issue at this point was simply one of nomenclature) reflected his deeply rooted conservatism on classificatory matters. After opposing the report Kroeber drafted, he indicated to F. W. Hodge that he would favor a simple statement that "among specialists who are working on linguistic stocks of America, the following names are at present in use, and therefore, for the time being, deserve recommendation," after which a list could be appended "made up by our California friends and other specialists" (BP: FB/FH 11/1/05). Perhaps more to the present point is the fact that Boas seems to have regarded an "analytic" treatment of language as essentially synchronic rather than diachronic. He suggested to Goddard that it made no difference that a substitute formulation which he had proposed lumped elements that differed in their origin. This was only to be expected in "any purely analytical treatment," in which elements that had become alike through the action of analogy or other causes would be part of a single grammatical category in the present (FB/PG 12/28/07; cf. Boas 1911a:82). Furthermore, despite Boas' editing of the Tlingit and Athapaskan, the *Handbook* is on the whole notably lacking in any sort of systematic comparison of one language to another. In the end, the comparative analysis that was to have been its capstone was never attempted.

During the next decade, when Boas' students went far beyond him in arguing genetic relationships among American Indian languages (Darnell 1990:107–31), he responded with critical skepticism, and perhaps in reaction, considerably elaborated the diffusional arguments that were already present in the Introduction to the *Handbook* (1911a:47–53). Even in the *Handbook* itself, Boas was not willing to assume that the structural similarity of Tlingit, Haida, and Athapaskan was the result of common origin, despite the fact that he was at this point still inclined to minimize the possibility of a "radical modification of the morphological traits of a language through the influence of another language" (49). By 1920 his position on this issue had changed drastically, and he was inclined to believe that diffusion of morphological traits could "modify the fundamental structural characteristics" of a language, and specifically disavowed his suggestion in 1893 that the morphological similarities of certain Northwest languages were "a proof of relationship of the same order as that of languages belonging, for instance, to the Indo-European family" (1920a:367–68; cf. Boas 1917, 1929). If, as this evidence suggests, the extreme linguistic diffusionism associated with Boas is in fact to be understood in the context of his later disagreements with certain of his students, then it seems unlikely that the *Handbook* was specifically designed to meet the felt need of diffusionary linguistics for "structural similarities among languages, whether related or not," rather than for "cognates among morpheme lists" (Voegelin 1952:439). On the contrary, it seems to have begun at least in part as an attempt to approach the problem of genetic relationship in morphological terms. But this goal was from the beginning subordinated to the goal of providing adequate "analytic" descriptions of the languages themselves, and by the time the Introduction was written in 1908, the whole problem of "the final classification of languages" was already postponed for an indefinite future time (Boas 1911a:58, 82). Just as the possibility of deriving laws for the development of culture constantly receded behind the horizon of mounting empirical data of American cultures, so the possibility of a genetic classification of languages—even on morphological as opposed to lexical grounds—seems already to have begun to recede behind the empirical complexity of American Indian languages (cf. Kluckhohn & Prufer 1959:24; Kroeber 1960:656; GS 1968a:210–12, 1974e).

The relation of the *Handbook* to the tradition associated with Wilhelm von Humboldt is also somewhat complicated. Boas later suggested that his greatest contribution to linguistics was to present each language in Steinthal's terms by analyzing it in relation to its own internal system rather than to categories imposed from without (Lowie 1943:184). Steinthal was perhaps the leading European disciple of Humboldt, and this would seem to suggest a fairly clear lineage through Boas to Sapir and Whorf for the "promissory note" of a comparative study of languages and *Weltanschauungen* (cf. R. L. Brown 1967:14–16; Hymes 1961a:23).

On the other hand, there is evidence to suggest that Boas' psychological approach to language was at least in part a response to the experience of his own fieldwork rather than simply an importation of a Germanic tradition. In a letter to the head of the Carnegie Institution in 1905, he suggested that:

> One of the remarkable features of American anthropology is the multiplicity of small linguistic families the origin of which is entirely obscure to us. The investigations made during the last ten years suggest that there may be larger unities in existence based rather on similarity of the psychological foundations of language than on phonetic similarity. This hypothesis is based on the observation that in several regions neighboring languages, although quite diverse in vocabulary, are similar in structure. The psychological significance of this phenomenon is still entirely obscure and would very probably be cleared up by a thorough study of those regions in which the greatest differentiation of language occurs. (BP: FB/Woodward 1/13/05)

Furthermore, Humboldt's leading American disciple was Brinton, who cited Steinthal at length on the "incorporative" character of all American Indian languages, and who was upon occasion inclined toward a rather extreme racial determinism and evolutionary dogmatism (Brinton 1895). The point is that in the late-nineteenth-century milieu, Humboldt's thinking had become linked with a melange of evolutionary and racial assumptions whose rejection was the cornerstone of Boas' own anthropology. More than any other single individual, it was in fact Brinton who was the target of the Boasian critique (cf. Darnell 1988).

In this context, it is not surprising that Boas' comments in the *Handbook* on the relation of language and culture were not without elements of ambiguity and even of apparent contradiction. To begin with, Boas, in line with his general scepticism of artificial classifications, devoted the first ten pages of his Introduction to an argument that the independence of their historical development ruled out any correlation between race, language and culture, not only in the present, but even in an hypothesized primitive state (1911a:5–14). When it came to considering specifically the relation of "language and thought," he explicitly rejected as *not* "likely" any "direct relation between the culture of a tribe and the language they speak." On the contrary, if primitive men lacked certain grammatical forms, it was because their mode of life did not require them. If this mode changed, these forms would doubtless develop, since "under these conditions the language would be moulded rather by the cultural state" than vice versa (67).

At the same time, Boas went on to argue that linguistic processes offered an important insight into the processes of cultural determinism. Like linguistic categories, major cultural categories, values, and norms arose unconsciously. They differed only in that they were subsequently subject to secondary rationalization. This argument was an important link in Boas' critique of traditional racial assumptions (cf. GS 1968a:222, 1974e). However, it also provided a means for reintroducing indirectly a portion of the linguistic determinism he had previously rejected. If the occurrence of "the most fundamental grammatical concepts in all languages" was proof of the essential psychological unity of man, it was also true that we think in words, and the words available to us could not but condition our thought. Thus it was an "open" question how far "linguistic expression" was secondary to the "customs of the people," and whether the latter "have not rather developed from the unconsciously developed terminology." Anticipating an argument his student Kroeber was to advance in 1909, Boas referred to kinship classes as an example. Coming then almost full circle, Boas concluded this section of the introduction by arguing that "the peculiar characteristics of languages are clearly reflected in the views and customs of the world" (1911a:67–73 [written in 1908]).

This argument is not intended to minimize the relation of Boas to the German tradition of Humboldt and Steinthal. His emphasis in the Introduction on "inner form"—which for both men was a technical term—is enough to suggest an important tie. But the primary impact of Boas' thought was to support a thoroughgoing linguistic relativism, and to reject any form of linguistic determinism that might be used to bolster either racial determinism or an evolutionary hierarchy. To enlarge somewhat on a suggestion by Dell Hymes, it may be that it was, in a retrospective sense, necessary at this point in the lineage of Humboldtian thought to purge it of

"Procrustean typological and evolutionary categories" (1961a:24). In the late-nineteenth-century context, these had racialist implications which were clearly incompatible with the general thrust of modern anthropological thought. If the subsequent anthropological concern with linguistics and worldview can legitimately be traced through Boas to Humboldt, there is nevertheless at this point a discontinuity some commentaries have perhaps passed over a bit too easily.[7]

As far as Boas' relation to subsequent structural linguistics is concerned, it should be clear from what has gone before that Voegelin went too far in subsuming Boas within the framework of what came after him. There may be a sense in which it is useful to regard Boas as exemplifying "monolevel structuralizing" (Voegelin & Voegelin 1963). But insofar as the notion of structure implies (as it seems to me to do) "inferences from the internal relations of a system more than inferences from discrete pieces of reality," then it seems to me that Hymes was correct in suggesting that Boasian grammars "itemize," but "on the whole, they do not structure" (1961b:90; cf. Hockett 1954). Doubtless Boas was interested in "observed regularities, recurrences, and reduction of redundancies" (Voegelin & Voegelin 1963:14), and his indication in 1908 that an "analytic" study of language was purely synchronic suggests an interesting parallel to Saussure. But it is also clear that he hesitated to carry the reduction to system too far. Indeed, his instructions to collaborators cautioned them against trying to make their analyses too tidy. Redundancies and inconsistencies would doubtless occur, since "in no language can be found a psychological system which is carried through logically" (BE: FB/collaborators 7/16/04). As Hymes suggested, Boas is best seen as "clearing the way for, but not quite occupying the ground of, his structurally-minded successors" (1961b:90; cf. 1970; Jakobson 1944:195, 1959).

Hymes advanced this interpretation in the context of arguing the consistency of Boas' approach to language with his approach to folklore. This consistency is in fact one of the most striking characteristics of Boas' anthropology as a whole. Thus his argument that classification of humankind according to race, according to language, and according to culture would not lead to the same results because each of these aspects had been differentially affected by historical processes is exactly parallel to his argu-

7. This discontinuity would seem to be particularly relevant in evaluating the suggested role of Brinton in this lineage. In view of the fact that Brinton was the implicit critical target of so much of Boas' anthropological thought (whether in linguistics or in culture theory generally), and of the fact that the Humboldt tradition was more directly available to him through Steinthal—whom he clearly read if he did not study with—it seems to me unlikely that Boas was linked to Humboldt through Brinton in any positive way (cf. Hymes 1961a; Darnell 1988; R. L. Brown 1967; GS 1968).

ment in regard to lexicon, phonology, and grammar as bases for the "Classification of Languages" (1911a:5–14, 44–58). And although there are aspects of his thought on culture that suggest the basis for an approach in terms of "system," his own orientation, in this area as in others, was antisystematic (cf. GS 1974e).

And for good reason. Boas' whole anthropology was a reaction against the simple typological thinking and "premature" or "arbitrary classification" that he felt was characteristic of evolutionary thought about man. His criticism of racial "types" and cultural "stages" carried directly over into his thought on language, which was a consciously relativistic reaction to traditional evolutionary assumptions about so-called primitive languages. Like the rest of Boas' anthropology, it shared with evolutionism the goal of elucidating development in time, but it did this by focussing in the first instance on processes observable in the present. It was—or attempted to be—rigorously empirical, and was above all concerned with the development of adequate methods of description.

Here we return to the title of the work itself. It was a *Handbook;* and whatever its later usage actually was, it was conceived, at least in part, as a guide to the study of Indian languages in the field. As Boas suggested to Holmes in 1903, "the principal point to be borne in mind is, on the one hand, to make a book which will show collectors how to proceed in recording Indian languages; and, on the other hand, to show by these ten examples what American languages really are" (BP: FB/WH 5/9/03).

In realizing the goal of adequate description, Boas placed great emphasis on the collection of texts, the utility of which has been questioned by some later writers on the grounds that the process of their dictation led informants artifically to simplify their sentence structure (C. F. Voegelin: personal communication). Although it may seem tangential to introduce this issue at this late point, it in fact helps to place Boas' linguistic orientation—and indeed his whole anthropology—more firmly in context. On several occasions Boas wrote in defense of texts to the Bureau, which tended to regard their publication as uneconomic. No one, he suggested to Holmes, would advocate the study of the "antique civilizations" of the Turks or Russians without a thorough knowledge of the "literary documents in their languages." For the American Indian, practically no such literary material was available, and to make it available was a crucial task for anthropology.

> My own published work shows that I let this kind of work take precedence over practically everything else, since it is the foundation of all future researches. Without it a control of our results and deeper studies based on material collected by us will be all but impossible. . . . What would Indo-European philology be, if we had only grammars by one or two students

> and not the live material from which these grammars have been built up, which is, at the same time, the material on which the philosophic study of language must be based? (BE: FB/WH 7/24/05)

The point was nowhere clearer, suggested Boas, than in studies based on the "old missionary grammars," in which the characteristic features were so obscured that without new and ample texts our understanding would always be inadequate. "As we require a new point of view now, so future times will require new points of view, and for them the texts, and ample texts, must be available" (BE: FB/WH 7/24/05; cf. BP: FB/WH 11/2/03). The passage is particularly revealing in that it suggests that despite his lack of training in European philology, Boas still tended to conceive of linguistics (and indeed cultural anthropology) as the study of *written* documents. If these were lacking, then one provided them. But he was not unaware that the method of text recording involved certain distortions—his experimentation with phonographs makes this quite clear (BE: FB/WH 11/3/06).

More to the present point, however, is the transformation of traditional approaches that took place in the process of achieving a rather traditional goal. It is not merely that Boas was, "in cold and sober fact, the agent who . . . more than any other" focussed "the attention of scholars on those unfamiliar languages that are the vehicles of the lowly and despised cultures of 'our primitive contemporaries.'" More than any other man, he transformed the negative evolutionary evaluation of these languages in the very process of defining the methods of their study. It is at this level of what modern American linguists take *most* for granted that Boas was "the *guru*, the ancestor in learning, of all those in this country who work in descriptive linguistics." It is at this level of attitude, assumption, and method that the *Handbook* was "the 'manifesto' for this study" (Emeneau 1943:35).

3

Anthropology as *Kulturkampf*

Science and Politics in the Career of Franz Boas

This essay was solicited by Walter Goldschmidt, then president of the American Anthropological Association, with the approval of its Executive Board, at the initiative of the Planning and Development Committee, which was anxious to encourage the nonacademic employment of anthropologists. The volume in which it appeared was clearly a response to the sense of crisis widespread in anthropology in the late 1960s and early 1970s. Its impulse, however, was not a radical "reinvention" of anthropology (Hymes 1972); as editor, Goldschmidt took pains to insist that he was *not* "raising here that recently popular shibboleth, 'relevance'" (1979:11). It was rather that "academic opportunities [were] declining to the vanishing point and because ethnographic work in the third world countries and in tribal America [was] increasingly difficult to engage in" (8).

In this context of present concern, the volume sought to overcome the anti-utilitarian bias which, since the "flight from Washington" after World War II, had made anthropology the most highly academicized of the social sciences (Solmon et al. 1981:157–58). If anthropologists were not engaged in "public involvements," it was because academic anthropologists, believing "that pragmatic activities are of little or no worth" (Goldschmidt 1979:9), did not "train them to be there—more accurately, perhaps, [have] trained them *not* to be there" (8). The purpose of the book was thus explicitly "to establish the legitimacy of the [present] use of anthropology by reference to its past applications" (1), because "this was seen as necessary for the preservation of a viable anthropology in the last quarter of the 20th century" (10). Most of the authors were practicing anthropologists, "recognized leaders in anthropology, themselves directly involved in its application," who had been encouraged to mention the names of "all known anthropologists" likewise involved, in the belief that "the sum of such lists would read like a Who's Who of anthropology today" (1). The goal, in short, was to encourage "the return of anthropology to the world of affairs" by recording "the degree to which anthropologists have historically engaged in public affairs and to show that these activities were both valuable and valued, and to assert through historical charter the legitimacy and propriety of such activities" (2, 9).

Goldschmidt found it anomalous that serious "historic examination of our discipline had [had] to be initiated from outside by historians" (Goldschmidt 1979:10); the anomaly was perhaps confirmed by the fact that the two historians recruited to cover "the earlier phases of our development" (10) both chafed somewhat in the harness of present purpose. Curtis Hinsley was reported as believing that there had been "a long-term secular trend in anthropology" away from public involvement, and "that the brief reversion sponsored by the New Deal and inspired by World War II may well have been a kind of anomaly" (7). And my own review of the career of Franz Boas focussed on the tensions and contradictions of Boas' characteristically academic "scientific activism." Emphasizing, in the words of the editor, "an appreciation of his attitudes and orientations rather than his specific performance," it was not exactly what he had anticipated (personal communication, 2/21/1977).

Fifteen years on, it is clear that, in terms of numbers, anthropology is much less "academic" than it once was: although the "modal" anthropologist of the latest doctoral cohort went on from fieldwork on a "nonapplied topic" to an academic position, 59 percent of her cohort had taken nonacademic jobs, which although lower in disciplinary status, were somewhat better paying (*Anthropology Newsletter* 5/91, p. 1). Whether such numbers will soon translate into changing professional norms or the more significant involvement of anthropology in the public realm is an open question. What will turn out to have been long-term secular trend and what merely short-term anomaly—or what short-term revolutionary change and what long-term evolutionary survival—is not simply a matter of historical perspective but of the outcome of present processes, involving human agency, whose effect may turn out to have been transformative.

As an historian of late-nineteenth- and early-twentieth-century anthropology, I have chronicled two such major transformations. But as a by-product of that historiographical experience (and the limits of my own anthropological training), I identify very strongly with the anthropology that emerged in what may be called the "classical" period (c.

1920–c. 1965). In treating developments since then I tend in certain fundamental respects to privilege continuity over change. This disposition has perhaps been strengthened by long residence in a department that remains staunchly academic, and whose response to present concerns has been intellectually grounded in what might be called the deeper structures of anthropological inquiry.

Strongly identifying with Boas, I have no doubt read him in terms consonant with my own experience. And the experience of that reading has now itself receded into the past, to be refreshed only occasionally since it was originally carried on in the two decades before 1976. The biography that I once contemplated is, for me, another unwritten book—and by this time others have taken up that daunting task (Cole 1988; cf. Hyatt 1990). In the meantime, this essay is the closest I have come to a general treatment of his full career. Focussing on the ironies and ambiguities of his lifelong fight for culture, it may perhaps contribute to our understanding not only of Boas but also of the anthropological tradition itself.

From the time of his entry into science in Bismarckian Germany until his death in the midst of the military struggle against German Nazism, the anthropology of Franz Boas evolved in a political milieu, and during much of that time he sought to use it to modify that milieu. Consideration of the reciprocal relation of science and society in his work may help to ground our understanding of Boas in particular historical contexts. But it may also have a more archetypical meaning. For just as the relation between science and history in his anthropological thought illuminates an enduring tension in the intellectual structures of the discipline, so may that between his scientific work and his political activity tell us something more general about the relation of anthropology and public life (cf. Hyatt 1990; Levenstein 1963; Wolf 1972).

From Bismarckian Germany to America in the Gilded Age

Boas was born in 1858, a decade after the liberal revolution and thirteen years before the emancipation of German Jewry was finally formalized in the constitution of the German Empire in 1871. His family were assimilating Jews who had broken "the shackles of dogma" and embraced "the ideals of the Revolution of 1848" (GS 1974c:41).[1] In Boas' own version of

1. In writing this essay I drew on previously published work, and on many points there is fuller documentation in the sources indicated. In citing Boas materials reprinted in GS

Franz Boas (second from left) during his year of compulsory military service in the *Infanterie-regiments 15 Prinz Friedrich der Niederlande,* 1881–1882. (Courtesy of the American Philosophical Society)

those ideals, education and equality of opportunity, political and intellectual liberty, the rejection of dogma and the search for scientific truth, the identification with all humanity and devotion to its progress were all part of a single left-liberal posture similar to that of his anthropological men-

1974c, I referred to the collection rather than the originals, and followed this policy also in the case of those early Boas essays reproduced in Boas 1945. To reduce the burden of parenthetical documentation, I referred to materials in the microfilm edition of Boas' professional papers (1972) only by date, since they are there organized chronologically, and virtually all of my quotations are from Boas himself.

tor, Rudolf Virchow. At the time that Boas came of age, however, these ideals seemed seriously compromised in Germany. The struggle for a culturally unified national state against the traditional religious authority of the Catholic Church—which Virchow himself had dubbed the *Kulturkampf*—had led in practice to religious division and the violation of liberal principles. Bismarck, turning from the liberals, was forging a new alliance of Junkers and big industry with the passage of a protective tariff and antisocialist legislation. Boas' university years witnessed the climax of an anti-Semitic upsurge that had begun during the depression of 1873, and his face bore the scars of duels he had fought over anti-Semitic remarks. Despite a profound identification with classical German culture, the German national state, and the tradition of German liberalism, Boas felt a strong sense of alienation from the Germany of his own day when he left for Baffinland in 1883 to do ethnogeographic research among the Eskimo. When he returned from the Arctic to find Bismarck laying the foundations of German colonial empire over other "primitive" peoples in Africa and New Guinea, his cultural identity seemed even further compromised (Holborn 1969; GS 1968a:135–60; Tal 1975).

In this context, Boas began to think of leaving Germany. His uncle Abraham Jacobi, whom he later described as having been "an enthusiastic adherent of Marx" (9/24/41), was a "forty-eighter" whose successful medical career in the United States offered the personal embodiment of a vision of America as land of political freedom and scientific opportunity. Discussing his future in a letter to his uncle, Boas declared that science alone was not enough for him: "I must be able to livingly create." As a member of the German professoriat, he would never be able to keep his "mouth shut politically against impure self-seeking, and be condemned to absolute inactivity." In the United States, where geographical science did not yet really exist, he saw the prospect of a work so rewarding that he could see "nothing equally worthwhile in Germany" (GS 1968a:150). Within two years Boas—by then having completed his trek from physics to ethnology—did in fact settle permanently in America (cf. ibid. 133–60).

At the very threshold of his scientific career in the United States, several themes were already established that resonate throughout Boas' later professional life. Fundamental to his viewpoint was the commitment—which Virchow had seen as basic to the *Kulturkampf*—to science and rational thought against the irrational authority of tradition. Boas' early experience, however, gave a certain ambiguity to each of the terms of the opposition. A German national state presumably committed to a rational and scientific worldview had produced a self-serving science and an emotionally unsatisfying culture that threatened to exclude Boas himself; in contrast, a "primitive" Eskimo society, presumably governed by inferior rationality, had produced a culture that was "relatively speaking" a fuller embodiment of human potential. In this context the political meaning of Boas' scientific life may be seen as a transvalued and dichotomized *Kulturkampf:* on the one hand, as a struggle to preserve the cultural conditions of the search for universal rational knowledge, and on the other, as a struggle to defend the validity of alternative cultural worlds. To Boas, however, any ethical and epistemological issues involved in the implicit opposition between what might be called the progressivist and the romantic anthropological attitudes never seemed a serious problem. Science for him remained always an ethically self-justifying activity. Retrospectively he saw his work as the expression of a unified scientific and political position: the scientific search for the "psychological origin of the implicit belief in the authority of tradition" would be fulfilled politically when, recognizing tradition's shackles, we were able to break them (GS 1974c:42). In the 1880s, however, there seemed little prospect of realizing such a goal in Germany, and his solution was in effect a withdrawal from the harsh reality of his native social world and entry into what seemed a more open and expansive political and economic sphere—a land whose many opportunities included the chance for an ambitious young scholar to pursue a double quest for scientific truth and personal advancement.

Paradoxically, the United States to which Boas emigrated had also entered a crassly materialistic and self-serving Gilded Age. Unrestrained capitalist expansion and increasing concentration of economic and political power were creating major social inequities, leaving many groups at the mercy of the cyclical forces of economic growth—and without the social insurance Bismarck had enacted to win the German working class from socialism. If opportunity still beckoned to Europe's oppressed peoples, the dominant American tradition impinged on its minorities with culturally destructive force; the noble American savages whose lives Boas must have known as a child in Leatherstocking tales had been reduced to the half-life of the reservation (Washburn 1975); the economic and political position of American blacks was approaching its postemancipation nadir (Logan 1965). American xenophobia was in the early phases of a long-term upsurge against the "new" immigration from eastern Europe (Higham 1955). Its internal expansion virtually completed, the country was shortly to embark on its own version of overseas imperialism (La Feber 1963).

Boas felt the impact of some of these forces personally. In 1890 his duel-scarred face was the focus of xenophobic attack by the Worcester, Massachusetts, press against the "docents" at Clark University who were vivisecting dogs and stripping schoolchildren naked, ostensibly to measure their growth (*Daily Telegram,* 3/12/90). The aggressive entrepreneurialism that penetrated even the world of science affected the conditions of his scholarly life, as he bounced from job to job in the early 1890s, spending more than a year without regular employment, until family and personal connections with a major academic entrepreneur, F. W. Putnam, finally helped establish him permanently in New York. During this period, when he struggled to win a place for himself and his discipline in American academic life, Boas' science was not only self-justifying, but to a very great degree self-centered. And understandably so, in view of his recent immigrant status—he felt it remarkable that he, "a *foreigner*," was chosen to give the sectional address at the American Association for the Advancement of Science in 1894 (BP: FB/parents 6/22/94). The talk he gave on "Human Faculty as Determined by Race" contained in germ the substance of most of his later public writings on race. But though he gave it at what he regarded as a "popular" level, it was buried in the pages of the Association's *Proceedings* (GS 1974c:221–42). Save for some letters to the Canadian press defending the Kwakiutls' right to potlatch, this seems to have been his only entry into the public arena before 1900 (La Violette 1961: 67–75).

Pragmatic Academic Activism in the Progressive Era

It was not until he was firmly established at Columbia that Boas began to respond more actively to public issues, and his first response casts an interesting light on some ambiguities of his own position, as well as that of anthropology generally. Boas was later to locate the moment of his disillusion with the promise of American life in 1898, "when the aggressive imperialism of that period showed that the ideal had been a dream." Recalling "heated discussions" with German friends in which he argued that "the control of colonies" was inconsistent with basic American values, he echoed his "profound disappointment" when "at the end of the Spanish war, these ideals lay shattered" (GS 1974c:331–32). His active response at the time, however, was much more pragmatic.

In January 1901 the German-Jewish financier Jacob Schiff, head of the banking house of Kuhn, Loeb & Co., gave $15,000 at Boas' behest to the American Museum to develop a Chinese collection—with the understanding that expenditures should be in the charge of a committee of seven, including the "robber barons" E. H. Harriman and James J. Hill, who were even then contending for control of the Northern Pacific Railroad (4/7/02). As secretary of the East Asiatic Committee, Boas for the next few years committed a good deal of effort to furthering research and instruction in East Asian cultures, as well as other projects relevant to the new "dependencies of the United States" (including a training program for "the Consular and Commercial Service" jointly sponsored by Columbia and Yale).

He frequently referred to the "practical" value of this work for "the business interests and the diplomatic service of our country" (10/12/01); and one may perhaps assume that such considerations carried some weight with Hill, who had long been interested in the East Asian trade as a means to fill empty boxcars travelling westward. Not, however, very much weight, if one may judge from the willingness of committee members to contribute hard cash. Boas, who was thinking ultimately in terms of two and a half million, a dozen professorships, and a new wing for the museum, was able to raise only $7,800 in an appeal for Philippine research in 1904 (2/15/04). Lacking adequate funds, and caught in the middle of Boas' battles with the museum administration, the committee went out of existence at the end of 1905 (12/28/05).

Although the episode scarcely sustains an oversimple view of anthropology as the "handmaiden" of imperialism, it does cast light on the situational determinants of anthropological research. Boas clearly responded to "external" events and processes, but his activity would seem to have been motivated largely by an "internal" disciplinary dynamic of intellectual and institutional development. His overseas research interests were a direct outgrowth of the diffusionist theoretical rationale underlying the Jesup North Pacific Expedition, which had been undertaken in 1896 to study cultural interrelations between North America and East Asia. His own "practical" goals had to do primarily with forwarding that research and strengthening the position of anthropology—Boasian anthropology—both intellectually and institutionally. As has often since been the case, the crucial factor mediating the relationship of anthropology and society was the problem of financing research, and situational determinism operated in an indirectly constraining rather than a positively directive fashion. In the present instance, Boas could get money for collecting Chinese artifacts but not for fieldwork among the Tagalog. Both were goals he defined, but he was at the mercy of his benefactors in pursuing the one rather than the other at a given point in time.

Pragmatic disciplinary concerns, however, were not the sole motivation for Boas' East Asiatic work. There was an "ethical purpose" as well. One could not deal with "representatives of foreign cultures" without understanding "their mode of thought" (6/18/02). This in turn required "a just appreciation of the achievements of various races" (4/7/02)—which was impossible so long as we persisted in our present "one-sided" emphasis on scientific culture, which led us "to undervalue lines of thought that have led to cultures different from our own" (6/18/02). But if Boas would have substituted intercultural understanding and cultural self-criticism for "the white man's burden," there is no denying a certain naiveté or unconcern with the nature of American economic and political interests overseas. He clearly assumed that the anthropological worldview might, if appropriately propagated, override forces of economic or diplomatic self-interest.

Some of the difficulties facing such a detached and idealist conception of the professional anthropological mission were manifest in Boas' attempt to develop anthropology in Mexico after 1905, when his East Asiatic undertaking ran aground (Godoy 1977). With the support of important officials in the Diaz regime, Boas was able to mobilize the resources necessary to establish the International School of American Archaeology and Ethnology in 1910. Although the school was staffed largely by American and German scholars, Boas realized that anthropology must become indigenous if it were to be propagated in Mexico. Mexican students must be trained, research reports must be published locally, and all artifacts and specimens (except duplicate materials) must remain in the National Museum to inspire native scholars and "to educate public opinion." Preoccupied with the propagation of professional anthropology, however, Boas never really understood the revolutionary political turbulence that swirled around the school almost from its opening—and which he likened to "a pitched battle between a Sheriff's posse and robbers" in the Kentucky mountains. Although he defended Mexico in the New York press and opposed Wilson's intervention, his solution was in fact quite authoritarian: "only a strong hand can bring relief—a Cromwell, or a Napoleon, or a Diaz" (11/12/13). This failing, the school was forced to shut its doors in 1914.

In addition to these extraterritorial initiatives, Boas' anthropological work at home was much more outwardly focussed in the decade and a half after 1900. A high proportion of the Columbia faculty were involved in public service activities external to the university during the Progressive Era, and Boas was no exception. Even so, Boas' response to domestic public issues tended to have a rather narrowly professional focus, and there was a touch of elitism in his approach to the propagation of anthropology. His resignation from the American Museum in 1905 was a protest against "the policy of subordinating all scientific work entirely under 'kindergarten work'" (6/15/05), and the theme that science was catering too much to public taste is recurrent in his letters of this period. A large proportion of his research, however, was oriented toward a critical national issue: the ability of various "racial" groups to assimilate to the conditions of life in the environment of modern American industrial civilization. With mounting concern over the problems posed by the "new immigration" and the outbreak of race riots in the years after 1900, the status of the immigrant and the Negro were issues agitating many liberals. Given Boas' personal background and the network of connections he had formed by this time in the New York philanthropic community—as well as the thrust of his own scientific work, which for some time had been concerned with issues of heredity—it is scarcely surprising that he should have become involved. Characteristically, he approached the problem primarily as one of the development and propagation of anthropological research.

Although he wrote several general articles on Negro cultural achievements and at W. E. B. Du Bois' invitation had given the commencement address at Atlanta University in 1906, Boas' serious interest in these issues developed only when his resignation from the American Museum forced him to seek new sources of research funding. Writing to Felix Adler, the leader of the Ethical Culture movement (in whose schools some of the Boas children were educated), Boas proposed the establishment of an "African Museum" to present to the public "the best products of African civilization," in which extensive cultural, anatomical, and statistical researches on the American Negro might be carried out (10/30/06). Financial appeals to Rockefeller, Carnegie, and the Sage Foundation failed to raise the half-million-dollar building costs and $40,000 annual expenses Boas envisioned, and when the founding of the U.S. Immigration Commission suggested an alternative means of funding work in the same general area. Boas turned to research on changes in immigrant bodily form (GS 1974c: 202–14, 316–38). He continued, however, to write and lecture on racial problems for an educated popular audience, culminating in the series of lectures on *The Mind of Primitive Man* that he gave in Boston and Mexico City in 1911.

Boas' analysis and prognosis regarding the "race problem" in the United States were heavily conditioned not only by his general view of the anthropologist's mission as critic of traditional assumptions but also by the very body of contemporary racial assumption he criticized. Despite his affirmation of the possibility of other equally valuable civilizations based on "a different equilibrium of emotion and reason" (1911b:208), he assumed that the critical issue in the present was the ability of immigrants and blacks to assimilate to the cultural standards of American life. Furthermore, he shared much of the prevailing perception of the American Negro: the basic question was "how far the undesirable traits that are at present undoubtedly found in our negro population are due to racial traits." Where he departed from prevailing assumption was in arguing that the evidence of cultural achievement in black Africa showed that these disabilities were largely "due to social surroundings for which we [whites] are responsible" (271). Similarly, Boas assumed that there would be "differences in the mental makeup of the negro race" corresponding to observed anatomical differences; but he felt these "trifling differences" (5/11/07) did not justify the assumption that "any demand made on the human body or mind in modern life" would prove "beyond the powers of the negro" (1911b:272). Like many writers of his day, Boas tended to see the problem of the "melting pot" ultimately in biological terms. Physical amalgamation, both for the immigrant and for the Negro, was the ultimate solution of the "race problem." The immigrant would be largely incorporated within a hundred years; and though recently passed antimiscegenation laws might "retard the influx of white blood" among blacks, they would not "hinder the gradual progress of intermixture" (GS 1974c:329). In the meantime, science supported the basic American value that each individual should be judged on his own merits, since the large overlap in the frequency distribution of particular traits made it impossible to make any assumption about individual characteristics simply on the basis of race. For the present, however, blacks must strive to work out their own salvation "by raising the standards of [their] life higher and higher, thus attacking the feeling of contempt of [their] race at its very roots" (315) – while anthropology carried on the same struggle of "fact" against "feeling" (cf. Meier 1963; Willis 1975).

Emotional Nationalism and Rational Universalism in World War I

The opposition of reason and emotion, now even more profoundly charged with personal meaning, runs like a leitmotif through Boas' writings on public issues during the years of World War I. Despite his generally critical posture toward evolutionary assumption, Boas in 1912 had still spoken of the development of ever-larger social units internally at peace as an "inexorable law of human history," which would necessarily override the "practical difficulties" of modern nationalism and the "so-called race instincts" of European whites. National solidarity was not based on "objective traits" but on "subjective ideals," whose "constant variation" throughout history was itself evidence for the possibility of their supercession (1945:100–3). The war, however, cast the problem of nationalism in a somewhat different light. Boas' early pain at Germany's role in the "wrong and egoistic strife" of European states was complicated by the intense anti-German feeling that developed in the United States as the Wilson administration moved toward entry on the Allied side (Rohner 1969:274). Outspoken in his opposition to American involvement and his criticism of the professedly universal values used to justify it, Boas defended both the cultural tradition and the military policies of his native land, whose submarine warfare he saw as the only effective means to counter a blockade threatening its very existence (3/30/17).

In this context, Boas began to place a greater emphasis on the localized solidarity of sentiment as opposed to the universal solidarity of reason – although he still distinguished between "the nationalism of ideas" and "the imperialistic nationalism of political and economic power" (1945:122). As a scientist, he knew that men were more likely to use human reason "to justify their way of feeling and acting" than to "shape their actions and to remodel their emotions" (157). His very skepticism as to the "absolute value" of historically evolved national ideals led him, however, to defend their continued existence: "as long as we know that the mass of mankind would never free itself from the fetters of tradition, progress requires the persistence of national characteristics"—since it was only "by comparison with foreign types of thought" that we could "recognize the traditional basis of our own" (182). Only thus could we arrive at "truly human ideals," which like science were "based on generalized concepts, free from the specific social setting that determines their form in each particular case" (183). In the meantime, Boas accepted the right of a nation to restrict immigration "of a cultural type entirely distinct in character," even though from "a general human point of view" he might wish all barriers to migration abolished (181). He adopted a similar double standard of patriotism—his own, which was "subordinated to humanism," and that of "the majority of mankind" (156). If rational "retrospect upon the history of mankind"—which was "the business of my life"—taught him that the former had a "higher value," it did not give him "the right to stamp everything as heinous crime that for well-nigh three thousand years has been counted as the highest virtue" (159). It did, however, give him the duty to defend and enlarge the realm of universal and scientific values—which in fact involved a critical reevaluation of certain ideals of American democracy and of his own personal value system (cf. Purcell 1973).

The nineteenth-century liberalism that had led Boas toward America was modified during the war years by collectivist influences that turned him once again toward Europe. He felt that American democratic electoral forms had in fact developed under particular historical conditions and were not to be equated with the "fundamental principles" of democracy. The latter had to do with the subordination of the state to the "rights and well-being of the individual citizen" (1945:147) and might be achieved by means quite different from the "free institutions" Americans sought to impose upon the world along with their religion, their ethics, and their standards of living (GS 1974c:332). Nor did true democracy necessarily imply the virtually unrestricted freedom of individual action that had developed in this country as a consequence of the abundance of resources in a "thinly settled young country"—a condition that was now rapidly passing, as it had long since passed in Europe. "Maturer years" had made Boas realize that individual freedom must be coordinated with the needs of the community as a whole (334). Indeed, he now felt that the demands of social justice were "higher than those of individual freedom"—which was "a recompense for the ability to do fruitful work"—and that the state had the right "to demand services to the community" (1945:162, 166). In reconciling the freedom of the individual with such collective demands, Boas tended to draw a line between action and thought—between the obligation to obey the law and the right and duty to criticize it—although he still allowed withholding active obedience when a law violated "the fundamental convictions of individuals" (160).

The failure of American intellectuals generally to adopt this critical role and the intensity of patriotic sentiment and anti-German feeling "even in our Eastern universities" were apparently a great personal shock (12/15/16; cf. C. Gruber 1975). Boas, who before the war had spoken in elitist terms of the "credulous public" and the "apathetic masses," now concluded that "the mental attitude of the educated classes," by virtue of training that required an extended "infusion of historically transmitted ideas," was in fact "much more strongly influenced by special traditional ideas than is the mass of the people"—whose desires were "in a wider sense more human than those of the classes" (1945:64, 136–39). The only political movement that stood for free expression of opposition to the war was in fact the Socialist Party, and in 1918 Boas, who had voted for McKinley and for Hughes, announced his intention to vote socialist (GS 1974c:335). Despite an earlier statement to a group of socialists that he "could not possibly be under any party discipline" (1915), he became for a time a member of the party and received letters from the local organizer addressed to "Dear Comrade Boas" discussing political activities in relation to the school system of his Grantwood, New Jersey, home (2/20/18).

In this context, Boas shortly after the war's end made his only important public statement on the issue of colonialism. Although his motive was in part to defend the record of German colonial administration and to show that the evils "inherent in the system" were "not peculiar to any one nation," Boas now offered a general condemnation of colonialism as a form of economic exploitation which, wantonly destroying the cultural forms "sacred and dear to the native," led to the "death of hundreds of thousands by starvation." Attacking the proposed mandate system on the grounds that "temporary charges" would tend to become "permanent property," Boas endorsed the British Labour Party's scheme for international control, which would "take account" of expressed native wishes, preserve native ownership of the soil, and devote revenues of the colonies to native development—which Boas, in common with many advocates of "indirect rule," felt should proceed by a "careful building up on the basis of native cultural life." Although the time had passed for such a preservationist policy in most parts of the world (including the United States), Boas felt it could still be applied in areas where "Europeans are not likely to settle in large numbers" (1919).

As his colonial views suggest, Boas' move toward socialism was heavily conditioned both by his growing pessimism and by certain more deeply rooted value assumptions. He regarded the complete elimination of human suffering as a delusory goal produced by the special conditions of modern civilization. The work of the world and the conflict of ethical obligations would always inflict pain, which "men must be willing to bear" (1928:120). Although he advocated the "radical social readjustment" necessary to provide equal opportunity for every child. Boas felt that full individual equality was "unattainable"—the achievements and rewards of human beings would and should vary with their "industry, energetic concentration, and strength of character" (1945:162–63). He was indeed as much preoccupied with the abolition of protective tariffs as with the imposition of inheritance taxes. And despite his identification with the needs of the masses, it is clear that he still saw intellectuals as the only source of significant cultural change—which could never entirely "cast away the past" (140). His public activity continued to be directed largely toward the maintenance of the conditions of cultural criticism, particularly within the institutions of education and science.

During the war years, these conditions were seriously degraded, and anthropology itself seemed in danger of subversion by enflamed nationalism (GS 1968a:273–95). To the waspish hard-science leaders of the National Research Council, the relevant anthropology was a physical anthropology strongly tinged with racialism, and their wartime Committee on Anthropology in fact included the racist polemicist Madison Grant. Although Boas and his followers resisted the "scientific reaction against cultural anthropology," the period of intense xenophobia and antiradical hysteria after the war witnessed a brief nativist movement within the discipline's professional organization. Precipitated by Boas' attack on certain anthropologists who had used Mexican connections established under his patronage as a cover for espionage work for the United States government, the attempt to "Americanize" the profession led to Boas' censure and removal from office in the American Anthropological Association.

From Boas' point of view, the issue was the preservation of science as the one human activity uncompromised by the forces of particularist tradition. He recognized the claims of the state upon the individual citizen in time of war—and in fact waited until the war's end to raise the matter. But if politicians, diplomats, and soldiers would "owing to their callings" conform to particularistic conventional standards of ethics, the independence of the scientist in his scientific role must be preserved: "If we cannot make up our minds to consider as the first and fundamental demand to be made upon the scientist, absolute truthfulness in relation to scientific work, we might just as well give up the hope of ever accomplishing anything that is worthwhile for mankind" (1/21/20; GS 1974c:336). The clash, as Alfred Kroeber noted, was one between "scientific" and "patriotic solidarity": and by a vote of two to one, the latter was upheld (1/18/20). Here then was the low point of Boas' disillusion with the land of his adoption; he later recalled that "after the war, I felt that I was emotionally through with America" (Rohner 1969:296).

The Struggle for Democracy and Intellectual Freedom

If history—which "is never rational" (1945:182)—seemed to have betrayed his optimistic liberal hopes for the promise of America and his qualified but nonetheless real belief in the general progress of mankind, it had not destroyed the *vorwärts* spirit of Boas' personal commitment to the struggle for human culture, in both its particularistic traditional and universal rational manifestations. Throughout the early 1920s he worked to reestablish the cultural institutions of his native land through the Emergency Society for German and Austrian Science and Art, and from time to time he spoke out against the "Nordic nonsense" then rampant in his adopted home. But although he published his major statement on *Anthropology and Modern Life* in 1928, for the most part the focus of Boas' energies in the postwar period was still internal to the discipline itself.

Paradoxically, one of the side effects of the nativist upsurge culminating in the "tribal twenties" was the provision of funds for research on racial issues. Despite the brief reactionary movement within anthropology, the Boasians had been able to maintain their dominance in the discipline (GS 1968a:296–307). In this context Boas was able to take advantage of the interest in racial problems to further research along the lines of his own point of view. Under the fellowship program in the biological sciences established by the National Research Council in 1923, three of his students won support for research on questions of race and culture. It is clear from Boas' correspondence that he saw the work of Herskovits on the physical anthropology of the Negro, of Mead on Samoan adolescence, and of Klineberg on racial mental differences as part of a coordinated attack on the problem of the cultural factor in racial differences. Boas' influence, furthermore, extended beyond the work of his own students. By 1926 he was playing a major role on the NRC Committee on the American Negro, and in 1928 he was one of the initiators of the Conference on Racial Differences sponsored jointly by the NRC and the Social Science Research Council. In the context of endogenous developments within the other social scientific disciplines and the flow of intellectual influences facilitated by the interdisciplinary movement of the period, the Boasian viewpoint on issues of race and culture, which in 1919 was still distinctly a minority current, by 1934 was on the verge of becoming social scientific orthodoxy (cf. Barkan 1988).

By that time Boas' own position on certain of these issues had undergone modification. Herskovits' researches, which to Boas' surprise had shown a tendency toward "the darkening of the whole colored population" (Boas 1928:177), had undercut his assumption that the ultimate solution of the race problem would be biological. At the same time, Boas' conception of cultural determinism had also evolved, as he became more sensitive to subtle differences of social environment and the effect of culture on motor habit and physiological function (55, 138). In complex modern civilization, however, cultural determinism in fact operated to reinforce individual freedom and the possibility of change. In a "diversified culture," the child was exposed to "conflicting tendencies," which prevented traditional behaviors from becoming "entirely automatic" and served as stimulus for "critical self-examination" (154, 158). In this context, Boas became more and more convinced that race had little or nothing to do with human behavioral and mental differences (1938a:v); and, biological assimilation having for the moment failed him, he turned to the hope that by the conscious control of the cultural process itself mankind might yet eliminate racial prejudice—through education and the creation, especially among children, of social groups in which other principles of cohesion would override race (1928:8, 1940:16). The defense of intellectual freedom became thus more critical than ever before, and the course of events was soon to give a heightened urgency also to the preservation of democratic forms.

The final phase of Boas' public life began with the establishment of the Nazi dictatorship in the spring of 1933 (cf. Purcell 1973). Boas had numerous relatives and friends in Germany, whom he had visited as recently as 1931; and he had long been active in supporting German cultural institutions—most recently in the gift of a portion of his personal library to his old university at Kiel. Now suddenly these fundamental cultural ties were placed in jeopardy. Although Boas was shocked by the "ruthless elimination" of Jews and liberals from intellectual institutions (4/25/33)—and by the news, later disconfirmed (1/18/37), that his own books had been burned—he was reluctant at first to believe that the extreme violence was more than mere "ruffianism" (4/21/33). Further reports of the attacks on German Jews and the evidence that the Nazi regime was fomenting anti-Semitism in the United States convinced him that the threat against "the old cultural values of Germany" was much more profound (11/14/35). It was not until late in 1935 that he could bring himself to resign from the Germanistic Society of America, which he had been instrumental in founding shortly after 1900, but whose cultural exchange activities involved a certain degree of cooperation with the German government. By that time, however, he had for two years been involved in a variety of activities in opposition to the Nazi regime and in support of its victims.

Boas' emphasis was on attacking racial propaganda, and, characteristically, he felt that "the only way to attack the racial craze that is sweeping the world nowadays is to undermine its alleged scientific basis" (10/4/33). To this end, he succeeded in raising money to push a two-pronged research program. On the one hand, by studying the "amount of variability" in human populations, Boas sought to demonstrate that heredity was a matter of "familial lines" and that "as a racial term" it had "no meaning whatsoever" (12/29/33, 4/24/37). On the other hand, he organized a series of studies patterned after his earlier work on immigrant head form, which were designed to prove that a variety of human characteristics usually presumed racial – bodily build, gesture, criminality, insanity, intelligence, and personality – were heavily influenced by "outer, particularly cultural conditions" (10/4/33). Paralleling this research effort was an attempt to popularize the results of anthropological inquiry through the public press, through radio broadcasts, even (though unsuccessfully) through motion pictures. His pamphlet "Aryans and non-Aryans," printed on tissue-thin paper, is said to have been widely circulated by the anti-Nazi underground in Germany (Herskovits 1953:117).

As the tempo of fascist aggression quickened in the period after his retirement from active teaching in 1936, Boas' attempt "to salvage cultural values" (3/18/38) and "stem the assault upon the basic principles . . . of civilized life" (3/17/38) gradually entered a more overtly political phase, culminating in 1939 with the founding of the American Committee for Democracy and Intellectual Freedom. Although he distinguished between "ideal" and "bigoted" democracy – which might be "as hostile to intellectual freedom as the modern totalitarian state" (1945:216) – Boas was once again inclined to emphasize the universal values underlying the particularistic forms of American political life. If the freedom embodied in our foundation documents had "not yet been fully achieved," Boas still felt that "democracy as conceived in our Constitution and as expressed in our daily life is a treasure that we are determined to guard under all circumstances" (177). This was possible only if the masses – among whom Boas now included intellectuals – were able to resist demagoguery and judge issues for themselves. Toward this end the work of the American Committee focussed "very largely on questions of education" – notably through the organization of scientific opposition to racism and the defense of "progressive educators" against attacks by conservative university administrators and legislative witchhunts (9/11/39, 6/4/42).

In this context Boas was inevitably forced to consider the question of communism (Iverson 1959:201). Privately he acknowledged that the methods the Soviets used to achieve the socialist ideal of "equal rights for every member of humanity" had "much in common" with those of fascist totalitarianism (7/20/39), and he was painfully aware of the limitations of in-

Franz Boas near the end of his lifetime personal *Kulturkampf.* (Courtesy of the American Philosophical Society)

tellectual freedom in a land where "anthropology must be Marxian and Lewis Morgan, otherwise it is not allowed" (2/21/39). Publicly, however, his posture was that of the "united front"—even in the period of the Nazi-Soviet pact and even to the jeopardy of funding that the American Jewish Committee had been providing for his research on race. Boas rationalized his position on the grounds that he could not "influence foreign countries"—though in other contexts he had attempted just that—and that in *this* country the real danger was not radical totalitarianism but "the spread of fascist ideology" (7/20/39). So long as people agreed with him "in regard to one specific problem on which we wish to cooperate," their views on other matters were irrelevant (1945:202). If young people "with a keen feeling of social obligations and lack of practical experience" were likely to take "extreme views" (4/27/41), their "emotional devotion to ideals should not be suppressed, but controlled by healthy, critical thought" (1945:191).

Whatever ambivalence this posture may have entailed was resolved for Boas first by the Nazi invasion of the Soviet Union and then by Pearl Harbor. His commitment to the universal ideals imperfectly embodied in American political democracy, Soviet socialism, and classical German culture could now be integrated in the "enthusiastic support of the fight against

Hitlerism and all it stands for" (12/12/41). This did not, however, mean a relaxation of domestic struggle. Throughout 1942 Boas mobilized the flagging energies of his eighty-fifth year in the continuing fight against bigotry—including "any cultural chauvinism" that might be directed against "any of the enemy countries" (12/15/41)—as well as in the campaign to free Earl Browder. The continuity of his public life was maintained until the end, which came at a luncheon on December 29, when in midsentence ("I have a new theory about race . . .") he fell over dead (Mead 1959a:355).

Cultural Relativism and the Ice-Cold Flame of Truth

Although it would be presumptuous in the space available to attempt systematic evaluation, one can scarcely avoid a few general comments on Boas' career as a scientific activist. Let us take as reference point certain limitations to Boas' activist role (cf. Levenstein 1963; Hyatt 1990; Willis 1972). Even after his move toward socialism, he was not much concerned with the redistribution of economic resources and political power. Nor was he ever much involved in the problems of the American Indian—though he was quite active privately in opposing John Collier's appointment as Indian Commissioner, regarding him as an "agitator" who would "make more acute the difficulties of the Indians which are inherent in their economic relations to their White neighbors" (1/16/33, 3/17/33; cf. Hertzberg 1971: 305). Although various reasons might be advanced for these neglects, one common factor underlying them would seem to be a certain fatalistic attitude toward technologically based historical processes—on the one hand, the movement toward more collectively oriented economic systems within Western European civilization, and on the other, its overpowering of more technologically primitive cultures in areas where the two were in direct confrontation.

If this seems paradoxical, in view of Boas' well-known opposition to economic determinism, it is not inconsistent with his general historical outlook. Boas never abandoned entirely a nineteenth-century liberal belief in a singular human progress in "civilization" that was based ultimately on the cumulation of rational knowledge—of which technology was the single most clearcut manifestation. Certain values deeply embedded in his own enculturative experience—scientific knowledge, human fellowship, and individual freedom—had in fact been cumulatively realized in human history, not merely in a generalized sense, but in the specific form of "modern" civilization, which Boas' language often made clear was "our own" (1928:206). Boas was far from satisfied with that civilization, and his alienation was ultimately expressed in his contribution to the modern pluralistic concept of "culture," which was founded on the legitimacy of alternative value systems. But anthropology, for Boas, did not lead to a "general relativistic attitude" (2/17/41). Quite the contrary. Not only were there general values that were cumulatively realized in the history of human civilization, there were also general values that were variously realized in different human cultures—"fundamental truths" that, notwithstanding their form in "particular societies," were "common to mankind" (2/17/41). Boas did not himself undertake the systematic comparison that might have revealed these values empirically, however, and his occasional specific references to them suggest that they, too, were rooted in his own enculturative experience. Thus the common moral ideas he saw underlying the varied ethical behavior of mankind turn out to be respect for "life, well-being, and property" within the range of the recognized social group (1928:225).

Despite this deeply rooted optimistic and universalistic rationalism, there was a repressed emotional-aesthetic undercurrent in Boas' personality, and his life experience had made him painfully aware of the role of irrational factors in human life. Positively, these tendencies were realized in the variety of human cultural forms; negatively, in the way emotionally rooted customs within particular groups were retrospectively rationalized and given pseudo-universalistic valuation. This opposition—and the broader one underlying it, which resonates of the traditional Germanic opposition between "civilization" and "culture" (cf. Kroeber & Kluckhohn 1952)—runs throughout Boas' career, expressing itself during certain extended historical moments in a rather deep pessimism.

Within these attitudinal parameters, Boas confronted the problems of the modern world. Although science had a hand in these—generating both technological progress and value conflict—they were essentially the product of emotion rather than reason and had primarily to do with the ways that men delimited the groups within which general human values were applied or the fruits of technological progress were distributed. Appropriately, Boas' scientific life was devoted to studying two phenomena in terms of which such exclusivity was defined—race and culture—and the gist of his scientific message was that groupings defined in these terms were profoundly conditioned by history. If he was willing to grant a certain contingent value to such particularistic groupings, which in the present phase of history might long endure, they could have no permanent place in the noncontingent realm of scientific truth.

Although there are moments in Boas' writings when scientific rationality itself is viewed in relativistic terms, in general he retained all his life a rather idealized and absolutistic conception of science. At the very end, he rejected the idea that scientists must lay aside their studies to devote themselves full-time to the anti-Nazi struggle: "the ice-cold flame of the passion for seeking the truth for truth's sake must be kept burning" (1945:1).

And despite the frequently utilitarian tone of his appeals for research funds, he had—or came to have as he grew older—a rather limited conception of the practical utility of anthropological research. The "usefulness of the knowledge gained" by "pure science" was an "entirely irrelevant" question (1928:16). True, anthropology might "illuminate the social processes of our own times"—might show us "what to do and what to avoid" (11). But given Boas' increasingly pessimistic view of the possibility of finding general social laws and his feeling that the variation of socially based ideals would make the application of social scientific knowledge always problematic, the practical utility of anthropology was somewhat limited. It told us much more what to avoid than what to do. Its posture vis-à-vis society was defensive rather than constructive. However, in fighting prejudice and intolerance, and in defending cultural variety, it sought also to defend the cultural conditions of scientific activity itself. And by these means, it sought also to provide the basis for systematic criticism of the particularistic cultural assumptions and the pseudo-universals that still pervaded "modern civilization." Its ultimate application was to "see to it that the hard task of subordinating the love of traditional lore to clear thinking be shared with us [scientists] by larger and larger masses of our people" (1945:2).

On the bottom line, the tension in Boas' thought between emotional particularism and universalistic rationality was thus resolved in favor of the latter. But particularism nonetheless played a critical role in its achievement. The fundamental Eurocentrism of Boas' attitude toward "the mind of primitive man" may best be understood in this context. On the one hand, in defending the mental capacity of non-European peoples, he was defending their capacity to participate fully in "modern civilization"; on the other, in defending their cultural values, he was establishing a kind of Archimedian leverage point for the criticism of that civilization. The need for such an external reference point was one of the leitmotifs of Boas' career, and it tended to carry with it a double standard of cultural evaluation: a universalistic one in terms of which he criticized the society in which he lived and a relativistic one in terms of which he defended the cultural alternative. Whatever the emotional roots of this need, the external cultural alternative was for Boas an essential precondition for the achievement both of scientific knowledge in the social sphere and of the freedom of the individual in society. Just as the "scientific study of generalized social forms" required that the student "free himself from all valuations based on our [own] culture" (1928:204), so also did true freedom require that we be "able to rise above the fetters that the past imposes upon us" (1945:179). Without an external cultural reference point by which to bring these valuations and fetters to the level of consciousness, both scientific knowledge and true freedom would be impossible. This then was the ultimate meaning of Boas' lifelong fight for culture.

From the perspective of today, one may well question just how far Boas was able to bring the shackles of his own tradition fully to consciousness. Many of the values that late-nineteenth-century liberals assumed were universal seem now to be anchored in a particular cultural historical context. To many present anthropologists, Boas' outlook must surely seem naively idealist, in both an ethical and an epistemological sense. Its tacit Eurocentrism cannot help but offend many in a postcolonial world. Its limited and defensive conception of the anthropologist's political role – which by World War II was already undergoing modification (below, pp. 165–68) – must seem quite inadequate to many of those who have come of age in the 1960s and 1970s. Questioning the assumptions underlying Boas' activism, one may question its achievements as well. Forty years of education in tolerance seem neither to have eliminated prejudice nor greatly to have strengthened "the power of clear thought" – nor to have fundamentally modified the social order of the United States.

But if he never transcended them, Boas nonetheless represents nineteenth-century liberal values at their most generically human, and we may still today appreciate his contribution to our cultural life. There is a sense in which he transmuted personal history into scientific paradigm: the experience of Jews in Germany provided him the archetype of an ostensibly racial group that was in fact biologically heterogeneous, which had assimilated itself almost completely to German national culture and which in multitudinous ways had enriched the general cultural life of modern civilization. Transported to the United States, the scientific viewpoint founded on that archetype offered strong support for certain fundamental American values that in the early twentieth century were much in need of reinforcement. By the time of his death, Boas' critique of traditional racial assumption and his contribution to the modern concept of culture had contributed not a little to that end. And if today his critical perspective and his anthropological activism may seem somewhat limited in scope, the standpoint from which he approached the issues of anthropology and public life is surely as sound as ever: "the whole basis of the anthropological viewpoint is the willingness to take the position of the non-conformist, not to take anything in our social structure for granted, and to be particularly ready to examine critically all those attitudes that are accompanied by strong outbursts of emotion, the more so the stronger the accompanying emotion" (1945:179).

4

Ideas and Institutions in American Anthropology

Thoughts Toward a History of the Interwar Years

Like others in this volume, this essay was written from an ambiguous disciplinary standpoint—assuming in the beginning an identification with "our" tribe, apologizing toward the end for "the historian's" lack of personal enculturative experience in the recent history of the discipline. But like the essay on Boas, it was in fact commissioned by anthropology's professional association, serving as introduction to one of three volumes of *Selected Papers from the American Anthropologist* published on the occasion of the association's seventy-fifth anniversary.

The volume I edited was bracketed between two edited by anthropologists: one treating the period from 1946 to 1970 (Murphy 1976); and the other a reissue of an earlier volume covering the years before 1920 (De Laguna 1960). The latter included a long essay, "The Beginnings of Anthropology in America," which was the major contribution made to the history of anthropology by the man who introduced me to the field: A. Irving Hallowell. Although the span assigned to me was shorter and my essay was less ambitious, I had in mind the model of Hallowell's breadth of coverage, which, in contrast to many more recent histories of anthropology, included all of the currents of inquiry that came together in the American tradition (Hallowell 1960; cf. 1965).

Although in 1975 the American Anthropological Association was already feeling the centrifugal strains that were to lead in a few years to a more loosely federative restructuring, it still embraced in principle (as, somewhat more tenuously, it does today) the "four fields" that certain unbelieving colleagues at Chicago have called "the sacred bundle": archeology, linguistic anthropology, biological (née physical) anthropology, and cultural anthropology (née ethnology). Because I came to the discipline through the study of the idea of race, in which all four were implicated, in a period when evolutionism and the critique thereof made their relationship theoretically meaningful, I have retained a certain predisposition in favor of the "unity of anthropology." This, despite the fact that Franz Boas, the anthropologist with whom I identify most closely, had already foreseen in 1904 the fragmentation of the discipline as its subdisciplinary components developed along substantively and methodologically specialized lines (below, p. 148). The problematic unity of the four fields became, then, the organizing theme of my essay.

Its frame was provided by two episodes in the history of the American Anthropological Association which nearly coincided with the termini of the period assigned to me—and this not entirely by coincidence, since wars and their aftermaths are moments when the ideas and institutions of anthropology are likely to be in interactive ferment. Although much of my work has dealt with the history of anthropological ideas, I have never thought of myself as an historian of ideas *per se*, but rather of ideas as manifested by human actors within ever-broadening circles of context. Of these, the specific institutions through which these actors come together to promote ideas seem to me especially privileged, both conceptually and methodologically—on the one hand, because they constitute a nexus through which are channelled many forces, inside and outside the discipline; on the other, because they provide a focus for inquiry that might otherwise go off in countless directions.

As a first attempt to carry the history of anthropology forward from the early twentieth century, the essay incorporated in summary form much of the work on Boas that had preoccupied me during the first decade or so of my academic career. It benefitted also from one of the most successful graduate seminars I have conducted, which helped to focus and to complement my own research in a period whose history had not yet been systematically explored. My own effort was frankly tentative and strikes me now as perhaps in some respects dated or problematic—notably, in the use of the paradigm and genetic metaphors. More important, perhaps, I have had some second thoughts about the conclusion. After leading graduate seminars in each of the last three years on "Anthropology Yesterday"—the self-confidently positivist era that was formative for the currently passing generation of anthropological elders—I am inclined to see the period between World War II and the "crisis of anthropology" as a distinctive phase in the history of the discipline, in which the emergence of the United States as world superpower was reflected in the internationalization of American anthropology (cf. Cohn 1987:26; Wolf 1964). As far as the interwar era itself is concerned, a considerable body of work has been published since my essay first appeared. However, I know of no other attempt to draw together all the major threads of American anthropology in this period; given that the continuing subdisciplinary fragmentation of anthropology has a tendency to replicate itself in the historiography of the field, it may be some time before an inclusive "four-field" interpretation is ventured again.

A Role for the History of Associations

Those who suffer the annual anomie of American professional association meetings may doubt they could ever really be significant in the development of an intellectual discipline. Nonetheless, their present disjointed multiplexity is itself an historical phenomenon. Some elders of our tribe can recall an age when most anthropologists knew each other personally, and corroborees could be held, if not around a single campfire, then at least in one meeting hall of modest size. No doubt many gatherings of the good old *Gemeinschaft* days had something of the timeless rhythmic character of the tribal rite. Surveying the proceedings of the American Anthropological Association during the interwar years, one gets a sense that any given annual meeting was pretty much like all the rest. And yet there are clearly points at which the organizational history of the discipline becomes the focus for significant historical change—the place where the divergent threads of intellectual and institutional development, embodied in the interaction of particular individuals, responding to the impact of broader forces from "outside" the discipline, can all be grasped at once. Whether by happy historical coincidence or determinist design, two such moments come very near to marking the interwar period: the censure of Franz Boas at the meeting of 1919, and the reorganization of the Association after the meeting of 1946.[1]

1. Drawn largely from my own work at a time when the history of anthropology literature for the period was minimal, this essay had originally no parenthetical citations, but was documented by a brief bibliographical reference note for each section, with a few specific footnotes for quoted passages, and internal references to the articles in the anthology for which it served as introduction—all of them from the *American Anthropologist.* Since then, the literature of the history of anthropology has grown tremendously, and some of the earlier references are dated. At the time, I noted my obvious debt to Kuhn 1962, and a less obvious one to Shils 1970. In the section that follows, the account of the censure episode and its aftermath is drawn from GS 1968a:270–307, where fuller documentation may be found.

The Boas Censure as Microcosm

The Boas censure and its aftermath mark the culmination of a major phase in the history of American anthropology: the rise and consolidation of what its adherents then spoke of as "the American historical school," founded and led of course by Boas himself. Although from an intellectual point of view the paradigm shift in American anthropology had begun a generation before and had surely been accomplished by 1911, when Boas' most important works in cultural anthropology, linguistics, and physical anthropology were published (GS 1974d), the resolution of this disciplinary revolution took somewhat longer to achieve. During the next decade the Association was an important arena for the struggle, and "every mother's son of us who stood for the Right," as Robert Lowie remarked, was annually exhorted to attend prepared to do battle if necessary against the Washington anthropologists associated with the older social evolutionary viewpoint. Whipping the "weaker brethren" and the "half-breed" Harvard archeologists into line, the Boasians succeeded in maintaining their control of the Association and its publication outlets until late in 1919, when Boas sent a letter to *The Nation* revealing that certain unnamed anthropologists working in Central America had actually served as spies for the United States government.

Coming in the context of the intense postwar xenophobia and antiradical hysteria that was shortly to lead to the Palmer Raids, Boas' letter served as the unintended catalyst for an abortive counterrevolutionary movement. Fired by patriotic indignation against the pacifist-oriented and predominantly immigrant Boasians, reinforced by a reaction against cultural anthropology in the waspish "hard"-science establishment, the forces of resentment accumulated in the course of the Boasian redefinition of American anthropology exploded in brief eruption. For a time they threatened, if not to reverse the paradigm shift, then at least to fragment the somewhat problematic and historically conditioned unity of American anthropology, with serious potential consequences for the scientific status and the funding of cultural anthropological research.

The critical issue was the representation of anthropology on the National Research Council that was established in 1916 to support the preparedness effort. During the war, the functions of its Committee on Anthropology had been defined in physical anthropological terms, and its personnel included several racialist anthropologists—as well as two leading eugenicists who had been given places at the insistence of leading biological scientists on the NRC. The issue of by whom and to what end anthropology would be represented on the Council surfaced again in the course of its conversion to permanent peacetime status. The then Council chairman, John C. Merriam, felt that American anthropology could no longer afford to occupy itself solely with American Indians. Instead, it must follow American interests overseas, and at home must deal with the pressing problem of the racial composition of the American population, studied in close cooperation with psychology, biology, and neurology. As the Boasians interpreted the message, it was that "our cultural stuff was getting nowhere, that we weren't scientists anyway, that it is time to take things out of our hands and really get down to business." From their point of view, the issue was the "self-determination of science." They had fought hard for what they regarded as professional standards within the discipline, and they insisted on the right of the discipline, which at this point they controlled, to define these standards for itself. These standards were broad enough to include men quite antagonistic to the Boasians, but they were not so broad as to include Madison Grant, the racist amateur paleontologist who had been coopted to the NRC Committee on Anthropology.

For a time, Boas was able to maintain a professional united front in the face of this outside challenge, and early in 1919 won the principle that representatives to the NRC should be elected by the Association. However, in the hysterical aftermath of his *Nation* letter, this somewhat fragile unity was fractured. At the December annual meeting the "breeds" and the "weaker brethren" combined with Boas' enemies to censure him, strip him from office, and force his resignation from the NRC. The following year, the counterrevolutionaries attempted to complete their coup by capturing control of the *American Anthropologist.* However, this time the Boasians—by mobilizing all their forces, adeptly politicking with the neutrals, and seizing a critical moment to force a compromise—were able to split the so-called Maya-Washington crowd and save the unity of the Association. Pliny Goddard, whose policies had been somewhat controversial, was replaced as editor of the *Anthropologist* by the placid and marginally Boasian John Swanton until 1923, when the Boasians regained control and Robert Lowie took over.

The maintenance of the organizational unity of the discipline—which had they been defeated completely, some of the Boasians were quite willing to sacrifice—had important consequences. The "scientific" status of anthropology, which was to a considerable extent the heritage of its association with the evolutionary tradition and its ties to the biological sciences, was sustained—not just for physical anthropology, but for all the component subdisciplines, and most important, for the cultural anthropological orientation that was to dominate the profession.

The Worldview of Boasian Anthropology

This orientation derived of course from Franz Boas, who more than anyone else shaped the character of American anthropology in the twentieth century.[2] This is certainly not to say that, even in 1920, all the characteristics of American anthropology were due to Boas' influence. Aside from the numerous continuities in his own work with what had gone before, or the perpetuation in Washington and Cambridge and elsewhere of lines that fall outside a strictly Boasian framework, or the input of other specific intellectual influences, much that was characteristic of the Boasians was simply a reflection of the prevailing circumstances of anthropological work in the United States. Thus the special character of "salvage ethnography" was largely the product of a generalized tradition of ethnographic assumption, the limitations of funding, the object-orientation of museums, the document-orientation of humanistic disciplines and the hard-"fact" elementalist empiricism of much contemporary science—as well as the condition of American Indians, who after three centuries of ethnocidal conflict had been reduced to a marginal reservation existence, their traditional cultures surviving more vividly in memory than in the drab reality of daily life (cf. J. Gruber 1970). No doubt the character of salvage ethnography would have retroacted upon anthropological theory whether or not Boas had settled in the United States. But even making such allowances, it is hard to overstate the weight of Boas' influence, and absolutely necessary to have an understanding of its underlying assumptions.

Boas' anthropological views are perhaps most easily described negatively, in terms of what he rejected. His intellectual journey from physics to ethnology under the influence of neo-Kantian philosophy in the 1880s had involved a rejection of his own early materialism and geographical determinism. By 1896, when his anthropological posture was fairly well set, he had begun systematically to confront the dominant evolutionary orientation. At once a kind of disciplinary paradigm and an expression of general cultural ideology, this more or less integrated body of assumption attempted to explain in scientific terms the presumed superiority of white-skinned civilized men to dark-skinned savages by placing them both on a single developmental ladder extending upward from the apes. Comparing existing cultural forms, evolutionists tried to reconstruct the process of development and to subsume it within a deterministic scientific framework, thereby legitimating the cultural superiority that had been assumed at the outset, as well as the physical domination on which that assumption had been based (cf. GS 1987a).

For those who felt no serious alienation from the machine-driven civilization celebrated at universal exhibitions, there was apparent reason enough for such an assumption. But Boas' cultural marginality as Jewish

2. The discussion of the Boasian viewpoint is based largely on GS 1974d, where fuller documentation may be found; unless specifically indicated, quoted passages may be found in GS 1974c.

German, his early field experience, and his difficulties establishing himself professionally in the United States helped to create an experiential standpoint from which a systematic critique could be developed. Arguing that the minds of savages and civilized men were alike not only in underlying principle but in present practice, Boas saw human psychic unity less as a process of ever-growing utilitarian rationality than as the retrospective rationalization of unconsciously derived categories and emotionally charged and largely automatic customary behavior. Rejecting the regularity of rational response to external stimuli, he questioned also the regularity of human cultural development. Cultural "achievement" was not so much a function of cumulative reason, preserved in an ever-expanding braincase, as of historical processes of diffusion, borrowing, and reinterpretation. Because cultural phenomena were affected by diverse historical influences, they did not march in lockstep. Their development followed no uniform sequence, nor could it be correlated with any presumed hierarchy of racial types. Although general evolutionary processes no doubt existed, the attempt to reconstruct their course or define their laws by comparison must depend on a prior study of their specific historical manifestations. It must not be forejudged by the easy assumption that one single cultural type provided a standard by which to evaluate or classify all others.

Boas' thinking about the problem of classification may in fact be interpreted as containing in germ most of the assumptions of his anthropology, both in its critical, and less obviously, in its constructive aspects. In response to the evolutionists' insistence that in human culture, as everywhere else, "like causes produce like effects." Boas argued that this axiom could not be converted—that one could not reason from the likeness of effects to the likeness of causes, since apparently similar phenomena might in fact be the outcome of dissimilar processes. Boas' anthropological writings ring changes on this problem: the same cultural form might have different functions; a given normal distribution might conceal two different "types"; the same sound might actually be heard differently by observers of different nationalities. In ethnology, Boas insisted, "all is individuality." Individuality, however, was not something that inhered in the single cultural element; it, too, was a reflection of historical process, and could only be understood in the context of the total culture of a given tribe.

For Boas, the greatest danger confronting the student of man was "premature" or "arbitrary" classification. On the one hand, classification was complicated by the prior experience of the observer; on the other, by the historical processes conditioning the phenomenon observed. Because the latter were various and not necessarily correlated, classification would be the more arbitrary the larger the number of factors it attempted to include, and classification in terms of one factor might produce quite different results from classification in terms of another. Only once one had gone behind appearances and untangled the historical complexity of the processes affecting human life to arrive at categories that were not founded "in the mind of the student" but were somehow derived from and in a sense internal to the phenomena themselves—only then could one turn to comparison and generalization about causal processes.

Building from assumptions such as these, Boas developed the systematic critique of evolutionism which, along with the puritanical methodological posture implicit in it, is often seen as comprising almost the whole of his anthropological viewpoint. But although never systematically elaborated, there was implicit in this negative critique a more positive orientation. By a kind of inversion of the process of anthropological understanding, one could generate a picture of the fundamental processes of culture. The phenomenal world revealed to human senses was essentially a continuum, on which order was imposed by unconscious processes of categorization. Although reflecting at a certain level universal psychic processes, the categories thus produced would vary in their content from group to group, and once established would constitute a distinctive screen or sieve through which new experiences must pass to be assimilated. Cultural process was thus both divergent and reintegrative; similarly, cultural categories were in a sense both *a posteriori* and *a priori.* Although they were historical products, they "develop at present in each individual and in the whole people entirely sub-consciously, and nevertheless are most potent in the formation of our opinions and actions." The resulting integration of culture was a psychological phenomenon, founded essentially on ideas rather than on external conditions. Basically nonutilitarian, its obligatory character was the result of unconsciously internalized categories, of processes of imitation and socialization, and of deceptively self-conscious secondary explanations. Furthermore, the integration of culture was an historical more than a logical phenomenon. The accidental accretions of culture contact, the constant manipulation of elements, and the retrospective systematization of secondary explanation pulled in various directions to create a dynamic, processual integration which was never fully stable, but subject to movement and drift. Its character might best be described in such terms as "theme," "focus," "style," or "pattern," rather than those of "structure" or "system." In all of this it reflected its origin in the romantic conception of the "genius" or *Geist* of a people.

Boas' scientific orientation must be understood in terms of his peculiar relation to the two traditions of inquiry that he described in "The Study of Geography" at the very beginning of his career as an anthropologist: the physical and the historical (1887). The physicist did not study "the whole phenomenon as it represents itself to the human mind, but resolves it into its elements, which he investigates separately." Similarly, facts were important to him only as they led to general laws: by comparing a series of similar facts, he attempted to "isolate the general phenomenon which is common to all of them." In contrast, the historian insisted on the equal scientific validity of the study of complex phenomena whose elements seemed "to be connected only in the mind of the observer." He was interested not in the elements, but in the "whole phenomenon," and in general laws only insofar as they helped explain its actual history. He sought the "eternal truth" through the method of "understanding," seeking, like Goethe, "lovingly to penetrate" the secrets of the whole phenomenon, "without regard to its place in a system," until its "every feature is plain and clear."

By inclination and training Boas was a natural scientist, grounded in the tradition of atomistic analysis of elements and mechanistic causal determination. He came of age, however, in a period when this tradition was beginning to undergo a process of epistemological self-examination, of which his own early work may be seen as an expression; and he was also profoundly influenced by the historicist tradition, which was simultaneously undergoing reformulation. But though he must have read Mach and surely read Dilthey, he did not accept a conventionalist view of scientific law or an unqualified assertion of the independence of the *Geistes-* from the *Naturwissenschaften.* The physical and the historical approaches, each conceived in rather traditional terms, remained in tension, if not mutual inhibition, in his work. Scientific laws must await the study of histories of growth; but history, pursued in rather positivistic terms through the study of the distribution of elements, was in practice so difficult and complex as to be almost impossible to realize. In the long run, Boas retreated both from scientific law and historical reconstruction, until in the mid-1930s Robert Redfield could say with justice that "he does not write histories, and he does not prepare scientific systems."

Despite his reaction against evolutionism, Boas' anthropology was deeply rooted in nineteenth-century tradition. As he himself was aware, its goal was essentially that of pre-evolutionary diffusionist ethnology, refashioned in the context of late-nineteenth-century science: "the genesis of the types of man" (GS 1973a, 1987a). Its basic orientation was historical, but the history it sought to reconstruct (and hopefully to subject to scientific law) was the history of human variability in all of its aspects. Boas' anthropology was therefore in principle embracive, including within its scope linguistics, physical anthropology, and archeology as well as the study of human culture—although in practice cultural analysis (or ethnology) was the central Boasian domain. Above all, Boas' anthropology was empirical. Although ultimately it sought to explain why "the tribes and nations of the world" differed, it must first trace how "the present differences developed"

—and before that it must accurately describe and if possible classify them. At this level, too, there was considerable continuity with what had gone before: on the one hand, the oft-noted "natural history" orientation of Boasian fieldwork; on the other, the substantive continuity, down to about 1920, implicit in completing the Powellian program of basic ethnographic description and "mapping" of the North American continent (cf. Darnell 1969).

In contrast, however, to the nineteenth-century anthropological tradition, Boas' empiricism was systematically critical, attacking prevailing classificatory and typological assumptions in all areas from a relativistic point of view, both in the methodological and evaluative sense. The privileged cases were the complex ones, or the ones offering the single exception that would, from Boas' point of view, invalidate a law. In science, if not in politics, Boas was staunchly conservative. In this context, there is no denying that his rigorously inductive approach had the effect of inhibiting not only scientific generalization, but even the establishment of a systematic conceptual framework. But there is also little doubt that his puritanical preoccupation with method was a "great reformatory movement" in American anthropology (Harris 1968:261).

Indeed, one is tempted to go beyond "reform" to "revolution," and to suggest that this was one of those moments in the history of the social sciences that may, up to a point, be illuminated by the concept of "paradigm" change. Certainly, the Boasians saw themselves as scientific innovators—paradoxically, in view of the antiscientific current in their thinking, as the *only* propagators of a really "scientific" anthropology. Their recruitment from outside, their youth, their creation and capture of institutional bases, their close community life, their tendency to rewrite the history of the discipline—in these and other "sociological" dimensions, their innovation had a definitely Kuhnian character. Substantively, the conception of culture and of cultural determinism implicit in Boas' critique of evolutionism provided the basis for a radically different disciplinary worldview, although its implications were slow to be developed. And although at this level Boasian anthropology may be seen as simply one manifestation of a broader intellectual movement that was revolutionizing almost every area of social scientific inquiry, its assumptions are clearly differentiable from those of its most important congener within that movement: the tradition flowing from Emile Durkheim through A. R. Radcliffe-Brown into modern British social anthropology. In contrast to Boasian assumption, the latter was built on the principle that like effects have like causes, that social facts could be "defined in advance by certain common external characteristics," that social "species" could be classified in terms of "the nature of the component elements and their mode of combination," and that "one well-constructed experiment often suffices for the establishment of a law."

Without going into detail, it is perhaps enough to suggest that Alexander Goldenweiser's review of Durkheim's *Elementary Forms* and Alfred Kroeber's dispute with William Rivers over the meaning of kinship terms are clearly retrodictable in terms of differences in paradigm assumption—although in the latter case, it is the Morganian current within British anthropology that was the antagonist, and not all Boasians would have agreed with Kroeber (GS 1974d).

Going beyond the revolution to its resolution, however, it seems clear that Boasian anthropology had only an imperfectly paradigmatic character. There is no doubt that it tended to develop in terms of the realization of programmatic positions laid down by Boas, first by carrying the critique of evolutionism into specific areas, then through a series of research problems that in many cases he defined. The underlying goal was to account for human variability in all its aspects, and often one can clearly see a unity of approach crosscutting particular subdisciplines. More specifically, Boasian field investigation was designed to produce evidence that would at once throw light on the "sociopsychological nexus of form and meaning" and provide a kind of documentation for historical reconstruction. The observation of behavior in the present was less important than the informant's memory of the way things were, or the details of psychic life as they "had become fixed in language, art, myth and religion" (Voget 1968:333–35). Similarly, one can find in the analysis of cultural phenomena a common mode of attack in terms of "elements," "processes," and "patterns." Developed in Boas' folklore studies in the 1890s, it was manifest also in his grammars of the next decade, as well as in the work of his leading students: "with each the grammars can be seen to have been written by the [same] men who wrote the ethnographies" (Hymes 1970:257).

There were even moments when anthropology for the Boasians had something of the "puzzle-solving" character of "normal science"—as when Kroeber wrote to Sapir suggesting that if he would prefer to be relieved of the task of proving Washo to be Hokan, then Kroeber and Roland Dixon would handle the job. By that time, however, the attempts of his students to establish genetic connections among American Indian languages were already causing methodological discomfort to Boas, whose approach to language tended more and more to be constrained by the diffusionary assumptions of his cultural anthropology. The case thus suggests in fact the limits of the paradigm metaphor. At Kroeber's suggestion, Edward Sapir offered a codification of the rules of historical reconstruction in 1916, and the next few years saw a series of attempts to synthesize in textbooks the results of an inquiry that until then had been carried on in articles and monographs (Sapir 1916; Lowie 1917; Kroeber 1923; Goldenweiser 1926). However, any tendency among the Boasians toward the development of "normal science" in the sense of the theoretical articulation of a paradigm was frustrated by Boas' methodological puritanism and generally atheoretical stance, in the context of the tension between the scientific and the historical currents in his thinking.

It is in this framework that one should view the pseudo-issue of whether or not the Boasians constituted a "school." At least through the period of the censure episode, there is no doubt that they thought of themselves as such. Their resistance to the identification dates from the 1930s. By then, the revolutionary phase had passed in which they had been united in the critique of evolutionism, the establishment of a sounder empirical base, and the winning of institutional control. The inadequacy of the Boasian paradigm to provide the basis for "normal science," the consequent (perhaps "natural") tendency of the group to develop in divergent directions, and the emergence of alternative, critical, orientations from outside, as well as the institutional developments in which these were reflected, all combined to redefine the group identity. Kroeber, who in 1931 had himself spoken of "the Boas school," protested in 1935 that such a thing had never existed (cf. L. White 1966:3).

Perhaps a more illuminating metaphor is suggested in Kroeber's comment that Boas was "a true patriarch"—a powerful and rather forbidding father figure who rewarded his offspring with nurturant support insofar as he felt that "they were genuinely identifying with him," but who was indifferent and even punishing if the occasion demanded it. In short, the Boasians may perhaps be better understood, as their own usage would imply, in terms of a different model of human group identity: the family. There are obvious analogies to the psychodynamics of a large late-Victorian family: the oedipal rebellion of certain older male offspring, the rejected sons, the sibling rivalries, the generational and sexual differentiations—most notable in the softening of the patriarch toward the younger generation of daughters, who called him "Papa Franz" and accepted the sometimes ambiguous benevolence of a man who facilitated the entry of many women into the discipline, but who still tended to assume that, in the world as it was then constituted, wives and secretaries could not enjoy all the prerogatives of professionalism (Modell 1974).

Quite aside from psychodynamics, however, there is another, quasi-biological, analogy to the family that may be helpful in understanding the Boasians—and perhaps some other intellectual movements as well. Thus Boas' basic anthropological viewpoint may be seen as a kind of intellectual gene-pool, containing a limited number of traits, some dominant, some recessive, whose manifestation in his descendants was affected by the genetics of their affinal intellectual relationships and the environments in which their phenotypes developed. The outcome might be a considerable

"Papa Franz" and a group of Boasians at a Columbia University anthropology picnic, c. 1925 (left to right): Nels Nelson, whose arm is held by an unidentified woman, Franz Boas, whose face is partly obscured by Esther Goldfrank, who along with Gertrude Boas obscures a second unidentified woman, Robert Lowie, Pliny Earle Goddard, William Ogburn, Gladys Reichard, Mrs. Nelson. (Courtesy of the National Anthropological Archives, Smithsonian Institution)

divergence within the patriline, but this divergence was limited by the original genetic makeup of the intellectual father and by his continuing presence in the disciplinary environment, as well as by a certain tendency to intellectual endogamy.

In this context, one may perhaps see the basic Boasian tension between history and science in terms of opposing pairs of genetic traits. At the theoretical level, scientific generalization contrasts with historical understanding; at the methodological level, rigorous induction from elements contrasts with the loving penetration of whole phenomena. In Boas, all four genes were present, although the first and last were clearly recessive. In his students, these traits were variously manifest. The most characteristically Boasian tended to be heterozygous, either at the theoretical level (Goldenweiser), or the methodological (Leslie Spier), or both (Melville Herskovits). Some, however, seem to have been homozygotically historical (Paul Radin and Ruth Benedict). Some (notably Kroeber) went through phases in which now one, now another genetic tendency was most clearly manifest. Straining the metaphor slightly, we may perhaps speak of genetic influences from outside the patriline. Lowie, under the influence of Ernst Mach, received a double dose of neopositivist empiricism; Kroeber and Sapir, under the influence of Heinrich Rickert and Wilhelm Windelband, received a second input of German historicism. Radin had a kind of affinal relation to American pragmatism; Margaret Mead established ties with British functionalism. Whatever their individual genetic makeup, all were affected by their Boasian upbringing—one feels in Kroeber a Spengler struggling to break loose from the inhibitions of inductivism, which were at best recessive in his intellect, and may simply have been imposed by early familial environment. Most of them continued to respond—although in some cases reactively—to the patriarch's continuing critical presence. None of them, however, was untouched by the historicist strain, although its phenotypic manifestations were quite varied. In none did the tendency to scientific generalization manifest itself in undiluted form. When a changeling like Leslie White was placed within the Boasian nursery, his true genetic makeup eventually asserted itself (cf. Barrett 1989).

No doubt this somewhat tenuous analogy should not be pushed too far—although viewed in the context of the psychodynamics of the Boasian family, it may place in better perspective such family squabbles as that precipitated by Kroeber's dogmatic pronouncements on the superorganic (below, p. 135), or Radin's later historicist assault on all his confreres (1933). The important point, however, is that the students of Boas manifested in different forms the body of Boasian assumptions that has been elaborated here, and that their work developed largely along lines implicit in it—although sometimes to the point of carrying a particular line further than Boas' own scientific and historical asceticism would allow. The history of American anthropology between the wars may thus be seen as the working out, in a changing intellectual and institutional context, of various implications of the position Boas had defined at the beginning of his anthropological career.

The Evolving Institutional Framework

The important thing to keep in mind about the institutional framework of American anthropology in 1920 is the extent to which research was carried out in non- or quasi-academic contexts.[3] Only about half the professional anthropologists were employed as college or university teachers; furthermore, the half dozen or so academic departments of anthropology all existed in some kind of relation to an anthropological or general museum. In several cases friction had attenuated these relations, but in the one in-

3. This account of changing institutional structure starts from the last chapter of GS 1968a, and builds largely on materials in the *American Anthropologist*—the proceedings of the Association and other societies, material in the "Notes and News," etc.—as well as on the publications of the institutions involved, some of which were researched by the students in my seminar in the fall of 1975; see also Frantz 1975.

stance where no close relation ever developed (the University of Chicago), academic anthropology before 1920 never got off the ground (GS 1979a). Even the government Bureau of American Ethnology, which since its founding in 1879 had probably sponsored more anthropological research than any other single institution, carried on its work in relation to the National Museum (Hinsley 1981; Darnell 1969). Aside from the money appropriated for government anthropology, research was supported largely by individual philanthropy, channeled through the museums; universities provided little if any money for anthropological research (Darnell 1970; Thoresen 1975).

At the same time, research institutions, although providing certain training functions, were consumers and not producers of anthropological personnel. From this point of view, the role of the Columbia and Harvard departments was critical in the overall institutional life of the discipline. Between them there was a *de facto* division of labor, Harvard specializing in archeology and physical anthropology, while Columbia took care of ethnology and linguistics. Together they produced thirty of the forty doctorates granted by 1920, with the others scattered among six different institutions, of which only the Universities of Pennsylvania and California (Berkeley) then maintained active instruction at the graduate level (Thomas 1955).

Mapping the institutional terrain as a whole, one can see three major centers of anthropological work—New York, Cambridge, and Washington—each with its complex of interrelated institutions, its locally based disciplinary society, its publication outlets, and to a certain extent its subdisciplinary emphasis. Each of the three was linked in complicated ways to the other two, and to institutions in other areas. Two of the latter—Berkeley and Chicago with its Field Museum—could be regarded as separate, independent institutional and research foci. Others—among them Yale and the several institutions in Philadelphia—are perhaps better viewed as satellites to one or another of the three major centers. Off in the hinterlands, many of them without even satellite connections to the major centers, were the great majority of the rest of the thirty-nine small private colleges and state universities in which some anthropology was taught in some other departmental context (MacCurdy 1919). More often than not, this teaching was by people without degrees in anthropology, most frequently by sociologists—in striking contrast to the major anthropological departments, which were rather slow in developing ties to the social sciences.

This institutional framework had certain implications for the development of the discipline. The relatively diversified structure concentrated in three major centers made it possible for a small but coherent and commit-

Staff members of the Anthropology Department, University of California [Berkeley], c. 1921, standing (left to right) in front of the "tin shed" which housed both the department and the Museum of Greek Sculpture: Robert Lowie, Monica Flannery (teaching assistant), T. Gray (teaching assistant), A. L. Kroeber. (Courtesy of the P. A. Hearst Museum of Anthropology, the University of California at Berkeley)

ted group to have great influence in an Association that until 1920 had no more than three hundred individual members, only a very few of whom were likely to attend meetings of the Council in which the major business was carried on. With the passing of the older evolutionary generation and the penetration of Boasian influence into Washington and Cambridge, no coherent alternative grouping emerged except momentarily around the censure motion. The establishment of a Central States Branch in 1922 provided a lively regional forum for the midwestern schools, which were a major growth area for academic anthropology in the interwar years. During the same period, individual membership of the Association more than doubled, with the Council growing by a gradual cooptation of newly trained Ph.D.'s. Neither development, however, affected the control of the discipline. Once the Boasians had reestablished their position after the abortive counterrevolution, power in the Association tended to concentrate in the hands of "old-timers"—either Boasians or neutrals deprived of any alternative reference group—who one after another filled the largely honorific national offices. The most significant positions were those which actively represented the intellectual or professional interests of the discipline—most particularly, the editorship of the *Anthropologist*, and representation on the three national interdisciplinary research councils. In all of these, the Boasian influence was especially strong, with Spier succeeding Lowie as editor in 1933 and Boasians dominating the anthropological representation on the councils save for a brief period in the early 1920s. The effect of all of this was not simply to sustain Boasian power—to which there was perhaps no real alternative. More important, in the context of other trends which we shall consider, it facilitated the domination of the discipline by "ethnology."

The character of ethnology, however, was itself affected by the institutional framework through which anthropological research was carried on. Although archeology was a secondary activity for Boasians, the customary linkage of archeology and ethnology in the museum context surely reinforced the historical orientation of anthropological theory, just as the object-orientation of museum collections sustained a particular attitude toward ethnographic data. More important, the whole culture-area approach, although in a sense the natural outgrowth of the Bureau of Ethnology program for mapping the continent, was very heavily conditioned by the problems of museum exhibition. Beyond this, the museum context, in which all the subdisciplines save linguistics were visually represented, obviously helped to reinforce the embracive tendency of the discipline, as well as its ties to the natural rather than the social sciences. The impact of the museum orientation continued to be felt throughout the 1920s, which were still a period of museum growth—although by the time the Depression forced a sharp cutback in museum activities, their importance was already being undercut by other institutional developments.

Some of these were already in evidence at the time of the censure episode. The so-called Maya crowd was a group centered around the Department of Archeology that the Carnegie Institution of Washington had founded in 1913, and which it funded on an increasingly liberal scale in the 1920s. During that period, the peacetime National Research Council, funded largely through grants from the Carnegie and other philanthropic foundations, supported a considerable amount of anthropological research. At the same time, the rising interdisciplinary movement in the social sciences had led to the founding of the Social Science Research Council, supported largely by Rockefeller philanthropic foundations. In 1925 anthropology accepted an invitation to join, and by 1930 the Association was admitted also to the American Council of Learned Societies. Along with other foundation activities—such as the Rockefeller subvention of university departments, or their founding of the Laboratory of Anthropology in 1928 (GS 1982a)—the result of all this by 1930 was a considerable modification in the economic basis of anthropological research. Government money continued to play a role, shortly to be heightened by the social welfare policies of the New Deal. But there was a marked decline in the role of the individual benefactor, whose interest in anthropology had largely been channeled through museums—a traditional meeting ground for the philanthropic and the acquisitive instincts. Henceforth, the philanthropic contribution to anthropological research was to be channeled largely through foundation directorates, committed to more general cultural or social welfare goals, and acting often through intermediate bodies in which professional representatives were influential (below, pp. 179–211).

Another institutional change, which was only beginning in 1919, was to have a considerable impact along similar lines: the academic expansion of the discipline, and the reorientation of its intra-university ties away from museums and toward the social sciences. By the early 1930s new departments had emerged or were emerging at Chicago, Northwestern, Michigan, Wisconsin, and Washington—almost all of them in relation to departments of sociology. By the end of that decade the number of separate anthropology departments had risen to over twenty, with another dozen or so combined departments of anthropology and sociology (Chamberlain & Hoebel 1942; Thomas 1955). At Yale, anthropology was reorganized in 1931 in close relation to sociology, and the establishment of a sociology department at Harvard the same year helped to reorient anthropology there. In the context of the discipline's participation in the various research initiatives of the Social Science Research Council, the effect was greatly to reinforce the social science component of American anthropology, which had been somewhat attenuated during the period of the Boasian critique of evolutionism. One aspect of this development was the direct influence of British functionalism. Radcliffe-Brown spent six years at Chicago and Malinowski later three at Yale (GS 1984b, 1986b); Lloyd Warner, a student of Lowie's who came under Radcliffe-Brown's influence while doing fieldwork in Australia, was quite influential at Harvard in the early 1930s (Warner 1988). At the same time, the filling of many new academic positions by Boasians and their continued presence in all the major departments helped to constrain the social science impulse within channels which, if not always traditionally Boasian, were nonetheless clearly distinguishable from British functionalism.

These institutional developments had a definite impact on the focus and character of anthropological research. In the context of the hard-science reaction against cultural anthropology and the widening arena of American interests overseas, certain already incipient tendencies toward broadening the traditional North American focus of anthropological research were greatly strengthened. The first Pan-Pacific Science Congress and the Bayard Dominick Expedition of 1920 opened up a continuing series of investigations in the Pacific extending as far east as the Philippines and Dutch New Guinea. Although American anthropological research in the Pacific was extremely unevenly distributed geographically, by the end of the interwar period Polynesia was an important research area, in which the Bernice Bishop Museum played the central institutional role (Bashkow 1991).

The 1920s also saw research initiatives toward Africa by Harvard, the Field Museum, and Columbia – although it was not until after 1930 that Herskovits began the African fieldwork which helped to establish African studies as a significant component of American cultural anthropology (Jackson 1986).

By 1934, Lowie's figures on the distribution of articles in the *Anthropologist* over the previous decade indicated that approximately one-fifth dealt with areas outside the New World. However, a number of these were not based on field research, and an impressionistic analysis of doctoral dissertation topics suggests that despite the new initiatives, overseas research did not bulk very large in American anthropology in the interwar period as a whole. There were exceptions – notably Northwestern (which gave only five doctorates in the whole period) and Harvard, where a number of physical anthropological and archeological doctorates were done outside the Americanist orbit, and in the early 1930s an anthropological survey of Ireland combined the community studies approach of Lloyd Warner with archeological and physical researches (Arensberg 1937). In general, however, Americanist interests predominated, and the most important single ethnographic area, both in terms of the amount and the significance of research, was probably the southwestern United States (GS 1982a).

At the same time, the range of Americanist activity was considerably broadened with a great expansion of archeological work in the civilizations of Central America (Brunhouse 1971; Willey & Sabloff 1974) and the opening of these and other regions by North American ethnographers (Sullivan 1989). As early as 1932, the project of a *Handbook of South American Indians* was broached in the National Research Council, although the goal was then frankly as much to stimulate research as to summarize it, and lack of funds forestalled the whole undertaking until the Smithsonian Institution revived it in 1939. By that time, it is clear that a basis had been laid for the vast expansion of research interests that was to take place after the war. While American anthropology was still overwhelmingly Americanist, and with a few exceptions overseas research by American anthropologists did not have a major impact on method and theory, the discipline was no longer constrained within the Powellian framework that by and large defined the interests of the Boasians before 1920.

During this same period ethnographic work, which at critical moments in the 1920s was sustained by the *ad hoc* benefactions of Elsie Clews Parsons (Hare 1985), was placed on a much firmer economic foundation. As the lengthy annual summaries in the *Anthropologist* by the NRC's Committee on State Archeological Surveys testify, the major portion of anthropological research in the 1920s was archeological. And although the hard-science attempt to reshape anthropology was unsuccessful, the rest of the early anthropological work initiated by the NRC tended to be oriented toward practical "racial" problems, conceived of in biological terms. The careers of several prominent cultural anthropologists who began in archeology (Ralph Linton [Linton & Wagley 1971] and Fred Eggan) or physical anthropology (Herskovits) perhaps reflect the research priorities of this era. By the end of the decade, however, the Boasian influence within the NRC and that of the new national interdisciplinary social science establishment outside it had succeeded in redefining the "racial" research of the NRC in social or cultural terms. Simultaneously, the SSRC provided an additional basis of support for cultural research, and by 1930, the Carnegie Institution had decided to broaden the purely archeological focus of its Central American researches. Taken together with the Rockefeller contributions to cultural research and the linguistic research supported through the ACLS, these developments placed the funding of cultural studies on a somewhat firmer basis. The decision of the Rockefeller Foundation in 1933 not to underwrite a worldwide program of salvage ethnography was certainly a blow, but Rockefeller money continued to flow into already existing programs for several years more (below, pp. 200–201). In this context, ethnology seems to have done rather better in the Depression years than it had in the early 1920s. The proportion of doctorates in archeology and physical anthropology, which had been nearly half in the 1920s, fell sharply in the next decade. Of the approximately 340 doctorates in anthropology granted by 1945, at least 230 were in ethnology, with another 20 in linguistics (Thomas 1955).

In addition to these changes in the areal focus and subdisciplinary balance of the profession, it seems quite likely also that institutional developments helped to mediate changes in the substance and methods of anthropological research. The shift from museum to foundation and research council funding would by itself have tended to undercut somewhat the institutional basis for the older object-oriented, historical ethnology (below, pp. 207–11). But the change also had a more positive impact. The early interest of the NRC and the SSRC in practical social problems relating to race and immigration clearly influenced the substantive focus of anthropological work. Herskovits' extended program of Afro-American research, beginning with the physical anthropology of the American Negro and eventuating in an intercontinental program for the study of acculturation, was developed in this context (Jackson 1986); so also, Redfield's Tepoztlán project was first formulated as a background study of a particular immigrant group (Godoy 1978). If acculturation studies may thus be viewed as the outgrowth of a practical interest in problems of race contact, the early culture-and-personality work may be seen as a transformation of NRC and SSRC interests in "racial" mental differences, in an interdisciplinary situation that brought anthropologists into closer association with psychologists of various persuasions (GS 1986a). Similarly, changing ethnographic areal orientations, the influence of British functionalism, and the closer relations of anthropology to an increasingly empirically oriented sociology both in the SSRC and the universities may all have contributed toward a more behavioralist research in present-day communities—although the roots of a more active participant observation were surely present in the Boasian tradition itself.

In short, there is considerable evidence to suggest that changes in the institutional framework of anthropology in the years after 1920 were not simply the reflection of internal intellectual processes within the discipline, but in fact helped to shape them. On the one hand, they created channels that slowed or encouraged the flow of certain intradisciplinary developments and interdisciplinary influences; on the other, they provided an important channel through which external social and cultural processes impinged upon anthropology as an intellectual endeavor. One of the more important developments mediated by these institutional processes was a profound change in the character, orientation, and intradisciplinary role of what we would call today "cultural anthropology," but which the Boasians still normally referred to as "ethnology."

From Ethnology to Cultural Anthropology

The central concept of ethnology was of course "culture," which provides a convenient focus for a brief treatment of ethnological theory in the interwar years.[4] Given Boas' resistance to systematic conceptualization (as opposed to the criticism of concepts), his students had some difficulty extracting constructive principles from his work—or in recognizing the Boasian component once they had. The situation at the beginning of our period is strikingly illustrated in Lowie's *Culture and Ethnology*, one of the first ethnological syntheses attempted by the Boasians. After arguing that culture (as E. B. Tylor had defined it in 1871) was "the sole and exclusive subject matter of ethnology," and then rejecting psychological, racial, and environmental determinism of cultural phenomena, Lowie was "a bit flabbergasted to discover that I did not even know what the determinants [of culture] were, and it required a long talk with Pliny Goddard to clarify my notions and to make 'diffusion' the hero of the plot" (1959:128). For

4. In addition to those cited in the text, useful sources on the development of ethnology include J. Bennett 1944; Eggan 1968; Goldenweiser 1941; Harris 1968; Kroeber & Kluckhohn 1952; Lowie 1937; Radin 1933; Singer 1968; Vincent 1990; and Voget 1968.

the next decade and a half, diffusion continued to play the central role in American ethnological thought, although as time wore on, its dimensions began to seem rather less heroic.

Already by the time Lowie wrote, certain issues in cultural theory had begun to surface that in the longer run were to assume much greater significance. When Kroeber had argued the autonomy of culture in even more extreme terms, several fellow Boasians reacted quite sharply to his conception of the "superorganic." Although at one with him on the importance of culture, Goldenweiser and Sapir nevertheless felt that Kroeber had gone much too far in arguing the separation of history and science, in denying the psychological aspect of ethnological inquiry, in eliminating entirely the influence of the individual upon cultural development, and in reifying what was in fact merely a name for a certain selection of phenomena (Kroeber 1917; Goldenweiser 1917; Sapir 1917b). It was some time, however, before the implications of these conceptual issues were to be fully felt. The immediate pressures to which anthropology was subject in the next few years led not to conceptual clarification but rather to what Boas would call "premature classification." Kroeber clearly felt these pressures when he reviewed the work that marked the culmination of the critical phase of Boasian anthropology—Lowie's book-length critique of Morganian assumption, *Primitive Society* (1920). Despite the soundness of Boasian method, its products seemed to Kroeber "rather sterile": "as long as we continue offering the world only reconstructions of specific detail, and consistently show a negativistic attitude toward broader conclusions, the world will find very little of profit in ethnology" (1920:380).

Building on assumptions developed in the arrangement of museum collections and in ethnological discussions over the previous several decades, and putting to one side some of the methodological cautions that guarded the pages of Sapir's *Time Perspective in Aboriginal American Culture*, Kroeber and Clark Wissler led an attempt to raise Boasian historical ethnology to a level of generality that would validate its status "to the worker in remote fields of science, and to the man of general intellectual interests" (Kroeber 1920:380). Starting from the geographical distribution and association of cultural elements in space, and assuming that the pattern of diffusion was uniformly from the center to the periphery of a "culture-area," so that the more widely distributed traits were necessarily the older, they attempted to recreate sequences of development in time. The "age-area" principle, supplemented by traditional evolutionary notions of typological complexity and by the limited archeological evidence then available, provided the basis for arranging the cultures of the western hemisphere in stratigraphic layers, with peaks in Central America, Peru, and the Northwest Pacific Coast. Despite Kroeber's earlier insistence on the complete separation of scientific and historical inquiry, the whole approach was considerably influenced by biological assumption, and led both Wissler and Kroeber to study the interrelations of cultural and environmental areas. By 1929, Wissler had gone off in a more sociological direction, but Kroeber's culture-area interests were more systematically pursued (Driver 1962; Freed & Freed 1983; Reed 1980; GS 1974f). In the later 1920s several of his students attempted to develop quantitative approaches to the problem, and in the 1930s a number of them were employed under Kroeber's direction in the "culture element survey"—most of them rather reluctantly, for lack of alternative research support (GS 1991b). By that time, the changing climate of anthropological opinion made the "laundry-list" approach to culture seem very much a dead end to an ambitious graduate student, and Kroeber's own underlying holistic historicism had reasserted itself.

One may doubtless elicit a variety of statements about the nature of culture from the culture-area syntheses of the 1920s, which were indeed influential in diffusing an anthropological orientation to the neighboring social sciences. Wissler's *Man and Culture,* for instance, offers in its "universal pattern" a framework of sorts for comparing the "plan" or "pattern" of individual tribal cultures (1923). In general, however, the methodologically significant units of this approach were the individual "traits" and the "trait complexes" that helped to define culture-areal "types"—rather than the "mere social unit," which Wissler suggested at one point had "little value as a culture unit" (1922:269). By objectifying cultural entities whose epistemological and ontological status was in fact rather questionable, the culture-element approach may have sustained a kind of culturological orientation, and it could and did lead indirectly to a holistic or configurationalist view. It contributed little, however, to the understanding of cultural process, beyond the demonstration of diffusion, which in any case by 1920 had already been accomplished. No doubt the culture-area notion provided a stimulus to ecological thought, and continues still to be a useful general taxonomic device, but the attempt to arrive at genetic classifications from the analysis of essentially synchronic data was already undergoing sharp criticism by the mid-1920s. Boas and Wilson Wallis attacked the assumptions underlying age-area analysis (Boas 1924; Wallis 1925); and by 1929 Leslie Spier, whose doctoral dissertation on the sun dance had provided an important model for the whole approach, had explicitly rejected its utility for historical reconstruction. Dixon's moderate and somewhat critical presentation of the viewpoint the previous year (1928), instead of placing it on a surer foundation, was itself left stranded on the mudflats of history.

The rather musty aura of the ethnology of the 1920s is largely an emanation from the sort of work just discussed, and reflects perhaps the institutional prominence of Kroeber, Dixon, and Wissler—who were the central figures at Berkeley, Harvard, and the American Museum respectively, and who were each moreover particularly responsive to the hard-science critique of cultural anthropology. Already by 1920, however, alternative lines of development had been suggested by Boas, who was shortly to pronounce that "diffusion was done." His "Methods of Ethnology" signalized a shift (which Boas later suggested had begun as early as 1910) from the study of dissemination of elements to the more difficult problem of the "inner development" of culture, conceived in terms of the study of "acculturation," the "interdependence of cultural activities," and "the relation of the individual to society" (1920b). In retrospect, this formulation may be seen as a prospectus for much of the anthropology of the interwar period, although it was also to be informed by exogenous scientizing impulses of a non- or even anti-Boasian character. What was in effect occurring was a change in emphasis between the central components of Boasian analysis—from "elements" to "processes" and "patterns"—in the context of a simultaneous shift in analytic perspective from the diachronic to the synchronic. Henceforth, the focus was to be on "the dynamic changes in society that may be observed at the present time." At the end of the decade Boas was in fact to suggest that "if we knew the whole biological, geographical, and cultural setting of a society completely, and if we understood in detail the ways of reacting of the members of the society and of society as a whole to these conditions, we should not need historical knowledge of the origin of the society to understand its behavior" (1930b:98).

Even after 1920, however, the shift was not precipitate. As Mead has suggested, "Boas had strict, puritanical views about the sequence in which problems should be investigated" (1959a:269). A number of the newer orientations that flowered in the 1930s had their roots in doctoral dissertations carried on within a trait-distribution framework. Benedict, Herskovits, A. I. Hallowell, and Mead all followed this pattern—as in fact did Julian Steward and Leslie White, though they worked under Boas' students, rather than Boas himself (GS 1974a; Jackson 1986; Darnell 1977b; Mead 1928a; Hanc 1981; Barrett 1989). Although their manifest targets were latter-day evolutionists or the diffusionist extremists of the German and British schools, each of the former four treated theoretical issues raised by trends in American diffusionary ethnology: the stability of cultural elements, the character of their interrelation, their reinterpretation in particular cultural contexts, the applicability of the culture-area concept to other regions, the problem of culture-area boundaries, the psychological nature of the man/environment relation. In each case there are hints of the direction which future research was to take, but in each case one feels the limitations imposed by the secondary nature of the analysis. All four were library dissertations, and in each case fieldwork provided a catalyst for the development of more integrative or processual approaches.

The first of these to have major theoretical impact was Benedict's configurationalism (GS 1974a; Modell 1983; Caffrey 1989). Although for Benedict the processes of cultural differentiation were quite traditionally Boasian, her approach—informed by Nietzsche, Dilthey, Spengler, Haeberlin, and Sapir—focussed on the historically emergent "configurations in culture that so pattern existence and condition the emotional and cognitive reactions of its carriers that they become incommensurables, each specializing in certain selected types of behavior and each ruling out the behavior proper to its opposites" (1932:4). Benedict had been touched by some of the psychological fashions of the 1920s (Jung and Gestalt), and was particularly concerned with the problem of individual deviance, but she was more interested in characterizing cultures in psychological terms than in the processes by which human personalities were determined within particular cultural contexts (Handler 1986). Her work helped to establish an integrationalist view of culture, and by focussing attention on culturally defined emotional and value orientations offered a broad framework for the explanation of human behavior. But although Benedict allowed in principle at least for differences in the degree of integration of different cultures, she left unanswered numerous questions as to the factors determining their development, their influence on human behavior, and the variability of individual behavior within any particular cultural context. Furthermore, except at a rather broad contrastive level, her work did not facilitate cultural comparison or generalization about cultural processes. Although her own research lacked any significant temporal dimension, Benedict was very much on the historicist side of the Boasian dualism.

As the culture-and-personality movement developed in the 1930s, some of these issues began to be more systematically explored—partly in reaction to Benedict's work, partly in response to other influences. Sapir's contrasting emphasis on the individual as the dynamic focus of cultural process (a focus shared by Boas himself) was quite influential in the interdisciplinary seminars organized by the SSRC, and was important especially in defining Hallowell's more differentiated and dynamic approach to culture and personality (Darnell 1960, 1990). At the same time, models of method and theory drawn from psychology began to play a more explicit role. The contribution of Freud—who had been something of a whipping-boy for the Boasians in the 1920s—asserted itself in more acceptable neo-Freudian form in the work of Margaret Mead and in the seminars conducted by Abram Kardiner at Columbia in the late 1930s (Manson 1986). Psychiatric orientations toward the problems of mental abnormality and deviance were an important influence, and neobehaviorist learning theory also had an impact, especially through the Institute of Human Relations at Yale (Morawski 1986). In contrast to the 1920s, when the intelligence test was the psychological method of greatest salience, a wider range of psychological measures and techniques began to be employed. Paralleling the influence of psychology, functionalism in both its Malinowskian and Radcliffe-Brownian variants contributed to the "scientizing" trend—on the one hand by emphasizing the biological factors conditioning cultural behavior, on the other by focussing greater attention on social structure as a mediating variable between culture and personality. At the end of the period, such developments seemed to offer the promise of a more differentiated, systematically comparative approach to the old Boasian problem of the "genius of a people," as well as an alternative to racialist interpretations of human mental difference. The cultural malleability of human nature was still fundamental anthropological dogma, but increasing emphasis was being placed on its more enduring aspects and on the general processes by which it was modified. Taken together, the varied manifestations of the culture-and-personality movement played such an important role in American anthropology that certain culturological critics feared that the independence of the discipline was threatened by subordination to psychology (cf. GS 1986a).

So far we have followed the integrationalist impulse along a line that led toward psychology. It can also be traced along a sociological line, again in the context of the reassertion after 1930 of more "scientific" approaches to the study of man. Despite Boas' retreat from general law, the scientific impulse within the Boasian dualism had never died out entirely. Quite aside from the dalliance of certain Boasians with biology in the 1920s, there was a continuing interest in problems of social organization in which the scientific component was clearly manifest. Even the criticism of Morganian assumption (as in the continuing stream of articles on Indian hunting territories [cf. Feit 1991]) helped to sustain his relevance; and by the end of the decade, historically oriented studies by Hallowell and others suggesting the prior widespread existence of cross-cousin marriage in fact provided confirmation of an important Morganian (and Riversian) hypothesis (Hallowell 1937). However, the continuity of interest in the general processes of the development of social organization was largely due to the influence of Robert Lowie—who, significantly, felt it necessary explicitly to reject the Boasian assumption that like effects need not be referred to like causes. Although he was Morgan's severest critic, it was Lowie more than anyone else (with the possible exception of Wissler) who during the 1920s preserved the ultimate goal of a systematically comparative social scientific anthropology (Murphy 1972).

By 1932 the attenuated sociological impulse in Boasian anthropology began to receive outside support. Social evolutionary ideas had lingered on for some time in sociology, despite the diffusion of anthropological thinking about culture in the early 1920s. Toward the end of the decade, the channels of influence were to some extent reversed, and the residual evolutionism of sociology had an impact back on anthropology. Redfield's intellectual debt to his teacher (and father-in-law) Robert Park is abundantly evident in *Tepoztlán,* which provided an instance of "the general type of change whereby primitive man becomes civilized man, the rustic becomes the urbanite" (1930a:14; cf. GS n.d.). George Murdock's background in the tradition of William Graham Sumner is obvious in his eclectic approach to the "science of culture" (1932), where Kroeberian superorganicism, behaviorist psychology, Wissler's universal pattern and Sumner's cross-cultural comparative approach were brought together in a postevolutionary framework stressing the adaptive value of social habits transmitted through time and space by the medium of language. The new sociological input into anthropology also helped to open the way for another major line of integrationalist thinking: British functionalism, which had little impact in the reconstructionist milieu of the 1920s. Malinowski's psychobiological utilitarianism fitted quite well with Murdock's orientation, and it was not inappropriate that he should have spent his last years in New Haven, which in the 1930s also hosted Richard Thurnwald, Charles Seligman, and Edward Evans-Pritchard (GS 1986b).

The more important functionalist influence, however, was that of Radcliffe-Brown, who came to Chicago in the fall of 1931, fresh from his comparative synthesis of the types of Australian social organization. Although his assumption that a similar order could be quickly introduced into American Indian data proved unduly optimistic, there is no doubt that Radcliffe-Brown's presence among the Boasians had considerable impact, both on their thinking and his own. For some time he had been insisting on the distinction between "ethnology," which attempted to give a "hypothetical reconstruction of the past history of civilization," and "social anthropology," which sought to "discover natural laws of human society." As Redfield suggested, "no one in America [had] offered a strictly nonhistorical scientific method, equipped with a self-consistent body of concepts and procedures for getting specific jobs done in relation to ultimate scientific objectives" (1937:xii). Radcliffe-Brown's presumption that he could offer just that did not sit well with the majority of American anthropologists, but it did contribute to an already on-going reconsideration of the relations of history and science in anthropology (Kroeber 1935a; Boas 1936; inter alia). Simultaneously, the tendency of common terminology to create conceptual confusion helped push Radcliffe-Brown toward the final clarification of his mature social structure orientation. In order to differentiate his own approach, he abandoned the idiom of "culture" for that of "social structure" and "social system"; in reaction to the looser usage of American anthropologists, he insisted on a specifically Durkheimian view of "function" as the inner consistency of the social system conceived of in organic terms. In this context, Radcliffe-Brown presented to American anthropology a prospectus for a "natural science of society." It was to be in no sense a psychology, and its subject matter was not "culture," which had no concrete existence. Its significant integrative units were rather "societies"—the "structural systems observable in particular communities"—whose "systematic comparison" would lead to laws of social morphology, social physiology, and ultimately of social evolution (GS 1984b).

Many American anthropologists were alienated by what they perceived as Radcliffe-Brown's self-centered messianic style; and even at Chicago he won few, if any, unqualified disciples (Steward 1938). The work of his most important student, Fred Eggan, who previously had been influenced by Leslie Spier, was an attempt to reconcile the methods of ethnology and social anthropology (1937). Nevertheless, in a diffuse way Radcliffe-Brown clearly had an impact, especially in the context of the more general reorientation toward sociology. The most influential textbook of the period, Ralph Linton's *Study of Man* (1936)—with its emphasis on such sociological concepts as "status" and "role," and its conceptual separation of "society" and "culture"—owes a good deal to Radcliffe-Brown, with whom Linton had various informal (and not entirely friendly) ties in the early 1930s (GS 1978a). More generally, Radcliffe-Brown's American sojourn clearly reinforced the scientizing trend in American anthropology, offering support for a more utilitarian, adaptive view of culture, and contributing from a particular perspective to the renewal of the Morganian tradition.

In this context, one may view certain developments of the late 1930s as representing a third expression of the integrationalist and scientizing impulses (Hatch 1973b). In contrast to the psychological and the sociological, it might be called the "economic" line—although only Herskovits, who remained essentially Boasian, worked with the categories of academic economic analysis. Marvin Harris' "techno-environmental" is perhaps a better term, since what was involved was a reassertion of environmental and technological determinisms that had been submerged during the Boasian critique of evolutionism (Harris 1968). The two spokesmen of the repressed determinisms—Steward and White—both wrote trait-distribution dissertations under students of Boas, and then moved toward a more integrationalist view of culture. Steward's ecological interpretation of the development of political and social organization clearly reflected his training under Kroeber, Edward Gifford, and Lowie (Hanc 1981). However, like White he conceived of the integration of culture as an adaptive utilitarian response to external forces, rather than in subjective emotional or ideational terms. White, whose epistemological assumptions were from the beginning in a profound sense anti-Boasian, represented a more radical departure—although he assimilated his materialistic "culturology" to Kroeber's

Leslie White (University of Michigan), with a graduate student fieldwork party of the Laboratory of Anthropology at the Hopi pueblo of New Oraibi, 1932 (left to right): Ed Kennard (Columbia), Jess Spirer (Yale), White, Fred Eggan (Chicago), Mischa Titiev (Harvard). (Courtesy of Joan Eggan)

idealist superorganicism (Barrett 1989). Having rediscovered Lewis Henry Morgan even before 1930, White took advantage of the rising current of scientism in the late 1930s to launch a scathing attack on the Boasians for rejecting the generalizing "materialist" evolutionism of Morgan and Tylor for a philosophy of "planless hodge-podge-ism" (cf. L. White 1987; Carneiro 1981).

Although there were other manifestations of a materialist orientation in this period, the influence of Steward and White was largely a postwar phenomenon. White was somewhat isolated at Michigan, which had not yet become a center of graduate training, and Steward was not able to establish himself in academia until 1946, when he replaced Linton at Columbia after the latter moved to Yale. Despite the rising interest in more generalizing approaches, the most influential of the newer anthropological currents still strongly reflected their roots in Boasian historical ethnology. This was surely true of the culture-and-personality movement; it was equally evident in acculturation studies, in which many of the newer currents came together.

The interest in acculturation had varied manifestations. One of the earliest and most interesting studies was done by Mead under the aegis of Wissler during an interval between her expeditions to the South Pacific (1932). The most important individuals, however, were Redfield, Herskovits, and Linton—all key figures in the late 1920s and early 1930s in the sociologically oriented midwestern institutional network. Redfield's interest developed through a Parkian reading of Wissler in the context of his fieldwork in Tepoztlán and Yucatan: "in understanding culture process, the mode and character of communication should be the center of attention, not the geographic distribution of the culture traits" (1930b;148). Strictly historical study could never sort out the "closely integrated body of elements" in present-day Yucatan. However, the historical process of culture change might be approached through the observation of four contemporary cultural situations whose spatial arrangement could be transformed into a typological temporal sequence (1934).

Herskovits' approach to acculturation developed out of his Boasian concern with disproving theories of Negro inequality, and he in fact began by defining acculturation as the total acceptance of an alien culture—illustrated, he then felt, by the Negro in the United States (Jackson 1986). However, his Surinam fieldwork, in which "Africanisms" were noted in the city as well as in the bush, led him to formulate an interhemispheric program for comparative research in which he arranged various Negro cultural groups in the Americas along a scale of intensity of Africanisms. Arguing that the character of contact situations had a differential impact on various aspects of culture, he came to revise his earlier views on American black acculturation. Rather more than Redfield's, his work thus reflected its origins in the "culture element" historical tradition. He tended to emphasize the role that acculturation studies could play in mediating between the historical and functional orientations, and the variety of anthropological approaches that could be integrated in the study of acculturation problems.

Linton came to acculturation studies somewhat later, after he had absorbed a good deal of Radcliffe-Brown's influence in the early 1930s, but his approach to acculturation was embracively eclectic (1936; Linton & Wagley 1971). Although focussing on the transmission of elements, he emphasized the modifications of their meaning and form, the reciprocal social and psychological factors conditioning their integration into pre-existing cultural patterns, and the varied outcomes of the whole process—including the reassertion of traditional cultural values in "nativistic" movements, as well as the "fusion" of two cultures in a "chemical" rather than a "mechanical" mixture. In this context, the schematic memorandum on acculturation which the three men authored for the SSRC in 1936, although later subject to criticism and modification, is one of the most representative documents of American anthropology in the interwar period. With its movement from elements to transmission processes to integration conceived of in psychological terms, it is an archetypical manifestation of the transformation of Boasian historical ethnology (Redfield et al. 1936).

The reaction of some of the older Boasians to this transformation helps further to illuminate its character. Without attempting to sort out responses to each new trend, it is fair to say that Boas himself was generally supportive, and his last general methodological formulation may in fact be read as a reassertion of the "scientific" aspect of his epistemological dualism (1938b). Among the first generation of his students Wissler—ever the eclectic—encouraged many of the new initiatives, and Goldenweiser was on the whole sympathetic. Sapir, of course, was a seminal figure in the culture-and-personality movement, and more generally in the area of cultural theory. The resistance—which came primarily from Kroeber, Lowie, Spier, and Radin—took varied forms. There was a tendency toward a patronizing assimilation of newer trends to traditional orientations. Thus Kroeber and Lowie were inclined simply to equate functionalism with an integrationist viewpoint, and to suggest that in this sense Boasian ethnology had always been basically functionalist (Kroeber 1943; Lowie 1937: 230–49; GS 1976a). One might also argue that what was "true" was not "new," and vice versa. Thus Radin and Lowie insisted on the one hand that the best American fieldworkers had always been interested in the "implicit" elements in culture, and on the other that it simply was not possible really to learn a language or a culture in a single fieldwork expedition. The resisters were by no means a coherent group—Radin was scathing in his criticism of Kroeber's quantifying reconstructionism. But they were each, in their own way, strongly committed to an historical conception of ethnology. Thus Lowie, although in some respects quite close to Radcliffe-Brown, made a special point of assimilating portions of the latter's work to the historical point of view. Despite his own switch on the utility of culture-element reconstruction, Spier still resisted acculturation studies as essentially "sociological" rather than ethnological (Meggers 1946). Kroeber's review of Redfield's *Tepoztlán* implied a similar distinction between sociological studies of present societies and ethnological studies of historical ones (1931). And for Radin—the historicist pluperfect—all the "reactions against the quantitative method" of the 1920s were vitiated by a failure to recognize the true historical vocation of ethnology (1933).

At the time, it seemed to some that a sorting out was taking place between the scientific and historical orientations (Kroeber 1936). Retrospectively, we may perhaps see a kind of differentiation among varieties of historical anthropology—with Kroeber attempting to free history from the dimension of time, and Radin standing out as the archetype of an enduring historicist and hermeneutic countercurrent within Boasian anthropology. No doubt the various manifestations of historical ethnology remained a force within the discipline. Thus Wissler's seminars at Yale contributed to the development of a more document-oriented ethnohistorical approach foreshadowed earlier by Swanton and Frank Speck (cf. Payne & Murray 1983). However, the more significant contemporary trend was expressed by those who sought to fuse the historical and functional approaches. Retrospect suggests that the overall development is best seen as a kind of acculturative incorporation of certain newer scientizing trends within an internally evolving Boasian tradition, in which the diachronic dimension tended to be reduced to "process in the present."

Lowie's defense of "horse and buggy" ethnographers notwithstanding (1940), the newer fieldwork methods and theoretical orientations had developed in reciprocal relation to each other, and by the end of the period there were signs of an increasingly sophisticated concern with culture theory, in which the newer trends were variously manifest. Clyde Kluckhohn, whose roundabout road to anthropology had brought him into contact with a wide range of theoretical viewpoints, was an early figure in this movement. But under the editorship of Ralph Linton—perhaps the best single candidate for "representative man" in the World War II period—the *Anthropologist* published a number of articles treating in some general theoretical way the nature of "culture" (Kroeber 1946; cf. Kluckhohn 1943a; Bidney 1944). There was no single generally accepted conceptualization, and Kroeber still wondered "if we know *anything* very fundamental about the nature of culture and how it works" (1944:88). Nevertheless, a range of issues that had been raised in the two decades since Kroeber's "Superorganic" were given more explicit formulation; and one can specify a number of emergent trends, which within a few years were to be more systematically treated in Kroeber and Kluckhohn's encyclopedic review (1952).

Although culture was still conceived as an historical precipitate, the primary focus was on the analysis of its synchronic or micro-diachronic processual aspects. Its *sui generis* nature was still maintained, but in more philosophically sophisticated terms of abstraction rather than reification; and a clearer distinction was made between culture and society. In studying human behavior in all its manifestations, formal and informal, a distinction was now insisted upon between actual and ideal behavioral norms. Increasingly, the realm of the cultural was conceived in ideational or symbolic terms, and the very idea of "material culture" began to be considered something of a misnomer. There was a growing interest in the units of culture, and a growing dissatisfaction with a purely enumerative approach to its content. Culture was a matter of the communication of designs for living. But while there was still considerable emphasis on the processes by which it was learned or transmitted, an increasing role was allowed for individual human creativity. At the same time—and most important—there was a strongly emergent sense that culture had some kind of enduring internal structure, not at a level immediately evident to its carriers, but rather an inner core of values that underlay their actual behavior. And while the commensurability of these structures was still an unsolved problem, the concern for the conceptual clarification of the idea of "culture" was itself evidence of an impulse toward the development of uniform categories that might provide the basis for more systematic comparison.

There were anthropologists, like Leslie White, who in some respects fell outside the framework just described, or who emphasized other facets of the newer trends—insisting on the adaptive or adjustive aspect of cultural behavior. But it is nonetheless true that the most influential figures in American anthropology shared a general approach to the nature of culture. Furthermore, despite Kluckhohn's complaint that psychologists, economists, and sociologists reading Boas' article on "anthropology" in the *Encyclopedia of the Social Sciences* (1930b) usually came away feeling "disappointed" and "empty-handed" (1943b:30), the core of this consensus was still essentially Boasian. Although anthropologists now talked in terms of "structure" and even of "system," the roots of the newer integrationist orientations in the Boasian element, process, and pattern schema were clearly manifest.

To appreciate this, it may help to pose an abstract contrast between the ideas of "pattern" and of "system" as integrative modes. Although the notion of "structure" is compatible to both, and may provide a kind of bridge between the two, it can still be argued that "pattern" and "system" represent quite different and even in a sense polar conceptions of integration. Connotatively, the two words suggest a series of antitheses: repetition vs. differentiation; justaposition vs. interdependence; openendedness vs. closure; contingency vs. necessity. Etymologically, one notes that "pattern" derives from the Old French "patron," and was not finally distinguished from its English congener, either in form or sense, until after 1700—a pattern, like a patron, being something worthy of imitation. There would seem thus to be a psychological, aesthetic, and humanistic bias in a sense inherent in the pattern notion, just as the core meanings of the term "system" are characteristically natural scientific. In the former case, the aspect of holistic integration is problematic and *a posteriori*—the result of historical process; in the latter, it is inherent in the concept itself.

Boasian ethnology, though it took cultural integration for granted from the beginning, in practice moved toward that integration from a study of the distribution of elements over cultural areas. The significant units of analysis were on the one hand smaller and on the other larger than the specific socially bounded groups of people that Radcliffe-Brown assumed as his analytic entities. For a variety of reasons—the lack of obvious boundaries, the underlying historical and psychological conception of the integration process, perhaps also the basic orientation toward analysis in terms of "item and process" rather than "item and arrangement"—"pattern" was a more likely mode of integration to emerge from this approach than "system" (cf. Hymes 1961b). Starting in 1923 from the "ultimate fact of human nature that man builds up his culture out of disparate elements," and rejecting as "superstition" the notion that "the result is an organism functionally interrelated," it is hardly surprising that the integration Benedict ultimately achieved had an *a posteriori*, *un*systematic configurative character (1923:84–85). Not all Boasians in 1923 would have insisted that organic interrelation was a "superstition"; but in general it seems fair to say that Benedict represents the movement of Boasian anthropology. Boasians did not start, like Radcliffe-Brown, with the *a priori* Durkheimian assumption of system. They moved *from* elements *to* patterns. Along the way, they came into cultural contact, as it were, with conceptions of integration in terms of functional interdependence within a bounded system, and some of the elements of these viewpoints became integrated into the pattern of their own thought—as Boas suggested, "some kind of formalization always develops that makes apparently contradictory ideas compatible" (1938b: 672). But the enduring core of their "culture" remained essentially Boasian. Even after they began to speak of patterns *as* systems, of culture as "a system of patterns," their formulations frequently betrayed an origin in a different integrative mode. Thus when Clyde Kluckhohn suggested that "every culture is a structure—not a haphazard collection of all the different physically possible and functionally effective patterns of belief and action but an interdependent system with its patterns segregated and arranged in a manner which is *felt* as appropriate" (1943a:226) his implicit privileging of an affective appreciation of wholeness harked back to the epistemological dualism Boas had articulated more than fifty years before.

Centrifugal Forces of Specialization

Despite this underlying unity of cultural assumption, the transformation of Boasian ethnology had by 1945 created some problems for the self-conception of the field.[5] Insofar as they were interdisciplinary in character,

5. Since this was written, the history of the subdisciplines of anthropology has developed apace with that of anthropology itself. In addition to other titles mentioned in the text, see the following: for physical anthropology, Spencer 1981, 1982; Boaz & Spencer 1981; and *PAN* (*Physical Anthropology News*); for linguistic anthropology, Hymes 1983; Murray 1989; Cowan et al. 1986; Hall & Koerner 1987; and *Historiographia Linguistica;* for archeology, Meltzer et al. 1986; Patterson 1986; Willey 1988; and *BHA* (*Bulletin of the History of Archaeology*); and the activities sponsored by the Society for American Archaeology's Committee on the History of Archaeology.

the newer trends tended to develop at its intellectual margins. Articles on culture and personality were likely to appear in journals that were infrequently read by anthropologists. Furthermore, insofar as they were resisted by the older anthropologists, the new trends also tended institutionally to be forced to the margins. The *Anthropologist* published little on culture and personality, was apparently unreceptive to the work of Julian Steward, and for a time resisted even acculturation studies. Their very marginality, however, made these trends seem disturbing to some anthropologists committed to a diachronic viewpoint, and fears were expressed that the field was losing its center. Retrospectively, it seems clear that in a certain sense this was indeed the case. As Dell Hymes has suggested in another context, "the two activities that had sustained a common frame of reference—the study of the American Indian, and the problems of historical ethnology"—were already becoming peripheral (1970:270). Although the fulfillment of this process was a postwar phenomenon, it was reflected in changing terminological emphases by 1945. "Ethnology" no longer held the field as the rubric encompassing inquiry into human cultural variability. Many anthropologists now distinguished between "ethnology" and "social anthropology"— not so much in Radcliffe-Brownian terms, but rather as receptacles for the traditional and the newer trends respectively. Within a few years, "ethnology" would in fact be largely replaced by the term "cultural anthropology."

Such problems of subdisciplinary self-image was perhaps more disturbing in the light of more fundamental centrifugal tendencies in anthropology as a whole. Although it had survived the censure episode, the embracive unity of anthropology was, as Franz Boas had argued in 1904, an historical product. Boas felt even then that there were "indications of its breaking up" under the stress of increasingly rigorous demands for specialized training in particular subdisciplines. Indeed, the "biological, linguistic, and ethnologic-archaeological methods" were already "so distinct" that it was difficult for one anthropologist to handle them all (1904b:36). His own archeological activities were limited, but Boas did in fact play a role in the methodological development of that subdiscipline; and his control of the other areas, although reflecting his autodidactic professionalization, was nonetheless indisputable. A number of his students made important contributions in two or even three of the subdisciplines, and by and large departmental anthropology programs continued to be conceived of in embracive terms, with faculty often required to teach in more than one subdiscipline. Radcliffe-Brown's stay at Chicago did not break up the sacred bundle, but merely added "social anthropology" as a fifth component (GS 1979a); Kluckhohn continued throughout the period to teach each of the four subfields as defined at Harvard. Even so, at the level of professional identification, the bridging of subdisciplines was somewhat problematic in the interwar period.

In part, this was due to continuing methodological specialization, institutional diversification, and shifting reference groups; but it was also related to changing theoretical orientations. The unity of anthropology was an historical product in more than one sense. It was not simply that a number of methodological approaches had come together historically in the study of non-Western man, but that the overarching interpretive frameworks were in a broad sense historical. Both the evolutionary and the ethnological traditions, each in its own way, were concerned with the history of humankind in all aspects. In this context, any movement in ethnology away from historical reconstruction could not help but have implications for the unity of anthropology. Furthermore, though the traditional historical orientation of anthropology had provided a kind of umbrella under which all the subdisciplinary interests could be kept together, in point of fact it had a rather different and ambiguous status within each of the subdisciplines, whose specialized substantive and methodological concerns were by no means uniformly historical.

The centrifugal tendency was first manifest in physical anthropology, which in continental Europe had in fact preempted the title "anthropology" and tended to develop as a separate discipline for which medical or biological training was prerequisite. To a considerable extent this was also the case in the United States. It is true that Powell in principle included the physical study of man within a broader rubric of "anthropology," the title of his Bureau of Ethnology notwithstanding, and Boas after him gave some substance to the integration. But despite the more embracive concept of anthropology in this country, the fact was that most practitioners of physical anthropology were drawn from and remained oriented toward other sciences.

The most important figure among them was Aleš Hrdlička (Stewart 1981). In contrast to Boas, whose work on immigrant headform had far-reaching revolutionary implications, Hrdlička was influenced by the static anatomical European tradition, with its emphasis on osteological and especially craniological determination of racial "types," and its lack of concern for biological process. Early in his career, however, Hrdlička became involved in a controversy which had a more positive significance for Boasian historical ethnology: the dispute between F. W. Putnam and W. H. Holmes over the antiquity of man in the Americas. Although he began under Putnam's influence at the American Museum, Hrdlička became a staunch supporter of Holmes once he entered government anthropology in 1903. Attacking every alleged "find" on the basis of morphological arguments, he succeeded in exiling early man from the hemisphere — so successfully that until 1930 it was almost heretical to claim an antiquity greater than two or three thousand years. Given such a limited time perspective, and in the absence of an adequate historical archeology, ethnology perhaps seemed a more likely approach to the history of man in the Americas than might otherwise have been the case.

Be that as it may, there is no question about Hrdlička's role as the advocate and leader of an increasingly self-conscious physical anthropology — although his orientation was toward the science of anatomy rather more than toward the rest of American anthropology. He had begun to work toward the founding of an independent journal as early as 1908, and in 1918, in the context of the events leading to the Boas censure, he succeeded in establishing the *American Journal of Physical Anthropology* (1918). His attempt to form a separate professional organization in 1924 was frustrated by anatomists who viewed it as a separatist movement, but by 1930 the American Association of Physical Anthropologists had held its first meeting, in conjunction with the American Association of Anatomists. Hrdlička was the new organization's first president, and his journal was designated as the official organ (M. Trotter 1956; Boaz & Spencer 1981).

At the founding meeting, Hrdlička took aside Harry Shapiro, one of the younger Harvard-trained physical anthropologists, and told him to eschew statistics like the plague (Shapiro 1959). In several ways, the incident is suggestive of trends which in the next decade or so were to have far-reaching impact on the subdiscipline. By 1930, men trained in anthropology departments were beginning to play a role in physical anthropology (Spencer 1981). Most of them came out of the Harvard department, where they were taught by Earnest Hooton, an anthropological eclectic who had in fact originally trained in cultural anthropology as a Rhodes Scholar at Oxford (Hooten 1935). Although a typologizer and a biological determinist, Hooton employed statistical methods, and some of his students were inevitably affected by Boas' more dynamic and processual statistical approach to physical anthropology. Shapiro in fact went on to do a study that confirmed Boas' work on environmental modification of headform. Hooton was also very much interested in the "correlation" of biological and sociological inquiry, and his students — trained in a department where the subdisciplinary bundle was still intact — tended to be oriented toward the trends that were transforming ethnology. This was of course true also of several men trained by Boas himself, and of Wilton Krogman, who received his doctorate at Chicago.

There were other omens, however, besides the emergence of a new breed of physical anthropologist. In 1929 the biometrician Raymond Pearl founded *Human Biology*, in which the distribution of articles approxi-

Harvard anthropologists of the later 1920s (left to right): (seated) A. M. Tozzer, C. C. Willoughby, E. Reynolds, R. B. Dixon; (standing) E. A. Hooton, C. S. Coon, H. J. Spinden, A. V. Kidder, F. R. Wulsin, S. J. Guernsey. (Courtesy of the Peabody Museum of Archaeology and Ethnology, Harvard University)

mated that of a "biological anthropology"—in sharp contrast to the overwhelmingly anatomical and anthropometric emphasis of Hrdlička's journal. In the course of the next decade, physical anthropology began to feel the impact of trends that were to lead by 1942 to a new synthetic evolutionary theory in biology, and eventually to a "new" physical anthropology as well (Goldstein 1940; cf. Haraway 1988). A rapidly growing body of evidence of fossil man brought evolutionary issues once more to the fore, and genetic thought began to have an impact, especially through the analysis of human blood types.

By the middle of the decade, the younger men were beginning to chafe under Hrdlička's domination. The finds at Folsom, New Mexico, when dated by geological criteria, offered quite convincing evidence of a much greater antiquity of man in the Americas, and by 1937 Hrdlička was almost alone in resisting it on morphological grounds (Stewart 1949). Human skeletal material continued to be used, as it had been by both Hrdlička and Hooton, to reconstruct historical ethnic relationships and migrations. But there was a tendency on the one hand for diachronic concerns to be stretched out to the macro-evolutionary level, and on the other for them to be reduced to the physical anthropological equivalent of Boasian process in the present. The latter tendency was particularly strong among some of the younger men. Suggesting a correspondence between the culture-area concept and the "physical-type assessment of early morphological anthropology," Krogman called for a study of "the dynamic march of unfolding pattern." Osteology and craniometry were not enough; in Shapiro's words, what was required was an investigation of man as a "living dynamic, functioning organism" (quoted in Goldstein 1940:204–5).

By 1942, when the membership of the AAPA had reached 150, the new tendencies were strong enough to force an institutional readjustment. An arrangement was arrived at whereby Hrdlička retired as editor of the *AJPA* and its control passed more directly into the hands of the Association. Although the new editor, T. D. Stewart, was rather traditionally oriented, he acknowledged the Association's desire for "liberalizing changes," promising to rectify the heavy leaning to craniometry, and to give recognition to applied physical anthropology and "other progressive subjects" (1943).

In linguistics, too, centrifugal tendencies may, up to a point, be viewed in relationship to European traditions of inquiry. Here, also, Boas' work had revolutionary implications. Its focus on unwritten languages and its insistence on the analysis of each in terms of its own internal categories in fact laid the basis for modern descriptive linguistics (above, p. 91). But in approaching the problem of the historical development of language, Boas tended with passing years to take a more and more conservative view, in effect denying that the assumptions of European comparative linguistics could be applied to American Indian languages, because the accumulation of diffusionary influences made it difficult to trace similar languages back to a single *Ursprache.* Before one could use similarities to establish genetic relationships, one must solve the prior problem of sorting out borrowed from archaic elements.

Edward Sapir, Boas' most brilliant student, came to him from a background in Germanic studies, and was not subject to the same temperamental-methodological inhibitions (contrast Boas' "ice-cold flame of the passion for seeking the truth for truth's sake" with Sapir's "passionate temperament cutting into itself with the cold steel of intellect" [Boas 1945:1; Sapir 1920:498]). During the 1910s, Sapir joined Kroeber and several other Boas students in a movement to reduce the fifty-five American Indian language stocks of the Powell 1891 classification by establishing genetic connections among them—which in Sapir's own case eventually led to the hypothesis of six "superstocks" (Darnell 1971b). Not surprisingly, this approach led Sapir into controversy with his mentor, and it is possible to interpret their respective viewpoints in terms of two models of historical process: one, derived from comparative linguistics, emphasizing *divergence* from a common source; the other, derived from Boas' folklore studies, emphasizing *convergence* from diverse sources (Darnell 1974; Hockett 1954). Given the very large overlap—indeed, the essential underlying community of assumption—in Boas' and Sapir's thought, it is perhaps better to regard these two "models" rather as emphases on different phases of cultural process (the divergent and the reintegrative) within the single Boasian paradigm. Nevertheless, it was a matter of some import where one placed the emphasis. Sapir's focus on "archaic residues"—those "fundamental features of structure, hidden away in the very core of the linguistic complex," which were immune to superficial diffusional influence—not only facilitated a reconstruction of more remote linguistic relationships and cultural history (Swadesh 1951). It also implied a more "structuralist" view of language and by extension of culture itself. Thus Sapir's thinking in the early 1920s on language ("the most self-contained, the most massively resistant of all social phenomena") was gradually generalized, until he came to insist on the "extraordinary persistence . . . of complex *patterns* of cultural behavior regardless of the extreme variability of the content of such patterns" (1921, 1929:82).

The impact of Sapir's thinking on ethnological thought about culture has already been suggested (Sherzer & Bauman 1972); and it is impossible to treat here all aspects of his linguistic thought (cf. Darnell 1990). The point to be emphasized is his role in the emergence of structural linguistics, of which, along with Leonard Bloomfield, he may be regarded as the founder. Although the essential principles of phonemic analysis would seem to be derivable from Boas' work on "Alternating Sounds" (1889) his own concern was with grammatical categories and processes, not with sound systems. Sapir, and Bloomfield even more, went far beyond Boas in conceiving of languages as composed of a limited number of elements in ordered relations within a bounded system. By the end of the interwar period, this development had led to a rejection of the Boasian "item and process" model of description for one of "item and arrangement." By that time, later Bloomfieldians—repressing both Sapir's contribution to structuralism and Bloomfield's own early historical interests—insisted that a "scientific" approach in linguistics could only be made in terms of a purely "synchronic, static arrangement and classification of the observed," rather than a "representation and imputation in terms of diachronic or dynamic process" (Hymes & Fought 1975:958). In the 1930s, however, the approach of Sapir and some of his early students—in contrast both to subsequent Bloomfieldian structuralism and to antecedent Boasian descriptivism—was quite historical, in the comparative linguistic mode—although Benjamin

Whorf is better known for his elaboration of Boas' and Sapir's ideas on the relation of language and worldview (Sapir 1936; Whorf 1935). In certain respects, the situation in mid-decade was analogous to that in ethnology, as Carl Voegelin suggested in arguing the need to combine both synchronic and diachronic viewpoints (1936). By the end of the period, however, the antihistorical trends were even more pronounced in linguistics than in ethnology, and the general outcome was an attenuation of relations between the two fields.

This process was reflected also in institutional developments. Through much of the period Boas himself played an important role. The *International Journal of American Indian Linguistics,* which he founded in 1917, continued to appear somewhat irregularly until 1939, when it lapsed until the end of the war; and Boas also chaired the ACLS Committee on Research in American Native Languages, which dispensed over $100,000 for the study of eighty-two languages between 1927 and 1937 (Flannery 1946). Increasingly, however, Boas' influence was diluted by the development of alternative orientations and institutions. In terms of sheer numbers, more linguistic dissertations were done at Columbia than elsewhere; but once Sapir established an academic base, first at Chicago and then at Yale, his students were clearly the more influential. Furthermore, after the founding of the Linguistic Society of America in 1925, anthropological linguistics took its place within a broader community of scholars committed to the "science of language" as the connecting link between the natural and the human sciences (Joos 1986). Although it was another generation before linguistics would achieve separate institutional recognition in the universities, the Society, with its journal *Language* and its summer Linguistic Institutes, provided a basis for a professional identity distinct from philology, modern language study, or anthropology. Although Boas was an early president of the Society, Sapir and Bloomfield were more important figures in its affairs, and anthropological linguists in general were but a tiny fraction of its membership. The early summer institutes were neither anthropological nor structuralist in orientation, and it was only in 1937 that anthropological work with informants in the analysis of unwritten languages was introduced by Sapir and then carried on by Bloomfield. This anthropological input had a permanent effect on the methodology of descriptive linguistics. However, the deaths of Sapir and Whorf (as well as Boas) left Bloomfield and his disciples to define the character of the triumphant structuralism, which had an extreme synchronic and "antimentalistic" scientific cast. Signalized by a change in the editorship of *Language* in 1940, the Bloomfieldian ascendancy was reinforced by the priorities of wartime linguistics work, which also helped to direct attention away from American Indian languages. Thus while the issues involved were generally analogous to those in the debate in ethnology between Radcliffe-Brown and the Boasians, in linguistics the advocates of a synchronic scientific approach achieved a clearcut victory.

It has been suggested in this context that the end of the interwar period marked "something of a low point for the relations of linguistics to cultural anthropology" (Hymes 1970:269). The development of the sophisticated structuralist methods of linguistic analysis had left more broadly trained anthropologists of the 1930s somewhat behind the development of the field; and those few who had participated in the process were, ironically, isolated from anthropology by their preoccupation with American Indian work in a period when anthropology was turning overseas. The very end of the period in fact saw foreshadowings of later rapprochement—such as Lévi-Strauss's participation in the Linguistic Circle of New York, which in 1945 began to publish *Word* in part as antidote to the Bloomfieldian approach dominant in *Language.* But when Ralph Linton defined the scope of anthropology for a symposium in 1945, he described linguistics as its "most isolated and self-contained" subdiscipline. Although he held out hope for its eventual relevance, he nonetheless felt it appropriate to ignore linguistics "in the present volume" (Linton 1945:7–8).

The development of archeology in the interwar years followed a somewhat different pattern from that of physical anthropology and linguistics, although the end result was again to raise serious questions about its subdisciplinary status. In archeology, what might be called endogenous factors were more important, insofar as there was no significant substantive or institutional focus of professionalization external to the dominant American anthropological tradition. Despite the already emerging division of labor between Columbia and Harvard, Boas felt no need to distinguish between the ethnological and the archeological method when he spoke of the centrifugal specialization of the discipline in 1904. As the name of the Peabody Museum of American Archaeology and Ethnology implied, the two fields of inquiry had been closely associated in this country for some time (Hinsley 1985). This was true, of course, only for the archeology of aboriginal America, which was fairly sharply separated from that of classical and Middle Eastern civilizations. True, the Archaeological Institute of America founded in 1879 had for a while published a series of Americanist papers, had set up a Committee on American Archaeology in 1899, and had even established a School of American Archaeology in the Southwest in 1907 (Elliott 1987; Chauvenet 1983). Nevertheless its focus was predominantly toward the Old World, and leading Americanist archeologists remained oriented toward the American Anthropological Association. However, in contrast to Europe, where the anthropological character of non-Mediterranean archeology reflected the emergence of prehistoric studies within an evolutionary framework, Americanist archeology up to the eve of World War I developed along lines that were neither evolutionary nor significantly historical. On the one hand, Holmes and Hrdlička squelched all attempts to extend the antiquity of man in this hemisphere; on the other, there was no significant temporal orientation even in regard to the accepted remains of aboriginal America (Wilmsen 1965; Meltzer 1983). The approach was essentially descriptive, excavations were directed toward the augmentation of museum collections rather than the solution of historical problems, and with a few isolated exceptions, there was no attempt to apply the stratigraphic methods that had been in use in Europe for over fifty years (Willey & Sabloff 1974).

The years after 1910, however, witnessed a methodological revolution in American archeology. Rigorous stratigraphic excavational methods were introduced by Manuel Gamio in the Valley of Mexico and by Nels Nelson in the southwestern United States; seriational studies of potsherds were undertaken by Kroeber and Spier; more systematic approaches to the typological classification of artifacts were developed. By 1924 A. V. Kidder's long-term excavations in the Upper Pecos Valley of New Mexico had provided the basis for the first detailed areal synthesis. Building on a chronological treatment of the remains in each southwestern subregion, Kidder was able to offer an outline of the history of Pueblo culture in general. Three years later, he organized the conference that produced the "Pecos Classification," which was to guide research in the area for the next generation (Woodbury 1973; Givens 1986; Taylor 1954). By that time, other developments were taking place that were to give the new chronological orientation both a greater depth and a greater precision. Almost contemporaneously with the Pecos Conference, the Folsom finds had begun a radical revision of notions of man's antiquity in America; and Kidder's synthesis had already referred to the dendochronological methods of A. E. Douglass, the first of several techniques from other sciences which over time were to make possible an absolute as well as a relative chronology (Kidder 1924). By the mid-1930s, the new archeological approaches developed in the Southwest were being applied in many other areas of North America (Fitting 1973). Thus archeology, which had scarcely figured at all in Sapir's *Time Perspective,* had within two decades largely realized his hope that it "would throw far more light on the history of American culture than it has in the past" (1916:398; cf. Griffin 1959).

Although much of this work was carried on by men without doctorates in anthropology, the leading figures tended to be oriented toward academic anthropology in its Boasian guise. Gamio was a student of Boas, who helped plan the work in the Valley of Mexico, and Nelson came to the Southwest

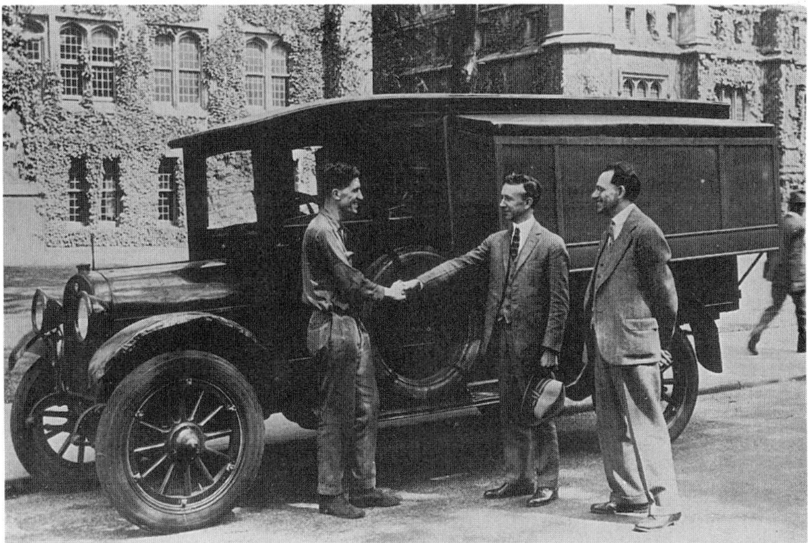

Fay-Cooper Cole and Edward Sapir wishing bon voyage to Paul Martin and John Blackburn (in the University of Chicago archeology truck), 1926. (Courtesy of the Department of Special Collections, University of Chicago Library)

from the Berkeley department. Kroeber and Spier were of course Boas students, and Kidder had studied under him. Whatever their feelings about Boas' politics, the Harvard archeologists all came from a department in which two of the three leading figures (Dixon and Alfred Tozzer) were in a broad sense Boasian. And as we have already noted, when Kidder took over the Carnegie Maya program in 1929, its focus was broadened to include contemporary ethnological work as well. Given this orientation toward academic anthropology, it is not surprising that in the 1920s American archeology was heavily influenced by Sapir's *Time Perspective* and the culture-area thinking of Kroeber and Wissler, or that in the 1930s it began to reflect the newer trends in ethnology. Archeologists then contributed to the criticism of culture-area assumption (Strong 1933), and some of them began to advocate the newer configurational and functional approaches. Several of the younger men were concerned that, despite its new chronological dimension, American archeology remained at an essentially descriptive level, mired in minutiae, with little to contribute to the general theory of cultural behavior or cultural process. In this context, signs of an emerging synchronic functionalist point of view were quite widespread by the end of the interwar period (Taylor 1948).

By that time archeology, too, had felt the effect of centrifugal institutional tendencies, although in response to rather different pressures from those in linguistics or physical anthropology. There, the push to institutional separation had reflected a sense of distinctive intellectual identity. In contrast, the archeologists "accepted their marginal position and second-class status" within anthropology for the most part "with becoming humility" (Willey & Sabloff 1974:131). Their concern with problems of professional self-identification was rather a defensive reaction against what they perceived as a massive threat from outside—what one of them has since characterized as the "rapidly spreading conflagration" of amateur archeology (Guthe 1967:434). Relatively speaking, archeology in this period suffered from an abundance of resources and a dearth of professional personnel. The NRC Committee on State Archaeological Surveys attempted to offer both a clearinghouse and a guiding hand for the various local activities it helped to foster. The late 1920s and the early 1930s, however, saw a proliferation of state archeological societies; and despite the organization of regional conferences on common problems, there was a sense among the professional archeologists that they were losing control. The problem was accentuated when the New Deal decided that unemployed men could be put to work on archeological digs. Suddenly in 1934 archeologists who had thought in terms of a few thousand dollars and less than a dozen laborers found themselves in charge of surveys with more than a thousand men working under them (Fagette 1985; Lyon 1982).

In this context professional archeologists, although still closely identified with anthropology, moved toward the founding of their own organization in order to integrate amateurs within a framework in which they could be guided and controlled by professionals. In December 1934, the Society for American Archaeology was organized with separate categories of membership for the two groups. In terms of numbers, the organization was a great success, and rapidly approached the American Anthropological Association in size. However, the problem of amateur/professional relations was a recurring concern within the Society, and never in this period achieved satisfactory solution. Furthermore, despite the insistence of the founders that the Society was in no sense a separatist movement, it could not but contribute to centrifugal tendencies within anthropology, if only because significant archeological articles tended to appear in the newly founded *American Antiquity* (Guthe 1967; Meltzer et al. 1986).

By 1945, these centrifugal tendencies in the subdisciplines were a matter of serious concern to many anthropologists who, whatever the focus of their own specific intellectual activity, still tended in principle to conceive of their enterprise in embracive Boasian terms. True, intellectual developments in the subdisciplines had in a rough way paralleled trends in ethnological thought in the interwar years. However, this was not necessarily an integrative factor, since ethnology itself was losing the historical focus and unity of subject matter which traditionally had been so important in sustaining the integration of American anthropology. Subdisciplinary trends had in fact contributed to the reorientation toward synchronic study in ethnology. Thus, on the one hand, the extension of human antiquity made an ethnological approach to the reconstruction of American culture history seem a less likely project; on the other, the newer archeological methods provided surer approaches to the same problem. And whatever the thrust of their intellectual endeavor, it was now a fact that one-third of the anthropological professionals in this country were in subdisciplines oriented toward their own professional associations. Furthermore, if academic anthropological departments still provided a framework that united the subdisciplines, developments were taking place in the world at large which were to have serious implications for the academically oriented anthropology that had flowered in the interwar period.

From Cultural Criticism to Applied Anthropology

It has been suggested that the half century between 1895 and 1945 constituted a single phase in the relationship of "American Anthropologists and American Society."[6] Following that of "Capitalism Triumphant," and preceding that of the "Military-Industrial Complex," the period of "Intermittent Liberal Reform" witnessed the reassertion of the claims of society against untrammelled capitalist individualism and the opening of the social and political arena to racial and cultural minorities previously excluded (Wolf 1972; cf. Vidich 1974). Appropriately, the anthropology of the period —which was very nearly that of Boas' preeminence—emphasized human plasticity and found its characteristic expression in the culture-and-personality movement. Such broad schematizations have their uses, and one can of course view the Boas censure vote in this framework. On the one side were the hard-core Boasians, a number of them of recent immigrant, usually Jewish background, mildly radical in their politics, pacifist or at best lukewarm toward the war, and in general critical of the values of their adopted culture. On the other side were the much more "old American" Harvard archeologists and Washington ethnologists, whose patriotic zeal, if not their ethnocentric cultural commitment, was manifest in the censure vote itself. Some of the latter group were no doubt holdovers, as it were, from the evolutionary era, just as the Boasians many be seen as representatives of the cultural pluralism that succeeded it. Even so, the fact

6. On the development of applied anthropology see Van Willigen 1980, in addition to sources cited in the text.

that the Boasians lost by two to one would suggest the need to look in a more differentiated way at the general historical processes conditioning the development of anthropology (GS 1968a:270–308).

To begin with, it might help to distinguish between critical and constructive phases in the development of the anthropology of liberal pluralism. In the first phase, the contribution of anthropology was largely critical and methodological: attacking the evolutionary synthesis, it suggested what may be regarded as an alternative world historical framework in which to place the development of American industrial civilization. Our concern here, however, is primarily with the later constructive phase, in which approaches to culture and personality, cultural values, and other integrative problems were more systematically developed. Within this later phase—roughly the interwar period—there were three extended historical moments that had an important conditioning effect on the character of anthropological inquiry: the return to "normalcy" after World War I, in which the conflict of cultural values between traditional rural and modern multi-ethnic urban America was particularly sharp; the subsequent economic breakdown and the political response of the New Deal, during which value concerns continued to be expressed, but more "adaptive" aspects of the integration problem came somewhat to the fore; and finally the rising menace of Nazism and the American entrance into World War II, in which the problem of cultural integration tended once more to be posed in ideational terms of national character and value commitment, although the adaptive issues were by no means obscured (Carter 1968; Pells 1973).

Running through all three of these cultural moments, however, are two distinguishable attitudinal modes, which represent enduring alternatives within the Western anthropological tradition, as well as a profound ambivalence toward the civilization that produced it: the "romanticist" and the "progressivist." Although never really escaping the bounds of its own cultural identity, the romanticist is nonetheless impelled by alienation toward an identification with the culturally exotic, seeking to *preserve* its "otherness" as an affirmation of the possibility of cultural worlds more harmoniously fulfilling of the potencies of the human spirit. In contrast, the progressivist dissolves any residual ambivalence toward its own civilization in the balm of ethnocentrism, seeking to *assimilate* the threatening "otherness" of the culturally exotic within a single progressive world process that would allow it at most only a precursory historical validity. Insofar as they express themselves in activism, the romanticist attitude finds its characteristic outlet in social criticism; the progressivist, in social engineering. In terms of the Boasian dualism, the romanticist mode is historicist; the progressivist, scientistic. But just as the Boasian dualism could be contained within a single intellectual orientation, so the attitudinal modes of romanticism and progressivism may co-exist in a single individual or a single school. Doubtless one may envision the possibility of a radical synthesis; but in understanding the interwar period it seems more helpful to maintain the distinction of the ideal types. From this point of view, it seems fair to say that in terms of their dominant tendency, Powellian evolutionism was progressivist and Boasian ethnology was romanticist.

Various factors, however, have tended historically to mediate the opposition between the two modes. Thus until World War I the contrast between the Powellian and the Boasian orientations was obscured somewhat by the fact that the activist impulse within American anthropology was never very strong. The relevance to reservation policies that Powell promised in establishing the Bureau was realized only in the most general way (Hinsley 1981); Boas' activism on behalf of minorities was slow in emerging and clearly subordinate to his professional role until the later stages of his anthropological career (above, pp. 98–100). Although he began around 1900 to insist on the relevance of anthropology to both racial problems at home and national interests overseas, his own efforts in each case were directed primarily toward the advancement of anthropological knowledge itself. Indeed, both Powell and Boas, each in his own way, were in the first instance concerned with establishing the autonomy and scientific status of their discipline. For both of them the underlying consideration in arguments of relevance was often the problem of financing anthropological research—which in all phases of the modern history of the discipline has been a crucial factor mediating the relationship of anthropology and society.

In this context we may briefly consider interwar trends in the latter relationship. On the whole, the period was one of increasing anthropological activism (Goldschmidt 1979; Partridge & Eddy 1978). Already in the censure episode, certain issues of involvement were sharply posed. True, what concerned Boas was not the misapplication of anthropology so much as the misuse of the scientific role—by making their identities as archeologists a cover for intelligence work the four men he attacked had violated the essential scientific commitment to "the service of truth." Nevertheless, both the censure vote itself and the issues implicated in anthropology's relations to the NRC suggest that the romanticist and progressivist modes stood in sharper opposition in the early interwar period. In the context of wartime xenophobia, the drive for "Americanization," and the immigration restrictionist movement which climaxed in the early 1920s, the progressivist current, in a distinctly racialist guise, was greatly strengthened. Several anthropologists trained by Boas in fact were either caught up by it momentarily, or swam along within it as their natural medium. Those who have not read the literature of the period would be surprised by the manifest racialism of Wissler, or by Kroeber's accommodations to hereditarian argument—although the historically significant Boasian response was probably Boas' own, which was to take advantage of funding available for "relevant" research to buttress his critique of racialist assumption (GS 1968a:270–308).

Other trends in the early postwar period, however, greatly strengthened the romanticist current, if not in American culture generally, then certainly among the intellectuals, who were for the first time perhaps fully conscious of their own group identity (below, pp. 284–90). In the backwash of the prewar progressive movement and the disillusion of the war's aftermath, intellectuals began to turn from politics to cultural self-criticism. Alienated equally from the consumer values of the dominant business culture and from the last-ditch puritanism of rural America, rejecting traditional "American civilized morality," but still sustained by the earlier "promise of American life," they struggled to find values upon which a genuine national culture could be founded. In various ways, Boasian anthropology of the 1920s was embedded in this intellectual context. The Greenwich Village of the New York *avant-garde* and the Southwest of D. H. Lawrence and Mabel Dodge Luhan were both important Boasian milieux; Boasians wrote poetry for the little magazines and articles for the liberal weeklies. One can scarcely understand Sapir's "Culture, Genuine and Spurious" or Mead's *Coming of Age in Samoa* without keeping this background in mind. There is in fact a manifest thematic continuity between *Our Changing Morality* and *Civilization in the United States*—two major intellectual symposia of the early 1920s in which Boasians participated—and the concerns of the emerging culture-and-personality movement: the problem of cultural integration in a multi-ethnic nation; the problem of personality in a period of rapidly changing sex-roles; the problem of values once "right and wrong finally followed the other absolute monarchs to an empty nominal existence somewhere in exile" (Kirchway 1924:vi).

The culmination of this romantic trend was of course Benedict's *Patterns of Culture,* which appeared in 1934. The single most influential anthropological work of the interwar period, Benedict's book offered to the American reading public a Boasian view of cultural determinism that seemed to carry the doctrine of cultural relativity to its logical conclusion in the ultimate incommensurability of each human mode of life (Hatch 1983). But in the aftermath of economic collapse, some of the inherent ambiguities of cultural relativism began to manifest themselves. Clearly, for Benedict relativism did not necessarily imply a nonjudgmental attitude toward all cultural forms. Two of the three cultures she studied in order "to pass judgment on the dominant traits of our own civilization" could easily be read as pathological parodies of the worst aspects of the puritan and robber-baron traditions; and the Apollonian integration of the Zuni was obviously posed against the "wanton waste of revolution and economic and emotional disaster" that seemed to threaten Western civilization (1934:248–49). In short, while the essential attitudinal posture of Benedict's *Patterns* was still romanticist, one can see in it hints of a reemergent social engineering impulse, which in some Boasians, like Margaret Mead, had always been quite strong (Yans-McLaughlin 1986).

By 1934, in the midst of economic chaos and reemergent political reform, the progressivist impulse, now largely cleansed of its earlier manifest racialism, had clearly reasserted itself. Some of the more scientific approaches to cultural integration of the 1930s should doubtless be viewed in this context. There is an obvious consonance between the increasing emphasis on functional integration and the adaptive aspects of culture and the issues facing American society in this period—although given the upsurge of radical politics in the thirties one might have expected the explicitly materialist current and the activist impulse to be somewhat stronger than they were (cf. Vincent 1990:152–224). Be that as it may, the early New Deal did witness two projects for the "application" of anthropology by the federal government: one in the Soil Conservation Service of the Department of Agriculture, the other in the Applied Anthropology Unit of the Bureau of Indian Affairs (Kimball 1979; McNickle 1979). Neither of these attempts to involve American anthropologists in problems of "native administration" along lines similar to the experience of British "indirect rule" seems to have been an unqualified success, however, and the experience of the Indian Service indicates that tension between the progressivist and romanticist impulses was a factor in the situation.

Significantly, the initiative had come from the newly reorganized Indian Service, and not from American anthropologists. With a few exceptions, the latter had long stood aloof from any activist involvement on behalf of American Indians, whose cultures they tended to regard tragically as inevitably doomed (Kelly 1980). However, the new Commissioner of Indian Affairs under Roosevelt, John Collier, had been influenced by Boasian anthropology; and in a general way, the Indian Reorganization Act of 1934 marked a shift from the dogmatic enforced assimilationism of the Dawes Act toward a policy that to many seemed actively preservationist. There was some resistance to direct involvement—Kroeber, although one of the few anthropologists to participate in Collier's Indian Defense Association in the 1920s, is said to have refused to recommend his students for employment under Collier after he became commissioner. In general, however, the anthropological community responded favorably when Collier carried his initiative to several professional meetings. Even so, the Applied Anthropology Unit lasted less than three years. Despite the shift away from a rigid progressivism, the Indian Service still pushed for more rapid change than anthropologists found congenial; the latter, in contrast, were still more interested in studying the surviving aboriginal patterns than the "new social values emerging under reservation life" (G. Foster 1969: 201). Undaunted, Collier in 1941 launched a large-scale project on "Indian Personality and Administrative Research" in cooperation with the University of Chicago, out of which came important monographic studies of five tribes (McNickle 1979:58). Again, however, the results were ambiguous. A change in Bureau policy and personnel (including Collier's resignation) limited the practical impact of the program, which was prematurely terminated in 1947; and from a theoretical point of view, its impact may be seen as buttressing a preservationist orientation. Although anthropologists no longer thought in terms of "the vanishing Indian," the effect of their direct involvement in problems of acculturation paradoxically was to reinforce the sense of the enduring stability of the inner value-core of each culture.

The years that witnessed the early initiatives toward direct involvement in applied anthropology were also those in which anthropologists began to respond to the racialist and antidemocratic threat posed by Hitler's ascension to power in Germany. Faced with a very different situation as Jewish German-American than he had faced in World War I, Franz Boas threw himself into the struggle against Nazism (above, pp. 107–8). In addition to his regular anthropological work, which now focussed more and more on the question of race, he undertook a variety of political activities, in which Ruth Benedict—overcoming her strong temperamental disinclination to activism—served as his second-in-command (Modell 1983; Caffrey 1989; Mead 1959a). By 1938, the Association, which had rarely spoken out as a body on other than narrowly professional matters, passed a resolution condemning German "scientific" racialism (Barkan 1988).

The contrast to the early 1920s was quite sharp. By this time the Boasian doctrine of cultural determinism, reinforcing endogenous trends in the other disciplines, had redefined the internal intellectual milieu of the social sciences, and was carrying increasing weight within the biological sciences as well. The new era had begun in which Boasian anthropology was to speak to educated Americans as "the voice of science" on matters of race and culture. Whereas in the 1920s racialist trends impinging on anthropology from outside had led to an accommodation to hereditarian assumption by some anthropologists, Mead now suppressed certain speculations about inherited temperamental differences in individuals on the grounds that they might be interpreted as supporting Nazi racialism (Yans-McLaughlin 1986:204). On the other hand, as the fight against Nazism intensified, the doctrine of cultural relativism, which had always been the dove of liberal tolerance, began to assume certain albatross traits. It was one thing to use it to defend racial equality and cultural pluralism in a democratic culture; but when that culture itself was threatened, Benedict herself felt it was necessary to go "beyond relativity" to "discover the ways and means of social cohesion," and to find a common ground for cultural values in the universal human desire for freedom (Mead 1959a:385).

Begun within the more congenial tradition of social criticism, the anti-Nazi activism of Boasian anthropologists led them inexorably into direct involvement as the ideological struggle became a military one (Yans-McLaughlin 1986). In this context, there was no fundamental division among American anthropologists over United States participation in World War II. Although the younger generation of leaders of the profession came from cultural backgrounds much more central to the "old American" tradition than had the earlier Boasians, both were at one in their opposition to Nazism. This is not to suggest that there were no political disagreements. The same Ralph Linton who in 1919 had alienated Boas by returning to graduate school in his AEF uniform was now, as Boas' successor at Columbia, more than a bit disturbed by what he felt were Communist influences toward which Boas had been quite tolerant (McMillan 1986). But as far as the war effort itself was concerned, anthropologists seem to have been as united as the American population generally.

That commitment dovetailed with the needs of government to produce a tremendous upsurge after 1941 of "applied anthropology" (Goldschmidt 1979: Pt. III). By early 1943 it was estimated that over half of the professional anthropologists were devoting their full time and energy to the war effort, with another 25 percent involved part-time (Beals 1943). The estimate may have been a bit liberal, but there is no doubt that a large number of anthropologists were involved in a broad range of war-related activities. Benedict and Mead worked on a study of food habits for the NRC. John Embree, John Provinse, and other were involved in the analysis of troubled communities of forcibly evacuated Japanese for the War Relocation Authority (Spicer 1979; cf. Starn 1986). A jointly sponsored Ethnogeographic Board was organized as a clearinghouse to provide the military and other war agencies with regional information and personnel data, and to encourage the promulgation of research projects. Julian Steward organized the Institute of Social Anthropology at the Smithsonian Institution to capitalize on (and to further) the State Department's "good neighbor" policy by sending anthropologists to teach and organize research in a number of Latin American countries (W. Bennett 1947; Foster 1979). Benedict, Kluckhohn, Alexander Leighton, and others were involved in the Foreign Morale Analysis Division of the Office of War Information, where they carried on a variety of researches, including studies of Rumanian, Thai, and Japanese national character, and investigations of the effects of strategic bombing on Japanese morale (Mead 1979). Outside of Washington, anthropologists still in the universities participated in language-training programs and in the preparation of personnel for military government, as well as in war-related research (Cowan 1979). Fred Eggan, for instance, directed the Far Eastern Civil Affairs Training School for the army at the University of Chicago (GS 1979a); Linton at Columbia helped train naval officers for military government in the Pacific Islands (Linton & Wagley 1971:61); Murdock at Yale directed a navy project to assemble data on Pacific peoples (Bashkow 1991). And of course a number of anthropologists were actually serving with the army or navy in the field.

All of this wartime activity had a considerable impact on the anthropological profession. Even before the United States entry into the war, several Harvard-trained anthropologists influenced by the early industrial research of Elton Mayo and the community studies of Lloyd Warner joined with Margaret Mead and others in the formation of the Society for Applied Anthropology. Within a few months, the Society began publishing a journal (*Applied Anthropology*) designed to propagate an action-oriented "science of human relations" that would study the way human organisms adjusted to each other and their environment in order to eliminate the "maladjustments in human relations resulting from technological change" (1941[1]:1–2). For the next several years, however, the journal was devoted largely to war-related topics: problems of industrial anthropology, relocated populations, military government, and in the immediate postwar period, "applied anthropology in dependent areas."

From a longer-run point of view, the wartime experience laid the basis for the tremendous growth of anthropology that took place in the postwar years. Anthropologists, who had difficulty finding jobs even in the late 1930s, when a number of new academic opportunities had begun to open up, could now look forward to a period in which the demand for anthropologically trained personnel would exhaust the supply. The wartime experience of applied anthropology stimulated visions of a wide range of new uses of anthropology that would require a great expansion of university training programs. And in fact the "area programs" that later became so important for the growth of the discipline were themselves largely the outgrowth of the wartime university experience in the training of military personnel (Fenton 1947; Steward 1950). Similarly, the extraterritorial fieldwork that had been developing in the interwar period received a great push, particularly in Latin America and the Pacific Islands, where the immediate postwar experience of military government provided the context for a great deal of field research (Embree 1949; Bashkow 1991).

At the same time, the war experience of applied anthropology raised or sharpened certain questions about the nature of the discipline (Embree 1945). The progressivist impulse toward social engineering now seemed to be running very strong, and was paralleled by what was in fact a more enduring push toward a more "scientific" anthropology. From this point of view, the doctrine of cultural relativism began to seem to some a methodological, theoretical, and ethical embarrassment. At the ethnographic level, anthropologists who took for granted the necessity of relativism as a basic prerequisite of field research could not but be disturbed by the different sort of relativism suggested when different anthropologists studying the same culture—notably Benedict's Zuni—came up with contrasting views of its central values and psychological integration (below, pp. 320–21). At the theoretical level, relativism was not a very satisfying basis for a generalizing science of man whose discoveries were to "become a part of the regular working equipment of other sciences." And at an ethical level, cultural relativism surely created problems for the "intelligent planning of the new world order" that seemed "inevitable" to Linton as the editor of the symposium volume on *The Science of Man in the World Crisis* (1945: 7–8). Not all anthropologists, however, perceived the issues of cultural relativism the same way—as the debate on the Association's "Statement on Human Rights" in 1947 was to reveal (Downing & Kushner 1988:126). Nor were they all equally comfortable with the "applied anthropology" that had developed during the war. Laura Thompson expressed concern lest anthropologists be merely "technicians for hire to the highest bidder" (1944:12); Herskovits spoke of the "dim, treacherous path" of the "social engineer" and appealed for a different kind of applied anthropology which was in effect a return to the old Boasian tradition of social criticism (1946: 267).

The truth would seem to be that the center of gravity of anthropology—weighted in the long run by the wartime training programs—was still in the universities. Despite the progressivist upsurge of the war years, the romanticist impulse remained very strong. As Mead has suggested, the general trend of anthropology in the postwar years was toward withdrawal from direct involvement and an "exodus from any situation connected with national policy" (1972b:9). No doubt some of the tracks that led eventually to Thailand were laid in the war and postwar years (Wolf & Jorgensen 1970), but they were obscured by the more general tendency to retreat into an academic world in which the relationship of anthropologists and society at large was mediated by the research grant and the interdisciplinary conference. True, there were other (and rapidly changing) worlds that anthropologists experienced in their fieldwork. But that contact was highly episodic, and despite scientizing tendencies of the discipline back home, or the grant-mediated concern with problems of modernization, anthropologists still tended to experience these worlds of others in the romanticist mode. In the event, it was not so much the brave new postwar world, but the many still alien peoples in it that truly engaged the anthropological imagination.

The Association Reorganized

In 1945, however, the withdrawal into the academy lay yet in the future. In contrast, the wartime experience was still fresh and the postwar visions still compelling. A number of anthropologists, however, felt that the institutional structure of the discipline was a barrier to their realization. After two decades during which its history might almost be reduced to chronicle, the American Anthropological Association became once again the focus of significant historical change.[7]

There is surely no denying that the Association in this period was in some ways a rather conservative organization. In 1940, a committee was established to revise the constitution, no action having been taken on the report of a similar committee in 1934. The concern, however, was simply to bring back into harmony the formal rules and the actual practices of the Association—for example, to legitimize the position of the associate editors of the *Anthropologist,* and the election of delegates to the research councils, which had not existed when the constitution was last revised in 1916. Although libraries were reduced from the status of "members" to simple "subscribers," no action was taken on a more drastic constitutional change: to dissolve the Council on the grounds that in practice there was no difference between it and the general business meeting of the Association. Between the annual meetings there was little activity. The main function of the Association as such was to carry on its publication work, which was in effect delegated to the editor. Any further business was carried on by mail under the guidance of the Association's secretary, whose *de facto* longer term provided an element of organizational continuity, and who often prompted the annual president on matters that required attending

7. In contrast to the rest of this essay, the major sources for the discussion of the reorganization of the American Anthropological Association were manuscript materials, provided for me by Sol Tax from his files, which have since then been deposited in the Regenstein Library (TaP); all quoted passages relating to this episode come from this source, or from the published accounts in the *American Anthropologist.* My comments on the AAA officers are based on materials provided to me by John Sorenson.

to. These had primarily to do with planning the next meeting, and with the replacement of the current crop of honorific leaders, who in this period tended a bit toward gerontocracy. Of the thirty-five different individuals who held office between 1923 and 1943, only ten had come of age in the profession in the 1920s and only three after 1930—despite the fact that four-fifths of the doctorates had been granted after that date. Not one president had received his doctorate after 1920, and the modal age of assuming highest office was well over fifty (Sorenson 1964).

Although the senior anthropologists who controlled the Association did not oppose the war, there was some feeling among the younger generation that the Association as a body had dragged its feet in giving active support. At the 1941 meeting, which took place in the aftermath of Pearl Harbor, Julian Steward and Ralph Beals organized an *ad hoc* discussion on the war effort, at which Benedict and Mead gave papers; but the Council declined to set up a national committee on the use of anthropologists in wartime, apparently out of fear that the Association might be reduced to a propaganda agency. At the next meeting—which on account of transportation problems was held in Washington, where about a hundred anthropologists then resided and a quorum was easily obtainable—a formal discussion of anthropology and the world crisis was held. Upon the motion of several younger members, a Committee on Anthropology and the War Effort was appointed. However, there were still hesitations among older members about just how much the profession should commit itself. When the Association met again in Washington in 1943, a letter was read from the absent president, Leslie Spier, expressing concern lest preoccupation with war work lead to the total neglect of anthropological science. Although a proposal was made at that meeting that the next should include a program devoted to problems of the war effort, the elder statesmen of the executive committee, deciding this time to find their quorum in New York, preferred simply to have a "discussion meeting" with the American Ethnological Society.

In this context, the spring of 1945 witnessed the beginning of a movement to found a new professional organization. The idea was first broached by Julian Steward at the meeting of the Society for American Archaeology—perhaps significantly, the one subdisciplinary organization where the distinction between amateur and professional had been a persistent problem and which itself had undergone reorganization in 1942. During the early summer a series of meetings were held in Washington, involving in all about twenty-five anthropologists, out of which came a Temporary Organizing Committee for an "American Society of Professional Anthropologists": Steward, Kluckhohn, Provinse, Frank Roberts, and Homer Barnett as chairman. A programmatic statement, along with a draft constitution and a questionnaire, was then sent to anthropologists around the country.

According to that document, there were then six hundred people in the United States who made their living as anthropologists, but there was no one organization where they could discuss "strictly professional [as opposed to scientific] problems and act for the profession as a whole." Although the American Anthropological Association performed useful functions, the majority of its members were amateurs, and insofar as it was representative of professional anthropology, it was "really, in fact, the association of ethnologists, and to some extent, of social anthropologists"—archeologists, linguists, physical anthropologists, folklorists, and applied anthropologists having transferred their allegiance to their own societies. As a result, the "common ground" that all should feel in "general anthropology" was no longer exercising its "desirable unifying force." No organization could speak for or protect the interests of anthropology as a whole, or set professional standards in a period when (as one advocate put it) "dozens of jerkwater colleges" were teaching "something called anthropology." Rejecting the possibility of revamping the Association—to which many professional anthropologists were alleged to be antagonistic—rejecting also any idea of federation, the writers argued the need for a new society which, by broadly defining the "essential core" of anthropology ("the comparative study of human biology, culture, and language") could counteract the centrifugal tendencies in the discipline and mobilize the resources of the whole profession for a broad range of both internally and externally oriented activities. Its provisional constitution required all members to have either the doctorate, or (having a degree in an allied field) to be employed as anthropologists; their membership would have to be approved by both a membership committee and two-thirds of a proposed Executive Board, which could subsequently disqualify them for "violation of scientific ethics."

Although the response of one hundred anthropologists to the questionnaire was taken by Steward to indicate a "deep interest," the fact that he felt it necessary in October to reassure certain colleagues that the plan was *not* an attack on the Association, or a secessionist movement, and that no attempt to railroad it through was intended, would indicate that considerable opposition had been aroused in the major anthropological centers outside Washington. At Berkeley, Kroeber and several others were opposed, as were the anthropologists at the University of Washington. At a meeting of the Chicago Anthropological Society held in October to consider the plan, no one from the midwestern schools would volunteer to defend the proposal even as devil's advocate. The New York anthropologists were reported to be "sizzling," and when Steward presented his plan to a meeting there late in November, the vote was 39 to 4 in favor of supporting the Association. Even the New England meeting was opposed to any separate organization until all possibilities of working in the Association had been explored.

There would thus seem to have been some difference in outlook between those who were caught up in what one now senior anthropologist recalls as "the Washington mixmaster" and those who remained on university campuses. Even so, the outcome would suggest that Steward had in fact touched on issues of considerable concern to the majority of what was by then a demographically very imbalanced discipline. By the time the question of reorganization came before the 1945 meeting in Philadelphia, a consensus seems to have been worked out that would avoid any fight on the floor. Hallowell, who had been one of the opponents of Steward's original plan, made a motion that the president-elect appoint a committee to canvass opinion and make recommendations on the reorganization of the Association and other matters pertaining to its "professional interests." After this had carried without dissent, a second motion was passed to establish a committee of "anthropologists living in Washington" to "report on matters of interest to the Association." Linton, the incoming president, made Steward the chairman of the nine-man Committee on Reorganization, and filled both committees with younger anthropologists; but on the whole he seems to have selected them from outside the original group who had proposed the establishment of a new organization. The results of the Reorganization Committee's questionnaire the following April made the mandate perfectly clear. Despite the fact that the 500 anthropologists receiving it included 160 who were not members of the Association and another 90 who were not members of its Council, there seems to have been no significant difference of opinion between members and nonmembers. And although only about a quarter of the total responded, there was an overwhelming consensus (105 to 10) favoring reorganization of the Association rather than founding a new society.

A revised constitution reflecting this consensus was presented to the Association's membership for approval at the Chicago meeting in 1946. In the reintegrative spirit of the reorganization scheme, Sol Tax, the chairman of the local arrangements committee, took the initiative in inviting the professional societies of the linguists, the physical anthropologists, the archeologists, the folklorists, and the applied anthropologists to meet concurrently. All of them accepted, and the large scale of the meetings—which departed from the old *Gemeinschaft* pattern, in which all the sessions were held in a single room—presented certain logistic problems. It seemed advisable to meet at a downtown hotel, not only because of the size of the gathering, but because it was feared the Chicago and Northwestern campuses might not be perceived by all anthropologists as neutral ground. The hotels, however, had recently adopted a policy of charging rentals for meeting rooms; what was worse, they had not yet abandoned their traditional policy of *de facto* Jim Crow, which allowed Negroes as daytime participants but not as overnight guests. The former problem was resolved when the Palmer House offered meeting rooms for half price and suggested that their cost be met by charging each person attending the meeting a twenty-five cent registration fee. The latter issue was more disturbing, and despite their earlier policy decision, the arrangers considered withdrawing to one of the local university campuses. In the event, however, the Northwestern downtown campus was not available, and logistic considerations prevailed—it being uncertain whether out-of-town blacks would attend the meetings in any case.

At the meeting itself, the constitution and by-laws proposed by the Committee on Reorganization were adopted with only minor changes. Aside from revised rhetoric regarding the purpose of the Association and certain more highly specified details of its organization, the new constitution differed from the old in only three essential points, the first of which was by no means clearcut. There was a reclassification of membership to dinstinguish between ordinary members with no voting privileges and "Fellows," whose professional qualifications were defined along lines suggested in the original proposal for a new society. Although the legal control of the Association was now lodged exclusively in the hands of the Fellows, the committee itself noted that the effective control had previously been in the hands of the Council, whose selection under the old constitution was governed by criteria little different from those for the new Fellows. The second major change was an enlarged and strengthened Executive Board to replace the old Executive Committee, and the transfer to it of various powers previously in the hands of the president. Finally, there was provision for the election of all officers (except the secretary, treasurer, and editor, who now became appointive officers of the Executive Board) by mail ballot of all fellows from three nominees chosen by the Board for each vacant office—as opposed to the traditional rubber-stamping at the annual meeting of a single slate presented by a three-member nominating committee. From a constitutional point of view, the reorganization would seem thus to have been essentially a demographic readjustment in which, after an initial revolutionary impulse, the older generation gracefully transferred power to the younger. The results of the first election under the new constitution seem to confirm this interpretation. Although the interim nominating committee appointed by Linton was slightly weighted toward the older age grades, only five of their twenty-four nominees had received doctorates before 1930, and of those only one was elected in the balloting of May 1947.

Clearly, however, something more important was going on. Some of the concerns expressed in the reorganization discussion are not easy to explicate. It is not evident, for instance, that there were any specific issues of "scientific ethics" underlying the reference to that problem in the original proposal for a new society; and the matter of differentiating professionals and amateurs seems to have been primarily a concern of archeologists, for whom some amateurs apparently had spoken at congressional hearings on river valley legislation. The problem of centrifugal tendencies was clearly a matter of general concern, and it is perhaps significant that neither Benedict's idea of a federative structure nor Mead's proposal for a new society of cultural and social anthropologists received much support at all. Although both in their way spoke to the centrifugal problem, they did so by further institutionalizing diversity; apparently, the reorganization of the Association seemed to most anthropologists a stronger statement for the importance of an embracive general anthropology.

That after several decades of centrifugal movement they should have felt it necessary to reassert this is a matter of no little historical significance. There is evidence to suggest that this concern was not simply a matter of tradition, or a reflection of purely intellectual considerations. Especially among the Washington anthropologists, there was a feeling that despite all the activity noted here, anthropology had not realized its maximum utility during the war. The problem, however, was not only one of application, but also of resources. As one of them put it, the discipline was not "pulling its weight" in the several research councils. There is no denying, for instance, that anthropology received only a small proportion of the total fellowships granted by the National Research Council, the Social Science Research Council, and the American Council of Learned Societies. Whether disproportionately small would require further study, but the justness of proportion is perhaps not especially to the point. What one historian of science has called the "Great Instauration of 1940" had brought to scientific research an "undreamed flow" of government support (Dupree 1972), and the immediate postwar period witnessed the attempt to place this support on a continuing peacetime basis through the establishment of a national science foundation (NAS 1964). Although political difficulties were in fact to delay the founding of the present National Science Foundation until 1950 (Lyons 1969:126–36), the issue was a matter of great concern in the scientific community during the period of the Association's reorganization, and this concern was manifest in the Association as well. Aside from the two already mentioned, the 1945 meeting had seen the appointment of a committee to "promote anthropology in national science legislation," which reported the following year that at its recommendation President Linton "at two critical points wrote to key members of Congress in advocacy of the inclusion of the social sciences in the proposed bills."

In this context, the more significant aspects of the 1946 reorganization were not the constitutional changes so much as the instructions given to the Executive Board at the recommendation of the Committee on Reorganization and the Committee of Washington Anthropologists. These involved such matters as supporting the proposed national research foundation and seeing to anthropology's place in it; developing a "comprehensive plan of research that is likely to meet the requirements for participation in the benefits" of such a foundation; expanding areal studies; seeking representation in consulting groups planning research in the Pacific; making contact with the United Nations Organization to "explore the possibility of applying anthropological viewpoints" in their research and policy-making units; surveying anthropological personnel and university curricula; developing the "public relations" of the discipline; and investigating the possibility of establishing a "permanent secretariat" to serve the "professional interests" of anthropologists—which, with Carnegie Corporation support, was in fact set up the following year.

The concern for "professional interests" that ran like a leitmotif through the reorganization discussion becomes much more understandable in this context, as does the concomitant commitment to an *embracive* anthropology conceived in *scientific* terms. The problem was not some threatened takeover by amateurs which required their exclusion from the policy-making bodies of the Association; that exclusion was already in effect. The issue of "professional interests" would seem rather to have been primarily a function of certain characteristics of the discipline in relation to its collaborators —and competitors—in the quest for government support for research in the social sciences. Numerically, anthropology was the smallest of the social science disciplines. Furthermore, its potential for application was limited at best, and its research costs were high relative to the resources readily provided by its institutional base. Finally, its professional structure was indeed more conservative than certain of its immediate competitors—notably the psychologists, who were felt by some to have dominated the joint NRC division of anthropology and psychology during the war, and who had themselves just gone through a major organizational restructuring.

The war had opened up broad new vistas, and the problem of "professional interests" was how to capitalize on them. To this end, an integrated embracive discipline claiming for itself the status of a "science" would clearly be more effective than a congeries of subdisciplines in some of which the humanistic orientation was quite strong. Whether the intellectual basis in fact existed for this integration remains to this day a somewhat moot point; likewise, the question whether the reorganization was in fact critical to achieving the implicit goals of its proponents. But there can be no doubt that several decades after its withdrawal to the academy American anthropology—for better or for worse—was still sustained in large part by research resources which, in a general historical sense, originate in the "Great Instauration of 1940," and were a central (although surely not the sole) concern of the reorganizers of the American Anthropological Association in 1946.

Evolution or Revolution in American Anthropology?

In the early stages of the reorganization episode, one of the small group of vocal defenders of the Association among the Washington anthropologists suggested that "given the revolutionary shifts in anthropological approaches of the last two decades, the transition period, now almost entirely a matter of the past, was astonishingly free of friction." Similarly, defenders of the *American Anthropologist* argued that aside from a few "minor incidents" such as the discussion in the Association in 1936 over whether acculturation studies should be printed in the journal, no obstacles had been placed in the way of newer ideas (Kroeber 1946; Opler 1946; cf. Meggers 1946). Recalling our earlier use of the metaphor of scientific revolution to characterize the emergence of Boasian anthropology in the United States, the quoted passage suggests a final comment on the interwar years. It has been argued that the development of American sociology between 1930 and 1945 is appropriately understood as a "scientific revolution" in which the older Chicago "ecological-interactionist paradigm" was faced by competing alternative paradigms of "functionalism" and "operationalism"—the former triumphing in the discipline as a whole, the latter within a particular subsection in which research methodology was more or less an end in itself (Kuklick 1973). Be this as it may in sociology, the question suggests itself: to what extent is it helpful to view the interwar years in anthropology in similar terms? (cf. Wolf 1964; Ottonello 1975).

It is difficult to characterize a process of change unless one can characterize its outcome. For the historian—who cannot take for granted any personalized picture of the recent history of the discipline such as anthropologists often carry with them as part of the baggage of their graduate training and theoretical orientation—a more systematic inquiry into the decades *after* 1945 would be necessary to answer this question with any degree of confidence (cf. Murphy 1976). Limiting oneself, however, to the reorganization and its immediate aftermath, it would seem that this is *not* an instance when the metaphor of scientific revolution is particularly illuminating historically.

In sociology, theoretical reorientation seems to have been clearly expressed at the institutional level. The young rebels who took over the American Sociological Society in 1935 founded the *American Sociological Review* to replace the old semi-official *American Journal of Sociology* as the publication of the Society, and analysis of their respective contributors in the late 1930s suggests a fairly clearcut differentiation into two groupings. In anthropology, however, the opposition seems much less clearcut, and the institutional outcome more evolutionary than revolutionary. Although the *Southwestern Journal of Anthropology* was in fact founded at this time, that event seems to have had nothing to do with the reorganization of the Association. No doubt one might say that the instigators of the abortive new society tended to be younger men resident in Washington, among whom there were a number of archeologists and applied anthropologists, a high proportion of whom seem to have been trained at Chicago, Harvard, or Berkeley. But it is not clear that these characteristics sharply distinguish them from many of the defenders of the Association. No doubt the latter tended to be more directly tied to the Boasian tradition. But despite an attempt to sidestep Ruth Benedict in the transition from the old constitution to the new, and the consequent termination of her presidency in midyear, it does not seem appropriate to characterize the reorganization movement as "anti-Boasian." Her predecessor's animosity toward Benedict is well known; nevertheless, Linton's anthropology was, in a broad sense, quite within the Boasian stream, as was that of Benedict's successor Kluckhohn. Even at a local institutional level, there seems to be little evidence of sharp break. When it was later suggested that at this point Columbia "had been sedulously swept bare" of "any signs of the Boasian tradition," one of the chief presumptive broom-wielders, Julian Steward, insisted that the reorganization there after Boas' retirement "meant a diversification of the tradition, not a break in it" (Mead 1959a; Steward 1959; cf. Murphy 1991).

On the whole, a model of evolutionary diversification rather than revolutionary disjunction seems more adequately descriptive of the development of American anthropology in the post-Boasian epoch. From about 1932 on, when the newer trends first began to be clearly manifest in the *Anthropologist* (Stern & Bohannan 1970; cf. Erasmus & Smith 1967), American anthropology became gradually more heterogeneous, until in the present day one does indeed wonder if the center has not gone (Wolf 1980). This diversification has been reflected institutionally—whether in "invisible colleges" or more overt forms—and in some cases the newer viewpoints may function as paradigms for particular groups of investigators, many of whom are working in terms of assumptions quite different from Boas'. No doubt at a broader level one may point to general trends within the discipline that have carried it in some respects quite far from the anthropology of the interwar period—which personal experience would suggest seems to many contemporary anthropologists far removed and of little value. Eric Wolf in 1963 commented on the repression of the romantic motif, the retreat from the unlimited flexibility of human nature, the growing interest in the development of civilization, the de-emphasis of cultural relativity, and the shift in perspective on the role of the individual in the maintenance of culture. No doubt culture theory has undergone considerable elaboration since the late 1930s, when the critical consciousness that produced Kroeber and Kluckhohn's analytic inventory (1952) was only beginning to manifest itself. In terms of the contrast posed here between pattern and system thinking, it is clear that American anthropologists—whether influenced by Parsonian sociology, or cybernetics, or biology, or linguistics—now speak much more consistently the idiom of "system" than they once did. But Robert Murphy's introduction to the succeeding volume (1976) would suggest that there has been no sharp break. Most of the diversification of the 1950s and 60s had its roots in developments already in evidence before 1945, and while the varied currents of the recent "theoretical flux" are by no means all Boasian, neither has any single anti-Boasian paradigm been generally accepted in the discipline. If anything, the Boasian tradition would appear to have reasserted itself in the last few years, even among some of those who, facing what does indeed seem like a general crisis of the discipline, argue the need for "reinventing anthropology" (Hymes 1972).

5

Philanthropoids and Vanishing Cultures

Rockefeller Funding and the End of the Museum Era in Anglo-American Anthropology

As an erstwhile Marxist of a rather activist and atheoretical sort, who moved back toward a patrimonial academic liberalism disillusioned but without regrets, I view the past from an eclectic interpretive standpoint, and am somewhat ambivalent about radical historical interpretations, as I am also about radical politics in the present. But if I eschew "causation" for "contextualization," I am still inclined to regard the ideational life of humankind as grounded in and constrained by more material realities, and therefore to see such phenomena as the class background of anthropologists, the funding of their research, the colonial circumstances of their fieldwork, and the institutional arrangements of their academic life as significant aspects of historical contextualization. On the other hand, the processes of history seem to me a complex interplay of conflicting (though unequally powerful) human intentionalities, each affected by a melange of variously potent external (or internalized) constraints; and I am indeed rather suspicious of the attempt to reduce that complexity by anything that smacks of monocausal determinism, however muddle-clarifying it may seem at first glance.

These rather mixed interpretive predispositions will be quite evident in the essay that follows, which touches on some of the more controversial issues implicated in the "crisis of anthropology," notably, its relation to the colonial interests of corporate capitalism. Like several other essays, it is based to a very considerable extent on research in a particular body of primary source materials, in this case, the files of the Rockefeller Archives Center relating to specifically "anthropological" activities in the interwar period, and the staff and trustee records immediately relevant to them, as they were available in 1977. My interpretive perspective was constrained by the limitations of that material, including the potentially very significant facts that records of declined grants were not preserved by the Rockefeller Foundation and that only a tiny fraction of relevant oral communication is reflected in the documentary record.

This essay was first drafted during a year I spent at the Center for Advanced Study in the Behavioral Sciences. It lay for a long time in a file drawer, from which it was removed on one occasion for presentation to the now defunct Chicago Group in the History of the Human Sciences and on another for submission to a journal whose editor, even more actively interventionist than I subsequently turned out to be, tried to redirect it along lines congenial to a long-term research interest of his own. I refused his suggestions, and the essay went back into a drawer, where it remained until 1984, when I was editing a volume of *History of Anthropology* on museum anthropology. Reframed in this context as a case study in the political economy of anthropological inquiry, the essay took on a somewhat different significance as an episode in the transformation of ethnography from a museum-based, object-oriented inquiry into the human past to a university-based, behaviorally oriented inquiry into the "ethnographic present." The impetus to that transformation antedated the infusion of Rockefeller funding; but Rockefeller funding decisions, themselves affected by the input of certain key anthropological advisors, considerably facilitated the process.

The Commodity Economy of Evolutionary Anthropology

Despite its implicit nominal assertion of generalized human relevance, anthropology throughout most of its history has been primarily a discourse of the culturally or racially despised. The marginality of its human subject matter has not for the most part strengthened anthropology's claim on the limited resources society makes available to support the pursuit of nonutilitarian humanistic knowledge. And while anthropologists have attempted in various ways to argue the social utility of a knowledge of "others," such claims have only occasionally been honored. As a result, the resources that sustain and constrain the creation of anthropological knowledge have been limited. They have also often been indirect and mediated, in the sense that anthropological activities have been incidentally or adventitiously supported by funds intended for some other purpose, channelled often through institutions not specifically anthropological. Characteristically, this mediation has involved a complex negotiation of not fully comprehended cross-purposes.

This often implicit mediation is variously evident in the late-nineteenth and early-twentieth centuries, when the discipline had barely got a foothold in universities—whose presidents and trustees were in any case little able (or inclined) to support research in the human disciplines. Although Lewis Henry Morgan devoted $25,000 of his own funds to the single-minded pursuit of data on kinship systems (Resek 1960:106), and General Pitt Rivers was able to hire crews of workmen to dig barrows on his own estate (Chapman 1981, 1985), those who wished to carry on more-than-avocational anthropological research had for the most part to rely on resources other than those under their personal control. In the United States, government support proved to be a possibility. John Wesley Powell's success in 1879 in convincing Congress that anthropology would be useful in getting Indians peacefully allocated to reservations made it possible for the Bureau of Ethnology to underwrite a large amount of research on topics somewhat tenuously related to that end (Hinsley 1981). So also, Franz Boas in 1908 managed to fund environmentalist physical anthropological research under the umbrella of a congressional commission devoted to the restriction of the immigration of "racial" groups presumed to be genetically inferior (GS 1968a:175). But in Great Britain (Van Keuren 1982), government was much less forthcoming; and in both countries the golden age of government funding still lay far in the future.

In this context, anthropologists had to turn to wealthy individual benefactors, and to a particular cultural institution—the museum—which was in turn supported largely by their benefaction (cf. Kusmer 1979; GS 1985). Here, again, the mediation of cross-purposes was often in evidence. Support for the establishment of anthropological work at the University of California may be seen as a well-intentioned subversion of Mrs. Hearst's instinct of aesthetic accumulation from the artifacts of classical culture to the languages of digger Indians (Thoresen 1975). So also, in seeking support for Far Eastern research in the aftermath of the Spanish American War, Franz Boas appealed to the commercial interests of the entrepreneurs of transcontinental railroads; but he also justified his request to these archetypes of the American way in terms of a relativizing appreciation of the achievements of distinctive civilizations (GS 1974c:294–97). Such attempts to build bridges of enlightened self-interest were always problematic; try as he might, Boas could not raise money from Andrew Carnegie and others for a museum of Afro-American culture (ibid.:316–18).

Insofar as support was forthcoming, it was facilitated by the fact that material objects served as both commodity and medium of exchange within the restricted political economy of anthropological research. From the perspective of donors whose beneficence was sustained by success in the world of commodity production, palpable and visible objects could be seen as a return on investment, even if their aesthetic or utilitarian value was minimal by conventional cultural standards. From the perspective of anthropologists, the collection of objects for sale to museums was an important if somewhat tenuous means of capitalizing research on less marketable topics (cf. Cole 1985). Between them, at the center of the political economy of anthropological research, stood the museums, institutions premised on the collection and display of objects. Although not often devoted solely to anthropology, they were, before World War I, the most important single institutional employers of anthropologists, and channelled into anthropological research an amount of support that has yet to be calculated—the return for which was most quickly evident in the boxes and bundles of cultural objects sent back for warehousing and display (cf. Darnell 1969:140–235).

Quite aside from the nature of its political economy, a number of intellectual factors also conspired to sustain an object orientation in anthropological research. To a much greater extent than today, knowledge itself was thought of as embodied in objects; William Rainey Harper took it for granted that a museum was as essential as a library to the creation of a great university (GS 1979a:11). As a discipline organized around the principle of change in time, and devoted primarily to groups that had left no written records, anthropology had a strong internal intellectual push toward the collection and study of material objects permanently embodying moments of past cultural or racial development. Within an evolutionist framework, human physical remains, archeological finds, and contemporary material culture were the most ready means of graphically illustrating the development of mankind; and though they were not convenient for public display, even the texts collected by linguists had a somewhat "object" character (GS 1977b). Indeed, it might be argued that the existence of an object orientation within each of its major subdisciplines was one of the strongest factors sustaining their rather problematic presumptive unity in a general "anthropology."

While Boas might have questioned whether the tendency is inherent in museum display *per se*, it seems likely that in an ideological milieu befogged by evolutionary racialist assumption such an object orientation often contributed to a degrading and distancing objectification of the "others" who had made the objects, and who were themselves literally objectified in museum displays. Be that as it may, there seems to have been some tendency for the more object- and museum-oriented anthropologists to be more closely identified with the dominant groups in American culture, and with the cultural ideology that justified their dominance (GS 1968a: 270–307).

Already before the outbreak of World War I, however, the evolutionary viewpoint had been brought seriously into question, first in American and then in British anthropology (below, pp. 352–56). The historically oriented diffusionisms that immediately succeeded it still sustained to some extent an object orientation insofar as they conceived of culture as a collection of easily transportable thinglike "elements." But even within the "historical school" certain leading figures in both countries had already begun to move away from an object-oriented, museum-based anthropology. By 1905, when he severed his connection to the American Museum of Natural History, Franz Boas had clearly decided that the psychological issues that had always been central to his concern could not be effectively pursued in a museum context (Jacknis 1985). In England, the emerging social anthropological orientation of Radcliffe-Brown and Malinowski strained not only against the object-oriented museum tradition, but against historical anthropology itself (GS 1984b, 1986b; Kuper 1983). In Boas' case, this movement was associated with a more general critique of racialism; in the British case, it reflected at least a more positive valuation of the culture of "savages." While "others" themselves might in a metaphoric sense still be objectified by the scientizing orientation that long survived the demise of evolutionary anthropology, in both countries "objects" as such were soon no longer to provide a focus for the unity of anthropology.

But if there was an endogenous intellectual movement within anthropology away from objects and museums, it was by no means evident to all at the time that this trend was to become dominant in the Anglo-American tradition. On the contrary, the immediate postwar period was one of considerable ferment and even disarray. In the United States, there was a brief reaction against the newly dominant anti-evolutionary cultural anthropology of Boas and his students, and an attempt to redefine anthropology in "hard" scientific racialist terms (above, pp. 117–18). In Britain, where the movement away from evolutionism had been later and less cohesive, the groupings within the discipline were more diverse. Although an elder generation of museum-oriented anthropologists still dominated the Royal Anthropological Institute, a strongly diffusionary school had emerged under the leadership of the neurological anatomist-cum-Egyptologist Grafton Elliot Smith, who sought to derive all human culture from a group of seafaring, sun-worshipping builders of megalithic monuments. Somewhere in between were the ethnographically oriented anthropologists who occupied the important positions at Oxford, Cambridge, and the London School of Economics. In this situation of lively intellectual competition, the commitments made by a major new funding alternative—the private foundation—could be a powerful selective influence. And indeed Rockefeller philanthropy, which did so much to reshape the whole range of human science in this period, was also to play a major role in determining the outcome of the postevolutionary reorientation of Anglo-American anthropology.[1]

From Human Biology to Cultural Determinism

By 1920, the vast bulk of the $450,000,000 which the ambiguous dynamic of robber barony and protestant ethic had set aside for "the well-being of mankind" had already been received by the four institutionalized Rockefeller philanthropies—the Rockefeller Institute for Medical Research, the General Education Board, the Rockefeller Foundation, and the Laura Spelman Rockefeller Memorial (Fosdick 1952:ix). Their organization and administration, however, did not reach mature form until 1928, and the early 1920s were a period of redefinition of philanthropic priorities and of transition in administrative style. Before this time, the dominant role in the definition of philanthropic policy had been played by Frederick T. Gates, the Baptist minister who long served as the elder Rockefeller's philanthropic aide-de-camp, and whose primary interest lay in the field of medicine and public health. When John D., Jr., decided in 1910 to devote himself almost full time to philanthropy, his somewhat broader vision of social welfare tended to encounter Gates's resistance (Fosdick 1956:138–42). Although early initiatives in the social sciences ran aground upon the conflict of corporate and philanthropic interest in the aftermath of the "Ludlow Massacre" in 1914 (Grossman 1982), the elder Rockefeller's creation of the Laura Spelman Rockefeller Memorial in 1918 to further his late wife's social reform interests reopened the possibility of social scientific research (Bulmer & Bulmer 1981). After 1920, in the context of a broadening of Rockefeller philanthropic activity overseas and an increasing focus on the support of institutions of higher learning, there was a general shift toward the encouragement of research as the best means of promoting human welfare (Fosdick 1952:135–45; Karl & Katz 1981; Kohler 1978; Bulmer & Bulmer 1981).

The movement toward academic research reflected the greater prominence within Rockefeller (and other) philanthropies of a group of academically trained foundation bureaucrats who came to play a very influential

1. Except where otherwise indicated, all manuscript citations are to materials in the Rockefeller Archives Center (RA), which form the primary research base of this essay.

role in the determination of policy (Kohler 1991:233–62; Bulmer & Bulmer 1981:358–59). In relation to anthropology, the key figures were Beardsley Ruml (who had received a Ph.D. in psychology at Chicago under James Angell), Edwin R. Embree (who had studied philosophy and served in administrative posts at Yale), and Edmund Day (who had been professor of economics at Harvard and Michigan). As the intellectually free-wheeling director of the Spelman Memorial, Ruml was instrumental in convincing its trustees in 1922 that practical social welfare must be grounded first on a firm foundation of social scientific research. When the Foundation proper established a Division of Studies in 1924, Embree played a key role in organizing a program of research into "Human Biology." Day was subsequently to become director of the Division of Social Sciences when all the research activities of the various Rockefeller philanthropies were consolidated within the reorganized Rockefeller Foundation in 1928. All three men shared Ruml's conviction that practical social welfare depended on developing first a more rigorously "scientific" and empirical social science, based on first-hand observation of living human beings rather than on historical materials, classificatory systems, or general theoretical speculation—a social science that would produce "a body of substantiated and widely accepted generalisations as to human capacities and motives, and as to the behavior of human beings as individuals and groups" (quoted in Bulmer & Bulmer 1981:362).

For Ruml, biology was one of the social sciences, and as Embree's program title suggests, a generalized "psychobiological" orientation was very influential in Rockefeller philanthropic circles in the early 1920s. Heavily influenced by racialist and evolutionist assumption still widely prevalent in the natural and social sciences—and momentarily resurgent in anthropology—it implied a kind of theoretical unity underlying a number of issues of practical social concern, ranging from immigration and crime to public health and mental hygiene to fertility and child development. Insofar as it expressed a generalized concern with the composition, quality, and control of the population of a complex industrial society, this postwar distillation of the progressive impulse may easily be interpreted as an ideological expression of the class interests of leading groups within a maturing corporate capitalist system (cf. E. Brown 1979; Fisher 1980). To a considerable extent, however, the story of Rockefeller anthropology in the interwar period is that of the redirection of the interest in "human biology" toward the study of human sociocultural differences.

Although it was in Day's division that a program in cultural anthropology was eventually to develop, the earliest Rockefeller involvement in anthropology developed willy-nilly out of the research of Davidson Black, a Canadian army surgeon who took the chair in embryology and neurology at the Foundation's Peking Union Medical College in 1918 (Hood 1964). Black had become interested in human paleontology while studying comparative anatomy in 1914 with Elliot Smith, who was then working on the "remains" of Piltdown Man (Spencer 1990). Despite the fears of Foundation officials that Black's anthropology would distract him from teaching (R. M. Pearce/DB 4/4/21), he was able to carry on the work that led to the discovery of Peking Man in 1926, and over the next decade the Foundation's previously limited support reached a total of almost $300,000 to Black and his successor Franz Weidenreich.[2] In 1920, Elliot Smith himself was a principal beneficiary of some $5,000,000 the Foundation gave to support medical research at University College, London (Fosdick 1952: 109; cf. Fisher 1978)—and which incidentally sustained the institutional base from which Elliot Smith and his disciple William Perry propagated their controversial diffusionist notions. In this context, Elliot Smith for a while seems to have been cast in what was to become an informally recognized role in the Rockefeller philanthropies: that of "expert anthropological advisor."

Davidson Black's work, like the China interest generally, had a somewhat special status within Rockefeller philanthropy. With the development of the psychobiological research orientation of the early 1920s, however, several interdisciplinary proposals put forward by scholars in the United States were to lead toward a more systematic program in anthropology. The first two of these came to the Spelman Memorial, and their fate reflects the influence of Ruml's personal, institutional, and intellectual affiliations in academic psychology. Ruml's own psychological research had been in mental testing, and during World War I he had worked on the large-scale psychological testing program carried on for the U.S. army (Bulmer & Bulmer 1981:354). One of the leaders of that program, Robert Yerkes, went on to take a leading position with the National Research Council, which was heavily funded by the Foundation; and when Yerkes approached the Memorial in 1923 for money to support the NRC's new Committee on Scientific Problems of Human Migration, Ruml was immediately receptive (RY/BR 2/26/23; Haraway 1989:71). Although the Committee began as a *de facto* research arm of the immigration restriction movement, the $132,000 contributed by the Memorial over the next four years in fact helped to undermine traditional restrictionist assumptions. The work of the Com-

2. Although there is no single overall summary of dollar figures for Rockefeller support of anthropology, an internal office document (Program and Policy, folder 910), initialed NST and dated 3/31/33, lists "Anthropology appropriations made by LSRM and RF" to that date, by institution (or in some cases, individuals). In arriving at overall totals for the period, I have supplemented these figures with later appropriations, as indicated in particular institutional files, or in the *Annual Reports* of the Rockefeller Foundation, 1934–38.

mittee was heavily influenced by Clark Wissler, whose own mildly nativist leanings enabled him to mediate between the racialism of the hard-science establishment and the cultural determinism of the Boasian school, with which in general he identified (Reed 1980). In this context, Rockefeller support for the NRC (which included a major fellowship program in the biological sciences), had by the early 1930s sustained a considerable amount of Boasian anthropological research, including Margaret Mead's work in Samoa, Melville Herskovits' physical anthropological studies of the Negro, and Otto Klineberg's studies of the intelligence of Negro migrants—each of which was a major building block of the emerging antiracialist scientific consensus (GS 1968a:299–300; cf. Coben 1976).

Later on in 1923, Ruml received a second psychobiological initiative that was to lead toward cultural studies. His mentor Angell, who became the president of Yale in 1921, proposed the establishment of a "Psycho-Biology Institute" that would study psychic life from a comparative point of view with emphasis on man and the higher primates (JA/BR 5/4/23; cf. Morawski 1986). The plan fitted well with Ruml's policy of developing a few major social scientific research centers, and by the following June, when Angell had succeeded in attracting both Yerkes and Wissler to Yale, the Spelman Memorial voted $200,000 to support the Institute of Psychology over a five-year period (BR/JA 6/27/24). Reorganized in 1929 as the Institute of Human Relations, the Yale project was ultimately to receive many millions from the various Rockefeller foundations. Although the major anthropological item was $550,000 for Yerkes' primate researches (Haraway 1989: 59–83), there was a small but significant flow of support to more culturally oriented studies under Wissler, and over the long run the Institute was heavily influenced by the increasingly dominant environmental and cultural orientation within the social sciences generally (M. May 1971).

A third psychobiological initiative in 1923 led, in an even more dramatic transformation of motive, to the first major Rockefeller programs in cultural anthropology *per se*. In December of that year, the racial polemicist Madison Grant forwarded to the Rockefeller Foundation a proposal from the eugenicist Galton Society for a study of the effects of natural selection among Australian Aboriginals as "the best approach to a proper understanding of the artificial conditions of selection now operating in civilized communities" (MG/R. B. Fosdick 12/29/23). When the proposal was referred to Embree in the newly organized Division of Studies, he followed up already established anthropological connections within the Foundation by writing for advice to both Davidson Black and Elliot Smith, who had just been invited to lecture at the University of California in 1924 (EE/DB 3/19/24; EE/ES 3/19/24). En route, Elliot Smith stopped off to consult with Embree, Wissler, and C. B. Davenport, another leading Galton Society racialist (EE/CD 4/10/24). Somewhat to the consternation of the Society, which felt control of the project slipping away, Embree sent Elliot Smith on to Australia to investigate the local anthropological situation—following a general Rockefeller Foundation policy that its own initiatives must always be linked to some local commitment of resources and personnel (EE/GS 5/7/24, 5/8/24).

The Australian scene was at that point in some confusion. A plan to found a university chair in Sydney in anthropology, which was developed at the second Pan-Pacific Science Congress in Sydney in 1923, had been undercut when a British colonial officer sent out to advise the government on the administration of its island mandates told them that "special training in anthropology was not advisable" for colonial administration (ES/EE 5/19/24, 5/21/24). Encouraged by Rockefeller support, however, the prime minister agreed to reconsider his opposition, and within the next several months Elliot Smith was able to report that two of the state governments had voted financial support (ES/EE 9/30/24, 11/5/24). In the meantime, the sudden death of the Sydney professor of anatomy, and the refusal of Davidson Black to leave Peking to replace him, undermined the biological aspect of the scheme, which the Australian National Research Council had in any case from the beginning conceived of in social anthropological terms (ES/EE 6/17/25). Late in November 1925, the Foundation received news that Elliot Smith, A. C. Haddon, and a third elector had chosen for the chair A. R. Radcliffe-Brown, one of the two leading exponents of "functionalist" social anthropology, over the historical diffusionist A. M. Hocart (Office memo 11/28/25). Although Radcliffe-Brown was completely unknown to the Rockefeller people, they invited him to tour American anthropological institutions on his way to Australia (G. Vincent/RB 1/7/26).

By this time, the Australian scheme had become linked with other research initiatives that had developed in the Pacific in the postwar period. In 1919, the NRC had established a Committee on Pacific Exploration (later, Investigations), which took the lead in organizing the first Pan-Pacific Science Congress; and about the same time Yale University and the American Museum of Natural History had joined in a cooperative scheme designed to revitalize the Bernice P. Bishop Museum of Honolulu. H. E. Gregory, the Yale geologist who became chairman of the NRC Committee, was appointed director of the Bishop Museum, fellowships were established for Yale graduate students, and $40,000 given to Yale was channelled through the Museum to support four anthropological field parties of the Bayard Dominick Expedition to Polynesia. Wissler, a member of the NRC Pacific Committee, became "Consulting Ethnologist," and a physical anthropologist was sent from the American Museum to round out an anthropological staff that had jumped from one to seven (GS 1968a:297–98). By the time the Rockefeller Foundation became interested in Australian anthropology, Gregory was looking for further sources of support for the Bishop Museum program (EE/HG 5/29/25).

Almost simultaneously, the Foundation received another initiative from Hawaii, when the president of the university there forwarded a memo on the study of racial differences written by S. B. Porteus, an Australian-born educational researcher who had just come from the Vineland, N.J., training school for mental defectives—another stronghold of the eugenics movement (EE/A. L. Dean 1/5/25; Porteus 1969; Kevles 1985:77). Faced with all these possibilities in the Pacific, Embree went out himself to investigate, travelling first to Australia with Wissler, and then returning to Honolulu, where they were joined by E. G. Conklin, a leading biologist associated with the Galton Society (EE/A. L. Dean 5/29/25; EE/Vice Chancellor, Univ. of Sydney 7/1/25; EE/HG 7/1/25). Despite the turn away from biology, Embree sent back a favorable report on the Australian plans (EE/G. Vincent 12/20/25); and while the Wissler and Conklin reports from Hawaii were oriented toward human biology and racial psychology, they also emphasized the need for institutional cooperation, in line with Rockefeller policy of developing regional research centers ("Rept. on Res. in Biol. in Hawaii" 3/n.d./26).

In this context, the Foundation voted in May 1926 to make five-year grants to support all three Pacific research proposals. The smallest ($50,000 on a matching basis, later supplemented by $14,000 more) was for the Bishop Museum's continuing research program, which had been primarily cultural from the beginning—although its traditional ethnological focus on Polynesian migration could be interpreted in racial terms (BPBM 1926: 25). In contrast, the support given to the University of Hawaii, totalling $215,000 over the next ten years, at first supported researches like those on racial temperament by Porteus and the anatomist Frederick Wood Jones. But when Jones left in 1930, the biological researches carried on by H. L. Shapiro were thoroughly in the Boasian tradition, and a series of visiting Chicago sociologists gave the whole program a decidedly culturalist turn ("Appraisal, U. of Hawaii, Racial Res." 8/n.d./38). In Australia, the money funnelled through the Australian NRC did support some physiological researches, as well as fieldwork by Porteus on the intelligence of Australian Aboriginals. But the bulk of the almost $250,000 granted by 1936 went for social anthropological fieldwork there and in the nearby southwestern Pacific (RB, "Rept. on Anthro. Work in Aust." 6/28/30).

The general pattern was clear enough: a number of "psychobiological" research proposals, several of them initiated by people with close ties to racialist doctrine, immigration restriction, or the eugenics movement, were favorably received by the new generation of administrator/academics, who were interested in furthering empirical social scientific research into human capacities, motives, and behavior. In almost every case, however, these initiatives were partly or totally transformed, as Rockefeller administrators accommodated to the rising current of sociocultural and environmental determinism within anthropology and the surrounding social sciences.

The Turn to British Functionalism

Although there were to be several later grants in support of research in human biology, these occurred within the framework of the cultural orientation that increasingly characterized Rockefeller anthropological activities in the later 1920s. Its somewhat tentative and *ad hoc* growth may be illuminated by considering the development of several more specifically anthropological initiatives within Ruml's social science program at the Spelman Memorial. In the United States, the earliest of these was an appropriation of $13,500 to the University of Chicago in 1926 to cover the first three years' salary of Edward Sapir, the brilliant linguistic anthropologist (A. Woods/J. H. Tufts 5/19/25; Darnell 1990). When Sapir joined his colleague Fay-Cooper Cole in forwarding a program for field research (FC/L. K. Frank 3/5/26; JT/BR 3/29/26), however, the matter was sidestepped, despite favorable evaluations from Wissler and two Memorial staff members (L. Outhwaite, Memo 4/9/26). Ruml apparently preferred at this point to work within the interdisciplinary regional social science centers the Memorial was already funding. Since these centers were given discretionary power over block-grant funds, anthropological work received support within the limits of the local definition of purpose and balance of disciplinary power. Thus when the Sapir-Cole request was channelled to the University of Chicago's Committee on Local Community Research, its mandate was stretched to cover Cole's archeological work in Illinois (L. C. Marshall/BR 5/31/26; cf. Bulmer 1980). Similarly, at Columbia, where Boas carried weight in the Committee for Research in the Social Sciences, anthropology was the indirect beneficiary of significant Spelman Memorial support (A. Woods/N. M. Butler 5/28/26).

In the meantime, a spin-off of the Cole-Sapir initiative was to lead toward further Rockefeller involvement in anthropology. The archeological training program Cole ran in the summer of 1926 stimulated more general interest among anthropologists in the NRC in an "intercollegiate field-school" in the Southwest, where, coincidentally, local archeological interests had made a direct personal appeal to the younger Rockefeller during a visit he made there in 1926. Successfully co-opting or overriding the local interests, the nationally oriented anthropologists were instrumental in establishing a Laboratory of Anthropology modelled on the Marine Biological Laboratory at Woods Hole, Massachusetts. Over and above Rockefeller's large personal gift for the physical plant, the Museum and Laboratory of Anthropology in Santa Fe received a total of $92,500 in Memorial and Foundation support during the next ten years, the great bulk of which went to support summer fieldwork parties sent out from established university departments of anthropology (GS 1982a).

Although more than half of the Laboratory's fieldwork was to be in ethnology and linguistics, the impetus that led to it had come from anthropologists whose orientation was still rather traditionally "historical." Developments during this period in England, however, were to lead to Rockefeller involvement in a more "functional" anthropology. As part of Ruml's policy of supporting regional social science centers on a worldwide basis, the Memorial gave substantial support to the London School of Economics, where investigations into the human and environmental bases of economics and politics fitted well with the psychobiological orientation then prevailing among Rockefeller officials (Bulmer & Bulmer 1981). Indirectly, this support helped to further work in anthropology, which had been augmented in 1923 by the appointment of Bronislaw Malinowski, protégé of Charles Seligman, the LSE's professor of ethnology—an appointment which, paradoxically, had been designed to counter the development of Elliot Smith's rival (and also Rockefeller-funded) school of anthropology at University College.

Although Malinowski was the beneficiary of Rockefeller-funded research assistants, large-scale direct support to anthropology in Britain developed outside the LSE in relation to attempts to apply anthropology to practical problems of colonial administration (cf. Kuklick 1978). British anthropologists were quite active at this time in trying to counter unfriendly official attitudes like those evidenced in the matter of the Australian chair. Emphasizing the importance of racial psychological studies in colonial administration, Seligman and others sought to reform the rather stodgy Royal Anthropological Institute so that it might take on the more utilitarian functions of an imperial Central Bureau of Anthropology modelled after the U.S. Bureau of American Ethnology (CS/W. Beveridge 3/13/24). Although an appeal for funds to Ruml in May 1924 elicited no immediate action (J. Shotwell/BR 5/6/24), the Australian matter kept the issue of applied anthropology before the attention of Rockefeller officials. Early in 1925, Elliot Smith sent Embree clippings from the London *Times* in which he and others argued the importance of anthropology for empire (ES/EE 1/20/25). In the meantime, men more directly involved in colonial affairs were also interested in furthering research initiatives.

At a conference in September 1924, a group of world missionary leaders and others critical of native policy in Africa advanced the idea of a

"Bureau of African Languages and Literatures" to further native education through "the medium of their own forms of thought" (E. W. Smith 1934:1). Among them was Dr. J. H. Oldham, who had close relations with several American philanthropies interested in promoting the ideas of the Tuskegee Institute as a model for African education, and also with highly placed British colonial officials who shared his view that research into "the human factor" was the key to preventing the "impending racial conflicts" threatening Africa (Bennett 1960; King 1971). Early in 1925 Oldham went to New York to drum up financial support, and when he subsequently forwarded more detailed plans to the Rockefeller people, they were favorably received (JO/A. Woods 6/9/25). At a conference that September, the planners of the African Bureau broadened their project to include the study of African social institutions, "with a view to their protection and use as instruments of education" (E. W. Smith 1934:2). Returning to New York for further discussions with Ruml, Oldham argued that a nation with so many of the "African race" within its own borders could not afford to remain indifferent to the economic and social problems created by the rapid movement of capital into the African continent (JO/BR 11/9/25). At the same meeting in which it appropriated $17,500 for the Royal Anthropological Institute over the next five years, the Spelman Memorial also voted support "in principle" for Oldham's scheme (BR/JO 11/7/25), although it was not until a year later that it actually allocated $25,000 over a similar period to what had by then become the International Institute of African Languages and Cultures (BR/JO 10/26/26).

Having made this commitment to British anthropology, Rockefeller officials apparently decided to establish closer contact with its prospective leaders. The Memorial invited Malinowski for an anthropological tour of the United States that overlapped Radcliffe-Brown's similar tour for the Foundation (BR/BM 11/12/25). Although neither venture led to the mass conversion of the American "historical school" to "functionalism," Malinowski's, especially, was viewed as a great success. Crisscrossing the continent, he met leading "gentlemen of colour" in the South, visited Indian reservations in the Southwest, taught summer school at Berkeley (where he had earlier left a "meteoric trail"), and gave joint seminars with Radcliffe-Brown to Boas' students at Columbia. Everywhere he went, Malinowski urged the behavioral study of "the cultural process" in the on-going present, insisting that it was "high time" anthropology took up earnestly "the economic problems and legal aspects of the present blending of human strains and cultures" (BM, "Rept. of American Tour" n.d.). The climax of his tour came when Malinowski joined Wissler in discussing the present state of anthropology at the Hanover Conference of the Rockefeller-funded Social Science Research Council. After Wissler opened the conference by predict-

Bronislaw Malinowski, c. 1925. (Courtesy of Helena Wayne Malinowska and the Department of Anthropology, London School of Economics)

ing a "revolt" within the discipline in favor of "what my friend Malinowski calls functional anthropology," Malinowski went on to discuss the method of the new anthropology, its relation to the other social sciences, and its relevance for contemporary social problems (SSRC 1926:I, 26, 42–54). The assembled social scientists and foundation officials were very impressed (54–71). As Charles Merriam had earlier suggested to Ruml, Malinowski was the first anthropologist he had met who wanted to bring the old antiquarian discipline into close relation to "living social interests" (CM/BR 4/24/26).

Even so, the Rockefeller philanthropies made no further commitment to British anthropology at this time, apparently because of "internecine strife" centering around the personality and theories of Elliot Smith (J. Van Sickle diary 10/6/30)—who by this time was losing his earlier position of influence with the Foundation, which in 1927 rejected a proposal to support cultural anthropology at University College (ES/EE 6/18/27). Indeed, after the opening of 1925–26, there seems to have been a momentary drawback from anthropology within the Rockefeller philanthropies. Aside from a small grant to the International Congress of Americanists in 1928, the only further direct support before the reorganization of 1928 was to the Institute for Comparative Research in Human Culture at Oslo, which received support totalling $45,000 by 1934. Nonetheless, it was clear that when major anthropological funding was resumed, "functional" anthropology would have an inside track.

Malinowski, Oldham, and the Prevention of Race Wars in Africa

With the reorganization of the Foundation accomplished at the end of 1928, the advancement of knowledge was now defined as its central function. Although it was still assumed that research should eventuate in practical reform, the trustees had accepted the position that "the margin between what men know and what they use" was "much too thin" (Fosdick 1952:140). The new divisional structure was oriented toward the major areas of human knowledge, with the humanities and the natural sciences each for the first time given independent recognition, and E. E. Day as director of the Division of the Social Sciences. Day's first grants were carried out without much ado along already established lines. In May 1929 the Foundation made a five-year grant of $75,000 to the Chicago Department of Anthropology (N. S. Thompson/F. C. Woodward 5/27/29); the following fall it voted $125,000 over the same term to the German association of scientific workers, which the now-defunct Spelman Memorial had supported on several occasions. Although the latter grant was in fact for a eugenically oriented study of the German people (F. Schmidt-Ott/ED 9/5/29), and the Foundation subsequently gave a small grant to support research on twins by the physical anthropologist Eugen Fischer (R. A. Lambert/A. Gregg 5/13/32), Day's primary interest was clearly cultural, and over the next several years he moved toward a unified program in this area.

The first major input came from Malinowski, whose performance at the Hanover Conference Day had witnessed in 1926. Although he had established a cooperative relation with Radcliffe-Brown at Sydney, Malinowski was not inclined to rest satisfied with only indirect access to fieldwork support. Since the Southwest Pacific was in Radcliffe-Brown's hands, Malinowski moved toward Africa, where little professional fieldwork had been done apart from the surveys of his colleague Seligman. By the end of 1928, Malinowski had joined forces with Oldham in a campaign to win major Foundation support.

The opening salvo was Malinowski's plea for a "Practical Anthropology" that would study the pressing problems of land tenure and labor as they affected the "changing Native" and the colonial administrator fearful of "what might be called 'black bolshevism'" (1929b:28). When Day came to London in June 1929, Malinowski pursued similar themes in both conversation and a memorandum on "The State of Anthropology . . . in England" (MPL:n.d.; ED/C. G. Seligman 6/24/29). Although functional anthropology offered "a special technique" of "rapid research" to solve such problems as how much labor must be kept in a tribe to maintain its economic base, the British universities (save LSE) lacked an effective fieldwork orientation. The critical problem was therefore to provide fieldwork money, and the most likely channel was the African Institute, which had already inspired favorable interest from the Colonial Office. At the same time, Malinowski forwarded to Oldham a confidential "Report on the Conditions in the Rockefeller Interests" by an unnamed "American Observer" suggesting that they would be receptive to a large-scale appeal stressing "the mutual unification of knowledge by practical interests and vice-versa"—especially if it had to do with "problems of contact between black and white and the sociology of white settlement" (MPL:n.d.). Fearful that the Royal Anthropological Institute and Elliot Smith at University College might be developing competing plans that would sacrifice "sound" anthropology for the study of fossil man and the diffusion of Egyptian cultural influences to Nigeria, Malinowski urged Oldham to "play any trump cards" he held "with a clear conscience" (MPL: BM/JO 6/11/29). His concern, however, was needless. Previously briefed by Ruml, Day already felt that Malinowskian functionalism was the coming thing in British anthropology, although he cautioned the Rockefeller European representative not to let Malinowski know of "our favorable prejudice" (ED/J. Van Sickle 11/16/29).

The first fruit of that prejudice was an arrangement whereby anthropological fieldwork was supported under the existing Rockefeller scheme of international postdoctoral fellowships (BM/ED 8/3/29; J. Van Sickle/ED 12/23/29). In the meantime, Malinowski and Oldham worked to develop a "million dollar interlocking scheme for African research"—interlocking, because a parallel initiative on behalf of the new Rhodes House at Oxford was supported by men so powerful politically that the Institute felt forced to coordinate planning (H. A. L. Fisher et al./Pres., RF 3/28/30). In their private communications to Rockefeller officials, however, Malinowski and Oldham made it clear that their own plans took priority (BM/ED 3/26/30). These were developed largely by Malinowski, who had begun to get an indirect practical familiarity with the African scene through a series of informal "Group Meetings" beginning in December 1929, in which missionaries, interested colonial officials, and anthropologists—sometimes confronting each other from separate sofas—discussed the problems created by culture contact (MPL: BM/JO 2/9/30). At the end of March 1930, a printed appeal was forwarded to the Foundation in separate letters from Malinowski and Lord Lugard, the retired colonial proconsul and ideologist of "Indirect Rule" who presided over the African Institute (MPL: BM/ED 3/26/30). In order to meet the dangers threatening "to defeat the task of Western Civilization" in Africa and to protect the "interests of the native population" in a period when world economic conditions foreshadowed "rapidly increasing exploitation," it was essential to carry on systematic field research along the lines of Audrey Richards' on-going study of the tribal context of native mining labor in Rhodesia. Toward this end, and the training of administrators and missionaries in a more enlightened understanding of African cultural values, the Institute was requesting £100,000 over the next ten years (MPL: Mem. Presented to RF 3/30/30).

Despite opposition from biological scientists in the Foundation and the threat of competing initiatives in Britain, Malinowski and Oldham were successful in gaining Rockefeller support. After entertaining one of the European representatives at his Italian alpine villa, Malinowski told Oldham that the key was to win over Selskar Gunn, a biologist in charge of all the Foundation's activities in Europe (MPL: BM/JO 9/17/30). Warning Gunn of the "possibility of racial wars of considerable magnitude," Oldham recounted Malinowski's "enthusiastic" reception by a group of colonial governors at a meeting in London (SG, diary 9/25/30). With the biological opposition thus effectively neutralized, the Foundation voted the following April to allocate $250,000 in matching funds to the Institute over a five-year period. At the same meeting it rejected the Rhodes House plan on the grounds that the Institute was more international, less compromised by political considerations, and therefore more likely to secure additional matching funding (RF minutes 4/15/31).

Although there were later to be small grants to the Institut für Völkerkunde in Vienna and the Institut d'Ethnologie in Paris, and a somewhat reluctant renewal of the earlier small grant to the Royal Anthropological Institute (J. Van Sickle/ED 5/29/31), the Foundation seemed clearly to have committed itself to Malinowskian functionalism, at least as far as the British sphere was concerned. But at the very moment when his influence was firmly established, Malinowski began to feel it threatened by the man whom he had been inclined to regard as his collaborator in the functionalist movement.

"The Biggest Anthropological Pie Ever Concocted"

When the impending termination of the original five-year grant and the rapidly deteriorating financial situation of the Australian state and federal governments threatened the continuation of the Sydney program in 1930 (A. Gibson/ED 3/3/31), Radcliffe-Brown approached Rockefeller officials with an omnibus plan that would combine an extension of the Australian grant and a proposal of his own for South African research with the Rhodes House and African Institute proposals then under consideration (RB/ED 9/17/30; RB/M. Mason 11/17/30). Suggesting that the time was ripe for more general consideration of Rockefeller anthropological policy, Radcliffe-Brown argued that no other science was faced with so dire a threat as that involved in the rapid disappearance of "the lower forms of culture," which might well vanish entirely "within the next generation." Fortunately, in the few years left, the "newer anthropology" based on the "functional study" of cultures as "integrated systems" might still formulate "general laws of social life and social development." Focussing on the present and future rather than the past, it might even approximate an "experimental science" that would be of "immediate service to those who are concerned with the administration and education of native peoples." What was needed was "the establishment of a number of research institutions around the world" to undertake cooperative investigation of the surviving native peoples "area by area and tribe by tribe" (RB, "Memo. on Anth. Res." 11/17/30). Radcliffe-Brown, who was leaving Sydney to take up an appointment at the University of Chicago, proposed to make his visit to London for the centenary meeting of the British Association in September 1931 the occasion for a concerted effort toward this goal (Radcliffe-Brown 1931).

Although Radcliffe-Brown had asked for Malinowski's aid in pushing his "vanishing cultures" plan (MPL: RB/BM 9/17/30), Malinowski seems to have viewed his return from the antipodes as a threat to his own planning (cf. GS 1984b). Vacationing in France, he received reports that Radcliffe-Brown was offering Oldham advice on how to implement the Institute's "five-year plan," and that Oldham was taking seriously Radcliffe-Brown's argument that studies focussing on economic life in terms of "social cohesion" were preferable to more comprehensive ethnographic inquiries (MPL: A. Richards/BM n.d.; JO/BM 9/9/31). Equally disturbing was Radcliffe-Brown's suggestion that the School of Oriental Studies, which at this point also had an application before the Foundation for massive aid, was a more logical institutional center than the LSE for anthropological research throughout the empire—a center that Radcliffe-Brown indicated his willingness to head (MPL: RB/BM 9/27/31, 1/30/32, 5/25/32). However, Malinowski was influential in getting the School of Oriental Studies grant scaled down to $36,000 and redefined in complementary rather than competitive terms (S. Gunn, interview with BM 3/4/31; SG/ED 12/7/31, 2/1/32), and Radcliffe-Brown settled in Chicago for the next six years. Once broached, however, the idea of a comprehensive re-evaluation of its work in anthropology was pursued within the Foundation itself.

By 1931, the Foundation's commitments in this area were fairly numerous. In addition to the program in Britain, those in Hawaii and Australia then being renewed, and the on-going support to the Chicago department, the Foundation was in the process of making grants to two other American departments: Harvard, where support for anthropology complemented a major commitment to Elton Mayo's researches in industrial psychology at the Business School (A. W. Tozzer/ED 11/22/30); and Tulane, where the personal intervention of an elder statesman of the General Education Board, Abraham Flexner, won a somewhat reluctant support for a bibliographical project in Middle American research (E. Capps, "Memo. on Proposed Inst." 6/9/30).

Faced with these rather disparate activities, Day was quite receptive when Radcliffe-Brown pushed the case for cooperative systematic research while he was teaching at Columbia in the summer of 1931. At a staff meeting late in July, Day argued that Radcliffe-Brown's memorandum established "a strong presumptive case" for a more unified program in cultural anthropology, which would provide comparative data for a contemplated Division in Behavior and Personality that Day hoped might be funded at $300,000 a year over the next fifteen years (ED, "Foundation's Interest in Cult. Anth." 7/30/31). In this context, the Foundation formally recognized cultural anthropology as "a special field of interest, the development of which presents an element of urgency" (RF Rept. 1931:249). After extended discussion at another staff conference the following January ("Staff Conf." 1/21/32), the Foundation's officers decided to undertake a full-scale survey of anthropological activities throughout the world (ED/S. Gunn 1/25/32).

Although Day considered asking Radcliffe-Brown himself to take charge of the survey (ED/SG 1/25/32), it was decided instead to hire Leonard Outhwaite, a currently unemployed former staff member of the Spelman Memorial who had studied anthropology at the University of California. Over the next few months, Outhwaite travelled throughout the United States and Europe, interviewing over two hundred anthropologists at fifty-one different institutions. Although he made it a point to start with a blank

A. R. Radcliffe-Brown, Sydney, Australia, c. 1930. (Photograph by Sarah Neill Chinnery; courtesy of Sheila M. Waters)

slate – spending time in the beginning attempting to define the word "primitive" (LO/ED 4/19/32) – Outhwaite's ties to the Boasian tradition inevitably gave the survey a different character than it might otherwise have had. He found Radcliffe-Brown "challenging" but "extreme" (LO/ED 4/19/32); and while he thought Malinowski was "reasonable," he was disturbed by his tendency to act as the "Tsar" of anthropology (LO/ED 6/10/32). Outhwaite could see no essential distinction between the two, and concluded that their differences were "not strictly scientific" (LO, "Anthro. in Europe").

The clearly evident theoretical differences between British functionalists and American historicists he saw as reflections of the differing cultures they had studied – and was therefore inclined to favor an essentially atheoretical approach to fieldwork. He was opposed to the functionalists' "narrowing" of anthropology, and while he accepted their notion of the systemic integrity of cultures, he insisted that this, too, must be understood as an historical phenomenon. In the end, he associated himself with the "best and most conservative workers in each country" – among whom he included Cole, Kroeber, Lowie, Wissler, Haddon, Seligman, and the Viennese diffusionists (LO, "Condensed Rept." 23).

In the meantime, the American Anthropological Association, apparently at Day's urging, had established a research committee to develop its own plans for the study of vanishing cultures. The preliminary draft circulated by the Association's secretary, John Cooper, before the committee's first informal meeting, gave major priority to a trait-oriented study of the North American continent (UCB: JC/A. Kroeber 4/21/32). As the proposal was refined at committee meetings, however, the initial Americanist bias was dropped for a cooperative worldwide orientation and a "catholicity of ethnographic approach" which even envisioned studies of the same tribe by functionalist and historical ethnographers (UCB: JC/AK, n.d.). The scant evidence of the committee's proceedings (NAA) suggests that the modification was engineered by Radcliffe-Brown and Alfred Kroeber – the former walking with deliberate caution and the latter by nature a compromiser. The final version was delegated to a subcommittee of five, in which Edward Sapir and Alfred Tozzer were aligned against Radcliffe-Brown and Wissler, and a major input in fact came from Boas, who later on was to side with Radcliffe-Brown against his Americanist colleagues on the relative importance of fieldwork and "source study" (UC: JC/F. Cole 1/25/33).

On June 24, 1932, the committee forwarded to the Foundation a twelve-year research proposal, including fieldwork on three hundred tribes throughout the world, at a total cost of $5,000,000 (UCB: [JC]/RF; [JC]/ED). The Foundation, however, delayed consideration pending the completion of Outhwaite's survey (UCB: JC/Res. Comm. 7/1/32). Comparing his own with the Association's scheme, Outhwaite noted that their "general conclusions" as to the scientific urgency of a global salvage program and their overall methodological approach were essentially the same, although his own was smaller in scope. Accepting Wissler's view that major fieldwork in North America could be completed in five years[!], Outhwaite estimated total expenses averaging only $250,000 annually over a fifteen-year period. Outside the North American area, Outhwaite felt that the less professionalized and relatively "poverty-stricken" state of European anthropology necessitated a gradual "strategic" approach, beginning with surveys of the major cultural areas to define specific research programs. Although emphasizing the importance of individual fieldwork by "general anthropologists" with "all-round" training, he was critical of the traditional one man/one monograph approach, urging also the possibility of interdisciplinary, regional, and comparative studies. The major difference, however, was one of governance. Internal and international jealousies made Outhwaite dubious of the Association's plan to have the program supervised by an executive committee dominated by Americans. Although he was optimistic that theoretical rivalries need not "in practice" be a serious problem, he favored centralized control by an internationally oriented nonpartisan body—namely, the Social Science Division of the Rockefeller Foundation. In this context he recommended that the Association's proposal be turned down, at least in "its present form," while the Foundation pursued its own planning (LO/ED 10/12/32; UCB: JC/Res. Comm. 11/28/21).

At Outhwaite's suggestion, however, the Association's committee was asked to develop plans for the American Indian field that might be incorporated into subsequent Rockefeller planning (UC: JC/M. Mason 3/6/33). After several months of discussions, the committee reached an impasse over the relative importance of further fieldwork as opposed to the systematization and publication of existing North American data. When the president of the Foundation notified the committee on April 26, 1933, that no support was feasible at that time, Cooper suggested that his letter seemed "to settle the tie vote" (UCB: JC/Res. Comm. 4/28/33; M. Mason/JC 4/26/33). By this time, the Foundation had in fact decided not to pursue a major program in anthropology.

The anthropologists were somewhat at a loss to understand what had happened. One contemporary nonparticipant suggested that there had been a "series of undercover battles" between Malinowski and Radcliffe-Brown, and between each of them and the Americans (W. L. Warner/ED 9/15/33). While we have seen some evidence of this, there is also evidence of a spirit of compromise in the Association's committee; and toward the end Malinowski and Radcliffe-Brown also seem to have joined forces in the attempt to win "the biggest anthropological pie ever concocted" (MPL: BM/W. Beveridge 11/19/32). By that time, however, the decision was already being made, on larger grounds than the internecine bickerings of anthropologists.

The essential context was the world economic crisis of the early 1930s, which not only presented the Foundation with an overriding immediate problem of human welfare, but also drastically reduced the income from its endowment. When the trustees met in the fall of 1932 to review the program in the social sciences, Day proposed a concentration on certain major practical problems of social engineering, and especially on economic stabilization ("Verbatim Notes, Princeton Conf." 10/29/32). Although Day himself was still inclined to support cultural anthropology, the trustees were moving toward a major policy reorientation in which anthropology would find little place. The early months of 1933 in fact marked the nadir of depression in the United States, and by the time the trustees met again in April, the decision had already been made to shelve Outhwaite's report (S. H. Walker/J. Van Sickle 4/4/33). For the next year, while the trustees carried on a ponderous reappraisal of the whole Foundation program, Day somewhat reluctantly declared a "moratorium in the field of cultural anthropology" (ED/D. H. Stevens 11/24/33; ED/A. Gregg 12/19/34). Early in 1934, the decision was made to terminate it entirely, as far as the Social Science Division was concerned, and let the director of the Humanities Division "pick up any part he wants to salvage" (Staff Conf. 3/8/34).

As it happened, the Humanities Division did not pick up very much. Before that time, its orientation had been quite traditional, emphasizing the preservation of source material. Its only support to anthropology was to linguistics – directly by the grant to the School of Oriental Studies, and indirectly through the American Council of Learned Societies, which in the ten years after 1927 funnelled $80,000 to the Committee on Research in American Native Languages (Flannery 1946). But the Humanities Division was also affected by the policy reorientation of 1933–34, moving away from the "aristocratic tradition of humanistic scholarship" toward the problems of mass communication, international cultural relations, and cultural self-interpretation in a democratic society – in which anthropology, as then conceived, was felt to have little place (D. H. Stevens "Humanities Program . . . : A Review" 1939). The discipline continued to receive Foundation support through general fellowship programs, through grants for interdisciplinary social science programs, and through a renewed program in "psychobiology" in the Division of Natural Sciences (cf. Kohler 1991). And for some time there were traces in the annual *Reports* of the "former program" in cultural anthropology, as payments continued to be made to a few major institutional recipients under tapering terminal grants. But by 1938 these had all ended. Two years later, the discipline reentered the Foundation through the side door, when the National Institute of Anthropology and History in Mexico City was funded by the Humanities Division under its program of Latin American cultural exchange (D. H. Stevens/R. Redfield 12/5/40); but this belongs to the postwar phase of Rockefeller Foundation history.

Social Scientific Knowledge and Corporate Self-Interest

Having traced in some detail the development of Rockefeller anthropological activities in the interwar years, it remains to consider more generally the forces influencing them, and their influence on the history of anthropology. In many other areas of Rockefeller activity, radical historical critics have found patterns of research reflecting the dominant ideology of corporate capitalist society or the class self-interest of its leading groups. Yerkes' primate studies have been treated as "Monkey Business," or "Monkeys and Monopoly Capitalism" (Haraway 1977, 1989); Rockefeller medicine as a conscious "strategy for developing a medical system to meet the needs of capitalist society" (E. Brown 1979:4); Rockefeller social science as a "way of distributing surplus wealth, which might otherwise go to the state in taxes," to produce "knowledge that would help preserve the economic structure of Western society" (Fisher 1980:258). Especially in view of recent concern with the "colonial formation" of anthropology (Asad 1973), the question therefore arises as to what extent and in what ways the anthropological research agenda may have been shaped by the self-interest or ideology of "the Rockefellers" as representatives of corporate capitalism or western colonialism. Given the limitations of the present source material,[3] it will not be possible to answer such questions in a fully satisfying manner. But having narrowed the angle and sharpened the focus of the historical lens, we may suggest some of the complexities of the historical processes by which anthropological research priorities seem to have been negotiated.

It will help to begin by formulating a criterion of scale. In appraising activities in the social sciences in 1934, a trustees' committee estimated that of the $298,000,000 disbursed by the Foundation's constituent bodies, $26,225,000 had gone to support social science research (Rept., Comm. Appraisal & Plan); when direct support to anthropology was completed four years later, the total allocation approximated $2,400,000 disbursed among some two dozen institutions (cf. note 2). Given what is known of Rockefeller decision-making processes in this period, it seems likely that the effective decision was in the hands of key staff members, within the framework of an overall philanthropic strategy. This is not to say that trustees limited themselves to approving staff decisions. Outsiders sometimes initiated proposals by direct appeal to the younger Rockefeller or close personal associates such as Raymond Fosdick, Abraham Flexner, or Colonel Arthur Woods; and their initialed comments on such correspon-

3. Among the relevant limitations are: the fact that records of declined grants were not preserved by the Rockefeller Foundation; that the present research was restricted largely to Rockefeller files relating to particular anthropological activities and staff and trustee records immediately relevant to them, as they were available in 1977; and that it included only a portion of the potentially relevant personal and institutional manuscript collections elsewhere —as well as the fact that only a small fraction of oral communication is reflected in the documentary record.

dence carried great weight—as in the instance of Mayan bibliography at Tulane. But for the most part, key staff members had the major input, not only at a grant-to-grant level, but also in defining programs in particular areas. When the trustees reevaluated the overall program in 1934, the social science program was clearly identified with Day personally, just as it had previously been with Ruml, and the human biology program had been with Embree.

Except at moments of general reevaluation, then, the forces most directly influencing program in anthropology seem primarily to have been those affecting the thinking of a rather small group of reform-minded academically oriented foundation bureaucrats, whom some in foundation circles jokingly referred to as "philanthropoids" (G. E. Vincent, Office diary 1/10/28), and the succession of anthropologists who advised them. No doubt their general ideological orientation was not radically antithetical to those of the Rockefeller trustees, and their receptivity to specific anthropological initiatives was not unaffected by more general economic, social, and political considerations. But it was perhaps even more strongly influenced by their vision of social science, and by their response to the play of influences endogenous to the discipline itself, in the context of certain Rockefeller administrative policies (the reliance on local academic institutions, on block grants, on surveys of current work, and on expert scientific advisors).

It was in such a context that a number of "psychobiological" and even racialist initiatives became vehicles for cultural determinist research. While the control of the Boasians was briefly threatened in the immediate postwar period, they still represented, both intellectually and institutionally, the dominant force within American anthropology. Given the Rockefeller policy of relying on professionally acknowledged disciplinary expertise, the shift away from racialist psychobiology, mediated through the role of Clark Wissler as expert advisor, followed from the fact of Boasian disciplinary dominance—even though Boas himself was never especially favored by Rockefeller philanthropoids, who were inclined to look instead to younger anthropologists with a more present-oriented, functionalist approach. This is not to suggest that Rockefeller support could not be an important selective factor in a situation where there was a more balanced competition of disciplinary trends. Ruml's and Day's "prejudice" in favor of Malinowski surely contributed to his rise at the expense of the diffusionists at University College. Neither is it to suggest that an antipsychobiological thrust is to be found in all areas of Rockefeller activity. Quite the contrary, the present analysis assumes that in areas where the internal intellectual thrust of a discipline was less clearly marked, or the role of an established scientific advisor exerted a strongly countervailing force, then the outcome might be different—as the continued support of Yerkes, and the reassertion of psychobiological interests in the natural science division under Warren Weaver suggests (Kohler 1991). Nevertheless, it seems that within the social sciences the dominant thrust ran generally parallel to that in cultural anthropology, away from hereditarian viewpoints toward cultural determinism. It is of course possible to interpret the shift from instinct to culture itself in terms of changing ideologies of domination (Haraway 1977), but insofar as such arguments imply a conscious shaping of research agendas in the interest of some group outside the discipline, they do not seem to be substantiated by the present chronicle of Rockefeller anthropology.

The issue of the "colonial formation" of anthropology has been posed most sharply in relation to the Rockefeller role in supporting British social anthropology in Africa (Asad 1973). Again, it seems quite likely that the philanthropoids and anthropologists whose interaction largely determined research priorities shared a general orientation on issues of colonial policy. Whatever their personal feelings about its legitimacy or desirability, they accepted the post-Versailles colonial system as historically "given." The danger was that unenlightened exploitation, without regard to the welfare of the native populations, might lead to "racial wars." In this context, colonial anthropological research was indeed promoted as a means of making the system "work" more effectively, from the point of view of capitalist development and administrative efficiency, as well as native welfare: "The anthropologist's task is to convince the government officials and capitalists themselves that their long-run interests are in harmony with the findings of anthropology" (BM, in Van Sickle diary 11/29/29).

The present materials do not cast direct light on the extent to which Rockefeller Trustees might have been influenced by ulterior corporate or class interest in reacting to such appeals. But they do give a hint of ulterior disciplinary self-interest among the anthropologists making them. As Malinowski noted privately in 1931, anthropology was the least able of all academic disciplines to support itself. Academic anthropologists spent their time breeding young anthropologists "for the sake of anthropology and so that they in turn may breed new anthropologists." Yet there was "no practical basis to our science, and there are no funds forthcoming to remunerate it for what it produces." The Rockefeller money of the last several years had made fieldwork possible; what must now be done was to capitalize on this "almost surreptitious deviation" and establish the discipline as a special branch of Rockefeller endowment (MPL: draft memo, "Res. Needs in Soc. & Cult. Anth."). Similarly, the proposed research centers of Radcliffe-Brown's vanishing cultures scheme were intended to provide "assurance that there will be openings" for the students who were to be trained for fieldwork research (RB, "Memo. on Anth. Res.").

Sustaining such a "surreptitious deviation" was not easy in a situation where colonial authorities were by no means wholly convinced of the utility of anthropological research, and often more than a little worried that it would somehow contribute to native unrest (cf. Kuklick 1978). In the fall of 1931, Oldham wrote to Malinowski suggesting that Paul Kirchoff, who had previously done research in Latin America under Boas, should be given an African Institute fellowship for fieldwork in Rhodesia, with a view to convincing the Colonial Office of the practical value of anthropology in relation to Rhodesian mining developments (MPL: JO/BM 11/19/31). Shortly before Kirchoff's planned departure, the Colonial Office suddenly refused him entrance to any British colony, letting it be known that he was suspected of being a Communist agitator (MPL: JO/BM 1/22/32, 2/16/32). Although Malinowski momentarily contemplated resignation from the African Institute rather than accept the Colonial Office's "bald veto" (MPL: BM/JO 2/5/32), he was rather quickly swayed by Oldham's argument that "the large interests of anthropology and African research" should not be sacrificed in a "forlorn" crusade (MPL: JO/BM 2/18/32). Convinced that the whole matter was a misunderstanding, and that Kirchoff was at most guilty of youthful indiscretion, Malinowski tried to send him to New Guinea, where he felt that even "the most intensive communistic doctrines" would present "no great danger" (MPL: BM/R. Firth 9/26/32). But this plan, too, was forestalled at the last minute by the Australian National Research Council on the basis of confidential information from British governmental officials (MPL: D. O. Masson/BM 9/26/32).

Although the actual substance of Kirchoff's research does not seem to have been at issue, and the Foundation, at Malinowski's urging, did give him a small grant to write up his earlier Latin American research, the constraining influence of this incident should not be minimized. At the time, the major participants concluded that in the future there must be a "very careful scrutiny of the past records and personality" of all candidates (T. B. Kittredge, Memo, talk with JO & BM 10/24/32); and while Malinowski seems to have retained a tolerant attitude toward youthful political "indiscretion," oral testimony from this period suggests that he was not alone in warning aspiring young anthropologists that they must choose between radical politics and scientific anthropology.[4]

To some extent, then, shared historical vision and disciplinary self-interest may have conspired to shape portions of the Rockefeller anthro-

4. The oral testimony includes interviews with several senior anthropologists. Letters in the Malinowski Papers indicate that Malinowski did not feel that Meyer Fortes's avowed radicalism was a bar to Rockefeller support (MPL: BM/JO 2/5/32). Within the Rockefeller records proper, the only political reference of this sort that I noted related to Radcliffe-Brown: reporting on a conversation about anthropological matters, Van Sickle (somewhat out of

pological agenda to the "needs" of the colonial system; and at least one incident of active constraint—which may well have had archetypal, "once-burned, twice-shy" implications—helped to discourage research (or rather, a researcher) the British Colonial Office felt threatening to it. But if it seems likely that the attempt to "sell" anthropology in terms of its colonial utility may have helped gain Rockefeller support, it was not the only factor, nor in the end an overriding one. During the period when the trustees accepted the view that human welfare could best be achieved by the advancement of knowledge, the interaction of philanthropoids and anthropologists won the discipline a place within the Rockefeller social science program, giving it brief recognition as a special field of concentration, and for a moment even offering the prospect of sustained long-run support. Once it had been dissociated from the charge of antiquarianism, its very exoticism enhanced its appeal: by the unique methodology of fieldwork investigation, it offered an otherwise inaccessible knowledge of the generic impulses underlying human behavior. Day, who felt that anthropology had a more "scientific" technique than sociology, was clearly won over by its promise of an esoteric social scientific wisdom ("Verbatim Notes, Princeton Conf." 11/29/32). So long as the foundation had a program "in the field of human behavior," he felt that there were "values in the comparative data in ethnology that cannot wisely be ignored" (ED/A. Gregg 12/19/34). By 1933, however, the trustees had begun to wonder about a social science program that spent more than 95 percent of its funds collecting facts and less than 5 percent determining "whether these facts could with any degree of effectiveness be applied to contemporary problems" (Rept. Comm. on Appraisal & Plan): "Is Day's social science program really getting anywhere? Is it too academic—too little related to practical needs?" (R. B. Fosdick/W. Stewart 7/10/34). When they then reversed (in the event, only temporarily) the priorities of the 1920s and turned to the "immediate problems of the today," anthropology was among the nonutilitarian programs that fell by the wayside. What had sold the discipline to philanthropoids like Day was not so much its alleged practical colonial utility as its promise of esoteric scientific knowledge; when the trustees decided that serious practical concerns must be paramount, anthropology lost its place on the Rockefeller agenda. Whether things would have happened differently if

immediate context) noted that "R-B thinks that our present capitalistic system bears within itself the germs of its own destruction" ("Conversations with A. R.-B." 9/7–8/31). There is evidence, however, that Foundation officials were concerned that Boas gave too much fieldwork money to women, who were felt unlikely to pursue professional careers (ED/FB 6/14/32; FB/ED 7/26/32); and that the candidacy of Godfrey Wilson was seen (in part) as a counterbalance to the high proportion of Jews and women among Malinowski's students (JVS "Training Fellows in Cult. Anth." 6/8/32).

the prior "colonial formation" of anthropology had been more conscious, more consistent, more systematic and more thoroughgoing is perhaps a moot point.[5]

Rockefeller Funding and Museum Anthropology

To question over-simple notions of the exogenous determination of research agendas in anthropology is not, however, to deny the impact of Rockefeller funding on the development of the discipline in the interwar period. To weigh this impact, it may help to consider the scale of Rockefeller involvement from a different point of view. For if their appropriations in anthropology seem relatively small from the perspective of overall Rockefeller philanthropic policy, they loom somewhat larger when one considers their impact on the history of a rather small disciplinary community. Because the history of the political economy of anthropology is a virtually untouched field, no figures are available on its overall funding at different points in time. It may help, however, to keep in mind the budgets of two fieldwork enterprises interwar anthropologists took as exemplars. The Bureau of American Ethnology, which British anthropologists sometimes looked to as a model of enlightened policy, had in its heyday a budget of between $30,000 and $40,000 a year, only a minor portion of which went for fieldwork expenses (Hinsley 1981:276). The Jesup North Pacific Expedition of the American Museum of Natural History, which the American Anthropological Association Research Committee used as benchmark, had a budget totalling $100,000 over about a dozen years (UCB: [JC]/ED, n.d.). In this context, five million dollars would indeed have been a very large anthropological pie, and the two-plus million that Rockefeller philanthropy did provide was welcome nourishment in a period when institutional belts were tight.

On the basis of ten recent expeditions to such places as Samoa, Manus, Dobu, and Tikopia, the Research Committee estimated the average cost of extended overseas fieldwork among still-functioning tribal cultures at $5,500; for tribes "on the point of extinction in North America from which information can be obtained only by questioning," $1,500 for a single summer's work would serve (UCB: [JC]/ED, n.d.). In using these figures to make a rough estimate of the total Rockefeller contribution to anthro-

5. Or, one might add, if the alleged utility had been more effectively demonstrated: reacting to one paper by a Foundation fellow who had worked in Assam—as characteristic of the work of "most anthropologists"—one Foundation official commented in 1937: "Somehow such work seems of only slight importance to colonial administration, or the practical problems, and the responsibilities for making the connections seem to rest on someone other than the anthropologist" (S. H. Walker/T. B. Kittredge 12/1/37).

pological fieldwork, one is hampered by the difficulty of weighing such factors as the allocation between subdisciplines, or between the two styles of fieldwork, or the proportion for general institutional expenses—which in Australia apparently included the embezzlement of £30,000 by administrative personnel (A. Gibson/RF, cable, 5/31/34). But even if one assumes that only a quarter of the total Rockefeller support went to fieldwork, the Foundation's anthropological grants supported the equivalent of one hundred summers of informant fieldwork among American Indians and eighty periods of extended fieldwork overseas—a figure not including anthropological fieldwork done under the general Rockefeller fellowship program, or funded indirectly through the Social Science Research Council. Nor does it reflect support for fieldwork through general institutional grants in the social sciences (such as the Institute of Human Relations at Yale), or through specific grants for other social science projects (such as the contribution Elton Mayo's program in industrial psychology made to Lloyd Warner's fieldwork in Newburyport, Massachusetts). Neither does it allow for the stimulus of the "matching" provision that was frequently attached to Rockefeller institutional grants in anthropology. Considering that the total academic anthropological community in the Anglo-American sphere at the end of the interwar period numbered somewhere around four hundred, as measured by doctorates in *all* subdisciplines, then the Rockefeller contribution looms very large indeed. One has only to glance at the biographical information in the *Register of Members* of the Association of Social Anthropologists of the Commonwealth, or at the final summary of the activities of the Laboratory of Anthropology in Santa Fe (GS 1982a), to realize that Rockefeller money played a major role in underwriting the fieldwork experience of a large majority of the anthropologists trained in the interwar period.

That money was not readily available from other sources. In the British sphere, there was a relatively small amount of research money available from the South African and several other colonial governments. In general, however, the British colonial establishment seems to have been swayed by arguments for the utility of anthropological research only to the extent that someone else was willing to pay for it. Until the late 1930s, as the British colonial reformer Lord Hailey observed with a certain patriotic regret, American money provided the main support for anthropological research in Africa (R. Brown 1973:184). Although certain other agencies (notably the Rhodes-Livingstone Institute) picked up some of the slack when the Rockefeller Foundation withdrew, it was only after World War II that the British government began to support research on a large scale. In the United States, the major alternative support came from the Carnegie Institution, which was heavily oriented to physical anthropology and archeology; such general ethnographic work as it sustained was an outgrowth of its interest in Mayan archeology (CIW *Yearbooks;* cf. Woodbury 1973:64; Reingold 1979).

In contrast, Rockefeller money supported ethnographic work on a much broader geographic scale, playing a major role in opening up two areas (Africa and Oceania) where the disintegrative impact of culture contact had not gone so far as in North America. To the extent that the intellectual movement of the discipline is a reflection of its empirical base, it seems likely that this sustained the more behavioral, functional, and holistic currents emerging in the 1920s and 30s (above, pp. 138–44). Insofar as that movement reflects an institutional dynamic, the Foundation's particular institutional commitments contributed to a similar end. Despite its antiquarian orientation in the humanities, the Rockefeller orientation in the social sciences, both in its psychobiological and its cultural determinist phase, was consistently behavioralist. And although in the case of anthropology the Foundation did make grants to specific departments, the more general policy was to work through interdisciplinary social scientific channels, all of which sustained those tendencies in anthropology that were moving away from the traditional historical orientations. The pattern of Rockefeller institutional support reflected this: the London School of Economics was supported at the expense of Elliot Smith's University College; Chicago, Harvard, and Yale got much more money than the more traditionally Boasian Berkeley and Columbia.

Although the prior institutional structure differed somewhat in the two countries, the general institutional impact may be illuminated by the American case, where, as we have seen, the funding of anthropological research was before World War I channelled largely to (or through) museum collections. Even the researches of the Bureau of American Ethnology were strongly conditioned by its relation to the U.S. National Museum; and every early major university department developed in direct relation to a museum, either within the university itself, or already existing in the same city. It was clearly expected, both by university administrators and anthropologists, that research would be sustained by this connection. As the names of major expeditions testify, money for anthropological research was frequently raised on an *ad hoc* basis from individual philanthropists, who—like the younger Rockefeller, in his personal philanthropy—tended to be more interested in archeology than in other anthropological subdisciplines. In this context, getting money for nonarcheological research was always a problem. As we have seen, this institutional framework reinforced a certain intellectual orientation: anthropology tended to be conceived of as a study of the human past as it was embodied in collectible physical objects, rather than as an observational study of human behavior in the present; its important relationships were to the biological sciences represented in museums of natural history, rather than to the social sciences.

In this context, the impact of the Rockefeller program was considerable. For the first time relatively large amounts of money became available to anthropology through channels that were primarily controlled, not by private philanthropists or museum-men oriented toward the collection of physical objects, but by men oriented to social scientific research, for whom the past as embodied in the object was no longer a privileged form of data, and for whom the university was in general the favored locus of research. True, at least one-third of total Rockefeller support to anthropology went to physical anthropological work, and archeology continued to get a share of many institutional allocations. But in the negotiation of competing interests and conflicting cross purposes, the anthropological object was no longer a common denominator of intellectual interest or a primary medium of exchange in the political economy of anthropological research. Despite their support of ethnographic research through the Bishop Museum, Foundation officials made it clear at several points that they were not interested in museum work of the traditional sort, but in the various factors affecting human behavior in the present (ED/J. Van Sickle 7/1/31). In the context of a general contraction of museum budgets in the Depression years, Rockefeller support thus encouraged an on-going intellectual reorientation within the discipline toward the other social sciences and a more behaviorally oriented field research. In the British sphere, the impact of Rockefeller financing was very much the same. The relative neglect of the museum-oriented Royal Anthropological Institute, the central role of the London School of Economics, which had no museum connections, and the general posture of Malinowski and Radcliffe-Brown all contributed to the weakening of the historical tradition, and the strengthening of social scientifically oriented academic research.

A further consequence was the weakening of the unity of subdisciplines within a general "anthropology." True, the traditional hybrid character of the discipline in the Anglo-American tradition remained strongly in evidence in the American Anthropological Association and the Royal Anthropological Institute. But the interwar period saw a considerable heightening of subdisciplinary specialization; there were fewer "general anthropologists"; interdisciplinary interests were increasingly likely to carry cultural or social anthropologists toward the social sciences rather than toward the other traditional anthropological subdisciplines. Furthermore, the balance of subdisciplinary relations within anthropology had changed. "Ethnology" — the subdiscipline in which the others had been presumed to find, at least in principle, a retrospective historical unity — was being transformed or displaced (below, pp. 352–56). In the British sphere, "social anthropology" (whose opposition to "ethnology" had been proclaimed by Radcliffe-Brown in 1923) had by the end of World War II established itself as a well-defined and institutionalized inquiry whose practitioners were in most contexts disinclined to march under a general anthropological banner. In the more pluralist institutional and theoretical atmosphere of the United States, there was no analogue to the Association of Social Anthropologists founded at Oxford in 1946 (GS 1984b). But although an historical "ethnology" remained a viable form of anthropological inquiry, its use as the name for the dominant anthropological subdiscipline was passing in favor of "cultural anthropology"—a category which, like its British analogue, was oriented toward the study of human behavior in the present. Its practitioners were, for the most part, interested in objects primarily as personal keepsakes of transcultural experience, brought back to decorate the walls of their homes, or to distinguish their offices from those of other social scientists down the hall.

It is of course impossible to weigh the independent contribution of Rockefeller activities to the transformation we have been describing, if only because the Rockefeller program was defined in interaction between Foundation officials and leading representatives of change within the discipline. But there can be no doubt that it played a critical role in a major disciplinary transformation. Significant numbers of anthropologists continued to be employed in museums, which continued to support important anthropological research; but the museum era of anthropology had come to an end—at least for the remainder of the century.

6

Maclay, Kubary, Malinowski

Archetypes from the Dreamtime of Anthropology

This essay dates from 1984, when my wife spent six weeks as an exchange scholar in the Soviet Union. Drawn in part by the chance to experience May Day in what had once been for me a distant sacred site, I accompanied her to Moscow for a ten-day visit. As it happened, we were able to watch marchers and floats gathering on the radial avenue outside our rather drab Academy of Sciences hotel, but the closest we got to Red Square on the first of May was the militia cordons at the bridge over the Moscow River, and the march itself we could see only on television. Several days later, I visited the Institute of Ethnography, where I met with its long-time head, Academician Yulian Bromley, who, through an interpreter, gave me an hour-long lecture on the history of the Institute and the role he had played in defining its mission (GS 1984d). As we parted, he presented me with a copy of an English-language edition of the ethnographic diaries of the man after whom, in 1947, the Institute had been renamed: Nikolai Miklouho-Maclay.

In reading Maclay's diaries, I had in mind those of an ethnographer much better known to anthropologists outside the Soviet Union: Bronislaw Malinowski, who at one point seemed to identify himself with Maclay, in contrast to Jan Kubary, another precursor in the Melanesian field. Along the way to the present essay there were several shorter explorations, including an initial draft focussing only on Maclay, and a slightly longer version, in which I added material on Kubary. But Malinowski was always the comparative reference point, and I began to think of the project as a triptych, in which three different ethnographic experiences within a single region over a half century might, by contrastive juxtaposition, suggest ways of envisioning certain broader developments in the history of anthropology. In the end, the triptych was fractured by the much fuller material available on Malinowski, and an evident break between his ethnographic and his academic years. But the contrastive structure remained, emplotted as a kind of dialectic—Maclay's utopian vision, Kubary's real-politikal complicity, Malinowski's academic-liberal middle way—which no doubt echoed my own history of political disenchantment.

Of the broader developments the comparison was meant to illuminate, the most important is the "colonial situation" of anthropology, which became a focus of disciplinary concern in the later 1960s, when many disaffected or critical anthropologists began to speak of a crisis of anthropology. Although the deeply rooted relationship of anthropology and colonialism has come to be more widely acknowledged, serious historical research into the variety of colonial situations faced by particular anthropologists at particular times in particular places has not been exhaustively pursued. The seventh volume of the *History of Anthropology* series was envisioned as a contribution to that project, with this piece providing a broader temporal background for a series of more highly focussed studies. Like several others in the present collection, it was written from an ambivalently ironic stance. Identifying in a general way with the ambiguously humanitarian academic tradition that Malinowski represents, it may nevertheless provide grist for more critical millers, intent on the reinvention or the reformation of anthropology.

Methodologically, it is quite far removed from the study of representative samples, rather than representative men, which constituted my doctoral dissertation. From the beginning, however, I have been strongly attracted to what I sometimes think of as "juicy bits": particular passages into which more meaning than the author perhaps intended is now compressed, which by explication and contextualization may be made powerfully illuminating. Several such passages from Malinowski play a focally important role in this essay, and may doubtless be squeezed for other meanings by others with different interpretive predilections—one hopes, however, with some sensitivity to the contexts in which the words were originally inscribed.

It might well be asked at this point how the category "myth" fits into such an argument. And, as a matter of fact, my use of that notion was questioned by colleagues in the Fishbein Workshop in the History of the Human Sciences at the University of Chicago, to which a penultimate version of this essay was presented. In its subsequently published version I inserted a long footnote (herewith incorporated with slight modification) in which I acknowledged that my usage was questionable, from at least three different points of view. From the perspective of a more systematic literary-historical myth analysis, my references to the Garden and the Fall may seem casual and undeveloped (cf. Frye 1957; Gould 1981; E. Smith 1973). From the perspective of the deconstructively inclined (of whom there were several in the Workshop), the implication that there might be a defensible distinction between "myth" and "history" seemed not only questionable in itself, but counter to the thrust of the essay, insofar as it tended, deconstructively, to reduce a certain version of the "history" of British social anthropology to the status of "myth." Finally (though they were not represented in the Workshop), I am well aware of a reaction to my work on the part of senior British social anthropologists, students of Malinowski, who at times have been inclined to see me as simply another deconstructionist doubter. Thus the late Edmund Leach, speaking on behalf of those "few surviving British anthropologists who knew Malinowski in the flesh"—for whom he was "a great hero"—associated me with those who view Malinowski as "a fraud, a man who preached the gospel of 'participant observation' but did not practice it" (Leach 1990:56).

Regarding the issue of systematicity: I waver between, on the one hand, feeling that a more capable analyst of myth, and perhaps even I myself, might develop the mythical parallels of the Garden and the Fall in a more thoroughgoing way, and, on the other hand, feeling that those parallels are better left as unsystematized resonances, for readers to augment if they are so inclined—on the grounds that it is as resonances that such ideas are present in the minds of anthropologists and echo throughout the history of anthropology. Regarding the myth/history distinction: while I am conscious of its epistemologically problematic status, I am committed to a notion of the historian's craft which assumes that a distinction between myth and history, or between more and less mythical views of history, is worth attempting in the practice of historiography—at the same time that one recognizes that much of what we deal with as historians is perhaps irreducibly "mythistorical" (cf. McNeill 1986). Regarding Malinowski's contribution: I would appeal (as, apparently unnoticed, I have done previously) to Malinowski's own notion of the empowering-charter function of myth (above, p. 59), which makes it possible to "get on with the work" of that highly problematic process of participant observation and to produce ethnographies that, although of varying quality, are in many instances at least as valuable and permanent a contribution to our knowledge and understanding of the variety of humankind as the efforts of those who would deconstruct them. Of these, surely among the most valuable and most permanently interesting are those of Malinowski.

There is a further question that was not raised by the members of the Workshop, perhaps because they were already aware of changes in my views on presentism and historicism, but which here merits comment: How in any case may the category myth be employed by an historian who makes such an issue of sensitivity to past contexts? In response, I would reiterate my suggestion that Malinowski, at least, seems to have had a sense of his own role in terms resonant of his own theory of the chartering function of myth. Similarly, one might argue, as the present essay suggests, that a long previous tradition of European primitivism was part of the cultural baggage that these ethnographers carried into the tropics, that they were aware of this tradition, and that Malinowski, at least, clearly saw aspects of his own career in relation to it—including some of its darker Kurtzian aspects.

But aside from the mythic consciousness of actors in the past moment itself, and of a tradition preceding and extending beyond that moment, there is the mythic aspect of modern anthropology, born in such past moments and out of that continuing tradition, enduring to the present—and on into the future. One might argue that Malinowski, who helped to create it, was not unaware of this third and most present-oriented strand of mythic sensibility. Be this as it may, it is obvious that the interpretive dynamic of this essay is driven by the assumption of its continuing power.

It might be argued that this assumption is largely a reflection of my own romantic involvment in the tradition of European primitivism and of my status as anthropologist manqué. Granting this as a possibility, I can only say that my experience of anthropology and anthropologists—past and present, full-fledged and fledgling—suggests that the mythic element has long been a diffusely powerful motivating factor in the more prosaic task of generating ethnographic knowledge, and that it still retains some power, even in an era when the nature and the future of an ethnographic anthropology are highly problematic. I can also imagine critics of a colonially situated anthropology insisting that what the myth of fieldwork empowers is a hegemonic tradition which in the postcolonial present must be transcended and that the role of the historian should be to expose its fraudulence and its function. Granting this as an alternative, I can only suggest that while my essay does acknowledge some of the negative and inhibiting aspects of the mythic sensibility of anthropology, it assumes also the legitimacy and the utility of an approach to history that is not driven by present critical purpose. Having said this, I leave it to readers to gain such illumination as they can from the present essay, with the caution that, although it figures prominently in this volume, myth is by no means the only interpretive theme I would apply to the history of anthropology.

One of the functions of history, by traditional accounts, is to demythologize—myth being taken in the negative sense of self-interestedly or naïvely fabulous or archetypal account of origins (cf. McNeill 1986). But as Malinowski long ago maintained (1926a), myth can also have a positively empowering cultural function; and from this perspective, the historian may be justified in treating it in a less dismissive fashion. Especially, perhaps, the historian of anthropology. Other disciplines, of course, have their empowering (and inhibiting) myths—but not so easily as does anthropology (cf. Halpern 1989; Bensaude-Vincent 1983). Counting responses to a questionnaire may have a certain mythic susceptibility; but to define the condition of humanity in the encounter with the exotic "other" at the boundaries of civilization is, in that bare statement, already a mythic activity.

Beneath, behind, beyond, above, and within the history of anthropology, there is a mythic realm in which the European anthropological encounter with "otherness" is enacted, again and again (cf., inter alia, Baudet 1965; Todorov 1982; Torgovnick 1990). A set of archetypal situations and experiences, residues of several thousand years of Western history—including the Garden of Eden, the Rousseauian natural state, and the Columbian first encounter—define a kind of anthropological "primal scene" in terms of which the experience of fieldwork is pre-experienced in imagination. Its myth, like any other, will vary with the teller, but every hearer will recognize the plot: the anthropologist venturing bravely across the sea or into the jungle to encounter an untouched people, there to be stripped of the defensive trappings of civilization and reborn in the study of a simpler culture, and returning with a grail of scientific knowledge and a vision of alternative cultural possibility. A myth of modernity, it does not tell so well in the postmodern world; but if we no longer (or never did) really believe, we do not easily give up the fantasy. The most sober positivists or the most ardent reinventors must recognize this mythic vision of anthropology, even as they seek to deny or to transcend it. Worldly wise and cynical professors glimpse it in aspiring graduate students and recall it in themselves; it is what makes anthropology exciting to the general public; it defines the image against which any "truer" history of the venture can be written. In a word, one might say that this mythic vision inspires the history of anthropology, both as enacted and recounted (Sontag 1966).

There are, of course, other mythic inspirations. Against the Garden may be posed the Fall; against Rousseau, Hobbes; against Columbus, Cortez. Like European dominance, anthropology has at times been inspired also by variations on the theme of fallen man—the uplifting of savages lapsed into idolatry and indolence, who must be taught to worship God and to earn their bread by the sweat of their brow (cf. Lovejoy & Boas 1935; Pagden 1982; E. Smith 1973). And it is not simply a matter of inspiration: both the softer and the harder primitivistic myths are enacted (interactively) in "real" historical settings, the most powerfully charged of which is now often (mythically?) encompassed in the phrase "the colonial situation" (Balandier 1951).

From the beginning of the modern fieldwork tradition, anthropology was characteristically pursued under an umbrella of European colonial power (cf. Asad 1973; LeClerc 1972). This fact was implicitly acknowledged in 1913 by William Rivers, at that time the leading spokesman for the new mode of "intensive study" in British anthropology. The "most favorable moment for ethnographical work," Rivers suggested, was from ten to thirty years after a people has been brought under "the mollifying influences of the official and the missionary"—long enough to ensure the "friendly reception and peaceful surroundings" that were "essential to such work," but "not long enough to have allowed any serious impairment of the native culture," or to have witnessed the passing of a generation who had participated in any "rites and practices" that might have "disappeared or suffered change" (1913:7). Although colonialism threatened to destroy (by transformation) the object of anthropological inquiry, it was at the same time a condition *sine qua non* of ethnographic fieldwork.

Rivers' pragmatic acknowledgment of the enabling aspect of colonialism stands in sharp contrast to the treatment of colonialism by others among the early cohorts of professionalizing anthropologists. This is not to say that colonialism itself was never acknowledged. Coming to anthropology in the early 1890s, Rivers' Cambridge colleague A. C. Haddon found the map of the world splotched with "the red paint of British aggression," whose victims would "be less than men if they did not rebel"; it was in this context that Haddon first envisioned an Imperial Bureau of Ethnology that would both soften the effects and reduce the cost of "maintaining our ascendance" (HP: manuscript on imperialism, c. 1891). Here, however, the enabling relationship moved in the other direction, from anthropology to colonialism. And in the ethnographic accounts that might presumably have served that enabling purpose, the colonial system was characteristically unmarked and invisible.

Preeminent among the generation of Haddon's and Rivers' students—though formally a student of neither—was, of course, Bronislaw Malinowski. He was the one who most self-consciously, systematically, and successfully applied Rivers' "General Account of Method" to what Haddon called "the intensive study of a restricted area," in order to carry out a "revolution in anthropology." That it was with his name that an emerging style of fieldwork was henceforth to be associated no doubt reflected the excellence of Malinowski's own ethnography, as well as his institutional and pedagogical role. But as the disillusion following the publication of his field diaries attests, it also reflected the more or less self-conscious mythicization by which, in a book full of mythic resonance, he had made himself the archetype of "the Ethnographer." For the opening chapter of *Argonauts of the Western Pacific* was not simply a methodological prescription; in the terms of Malinowski's later anthropological theory, it was a "mythic charter" for what was to become the central ritual of social anthropology. A motivating myth for "apprentice ethnographers," it reassured them that a difficult and even dangerous task was possible, that those who would follow in Malinowski's charismatic methodological footsteps could in fact "get the work done"—even to the point where it would become a matter of disciplinary routine (above, pp. 57–59).

Malinowski's epoch-marking fieldwork in the Trobriand Islands came within the optimal period Rivers had defined—a decade after a permanent government station, a decade and a half after the last internal fighting and an abortive attempt at violent resistance to colonial power, two decades after the Methodist Overseas Mission headquarters had been established at Losuia (Weiner 1976:33–34; Seligman 1910:664–65). Such facts, however, went unrecorded in *Argonauts,* where the methodological stage is set in terms of the classic anthropological myth ("imagine yourself suddenly set down . . . alone on a tropical beach close to a native village . . ."), and the European colonial presence is reduced to annoying archetype (the "neighboring white man, trader or missionary") from whom the ethnographic novice is urged quickly to absent himself (Malinowski 1922b:4; cf. Payne 1981; Thornton 1985). The present essay is, among other things, an attempt to contextualize that mythicizing erasure.

To do so, it will help to consider Malinowski's fieldwork in relation to that of prior ethnographic ventures in the western Pacific, in somewhat different colonial situations from his own. Two earlier ethnographers, Nikolai Miklouho-Maclay and Jan Kubary, are of special interest, because their names occur, somewhat cryptically, at a critical point in Malinowski's Trobriand diary, when he was explicitly contemplating problems of ethnographic method:

> Yesterday while walking I thought about the "preface" to my book: Jan Kubary as a concrete methodologist. Mikluho-Maclay as a new type. Marett's comparison: *early ethnographers as prospectors.* (1967:155)

Posed here against some undefined "new type," the "concrete method" was Rivers' special contribution to ethnographic methodology, and Malinowski had begun his Melanesian fieldwork under Rivers' ethnographic aegis. But as he elsewhere indicated, Malinowski sought not just to emulate Rivers but to transcend him: "Rivers is the Rider Haggard of anthropology; I shall be the Conrad" (R. Firth 1957:6). In this context, we are perhaps justified in combining these statements into an archetypal programmatic proportion: "as Mikluho-Maclay was to Kubary, I shall be to Rivers." No longer surveying like a mere ethnographic prospector, Malinowski, as he suggested elsewhere in his diary, would dig down below the surface of difference to the native's "essential deepest way of thinking" (1967:119).

In relating himself to Miklouho-Maclay and Kubary, Malinowski chose two ethnographers who shared with him a connection with partitioned Poland, and who, although working in other areas of the western Pacific, had both briefly visited the Trobriands. The ethnographic biographies of all three men resonate to issues that have been much in the forefront of professional concern in the twenty years since the publication of Malinowski's diaries sent shock waves of reluctant recognition throughout the anthropological world. In the context of a heightened awareness of the colonial situation of modern anthropology, we may read those biographies today with greater sensitivity to issues of reflexivity and responsibility, of ethics, and of power in the practice of ethnography. As we shall see, the implicit programmatic proportion attributed here to Malinowski bears only a rather tenuous symbolic reference to what may be known of the ethnographic biographies of the three men, in the context of their differing relationships to the differing colonial situations of their ethnography. But by placing the ethnographic careers and changing colonial situations of all three anthropologists in juxtaposition, we may perhaps nevertheless illuminate that murky realm in which myth and history interact, and in the process cast light on the emergence of modern anthropology, both as a specific historical phenomenon and a generalized experiential archetype.

Tamo Russ: Defender of Paradise

Nikolai Miklouho-Maclay was born in 1846 in a village in the Russian province of Novgorod, son of a petty nobleman and engineer with the Cossack surname Miklouho. Glossing it as Maclure, one source has suggested that the family descended from Scottish craftsmen brought to Russia by Peter the Great (Greenop 1944:20) – which may have encouraged young Maclay to adopt a more recognizably Scottish name (perhaps that of his grandmother) when he was twenty-one.[1] Left fatherless at ten, Maclay was much influenced by his widowed mother, who was of Polish origin and apparently had some connection to the revolutionary circle of Alexander Herzen (Tumarkin 1982a:4). During adolescence Maclay was also inspired by Nikolai Chernyshevsky, another leader of the democratic movement, and at fifteen he was arrested in a student demonstration and briefly jailed. In 1864, he was expelled from St. Petersburg University and forced to seek his education abroad.

After studying natural science and political economy at Heidelberg, Maclay migrated to Leipzig and to Jena, where he worked under the leading German Darwinist, the zoologist Ernst Haeckel. In 1867, he accompanied Haeckel on a field trip to the Canary Islands, after which he journeyed alone through North Africa on foot. During a subsequent marine zoological trip to Sicily and the Red Sea, Maclay became interested in the anthropological variety of the latter region (where, like such other nineteenth-century anthropological notables as Richard Burton and William Robertson Smith, he travelled in Arab dress).

Maclay's incipient anthropological interests were further stimulated after his return to Russia in 1868, when he came under the influence of Russia's leading scientist, Karl von Baer. World-renowned as zoologist and embryologist, Von Baer was also active as an ethnographer and physical anthropologist. An ardent monogenist, he had proposed the need for more detailed study of the relations of the Papuans to other races in order to confirm the unity of the human species against the arguments of Anglo-American polygenists (Tumarkin 1982b:10–11). Although Von Baer was anti-Darwinian, the racial affinities of the Papuans were also an issue to evolutionary writers, including Alfred Russel Wallace, whose account of *The Malay Archipelago* drew a sharp distinction between the Malayan and

1. The transliteration of Maclay's name has been quite various: Miclucho, Mikloucho, Miklouho, Mikluka, Miklukho; Maclay, Maklai, Maklay. I have used the spelling adopted by the Institute of Ethnography of the Soviet Academy of Sciences, which was renamed for Maclay in 1947. The most reliable biographical source is Webster 1984, which includes references to a number of secondary accounts. Although Soviet writers have had access to materials unavailable in the West, they emphasize the heroic egalitarian aspect of Maclay's persona, and minimize his authoritarian Kurtzian side, rendering him more comfortably "progressive" than perhaps he was (Tumarkin 1982a, 1982b, 1988; cf. Butinov 1971). As a result, the accounts of several critical episodes come across quite differently than in Webster's account (cf. Webster 1984:250–52; Tumarkin 1982b:38). A similar idealizing tendency may also be at work in postindependence New Guinea publications (Sentinella 1975; cf. Webster 1984:350).

Miklouho-Maclay (seated) with Ernst Haeckel, at Lanzarote, in the Canary Islands, on their marine zoological field trip of 1867. (From *Ernst Haeckel im Bilde: Ein physiognomische Studie zu seinem 80. Geburtstage, herausgegeben von Walther Haeckel mit einem Geleitwort von Wilhelm Gölsche* [Berlin, 1914], pl. 6)

the Papuan races. Wallace assumed that the latter were remnants of the aboriginal population of a subsided continent, which the British geologist Phillip Sclater had called Lemuria, and which Haeckel suggested was "the probable cradle of the human race" (Webster 1984:28, 30; GS 1987a:100). Maclay had already been planning to do zoological researches in the Pacific when he read Wallace's book in 1868, and he now thought of pursuing anthropological questions as well, hoping perhaps to find Lemurians still living in the interior of New Guinea. Having brought himself to the attention of the president of the Russian Geographical Society (the Grand Duke Konstantine, brother of the tsar), Maclay was able to obtain free transport to the Pacific on the naval corvette *Vitiaz*.

After a ten-month voyage around Cape Horn, Maclay was set ashore in September 1871 at Astrolabe Bay on the northern coast of New Guinea, still weak from illness he had suffered while at sea. He had brought with him two servants, a Swedish seaman named Will Olsen, and a Polynesian Maclay spoke of simply as "Boy," who he thought would somehow serve as his intermediary with the Papuan natives. Boy soon died from malaria, and Olsen proved a constant burden. Maclay thus found himself virtually alone among previously uncontacted and totally "untouched" groups of the sort whose racial characteristics he had planned to study—an ethnographic situation often imagined in archetype, but rarely achieved in practice.

For the next fifteen months, Maclay made his home in a cabin built for him by the corvette's crew before their departure. He had chosen a site ten minutes' walk from a nearby native village, for reasons that illuminate his ambivalent and ambiguous ethnographic situation: lacking the natives' language, he was unable to ask their permission to settle within the village; fearing that he would be annoyed by the noise if he did, he felt more comfortable remaining outside. This mixture of panhuman tact and strongly asserted personal identity defined for Maclay a position in the Papuan world that was at once intimate and distanced. Although the salvos fired in honor of the grand duke's birthday and the swaths cut through the jungle by the corvette's crew set Maclay from the beginning somewhat above the natural course of Papuan existence, his considered policy was to bring himself close down to, though still above it—simultaneously asserting a common humanity and a powerfully alien identity. Going unarmed into the village, he faced arrows shot to see if he would flinch. His response was to put down his mat in the village square and go to sleep—using a natural human function to assert a more than natural strength of will (Tumarkin 1982b:82–83). From that time on, Maclay let the natives' curiosity lead them to his cabin, confident that in a moment of crisis the shotgun and revolver he kept hidden from them would set a "big crowd of natives fleeing" (126). Following a "policy of patience and tact" (112), he regularly blew a whistle before coming into the village of Gorendu, so that the men would know he did not come to spy and the women would have time to hide—until one day the women were all introduced to him, in order that henceforth life could go on normally in his presence.

At points, Maclay spoke of himself as "becoming a bit of a Papuan" (Tumarkin 1982b:187)—as when on impulse he caught a large crab and ate it raw. By disposition, however, he seems to have savored solitude, and when he was drawn forth from it, he preferred to be "a mere spectator and not an active participant in whatever is going on" (173). He never gave up his boots and gaiters, or moved into the village, and in several instances his considered policy clearly contributed to setting him apart from—and above—Papuan normality. To keep secret Boy's death—which would have belied the prevailing notion of the intruders' immortality—Maclay threw the weighted body into the sea at night, leaving the natives to believe that he had enabled Boy to fly to Russia, which in their minds soon became equated with the moon. Amazing them by burning alcohol and by the power of his "taboo" or shotgun, curing people who had been abandoned to death, refusing proffered sexual partners ("Maclay does not need women!" [225]), never allowing "any expression of familiarity" (388), he came to be "regarded as a really extraordinary being" (229). Rather than answer their direct question as to whether he himself could die—and unwilling to lie to them—Maclay offered his body for the natives to test; their unwillingness to do so became proof of his immortality (388). At once god and man, Maclay seems to have created for himself a remarkable position of trust and power, one which might well have been assumed to provide the basis for Malinowski's ethnography of a new type.

In retrospect, however, the anthropological purposes to which Maclay employed his unusually privileged position seem remarkably time-bound. They are suggested by a grisly operation he coolly performed on the still-warm body of Boy. Maclay—who at one point planned a five-volume work on the comparative anatomy of the brain—wanted "to preserve Boy's brain for research purposes." But lacking a "vessel large enough to contain a whole brain," and fearful that the natives might arrive at any moment, he removed only the speech apparatus—thus fulfilling a promise to his German professor of comparative anatomy, Carl Gegenbaur, to bring back "the larynx of a dark man with all the muscles" (Tumarkin 1982b:129). As a student of Haeckel and disciple of Von Baer, Maclay had research interests that were "anthropological" in the nineteenth-century continental European sense: it was, at least in the first instance, the physical characteristics of man that preoccupied him, and "ethnological" questions were to him those of "racial" relationship (below, p. 350).

While Maclay seems to have avoided taking positions on many of the major anthropological issues of the day (Webster 1984:343), his sympathies were in general monogenist. He rejected the notion that living races were closer anatomically to animal forebears; his purpose in collecting so many samples of Papuan hair was to show that it "grows in precisely the same way as ours, . . . and not in groups or tufts as one reads in anthropology textbooks" (Tumarkin 1982b:142). On the other hand, his dissections of executed criminals in Australia suggested that there were "peculiarities of by no means trifling import" in the brains of different races, and he was inclined to attribute his own inability to pronounce certain sounds in New Guinea languages to a racial difference in vocal organs (Webster 1984:240, 343, 350; cf. Sentinella 1975:291). But if Maclay could be naïvely ethnocentric in evaluating Papuan physical beauty, and took for granted an evolutionary view of their social development, he also felt that, at bottom, Papuan natives were just like Europeans—practical, hardworking, ready to "adopt and use European instruments at the first opportunity" (Tumarkin 1982b:214).

Maclay spent a great deal of time sketching—physical types, costumes, material culture, local settings. Indeed, he seems in general to have stayed at the surface of things, and to have expressed relatively little interest in penetrating the subtleties of religious life and social organization. While this clearly reflected the limitations of the anthropological perspective he brought from Europe, Maclay's focus on what was easily described from the outside may also have expressed a sensitivity to the extremely problematic character of any attempt to get beneath the surface. Although his background, personal history, and surviving correspondence indicate a facile multilingualism like that of Malinowski—who is said to have made his way in eleven languages—Maclay's diaries suggest also an acute sense of the difficulties of language learning in a pristine contact situation, in which there was not a single bilingual intermediary. After two months, he still did not know the Papuan words for "yes" and "no": "Anything that cannot be pointed at remains unknown, unless I learn the word by chance" (Tumarkin 1982b:117). It was only after five months that he finally figured out the word for "bad" (by giving the natives all sorts of salty, bitter, and sour substances to taste), and then by opposition, the word for "good"—having been for some time misled by the word for "tobacco" (150–51). Even then, it turned out that the word he had learned was specific to food preparation (491). Had he carried with him the "genealogical method," on which Rivers' "concrete method" was founded, Maclay could scarcely have made use of it, since he did not learn the words for "father" and "mother" until the eighth month (219).

Maclay's focus on readily observable surface phenomena can thus be interpreted not only in terms of conceptual predisposition but also as a reflection of methodological restraint. It was only toward the end of his first visit, when after fifteen months he had won the natives' "complete trust" and had a "pretty good command" of one dialect, that he felt that "he had cleared the ground" for the many years of research it would take to "get a real knowledge of these men's way of thinking and way of life" (Tumarkin 1982b:271). Even then, in promising that he would return, he could not tell them that it would be "many months," because he had not yet learned a word for "many" (278).

In December 1872, Maclay—whose death had been rumored at home—boarded a Russian clipper that had been sent in search of him by the Grand Duke Konstantine. When he took a group of natives on to the ship "for a bit of sightseeing," they were so frightened by the many Europeans and the "various devices whose purpose they did not know" that their clinging to him made movement impossible; wrapping a rope around his middle, he left the ends free for them to hold as he walked about the deck (Tumarkin 1982b:277). At this time, northern New Guinea had barely been touched by the expansive processes of European colonialism, and it was unfamiliarity rather than prior experience of contact that terrified them. But forces were already in operation that were to engulf Maclay's New Guinea Garden in the larger colonial situation of the southwestern Pacific. The first permanent mission had just been established on Murray Island in the Torres Straits, and in a few months Captain John Moresby was to discover the harbor which became Port Moresby (Biskup et al. 1968:20, 29). Australian interest in New Guinea had already been stirred by rumors of gold, which had led to the formation of a short-lived New Guinea Prospecting Association (Joyce 1971a:9). By this time the labor traffic to supply the plantations of Queensland, Samoa, and Fiji had already begun, and "blackbirders" were regular intruders in the region (Scarr 1969; Docker 1970). The consequences of such intrusions into his primal ethnographic scene were soon to distract Maclay from any systematic social anthropological goals he might have entertained.

After a circuitous trip—during which he made a three-day anthropometric study of Philippine Negritos he thought might be related to the Papuans—Maclay disembarked in Java, where he spent seven months as the guest of the governor-general of the Dutch East Indies, recuperating from the debilitation of his New Guinea experience. Early in 1874, he was off again, this time to the same southwestern Papuan coastal area Alfred Russel Wallace had refrained from visiting two decades before, because the natives were rumored to be "bloodthirsty" (Sentinella 1975:226). What Maclay found during two months in the area were groups of Papuans similar to those he knew already. Concluding that their differences in nasal structure were of no significance, he suggested that it was only "anthropologists who have never left Europe and divide the human race into races from their comfortable armchairs" who regarded the nose as a "characteristic feature" (Tumarkin 1982b:322). The "wretched" nomadic life led by these groups had been forced upon them by the recurrent raiding of Malay slave traders; their "treachery" toward strangers—which he himself on one occasion narrowly escaped—was a perfectly understandable human response.

This experience with a Papuan population suffering from culture contact seems to have heightened Maclay's awareness of the external political and social forces impinging on untouched Papuan life—which more and more took on an aura of Noble Savage innocence. But in the case of these already contaminated Papuans, his response was to suggest a more active European intervention. If his friend the Dutch governor would not agree to found a "military settlement" sufficiently strong "to enforce law and order," Maclay was willing himself to return "with a few dozen Javanese soldiers and one gunboat," provided he was given "complete independence of action, including the right to decide matters of life and death regarding my subordinates and the natives" (Tumarkin 1982b:442, 445).

When his offer was refused, Maclay undertook instead two difficult expeditions in the Malay Peninsula, measuring the heads of mountain Negrito aboriginals he thought might be related to the Philippine and Papuan groups he had previously studied, as well as the local representatives of those Malay pirates who had ravaged the Papuan coast. Ironically, it was in relation to the latter that, according to one source, he now adopted the policy of principled silence which, in the context of a developing activist commitment, was drastically to limit his published ethnographic output. Aware that the English were trying to extend their influence north from Singapore, and having enjoyed the hospitality of Malay rajahs only after assuring them he was "not an Englishman," Maclay felt it would be dishonorable to "communicate any information under the guise of benefit to science"—the Malays who trusted him would rightly have called "such behaviour espionage" (Sentinella 1975:231; cf. Webster 1984:368, n. 167).

When Maclay returned to Singapore late in 1875 from his second expedition into Malaya, the newspapers were debating the problem of British annexation of the eastern half of New Guinea, which Australians were pressuring the London government to do (Jacobs 1951b; Legge 1956:7–18). Determined to do what he could to forestall "the *terribly pernicious* consequences for the black population of their encounter with European colonisation" (Tumarkin 1982b:25), Maclay decided the time had come to keep his promise to return to the northeastern Papuan coast to which he had given his name. This time, however, he would come "*not just* as naturalist, but also as the *'protector'* of my black friends" (447). Once there, he intended to proclaim the independence of the "Papuan Union of the Maclay Coast"; if the attempt should prove abortive, at least his scientific studies would partly "compensate" him (26).

In February 1876, Maclay began his return trip to Astrolabe Bay aboard a vessel captained by the notorious David O'Keefe, a flamboyantly aggressive American trader who was later to style himself Emperor of Yap. While at Yap, Maclay made ethnographic notes on a hierarchical society for which he had a very limited empathy; he had even less for the natives of Kubary's Palau, whom he saw as corrupted by a long experience of European trade. Imagining them as once Noble Savages among whom the first white men walked "as gods," he dismissed their present warfare as "all ruses, deceptions and ambushes." After moving from the trade center of Korror to the larger island with which it was often at war, Maclay seems completely to have misunderstood the transferral of allegiances involved when he acquired two parcels of land on which he thought he might someday settle. But he willingly accepted another gift offered "to bind the white man's loyalty": the twelve-year-old niece of a native dignitary, who went on with him to Astrolabe Bay—but as one of three native servants, rather than as "temporary wife" (Webster 1984:180–85, 191).

Maclay's second sojourn in Astrolabe Bay (June 1876–November 1877) is less well documented, and it has been suggested that his journal entries were "short and fragmentary precisely for the reason that he did not want to facilitate . . . the 'appropriation' of this part of New Guinea by foreign invaders" (Tumarkin 1982b:29). Despite his status as *Tamo-boro-boro* (big, big man) his scientific work apparently did not go well: "secretiveness and superstitious fear"—along with continuing linguistic difficulties—forced him to become "a spy for science." Employing "stratagems to witness ceremonies 'accidentally,'" he learned "next to nothing" of "the natives' thoughts and beliefs" (Webster 1984:188, 194). Several attempted explorations into the interior and along the coast, undertaken in part to enlarge the area of his political influence, revealed instead the limits of his authority. Relying on his reputation for magical power, he never really did understand the local disputes in which he became entangled. He did, however, become aware that his own activities (including the illicit trade his servants carried on in goods stolen from his stock) were doing quite a bit to modify the pristine contact situation, and by the time he left in November 1877 he had decided that he would do "positively nothing, either directly or indirectly, to facilitate the establishment of communication between whites and Papuans" (Tumarkin 1982b:29). Before his departure, he called together representatives of nearby villages to warn them against other white men, with hair and clothing like his own, who might come in ships and take them into slavery—and gave the Papuans signs by which they could tell potential "friends from foes" (30).

Maclay's subsequent travels in New Guinea were all motivated as much by political as by scientific concerns. Settling in Australia, he was befriended by several prominent Scotsmen with scientific interests (one of whose daughters he was subsequently to marry). In March 1879 he undertook a ten-month voyage through the New Hebrides and the Solomons, combining scientific work with the attempt to gather more first-hand information on the "blackbirding" trade. After stopping briefly in the Trobriands on his return, he sailed along the southeastern coast of New Guinea on the London Missionary Society steamer, measuring heads and striking up an acquaintance with the missionary James Chalmers, who was to be an ally in the defense of native land rights and the opposition to labor recruitment.

By this time Maclay's exploits had given him a considerable public notoriety. Referred to as "Baron" in the Australian and European press, he tacitly accepted the title, and as "Baron de Maclay" spoke out publicly in defense of Papuan interests. He sent several open letters to Sir Arthur Gordon, the British High Commissioner of the Western Pacific, calling on the imperial government to "recognize the right of the aborigines to their own soil." Arguing on the basis of his own researches that every single piece of land on the Maclay Coast was already "entirely owned by different communities engaged in tilling the soil," he insisted that the natives had no understanding of "parting with their land *absolutely*" (Tumarkin 1982b:449, 453; Webster 1984:221).

When the killing of ten Polynesian teachers of the London Missionary Society at a village in southeastern New Guinea provoked a punitive expedition in 1881, Maclay wrote to the British naval commander of the southwestern Pacific, Commodore John Wilson, suggesting that such "massacres" were to be understood as a response to the blackbirding trade. In this case, however, his friend Chalmers was inclined to blame "sheer blood lust"; and although both he and Maclay were taken along as mediators, the outcome was a shooting affray in which, quite by chance, the village chief was killed (Webster 1984:250–52; cf. Tumarkin 1982b:38).

Later that year, however, Maclay wrote an "open, but very confidential" letter to Commodore Wilson attempting to enlist his support for a more ambitious plan for the controlled acculturation of the Maclay Coast. Politically, it involved the formation of a "Great Council," with Maclay himself as foreign minister and general advisor, in order to bring the Papuans gradually to a "higher and more general stage of purely native self-government" extending over a large area. Economically, Maclay proposed the establishment of plantations in which the natives would be employed at "reasonable remuneration and under fair treatment." After "having been for some time under the direction of competent overseers," they would "gradually acquire habits of greater industry" and "become possessed of sufficient knowledge to work for themselves." To raise the necessary capital of £15,000, Maclay hoped to obtain the cooperation of "some philanthropically-minded capitalists." On this basis, New Guinea might provide raw materials to Australia, receive manufactured goods in return, and perhaps eventually itself solicit Great Britain to set up a protectorate (Tumarkin 1982b:455–60).

Although Wilson and Gordon were personally sympathetic, Maclay's paternalistic dream of Papuan self-government within the British "empire of free trade" was quickly to be overwhelmed by the cresting wave of European colonial expansion, which in the middle 1880s tumbled over the whole of eastern New Guinea. Ironically, Maclay's own efforts on behalf of independent Papuan development were in the process turned to the advantage of the contending imperial powers.

Early in 1882, Maclay returned to Russia, hoping to persuade the new tsar to support his "Maclay Coast Scheme." While in Europe, he had several portentous meetings. In England, he consulted with Gordon, Wilson, and William MacKinnon, one of the chief movers of British colonial expansion in East Africa, whom Wilson had suggested as a possible supporter. In France, Maclay met the Russian novelist Turgenev, from whom he is said to have sought information about the Communards, some of whom he had visited in 1879 when he inspected a prison in New Caledonia, and whom he apparently thought of as models for his utopian venture (Tumarkin 1982b:43). In Berlin, he met the German anthropologist Otto Finsch, who unbeknownst to Maclay was to become an active agent in the establishment of German colonial power on the Maclay Coast. In Russia, Maclay was presented to the tsar, and became involved himself in a secret Russian plan to establish a naval station in the southwestern Pacific—apparently in the vain hope that this might help to sustain his proposed Papuan Union (Sentinella 1975:307, 345; cf. Webster 1984:271). But when he returned to the southwestern Pacific early in 1883, all of these efforts either came to nought or backfired.

Stopping off in Batavia on his return to the Pacific, Maclay transferred—apparently by prearrangement—to a Russian naval ship he was to accompany on a survey of suitable sites for the proposed naval station. While he was in New Guinea for a brief last visit, in which he brought farm animals and various shoots and seeds for his proposed plantations, his transfer in Batavia became known in Australia. The resulting publicity precipitated an attempt by Queensland to annex New Guinea, in order to forestall the threat of a similar move by the Russians—who in the meantime had decided that the area was unsuitable for a naval station. Opposed by Maclay and Chalmers in various communications to London, the Queensland attempt was overruled by the British government.

In the fall of 1883, when reports circulated that a Scottish adventurer named MacIver planned to colonize the Maclay Coast, Maclay again fired off a telegram to Lord Derby: "Maclay Coast Natives claim political autonomy under European protectorate"—although he privately acknowledged that his efforts "resembled a request to the sharks not to be so voracious" (Tumarkin 1982b:478; Sentinella 1975:310). But despite London's having already intervened to forestall MacIver (Webster 1984:293–94), eastern New Guinea was soon to be partitioned between the British and the then-emerging German overseas empire. Ironically, Maclay himself helped to sate the sharks' voracity: the Germans justified their claim to the northern coast by the fact that Otto Finsch had set up a station on the Maclay Coast in the fall of 1884, after presenting himself to the natives, in their own language, as Maclay's friend (S. Firth 1983:22). By the end of that year, the eastern half of New Guinea had been divided between the British and the Germans, with the exploitation of Maclay's coast (now part of Kaiser Wilhelmsland) placed in the hands of the newly founded *Neu Guinea Kompagnie* (Jacobs 1951a, 1951b; Moses 1977).

Even after the fact, Maclay persisted in resisting annexation. A telegram he sent to Bismarck ("Maclay Coast natives reject German annexation") was used by the Iron Chancellor to rally anti-British and procolonial feeling in the Reichstag. Once this move had backfired, Maclay sent a final appeal to London: "Kindly inform the British Government that I maintain my right to the Maclay Coast" (quoted in Webster 1984:307, 309). In 1886, leaving his wife and two sons in Australia, he returned to Russia to seek the tsar's support to form a cooperative colonization venture of his own on an island off the Maclay Coast. During his stay, a great deal of public attention was given to the man who called himself "the white Papuan" and whom the press called "The King of the Papuans." Maclay in fact received applications from hundreds of prospective colonists, who dreamed of a freer life on a warm South Sea island. He had two audiences with the tsar, who appointed a special committee to examine Maclay's detailed "Draft Rules," which combined direct democracy with a great deal of power reserved to him as premier or "elder." Maclay, however, was very vague about just which island he had in mind, and in the end the proposal was rejected, in part because the tsar, embroiled in Balkan controversies, was unwilling to jeopardize relations with Bismarck (Webster 1984:314–25).

Depressed in spirit, long plagued by ill-health and now suddenly grown old, Maclay returned once more to Australia to take his family back to St. Petersburg. Once there, he devoted himself to getting his diaries and scientific manuscripts in order for publication, dictating when neuralgia and rheumatism made writing impossible. However, the task remained still incomplete at the time of his death in April 1888; it was not until 1923 that his diaries were first published, and not until the early 1950s that a collected edition of his scientific writings was published (Tumarkin 1982b:54).

By that time, Maclay had long since stepped outside of history into the realm of myth. His exploits—enhanced by his obvious talent for self-dramatization—made him something of a legend during his own lifetime. After meeting Maclay in Paris in 1882, the French historian Gabriel Monod described him as "the sincerest man of ideals" he had ever met—"a hero in the noblest and broadest sense of the word" (Webster 1984:274). To Tolstoy, Maclay's work was "epoch-making": he was "the first to prove indubitably by experience that man is the same everywhere" (Butinov 1971:27). From an early point, it was Maclay's experience, rather than his scientific contribution, that formed his heroic reputation. Though he published over a hundred scientific papers, they were mostly nonanthropological or physical anthropological or travel accounts, appearing in what for most readers were obscure publications; the larger anthropological work he planned was never completed. But if his scientific work quickly receded into historical obscurity, Maclay's life experience—compacted by mythical elision—resonated to archetypes old and new. There was the age-old European dream of the Noble Savage, realized in a Papuan Paradise. There was the late-nineteenth-century fantasy of the White Man "who became the ruler and god of a primitive people" (Webster 1984:348). And when faith in Europe's civilizing mission was shaken in the early twentieth century, there was the alternative image of "the lone Ethnographer," and the memory of the nineteenth-century humanist who had fought against slavery and imperialism—most prominently in the Soviet Union, where in 1947 the Institute of Ethnography of the Academy of Sciences was renamed after Miklouho-Maclay. Back in New Guinea, Maclay, promethian bearer of metal axes and knives, had entered local mythology as a vague precursory figure of what later anthropologists were to call the "Cargo Movement" (Lawrence 1964:63–68; cf. Tumarkin 1982b:55).

Paralleling these mythic transformations were a series of elisions that helped to simplify an ambiguous historical complexity. There was the executed Australian Aboriginal criminal whose brain had confirmed the existence of racial differences (and whose body Maclay pickled and sent to Rudolf Virchow in Berlin)—standing in striking contrast to the antiracialist monogenism for which Maclay was to be remembered (Webster 1984: 243). There was the Chinese sawyer in the Malayan jungle whom Maclay threatened to shoot for disobedience—a striking instance of the "servitude of others" that was an unmarked but essential ingredient both of Maclay's own freedom and of his utopian visions (157–61). To think of Maclay as Conrad's Kurtz, alone in the jungle, surrounded by adoring natives he had come to uplift, would be to mythicize in a different mode; Maclay's self-empowering impulses were never reduced to Kurtz's horrific exterminating scrawl. But not to hear the Kurtzian resonances in the life of this "nineteenth century scientific humanist" would be tone-deafness to historical complexity.

Herr Kubary: Lord God of Astrolabe Bay

When Maclay first arrived in New Guinea, Jan Stanislaus Kubary was already doing ethnographic work in the Palau Islands, a thousand miles to the northwest. Although Maclay became aware of Kubary in 1876, when he stopped at Palau on his second voyage to the Maclay Coast, the two men seem never to have met. But in the aftermath of Maclay's final departure for Europe a decade later, their contrapuntal careers were brought into direct relationship, when Kubary arrived on the Maclay Coast, there to play a radically different role in the relations of Papuans and Europeans.

Kubary was born in the same year as Maclay, in Warsaw, Poland. His Hungarian father, butler to an Italian opera producer, died when he was six; his mother, a native of Berlin, remarried the Polish owner of a small footwear factory. As a student in high school, Kubary joined the uprising against Russian rule in 1863; but when his group gathered in the forest with only two rifles, twenty scythes, and some wooden staves, he decided that "to wage war in this manner only invites a beating"—and escaped across the border into Germany. After staying for two months with an uncle in Berlin, he returned to Poland, this time joining the underground civil administration in Cracow. But when he proved unable to carry out an assignment to collect taxes for the rebel government, he "submitted his resignation and was eventually dismissed." Retreating again to Germany, Kubary "broke down morally," confessed his revolutionary activities to the Russian consulate in Dresden, and in return for a promise to serve the Russian government faithfully, was allowed to return to Warsaw. When he was arrested upon his return, he revealed "the entire organization of the insurgents" in Cracow, after which he was allowed to take up medical studies. Soon, however, he was ordered by the Russian chief of police to go to Paris to persuade an émigré friend to act as agent provocateur to entrap several prominent political refugees—a venture which he then reported to the insurgents, with the result that he was imprisoned by the Russians and marked for deportation to Siberia. However, thanks to the intervention of his mother's family in Germany—and another denunciation of his insurgent friends—he was finally allowed to return to his medical studies (Paszkowski 1969:43–44; cf. R. Mitchell 1971).

After four years of this double life, Kubary decided in 1868 to begin anew, and fled again to Berlin. When this time his uncle refused to aid him, he served as an apprentice in a stucco works, stayed for a time with a stonecutter in London, and then returned to Hamburg, the headquarters of the commercial and shipping firm of J. C. Godeffroy and Sons. Since the establishment of their first Pacific factor in Samoa in 1857, Godeffroy had become the dominant traders in central Polynesia, exchanging nails, tools, cotton prints, and other manufactures for copra, bêche-de-mer, and pearl shell; by the late 1860s they were expanding their influence northwestward to the Carolines (S. Firth 1973:5). The Godeffroy firm had scientific as well as commercial interests, and when young Kubary visited their museum of the South Seas, he was introduced by the curators to the company patriarch. Impressed by Kubary's multilingual intelligence, Godeffroy offered him a five-year contract to collect specimens in the Pacific (Paszkowski 1969:44; Spoehr 1963:70).

After a year of island-hopping across the Pacific, Kubary arrived in Palau (now Belau) in February 1871, when Maclay was in Rio de Janeiro on his way to New Guinea. Kubary landed on the island of Korror (now Oreor), the center of European influence since Captain Henry Wilson had initiated the modern contact era in 1783. From that time on Korror had taken advantage of its access to firearms to become the wealthiest and most powerful Palauan people, exercising a limited hegemony over the rest. In the early 1860s, an Englishman named Andrew Cheyne tried to establish a trading monopoly by drafting a "Constitution of Pellow" to be signed by the *ibedul* of Korror, who had begun to style himself by the English term "king." When Cheyne later tried to expand his influence by selling guns to Melekeok, the major rival of Korror, he was murdered—to which the British responded by sending military vessels to burn villages, collect indemnities, and execute the *ibedul* (Spoehr 1963:71–72; Parmentier 1987:47, 192–93).

In this context of intergroup rivalry, the then king of Korror tried to enforce on Kubary a position of privileged vassalage, making it difficult for him to travel (lest his trade goods fall into the hands of enemies) and giving him permission to do so only in return for a suitable payment. To maximize his ethnographic mobility, Kubary had "to fight the King with trickery," playing off the factional divisions within Korror, and on a larger scale, the hostilities between Korror and other Palauan groups. Far from standing above Palauan life like a god, Kubary had to struggle to win a degree of freedom of action within a complexly human network of socio-

Johann Kubary, with Belauans, in the early days of his research for J. C. Godeffroy and Sons. (From Karlheinz Graudenz with Hanns Michael Schindler, *Die deutsche Kolonien: Geschichte der deutschen Schutzgebiete in Wort, Bild und Karte* [Munich: Südwest Verlag, 1982], p. 268)

political obligations—which he found "a great hindrance" to his activities, "for customs and usage would not permit this and that and the other, and in turn permitted things that I did not want" (Kubary 1873:6).

Seven months after his arrival, Kubary took advantage of the overthrow of the king by an opposing faction to settle three miles away on the small volcanic island of Malakal, where Cheyne had been killed in 1866, and which the natives avoided "because they were afraid of his spirit." Having the advantage of linguistic intermediaries, Kubary was by this time sufficiently adept in the Palauan language to say farewell to the assembled chiefs of Korror in the following terms:

> . . . though I am not angry at Korror, your manners and customs have deeply offended me. Your behavior is false throughout, and our good nature you take for stupidity. You call us *Rupak* (chief) to our face, and *Tingeringer* (stupid, crazy) behind our backs. You pretend to be friends and cannot protect us from harm. You want my goods but are too lazy or too poor to give me anything for them. I see through you. At first I did not understand, but now I know your language and will make an end to your doings. I shall be hard as stone. The time of gifts is over. I shall give nothing free. Those who try to force themselves on me I shall treat like enemies. Powder and shot I have enough; war I do not fear. If you wish to treat me like Captain Cheyne whom you murdered, then come. I now forbid every inhabitant to land on Malakal unless he has something useful for me, and no canoe may

> approach safely at night. That part of Malakal where I live is foreign land, and all your laws and customs end there. But I wish to be just, and to him who is friendly to me I shall be friendly also. (1873:6–7)

Distributing three pounds of tobacco as a parting gift, Kubary sailed off to Malakal, where he hoped to escape further "exploitation by the chiefs" (Spoehr 1963:75).

Despite his withdrawal from Korror, Kubary had still to negotiate relations with the new king, whom he regarded as a puppet of the "reactionary" chiefs, and who in various ways tried to prevent him from travelling among the traditional enemies of Korror on Babeldaob, the largest island in the archipelago. His freedom of action was greatly increased after an influenza epidemic early in 1872, which carried off all but one of the chiefs who supported the new king. Claiming a greater power than any Palauan *kalit* (spirit), Kubary vowed publicly that this man would never die. He took him into his own house, nursed him through a violent fever, and by "bloodletting, morphine, and other means" brought him back to consciousness after ten days (Kubary 1873:12–13). As a result, Kubary became the king's personal physician and took on the care of other patients; when none of them died, his influence was greatly increased, and he was able to carry out his "long cherished plan of visiting the hostile party" on Babeldaob—although not without a watchful retinue.

The next three months in the Molegojok (now Melekeok) area were extremely fruitful. Establishing a "very friendly and intimate" relationship with the *reklai* (the counterpart of the Korror *ibedul*), Kubary was able to use his speaking knowledge of the language to "hear a great deal that has long since vanished from the memory of the degenerate inhabitants of Korror" (1873:28)—as well as much about contemporary Palauan life. And because the local natives were "unspoiled," he was given a great many specimens of material culture for which he could not bargain—since the Korror people had discouraged him from bringing along trade goods. Kubary felt "more at ease in the midst of these cannibals and poisoners"—as they had been described to him by the Korror people—than at any time before (30); he left "deeply touched" by the tears in the eyes of the *reklai* (43).

Back in Korror the chiefs tried to force Kubary to agree never to mention his stay among their enemies in his reports, and to destroy all the drawings he had made among them. He refused, however, placating them with two of his six European shirts and the promise to photograph them. On this basis, Kubary was able to work in peace for another year, despite the fact that his feelings toward the Korror people were extremely negative:

> My relations with the natives have remained unchanged. . . . The advantages which I once won from them I have maintained, and my personal safety is not endangered, even if the ship should delay in arriving for a long time. My stay is not precisely comfortable, according to our ideas, for no one would want to live alone in the midst of these savages, whose good behavior was achieved only after long struggles. The bond that unites me to the natives is fear and the feeling of their own weakness. Unfortunately, I did not find the natives of Korror to be as Wilson describes them in 1783. They were no "ornament of mankind" as far as I was concerned. They had become insolent by virtue of the murder of Cheyne, and perhaps also because of their treatment by greedy white speculators. (1873:47)

Despite the various resistances he had to overcome, Kubary was able to accomplish – in Korror as well as Molekojok – an ethnographic description of a sort very different than Maclay achieved in New Guinea. His contract for Godeffroy required him to spend much of his time studying the natural history of the area, and collecting geological, botanical, ornithological, and conchological specimens, as well as numerous items of material culture for their museum; and he also spent time photographing racial "types." But his ethnography was much less grounded in contemporary issues of racial anthropology and much more akin to modern social and cultural anthropology. However inconvenient it may have seemed at the time, Kubary's involvement in the factional and intervillage struggles of Palauan life gave him an excellent perspective on matters of political and social organization. He also devoted considerable attention to religious matters, and collected a good deal of mythic material – in contrast to Maclay, who had argued against the missionary Chalmers that mythology could "never have the same significance" for ethnological classification as the "observation of anatomical type" (Tumarkin 1982b:402). More than a century later, Kubary's work remains a crucial benchmark for any student of the area: at several dozen different points, a recent study of "myth, history and polity in Belau" refers to Kubary's observations, usually in agreement with him, and on a number of occasions, with extensive quotation (Parmentier 1987:61, 77, 80, 161, 163, 172–73, 175, 177, 201, inter alia).

If the bond that tied Kubary to the Palauans was founded on fear – as well as on trade goods and other forms of material and nonmaterial self-interest – it was nonetheless real. On a later trip back to Palau early in 1883, he was made an honorary chief and given "a splendid community house" as a "gesture of gratitude" for his earlier services during the influenza epidemic; and when a British warship appeared in the aftermath of an earlier punitive bombardment, he played a role in negotiating peace between the *ibedul* and the *reklai* (Paszkowski 1969:54–57; Hezel 1983: 218–80). However, his bond to the Palauans was not one that impelled

Kubary to adopt a systematic policy of native advocacy; on the contrary, in contrast to Maclay, Kubary was to become an aggressive participant in the processes of colonial exploitation.

Although he travelled for Godeffroy for six years after leaving Palau in 1873, Kubary's main base was the island of Ponape, where he married the part-Polynesian daughter of a Methodist missionary, and where he managed his own plantation. When a typhoon devastated Ponape in 1882, Kubary's life entered its long, last phase of decline. After working briefly for museums in Tokyo and Yokohama, he returned to Palau to collect for the Leiden Museum. In 1884, he island-hopped on one of the ships of the notorious trader O'Keefe, collecting for the Berlin Ethnographic Museum. Although he had become a British subject in 1875 during a visit to Australia, a decade later he became involved in German imperial ventures under circumstances that suggest the connivance of the German government. A German warship visiting Yap brought notice of the sudden termination of Kubary's contract with the Berlin Museum on the grounds of "fraternization with the natives and extravagance in relation to them" (Paszkowski 1969:57). Stranded without means of livelihood, Kubary was compelled to accept employment as interpreter and guide on the same warship, which was in the Pacific "for the specific purpose of planting the German flag on various islands of the Carolines." When this venture brought Germany and Spain to the brink of war, a settlement mediated by the pope recognized Spain's hitherto tenuous claim (Sentinella 1975:324; Hezel 1983). By that time, however, Kubary had settled in the territories acquired by Bismarck the previous year.

For a year and a half, Kubary was in charge of a plantation in New Britain belonging to the firm of Hernsheim. Early in 1887, however, his odyssey of decline brought him to the very area where the departing Maclay had warned the natives about men with hair and clothing like his own who might come to exploit them. Entering the employment of the *Neu Guinea Kompagnie* as manager of the station at Konstantinhafen on Astrolabe Bay, Kubary became the primary agent of an aggressive policy of land acquisition. Over the next two years, he is reported to have "bought" virtually the entire coast of Astrolabe Bay "in the most cavalier manner, judged even by the standards which the New Guinea Company set itself." Sailing along the coast noting river mouths and prominent features, Kubary would dispense a few trade goods and then post "a sheet of paper on a coconut palm to conclude the 'sale'"—with the full knowledge that "he had not concluded straightforward purchases of land" (Hempenstall 1987:167–68; S. Firth 1983:25–27, 83; Sack 1973:138–40).

Land, however, would not work itself, and the labor problem plagued the *Neu Guinea Kompagnie* throughout its short, often violent, and unprofitable history—at "a cost of human suffering and death on a scale unknown on the British side of the island" (S. Firth 1983:43; cf. 1972; Moses 1977). Because local native labor disappeared into the bush, the *Kompagnie* had to recruit natives from the islands, and eventually turned to Chinese coolies. Even before Kubary arrived, the importation of laborers had provoked charges of "slavery" by an anticolonialist deputy in the Reichstag: "it has been confirmed to me by the well-known explorer, Baron von Miclucho-Maclay, that on German plantations in New Guinea labourers are employed by force" (quoted in Bade 1977:330). Once on the scene, Kubary himself became involved in recruiting, bringing back seventy-one laborers from New Britain in January 1888—twenty-eight of whom must have died during their service, according to overall mortality figures of the period (Paszkowski 1969:59; S. Firth 1972:375).

In addition to his land acquisition and labor recruiting, Kubary was a plantation manager. His daughter later recalled his being in charge of "big plantations and hundreds of labourers," to whom he was "severe," but "just" (Paszkowski 1969:58); company reports at the time described "Herr Kubary" as "energetic" (Sack & Clark 1979:6). Glossed in terms of the *Kompagnie*'s disciplinary regulations, this would have implied the supervision of floggings, which in practice were often much more severe than the statutory limitation of ten strokes a week (S. Firth 1983:29). According to one account (Spoehr 1963:95), Kubary took to drink, and led "a harassed vagabond existence." Meanwhile the natives of Astrolabe Bay, experiencing the terrible fulfillment of Maclay's last warning, withdrew (too late) into sullen noncooperation, refusing to work on plantations, rejecting the efforts of missionaries, and organizing several abortive rebellions.

By 1892, Kubary's own health was broken. Advised by a doctor that he must return to Europe or "choose a grave in New Guinea," he took his wife and daughter with him to Germany. He was unable, however, to find employment, and had to sell his collections for a pittance; within months, he was back for another stint in Kaiser Wilhelmsland. After the "dissolution" of his contract in 1895, he negotiated with the Spanish authorities in Manila to reclaim his plantation on Ponape—only to discover when he arrived there the following summer that it had again been devastated, this time by a native revolt. Within a few weeks, he was found lying dead upon the grave of his only son—victim of assassination, heart attack, or suicide in a fit of depression (Spoehr 1963:97; Paszkowski 1969:62).

In 1898, a committee of scientists and men with colonial interests was formed in Berlin to raise money to erect a small monument on Ponape to "the ethnographer who penetrated with deep understanding into the mentality and customs of the native population" (Paszkowski 1969:64). Eight years later, when Kubary's grave was opened, it was empty—the body having apparently been removed by native friends to a sacred graveyard.

It is said that during his New Guinea years Kubary boasted he was "the Lord God of Astrolabe Bay" (Sentinella 1975:327, 329). Recalling his youthful period of moral breakdown and political duplicity—and the moral schizophrenia endemic in so many colonial situations—it is not surprising that he should eventually descend into a Kurtzian darkness unrelieved by utopian visions, or that, having witnessed there "the horror," he might in the end have taken his own life. What cuts across the grain of mythical anthropological expectations is that such a man could also have been a fine ethnographer.

Dr. Malinowski's Less-Civilized Colored Brethren: "Why Does a Boy Sign On?"

Bronislaw Malinowski was born in Cracow in 1884, the year in which eastern New Guinea was partitioned by the Germans and the British, and close to a century after Poland had been partitioned among the Germans, the Austrians, and the Russians. A decade had passed since Maclay and Kubary had accomplished their major ethnographic work; twenty years, since the revolutionary moment in which their careers had taken the turn that led toward exile, exoticism, and ethnography. If Malinowski's career took a similar turn, it had a different starting point, and went on to a very different conclusion. Beginning in the academic situation of Habsburg Poland, passing through the colonial situation of Australian New Guinea, it ended in the academic situation of late imperial London.[2]

Malinowski's father exemplified a characteristic career pattern in mid-nineteenth-century Galicia, where—in contrast to the other two occupied areas of Poland—the Austrians had relaxed their earlier Germanizing efforts, and a more liberal administrative policy facilitated a flowering of Polish culture. During the same period, social changes in the countryside impelled the scions of the petty nobility into urban intellectual occupations, often of relatively high status and influence. In this social process, Lucjan Malinowski, after taking a Ph.D. at Leipzig, became professor of Slavonic philology at the Jagiellonian University of Cracow, where a new, modernizing nationalism found an outlet in linguistic, historical, philo-

2. In contrast to such largely forgotten figures as Maclay and Kubary (for whom a few paragraphs may offer the illusion of biography), Malinowski occupies a very large space in the history of anthropology; the secondary literature and the primary sources are extensive. Although the treatment accorded him here considerably outweighs that of the two other figures, it is, in relation to the material available on Malinowski, highly selective—from the particular comparative interpretive perspective of the present essay (cf. above, pp. 40–57; GS 1986b; a recent listing of other relevant materials may be found in Ellen et al. 1988).

sophical, and scientific studies rather than in revolutionary political activity. A member of the "exclusive clan" of a great "university aristocracy," he was recognized as "the founder of Polish dialectology" (M. Brooks 1985). Although this "stern and distant" father died when his only son was fourteen, the younger Malinowski was a product of this academic intellectual milieu (Kubica 1988:89). The family lived in an apartment in the Academic Dormitory, which Malinowski's mother apparently had charge of after her husband's death. When ill-health forced her son's withdrawal from the King Jan Sobieski gymnasium, she supervised his education at home and during several recuperative trips to the Mediterranean, Northern Africa, and the Canary Islands. In 1902 he entered his late father's university, where he studied physics and philosophy.

Although there has been some debate as to the relative importance of the "second positivism" and "modernism" (or, in one version, "the second romanticism") in Malinowski's intellectual formation (Flis 1988; Jerschina 1988; Paluch 1981; Strenski 1982), there is no doubt that he was affected by both. His philosophy professors were influenced by Machian positivism, and his doctoral dissertation was a friendly critique of Mach's principle of "economy of thought" (1908). In contrast, his summers were spent at Zakopane in the Tatras mountains, where his circle of intimate friends included several aspiring artists, novelists, and philosophers — one of whom, Stanislaus ("Staś") Witkiewicz, was to become a major Polish cultural figure as a painter, dramatist, and writer (Gerould 1981). Theirs, however, was more a cultural than a political radicalism, oriented beyond the modernism of the Young Poland movement to that of turn-of-the-century Vienna and western Europe generally. When Malinowski broke with Staś in 1914, he marked the rupture by reference to two heroic icons in European modernism: "Nietszche breaking with Wagner" (1967:34). Malinowski had in fact been profoundly influenced by Nietszche, whose *Birth of Tragedy* was the subject of his first serious philosophical essay in 1904 (Thornton n.d.).

One of two manifestly "anthropological" references in Malinowski's doctoral dissertation was Nietzschean in a more disturbing sense. In arguing for the "objective" validity of scientific laws, Malinowski chose a practical criterion: "even if in the world only one normal man remained, and everyone else lost the ability to give judgments which can be regarded as normal and logical, then even this one man would not have to despair of the values, both material and scientific, of the achievements of mankind," since their "enormous practical importance" would "allow him to destroy his adversaries outright": "the relation of the white man to his less civilized colored brethren illustrates this sadly and emphatically" (1908:56–57). Knowledge and power — the laws of science and the Gatling gun — in the hands of a "normal" individual (male, white, European, and civilized) – thus confirmed and sustained each other, sadly but emphatically.

But this insistence on the objective validity of European science and civilization should not drown out the elegaic undertone of empathic identification. Malinowski may have been more positivist than Staś, but his several preadolescent experiences at the cultural margins of Europe had inspired also a romantic fascination with the culturally exotic. Given his father's interest in Slavic linguistics and folklore, and his own social position in a subjugated nation, which made him sharply aware of the variations of cultural belief and behavior in different social strata, it is not surprising that Malinowski should have turned from physics to anthropology – although he himself later attributed his "enslavement" to anthropology to the reading of Frazer's *Golden Bough* when ill-health enforced a respite from physics (1926a:94; Kubica 1988:95).

Upon completing his university studies in 1906, Malinowski spent two further years in the Canary Islands, where he found social relationships "extremely primitive and Spanish" – "a hundred years behind in respect of culture" (BM/S. Pawlicki 1/4/07, in Ellen et al. 1988:203). After returning to Poland to receive his doctoral degree, he followed in his father's footsteps to Leipzig, where he studied *Völkerpsychologie* with Wilhelm Wundt; he also attended the lectures of Karl Bücher, an economist who had published a book on the nature of work among civilized and savage peoples. In Leipzig he began an affair with a South African pianist, whom he followed to London in 1910, where he received fellowship support from the University of Cracow – a venture he justified in terms that Frazer might have appreciated: "for there [i.e., England], it seems to me, culture has reached its highest standard" (BM/S. Pawlicki 1/5/10, in Ellen et al. 1988:204; Wayne 1985:532).

In England, Malinowski studied sociology and anthropology at the London School of Economics, where formal instruction in ethnology had recently been initiated by members of the new fieldwork-oriented "Cambridge School." Malinowski, in short, entered anthropology when two interrelated transformative processes – academicization and ethnographicization – were already underway. His first several years were spent attending the seminars and lectures of Edward Westermarck and Charles Seligman, and in the British Museum researching a library monograph on the family among Australian Aborigines. But it was from the beginning hoped, if not expected, that he would do what Alfred Haddon called an "intensive study of a restricted area" – following in Seligman's recent footsteps to the Sudan, or among the peasants of the Polish countryside, or, as it was in fact to turn out, along the southern coast of New Guinea, where the Cambridge School had won its reputation with Haddon's Torres Straits Expedition in 1898, and to which Seligman had returned in 1904 (cf. above, p. 42; GS 1986b).

But if Malinowski's anthropological situation was from the beginning academic, it was also colonial. When the British Association for the Advancement of Science went to Australia in 1914 for one of its periodic meetings in a white settler colony, Malinowski got free passage as secretary to R. R. Marett, the recorder of the anthropological section (Mulvaney 1989). Although he carried with him the promise of scholarship support from the London School of Economics and a letter from its director commending him as an "investigator of exceptional promise and ability," the outbreak of war while he was at sea meant that he disembarked in Australia as a somewhat impecunious "enemy alien," whose personal funds back in Austrian Poland were no longer accessible to him. For the entire period of his fieldwork during the next four years, he was therefore dependent upon the officials in charge of Australian colonial affairs, not only for permission to enter those areas of New Guinea under Australian rule since 1906 or then being taken over from Germany, but also for financial support, and even for his own continued freedom of movement in Australia. This dependency was mediated by members of the Australian scientific community, one of whom intervened to save Malinowski from incarceration in a "Concentration Camp" for enemy aliens when he neglected to get a pass for a trip from Melbourne to Adelaide (Laracy 1976:265). Throughout his fieldwork years, Malinowski's status was the subject of continual negotiations with Atlee Hunt, the secretary of the Australian Department of External Affairs, and Hubert Murray, the lieutenant-governor of Papua from 1908 to 1940 (cf. Young 1984).

Between them, these two men represent a considerable portion of the historical experience that helped to define the colonial situation of Malinowski's ethnography. Educated for the law in Sydney, Hunt became secretary of the Federal League of Australasia in the late 1890s, and was an insider in the campaign for united commonwealth status within the British empire. As permanent head of the new federal Department of External Affairs, he was closely involved in the final legislative implementation of the "White Australia" policy. Hunt played an important role in drafting both the racialist Immigration Restriction Bill of 1901 and the Pacific Island Labourers' Act of 1902, which provided for the termination of the importation of "kanaka" laborers by 1904 and for the deportation of any who on December 31, 1906, still remained on Queensland plantations (Parnaby 1964:196–97; Willard 1923; London 1970). When it came to European immigrants into the Pacific Islands, however, Hunt was a consistent supporter of the economic interests of white settlers in Papua, of whom there were about twelve hundred in 1914 (Rowley 1958:287–91; Young 1984:3).

As such, Hunt was sometimes at odds with Murray, who as both lieutenant governor and chief justice of a neglected and underfunded area had a freer reign than the normal colonial governor (Mair 1948:11; Legge 1956: 227–28; West 1968:104–9). Son of a rich Australian pastoralist fallen on hard times, Murray was educated at Oxford (where his younger brother Gilbert became Regius Professor of Greek) and at the Inns of Court. Turning away from white settler society to assimilate the "effortless superiority" of the British ruling class (West 1970:x–xi), Murray was to be known as the archetype of a paternalistic proconsul. Benevolent but authoritarian, he saw "the native problem" as a matter of both "preserving the Papuan" and "raising him eventually to the highest civilisation of which he is capable" (1912:360).

In achieving these ends, Murray opposed the punitive raids associated with name of Sir William MacGregor, the first British administrator after the annexation in 1884, and with the early-twentieth-century German regime to the north—which had "a reputation for brutality, especially in the unctuous eyes of Papua's Australian administrators." But the protectionist policy of the "Murray System" was in many respects continuous with that of MacGregor, and much more actively interventionist in native life than the Germans, who were "not overly concerned with the indigenes' longterm welfare" (Wolfers 1972:88–89; Joyce 1971b:130). The Australian Papuan administration sought to preserve traditional village life (and to keep it rigidly segregated from that of the few European urban enclaves); but it also intervened to change it in substantial ways. Village constables, selected by the resident magistrates without regard for traditional leadership, were expected not only to keep the peace and to report cases of venereal disease but to help enforce regulations against keeping the dead inside the village, and against lying or using threatening language or engaging in sorcery—or, positively, requiring the cleaning of the village and the planting of coconuts. More active developmentalists may have seen Murray as "pampering" and "coddling" the natives, but he did not discourage Papuans from "signing on"—though the Native Labour Ordinance required local magistrates to supervise the process. The native "chewing betelnut in his village" might be "more picturesque" than the same native "working in a plantation," but it was "to the advantage of the Papuan to learn to work," and the "the best available schools" were the plantation and the mining field (J. Murray 1912:362; Rowley 1966).

Murray was not without a certain sophistication in both evolutionary and postevolutionary anthropology: he had read Tylor and Maine, and works by members of the Torres Straits Expedition; he was a friend of Seligman's, and later hired F. E. Williams as "government anthropologist." But he was dubious of diffusionist and later of functionalist theory, and attributed to anthropologists a preservationist bias against social change. And though he respected Malinowski's ability, he considered him a German and disliked him personally (West 1968:211–18). Hunt, in contrast, was part of the same gentlemanly community in Melbourne that included Baldwin Spencer and the other Australian scientific men who had hosted the British Association and were now proponents of Malinowski's research plans. Although Murray somewhat ungraciously supported Malinowski's initial request for funds, it was Hunt who became his advocate, writing letters of introduction, securing free travel passes, arranging grants, defending him against charges of pro-German sympathies, facilitating his entry into and helping to extend his stay in the areas of his ethnographic research (Young 1984:5; Laracy 1976).

"Taking leave of civilization," Malinowski arrived in Port Moresby on September 12, 1914 (1967:5). After making the appropriate visit to Government House, he was introduced to Ahuia Ova, an ardent Christian convert (and advocate of "pacifying") who had served so well as village constable that he became Central Court Interpreter for Murray—and who a decade previously had served also as Seligman's primary informant (1967:9; F. Williams 1939; Young 1984:8). For a month Malinowski did a kind of linguistic and ethnographic cramming, "borrowing" Ahuia for periods at the Central Court, and for more extended visits to his nearby village—save for a few days of enforced idleness when Ahuia was busy at the trial of a European who had "hung up a native for five hours" (1967:17; Seligman 1910).

On October 13, Malinowski set off on the steam launch *Wakefield*, and headed for the island of Mailu, two hundred miles down the southeastern coast, on which the London Missionary Society had maintained a station since 1894. His "travelling companions" included several stereotypical figures of the Melanesian colonial situation: a "brutal" German captain, who was "continually abusing and bullying the Papuans"; the local planter Alfred Greenaway, an English Quaker of working-class background, from whom Malinowski was to get quite useful ethnographic information; and Mailu's resident aristocratic vagabond, "Dirty Dick" De Moleyns, the drunkard son of a Protestant Irish lord. De Moleyns was a "rogue" but a "noble thoroughbred," who though "cultured" lived a "completely uncivilized" life in "extraordinary filth" in a "house without walls," where Malinowski was to find occasional "lubrication" and camaraderie in the weeks to come (1967:25, 37, 40). Also on the *Wakefield*—though unmentioned as a travelling companion—was Igua Pipi, fluent in the lingua franca Motu, who was to serve as chief factotum in Malinowski's retinue of several native "boys." Once on Mailu, Malinowski became the paying guest of the Reverend W. J. Saville, who with his wife had served on Mailu since

1900, and who in 1912 had published "A Grammar of the Mailu Language" in the *Journal of the Royal Anthropological Institute.* It was from Saville's mission house that each day during the next few weeks Malinowski "went to the village"—accompanied on the first occasion by a native policeman.

In retrospect it seems clear that Saville became the negative archetypal focal point of Malinowski's ambivalent feelings about the "civilizing" mission of colonialism. Initially quite dependent on him, Malinowski was repelled by Saville's "underhanded dealings" with the resident magistrate of the region and by his "persecution of people unfriendly to the mission." Had he been aware of Saville's ten commandments for dealing with natives ("5. Never *touch* a native, unless to shake hands or thrash him"; "7. Never let a native see you believe his word right away, he never speaks the truth"), Malinowski might have been even more "disgusted" than he was by Saville's attitude of white superiority (Young 1988:44). In the beginning, he was willing to make a slight allowance for the fact that Saville played cricket with the natives and treated them "with a fair amount of decency and liberality"—were he a German, "he would doubtless be downright loathsome." But over the few weeks Malinowski's "hatred for missionaries" rapidly increased, and he began to ponder "a really effective anti-mission campaign" (1967:16, 25, 31, 37):

> these people destroy the natives' joy in life; they destroy their psychological *raison d'être.* And what they give in return is completely beyond the savages. They struggle consistently and ruthlessly against everything old and create new needs, both material and moral. No question but that they do harm—I want to discuss this matter with Armit [the resident magistrate] and Murray. If possible also with the Royal Commission. (41)

With its empathy for a threatened "savage" life, its ethnocentric presumption about the limits of "savage" capacity, its implicitly functionalist preservationism, and its ultimate appeal to the good intentions of established colonial authority, the passage suggests a great deal about Malinowski's characteristic response to the colonial situation in which his anthropological orientation matured.

More immediately, Malinowski began to see Saville as a distinct impediment to effective ethnographic work—and as a kind of antimodel to the emerging archetype of "the Ethnographer" (cf. above, pp. 55–56; Payne 1981).[3] Still an ethnographic novice, Malinowski carried into the field the fourth edition of *Notes and Queries on Anthropology,* and his published

3. In 1922, Saville in fact attended Malinowski's lectures at the London School of Economics; in 1926, Malinowski wrote an introduction, which has been described as "sincerely complimentary and faintly patronizing," to Saville's *In Unknown New Guinea.* Without referring to it once, Saville's book closely paralleled the structure and content of Malinowski's mono-

report on Mailu reflected quite clearly its topically interrogative categories (Young 1988). But *Notes and Queries* also contained Rivers' "General Account of Method," in which a much more "Malinowskian" fieldwork style was clearly enunciated (1912), and there are various passages both in the published Mailu ethnography and in Malinowski's diary and correspondence which indicate that his own ethnographic experience was leading along the same path toward a more participatory observational style. Foreshadowed even before he left Port Moresby, this process was linked to his dissociation from Saville. After staying several nights in a *dubu*, or men's house, during his return from a tour of the southeastern coast of Papua in December, Malinowski arrived on Mailu resolved that he "must begin a new existence" (1967:49; cf. above, p. 43).

This resolve was facilitated by the fact that Saville was absent from the island for an extended period. In a move presaging his later call for anthropologists to come down from the verandah into the open air (1926a: 146–47), Malinowski left the Savilles' house and took up residence in a previously abandoned mission house, where Igua Pipi and several Mailu men were wont to gather in the evening, talking in Motu—which Malinowski had quickly mastered (though not, apparently, the Mailu language itself). On one occasion Malinowski was left alone for a week when he refused to pay the Mailu to let him come along on a trading expedition (1967:62)—not out of methodological principle (for he systematically used tobacco to purchase cooperation)—but because he thought the price exorbitant. He was able, however, to accompany a second briefer expedition, and on the whole regarded the weeks of Saville's absence as by far his most productive period.

Reflecting on it later, Malinowski suggested that work done "while living quite alone among the natives" was "incomparably more intensive than work done from white men's settlements, or even in any white man's company" (1915:109). Explaining why it was that he had been able to elicit information about sorcery but not about "eschatological beliefs," Malinowski suggested almost incidentally the general principle of a more participant ethnographic method: "direct questioning of the natives about a custom or belief never discloses their attitude of mind as thoroughly as the discussion of facts connected with the direct observation of a custom, or with a concrete occurrence, in which both parties are materially concerned"

graph—although it has been described as "more reliable" on "matters of language," and "richer in quotidian detail" (Young 1988:49). And just as Saville's attitude to natives seems to have "mellowed" somewhat, so also did Malinowski's toward missionaries: in the later 1920s, he cooperated with the missionary J. H. Oldham in a campaign to win research funds from the Rockefeller Foundation for the International African Institute (above, pp. 194–95; below, p. 261).

(275). Judging from other passages, it is evident that in practice that mutual concern was usually somewhat asymmetrical. In one instance it involved pretending to be worried about protecting himself from ghosts (273); quite often it involved payment in tobacco, sometimes offered as bribery to test the strength of native belief in a taboo (185); more generally, it simply involved "witnessing an occurrence or seeing a thing, and subsequently (or previously) discussing it with the natives" (109). But if it had in many respects been foreshadowed programmatically in Rivers' "General Account" (which in turn probably reflected Rivers' prior collaboration with A. M. Hocart), Malinowski's ethnographic experience in Mailu was an important stage in the emergence of the ethnographic style for which he was later to provide a kind of mythic charter (cf. above, pp. 51–57).

The experiential and contextual reality of Malinowski's evolving ethnographic situation was, however, somewhat imperfectly manifest in the ethnography he wrote after returning to Australia at the end of February 1915. One must turn to his Mailu diary to find mention of the Kurtzian moment when his "feelings toward the natives" were "decidedly tending to '*Exterminate the brutes,*'" or of "the many instances in which I acted unfairly and stupidly" (1967:69), or of the pleasure of "having a crowd of boys to serve you"—which in Igua Pipi's case involved massaging him while telling stories "about murders of white men, as well as his fears about what he would do if I died in that way!" (40, 73).

This attitudinal elision—quite understandable in terms of the "scientific" ethnography Malinowski sought to practice—is paralleled by the very limited glimpses Malinowski provided of his "colonial situation." That situation is hinted at in his vain attempt to "exert a certain pressure through the village constable" when six sticks of tobacco to each of the actors failed to get them to perform a ceremony a second time in full daylight so that he could photograph it (1915a:300). More positively, from a postcolonial perspective, it is evident in his deliberate omission of certain passages in a magical incantation, lest they fall into the hands of a white man "eager to put down superstitions" and "unscrupulous enough to divulge the charm among the natives"—thereby destroying its efficacy (282). At a more general methodological level, it is evident in his encouraging informants to "compare native social rules with the introduced European system of administering justice" in order to determine if there was "any counterpart in native ideas" to the European distinction between civil and criminal law (194).

As that passage suggests, however, Malinowski's ethnographic purpose—like that of most if not all of his anthropological contemporaries, including anti-evolutionary diffusionists like Franz Boas—was to get behind the circumstances of European contact, in order to reveal the essential ethnic characteristics of the particular native group. Such ethnicity was not presumed to be pristine, and by 1915 not all anthropologists would have generalized it as "savage"—as Malinowski continued to do, if only in the titles of his books, until 1930. But if it was not pristine, it was definitely prior. In Malinowski's case, what was initially at issue were the characteristics that would enable him to solve a particular "ethnological" problem: to clarify ethnic relationships in an area of New Guinea about which Seligman had felt "very little is known" (Seligman 1910:24; cf. Malinowski 1915a:106). If his published monograph contained little further reference to what in the introduction was called "the Mailu problem," it is nevertheless the case that it was those underlying precontact ethnic characteristics and relationships that he sought to reconstitute.

Insofar as Malinowski's description departs from the sequence of categories of *Notes and Queries,* it is largely in the total omission of physical anthropological data and the relegation of technology to incidental treatment—both of which might have followed from Rivers' emerging conception of the nature of "intensive study"—as well as in the extensive separate consideration of "Economics." It has been suggested that Malinowski's emphasis on "land tenure and native attitudes to 'work'" reflected the fact that these "were all contentious topics in the colonial situation of 1914"—issues sparking "heated arguments," "ideological obfuscations," and "blatant racial bigotry" in the "after-dinner conversation on the planters' and mission house verandahs" (Young 1988:34). Although most of the conversations mentioned in Malinowski's diary in fact relate to ethnographic topics, some of his comments on Saville do sustain this interpretation. At one point Malinowski specifically discussed "native labor" with the inspector of native affairs in Port Moresby, and he later described himself as "obsessed by the thought of some ethnological government post in N. G."—which might well have pushed him in the same direction (1967:13, 64).

But Malinowski's interest in economic problems is also quite consistent with the prior trajectory of his intellectual interests, which—while no doubt subject to ideological conditioning of a more general sort—had turned to economic issues well before he entered the Melanesian colonial situation, or even into anthropology. Analogically foreshadowed in his doctoral dissertation on "the economy of thought," such concerns would have been a central topic of his study under Bücher. They were explicitly the topic of one of his very first anthropological publications, in which (frequent citing Bücher) Malinowski treated the Australian Intichiuma ceremonies as a first step in the "training of man in economic activity" in a "civilized" style—that is, foresighted, planned, organized, regular, continuous, and repetitive (1912:107).

But however his interest was motivated, Malinowski did make a point of mentioning to Atlee Hunt his emphasis on "the economic and sociological aspects of native life" and (though his ethnography did not show it) on "the process of adaptation of the natives to their new conditions" (Young 1988:12). Hunt was duly impressed with the "class of investigation which he has been conducting," which by emphasizing "the mental attitudes and peculiar customs of the people" rather than "measurements of bodies, etc.," was one "likely to be of much use to the Government in our dealing with natives." He quickly saw to it that Malinowski was funded for a second round of fieldwork in New Guinea (Laracy 1976:265–66).

Although Seligman wanted him to go southeast to Rossel Island to examine another ethnic boundary region (cf. above, p. 44), Malinowski decided instead to go to the Mambare district on the northern coast of New Guinea, the site of an earlier gold rush, where a series of prophetic cults were now causing government concern (Young 1984:13). In the event, however, Malinowski never arrived at Mambare, and the site of his major fieldwork seems clearly to have been somewhat adventitiously determined, without apparent regard for its administrative relevance. On his way to Mambare in June 1915, Malinowski stopped in the Trobriands, in order "to get an idea of what is going on among them" and to seek the help of the medical officer and resident magistrate, R. L. Bellamy, in securing some museum specimens before Bellamy left to serve in the European war (Young 1984:15–17). Bellamy was an enthusiastically paternalistic administrator, who after ten years in the Trobriands had finally got the natives to line the paths of Kiriwina with 120,000 coconut trees by imposing stiff penalties for failure to do so. With a jail, a hospital, twelve white residents, and a thriving pearl fishery in its lagoon, Kiriwina (the largest Trobriand island) was one of the "best governed and most 'civilized' places" in the region (Young 1984:16; cf. Black 1957).

It was also a lushly idyllic tropical island, little touched by the labor trade (Austen 1945:57; Julius 1960:5), whose chiefly aristocracies and erotic dances had already begun to sustain a certain popular image—"part noble savage, part licentious sybarite" (Young 1984:16). Malinowski was clearly captivated, and although for a time he kept assuring Seligman and Hunt that his stay was only temporary, by the end of September he had decided to remain, despite the fact that Seligman had already done some work there: "I am getting such damned good stuff here though, that you will forgive me anything I hope" (MPL: BM/CS 9/24/15). In the event, Malinowski remained in the Trobriands for eight months; and after a year in Australia, during which he made an initial analysis of his data, he returned for another ten months—Hunt having interceded with the reluctant Murray to extend an original six-month permit (Young 1984:22).

In reassuring Malinowski that territorial "encroachment" was no issue,

Seligman pushed him to the study of land tenure, which Malinowski had already told Hunt was one of several topics of "some practical interest" to which he was giving "special attention" (Young 1984:18). Land tenure was of course encompassed in the "whole system of 'ceremonial gardens,'" which Malinowski noted to Seligman as one of several areas of research remaining to be pursued; however, at this point Malinowski approached the system as an "agricultural cult" (in the Frazerian sense). In addition, he planned to focus on the reincarnation "beliefs and ceremonies about the spirits [called] Balóm," the annual harvest feast called Mila Mala, and the "'trading ring' called Kula." With the significant addition of Trobriand sexual practices (which were in fact implicated in the problem of reincarnation), these were to be the topics of his major ethnographic works (MPL: BM/CS 7/30/15). But while all these topics were certainly matters of current native practice and belief, Malinowski approached them in terms that had little direct relation to problems of present colonial administrative practice. Although he quickly moved beyond the ethnic boundary issues he inherited from Seligman, his ethnographies were still conceived as representations of a specific, precontact cultural system—universalized, for more general audiences, as that of "savages" generally. His magnum opus, *Coral Gardens and Their Magic*—published twenty years later, when the category "savage" had been largely excluded from the discourse of professional anthropology—was still presented as a study of "the essential Trobriander," exemplifying "the ways and manners of Oceania as it flourished for ages, unknown and untouched by Europeans" (1935:I, xix).[4]

According to the long conventional mythistoric account of British anthropology, it was Malinowski's Trobriand fieldwork that revolutionized ethnography. Before then, the "standard methods of ethnographic research"—in which the native was a specimen to be measured, photographed, and interviewed—"were such that the social superiority of the investigator was constantly emphasized." But by pitching his tent in the middle of the village, learning the language in its colloquial form, and observing native life directly "throughout the 24 hours of an ordinary working day"—something "no European had ever done"—Malinowski "changed all this." Sustained by the high estimate of his ethnographic work (well after his theoretical contributions had been called into question), this account still served in 1965 as preface to the reprint edition of *Coral Gardens* (Leach 1965:viii–ix).

Within two years Malinowski's ethnographic heirs were shaken by the

4. By this time Malinowski (in a context that will be noted briefly below) had begun to advocate the study of "culture change" under the influence of European civilization; however, such phenomena were only incidentally mentioned in *Coral Gardens* (cf. 1935:I, 479–81, in appendix 2, "Confessions of Ignorance and Failure").

striking contrast between the intimate revelations of his field diaries and the methodological injunctions of the first chapter of *Argonauts* (1967, 1922b; cf. R. Firth 1989). But if one makes a certain allowance for the exhortatory and prescriptive character of that mythic charter, it does not now seem that Malinowski grossly misrepresented his ethnographic practice. His "aloneness" among the Trobrianders was relative rather than "absolute": the pearl traders Billy Hancock and Rafael Brudo were never more than a few miles away from Omarakana, where Malinowski pitched his tent in the center of the village. But if his "Capuan days" with fellow Europeans and his bouts of novel reading were rather more frequent than methodological prescription would later imply, there is little doubt that his fieldwork method was in general consistent with that which Rivers (his methodological "patron saint") had called for in 1912, and which Malinowski himself had already begun to implement in Mailu (cf. above, pp. 37–40).

However, if the methodological contrast is probably more apparent than real, the attitudinal contrast is undeniable: there is nothing in *Argonauts* that prepares us for all those aggressive outbursts against Trobrianders. Nor were the frequent references to "niggers" simply an accident of mistranslation from the Polish "nigrami," as some defensive ethnographic heirs have suggested (Leach 1980); Malinowski also used the word in letters composed entirely in English. This, too, is at least in part a reflection of his colonial situation; absent from the Mailu diary, the epithet appeared only after Malinowski had been in the area long enough to pick up its racialist vocabulary. But without minimizing the psychological and ideological significance of the Kurtzian passages in the diary, it would be a mistake on this basis simply to dismiss Malinowski "as an anthropologist who hates the natives" (Hsu 1979:521; cf. above, p. 49).

To begin with, one must keep in mind that the surviving Trobriand diary (which covers only his second trip there) was not so much a chronicle of ethnographic work as an account of the central psychological drama of his life, and an attempt to locate what he called "the mainsprings of my life." That drama was a tale of oedipal conflict, of simultaneous erotic involvement with two women (both the daughters of eminent Australian scientists), and of unresolved national identity, symbolized by his mother back in Poland—the news of whose death brought the diary to a sudden conclusion, in which his commitment to his future wife was affirmed. Although some of his outbursts against the Trobrianders are manifestly expressions of ethnographic frustration, many of them occur in close relation to this psychological plot of sexual and cultural longing and ambivalence, and may perhaps be interpreted as displaced expressions of the frustrations implicated in it (cf. GS 1968b, 1986b).

Insofar as the diary casts light on his ethnographic practice, one must balance these outbursts against less dramatic quotidian passages, as well as the evidence of the ethnographies themselves. Malinowski had a somewhat confrontational fieldwork style and was perfectly willing to express disbelief in what the Trobrianders took for granted. On the whole, however, it would seem that his methodological insistence on the importance of "personal friendships" to "encourage spontaneous confidences and the repetition of intimate gossip" was realized in relationships which, although temporary, differentiated, asymmetrical, and instrumental (like the vast majority of ethnographic relations since then), were nonetheless characterized by a certain degree of positive affect.

As a European, he was set—and set himself—somewhat apart, and took for granted many of the perquisites of colonial power. He had momentary exultations of petty lordship ("delightful feeling that now I alone am the master of this village with my 'boys'" [1967:235]), cast sometimes as a foreshadowing of a later claim to ethnographic authority ("Feeling of ownership: it is I who will describe them or create them" [140]). When "irritated" by the natives, he was several times moved to exercise the ultimate colonial prerogative of direct physical aggression. Repressing that impulse in the case of one of his "boys"—"whom I could willingly beat to death"—he felt he could "understand all the *German and Belgian colonial atrocities*" (279); another time the same servant so "enraged" him that Malinowski in fact "punched him in the jaw once or twice" (250). But if on occasion Malinowski behaved in a manner consistent with Saville's "fifth commandment" of race relations, his status and relation to the natives were quite distinct from those of a missionary or a resident magistrate, and in general he seems to have made it a point to set himself apart from these more direct embodiments of European power. During the month or so he overlapped with Bellamy before the magistrate departed for the European war, they had a falling out—an event Malinowski was later to archetypify, by urging students to "pick a fight" with the district officer as a means of gaining rapport with the groups they were studying. And Bellamy is in fact reported later to have complained that in his absence at the front Malinowski had "undone" much of the work of his ten years in the Trobriands (Black 1957:279). How to gloss that undoing is of course problematic, but it probably referred to the subversion of "progressive" cultural innovations and the violation of the still fairly recently established etiquette of race relations (cf. Nelson 1969).

At a different level from that of everyday ethnographic and race relations, one must take seriously also those passages in the diary which suggest a more systematically sympathetic attitudinal/ideological posture. When in November 1917 Malinowski formulated the "deepest essence" of his ethnographic endeavor, it was in terms similar to those which motivated his own self-analysis. Just as he strove to watch himself "right down to the deepest instincts," so did he seek to discover the native's "main passions, the motives for his conduct, his aims . . . his essential deepest ways of thinking." At that level, "we are confronted with our own problems: What is essential in ourselves?" (1967:119, 181). At that level, Malinowski clearly felt that the "primitive" Trobriand "savages" who, in particular passional contexts, he berated as "niggers" shared the same "essential" human mental makeup as the Ethnographer who would later recreate them.

At this point, however, it is clear that Malinowski still thought of this shared mental makeup in rather traditional evolutionary terms. Between "aims" and "deepest ways of thinking" in the diary passage just cited, there was in fact a starkly disjunctive parenthesis: "(Why does a *boy 'sign on'*? Is every *boy*, after some time, ready to *'sign off'*?)" (1967:119). Recalling Malinowski's first contribution to anthropological literature, and looking forward to the argument of *Sex and Repression*, it is possible to integrate the elided passage into the broader themes of Malinowski's anthropology, and of his ethnographic experience. Like the disjunctive parenthesis, the essay on the "economic functions" of the Intichiuma ceremonies had to do with the transition from "savage" to "civilized" labor (1912); in contrast, *Sex and Repression* makes it clear that the passage from savagery to civilization was also a passage away from a relatively easy and harmonious genital sexuality (1927). For mankind as a whole, the long-run evolutionary consequence of "signing on" might be seen as loss as well as gain—and the loss might be even more sharply felt by a European living on a tropical island, who had vowed to deny himself the sensual pleasures often associated with such exotic realms. Denied the compensating gains of civilization, why, indeed, would the native "boy"—or anyone else—"sign on"? (cf. GS 1986b:26–27).

On the other hand, it is obvious that the question also had a pragmatic colonial economic aspect, which Malinowski had previously addressed in a more public context than his diary. In 1915 Australian government leaders, anxious to pick up their "due share of the trade formerly in German hands," established a parliamentary commission on "British and Australian Trade in the South Pacific" (Rowley 1958:47–49). Among the matters considered was the problem of plantation labor, which had recently been exacerbated by the prospect that the Indian and Chinese governments would end the system of indentured service that had helped to supply the needs of plantation owners in many areas of the British empire since the abolition of slavery in the 1830s (Tinker 1974). Despite the earlier termination of the importation of "Kanakas" into Queensland, the issue of Melanesian labor was still a live one, heightened perhaps by the emerging concern that the native races were "dying out" (Rivers 1922). Along with government agents, traders, planters and missionaries, Malinowski was called upon to testify before the commission in the fall of 1916. Although he had not made it a matter of special study, he felt that his researches might "throw some light on the labour question" (GS 1986c).

Generalizing, Malinowski felt that "the native Papuan is not very keen on working for the white man." Left under his own conditions, he had "plenty of work at hand"—work which, though "not of a purely economic description," nevertheless made "life worth living." If he "signed on," it was not out of "deep-seated" motives, but as a response to the "personality and behaviour of the recruiter" and the prospect of something new and different. After a few weeks, "any native would desire to leave if it were not for the penalty"; but after a year "he gets to like life on the plantation"—depending of course on the way "the natives are managed." Although he acknowledged in passing the necessity of "firmness," Malinowski emphasized the attempt "to make their lives pleasant." Speaking from "the natives' point of view," he suggested that they were "very sensitive on the matter of tobacco," and recounted how returning laborers recalled the times when they were allowed to have "corroborees" and to dance. While he was not sure just what the plantation sexual regulations were, he knew that even married natives went to plantations by themselves. And although the Papuan was "not very likely to expressly formulate an emotional state of mind or a defined feeling such as homesickness," he knew that married men "who have got into the habit of domesticity" did not readily "sign on," and when they did "always wanted to get back" (GS 1986c).

Malinowski, whose own extended sexual deprivation in the Trobriands was to be the potent experiential archetype of his later psychobiological functionalism, was particularly concerned with the sexual problem (GS 1986b:22–28). Contrasting Papuan sexual customs with those of Indian coolies, he felt that to allow married men to bring their wives would encourage disorder among the unmarried. Even if the Papuans themselves were undisturbed by "immorality," missionaries would object—and in this official testimonial context, Malinowski suggested that their "outcry" would be "quite justified." In a more instrumental mode, however, he went on to suggest that laborers often had access to local women, and "it was almost impossible to think that a young native would spend three years of his life without having sexual intercourse without degenerating into sexual abnormality." Nor would the separation of three or four thousand Papuan men from their wives decrease population, since the reproductive slack would be taken up by adultery—which in the area he knew best was a matter of relatively small social consequence. Although it was "extraordinary" that the Melanesians, who were "relatively high types of men," should share the ignorance Baldwin Spencer had found among Australian Aboriginals, they did in fact fail to appreciate "the natural connexion between intercourse and birth"—one young native, absent for two years, became extremely indignant when a white man suggested to him that his newly delivered wife might have been guilty of infidelity (GS 1986c).

Turning finally to the general problem of "development," Malinowski gave a favorable report of Bellamy's enforced coconut planting. He doubted, however, that "it would be possible to induce the natives to engage in any other form of industry." The native Papuan "cannot really see even seven or eight days ahead, though he may be very intelligent in other matters; he has no grasp of a further perspective. . . . there is no incentive to the native except some present desire." After a glancing attack against German colonial regimes—which never considered "the welfare of the races they govern" and by transplantation had "decimated" the tribes of Southwest Africa—Malinowski ended with a preservationist appeal. There was "not much likelihood of the native Papuans dying out if left alone, and if they do not come in contact with the white man's civilization." Broadly speaking, he felt that "it would be best to leave them to their own conditions" (GS 1986c).

Given the circumstances of presentation (and the exigencies of recording), one hesitates to take every phrase in this somewhat disjointed official testimony at interpretive face value—the more so since Malinowski, throughout his life, was quite capable of tailoring argument and rhetoric to instrumental ends. In other contexts he was not so inclined to cater to the sensibilities of missionaries. While portions of the implicit evolutionary argument (including the crucial matter of sexual ignorance) are quite consistent with his ethnography, it seems clear that evolutionary assumption also served as the medium for expressing Malinowski's ambivalence about colonialism as civilizing process—and about his role as "expert" witness. On the one hand, he offered advice designed to make a system of native labor "work" more effectively; on the other hand, the import of much of his testimony was to suggest that contract labor was alien and unsatisfying to the native psyche, and that all things considered, it would be better for them if they were not encouraged to "sign on."

Practical Anthropology and the Tragedy of the Modern World

In the later pages of his Trobriand diary, Malinowski referred to two essays he hoped to write after he left the field. Among the "main points" of the first, on the "Value of Ethnographic Studies for the Administration," were the standard developmental topics of "land tenure; recruiting; health and

Bronislaw Malinowski, with Togugu'a (identified in *The Sexual Life of Savages* as "a sorcerer of some repute and a good informant, who is wearing a full wig") and two other Trobrianders, each holding the limepot used in the preparation of the betel nut stimulant. (Courtesy of Helena Wayne Malinowska and the British Library of Political and Economic Science, London School of Economics)

change of conditions (such as getting them down from the hilltops)." But Malinowski insisted that what was important "above all" was "knowledge of a people's customs" that would allow one "to be in sympathy with them and to guide them according to their ideas." Characteristically, colonial government was "a mad and blind force, acting with uncontrollable force in unforeseen directions"—"sometimes as a farce, sometimes as tragedy," but "never to be taken as an integral item of tribal life." And since colonial government was incapable of a more enlightened view, he would cast his "final plea" in terms of the "purely scientific value" of "antiquities more destructible than a papyrus and more exposed than an exposed column, and more valuable for our real knowledge of history than all the excavations in the world" (1967:238).

This preservationist impulse ran even stronger in another essay advancing the idea of a "New Humanism" that might be promoted by a "kind of humanistic R[oyal] S[ociety]." In contrast to the "dead-petrified thinking" of the "'classics,'" it would be inspired by "living man, living language, and living full-blooded facts" (1967:255, 267). Although the "Society of Modern Humanists" was never realized, Malinowski recurred to the "new humanism" in an article drafted during a postwar interlude "far from the trouble and irritation of Europe" in the Canary Islands—the central site of those early ventures with his mother into extra-European otherness (MPL: BM/CS 10/19/20). It was during this idyllic year with his new wife—whose espousal was the unwritten conclusion of the psychodrama of his diary—that Malinowski crafted *Argonauts of the Western Pacific*, the most literary and the most romantic of his ethnographies (FP: BM/JF 5/8/21; cf. Strenski 1982; Wayne 1985:535). And just as the first chapter of *Argonauts* was the methodological manifesto of the "revolution in social anthropology" he had conceived of during that final period in the Trobriands (1967:289), "Ethnology and the Study of Society" was the first programmatic statement of his later psychobiological functionalism (1922a; cf. GS 1986b:27–28).

In arguing the theoretical utility of ethnology as the basis of a general science of man, Malinowski saw modern anthropology as the final step in the historical development of humanism. Given its first impulse in the Renaissance by the opening up of a new vista on a forgotten civilization, broadened in the eighteenth and nineteenth century by the discovery of Sanskrit, humanism had now to respond to the challenge of modern (i.e., evolutionary) anthropology, which sought "The broadest basis of comprehensive comparison of all civilization, including those of the savage races" (1922a:217). In contrast to the old, the "New Humanism" would be based on a really scientific, empirical knowledge of human nature, for what "*time* has hidden from us forever, *space* keeps preserved for a while," waiting for the "field ethnologist" (216). He was the only sociologist who could do anything like an experiment, by observing the "differences in human mental constitution and human social behavior under the various forms of physical and mental environment" (217). Avoiding sensationalism, seeking instead a "*comprehensive treatment of all aspects of tribal life and their correlation*," ethnology could become the "handmaiden" of "a general theory of human society" (218).

Ethnology, however, could claim more than a theoretical usefulness: the first half of Malinowski's essay was an appeal for its direct application in the "scientific management" of native populations—which, until recently, a colonial atmosphere marked by slavery and punitive expeditions had made impossible. Among contemporary colonial problems, the "most sinister" was the gradual dying out of native populations, which Malinowski explained in psychological terms as largely due to "destruction of all vital interest for the native" (1922a:209; cf. Rivers 1922). Berating convention-bound, middle-class "morality mongers" and parochial "petty inquisitors of primitive life" whose "fanatical zeal to prune and uproot" had choked off the natives' "joy of living" by suppressing the institutions that gave "zest and meaning to life," Malinowski offered one of his earliest published statements on the functional integration of culture:

> every item of culture . . . represents a value, fulfils a social function, has a positive biological significance. For tradition is a fabric in which all the strands are so closely woven that the destruction of one unmakes the whole. And tradition is, biologically speaking, a form of collective adaptation of a community to its surroundings. Destroy tradition, and you will deprive the collective organism of its protective shell, and give it over to the slow but inevitable process of dying out. (1922a:214)

The implication was clear enough: while there was much in native life that must or would "succumb" to processes that Malinowski still thought of in evolutionary terms, the better part of policy and of humanity was an attempt, justified in terms of an emerging functionalism, to "preserve the integrity of tribal life as far as possible" in order to prevent the "complete extinction" of native peoples (214).

However, more pragmatic developmental pressures, both colonial and personal, strained hard against Malinowski's preservationism. It was not simply native lives that were at stake; so also were "millions" in European money. In the South Seas, where white labor was not viable and "Yellow and Hindu" labor involved a "serious political danger," native survival was essential to the solution of the labor problem (1922a:209). Despite his reservations about "signing on," Malinowski was quite willing to appeal directly to European economic interest to strengthen the case for the practical utility of anthropology (cf. 1926b). And it is clear that in the inter-war period the advancement of practical anthropology was closely linked with the advancement of his own anthropological career.

During his Australian years, Malinowski's economic position had been as marginal as his cultural status; visiting his digs in Melbourne, his friend Elton Mayo found him living in "Slavonic squalor" (MPa:10/n.d./19). But although at points Malinowski seemed to envision a life of saintly anthropological poverty (1967:282), the motif of professional ambition was closely interwoven with themes of eroticism and national identity in the Trobriand diary: in the climactic moments of his despair at the news of his mother's death, he complained that "external ambitions" crawled over him "like lice": "F. R. S. [Fellow of the Royal Society] – C. S. I. [Companion of the Order of the Star of India], *Sir* [Bronislaw Malinowski]" (291). Earlier on he had thought of becoming "an eminent Polish scholar" (160), and in 1922 he still seriously considered the offer of a newly established chair in ethnology at Cracow. However, because "money for the new department was scant," and administrative and teaching burdens would have left him no time to write up his field materials, he declined to accept this direct inheritance of his academic patrimony (Wayne 1985:535). Although he and his Scottish-English wife both obtained Polish citizenship when the nation became independent after the war, the diary suggests that he had for some time felt that his academic anthropological ambitions might better be pursued in Britain—which, given the international stature of the British school, was where a "revolution in social anthropology" would have to be waged (1967:291).

But as a "penniless Pole" approaching forty, with a family under way, Malinowski had not yet in 1921 found an economically secure place in what was still a marginally institutionalized academic discipline. His prospects were best at the London School of Economics, where his mentor Seligman was active on his behalf, and it was in the journal of the LSE that his essay on the "new humanism" was published, after he had begun to lecture there in the fall of 1921. When a readership in anthropology was created in 1923, it was with Malinowski specifically in mind; in 1927, when a chair was finally created, he became professor (R. Firth 1963). Malinowski's professorship, however, was at that time the only one at the three major British universities; at Oxford and Cambridge, anthropology still merited only a readership. As a consequence, much of his energy was devoted to the propagation of anthropology and to strengthening its academic base at the LSE (Kuklick 1991: ch. 2).

The major means to this goal was the International African Institute, an organization of leading Africanist scholars, colonial administrators, and missionaries founded in 1926, largely at the initiative of Dr. J. H. Oldham, the secretary of the recently organized International Missionary Council, and one of a new breed of ecumenical and culturally oriented missionaries (E. W. Smith 1934; cf. above, pp. 190–91). The titular leader of the Institute was the retired elder statesman of British colonial proconsuls, Lord Frederick Lugard, whose career had taken him from India, where he served in Afghanistan, to East Africa, where he fought Arab slavers and opened up Uganda, to Nigeria, where as high commissioner and governor-general between 1900 and 1919 he was known as the architect of "indirect rule" (Perham 1956, 1960). When the British Empire reached its apogee under the "mandate" system established by the Treaty of Versailles (Louis 1967; Beloff 1970), Lugard served for more than a decade as British member of the Permanent Mandates Commission. In 1922 he published what was to be at once a classic defense of the British imperial role in Africa and a justification for the new mandate system: *The Dual Mandate in Tropical*

Africa. As "the protectors and trustees of backward races," the "civilised nations" had a responsibility both to develop the "abounding wealth" of the tropics for "the benefit of mankind," and to "safeguard the material rights of the natives, [and] promote their moral and educational progress" (1922:18). Fortunately, there was no necessary contradiction between humanitarianism and economic self-interest: in the very process of bringing "the torch of culture and progress" to "the dark places of the earth, the abode of barbarism and cruelty," mandating nations could at the same time minister "to the material needs of our own civilisation" (618).

At some point early in his involvement with Oldham, Lugard, and the Institute, Malinowski briefed himself by consulting Lugard's *Dual Mandate,* leaving a record of his reactions in some undated notes (MPL). Commenting on Lugard's justification for direct taxation, Malinowski felt that the argument might have been strengthened by an appreciation of the "psychology of the gift," which, if appropriately considered, would make it possible to introduce taxation without hurting native feelings, in fact creating "indigenous ambition" and "esprit de corps." Responding to Lugard's suggestion that "in order to develop a system suited to their [native] needs, the District Officer must study their customs and social organisations," Malinowski felt that this was "rather short shrift for the whole Anthropological point of view"—"he knows nothing of real Anthropology." When Lugard quoted colonial prognosticators on the inevitability of detribalization, Malinowski asked if it was in fact the case, and if it was necessary—suggesting that Lugard did not know how much law, order, and authority there actually was in a primitive tribe. But when Lugard proposed to "evolve from their own institutions, based on their own habits of thought, prejudices, and customs, the form best suited to them, and adapted to meet the new conditions," Malinowski thought this "excellent"—equating it with "the whole antiprogressive conception." Asking "what has been done toward it?" Malinowski dismissed with exclamation marks the previous efforts of Northcote Thomas and C. W. Meek, who had served as government anthropologists in Nigeria. On the crucial issue of land tenure, he noted that "my 'theory' teaches you [the] meaning of [the] words 'communal,' 'tribal', 'ownership': by the time you know that, you know how to collect in a few weeks all the facts necessary to answer the practical questions"—and reminded himself to "make it clear that I worked on *land tenure; economic value; exchange,* etc. long before I knew the practical interest." At points Malinowski was skeptical of Lugard's motives: "he is not free from hypoc[risy]—after all, it is not merely native welfare," but "because *we* are there that we must limit [?] them." But the conclusion was clear enough: "if he had wanted to control scientific Anthropology to fit into his imperial idea—he couldn't have done anything but to create

[the] Functional School"; "Indirect Rule is a Complete Surrender to the Functional Point of View."

Joining forces with Oldham, in 1929 Malinowski launched a campaign to win Rockefeller Foundation support for an International African Institute program in "Practical Anthropology" that would study the pressing problems of land tenure and labor as they affected the "changing Native." For the next few years Rockefeller money channelled through the African Institute supported the fieldwork of a substantial portion of the cohort that was to consolidate the "revolution in social anthropology" (above, p. 210).[5] While the details of Malinowski's own involvement in African anthropology and the study of "culture contact" and "culture change" would overleap the bounds of the present essay, it is clear that he did his best to sell the utility of anthropology to the colonial establishment (cf. James 1973; Kuklick 1991: ch. 5; Kuper 1983: ch. 4; Onege 1979; Grillo 1985). In doing so, he seems to have been motivated largely by his own interest in advancing the academic discipline in which he had finally succeeded in establishing himself. As he noted privately in 1931, academic anthropologists spent their time breeding young anthropologists in a situation where there was "no practical basis to our science," "no funds forthcoming to remunerate it for what it produces" (above, p. 204). In this context, Malinowski promoted anthropology in terms that might convince an ill-informed and reluctant buyer. It was surely he whom his student Audrey Richards later had in mind, in evaluating "Practical Anthropology in the Lifetime of the International African Institute," when she said that "it looks as though the Anthropologist had been advertising his goods, often rather clamourously, in a market in which there was little demand for them" (1944:292).

In selling anthropology, Malinowski spoke in different voices to different audiences. In the initial appeal for a "Practical Anthropology," directed to the Rockefeller Foundation and the colonial establishment, he warned that the attempt to "subvert an old system of traditions" and "replace it by a ready-made new morality" would invariably lead to "what might be called 'black bolshevism'"; in contrast, the anthropologist with no "vested interest" and a "cold-blooded passion for sheer accuracy" would be able, without causing alarm, to do a survey of land tenure which would reveal the "indispensible minimum" that must be preserved for the natives, who "would often be not even aware" of the goal of the study (1929b:28–32).

5. The "revolution in social anthropology" was of course to be at least as much the work of A. R. Radcliffe-Brown, to whom a number of Malinowski's students shifted their allegiance in the 1930s, and who upon Malinowski's departure for America succeeded him as the dominant figure in the British sphere (Stocking 1984b).

But in defending "practical anthropology" against criticism by a colonial officer who felt that anthropologists should stay in their academic laboratories and leave colonial administration to "practical men," Malinowski struck a somewhat different chord. Citing "the history of 'black-birding' in the South Seas," he argued that practical men, by their ignorance of native customs, had provoked punitive expeditions in which "the 'practical man' himself would act as the murderer" (1930a:411; cf. P. Mitchell 1930). In appealing to a "community of interests" among "practical men of goodwill" in the colonies, his critic had failed to recognize the "profound, indeed irreconcilable, differences" among them—the "greed and ruthless rapacity" of the white employer, the "mawkish sentimentalism, wrong-headed dogma or false humanitarianism" of the missionary—and had failed even to consider "the native African, 'savage' and detribalized alike" (1930a:424).

Malinowski's own approach to the native African evolved somewhat in the early 1930s, with slightly variant messages being offered around a common theme at each moment along the way (cf. Rossetti 1985; James 1973). In 1930 he warned against the dangers of a caste society such as was developing in South Africa and the American South—"where neither race displaces the other," and "the social disabilities weigh heavily on the lower and demoralize the higher stratum" (1930b, as quoted in 1943:663). The following year, in a symposium on "The Colour Bar," he in fact described segregation as "at present a necessity"—identifying himself with the positions taken by Lugard and the American racialist Lothrop Stoddard, as opposed to four others who had "merely belittl[ed] the importance of race prejudice" as "superstitious." But in taking a stand on the "bedrock of reality," Malinowski insisted (against Stoddard) also on the "bedrock of justice and wisdom." Arguing that the color bar should work both ways, he advocated not only the restriction of white immigration into East Africa—"at present the danger spot of the whole world's racial situation"—but the deportation of whites already there, in order to give the colored races "some elbow room" (1931:999–1001; cf. 1929c).

Three years later, when he made a two-month inspection tour of fieldworkers of the International African Institute, Malinowski had first-hand experience of the color bar in South Africa. While there, he gave several lectures, two of which, directed to audiences of white educationalists, were later published as "Native Education and Culture Contact" (1936). Malinowski insisted on the "difficulties and the dangers" of the "schooling of unblushingly European type" that was being "mechanically thrust" on "peoples living in the simple tribal conditions of Africa" (481). Depriving the native child of his "cultural birthright" to "his own tradition and his own place in his tribal life," such schooling did not offer him in exchange "the charter of citizenship in our own civilization and society." The "white community of South Africa," moved "not by any malice or racial viciousness" but by "the sheer force of economic necessity," was "not prepared to give a Native, however educated and intelligent, that place to which he is entitled by his training" (484). Unable "for political reasons" to recognize that more land and economic opportunities should be given to natives, the "friends of the African" within the European community instead offered "more and better education," as if it were "a panacea which can work by itself" (491). But those who "talk about 'segregation' and want to attach a positive meaning to that term must realize that unless some sort of political scope is given to the African he will not be satisfied with anything less than equal political rights with the white settlers" (498). In this context, Malinowski favored an education—carried on in the English language by speakers of the vernacular—that would not "estrange the African from his tribal culture" or "develop in him claims and desires which his future salary and status will never satisfy" (501). Now that the development of "modern anthropological technique in fieldwork" had enabled us "fairly easily to learn all there is to be learnt about Natives and their culture," there was no further excuse for "committing blunders or continuing in them" (507).

While he was in South Africa, Malinowski also gave a talk to an audience of blacks on "African (Negro) Patriotism." In it, he contrasted anthropologists with two groups of "pseudo-friends": sentimental "Negrophiles" like Norman Leys, and Christian friends of "Sable coloured brethren" who had in fact done little to prevent slavery, labor exploitation, and land grabbing. Acknowledging the existence of a racial school among anthropologists (and the "reality" of race as a topic of inquiry), as well as the tendency of all anthropologists to ignore or despise detribalized Africans, he insisted that anthropology was changing. Referring to his own articles of 1922 and 1929 to document the move, he argued that the focus of anthropology was shifting from the "naked African" toward the African "in trousers." For the former, functional anthropology had and still offered a "moderate but effective championship": recognizing the value of African culture (even to the point of defending such traditional practices as witchcraft and cannibalism), it resisted the taking of tribal lands, the perversion of tribal laws, or the imposition of an alien Christian morality, favoring political autonomy and economic development along "natural" lines. But it was now time for functional anthropology to face also the problems of the modern Negro—equality of status, freedom of competition in the labor market, and the protection of racial self-esteem; it was time, in short, to "recognize the reality of the detribalized African and fight for his place in the world." While there was clearly a level of substantive consistency between this talk and those to the white educationalists, the differences of emphasis and rhetoric were apparently quite dramatic. One African woman in the audience was "emotionally swept away," proclaiming that in an atmosphere of hypocrisy and humbug, Malinowski's "sympathetic understanding of an oppressed people" amounted "to sheer heroism" (MPL: Zamunissa Cool/BM 7/7/34, 8/28/34).

Not then inclined to play the same heroic role before audiences of fellow Europeans, Malinowski filed the talk away in a folder with the annotation "Nig Lec." (MPL: "African [Negro] Patriotism"). But behind a sometimes obscuring cloud of instrumental rhetoric, spoken in different voices to different audiences, his views on the future of native peoples and the responsibilities of the anthropologist continued to evolve. In 1936, when he appealed to Lord Lugard to support the work of Jomo Kenyatta, who had become interested in anthropology while earning money as a linguistic informant during the early part of his long stay in England (Murray-Brown 1972:180), Malinowski put the case in crassly instrumental political terms:

> Mr. Kenyatta proposes to devote himself to anthropological field-work from the practical point of view on his return to his native country. . . . Mr. Kenyatta started his work in my Department about two years ago. At that time he had a definitely political bias in all his approach. This, I think, has been almost completely eradicated by the constant impact of detached scientific method on his mental processes. The highly depoliticising influence of scientific anthropology has worked a remarkable change. Another two years of systematic study and the hall-mark on his type of approach provided by a Diploma in Anthropology; also the obligation under which he will feel himself towards the [International African] Institute, will, I am certain, complete the change. Since Mr. Kenyatta has considerable influence on African students, and also on the educated Africans in Kenya, the contribution will not only be towards the advancement of theoretical studies, but also towards the practical influence of anthropology. (MPL: BM/LL 12/7/36)

Unswayed by the brainwashing power of social anthropology, Lugard was the lone dissenter when the matter came to a vote in the Institute's governing bureau (MPL: [unsigned]/BM 12/21/36); Kenyatta, his mental processes still politicized, went on to become the leader of the independence movement and the first president of the Kenyan nation. But in 1938, he did publish his doctoral dissertation, to which Malinowski wrote an introduction wherein by implication he called into question the historical realization of Lugard's whole project, by commending Kenyatta for "help[ing] us to understand how Africans see through our pretences, and how they assess the realities of the Dual Mandate" (1938a:x). The year before, in the preface to a volume entitled *The Savage Hits Back*, he hailed the author as one who was "frankly the native's spokesman, not only of the native point of view, but also of native interests and grievances."

> It has always appeared to me remarkable how little the trained anthropologist, with his highly perfected technique of field-work and his theoretical knowledge, has so far worked and fought side by side with those who are usually described as pro-native. Was it because science makes people too cautious and pedantry too timid? Or was it because the anthropologist, enamoured of the unspoiled primitive, lost interest in the native enslaved, oppressed, or detribalized? However that might be, I for one believe in the anthropologist's being not only the interpreter of the native but also his champion. (1937:viii)

Although offered rather casually in a brief occasional piece, as an opinion he had "always" held, the passage may perhaps be taken as self-reflective commentary on Malinowski's evolving awareness of what it was to be "the native's spokesman." Enamored of "the unspoiled primitive" even before he came to anthropology, but taking for granted the overwhelming knowledge/power of European civilization, he had for much of his career been a spokesman of "the native point of view" of the precontact "savage"—preserved insofar as possible from enslavement, oppression, and detribalization. In the later 1920s, seeking the means to propagate his science, he greeted "indirect rule" as a policy compatible with this underlying preservationism, and offered in return a "practical anthropology" as the means by which the interests of natives, colonizers, administrators, and anthropologists could all be advanced. As he gained more systematic and direct experience with the processes of culture contact in the African colonial situation in the early 1930s, the "savage"—now often "so-called" or called into question by quotation marks—was pushed into the wings of "practical anthropology." The "detribalized native" was given center stage, at first as the object of administrative policy, then with a greater appreciation of native "interests and grievances," and finally with an incipient awareness of the emergence of Africans as a world historical political force (cf. Rossetti 1985; James 1973).

In the preface to Kenyatta's book, Malinowski found it "amazing" how Mussolini's Abyssinian venture had "organized public opinion in places and among natives whom one would never have suspected to having any complicated views on the League of Nations, on the Dual Mandate, on the Dignity of Labour, and on the Brotherhood of Man," and how the "Chinese incident" was "uniting the world of coloured peoples against Western influence" (1938a:x). That same year, in the introductory essay to the Institute's memorandum on *Methods of Study of Culture Contact,* he noted the emergence of a "new African type of nationalism, of racial feeling, and of collective opposition to Western culture" which had been aroused by the systematic denial of certain essential "elements of our culture": the "instruments of physical power," the "instruments of political mastery" ("even when they are given Indirect Rule, this is done under our control"); "the substance of economic wealth"; and admission "as equals to Church Assembly, school, or drawing-room" (1938b:xxii–xxiii).

The last essay Malinowski prepared for publication before his death, written after he had left England for the United States and was no longer directly involved in the colonial propagation of British anthropology, provides a final marker of the change. For the most part a reprinting of the earlier essay on "Native Education," it was substantially modified in the concluding sections, where he attacked segregation as amounting to "a complete political and legal control of Africans by whites" (1943:661). Malinowski suggested that "a complete transition of the whole of Africa to European standards" would require not only "the complete withdrawal of Europeans from Africa so as to restore the land, the political power, and opportunities which are now usurped at the African's expense," but also an infusion of capital from Europe "and the whole Western world," the fruits of which would not be "garnered, as now, by European capitalists," but "presented to Africans" (660). However, Malinowski still did not foresee emergent African nationalism as leading to the end of the colonial system. On the contrary, what was "actually occurring" was "the formation of a rigid caste system" in which "one of the two component cultures" was systematically deprived of the "fundamental necessities of a civilized human being" (662–63). And though he offered once again proposals for appropriate native education, he did so with the caveat that raising their level of aspiration without "any wherewithal to satisfy the resulting claims is the royal road to social catastrophe" (664). In the end, he could do no more than fall back on an analogy to his own early experience as a Pole within the Habsburg Empire:

> Speaking as a European, and a Pole at that, I should like to place here as a parallel and paradigm the aspirations of European nationality, though not of nationalism. In Europe we members of oppressed or subject minorities . . . do not desire anything like fusion with our conquerors or masters. Our strongest claim is for segregation in terms of full cultural autonomy which does not even need to imply political independence. We claim only to have the same scale of possibilities, the same right of decision as regards our destiny, our civilization, and our mode of enjoying life. (665)

The appeal to his Polish identity was a characteristic Malinowskian trope: "speaking as a Pole, on behalf of the African, I again can put my own experience as a 'savage' from Eastern Europe side by side with the Kikuyu, Chagga or Bechwana" (1936:502). But if this experience did not provide a very satisfactory model for the future of race relations in the colonial world, it may have helped him to understand what it was to have "a two-fold social personality"—as in the case of several students of "African extraction" who had been in his classes. One of these, of course, was Jomo Kenyatta, who had served as spokesman of the Kikuyu "before more than one Royal Commission on land matters" (Kenyatta 1938:xx); and it seems reasonable to suggest that Malinowski's changing consciousness of the changing aspirations of Africans may in part have reflected their relationship—that his own mental processes were, to some extent, remolded by the politicizing influence of African nationalism.

Malinowski, however, had no more been transformed by African nationalism than Kenyatta had been by social anthropology. The two men continued to move from different starting points, along different trajectories; their visions of the present world were as different as their visions of the future. There was a brief historical moment when the author of *Facing Mount Kenya* and his "friend and teacher, Professor Malinowski," could meet on common ground (Kenyatta 1938:xvii). In many respects Kenyatta's book could have stood as documentation for Malinowski's views on traditional African education. Its central chapter was devoted to showing that cliteroidectomy, or female circumcision, which was attacked by missionaries as "something savage and barbaric, worthy only of heathens who live in perpetual sin under the influence of the Devil," was not simply a "mere bodily mutilation," but "the *conditio sine qua non* of the whole teaching of tribal law, religion, and morality" (128, 147). The book's conclusion opened with a resoundingly functionalist affirmation "that the various sides of Gikuyu life here described are parts of an integrated culture," of which "no single part is detachable: each has its context and is fully understandable only in relation to the whole" (296).

However, the ground on which the two men met was not that of the "detribalized native" but that of precontact Kikuyu culture: the "system of education" Kenyatta described was that exising "prior to the advent of the European" (1938:95). If years in mission schools and British academic life had given him, like Malinowski, a "two-fold social personality," the two felt their psychic dualism rather differently. Thus when Kenyatta spoke of having to keep "under very considerable restraint the sense of political grievances which no progressive African can fail to experience" (xvii), Malinowski glossed the comment a bit patronizingly in terms of his own civilizational angst:

> In fairness to Mr. Kenyatta, and as a matter of wisdom in any co-operation between Europeans of goodwill and Africans who have suffered the injury of higher education, we have to recognize the fact that an African who looks at things from the tribal point of view and at the same time from that of

> Western civilisation, experiences the tragedy of the modern world in an especially acute manner (1938a:ix)

And in stark contrast to Malinowski's backward-looking Habsburg paradigm of cultural autonomy without political independence, Kenyatta's book ended with a ringing call for "unceasing" struggle toward "complete emancipation" (1938:306).

Malinowski never ceased to trumpet the virtues of "scientific anthropology" and its applicability to the solution of practical problems. But if his rhetoric was often a reflection of mood and moment, there is also evidence to suggest that he became increasingly disillusioned in the interwar period with the civilization that science had produced. Born "into a world of peace and order," to a generation that "cherished legitimate hopes of stability and gradual development," he had lived through a profound "historical demoralisation" (1938a:ix). By 1930, he had come to see " the aimless drive of modern mechanization" as "a menace to all real spiritual and artistic values" (1930a:405). In the middle 1930s, he spoke of our "ultra-efficient modern culture" as a "Frankenstein monster with which we are as yet unable to cope" (1934:406); in 1938, quoting the words of William James, of progress as "a terrible thing" (1938a:ix).

In 1908, Malinowski had defended the objective validity of scientific knowledge by an appeal to colonial power, and he continued to think of both forces in terms of a virtually irresistible inevitability. But by the 1930s, his attitude toward science had clearly changed: it was now "the worst calamity of our days" (1930a:405). What was needed was "not an acceleration of 'progress,' which we neither understand, nor master, nor even approve of, but, rather, the greatest possible slowing down." Rather than speaking of "the benefits of Western civilization as the ultimate goal of all humanity," we should be thinking of how "to prevent the spread of our own troubles and cultural diseases to those who are not yet affected by them" (1934:406). The pathos of the primitive—which since Rousseau had been a projection of self-pity—was now again strongly reinforced by the pathos of the civilized. Once problematic primarily for the Melanesians, "signing on" had become problematic for all mankind.

Ethnographic Archetypes, Motivating Myths, Colonial Power, and the Ironies of Ethnographic Knowledge

To compare the anecdotally recounted ethnographic experiences of three different anthropologists among three different peoples in three different colonial situations is a risky enterprise at best. But since Malinowski at one point placed himself in a kind of archetypal relation to the other two, let us treat the three in similar fashion. Without pretending to pursue the comparison systematically, we may see them as representing different moments in the more general colonial situation of ethnography, different phases in the development and institutionalization of anthropology, and different responses to its political and ethical dilemmas.

Maclay's arrival on the northern coast of New Guinea comes close to realizing the imagined primal scene of the anthropological encounter. Far from working under Rivers' umbrella of established colonial power, Maclay was, once the corvette sailed away, effectively alone in a lush tropic jungle among a previously "untouched" people. Although they were soon to be entangled in a rapidly developing colonial situation, it was still fluid enough so that a man of Maclay's richly romantic temperament could imagine resisting or reshaping it. His ethnographic interests were largely sacrificed to this foredoomed effort, and there were ambiguities as well in his ethnographic enterprise. Despite his unusual sensitivity to certain ethical and political implications of anthropological fieldwork, a darker Kurtzian impulse to power was clearly evident in Maclay's paternalistic protectionism; and the ethnographic knowledge produced in this context of power relationships was, by present standards, of a somewhat limited sort.

In contrast to the precolonial situation of Maclay on the northern New Guinea coast, the people Kubary dealt with on Palau had been in contact with Europeans for a century. Although European power was still somewhat tenuously manifest through buccaneering traders and occasional punitive gunboats, Kubary's ethnography was from the beginning enmeshed in a complex network of local politics and trade. Temperamentally pragmatic to the point of duplicity, he seems to have adapted in an eminently practical way to inequalities of power and influence. Far from imagining a resistance to the further encroachment of colonialism, when he found himself stranded in the Pacific without institutional support, he became an active agent in its implementation. And yet the ethnographic knowledge he produced is surely more recognizable to us today than that of Maclay.

When Malinowski began his ethnographic career, both the colonial situation and the institutional development of the anthropology of the southwestern Pacific were in a very different phase. At the time he first landed on Mailu, an Australian expeditionary force was already occupying German New Guinea, where Maclay had done his fieldwork and Kubary had served as plantation manager (Mackenzie 1927:xv). The establishment of European power was no longer problematic; what was at issue was rather the transfer of colonial power in spheres where administrative and economic structures were already in place—though any given area, like the

Trobriands, might still be within Rivers' window of optimum ethnographic opportunity. Although the institutionalization of anthropology was still precarious, the lineaments of its modern academic framework were already visible. If Malinowski, too, was an Eastern European émigré dependent on makeshift arrangements for his continued research, he had nonetheless come to the southwestern Pacific with money channelled through an academic department, and could realistically aspire to a university career back in Europe—which was where his "revolution in anthropology" would have to be consolidated. And despite the shock of his diaries, his ethnographic work remains a landmark in the history of anthropology—one of the relatively few rich lodes of ethnographic material that have been and will long be the foci of continuing theoretical discussion, one of the relatively few anthropological oeuvres that had a substantial impact on the intellectual and cultural movements of their era.

Against this brief summary sketch, we may consider Malinowski's own mythic view of his two predecessors. Assuming that they were not somehow reversed in transcription or translation, one wonders how much he really knew of the two "types" of the ethnographic proportion which by implication he established in 1917. As precursors in his ethnographic realm, and fellow émigrés from east of the Oder, they were certainly known to him by reputation. But his implicitly negative characterization of Kubary as a "concrete methodologist" suggests that he was not closely familiar with Kubary's Palauan work. It seems also unlikely that he would have had much direct familiarity with the published writings of Maclay, which had appeared in relatively inaccessible Russian journals, and in a Dutch publication in Batavia. Had he read them, he would scarcely have described Maclay as an ethnographer of a "new type," since his work was in fact "concrete" in a pre-Riversian sense, inasmuch as it focussed largely on physical anthropology, material culture, demography, and linguistics of the wordlist variety (Webster 1984:346).

But if it seems unlikely that Malinowski had a close familiarity with either archetype's contribution to ethnographic knowledge, he must have had an idea of their current reputation in the local arena of colonial power. And just as Maclay's influence was "always primarily a moral one" (Webster 1984:348), so would Kubary during World War I have been perceived in moral terms. Maclay—the Kurtzian resonances of his own unpublished diary hidden from view—could be romanticized as the European ethnographer venturing alone to live among uncontacted natives, who not only brought back the grail of scientific knowledge, but became their defender from the destructive impact of European power. Kubary—who ended his career in the active service of German colonialism in a nearby area recently occupied by Australian troops—could scarcely have avoided being touched by the responsibility for German "colonial atrocities." To a man who knew his Conrad (cf. Clifford 1988), the image of Kubary as Kurtz might easily have suggested itself; and if the Kurtz in Malinowski could at moments "understand" such atrocities, those recurring Kurtzian impulses had no place in the mythic charter he would write for the "revolution in anthropology." Like the ethnography it introduced, that charter was very much a product of the romantic primitivist side of Malinowski's persona.

In identifying himself archetypically with Maclay against Kubary, Malinowski may be said, metaphorically, to have gone behind the moral and methodologiocal complexities and ambiguities of his colonial situation to return to an imagined primal Garden of prelapsarian anthropological innocence. Having left behind the cultural baggage of civilization (though not of scientific anthropology), the lone Ethnographer there encountered the precontact Primitive, distilled the essence of a particular cultural "otherness," and brought back to civilization an exotic, esoteric knowledge of universal human import. In such a context, the colonial situation of ethnographic fieldwork finds a place in Malinowski's mythic charter only as a series of stock characters from whom the Ethnographer is encouraged to dissociate himself. In such a context, the Ethnographer could forestall a choice between Maclay's quixotic resistance to European power or Kubary's Kurtzian complicity in it: going behind the European presence to recapture a primitive precontact essence ethnographically, he could in a sense preserve it from the demoralizing and destructive impact of European contact without coming to terms with that process in the real world.

There was, however, another Malinowskian voice besides that of the romantic primitivist. There was also the Malinowski whose doctoral dissertation insisted on the power that scientific knowledge gave the European over his "less civilized colored brethren," who read Machiavelli while in the field, whose interest in the advancement of ethnographic knowledge was inseparable from the advancement of his own career, and who, despite his suspicion that natives might be happier if they did not "sign on," was not unwilling to offer advice as to how to make them work more efficiently once they had. Unlike his romantic primitivist alter ego, this other more real-politikal Malinowski chose, after his fashion, to come to terms with the colonial system.

In the real historical world, the Garden in which the Ethnographer encountered the Primitive had long since been violated (Wolf 1982). Expropriating the Garden, European power had imposed upon its inhabitants the labor demanded of all fallen humankind—the fruits of which were also subjected to expropriation. And in the real world, the Ethnographer, too, was subject to the demands of labor—not only to earn his own bread, but to nurture the marginally institutionalized discipline by which he earned it. He might carry back to Europe the knowledge of a prelapsarian ethnographic Garden, but the market for that rather exotic fruit was limited. A more utilitarian product seemed to be required, and this Malinowski sought to provide. He did not himself "sign on" for the "dirty work of Empire at close quarters"—as Kubary had perhaps felt forced to do at an earlier moment of the anthropology's institutional development; but neither would he tilt at the windmills of a colonial power now much more substantial than in the era of Maclay. Between these two archetypes, somewhere "within the limits of truth and *realpolitik*" (1931:999), he sought a middle course: to offer to the colonial establishment a new kind of anthropological knowledge—academic, but practical—that would facilitate a more effective, a more economical, a more harmonious, and a more humane administration of colonial populations, simultaneously promoting both European interests and native welfare (cf. James 1973; Rossetti 1985; Le Clerc 1972; cf. Onege 1979). In a market of few buyers, such a product could perhaps provide the resources to pursue ethnographic research and to further the institutional development of anthropology—as indeed it did (above, pp. 208–10).

Malinowski himself saw the move to "practical anthropology" as "deromanticizing": "romance is fleeing anthropology as it has fled many human concerns, [and] we functional anthropologists have to rely upon the other attraction which science presents, the feeling of power given by the sense of control of human reality through the establishment of general laws" (1930a:408). But while the power of scientific knowledge never lost its attraction to Malinowski, his somewhat opportunistic attempt to make it more "practical" did not by any means represent a complete transformation of his anthropology. Moving toward the historical world, Malinowski's anthropology remained imperfectly historical. Trumpeting its utility for the colonial establishment, it nevertheless distanced itself from the exercise of colonial power. Proclaiming its "deromanticization," it left plenty of room for the romantic impulse to operate in the space it created for ethnographic research.

In advocating the study of cultural contact as "one of the most significant events in human history" (1939:881), Malinowski urged the anthropologist to "train his vision forward rather than backward" (1938b:xxvi). But although he was critical of the idea of a precontact "zero point," his proposed study of contact situations as "integral wholes" had a somewhat statically ahistorical character. In the posthumously published columnar analyses of *The Dynamics of Culture Change*, active historical agency was firmly lodged in the first column of "white influences, interests and intentions" (1945:73). As he suggested in a paper forwarded to a conference on colonialism in Africa held in Rome in the aftermath of the conquest of

Ethiopia, colonization depended on "the effective demonstration of force," which made Africans both individually and collectively "completely malleable"; furthermore, it was the "duty" of the administrator "to initiate and control change" (1939:883). Thus the second column of Malinowski's contact chart, "the processes of culture contact and change," was a "translation" of white intentions "into practical action," which, despite the "vitality of African tribalism," was "sooner or later bound gradually to engulf and supersede" the "surviving forms of tradition" catalogued in the third column (1945:81). Although Malinowski acknowledged "new forces of spontaneous African reintegration or reaction," this category was incorporated analytically only as a fifth right-hand column, after that of the "reconstructed past"—and even then, it was actually utilized only "in some cases": in analyzing warfare, but not witchcraft, native diet, land tenure, or chieftainship (1945:73–76).

Despite Malinowski's move toward the study of change, the new space created for ethnography remained still in a certain sense outside the processes of world history. Though he had come to recognize and even identify with the stirrings of African nationalism, Malinowski did not envision the end of the colonial system, except perhaps in some "ultimate" (a)historical moment—and the same can probably be said for most if not all of his anthropological contemporaries (cf. R. Firth 1977:26). In the historical present, he sought to maintain a certain distance between anthropology and the actual processes of colonial policy and practice, both on the ground and in the metropole. For although Malinowski felt free to criticize the failures of existing colonial policy, and in a general way to suggest alternatives, he made a point of disavowing "academic men meddling in colonial politics" (1930a: 419). Limiting itself to "the study of the facts and processes which bear upon the practical problems," and leaving to statesmen "the final decision of how to apply the results," practical anthropology offered to the colonial establishment a putatively utilitarian cargo of unbiassed scientific understanding—but without being involved in either the determination or the implementation of colonial policy (1929b:23).

In the event, Malinowski's incipient move toward the study of social change in the colonial world was to a great extent forestalled by the shift, under the aegis of Radcliffe-Brown, back toward a more static analysis of social structures in the ethnographic present (Kuper 1983:34, 107, 112). And in the event, the position of the "practical anthropologist" proved more than a bit problematic. Commenting on "Applied Anthropology" several years after Malinowski's death, Evans-Pritchard emphasized the tension between practical and scientific concerns, arguing that the anthropologist would best employ his knowledge and his time in the solution of scientific problems, which might have no practical value whatsoever. Although allowing a role for the anthropologist as "advisor" to colonial governments, Evans-Pritchard was concerned that he be given full access to all documents that affected the interests of natives, in order to assure that they got a "square deal" within the limits of administrative requirements and imperial policy." But his main point was that the future of anthropology lay in its academic development: what was needed was "more and bigger university departments" (Evans-Pritchard 1946; cf. Grillo 1985).

The role of colonial research grants and colonial research institutes in the postwar period is beyond the scope of this essay; so also the much mooted issue of whether or not the work of Malinowski and his students actually provided information that facilitated colonial rule.[6] More to the present point is the nature of the discursive space created by the "revolution in anthropology." At a pragmatic methodological level, we may regard Malinowski's mythic charter as a critical move in the constitution of the privileged moment in the characteristically atemporal structure of much of twentieth-century anthropological discourse. In nineteenth-century evolutionism, the objects of ethnography existed as a series of static moments along a diachronic scale extending upward from the privileged moment of cultural origins at the beginning of human time (cf. GS 1987a). With the dehistoricization of anthropology—of which Malinowski's *Argonauts* was a major marker—that temporal scale was compressed into a single moment ambiguously situated outside the flow of time. Insofar as it was the product of the ethnographer's own participant observation, it was a "present" moment; but insofar as its constitution erased a present colonial situation in order to recapture a presumed precontact cultural essence or structural form, it existed in the "past"—and doubly so, since there was always a substantial interval between observation and publication. By a convention that was not named until 1942, this privileged moment of modern ethnography came to be called the "ethnographic present" (Burton 1988; Fabian 1983). Although closer perhaps to the real world than the "primal scene" of the archetypal anthropological encounter, it was an imagined space in which that encounter could, after the fashion of Malinowski's mythic charter, be reenacted again and again.

To suggest this is not to imply that Malinowski was "a fraud" or that those who followed in his footsteps did not make substantial contributions to ethnographic knowledge. At the very least, the present consideration of three ethnographic archetypes should hint at certain ironic complexities in the relationship of motivating myths, colonial power, and ethno-

6. On these issues see, inter alia, Asad 1973; LeClerc 1972; Huizer & Mannheim 1979; Hymes 1973; Kuklick 1978; Kuklick 1991; Kuper 1983; Loizos 1977; GS 1991a.

graphic knowledge. As the instances of Maclay and Kubary suggest, purity of motive and pristinity of situation have never been guarantors of the quality of ethnographic knowledge. Such knowledge has always been implicated in (i.e., both facilitated and constrained by) asymmetries of power.[7] There never was a moment of ethnographic innocence; all of anthropology is postlapsarian. But so long as it was possible simultaneously to operate under an umbrella of colonial power and to maintain a certain distance from the forces upholding it, variants of the myth of the primal encounter could serve as a powerful motivating agency in the production of ethnographic knowledge, helping several generations of anthropologists to "get on with the work" without too much worry about ultimate questions of knowledge and power.

That the Malinowskian archetype had some such mythic potency is suggested by the intensity of the reaction to the publication of his Trobriand diary in 1967; dismay, deprecation, denial all evidenced the depth of disenchantment (cf. R. Firth 1989). By that time, of course, the charmed colonial circle of the ethnographic present had been broken, and the real-world power relations that make ethnographic knowledge possible were being permanently altered (Holland 1985; Huizer & Mannheim 1979). As native nationalisms intent on defining the terms of their own development won a place in the equation of knowledge and power, the primitivist visions that long inspired European anthropology became increasingly an ideological burden (cf. Torgovnick 1990). But if they may no longer be seen as enabling ethnography, primitivist impulses will no doubt continue to motivate anthropologists for as long as contrasts of culture allow a space for the play of alienated imaginations—and for the shadowy dance of archetypes from the dreamtime of anthropology.

7. Lest the scope of the present essay be misunderstood, it is perhaps worth making explicit that it does not pretend to offer an exhaustive consideration of the effect of such constraints and facilitations on the ethnography of any one of its three archetypical figures; for an example of a more systematic analysis, see Bashkow 1991.

7

The Ethnographic Sensibility of the 1920s and the Dualism of the Anthropological Tradition

Written in 1988, during the year I spent at the Getty Center in Santa Monica, this essay draws on research carried on over a long period (1974a, 1980a, 1982b). Its specific genesis may be traced to early 1982, when the Harvard University Press asked me to comment on the historical portions of a manuscript by the Australian anthropologist Derek Freeman attacking Margaret Mead's Samoan ethnography and, by extension, the presumed development of cultural anthropology in the United States since 1900. Although I noted a tendency in the manuscript toward oversimplification for polemical purposes, the historical argument (which drew substantially on my own early work on Boasian anthropology) seemed to me adequate when considered in relation to other presentist histories, and occasionally even illuminating. Had I fully appreciated just how hotly debated the book would be, I might have spent more time reexamining the original contexts of quoted passages—later experience suggesting that nuanced contextualization is not Freeman's forte. But I doubt that would have altered my advice as to its publishability. Whatever its flaws—some more obvious to me today than at the time—it still seems to me a significant (though appropriately debatable) contribution to scholarly discourse about the historical development and current state of ethnographic practice and anthropological theory.

That I should persist in thinking this is perhaps a measure of my irreducible marginality to the discipline of anthropology. For the reaction of American anthropologists was at the time extremely critical, if not to say outraged. I became painfully aware of this at a session of the 1983 meetings of the American Anthropological Association, which I had been invited to chair, and also to give a paper evaluating Freeman's historical account. Well before the event, I decided against this topic—in large part, I suspect in retrospect, because it implied a defense, in what had become a highly charged atmosphere, of a confidential editorial judgment which, although it still seemed to me by and large valid, put me clearly at odds with my adopted discipline. To have dealt with the matter in a way that would do justice both to my original evaluation and to the issues as they had since been rapidly evolving, at a time when I was preoccupied with nineteenth-century British anthropology, seemed impossible. So I sidestepped the problem, and gave a short paper foreshadowing the argument of the present essay, under virtually the same title.

While mine and two other contributions to the session might have been glossed as implicitly supportive of aspects of Freeman's critique, the papers were in general highly critical of his position and defensive of Mead. During the discussion period, the temperature of the meeting became quite heated, as the audience was encouraged to support a letter to the editors of *Science 83* protesting the inclusion of Freeman's book in a short list of books suitable for holiday gift-giving. As session chair, I suggested that such an action might be more appropriate at the annual business meeting, in which the Association regularly takes positions on a wide range of issues. And later that day, such a motion was in fact passed: "consistently denounced by knowledgeable scholars as being poorly written, unscientific, irresponsible and misleading," Freeman's book "not only distorts the work of Margaret Mead, but it misrepresents the entire field of anthropology" (*Anthropology Newsletter,* 1/84, p. 5).

As a presumably knowledgeable scholar of the history of anthropology who had been involved (some would have said complicit) in the decision to publish a work officially so characterized, I felt my identification with the discipline seriously compromised. Although I had achieved a certain status as its historiographer, and both sides in the Mead dispute have in fact appealed to my work, I was reluctant to be called into service as arbiter of historical disputes with quite substantial implications for the definition of the discipline in the present. Preoccupied with the long-delayed completion of *Victorian Anthropology,* I deliberately tried to maintain a certain distance from the Samoa debate, in part because I still anticipated someday being its relatively objective historiographer.

Although the continuing priority of other projects now makes that prospect less likely, I still maintain files on the Samoan controversy as one of those infrequent episodes in the history of anthropology, like that of Malinowski's diaries, when the definition and the boundaries of the discipline are profoundly at issue. Methodologically, it seems particularly interesting as an exercise in levels of contextualization (much of the argument having involved a citing and counter-citing of quoted passages); substantively, as an exercise in the levels of discourse in different disciplinary arenas before different audiences (monographic discourse, informal professional interchange, introductory textbooks, books for the general public, etc.). But with a sequel to *Victorian Anthropology* still unfinished, the Mead/Freeman affair has not been high on my research agenda, and my only attempt so far to deal with it more systematically is in the present extended elaboration of that short paper I gave in 1983. In this form, it is only one of three episodes in what is still an occasional piece, written to provide a vehicle that would carry the sixth volume in the *History of Anthropology* on into the twentieth century and permit more general reflections on its unifying theme: "Romantic Motives: Essays on Anthropological Sensibility."

Composed after "The Ethnographer's Magic," and during a period when I was also working on the "dreamtime" essay, the present essay, too, makes use of the idea of myth. However, it certainly was not my intention to imply, as Freeman did, that the more general methodological or theoretical orientations of American cultural anthropology may be dismissed as founded ultimately on myth. Although I lack specific ethnographic competence, the evidence for the serious deficiencies of Mead's Samoan ethnography seems to me by now fairly convincing (though this, of course, is quite a different issue from that of her more general role in the history of anthropology or American cultural life). Nevertheless, the suggestion that her Samoan fieldwork was critical to the establishment of a culturalist paradigm, so that to discredit it was to undercut the paradigmatic foundations of post-Boasian American cultural anthropology, has always seemed to me single-mindedly oversimplifying—however one may feel about the present timeliness of an "interactionist" approach to the relationship of culture and biology.

But if I reject the notion that American cultural anthropology is *founded* on an anthropological myth, I am still inclined to believe that its central methodological values have long been *sustained* by stories and beliefs that have something of the character of myth. The idea that there were certain methodological values underlying the practice of cultural anthropology developed for me in the aftermath of a conference on the crisis of anthropology sponsored by the Wenner-Gren Foundation in 1976 and attended by a number of anthropological elders, each of whom was asked to invite a former student. The conference was thus composed of two generations: one trained before World War II, the other trained after 1960—the latter articulating in a mildly confrontational way the critical spirit of "reinvention," the former defending the legitimacy (and especially the moral legitimacy) of an anthropology that had not yet been fundamentally called into question. In doing so, David Mandelbaum enumerated four "basic postulates" of anthropology that he felt could be derived from the concept of culture (1982)—postulates which, by and large, seemed to me to be shared by both generations. Several years later, in the context of discussions on the formation and differentiation of disciplines carried on in the Fishbein Center Workshop in the History of the Human Science—and my own awareness that there were underlying and implicit differences of assumption between even the most historical of anthropologists and the most anthropological of historians—I began to toy with the idea that human science disciplines might be differentiated by quite disparate sets of implicit methodological values, which were, in a not fully articulated sense, conditions of their professional activity and identity.

Although I have never attempted to explore the idea systematically, I got far enough to suggest a modification of Mandelbaum's original quartet—holism, fieldwork, the comparative approach, and the movement from micro- to macro-theorizing (1982b)—and its augmentation into what became the two sets indicated in the text of this essay: one of them in a broad sense "scientific" and comparative; the other, "interpretive" and particularizing. For certain historiographical purposes, it has seemed appropriate to regard these two sets of methodological values as enduring precipitates of two distinct phases in the history of anthropology, the late-nineteenth-century evolutionary and the early-twentieth-century ethnographic. As such, they may be seen to be dominant at different historical moments or among different groups of anthropologists. But their relationship may be also be seen as one of enduring epistemological tension, both within a single individual, or more generally, within the anthropological tradition itself.

While this dualistic picture no doubt reflects my own epistemological ambivalence (as well as aspects of my disciplinary marginality) it is not without precedent in the history of anthropology. For me, the *locus classicus* is of course to be found in Boas, in an essay which he composed at the beginning of his career on the epistemological dualism inherent in the study of geography (1887), and which, at its end, he gave a prominent place in his collected essays (1940). There have always been anthropologists who would resolve this dualism by systematically privileging either of its poles—scientizers and literizers, as I have previously referred to them. It may be that one or the other will eventually sweep the field (there are in fact narrativists today in its traditionally more "scientific" subdisciplines): it could also be that the fragmenting subdisciplinary components of anthropology will sort themselves roughly between the two. But having entered the field historically through Boas, in a period when the tension seemed very real to him, I am inclined to see the anthropological tradition as inherently dualistic, enough so to encompass both Margaret Mead (whose own multifaceted career can scarcely by reduced to the Samoan episode) and Derek Freeman (whose critique must in principle be subject to a similar biographical and cultural contextualization).

Like individual memory, the recollected or reconstructed past of a human discipline reflects mythistorical processes of archetypification, which characteristically coalesce around nodes of person and of moment. Archetypically, the endeavors of pattern-making figures, at critical moments of discipline formation (or reformation), mold the models and write the rules of subsequent inquiry, embodying the discipline's fundamental methodological values in their own heroic efforts. In the case of psychoanalysis, the archetypifying forces are powerfully condensed around particular episodes in the career of a single individual (cf. Sulloway 1979; Pletsch 1982). But the process may be more diffuse and pluralistic: alternate (or competing) archetypes—not always tied to the personage of a single historical figure—may be associated with particular phases (or tendencies) within the discipline, or within the undisciplined chaos that preceded it.

In the most potent version of the mythistory of anthropology (cf. McNeill 1986), three looming archetypes contest the stage of the disciplinary past: the amateur ethnographer, the armchair anthropologist, and the academically trained fieldworker. Each of these archetypes can be linked to a particular moment, developmental and/or chronological, in the history of the discipline. Thus the defining moment of the ethnographic amateur is a vaguely temporal preprofessional phase, beginning with the accounts of early explorers, travellers, and missionaries, but persisting on into the twentieth century out beyond the margins of the academic realm in which professional values were domesticated. In contrast, the defining moment of the armchair anthropologist is the "late-nineteenth century," when E. B. Tylor and J. G. Frazer, at their desks in Oxbridge studies, synthesized the reports of ethnographic amateurs (to some of whom they offered an encouraging epistolary supervision) in comparative evolutionary studies of the customs and beliefs of the "Amongthas"—"Among the Watchandis of Australia . . . ," "Among the Esquimaux . . . ," "Among the Aryan nations of Northern Europe . . ." (Tylor 1871:II, 200–201). The defining moment of the archetypal academic fieldworker is harder to fix in time, because that role has been attributed to, or claimed by, more than one anthropological prometheus: Bronislaw Malinowski, William Rivers, Franz Boas, Frank Hamilton Cushing, Nikolai Miklouho-Maclay, even Lewis Henry Morgan, could be called forth as candidates. But a case can nevertheless be made that the emergent "moment" of the archetypal fieldworker is the decade or so following World War I.

This is not to say that the method of modern fieldwork, as promulgated by Malinowski in 1922 in the opening chapter of *Argonauts,* had in fact been "invented" by him in the Trobriand Islands seven years before. Indeed, as the above list of putative paters suggests, the emergence of modern fieldwork was a multifaceted process to which many individuals before and after Malinowski contributed (cf. GS 1983a). But Malinowski's deliberate archetypification of the role of "the Ethnographer" offered, both to prospective anthropologists and to various publics at the boundaries of the developing discipline, a powerfully condensed (yet expansive) image of the anthropologist as the procurer of exotic esoteric knowledge of potentially great value—an image potent even in the United States, where the students of Franz Boas were inclined to insist that they were already practicing what Malinowski preached (above, p. 144). The academicization of the discipline, which had gained its first real momentum in the decade after 1900, and survived a period of wartime and postwar retrenchment, was in the later 1920s reinforced by substantial support from major philanthropic groups (above, pp. 179–211). By that time, one could speak of a second generation of academic anthropologists—students of the students of those who brought anthropology into the academy. Although the doctoral dissertation based on fieldwork was not yet the norm, and academically trained fieldworkers were still few in number, those who went out from the university to the field in the 1920s were confident that they were doing ethnography in a different, more efficient, more reliable, more "scientific" way than the travellers, missionaries, and government officials whom they were pushing to the margins of the discipline. Expressed in the metaphor of the ethnographic field as a "laboratory," in which a distinctive method was employed to test previously assumed comparative (or merely culturally traditional) generalizations about human behavior, this disciplinary self-image was projected with considerable success outward to the surrounding social sciences, and even beyond to the general intellectual and literate public.

As the defining moment of the fieldworker archetype, the 1920s may be regarded also as the beginning of the "classical" period of modern anthropology. With the critique of social evolutionism already established, and the succeeding phase of historical diffusionism rapidly passing, a powerful movement had begun within the Anglo-American tradition toward a largely synchronic anthropology. Allowing for the temporal vagueness inherent in the idea of the "ethnographic present," the focus of ethnographic and theoretical concern was henceforth increasingly to be on the study of culture and social structure as manifest in current rather than remembered or reconstructed custom and belief (Burton 1988). It was during this defining moment that modern anthropology's fundamental "methodological values"—the taken-for-granted, pretheoretical notions of what it is to do anthropology (and to be an anthropologist)—began to be established: the value placed on fieldwork as the basic constituting experience both of anthropologists and of anthropological knowledge; the value placed on a holistic approach to the entities that are the subject of this form of knowledge; the value placed on a relativistic valuation of all such entities; and the value placed on their uniquely privileged role in the constitution of anthropological theory (GS 1982b:411–12, 1983b:174).[1] Method itself was still evolving—Margaret Mead's Samoan research was seen by Boas as marking "the beginning of a new era of methodological investigation of native tribes" (MMP: FB/MM 11/7/25); to more conservative historical diffusionists, Redfield's community study of Tepoztlán was a "sociological" departure from traditional ethnographic approaches (Kroeber 1931). But although "laundry lists" of cultural elements continued to be required tools in the ethnographic kits of Kroeber's students at the University of California on into the late 1930s, the more "sociological" (and psychological) approaches were clearly beginning to carry the day.

Given the sense of urgency that has characterized ethnographic endeavor since the early nineteenth century, and the consequent commitment to the importance of "salvaging" the (presumed) pristine human variety facing obliteration by the march of European civilization (J. Gruber 1970), it is scarcely surprising that the ethnography of academic anthropologists tended to follow a "one ethnographer/one tribe" pattern. The number of aspiring anthropological professionals was far fewer than the number of unstudied tribes, and the methodological values of the new ethnography encouraged

1. These methodological values of the "classical" period are a modification of David Mandelbaum's listing of basic postulates derived from the concept of culture: holism, fieldwork, a comparative approach, and micro- to macro-theorizing (1982:36). In addition to the four primary methodological values noted here, I have elsewhere suggested a secondary triad, herein enlarged to a quartet, products of an earlier evolutionary phase of the discipline, which still retain a considerable potency (GS 1982b; see below, p. 338).

a "my people" syndrome—the effects of which were reinforced by a strong sense of institutional territoriality among emerging academic centers. In areas of ethnographic concentration, several academic anthropologists might study closely related peoples, or different aspects of the same culture—sometimes for training purposes (cf. GS 1982a). But if the salvage imperative (and the ultimate vision of a comparative science of man) encouraged some academic ethnographers to work among more than one people, it did not encourage competition among academic ethnographers. In contrast, it did allow them to study peoples who had been studied previously by "amateurs," whose work might be mined for facts but was likely to be superficial and/or systematically flawed by ethnocentric assumptions. In this context, the problem of the reliability of ethnographic data—which might perhaps have been suggested by the laboratory metaphor and by the frequent self-identification of the new academic professionals as "scientists"—was largely forestalled by the archetypal distinction between the ethnographic amateur and the academic professional. University-trained fieldworkers might talk of a "personal equation," but they did not allow such concerns to keep them from "getting on with the work" of documenting the ethnographic variety of humankind before it was effaced.

A generation further on, when the distinction between amateurs and professionals was an accomplished historical fact, the problem of ethnographic reliability was not so easily sidestepped. As professional anthropologists increased in numbers, they became more differentiated theoretically, methodologically, and institutionally. Less inhibited by the forceful founding figures of earlier professional generations, they began occasionally to tread in each other's ethnographic territories, and sometimes to map them in rather different ways. Even so, when ethnographic reliability first presented itself as a serious issue to modern anthropologists, it did so indirectly, as a consequence of interpretive differences between students of groups in the same culture area (J. Bennett 1946) or as a by-product of the attempt to study culture change using a previous study as base point (Lewis 1951). And despite the growth of the discipline over the succeeding four decades, the "my people" ethic remains very strong. Although ethnographic method has upon occasion been the subject of systematic consideration (e.g., Lewis 1953; Naroll 1962; Pelto 1970; Werner et al. 1987), ethnographic data are still characteristically produced by individual investigators, using relatively unsystematic and subjective methods, whose reliability is only rarely at issue.

There are, however, a small number of classic "restudies" in which the problem of ethnographic reliability has presented itself in a compelling fashion—instances in which ethnographic work of particular significance in the development of the discipline has been called into question by another ethnographer studying the same people. Every anthropologist is aware of the differing interpretations of Pueblo culture in the American Southwest and the criticisms by Oscar Lewis of Robert Redfield's study of Tepoztlán in central Mexico. Given the recent furor surrounding Derek Freeman's critique of Margaret Mead's study of Samoa, it seems likely that in the future this will be regarded as a third such case.

There are of course compelling methodological and epistemological grounds for defending the idiographic character of ethnographic inquiry in contrast to that which is generally presumed to be characteristic of the natural sciences (e.g., Ulin 1984). But regardless of its methodological significance, the fact that different observers of what in a general sense may be regarded as the same phenomenon should have represented it in what seem to be radically differing ways does present an interesting interpretive problem, especially when major figures in the history of a discipline are involved (cf. Heider 1988). In the present instance, the interpretive significance is perhaps enhanced by the fact that all three classic cases originate in a single cultural historical moment: the 1920s—which, as has been suggested here, is also the defining moment of the academic fieldworker as a disciplinary archetype. From this point of view, an attempt to consider the three cases together, in historical context—even if it should leave many issues unexplored or unresolved—may still cast some light on the historical development and perhaps even the nature of anthropological inquiry.[2]

Culture and Civilization in the 1920s

If the emergence of the fieldworker archetype in the 1920s was one marker of the beginning of the "classical period" of anthropology, another was the recognition of "culture" as its focal concept and subject matter.[3] Prematurely proclaimed in an evolutionary form by E. B. Tylor in 1871,

2. A fourth case could easily be added: that of Malinowski himself, whose interpretation of the Trobriand oedipal complex has recently come under attack along lines that could be encompassed within the present argument (Spiro 1982)—and whose archetypical status as "the Ethnographer" has now for twenty years suffered from the self-exposure of his ethnographic diaries. But since I have discussed Malinowski's diaries elsewhere, and since his inclusion here would require a consideration of the postwar milieu in Britain as well as in the United States, I have not treated him in the present essay.

3. This statement requires qualification for one of the two dominant anthropological traditions of the "classical" period. Within British social anthropology, where Boas had little or no influence, the culture concept had an aborted development. Although current in the immediate postevolutionary moment in the work of Rivers and then of Malinowski, "culture" was by the 1930s replaced by Radcliffe-Brown's concept of "social structure" (cf. GS 1984b, 1986b).

intellectually grounded in the work of Franz Boas and the first generation of his students, "culture" burst into flower in the 1920s (cf. GS 1968a). As its analytic bibliographical chronologists have shown (Kroeber & Kluckhohn 1952), this was the moment when citations burgeoned: save for five precursory figures, whose usage they suggest may only have had a "formal or verbal resemblance" to the anthropological concept, without actually having "'meant' the same" (149–50), the opening entry in most of their categories dates from this period. It was at this time that, building on Boas' critique of evolutionary culture, anthropologists (e.g., Boas' student Clark Wissler [1923]) and sociologists (e.g., the Boas-influenced William Ogburn [1922]), joined forces in fashioning and making fashionable what was later described by one influential popularizer as "the foundation stone of the social sciences" (Chase 1948:59).

However, one need only consult an historical dictionary to realize that, like some other central concepts in the human disciplines, "culture" was from the beginning entangled with the categories, the discourse, and the experience of the "outside" world—and that it only gradually achieved a certain (inherently limited?) independent conceptual status. In the 1920s it was also still closely (and problematically) tied to its conceptual sibling "civilization"—which in Tylor's definition had been its synonym, and which Kroeber in 1917 had used as pseudonym to avoid the unpatriotic resonance of the German "Kultur" (Kroeber & Kluckhohn 1952:28–29). And in the 1920s, beyond (and at) the margins of disciplinary discourse, these linked concepts were the subject of widespread discussion and debate among American intellectuals.

To put the matter in a nutshell, world (and national) historical experience seemed no longer to sustain either the easy absolutism implied in the popular Arnoldian notion of culture ("the pursuit of perfection . . . the best that has been thought and known" [1869:69–70]), or the easy evolutionary synonymity of Tylor's "ethnographic" definition ("Culture, or civilization, . . ." [1871:I, 1]). For many intellectuals, the values to be cultivated by the individual in the pursuit of perfection could no longer be taken for granted; and the "permanent distinction and occasional contrast" between such cultivation and the idea of civilization—on which Coleridge had long before insisted (R. Williams 1958:67)—had become painfully evident.

There have been various attempts to encapsulate the values associated with the idea of civilization in the later Victorian era. One influential interpretation grouped them in a triptych, with "progress" and "culture" (in the Arnoldian sense) flanking the central panel of "practical idealism": "the reality, certainty, and eternity of moral values" (H. May 1959:30, 9). A more recently proposed trio included the "ethic of self-control and autonomous achievement, [the] cult of science and technical rationality, [and the] worship of material progress" (Lears 1981:4). But linked to (or implicated in) these triads were also other value commitments: the ethnic values of white Anglo-Saxon racial superiority, the political values of liberal representative government, the economic values of free capitalist enterprise, the religious values of Protestant Christianity, and—perhaps most centrally, in terms of the transmission of cultural character, the familial, gender, and sexual values of patriarchal respectability (cf. N. Hale 1971; GS 1987a: 187–237).

By 1920, many intellectuals had begun to question both these values and the idea of civilization in which they were embodied. The timing, extent, and thoroughness of this intellectual rebellion has been a matter of historiographical debate. The "revolution in morals" has been associated with flappers, jazz, speakeasies, and the "lost generation" as a characteristic phenomenon of the 1920s itself (Leuchtenberg 1958). In contrast, the "end of American innocence" has been associated with the "scoffers" and "questioners" of the turn-of-the-century decades, and with the "innocent rebellion" of younger American intellectuals between 1912 and 1917 (H. May 1959). More recently, the development of an antimodernist "revolt against overcivilization" (which in fact promoted "new modes of accommodation to routinized work and bureaucratic 'rationality'") has been traced throughout the four decades before 1920 (Lears 1981:iv, 137). Against all this has been argued the persistence of the older values and the constructive role of a "nervous generation" of American intellectuals in reshaping them during the 1920s itself (Nash 1970). But even a staunchly self-proclaimed revisionist has acknowledged that a "moral earthquake" shook Western civilization in the years after World War I (ibid.:110). Whatever questioning of Victorian values had taken place prior to the war's outbreak, it was the horrible spectacle of the civilized nations of the West engaged in the mutual slaughter of their youth that forced many intellectuals to wonder if there were not some alternative to the values of what Ezra Pound called "a botched civilization" (1915).

If Pound's adjective implied an alienated despair, the indefinite article could also imply a regenerative relativity, which in fact had been reflected previous in the prewar sense of cultural self-discovery epitomized in Van Wyck Brooks's *America's Coming-of-Age* (1915). Thus when "civilization" became "the center of interest" in the postwar decade (Beard & Beard 1942: 10ff.), the issue was not simply the content of a painfully problematic universal category, but the possibility of now, finally, realizing a civilization that would truly embody the maturing American experience—rather than the worn-out values of the "puritan" tradition, or the hypocrisy of small-town Babbittry, or the acquisitive commodity culture of big cities and their suburbs. In the fall of 1920, Brooks and Harold Stearns, responding to the "common enemy of reaction" in the "hysterical post-armistice days," got together a group of "like-minded men and women" who would attempt to "speak the truth about American civilization as we saw it, in order to do our share in making a real civilization possible" (Stearns 1922:iii–iv). Dividing the domains of American culture among themselves, they covered topics ranging from "the city" and "the small town" to "the alien" and "racial minorities," from "art" to "advertising," from "philosophy" to "the family," and from "science" to "sex"—with the notable omission of "religion," about which no one was willing to write, because they felt that "real religious feeling in America had disappeared, . . . and that the country was in the grip of what Anatole France has aptly called Protestant clericalism . . ." (vi). From these contributions, Stearns distilled three major themes: hypocrisy, the suppression of heterogeneity, and "emotional and aesthetic starvation" (vii).

Noting the "sharp dichotomy between preaching and practice" in "almost every branch of American life," Stearns suggested that rather than submitting the "abstractions and dogmas which are sacred to us" to "a fresh examination," Americans worshipped them "the more vociferously to show our sense of sin." Arguing that "whatever else American civilization is, it is not Anglo-Saxon," he insisted that "we shall never achieve any genuine nationalistic self-consciousness as long as we allow certain financial and social minorities to persuade us that we are still an English colony." Asserting that "we have no heritages or traditions to which to cling except those that have already withered in our hands and turned to dust," Stearns considered "the whole industrial and economic situation so maladjusted to the primary and simple needs of men and women," that it was futile to attempt a "rationalistic attack" on our "infantilisms of compensation":

> There must be an entirely new deal of the cards in one sense; we must change our hearts. For only so, unless through the humbling of calamity or scourge, can true art and true religion and true personality, with their native warmth and caprice and gaiety, grow up in America to exorcise these painted devils we have created to frighten us away from the acknowledgment of our spiritual poverty. (1922:vii)

The overlapping of anthropological discourse and the discourse of cultural criticism in the early 1920s is evidenced by the inclusion of two important Boasians among the thirty participants in the Stearns symposium: Robert Lowie, who offered Boas' "transvaluation of theoretical values in the study of cultural development" as the exemplar of modern anthropology's contributions to contemporary science (Stearns 1922:154); and Elsie Clews Parsons, who attacked puritan "attitudes of repression or deception" toward sex as an expression of "arrested development," in which women, classified "by men on an economic basis," were "depersonalized" as "creature[s] of sin" or "object[s] of chivalry" (ibid.:310, 314–15, 317). And there were other Boasians who, in other venues, were also important contributors to the discourse of cultural criticism in the early 1920s, in tones resonant of the Stearns volume.

The most notable of these was Edward Sapir, whose seminal essay "Culture, Genuine and Spurious"—as its publication history suggests—was at once a part of that critical cultural discourse and a major document in the development of the anthropological culture concept (cf. Handler 1983: 222–26, 1989; Kroeber & Kluckhohn 1952, where Sapir is the third most cited author). Published in part in two of the better known "little magazines" of the period (Sapir 1919, 1922a), the essay appeared in full in 1924 in the *American Journal of Sociology,* where it was perhaps the most important contribution to the sociological discussion of the anthropological culture concept in the middle and late 1920s (cf. Murray 1988). Although drafted a year before the Stearns symposium was conceived, it could in fact be viewed as a conceptual commentary on the relationship of the symposium's central concern ("civilization") to another concern which appeared occasionally and unsystematically throughout, and which Sapir (like Coleridge) insisted was quite a different matter ("culture").

Sapir began by distinguishing three different meanings of the term "culture": the "ethnologist's," which included "any socially inherited element in the life of man, material and spiritual" (in which terms "all human groups are cultured, though in vastly different manners and grades of complexity"); the "conventional ideal of individual refinement"; and a third which was to be his own concern. Sharing aspects of the first and second usages, it aimed "to embrace in a single term those general attitudes, views of life, and specific manifestations of civilization that give a particular people its distinctive place in the world" (1924:308–11). "Civilization," in turn, was the progressive "sophistication" of society and individual life resulting from the cumulative sifting of social experience, the complication of organization, and the steadily growing knowledge and practical economic mastery of nature. It stood in sharp contrast to "genuine culture," which was an "inherently harmonious" and "healthy spiritual organism," free "of the dry rot of social habit," in which "nothing is spiritually meaningless" for the human individual: "civilization, as a whole, moves on; culture comes and goes" (314–17). It was clearly gone from modern American life, in which the "vast majority" were either "dray horses" or "listless consumers":

> The great cultural fallacy of industrialism, as developed up to the present time, is that in harnessing machines to our uses it has not known how to

> avoid the harnessing of the majority of mankind to its machines. The telephone girl who lends her capacities, during the greater part of the living day, to the manipulation of a technical routine that has an eventually high efficiency value but that answers to no spiritual needs of her own is an appalling sacrifice to civilization. As a solution of the problem of culture she is a failure—the more dismal the greater her natural endowment. As with the telephone girl, so, it is to be feared, with the great majority of us, slave-stokers to fires that burn for demons we would destroy, were it not that they appear in the guise of our benefactors. The American Indian who solves the economic problem with salmon-spear and rabbit-snare operates on a relatively low level of civilization, but he represents an incomparably higher solution than our telephone girl of the questions that culture has to ask of economics. There is here no question of the immediate utility, of the effective directness, of economic effort, nor of any sentimentalizing regrets as to the passing of the "natural man." The Indian's salmon-spearing is a culturally higher type of activity than that of the telephone girl or mill hand simply because there is normally no sense of spiritual frustration during its prosecution, no feeling of subservience to tyrannous yet largely inchoate demands, because it works in naturally with all the rest of the Indian's activities instead of standing out as a desert patch of merely economic effort in the whole of life. A genuine culture cannot be defined as a sum of abstractly desirable ends, as a mechanism. It must be looked upon as a sturdy plant growth, each remotest leaf and twig of which is organically fed by the sap at the core. (316)

Despite Sapir's denial of "sentimentalizing regrets" for "natural man," a strong residual aroma of romantic primitivism hangs heavily over this rhetorically tangled bank of critique and concept. If "a genuine culture was perfectly conceivable in any type or stage of civilization," it was "easier, generally speaking," for it to "subsist on a lower level of civilization" (1924: 318). There was a "geography of culture," which reached "its greatest heights in comparatively small, autonomous groups"—not in the "flat cultural morass" of New York, Chicago, and San Francisco, but in Periclean Athens, Augustan Rome, the city-states of the Italian Renaissance, Elizabethan London—and the typical American Indian tribe, where the "well rounded life of the average participant" could not escape the notice of "the sensitive ethnologist" (328–31, 318). Sapir's thought on the idea of culture and its relation to personality departed in important respects from that of many of his fellow anthropologists in the 1920s and 1930s—including several who were most influenced by him (Handler 1986; Darnell 1986). But in these passages, he was clearly speaking for other "sensitive ethnologists" who were critical of the civilization of their day. From this point of view, "Culture, Genuine and Spurious" was a foundation document for the ethnographic sensibility of the 1920s, and it is perhaps more than coincidental that the authors of its three most problematic ethnographic cases were all strongly influenced by Sapir—who was an intimate poetic confidant of Ruth Benedict and Margaret Mead, and a teacher of Robert Redfield.

The Geography of Genuine Culture

For intellectuals searching for genuine culture in the postwar period, there were several localities in the cultural geography of the United States that were clearly marked off from the surrounding "flat cultural morass." In New York City, there was Greenwich Village, where just before the war the cheap rents of a disintegrating traditional neighborhood (Ware 1935: 93) had opened a cultural space for rebel-seekers who were by temperament (or by gender) excluded from "business, big-time journalism, university life, and other corporate pursuits" (Lynn 1983:89, 83). Finding "the traditional Anglo-Protestant values inapplicable and the money drive offensive," they set out on an evanescent urban frontier "to make for themselves individually civilized lives according to their own conceptions" (Ware 1935:235). Much of their rebel energy was spent in "free love, unconventional dress, erratic work, . . . all-night parties, . . . plenty of drink, living from moment to moment"—"rationalizing their conduct with the aid of Freud and art" (ibid.:95, 262). Their "counter-culture" was soon to a considerable extent coopted by middle-class culture, with the *New Yorker* adapting the style of the *New Masses,* and the Theatre Guild evolving from the Washington Square players (Lynn 1983:91). But if "the Village" offered more of individualistic escape than of "genuine" cultural alternative, it was also for a time a bubbling oasis of cultural modernism, in which intellectuals alienated from the spurious culture of contemporary business civilization could savor heterodox ideas, discover new aesthetic modes, and experiment with alternative life styles (cf. Lasch 1965)—directly, as residents or occasional habitués, or vicariously, through the various media of cultural criticism.

It has been argued that one "longing" that served to bring together all factions of the cultural rebellion was an "aesthetic" fascination with "the culture of poverty"—a manifestation of a more general "preoccupation with primitive vitality" among many intellectuals in this period (Lynn 1983: 87–89). For those intellectuals, like Mabel Dodge, whose primitivist urges required a more "genuine" culture than urban bohemia could provide (Lasch 1965:119), there was another oasis far out across the great cultural desert of middle America: the pueblo Southwest. Against a backdrop of arid ochre scarps and arching crystal skies, the crisp adobe lines of Spanish churches and Indian pueblos—artifacts of cultural traditions more deeply rooted than colonial New England—provided the setting for a resonantly exotic cultural life in the present (cf. GS 1982a).

Starting in the late 1890s, when the advertising department of the Santa Fe Railway began to "mine the landscape for culture" and to present the Santa Fe Indian as "a prototype of preindustrial society" (McLuhan 1985: 18), a small group of painters, playwrights, poets, and writers had settled in Santa Fe and Taos. Twenty years later Harriet Monroe, the editor of the "little magazine" which was the major outlet for the new American poetry, complained that "we Americans, who would travel by the many thousand, if we had the chance, to see a Homeric rite in Attica, or a serpent ceremony in old Egypt, are only beginning to realize that the snake-dance at Walpi, or the corn-dance at Cochiti, are also revelations of primitive art, expressions of that original human impulse toward the creation of beauty" (ibid.:41).

By 1924 the Santa Fe Railway was transporting fifty thousand tourists a year to the rim of the Grand Canyon, and two years later it had begun the "Indian Detours" in which Packard touring cars drove the richer and more venturesome to witness "spectacles which can be equaled in very few Oriental lands" (McLuhan 1985:43). Others found a deeper message of spiritual regeneration. When Mabel Dodge heard the singing and drumming at Taos pueblo, she felt herself suddenly "brought up against the tribe, where a different instinct ruled, and where virtue lay in wholeness instead of in dismemberment" (ibid.:156); within several years she had cast off her artist third husband to marry the Pueblo Indian Tony Luhan. For D. H. Lawrence, whom she lured to "the edge of Taos desert" in 1923, it was a matter of "true nodality":

> Some places seem temporary on the face of the earth: San Francisco for example. Some places seem final. . . . Taos pueblo still retains its old nodality. Not like a great city. But, in its way, like one of the monasteries of Europe. . . . When you get there, you feel something final. . . . the pueblo as it has been since heaven knows when, and the slow dark weaving of the Indian life going on still . . . and oneself, sitting there on a pony, far-off stranger with gulfs of time between me and this. And yet, the old nodality of the pueblo still holding, like a dark ganglion spinning invisible threads of consciousness. (Ibid.:162)

In the 1920s, the mapping of the cultural geography of cultural criticism overlapped that of cultural anthropology to an extent that we may not appreciate today, when the boundaries between academic anthropology and the outside world are more sharply imagined. The routinization of anthropological charisma had not yet reduced the careers of its devotees to years in the university punctuated by occasional episodes of fieldwork. A number of the New York anthropologists were frequenters of the culture of Greenwich Village, participants in the New School for Social Research, contributors to little magazines. When the same anthropologists went into the field, it was not into a generalized laboratory but into particular exotic places, some of them heavy with the musky scent of "primitivistic longing."

The single most-visited venue was the pueblo Southwest. With the post-evolutionary changing of the institutional and theoretical guard in American anthropology, this favored preserve of anthropologists associated with the Bureau of American Ethnology became more accessible to the Boasians. The pueblo at Zuni, which from 1879 on was studied by Frank Cushing, Matilda Stevenson, Jesse Fewkes, and F. W. Hodge, began to attract Boasians in 1915, when Elsie Clews Parson arrived, to be followed during the next nine years by A. L. Kroeber, Leslie Spier, Boas himself, and then Ruth Bunzel and Ruth Benedict (Pandey 1972). It may be that Boas' on-going shift from historical diffusionism toward the psychological study of the individual and culture made more attractive an area where the culture seemed still vibrantly "alive and well." But if there was a disciplinary dynamic that drew Boasians to the area, it seems also clear that some of them – sharing to a considerable extent the backgrounds, motives, sensibilities, experiences, and impressions of nonanthropologist intellectuals – also felt the pull of Lawrence's "invisible threads of consciousness."

The Delectable Mountains of the Apollonian Southwest

For Ruth (Fulton) Benedict, these threads ran back to a dark ganglion of childhood fantasy. As she later recreated it for Margaret Mead, the story of her life began when her father, a young surgeon interested in cancer research, died twenty-one months after her birth in 1887 (Benedict 1935: 97).[4] Her mother, a Vassar graduate who later supported herself as teacher and librarian, took tiny Ruth and her infant sister in to view her father in his coffin, "and in an hysteria of weeping implored me to remember"

4. The fact that this manuscript was prepared for Mead in 1935, "at a time when life histories were becoming a matter of anthropological interest" (Mead 1959a:97) – and after *Patterns of Culture* (Benedict 1934) was already in print – might cast doubt on its status as independent source material about that volume's genesis, since Benedict may have been consciously or unconsciously patterning her own life in relation to one of the patterns of her book. But if so, it can still be argued that the interpretation here given to these two sources has a basis in her own self-understanding. Although I have also drawn information from Modell's biography (1983), and have consulted Caffrey (1989), the interpretation here derives from my own long-standing concern with Benedict's career (1974a, 1976b).

(98).[5] Benedict later recalled it as her "primal scene": "Certainly from earliest childhood I recognized two worlds, . . . the world of my father, which was the world of death and which was beautiful, and [my mother's] world of confusion and explosive weeping which I repudiated" (99). Benedict marked that repudiation by "ungovernable tantrums" and "bilious attacks" (which followed the same six-week rhythm as her later menstrual periods) – "protests against alienation from my Delectable Mountains" (108). In her other, calmer world, she had an "imaginary playmate" who enjoyed "a warm, friendly family life without recriminations and brawls" in "the unparalleled beauty of the country over the hill" – until, at age five, she was taken by her mother to the ridge of her maternal family's upstate New York farm, and she saw that beyond it lay a territory that was "all familiar and anything-but-romantic" (100). From then on, her other world was "made up mostly out of my Bible," and peopled "by people of a strange dignity and grace," who moved like Blakean figures, "skimming the ground in one unbroken line" (107, 109). Her isolation heightened by partial deafness after an infant bout with measles, Benedict allowed no one to pass beyond her "physical and emotional aloofness." The one partial exception was Mabel Ganson (later Dodge), who went to the same girls' school in Buffalo; although Benedict was six years younger and their acquaintance was slight, she remembered "knowing that [Mabel Dodge] lived for something I recognized, something different from those things for which most people around me lived" (109). And, while she introduced this recollection with the comment "amusingly enough," the present context suggests a greater symbolic significance.

Their routes to the Southwest were, however, to be quite different. In 1905, Benedict matriculated at Vassar, where as a freshman she abandoned

5. Collecting information on the "perceptions of their parents" of eighty-eight Greenwich Villagers, Kenneth Lynn found that two-thirds of them "were raised in households which they considered to be female-dominated" due to the "personal force of the mothers" and "the absence or startling weakness of the fathers." Lynn used these data to attack the idea that they were rebelling against "patriarchal authority," and suggested that their family backgrounds had in fact encouraged them to be nonconformist, and to place a high value on personal freedom and self-realization: "Strong mothers taught their gifted daughters to believe that women in America could not be fulfilled unless they ignored restrictive definitions of their social role . . . [and] inflated their [gifted sons'] egos to the point where [they] were unprepared to accept the discipline of any organization not put together for their own benefit . . ." (1983:78–79). While this may represent an important sophistication of our understanding of the rebelling or questioning intellectuals, the image of all those "strong mothers" seeking vicarious release from "restrictive definitions of their social role" suggests that the issue of "patriarchal authority" may have been lurking somewhere in the background. Be that as it may, it is worth noting that Benedict, Redfield, and Mead all came from families with strong mothers (and grandmothers), although in the case of Benedict, her emotional relationship to her mother was markedly antagonistic.

Ruth Benedict, c. 1925. (Courtesy of Special Collections, Vassar College Libraries)

formal religious belief for Walter Pater's humanistic vision of culture, and as a senior lamented the loss of "the sense of reverence and awe" in the realistic "Modern Age" (Mead 1959a:116, 135). After a year in Europe, another doing charity work in Buffalo, and three more teaching in girls' schools in California, she tried to come to terms with the "very terrible thing [it was] to be a woman" (120) and to "master an attitude toward life which will somehow bind together these episodes of experience into something that may conceivably be called a life" (129). Putting aside, for the moment, the youthful idea that "we were artificers of our own lives," she decided that "a woman has one supreme power—to love" (130); in 1913 she married Stanley Rossiter Benedict, a brilliant biochemist, and tried to live the life of a housewife in a suburb of New York. There she dabbled with literary projects, including "chemical detective stories" she hoped to publish under the pointed pseudonym "Stanhope," and a manuscript on "New Women of Three Centuries." But when fate denied her the "man-child" who might "call a truce to the promptings of self-fulfilment," Benedict was unwilling to "twist" herself into "a doubtfully useful footstool" (135); "Stanhope" died, to be reborn later as "Anne Singleton" (the name under which she published poetry in the 1920s).

After armistice brought an end to "this tornado of world-horror," when it had "seemed useless to attempt anything but a steady day-by-day living" (Mead 1959a:142), Benedict searched once more for expedients to "get through the days." Although she rejected the advice of a friend to "move to the village and have a good time, and several love affairs" (7), she did in 1919 begain to attend lectures at the New School, where she was quickly attracted to Elsie Clews Parsons' course on "Sex in Ethnology," which offered a comparative study of the "distinctive distribution of functions between the sexes" (Modell 1983:111; cf. Hare 1985; Rutkoff & Scott 1986). She also took a number of courses from the brilliant Boasian maverick, Alexander Goldenweiser, who during this period was at work on "the first book by an American anthropologist which was to present cultures briefly as wholes" (Mead 1959a:8). To one whose psyche was grounded in an opposition between radically different emotional worlds, and whose life and marital experience had undercut the value-absolutes sustaining the central institution of her culture, the implicit relativism of the anthropological approach offered a principle of order; and in 1921, Benedict was taken uptown to Columbia by Parsons, to be introduced to Boas and to begin study for a doctorate in anthropology.

Quickly sensing the vigorously imaginative mind veiled by her "painfully shy" demeanor, Boas waived credit requirements to hurry Benedict through the Ph.D. Her dissertation, a library study of American Indian religion, was an analysis of the "observed behavior" of a single "well-recognized cultural trait," the guardian spirit concept, which she argued was "the unifying religious fact of North America" (1923:6, 40). Rejecting all generalized origin theories, Benedict found that the guardian spirit was associated with other cultural elements in a series of "essentially fortuitous" and "fluid recombinations" defying any single causal explanation (56, 82). The dissertation showed various precursory traces of the later Benedictine viewpoint. Thus, although she concluded with an attack on "the superstition that [a culture] is an organism functionally interrelated" (85), Benedict insisted that in any given culture area, the vision-complex was "formalized" into "definite tribal patterns" under the influence of dominant values and activities (41–43) – to such an extent that in the American Southwest, where every other element of the complex was present, the notion of the individual guardian spirit experience had almost totally disappeared "under the influence of group ceremonial as the proper way of approaching the gods" (35–40). For the most part, however, the dissertation remained within the conventional mold of Boasian historicism, in which the approach "toward a more just [i.e., nonevolutionary] psychological understanding of the data" depended first on an adequate reconstruction of the particular one "of all these indefinitely numerous plausible potentialities . . . [that] did actually and historically secure social recognition among a given people" (7).

Hampered by deafness and diffidence, Benedict did not find fieldwork congenial, and the small amount that she did (no more than eight months altogether) fell into a rather conventional early Boasian mold. In 1922, she combined a visit with her sister's family in Pasadena with a memory ethnography of the "broken culture" of the Serrano of Southern California, working primarily with one seventy-year-old woman (Mead 1959a:213). The following February, after some hesitation, she yielded to Boas' urging and accepted a fellowship for folklore research from Elsie Clews Parsons, who funded ethnographic work through her personal anthropological philanthropy, the Southwest Society (Mead 1959a:65; Hare 1985:148); but it was not until August of the next year that Benedict actually went to Zuni, at the same time that Ruth Bunzel (the second of Boas' departmental secretaries to turn anthropologist) was beginning her study of Pueblo potters (cf. Mead 1959b:33–35). A year later, Benedict returned to the Southwest for another six weeks of folklore research, divided between Zuni (where her stay again overlapped Bunzel's), and then Peña Blanca and Cochiti. Although she was subsequently to lead parties of students among the Mescalero Apache and the Blackfoot, the last fieldwork Benedict did on her own was among the Pima of Arizona in 1927 (Modell 1983:169–79).

Margaret Mead later suggested that Benedict had never seen a "living flesh-and-blood member of a coherent culture" (Mead 1959a:206), and Benedict herself commented on "the disintegration of culture" at the Rio Grande Pueblos. But she did so in the course of contrasting them with Zuni, which she was grateful to have gotten to "before it's gone likewise" (RB/Mead 9/16/25, in Mead 1959a:304). When Benedict arrived at Zuni, it was, as Bunzel later noted, "in one of its periodic states of upheaval": the "progressives," who were traditionally friendly to ethnographers, "had been ousted after unsuccessful attempts by [BAE] anthropologists to photograph the mid-winter ceremonies," and were now discredited, so that Benedict and Bunzel were forced to find informants "among the conservative and traditionally hostile group that was now in power" (as quoted in Pandey 1972:332). Assisted by interpreters, Benedict worked with paid informants, for eight or nine hours a day, taking down the myths and folktales they dictated to her. Although one "amorous male," ready to play the role of Tony Luhan, hoped she would be "another Mabel Dodge" (RB/MM 9/8/25, in Mead 1959a:301), most of Benedict's informants were old men, and it has been suggested (and indirectly acknowledged by Benedict herself) that the vision of Zuni culture that emerged through the double haze of memory and myth may have been somewhat idealized (Pandey 1972: 334; cf. Mead 1959a:231). Benedict herself clearly sensed the mythopoeic power of the place, remarking after leaving Zuni that she felt as if she had "stepped off the earth onto a timeless platform outside today"; after a walk with Bunzel under the "sacred mesa" along "stunning trails where the great wall towers above you always in new magnificence," she exclaimed: "when I'm God I'm going to build my city there" (RB/MM 8/29/25, 8/24/25, in Mead 1959a:295, 293).

While Zuni provided the site for a lapsed puritan's "city on a hill," the development of a conceptual framework for its construction took some time. Although Boas' intellectual shift away from historical reconstruction toward problems of cultural integration and the relation of individual behavior and cultural pattern had already begun, anthropologists were still, as Mead later noted, searching for a "body of psychological theory" adequate to the analysis of cultural materials (Mead 1959a:16). One of the most important searchers was Sapir, who, for Boas' more conservative taste, had "read too many books on psychiatry" (FB/RB 7/16/25, in Mead 1959a: 288), and to whom Benedict apparently sent a copy of a preliminary version of her dissertation (ES/RB 6/25/22, in Mead 1959a:49). Over the next several years, during which the mental illness of his first wife occasionally took him from Ottawa to New York in connection with her treatment, Sapir and Benedict developed a close relationship, carried on largely by correspondence, in which they discussed the "poetries of passion and despair" they were each writing "to express the agony of marriages unravelling": "Lovers have nothing left, the incomparable worth of flesh become a shifting ash that covers love's utmost grief with characterless earth" (in Mead 1959a:161; cf. Handler 1986:138, 143; Darnell 1990). Sapir offered detailed appreciative criticisms of Benedict's poems (in the puritan tradition, "but with a notable access of modernity"), and cautioned her against using a pen name: "you know how I feel about even toying with the idea of dissociation of personality" (ES/RB 2/12/24, 3/23/26, in Mead 1959a:166, 182).

He also seems to have encouraged her to move toward psychology, suggesting that "the logical sequel" to her dissertation would be a study of "the historical development of the guardian spirit in a particular area, the idea being to show how the particular elements crystallized into the characteristic pattern"—a task which he felt required "room somewhere from psychology," unless "you balk at psychology under all circumstances" (ES/RB 6/25/22, in Mead 1959a:49).

The psychology Sapir first commended to Benedict was Jung's theory of *Psychological Types,* which had just been translated into English (1923), and which was the subject of "continuing excitement" in conversations at the anthropological section of the British Association for the Advancement of Science meeting in Toronto in 1924 (ES/RB 9/10/23; MM/RB 8/30/24, 9/8/24, in Mead 1959a:54, 285–86; cf. 207, 552). Benedict did not fully share the enthusiasm Sapir and several others had for Jung, speaking disparagingly of Paul Radin's "lecturing" her about "the great god Jung" (RB/MM 3/5/26, in Mead 1959a:305; cf. 206, 546). And there were other important influences on her work—including the Gestalt psychologist Kurt Koffka, whose *Growth of the Mind* (1925) Sapir commended as "the real book for background for a philosophy of culture, at least your/my philosophy" (ES/RB 4/15/25, in Mead 1959a:177). However, it seems likely that Jung's book, which was heavily influenced by Nietzsche (whose *Zarathustra* Benedict had read twenty years before), was the immediate source of the Apollonian/Dionysian opposition which in 1928 was to structure her discussion of "Psychological Types in the Cultures of the Southwest" (cf. Benedict 1939:467, where she mentioned Jung's book as a starting point for the interest in culture and personality).[6]

Having earlier noted the hypertrophy of the vision quest among the Plains Indians, and its attenuation in the Pueblo Southwest, and having been strongly impressed by the contrast between the Zuni and the Pima, for whom "intoxication is the visible mirroring of religion, . . . and the pattern of its mingling of clouded vision and of insight" (1928:250; cf. Mead 1959a:206), Benedict now elaborated a contrast that echoed the two worlds

6. According to Mead, Benedict's characteristic conceptualization of culture as "personality writ large" was worked out during the winter of 1927–28, in long conversations the two of them had about "how a given temperamental approach to living could come so to dominate a culture that all who were born in it would become the willing or unwilling heirs to that view of the world" (Mead 1959a:206–12, 246–47), and was first applied by Mead in *The Social Organization of Manu'a.* Although the issue is not germane to the present argument, it is worth noting that the phrase ("personality writ large") was first used by Benedict in "Configurations of Culture in North America" (1932), which Mead suggests (and textual evidence confirms) was written after "most of *Patterns of Culture* [1934] had been completed" (Mead 1959a:208); although Benedict included "certain paragraphs" from "Configurations" in *Patterns,* they did not in fact include the phrase that was to be her theoretical leitmotif.

of her childhood. On the one hand, there were the Dionysian Pima, pushing ritual to excess in order to achieve "the illuminations of frenzy"; on the other, the Apollonian Zuni, distrusting of excess, minimizing to "the last possible vanishing point any challenging or dangerous experiences," allowing "the individual no disruptive role in their social order" (Benedict 1928:249–50). Separated by no "natural barriers from surrounding peoples," Pueblo culture could not be understood by tracing "influences from other areas," but only in terms of "a fundamental psychological set which has undoubtedly been established for centuries," and which "has created an intricate pattern to express its own preferences"; without such an assumption, "the cultural dynamics of this region are unintelligible" (261).[7]

Without implying that it had no basis in her own observations, or no confirmation in those of others, it seems evident that the picture Benedict painted of Zuni reflected the personal psychological set established at the moment the story of her life began, and the patterning and dynamics of her subsequent personal and cultural experience. The resonance is richest in *Patterns of Culture,* a work written for a popular audience, in which Benedict was, as it were, speaking to the culture in which, after much pain, her personality had found a suitable niche—"Papa Franz" having got her appointment at Columbia regularized after she and her husband finally separated in 1930. Not the least of these resonances is that of sexuality, which in Benedict's own life had moved from a passionless marriage through the distanced passion of a poetic intimacy to a settled lesbian relationship with a younger woman (Modell 1983:188). Thus one of the prominent features of the matrilineal Pueblo pattern was the ease of sexuality, in which menstruation made "no difference in a woman's life" (Benedict 1934:120), in which houses built by men "belong to the women" (106), in which marital jealousy was "soft-pedalled" (107), in which divorce was simply a matter of placing the husband's possessions "on the doorsill" (74), in which there was no sense of sexual sin and no "guilt complexes" (126), and in which homosexuality was an "honourable estate" (263). Just as sex was "an incident in the happy life" (126), so also was death "no denial of life" (128); never the occasion for "an ambitious display or a terror situation," it was got past "as quickly and with as little violence as possible" (109). Homicide was virtually nonexistent, suicide too violent even to contemplate (117); save for witchcraft and revealing the secrets of the kachinas,

7. Superficially, this position echoed Sapir's call for the application of psychology to make understandable the historical process by which "particular elements crystallized into the characteristic pattern"; but at a deeper level, Benedict's hypostatization of an underlying psychological set for each culture contrasted sharply with Sapir's developing thought on the relation of culture and personality, which was increasingly critical of any tendency to reify culture, or to view it as "personality writ large" (Handler 1986; Darnell 1986).

there were "no other crimes" (100). Economic affairs and wealth were "comparatively unimportant" (76, 78); controversies, whether economic or domestic, were "carried out with an unparalleled lack of vehemence"; "every day in Zuni there are fresh instances of their mildness" (106). Although Zuni was "a theocracy to the last implication" (67), everyone cooperated, and "no show of authority" was ever called for, either in domestic or religious situations. Save for the ritual whipping of initiation—which was "never in any way an ordeal" (103)—children were not disciplined, even by the mother's brother, and there was no "possibility of the child's suffering from an Oedipus complex" (101). There was no striving for ecstatic individual experience, "whether by the use of drugs, of alcohol, of fasting, of torture, or of the dance" (95), and no culturally elaborated "themes of terror and danger" (119); the Pueblo way of life was the Apollonian middle way "of measure and of sobriety" (79, 129). Small wonder, then, that the Pueblos did not "picture the universe, as we do, as a conflict of good and evil" (127).

Zuni society was "far from Utopian"; it manifested also "the defects of its virtues" (Benedict 1934:246)—most notably, from our own cultural perspective, "the insistence on sinking the individual in the group" (103): there was no place for "force of will or personal initiative or the disposition to take up arms against a sea of troubles" (246). But for one for whom the achievement of individual identity had been so painfully problematic, and at a cultural moment when "rugged individualism" had come up against the painful reality of massive economic disaster, even this defect had its attractions, especially in view of the broader purpose for which Benedict had written the book. Primitive cultures were "a laboratory of social forms" in which the "problems are set in simpler terms than in the great Western civilizations" (17). Studying them should teach us not only "a greatly increased tolerance toward their divergencies" (37), but could also train us "to pass judgment upon the dominant traits of our own civilization" (249). And when placed against the "cut-throat competition" of the paranoid puritans of Dobu (141) and the "conspicuous waste" of the megalomaniac Kwakiutl (188), there could be little doubt as to which of the three provided the positive reference point for that task of cultural self-criticism.

In reviewing the book, Alfred Kroeber emphasized that it was written for the "intelligent non-anthropologist," arguing that here Benedict had used "pattern" in a "wider sense" than in the article she had published for a professional audience (Kroeber 1935b). But as "propaganda for the anthropological attitude," *Patterns of Culture* was a powerful statement of the anthropological conception of cultural plurality, integration, determinism, and relativity, and it did a great deal toward accomplishing Benedict's goal of making Americans "culture-conscious" (1934:249). Selling well over a million copies during the next thirty years, it was widely used as a college text, and served for many later anthropologists as an introduction to the discipline, even after its portrayal of Zuni culture had come under sharp criticism (cf. A. Smith 1964:262).

The Long-Imagined Avatar of Tepoztlán

During the 1920s, the geography of United States cultural anthropology, which with a few exceptions had until then been coextensive with that of the nation itself, began to expand its horizons – although it was not until after World War II that it became substantially international. As ethnography moved tentatively into new areas, it encompassed other nodes of primitivistic longing, the nearest of which were the transfigured remnants of Aztec Mexico. Objects of ambivalent regard over the centuries, they were then entering a phase of rediscovery, in the eyes of both Mexican *indigenistas* seeking a more viable basis for national identity, and United States intellectuals yearning for a more "genuine culture" (Keen 1971:463–92; cf. Warman 1982:90; Hewitt 1984). One of the centers of *indigenista* interest was the village of Tepoztlán, on the southern side of the mountain rampart rimming the valley of Mexico, where the four thousand inhabitants ("Indians of almost pure blood") still spoke Nahuatl as well as Spanish, and the "folk culture [was] a fusion of Indian and Spanish elements" (Redfield 1930a:30, 13; Godoy 1978:61) – and where Robert Redfield undertook his first anthropological fieldwork late in 1926.

Like the cultural history of Tepoztlán, Redfield's personal history was a fusion of two traditions. In a biographical statement elicited in 1950 by Anne Roe for a comparative psychological study of prominent natural and social scientists, he described himself as "conscious from the first of belonging to two pasts": the "frontier tradition" of his father's "old American" family, and the "European tradition" of his mother, the "hyperrefined" daughter of the Danish consul in Chicago – where Redfield was born in 1897 (Roe 1950; cf. 1953a; GS 1980a). This dual cultural heritage was symbolized in the calendric cycle of his childhood: the six warmer months close to nature in the "clan community" that had developed on land his paternal great-grandfather had settled northwest of Chicago in 1833; the rest of the year in city apartments among Danish-speaking maternal kinfolk who kept alive a strong European tradition (reinforced by occasional trips abroad). Kept "secure from the world" by an "intensively protective father" (a successful corporate lawyer), the "inward facing" family life was marked by "intense intimacy combined with a certain aloofness from the ordinary world." A shy and timid boy, Redfield had little contact with children other than his younger sister, and was tutored at home throughout his somewhat infirm childhood. In 1910, he entered the University of Chicago Laboratory School, where his earlier natural historical interests took a marked literary turn, and he became part of a "somewhat precocious group of literati," before enrolling in the University of Chicago in 1915.

The only conflicts Redfield later recalled with his father were about his "over-protection," and in 1917 he "went down one day" without prior consultation to enlist in an ambulance unit being organized to support the French army—for which his father then arranged the purchase of an ambulance. In France, Redfield took a "salutary beating" from his "hoodlum" buddies, and heard about (though he did not join) their trips to Paris; he also saw "some hard service"—memorialized in poetry later published by Harriet Monroe: "Are all men dead but me, or is this Death by my side?" (Redfield 1919:243). When the unit was disbanded, Redfield returned to the United States "very confused and disorganized," and convinced that "war was unspeakably bad"—although he did make speeches for the Liberty Loan drive after a heart murmur kept him out of the army. Accepting his father's suggestion that he go to Harvard, Redfield briefly studied (and disliked) biology, and then joined his family in Washington, where he served as a Senate office boy and worked in the code room at Military Intelligence. When the family returned to Chicago after the war, Redfield again followed paternal advice and studied law. Upon taking his degree the year after his father's death, he went to work in what had been his father's firm, where he did ill-paid drudge work in the city records for cases involving the sewer system ("I knew more about manhole covers than anyone in the city of Chicago") (Roe 1950).

By this time, Redfield had married the daughter of the Chicago urban sociologist Robert Park, and (at his own father's expense) had enjoyed a honeymoon in the Pueblo Southwest. In 1923, when Redfield was in a "state of great restlessness" over his work, and had begun to be excited by his father-in-law's ideas about a "science of society," his wife suggested that they accept an open invitation to visit Mexico previously extended to the Park family by Elena Landazuri, a feminist *indigenista* who had studied under Park. While there, they met other *indigenistas*, including the artist Diego Rivera, the folklorist Frances Toor, who had recently done research in Tepoztlán, and Manuel Gamio, a Boas-trained anthropologist then carrying on archeological and ethnographic research at Teotihuacán. Observing Gamio at work in the field, Redfield decided to become an anthropologist—happily, at the very time when his father-in-law wrote to announce that the Chicago Department of Sociology and Anthropology was taking steps to develop a training program in the latter field (Godoy 1978:50–51).

Redfield began his studies in the fall of 1924, the second year of Fay-Cooper Cole's effort to revitalize Chicago anthropology, which under

Frederick Starr had been moribund for twenty years. Cole was an early Boas Ph.D. of rather traditional archeological and ethnological orientation; but he was also a talented academic entrepreneur, sensitive to changing trends within anthropology and to emerging funding patterns in the social sciences. Within a year he had succeeded in bringing Edward Sapir to Chicago. While most of Redfield's anthropological work was with Cole, he took several courses with Sapir, as well as courses in sociology with Ellsworth Faris, William Ogburn, Ernest Burgess, and his father-in-law. His early anthropological orientation clearly reflected Park's personal intellectual heritage, which was an amalgam of the pragmatism of John Dewey and William James, the sociological concepts of Georg Simmel, Ferdinand Tönnies, and William Graham Sumner, and the epistemological thought of Wilhelm Windelband. Accepting the Germanic distinction between idiographic and nomothetic sciences, and acknowledging the Boasian critique of evolutionism, Redfield associated himself with the emerging anthropological interest in "processual generalizations," which he felt was exemplified in the work of William Rivers, Clark Wissler, and Sapir (GS n.d., 1979a).

Perhaps his most significant experience, however, was in Burgess's practicum in sociological research, which in a department noted for its empirical work in the "laboratory of the city" was required of every student. During his first year of graduate study, Redfield made more than forty visits to the Chicago Mexican community, recording his experiences in a lengthy typed diary. After Redfield completed two years of course work and a year of teaching at the University of Chicago, his experience in Burgess's practicum became the basis for a research proposal that Cole forwarded to the recently formed Social Science Research Council, in the hope that field research might be made a standard part of graduate training in anthropology. Redfield's previous "survey of Mexicans in Chicago" suggested the need for a study of the "conditions under which the Mexican has been raised" in "semi-primitive village communities" in order to understand "the problems arising out of the growing Mexican immigration into the United States." To this end, he proposed an inquiry that touched the four bases of his own (and his father-in-law's) social scientific interests: a "nomothetic study" of the problem known "to sociologists as assimilation and to the anthropologists as culture-borrowing"; a more subjective understanding of native culture by entering "the lives of people and learn[ing] the problems which occupy their minds"; a functional study of the various social institutions and their interrelations; and a study of "comparative mentality" (Godoy 1978:54–60; cf. GS n.d.).

Aided by a $2500 Social Science Research Council fellowship, and accompanied by his wife, their two small children, and his mother-in-law,

Redfield left Chicago in November 1926 for Tepoztlán, which Gamio had suggested as a field site. After travelling the sixty miles from Mexico City by rail, they were met at nearby San Juan by Jesús Condé, a member of the expatriate "Colonia Tepozteco" formed in Mexico City during the latter days of the Mexican Revolution. Condé had subsequently returned to his native village to push a program of civil reform and Indian cultural regeneration, and was to be Redfield's primary informant. After a four-hour mountain trek to Tepoztlán, the Redfield family settled quickly into simple (but by local standards "elegant") domesticity in a one-room brick-floored house. Savoring the vista of the valley spread out before their doorway, and the visibly embedded history of the "stillest, quietest place" he had ever seen, Redfield and his wife filled their days with ethnographic work among barefoot people who moved "in crooked lanes, where never runs a wheel, like figures in a dream." It was so much what Redfield had "for so long imagined" that it felt like "a repetition of an experience in some earlier avatar" (RR: RR/R. Park 12/2/26).

But as Redfield also noted, Tepoztlán had been a focal point of revolutionary violence, and it was still "very Zapatista in sentiment." Beneath the surface of its "relatively homogeneous and well-integrated" society, the village was divided between religious and "bolshevik" factions, and the "Cristero" rebels in the surrounding region made the Redfields' position insecure almost from the first. On February 18, forty armed men rode into the village shouting "Viva Cristo el Rey," and before the "battle of Tepoztlán" was over, two locals had been wounded and one rebel left dead in the gutter (RP: RR/Clara Park 2/20/27; Godoy 1978:67–68). The Redfields retreated to sanctuary in the Federal District, from which Redfield carried on a commuter ethnography—despite fits of "profound depression," the serious illness of his wife, and continuing rebel activity that made his informants "reluctant to give information." By the end of June he was physically and emotionally exhausted, and over Cole's objections that it would not "look good" to his funders, he took his family back to Chicago (Godoy 1978:70–72).

Redfield looked back upon the rebellion as a "minor disturbance of a life as delightful as it is remote, and as scientifically provocative as it is delightful" (1928:247). He had collected a fair amount of rather traditional ethnographic information on such topics as festal cycles and the social organization of the barrios, as well as a large number of "corridos" (contemporary folk ballads), which he saw as playing the same integrative role his father-in-law (a former journalist) attributed to the newspaper in urban society. But in general Redfield's ethnographic corpus was somewhat thin and spotty, and the frankly sketchy synthesis he defended as a dissertation in the summer of 1928 (and published with slight revision two

Robert Redfield in Tepoztlán, 1926. (Courtesy of the Department of Special Collections, University of Chicago Library)

years later) showed at various points not only the influence of the personality and values that predisposed him to romanticize Tepoztecan life and to repress its less "enjoyable" aspects, but also the influence of prior conceptual and theoretical assumptions.

Redfield regarded Clark Wissler's *Man and Culture* (1923) as "the best piece of anthropological writing" he had read (RP: RR/Wissler 2/9/25), and *Tepoztlán* is clearly influenced by Wissler's concepts, which were quite congenial to the "ecological" approach Park had adopted for the study of the city. In interpreting the diffusion of culture traits in Tepoztlán, Redfield redefined the notion of the "culture area" in terms of a modification of the concentric ecological zones Burgess had laid upon the map of Chicago, with the central plaza serving as the "periphery of change" from which to trace "the diffusion of city traits." Like Park, Redfield conceptualized cultural units and processes in terms of different styles of mental life and personality types, transforming the Tepoztecan descriptive adjectives "tonto" and "correcto" into polar personality and class categories. Redfield's conception of the "folk community" as a type "intermediate between the primitive tribe and the modern city" (1930a:217) was strongly influenced by Park (and the German traditions on which Park drew), and by the modified social evolutionism that structured Park's thinking. Thus "the disorganization and perhaps the reorganization" of Tepoztecan culture "under the slowly growing influence of the city" was merely an example "of the general type of change whereby primitive man becomes civilized man, the rustic becomes the urbanite" (Redfield 1930a:14; cf. GS n.d.; Breslau 1988). But Redfield showed a greater tendency than Park to romanticize the *gemeinschaftlich* organicism of the folk community, and the relation to Sapir's dichotomy of cultures was subsequently suggested by one of Redfield's students: "To the degree that a culture is folk it is also genuine; and, to the degree that a culture departs from its folk attributes, to that degree is it moving toward a condition of spuriousness" (Tumin 1945:199).

By the time *Tepoztlán* appeared, Redfield had embarked on a long-term study of four communities in Yucatan, distributed "along the scale of modernization," which exemplified the process by which small, isolated, closely integrated folk communities underwent a regular process of disorganization, secularization, and individualization as they came in more frequent cultural contact with heterogeneous urban society (GS 1980a). Both the "folk-urban continuum" and the ethnography of Tepotzlán were to come under sharp criticism from a later generation of meso-American anthropologists. Even at the time, Ruth Benedict (who must have had in mind Malinowski and Mead rather than her own rather traditional memory ethnography) criticized Redfield for relying on informants rather than on his own "actual participation in the life of the community" (1930). But the leading Boasian historicist greeted Redfield's book as a "landmark" study, which might provide a "model" for future inquiry (Kroeber 1931:238). And although Redfield, unlike Benedict and Mead, did not direct his study to popular audiences, or himself use Tepoztlán for purposes of cultural critique, several of his readers did. For Stuart Chase, the influential cultural critic and popularizer of social scientific ideas—who drew extensively on Redfield's work—*Tepoztlán* became an archetype to be posed against *Mid-*

dletown (Lynd & Lynd 1929) as contrastive "other" in his on-going critique of "mechanical civilization."

> Middletown is essentially practical, Tepoztlán essentially mystical in mental processes. Yet in coming to terms with one's environment, Tepoztlán has exhibited, I think, the superior common sense. . . . These people possess several qualities the average American would give his eyeteeth to get; and they possess other things completely beyond his purview—human values he has not even glimpsed, so relentlessly has his age blinded and limited him. (Chase 1931:17, 208)

Lithe Brown Bodies Silhouetted against the Sunset

From the time that Captain Cook returned from Tahiti, the focal ganglion in the world geography of European primitivistic longing was the islands of the "South Seas," where handsome brown-skinned natives led untroubled lives, finding ready sustenance in the fruit of palm trees under which they made a free and easy love (Fairchild 1961; B. Smith 1960). But although the islands of the Pacific were also the locus of antiprimitivist missionary enterprise throughout the nineteenth century (Boutilier et al. 1978; Garrett 1982), and were touched by the United States Exploring Expedition in the 1840s (Stanton 1975), they did not become an object of serious American anthropological interest until immediately after World War I (Te Rangi Hiroa 1945). In a postwar context of cultural criticism, moral questioning, and sexual experimentation, it is scarcely surprising that this anthropological interest became entangled, in the work of Margaret Mead, in "invisible threads" of primitivist consciousness.[8]

Four years younger than Redfield, Mead was also the firstborn child in a family securely set off from the rest of the world; she later recalled taking "pride in living in a household that was itself unique," but also longing "to share in every culturally normal experience" (1972a:20). And while both her parents came from "old American" backgrounds, the rather dramatic contrast between the strong women and the weak men within her family environment must have reinforced a sense of the possibilities of culturally conditioned difference. But if her father's life had been "cut down"

8. Although they did not achieve the same degree of anthropological notoriety, Ralph Linton's observations on Marquesan sexuality were also based on fieldwork done in this period, and provide an interesting gender contrast to those of Mead in Samoa. Whereas Mead emphasized the freedom of female premarital sexuality, Linton emphasized the treatment of women as sexual subjects, and the man's "playing up to her erotic wishes" (1939:173)—a characterization that was to be called into question by a later ethnographer, on methodological grounds not dissimilar to those raised in the case of Mead (Suggs 1971).

to "the pattern of academic and social virtues in which [her] mother believed" (40), his marginal involvement in the entrepreneurial world as professor in the University of Pennsylvania business school and editor of *Railway Age* nevertheless assured the family a comfortable middle-class existence, and he found outlet for a somewhat anxious masculinity in occasional infidelities. Overprotective of his "fragile" and disaster-prone son, he left most of the supervision of his daughters to his wife. Mead resented his occasional "arbitrary intrusions into our lives" and his "conservative, money-bound judgments" (39), but she quickly learned how to get what she wanted from him—and as "the original punk" was easily able to dominate her younger brother. Her mother, a graduate student at the University of Chicago when she married at the age of twenty-nine, moved the family to Hammonton, New Jersey, in 1902 so that she could continue her never-completed dissertation research among Italian families. A feminist radical who combined "fury at injustice" with "deep personal gentleness" (25), she retained a strong Old New England sense of the distance between "people with some background" and the "common herd" (28)—but also "danced for joy" at the outbreak of the Russian Revolution (97). That Mead in her own life "realized every one of her [mother's] unrealized ambitions" (29) was in large part due to the "decisive influence" (45) of her paternal grandmother, a one-time school teacher, who was responsible for Mead's education until she entered high school, who taught her "to treat all people as the children of God" (54), and who set the ten-year-old Mead to work taking notes on the behavior of her younger siblings (just as Mead's mother had previously taken notes on Mead's). Within the "overriding academic ethos [that] shaped all our lives," in which "the enjoyment of the intellect as mediated by words in books was central," Mead was "the child who could make the most of this," and was never "asked to constrain or distort some other gift" (90).

Child of pragmatic rationality and confident privilege, Mead's only remembered experience with "a possibly punitive authority" came at the age of two when her mother made her show a stolen violet to a park policeman, who "only smiled" (1972a:120). Her archetypal experience of the formation of irrational prejudice came when midwestern sorority members at DePauw University in Indiana rejected her for her exotic eastern mannerisms and the ritualistic Episcopalianism she had embraced in mild adolescent rebellion against her agnostic parents—if not also for her feeling that "from this position of security" she could "dictate egalitarian behavior" (94). Although Mead responded characteristically "by setting out to see what I could do within this system" (98), she experienced her year at DePauw as a small-town "exile" from "the center of life" in New York City (100), and in the autumn of 1920 she transferred to Barnard College.

There she quickly found a subculture she could fit into: an unusually talented literary "intelligentsia" set off from their "mediocre" and "reactionary" classmates, who lived in an off-campus apartment and went down to "the Village" ("a most delightful place"), who refused to attend a dinner with Columbia's president "Nicky Butler" because evening dress was required, who (after some hesitation) "bobbed" their hair, who listened to Scott Nearing and "organized a meeting for two Italians framed up for murder because they are radicals," and who called themselves first the "communist morons" and then the "Ash Can Cats" (MeP: MM/E. F. Mead, 1920–23). Although they were "still remarkably innocent about practical matters relating to sex," they read Margaret Sanger, talked about Freud, and knew that "repression was a bad thing" (Mead 1972a:103). They also "learned about homosexuality"—as "Euphemia," Mead received passionate letters from a classmate who signed herself "Peter" (MeP: Box C1). Mead later spoke of her friends as "part of a generation of young women who felt extraordinarily free"—refusing to "bargain with men," delaying marriage until they felt like it, and carrying on affairs with older men who were somewhat perplexed by their freedom (1972a:108; cf. Fass 1971:260–90). She herself, however, had been engaged since shortly after her sixteenth birthday to Luther Cressman, whose own moral odyssey took him from army training camp into training for the Episcopal priesthood, and thence into graduate training in sociology (Cressman 1988). Until (both still virgins) they were married after her graduation, the major nonverbal outlet for her libidinal energy was apparently a persistent neuritis of the right arm (Mead 1972a:104; cf. J. Howard 1984:47–48; Cressman 1988:92). From the beginning, the emotional commitments in what she later called her "student marriage" seem to have been a bit asymmetrical. However, Mead did not have her own affair with an older man until her poetry had begun to reveal her marital discontent: "You could dampen my joy with your reason, My ecstasy cool with a glance" (MeP: Poems; cf. Mead 1972a:123). When she did, it was with "the most brilliant person" and the "most satisfactory mind I ever met" (1972a:50); but when Edward Sapir "implored" her, after the death of his wife, to "be mama" to "his three motherless children" (quoted in J. Howard 1984:52), Mead had by that time already committed her own life to anthropology.

At Barnard, Mead's ambitions had shifted from writing to politics to science, through which she hoped both to understand human behavior and "be effective in the world of human events" (1962:121). Although she majored in a rather scientistic quantitative psychology, at the beginning of her senior year she took two classes that were to lead her toward anthropology: Ogburn's course on the psychological aspects of culture, which—despite his strong statisticalist bent—was the first in which "Freudian psychology was treated with respect" (111); and Boas' introductory course in anthropology, in which Mead so impressed him by her "helpful participation in class discussion" that Boas excused her from the final exam (112). Despite Boas' anti-evolutionism, what moved her most about anthropology was the "sense of the millennia it had taken man to take the first groping steps toward civilization" (112)—and the prospect of studying one of the "primitive cultures" that were fast being killed off by "contact with modern civilization" (MeP: MM/M. R. Mead 3/11/23; cf. Mead 1959b). "Dr. Boas"—not yet "Papa Franz"—remained a somewhat distant and unapproachable figure, and it was Ruth Benedict who "humanized Boas' formal lectures" (Mead 1962:113) and recruited Mead for anthropology—and who, in the aftermath of a classmate's shocking suicide, Mead began to know "not only as a teacher but also as a friend," and later for a time as lover (115; cf. Bateson 1984:140).

Although Mead's master's thesis was formally in psychology, the problem was set by Boas, as part of his on-going critique of hereditarian racial assumption. Carried on in the same community her mother had studied two decades before, Mead's research on "Group Intelligence Tests and Linguistic Disability Among Italian Children" showed that test scores varied in proportion to the amount of English spoken in their homes (Mead 1927). Her doctoral research, eventually published as *An Inquiry into the Question of Cultural Stability in Polynesia* (1928a), reflected another part of Boas' developing agenda: the attempt, in response to the hyperdiffusionism of certain British and German ethnologists, to test the relative stability of different elements of culture. Like Benedict's dissertation, it was a library study of the association of cultural elements over a broad geographical area, and led toward a more integrative study—inasmuch as the form and meaning of elements was "particularly subject to reinterpretation in terms of the prevailing pattern of each group" (84).

At the end of her first year of graduate study, Mead was initiated into the then rather intimate world of professional anthropology at the Toronto meetings of the British Association. There she heard Sapir and Goldenweiser arguing about Jung's psychological types, met Erna Gunther (whose "avant-garde 'contract marriage'" with Leslie Spier in 1921 had occasioned shocked comment in the New York press), and discovered that everyone "had a field of his own, . . . a 'people' to whom he referred in his discussions" (1972a:124). Already immersed in the ethnographic literature of Polynesia, and no doubt aware that few professional claims had been staked in the area, Mead decided to do fieldwork there on the question of cultural change. Although Mead hoped that the psychogalvanometer (the forerunner of the lie detector) would enable her actually to measure "the individual's emotional responses" to change (125), Boas regarded such quantification as "premature" (Mead 1962:122). By this time his research agenda was shifting from diffusionary questions to "the set of problems that linked the development of individuals to what was distinctive in the culture in which they were reared" (Mead 1972a:126), and he proposed instead that Mead undertake a study of "the relative strength of biological puberty and cultural pattern" (Mead 1962:122; cf. Freeman 1991a).

In the era of "flaming youth," the phenomenon of adolescence was a center of cultural concern, and the discussion was strongly influenced by the recapitulationist evolutionary arguments of G. Stanley Hall (1907)—who had in fact been *persona non grata* to Boas since his acrimonious departure from Clark University back in 1892. Boas may have felt that adolescence was a particularly appropriate problem for Mead, who at twenty-three knew what it was to be a "flapper," and who still had a slight, adolescent figure and a childish gait. A bargain was struck, and Mead accepted Boas' problem, which they presented to the National Research Council as "A Study in Heredity and Environment Based on the Investigation of the Phenomena of Adolescence among Primitive and Civilized Peoples" (MeP: Fellowship application, 1925). In return, Boas—overriding Sapir's objection that she was "too high strung and emotional"—agreed that Mead might go to an area he himself regarded as "too dangerous," provided she chose an island "to which a ship came regularly" (Mead 1972a:128–29). Mead picked American Samoa, which since 1900 had been under the governance of the U.S. Navy, and where her father-in-law had contacts (cf. Cressman 1988:114). When April 30, 1925, brought the news that she had been awarded a Research Council fellowship, Mead and the Ash Can Cats were able to join its celebration to another they had already planned: a midnight visit to Greenwich Village, where they hung a Maybasket of flowers on the front door of a surprised and delighted Edna St. Vincent Millay—though they could not summon up the nerve to recite her verse in chorus (J. Howard 1984:56–57).

Three months later, Mead set off by rail across the country, accompanied part way by Benedict, who was returning to Zuni. Passing through Los Angeles (a city "run by real estate men for other real estate men"), Mead embarked from San Francisco for Honolulu (where "wandering mists" hid "all the signs of industrial civilization"). From there she sailed to Pago Pago, where she stayed in the hotel that had been the setting for Somerset Maugham's *Rain*, and went to dances aboard a naval cruiser (Mead 1977:21, 23; cf. MeP: "Field Bulletins"). During the next few weeks in Pago Pago and in nearby villages on the island of Tutuila, she practiced the language and saw "the principal social ceremonies," remarking the contrast between what was visible on the surface to the "transient white man" and the underlying "fabric of their culture," and concluding that it was "much easier to derive aesthetic pleasure from contemplating the ideas underlying their culture than from looking at the human embodiments of those ideas" (MeP: "Field Bulletins" 10/3/25). She decided to transfer in November to Ta'u, the easternmost island of the Manu'a district, which several years before had been the center of a rebellion against United States rule—"an insane procedure fostered by an unstable officer and a scheming carpetbagger" (MeP: "Field Bulletins" 10/31/25). "More primitive and unspoiled than any other part of Samoa," Ta'u nevertheless had a resident naval medical officer, with whose family Mead could live, so that she could be "in and out of the native homes" all day and "still have a bed to sleep on and wholesome food" (1977:28).

Although Boas felt that Mead's study was a methodological innovation, marking the "first serious attempt to enter into the mental life of a group in a primitive society" (MeP: FB/MM 11/7/25), he had given her only one half-hour of methodological instruction before she sailed for Samoa, emphasizing that she should stick to her problem and not waste time "studying the culture as a whole" (Mead 1972a:138). Mead did in fact collect general ethnographic material, but she concentrated on performing psychological tests and collecting systematic data on a group of fifty girls, twenty-five of them postpubertal (1928b:260; cf. MeP: MM/FB 2/15/26). The most problematic data were of course those on sexual behavior, which were collected by various means. Mead's notes on the Samoan language include a lengthy and highly explicit list of sex terms recorded sixty years before by the missionary George Pratt; her general notes include a long and vividly detailed interview with one adult male informant covering all aspects of Samoan sex life, including techniques of masturbation and foreplay, sexual positions, frequency of married and premarital intercourse, and female behavior at the height of orgasm; one of her bulletin letters home includes an account of an evening with adolescents that ended with one of the girls, amid much banter about her numerous lovers, picking out a boy to accompany her home; the records Mead kept of her fifty girls include a column headed "Sex," in which she made such notes as "admits a lover," "the other girls say she sleeps with . . . ," "promenades a great deal." Mead's bulletin accounts suggest that although she had some trouble with the language, she worked without an interpreter (being in fact coopted for that role by the chaplain), and that she was able to establish good rapport with young Samoans, who visited her from five in the morning until midnight. Indeed, a key component of her "method" seems to have been the kind of late-night gossip she must have enjoyed with the Ash Can Cats.[9]

9. Derek Freeman has suggested that the Samoan participants in these late evening sessions "plied Mead with . . . counterfeit tales" in order to "amuse themselves, and had no ink-

After five months in Ta'u — during which a severe hurricane had disrupted her work for two weeks — Mead felt that she had really experienced Samoan life from the inside. She had avoided entanglement in the "toils" of the rank system in her own village, where the children called her "Makelita" and treated her as "one of themselves." But elsewhere on the island, where she was treated as *taupou* (or ceremonial virgin), she had "rank to burn," and "could order the whole village about." At the end, she felt that she had not only watched Samoans, but had "been them":

> I have been dressed to dance by the whole village as they tied the ti leaves around my wrist and ankles and smeared the cocoanut oil over my arms and shoulders. . . . I haven't watched a group of boys flirt with the visiting lady, I've flirted myself as the visiting lady . . . and I've listened to my talking chiefs quarrel and scheme over the return presents and shared the humiliation of high chiefs too poor to properly validate their privileges. (MeP: MM/M. R. Mead 4/15/26)

When it came time to leave, Mead was ready to go home: "nine months of isolated labor in an uncongenial climate are quite enough for me." But as she told her grandmother, who had taught her "to appreciate the infinite detail of existence," she felt a deep sense of loss that soon there would be "no more palms, no more lithe brown bodies passing and repassing, silhouetted against the sunset": "if Samoa were nearer to you all, and there were no dull white people and mosquitos, it would be a pleasant paradise" (MeP: MM/M. R. Mead 4/15/26).

Two months into her stay on Ta'u, in a moment of methodological angst, Mead had written to Boas wondering how she might present her material so that "no reader should have to trust my word for anything," but would be offered "an array of facts from which another would be able to draw independent conclusions." The "Ogburns of science" would not be satis-

ling that their tales would ever find their way into a book"; they were simply manifesting the behavior called *tau fa'asse'e,* "the action of deliberately duping someone, a pastime that greatly appeals to the Samoans as a respite from the severities of their authoritarian society" (Freeman 1983a:290). More recently, he has offered evidence of interviews with several elderly Samoan women who recalled those evenings of sixty years ago in very much the same terms: "I think some girl told her a wrong story. The Samoan people you know wants to laugh to a foreigner or someone, so they told a wrong story to influence her to listen to the story but it's not a true story." "Yes, she asked us what we did after dark. We girls would pinch each other and tell her that we were out with the boys. We were only joking, but she took it seriously. As you know, Samoan girls are terrific liars and love making fun of people, but Margaret thought it was all true" (Freeman, personal communication, 11/22/88, quoting passages from the postproduction script of the film *Margaret Mead and Samoa,* by Frank Heimans; cf. Freeman 1989). There is little doubt that the matter of Samoan sexuality is one where Mead seems to have been particularly susceptible to scotomization (blind spots) and/or projection (cf. Devereux 1967) and she might also have been the victim of misinformation.

Margaret Mead and unidentified Samoan friend, Manu'a, 1926. (Courtesy of the Institute for Intercultural Studies, Inc.)

fied with anything other than a "semi-statistical" presentation, but this would be "misleading" because the sample was too small, and "isolated facts" had meaning only in the context of "my final conclusion as to submission and rebellion in the family circle." Alternatively, she could use case histories—but to fill them "with all the minutiae which make them significant to me when they are passing before my eyes is next to impossible," and it was not clear in any case that they would "prove a point" (MeP: MM/FB 1/5/26). In response, Boas suggested that a "statistical treatment of such an intricate behaviour" would "not have very much meaning." He recommended instead giving a "summarized description" of "the conditions under which the behaviour develops" and then setting off "the individual against the background"—which he compared to "the method that is used by medical men in their analysis of individual cases on which is built up the general picture of the pathological cases that they want to describe." While "complete elimination of the subjective attitude of the investigator is quite impossible in a matter of this kind," Boas felt Mead would undoubtedly "try to overcome this so far as this is possible" (MeP: FB/MM 2/15/26; cf. GS 1987b).

Mead returned from Samoa westward via Europe, and on the trip fell passionately in love with an aggressively masculine young New Zealand psychologist, Reo Fortune, who was on his way to England to study anthropology with Malinowski. For the moment, she "re-chose Luther," but the sense of "common vocation working with people within the framework of the church" was gone, and Mead, who had planned to have six children, was told by a gynecologist that a tipped uterus would prevent her ever giving birth. She continued to live with Cressman through an "odd winter," finishing an account of her Samoan research during time free from her new job at the American Museum of Natural History. But after another "tempestuous" month with Fortune in Germany the following summer, she decided to marry him, and wrote to Cressman insisting on a divorce (1972a:157–67; Cressman 1988:189–91).

Back in New York that fall, Mead worked on revisions of the rather prosaically titled manuscript on "The Adolescent Girl in Samoa" which she had previously sent to the publisher William Morrow. In that version, cross-cultural comparisons were relegated to a brief set of "conclusions" in which Mead suggested that "only by criticizing our own civilization in terms of the behavior of other human beings in civilizations having different patterns of behavior can we arrive at any knowledge of how great a part of our attitudes and behavior is due, not to the accident of humanity or even of sex, still less of race, but rather to the accident of being born in America, or in Samoa, in the America of 1927 instead of the America of 1729" (MeP): Morrow was interested in the manuscript, but he wanted something that might have the impact of the recent best-selling anthropological popularization *Why We Behave Like Human Beings* (1926) – whose author, George Dorsey, had introduced Mead to Morrow (J. Howard 1984: 87–88). Somewhat ambivalently, Mead "finally decided" to go along with a number of proposed revisions and provided Morrow with new material in which she pushed speculation "to the limit of permissibility" (MeP; MM/WM 1/25/27, 2/11/28).

The result was *Coming of Age in Samoa: A Psychological Study of Primitive Youth for Western Civilisation* (1928b).[10] The worrisome methodological issues Mead had discussed with Boas were now relegated to an appendix on problems of sampling and the "personal equation," where, accepting Boas' clinical analogy, she acknowledged that the "student of the more intangible and psychological aspects of human behavior is forced to illuminate rather than demonstrate a thesis" (260). In rather striking contrast, her new introduction confidently asserted the validity of the "anthropological method" as the only option for those "who wish to conduct a human experiment but who lack the power either to construct the experimental conditions or to find controlled examples of those conditions." By choosing "quite simple, primitive peoples," whose "fundamental structure" a "trained student" could "master" in a "few months," and in which "one girl's life was so much like another's," it became possible to answer the question "which sent me to Samoa" (7, 8, 11).

Mead's ability to do this depended in part on relegating another potentially troublesome issue to the back of her book, where "Samoan Civilisation as it is Today" (originally her final chapter) also appeared as an appendix. In it, she minimized the impact of missionaries and emphasized the naval administration's "admirable policy of benevolent non-interference in native affairs," concluding that while "the new influences" had "drawn the teeth of the old culture" (cannibalism, blood revenge, the "cruel defloration ceremony," etc.) they had not introduced "economic instability, poverty, the wage system, the separation of the worker from his land and from

10. For a suggestive analysis of Mead's rhetorical strategy in *Coming of Age*, see Porter 1984. During the same period when Mead was working on revisions of that book, she wrote a more conventional ethnography, *The Social Organization of Manu'a*, which was published in 1930 as a museum bulletin. While it seems evident that certain of the more questionable aspects of her interpretation of Samoa reflect the attempt to popularize her findings in response to Morrow's urging, it is doubtful that all the issues that have been raised regarding her Samoan ethnography can be resolved by compartmentalizing the "popularized" and the "professional." Although the substance and the style of the second work were clearly directed to a specifically professional audience, Mead did not at the time insist on the difference. She cited her earlier study (1930:126), and insofar as the two studies overlap, their interpretations seem consistent with one another.

his tools, modern warfare, industrial disease, the abolition of leisure, the irksomeness of a bureaucratic government," or the "subtler penalties of civilisation" such as neuroses, philosophical perplexities, and individual tragedies (1928b:270, 276–77). Granting that precontact Samoan culture had been "less flexible" and "less kindly with the individual aberrant," and cautioning the reader against mistaking the conditions she described for "aboriginal" or "typical primitive ones," Mead suggested that "present day Samoan civilisation" was simply the result of the "fortuitous" and "fortunate" impact of "a complex intrusive culture upon a simpler and most hospitable indigenous one" (272–73). But in the body of the book itself, such ambiguities of cultural historicity were subordinated to purposes of cultural archetypification.

The tone was set right at the beginning in a brief account Mead had inserted of "A Day in Samoa," which opened at dawn with "lovers slip[ing] home from trysts" and closed long past midnight with "the mellow thunder of the reef and the whisper of lovers" (1928b:14–19). This archetypifying sense of cultural contemporaneity was sustained throughout the next ten chapters by the consistent use of the "ethnographic present," except when Mead referred in the past tense to the behavior of particular individuals she had studied. Similarly, most of her infrequent comments on "former days" or processes of cultural change had the effect of accounting for anomalies in the pattern she was constructing—for example, the reference to rape as an "abnormal" result of contact with "white civilisation" (93), or the explanation of the "curious" attitude toward virginity as the result of the "moral premium on chastity" introduced by Christianity (98).

When at the end Mead undertook more explicit comparison of the "civilisation of America and the civilisation of Samoa," this archetypifying atemporality had (paradoxically, for a disciple of Boas) an evolutionary as well as a culturally particular aspect: what made the life of the Samoan adolescent girl different was partly the "shallowness" of Samoan (as opposed to other) "primitive civilisations," and partly the limitation of individual choice that was characteristic of "all isolated primitive civilisation" (1928b:198, 200). The presentation of cultural relativism in an evolutionary package ("A Study of Primitive Youth for Western Civilisation") made it possible to appeal simultaneously to motives of romantic primitivism and ethnocentric progressivism. On the one hand, Mead insisted that "our own ways are not humanly inevitable or God-ordained" (233) and that we "pay heavily for our heterogeneous, rapidly changing civilisation" (247). But in return, we gained "the possibility of choice, the recognition of "many possible ways of life, where other civilisations have recognized only one." By accepting the "downfall of a single standard" and educating our children for choice, "we shall have realised the high point of individual choice and universal toleration which a heterogeneous culture and a heterogeneous culture alone can attain" (248).

Mead felt that she had written a book about the cultural determination of individual choice, and that message was surely there. But a more specifically sexual message was suggested by the dust jacket illustration of a bare-breasted maiden rushing with her lover to a tryst beneath a moonlit palm. And the text itself, resonating to both contemporary cultural and Mead's own personal experience, did a great deal to sustain this reading: "romantic love as it occurs in our civilisation, inextricably bound up with ideas of monogamy, exclusiveness, jealousy and undeviating fidelity" was absent among Samoans, who "scoff at fidelity to a long absent wife or mistress, [and] believe explicitly that one love will quickly cure another" (1928b:104–5). When Robert Lowie suggested that the "free love" of modern Samoa might be the abnormal result of cultural contact and should not be offered as evidence for Mead's "pedagogical theses" (Lowie 1929: 533), Mead insisted that she had never intended to imply that "Samoans are free from conflict principally because they are 'sexually uninhibited'" (MeP: MM/RL 11/5/29). Similarly, she was amazed that the students of a professor at a Tennessee teachers' college should have thought that her book was "mainly about sex education and sex freedom," when "out of 297 pages there are exactly sixty eight which deal with sex" (MeP: MM/W. Brownell 3/10/30). But as the dust jacket comments, the almost uniformly favorable reviews in the popular press, and the many news accounts of Mead's adventure suggest, there were many others who got the same impression—including Edward Sapir, whose neo-conservative essay on the "discipline of sex" was written with Margaret Mead in mind (Sapir 1930; cf. 1928:523; Handler 1986:143–47).

Despite Mead's initial "amazement" that it had been used as a college text, *Coming of Age in Samoa* served that purpose from the moment of its publication. And although there was from the beginning an undercurrent of professional criticism of its ethnographic adequacy, it has been, like *Patterns of Culture,* one of the most influential anthropological works of the twentieth century. This, despite (or perhaps because of) the fact that it, too, was strikingly marked by personal and cultural concerns at once particular to an historical moment and resonant of a more general cultural tradition (cf. E. Jones 1988).[11]

11. Three decades later, Mead herself acknowledged the embeddedness of her book in the cultural context of the mid-1920s, which she recalled as both "young and hopeful," but filled with "the rebellion and self-criticism, the hatreds and the cynical despair which were nourished by the growing crisis of the post–World War I world." For many, her book was "an escape in spirit that paralleled an escape in body to a South Sea island where love and

The Critique of Apollonian Ethnography

Although their career patterns followed rather different trajectories, Benedict, Redfield, and Mead all became major figures in American anthropology. But over the decades each of their early ethnographic interpretations was to become the subject of systematic (and controversial) criticism. Widely spaced in time, these critiques were not themselves the products of a single cultural historical moment. Nevertheless, there are certain common threads that run through them, and by considering them here together, we may perhaps cast light not only on the "Apollonian" ethnography of the 1920s,[12] but on certain more enduring aspects of the modern anthropological tradition, regarded both as a professional discipline and as a cultural ideology.

The fieldwork on which the first of these critiques was based was actually begun before Benedict herself had gone to the Southwest, when in 1920 Franz Boas' young secretary, Esther Schiff, coaxed him to allow her to join him on a field trip to the Laguna pueblo, where the previous summer he had begun a study of the Keresan language. Born in 1897 to one of the German Jewish financial families from whom Boas occasionally sought research support, Schiff had taken his introductory course during her senior year at Barnard. Although she continued as his secretary after her month in the Southwest, she also attended anthropology classes, and the following summer was invited to accompany him again. This time she began fieldwork at Cochiti, where she was struck by the occasionally violent factionalism between the "progressives" and "conservatives." In 1922, she again accompanied Boas to Cochiti, where she was adopted into the clan of her hostess, and continued the research that eventuated in a monograph on social and ceremonial organization (Goldfrank 1927). In the fall of 1922, Schiff gave up her secretarial position (to Ruth Bunzel) in order to pursue an academic career. However, that career was interrupted by her marriage that December to Walter Goldfrank, a widower (with three

---

ease were the order of the day." Furthermore, this was a reading her own "inexperience" had encouraged: because she herself had "yet to come to terms with other primitive people, fear-ridden and hungry and harsh to their children, the Samoans inevitably stood for 'the primitive'"—despite the fact that she "was not advocating a return to the primitive but rather greater knowledge which would give modern man more control over the civilizing process itself" (1961:xi–xii).

12. Although I have used the term "ethnography" here to characterize the work of both the Apollonians and their critics, most of the works at issue are not in a conventional sense ethnographic monographs—and one of the authors has specifically disavowed the idea that his work constituted "an alternative ethnography" (Freeman 1983a:xii); from this perspective, "ethnographic interpretations" is perhaps the more appropriate term, since the problem of interpretation is undeniably at issue in every single case.

sons—although she did manage a trip to Isleta pueblo in 1924 (Goldfrank 1978, 1983).

When her husband died suddenly in 1935, Esther Goldfrank felt free to return to anthropology in the Columbia department, which was then sharply divided between the students of Ruth Benedict and those of Ralph Linton, whose hiring had forestalled Benedict's inheritance of Boas' mantle. Goldfrank became a participant in the extramural seminars on culture and personality in which Linton had joined the psychoanalyst Abram Kardiner, and in which a more differentiated and processual approach to culture and personality than Benedict's was being developed (cf. Manson 1986). However, Goldfrank took her theory courses from Benedict and joined Benedict's fieldwork party among the Plains Indians in the summer of 1939. Although Goldfrank found *Patterns of Culture* conceptually interesting, she argued vehemently with Benedict about her view of Zuni society, which Benedict tended to generalize to the pueblos Goldfrank herself had studied. By this time Benedict's interpretation had, somewhat tentatively, been called into question in print by the Berkeley-trained Chinese anthropologist, Li An-che (1937). But Goldfrank herself did not develop a systematic critique until after 1940, when she met and married the brilliant German Marxist sinologist Karl August Wittfogel, who had just left the Communist Party in the aftermath of the Hitler-Stalin pact. Long convinced that "the fundamental question" of social development was "the effect of water control on societal structure," Wittfogel had scarcely met Goldfrank before he asked her "What about irrigation among the pueblos?" (Goldfrank 1978:156, 146). In 1943 they produced a collaborative article in which pueblos were discussed as "miniature irrigation societies"—but which did not yet directly confront Benedict.

Following this joint effort, Goldfrank wrote a series of articles on different American Indian tribes, each challenging prevailing interpretations from a Marxist-influenced perspective. The first drew on historical accounts to argue (to Benedict's considerable displeasure) that among the prereservation Teton Dakota "wealth was important for status recognition; that warfare was no 'game'; and that in-group violence was well documented" (1978:161; cf. 1943). The second argued that "Navajo leadership, like Navajo community cooperation, had developed out of the requirements of agriculture in a semi-arid environment," and was "no mechanical replica of Pueblo organization" (1978:165; cf. 1945a). The third, an analysis of Hopi and Zuni child-rearing patterns, "called into question the image of Pueblo society and personality that Benedict had been so insistently presenting since 1928" (1978:171). Drawing on historical documents, autobiographical accounts, and psychological tests, Goldfrank argued that the achievement "of the cooperation necessary for a functioning irrigated agriculture" was "the end of a long process of conditioning, often persuasive, but frequently harsh, that commences in infancy and continues throughout adulthood." The anxiety-ridden adult Pueblo personality was "moulded not so much by parental permissiveness during infancy as by the severe disciplines imposed after infancy by external agents—by impersonators of the supernaturals and by the priesthoods" (1945b:527, 519, 523, 536).

Benedict herself never responded in print, or to Goldfrank privately, "except to say that the Pueblos 'bored' her" (Goldfrank 1978:171). But Goldfrank's critique, along with the previous one by Li An-che, did stimulate the first systematic consideration of the influence of personal values on ethnography, in an article by John Bennett, who had studied with Redfield while taking his doctorate at Chicago in the late 1930s. Reviewing "The Interpretation of Pueblo Culture" in 1946, Bennett drew a sharp contrast between what he called the "organic" and the "repressed" views. On the one hand, there had been several studies of Pueblo Indians (primarily Hopi and Zuni) which saw their culture as "integrated to an unusual degree, all sectors being bound together by a consistent, harmonious set of values," with "an ideal personality type which features the virtues of gentleness, non-aggression, cooperation, modesty, [and] tranquility"—"virtually a fulfillment of the ideal-typical folk-preliterate homogeneous, 'sacred' society and culture" (1946:362–63). On the other, the Pueblos had been viewed as "marked by considerable *covert* tension, suspicion, anxiety, hostility, fear and ambition," with children "coerced subtly and (from our viewpoint) brutally into behaving according to Pueblo norms," and with "authority in the hands of the group and chiefs, the latter holding the power of life and death," so that the adult individual must "repress his spontaneity, originality, enthusiasm, out-goingness, individualism, . . . and become neurotic" (363, 367). Although Bennett charged the organic approach with "the sin of omission of certain important sets of data," with "a tendency to distort or misrepresent some facets of the Pueblo configuration [and] to make the interpretation in the long run an entirely personal, subjective affair," he did not conclude that it was "wrong." Rather, he argued that it was not possible to say that "one side or the other is less- influenced by values," and left it to the sociologist of knowledge to "make a reflexive analysis of the meaning of the respective interpretations in the culture of which they are a part" (373, 374). Nevertheless, the effect of the article was to make it thenceforth rather difficult for Pueblo culture to be interpreted in systematically harmonious Apollonian terms.

Although Bennett called attention to Redfield's concept of the "folk society" as part of the context of theory in which the organic view should be understood (1946:364), he made no reference to Redfield's study of Tepoztlán. However, within several years that, too, was subjected to systematic criticism by a young anthropologist who had also received his training in the faction-ridden pre–World War II Columbia department. Born in 1914, Oscar Lewis (né Lefkowitz) was the son of a Polish immigrant rabbi who for reasons of health moved to a small town in upper New York state, where he managed a somewhat marginal subsistence by converting a farm into a summer hotel. Introduced to Marxism by a Communist Party organizer who summered nearby, young Lewis went on to a take a bachelor's degree in 1936 at the City College of New York, where he studied with the Marxist historian Philip Foner before going on to do graduate work at Columbia Teachers College. But he soon became disillusioned with the limited historical perspective he found there, and at the suggestion of his brother-in-law, the psychologist Abraham Maslow, had a long talk with Ruth Benedict, which led him into anthropology. However, Lewis, like Goldfrank, was also influenced by Kardiner and Linton, and while he greatly admired Benedict as a person, and for her critique of racism (1940), he, too, became somewhat critical of her approach. Although his doctoral dissertation was to be a library treatise on "The Effects of White Contact upon Blackfoot Culture," he had accompanied Benedict on the field school of 1939. Out of that experience came a study of the Piegan "manly-hearted women," in which Lewis expressed scepticism of "theories of culture which play down the role of economics and which stress homogeneity at the expense of the range of behavior and values" (Butterworth 1972:748; cf. Rigdon 1988:9–26).

During the early years of World War II, Lewis worked with the Strategic Index for Latin America of the Human Relations Area Files at Yale University and briefly as propaganda analyst for the U.S. Department of Justice. In 1943, he and his psychologist wife moved to Mexico City in connection with a large-scale comparative study of Indian culture and personality, and there also assumed administrative duties in the Inter-American Indian Institute headed by Manuel Gamio. Seeking a nearby site to study, and hoping to take advantage of Redfield's monograph as the ethnographic base for his own research, Lewis chose Tepoztlán, which by then had been linked by highway to the Federal District. With the help of his wife and more than a dozen native Mexican researchers, Lewis carried out a systematic investigation during seven months in 1944, with return trips during the summers of 1947 and 1948. The team collected extensive data on representative families from different income groups in each barrio, using schedules of questions that extended to a hundred pages. From the beginning, the project was oriented toward problems of rural development; and to overcome the resistance of villagers who were suspicious that he was an agent of the government, Lewis organized meetings at which he encouraged them to talk "about their needs and problems" in order that he might "draw up proposals for the improvement of conditions in Tepoztlán." This orientation "set the tone for the entire investigation," which soon suggested that while Redfield's material was "adequate" regarding religious and ceremonial matters, "the picture of Tepoztlán as written by Redfield and Stuart Chase has been highly romanticized" ("Progress Report," 2/44, as quoted in Rigdon 1988:32–35).

From the time he chose the Tepoztlán site, Lewis was in correspondence with Redfield, who wrote letters supporting his applications for funding, and (though he considered Lewis "probably not a man of first rank") also endorsing Lewis's candidacy for the job he got at the University of Illinois in 1948 (RP: RR/Carl Taylor 11/11/46; RR/J. W. Albig 4/26/48). By that time, however, serious "differences in interpretation and in field data" had arisen. Responding to the suggestion (made by Redfield's wife) that "if culture is seen as that which gives some order and significance to life," then Lewis's account of a particular Tepoztecan family had "very little of culture in it," Lewis argued that "much of the unity and bonds of family life in Tepoztlán flow from what might be called negative factors rather than positive ones":

> What I mean is that in a village where most people are withdrawn and suspicious and view the world as a hostile place to live in, the family unit by comparison with the non-family represents a relatively close in-group and in this sense is a haven. But it would be missing many of the crucial aspects of Tepoztecan family life and the quality of human relationships in Tepoztlán not to see the great amount of internal tensions and conflict that exists, as well as the frustrations and maladjustments. Nor do I believe that this is to be explained entirely in terms of the break-down of an earlier folk culture. The idea that folk cultures produce less frustrations than non-folk cultures or that the quality of human relationships is necessarily superior in folk-cultures seems to me to be sheer Rousseauean romanticism and has not been documented to my knowledge. (Quoted in Rigdon 1988:205)

Lewis in fact doubted that Tepoztlán was really a "folk culture": "It seems to me that Tepoztlán is not now and in all probability has not in the last four hundred years been a folk culture in the sense that you have defined the term in your writings." Rejecting the implication "that he was guilty of middle-class bias" because "my picture of family life turns out to be so similar to family life as it has been reported in our own culture," Lewis insisted that it was "possible to have valid standards which cut across all cultures without thereby being ethnocentric, by which the quality of human relationships can be measured and appraised," noting "Fromm's recent book 'Man for Himself' [as] a step in this direction" (RP: RR/OL 6/8/48; OL/RR 6/11/48, quoted in Rigdon 1988:205–6).

When it appeared in 1951, Lewis's book bore a dedication to Redfield, who in return offered a somewhat double-edged jacket comment: "In putting before other students my errors and his own [*sic*] in a context of intelligent discussion, he has once more shown the power of social science to revise its conclusions and move toward the truth." In the volume itself, Lewis drew a sharp contrast between Redfield's view of Tepoztlán as "a relatively homogeneous, isolated, smoothly functioning and well-integrated society" and his own findings, which emphasized "the underlying individualism of Tepoztecan institutions and character, the lack of cooperation, . . . the schisms within the village, and the pervading quality of fear, envy, and distrust in inter-personal relations" (428–29). Granting the influence of "the personal factor," and allowing something also for cultural change and differences in the "general scope" of the two studies, Lewis was inclined to emphasize instead "differences in theoretical orientation," and especially "the concept of the folk-culture and folk-urban continuum" which was "Redfield's organizing principle in the research" (431–32), and which since 1930 had been further elaborated in his study of *The Folk Culture of Yucatan* (1941).

Unlike Benedict, Redfield spent a good deal of effort, both in correspondence and in print, in responding to Lewis's critique, which in the early 1950s precipitated a considerable discussion of folk culture, peasant societies, and the folk-urban continuum (Miner 1952; G. Foster 1953; Mintz 1953; Wolf 1955; Wagley & Harris 1955; cf. Redfield 1953, 1955, 1956). Although Redfield insisted that it was not prior hypothesis, but "some experience with Tepoztlán" which led him to develop the concept of a "folk society," his general approach was to insist on the abstractive nature of his "ideal type," which was "a mental construction of imagined societies that are only approximated in particular 'real' societies" (RP: RR/OL 6/22/48; RR n.d., response to OL's "six objections"). And while he did not "recall any intention to suggest that everything about savages or about Tepoztecans has my approval nor that with civilization came the fall of man" (RR: RR/OL correspondence, n.d.), in the end Redfield was inclined to explain the empirical differences in terms which were clearly value-laden: the "hidden question" of his own research had been "What do these people enjoy?", whereas that of Lewis's had been "What do these people suffer from?" (Redfield 1955:136). On that basis, the two men were able to minimize their differences (RP: OL/RR 4/25/54; RR/OL 4/27/54)—though Lewis later insisted that *his* hidden question was "more productive of insight about the human condition, about the dynamics of conflict and the forces of change" (1960:179).

When a conference was held in 1952 to evaluate the general state of "anthropology today," Lewis was asked to present a paper on fieldwork method, in which he argued at some length for the importance of systematic restudy as an essential feature of anthropological method (1953). During the next few years there was to be a flurry of studies that were undertaken (or reconceptualized) as restudies. One of these was in fact a study of the same Samoan village in which Mead had worked—although, here, as in Lewis's own case, the work was apparently not originally intended as a restudy. Lowell Holmes, a graduate student of Melville Herskovits at Northwestern, had intended to do research in Rarotonga, but two weeks before his planned departure the University of Hawaii, which was funding his work, suggested that he go to American Samoa instead. Suddenly left "without a definite research problem," Holmes decided, in consultation with Herskovits (who had been Mead's contemporary under Boas at Columbia), to carry on an acculturation study of the Manu'a group, working in Mead's village, and using her material "as a base line." To facilitate this, he asked Mead for some of her field data (MeP: LH/MM 9/2/54). While she refused to divulge the real identities of the girls she had studied, she indicated that Holmes could determine them from her village census, which she would send if he would first send her a copy of one that she suggested he should make to provide an independent point of comparison (MeP: MM/LH 6/22/54). Holmes seems not to have taken up this offer (Mead 1969:xix), relying instead on Mead's published work as his base point. After five months in Ta'u, where he worked largely in English, and four in Pago Pago, Holmes came back ready to write a dissertation rather critical of Mead's work, but as he later recalled, "was forced by my faculty advisor [Herskovits] to soften my criticism" (LH/DF 8/1/67, as quoted in Freeman 1983b:134). Although Holmes disputed Mead on a number of factual issues—later suggesting that she had discovered "what she hoped to find"—he nevertheless concluded that "the reliability of Mead's account is remarkably high" (1957a:232). Holmes's posture was roughly that of the general anthropological community for the next several decades: whatever reservations may have been held in Oceanist circles about the quality of Mead's Samoan ethnography (cf. Mead 1969), these did not affect its public status, which was sustained by her own position as the single most visible American anthropologist (cf. McDowell 1980; Rappaport 1986).

By 1967, however, Holmes was warning Mead of the "present activities" of another Samoanist, Derek Freeman, who was seeking to "discredit you, me, Boas and all of American anthropology" (MeP: LH/MM 10/23/67). Mead had in fact been aware of Freeman's work since at least 1964, when after a somewhat heated debate in a seminar at the Australian National University over the significance of Samoan defloration ceremonies, Freeman told her he intended to do further research on "the realities of adolescent and sexual behaviour in Samoa" (MeP: DF/MM 11/11/64; MM/DF 12/2/64). Born in 1916 in Wellington, New Zealand—where during adolescence he developed a passion for exploration and mountain climbing – Freeman had attended Victoria University College and the Wellington Training School for Teachers. In 1938 he became a member of the graduate seminar of Ernest Beaglehole, who held a Ph.D. degree in sociology from the London School of Economics and who had come under the influence of Boasian anthropology as a postdoctoral student of Sapir's at Yale in the early 1930s. Like Beaglehole, Freeman was at that time very much a cultural determinist, concluding from a study of the socialization of school children that "the aims and desires which determine behavior" were all derived from the social environment (1983b:109). Under Beaglehole's influence Freeman began to think seriously of doing anthropological work in Polynesia, and in 1939, he obtained a position in the Education Department of Western Samoa, where he hoped also to carry on ethnographic research that would extend the work of Margaret Mead (Appell & Madan 1988:5). After two years during which he became fluent in Samoan, Freeman began intensive research in the settlement of Sa'anapu, where he was adopted into the family of a senior talking chief and given the title and status of the heir apparent (a young man whose name, John, was the same as Freeman's middle name, and who, fortuitously, had died just before Freeman's arrival on the scene). Gradually becoming aware of serious discrepancies between his own observations and Mead's, Freeman was at first inclined to explain them as due to the fact that he worked in Western and she in Eastern Samoa. But by the time he left in November 1943 to serve in the New Zealand navy, he had concluded that he would "one day face the responsibility of writing a refutation of Mead's findings" (1983a:xiv).

After the war (and a brief return to Samoa in the summer of 1946), Freeman went to the London School of Economics to study anthropology under the leading British Polynesianist, Raymond Firth. There he continued studies of manuscript sources on Samoa in the archives of the London Missionary Society, and in 1948 produced a diploma thesis on "The Social Structure of a Samoan Village Community." However, when Firth dismissed as "structure *ad nauseam*" a paper of Freeman's that was highly praised by Meyer Fortes, Freeman shifted his intellectual allegiance (Appell & Madan 1988:6). When he left Britain in 1948 to carry out research among the Iban in Sarawak – whom he had previously encountered during his war service – he was strongly under the influence of Fortes' more orthodox Radcliffe-Brownian structuralism, which continued to condition the analyses of Iban society that occupied him during the next decade.

After receiving his doctorate under Fortes at Cambridge in 1953, Freeman returned to New Zealand as visiting lecturer at the University of Otago, and was invited to the Australian National University in 1955. During the next few years, Freeman became dissatisfied with the way in which British social anthropology set up methodological barriers against most of the other behavioral sciences (cf. MacClancy 1986), which he found particularly inhibiting in the interpretation of the symbolism of the Iban headhunting cult. His dissatisfaction climaxed during the visit of Max Gluckman to ANU in the summer of 1960, and that fall Freeman wrote Fortes suggesting that social anthropologists should acquire "systematic training in psychoanalysis" (Appell & Madan 1988:12). The following February, he was asked by the vice-chancellor of ANU to alter his plans for study leave in order to go to Kuching, Sarawak, to investigate a problem that had arisen between the curator of the Sarawak Museum, Tom Harrisson, and a research scholar from the ANU. When he arrived, Freeman found himself "in the center of a complicated social situation in which he was able to study at first hand a whole series of deep psychological processes." Although the details of the situation have not been specified, the result was a "cognitive abreaction" so "momentous" that he "suddenly saw human behavior in a new light" (ibid.; cf. Freeman 1986).[13]

Departing from Sarawak in March 1961, Freeman broke off his fieldwork plans in order to embark on systematic reading in ethology, evolutionary biology, primatology, the neurosciences, psychology, and genetics. Writing to Fortes in October 1962, Freeman suggested that his approach to anthropology was now "very much that of the natural historian," and insisted that "anthropology, if it is to become the science of man, must be biologically based" (quoted in Appell & Madan 1988:13). In the aftermath of this conversion to a "naturalistic approach to human behavior," Freeman underwent certain other dramatic intellectual changes. Arguing that "dereistic thinking and irrational behavior are not one whit the less dereistic because they happen to be shared and accepted," he abandoned the doctrine of cultural relativism (1962:272; cf. 1965), embraced the scientific epistemology of Karl Popper, studied ethology under the guidance of Konrad Lorenz, and undertook a year's training and personal analysis at the London Institute of Psychoanalysis—although his later attempt to apply Popperian principles in a series of psychoanalytic papers led to his ostracization by the Australian Society of Psychoanalysts in 1965 (Appell & Madan 1988:15–16).

13. When this essay was originally in press, and past the point of alteration, I received from Freeman a copy of "Some Notes on the Development of My Anthropological Interests," which he had prepared in 1986, which includes two pages (26–27) of further detail on the "complicated social situation" he faced in Sarawak. Given the nature of the incidents described, and the lack of corroborating evidence, I refrain from going into the details here. For similar reasons, I also refrain from repeating here oral accounts from several sources, clearly relating to the same incident, which cast its psychodynamics in a rather different light.

It was in the context of these changes—and the rereading of Mead's *Coming of Age* when he was returning to Australia from Europe in July 1964—that Freeman decided he must reexamine and test the evidence Mead had offered for her conclusion that adolescent behavior could not be explained in terms of biological variables. Returning to Western Samoa in December 1965, he carried on further fieldwork in Sa'anapu, and in 1967 made a visit to the site of Mead's fieldwork in Manu'a. By the time he went back to Australia in January 1968, Freeman had concluded that Mead's work was "pivotal to the development and acceptance in the United States of the doctrine of cultural determinism" (Appell & Madan 1988:17). Turning to investigations of the historical background of Boasian anthropology, he soon became convinced that "these men were not really interested in dispassionate scientific enquiry, but rather in the dissemination and support of certain doctrines, of an idealistic, metaphysical and quasi-political kind, in which they passionately believed"—and he suggested to Mead that he might have to write a book devoted to the reexamination of "some of these doctrines" (MeP: DF/MM 3/20/69).

By 1971, Freeman was able to submit to an American publisher a summary of the proposed work, but the negative responses of anonymous reviewers led him to delay its completion while he carried on further research (Appell & Madan 1988:19). In 1978, Freeman offered to send Mead a preliminary draft of an "*acutely* critical" paper on Samoan sexual values and behavior (MeP: DF/MM 8/23/78). But her illness and death intervened, and to Freeman "made it obvious that the publication of [his] refutation would have to be deferred"—presumably in order to let a decent interval elapse (as quoted in Appell & Madan 1988:21). It was only late in 1981, after Freeman had gained access to the archives of the High Court of American Samoa, that the manuscript was finally sent off to the Harvard University Press.

Even before its publication in 1983, Freeman's book had become a cause célèbre. Despite (or perhaps because of) her immense public stature, Mead had always been somewhat ambivalently regarded by professional anthropologists, and her work had been controversial at least since the early 1950s debate around the "swaddling hypothesis" interpretation of Great Russian personality (Mead 1954). Had Freeman's critique been limited to what he described as a "formal Popperian refutation" of her Samoan ethnography, the professional response might have been much more restrained—although many anthropologists would surely have been put off by his strident scientism. But his book was quite explicitly a frontal attack—in a rather abrasively polemical style—on what he insisted was the evidential linchpin of the paradigm of "absolute cultural determinism" that he alleged had dominated American anthropology for fifty years.[14] While for the most part rejecting Freeman's characterization of their discipline's history, American anthropologists were clearly concerned that a critique of cultural determinism might support a resurgence of hereditarian thought and racialist politics. Although Freeman insisted that his goal was to clear the way for a new "interactionist" paradigm that would give appropriate weight to the influence of both biological and cultural factors and had himself been somewhat critical of sociobiology (1980), his book was seen by many as giving aid and comfort to the ideological enemy. In this context, American anthropologists rallied to the defense of their discipline and of the figure who was publicly most prominently identified with it.[15]

For present purposes, however, the broader issues of the controversy are less germane than some of the specifics of Freeman's critique, which resonates strongly of the earlier critiques of Benedict and Redfield. Charging that Mead had failed to appreciate the "bitter rivalries" generated by the rank system (1983a:135), Freeman insisted that far from eliminating "interest in competition," Samoans showed an intense competitiveness not

14. Since my own work has been drawn on to buttress this characterization (Freeman 1983a:passim), I offer here a brief comment on this issue. There is no doubt that cultural determinism (in some sense) was an essential feature of the anthropological idea of culture, which since the 1920s has had a pervasive influence in the social sciences and in American culture generally (cf. GS 1968a). There is no doubt also that Mead's study was conceived as an inquiry into the power of cultural determinism, and that it played an important role in the dissemination of that notion. On the other hand, the addition of the modifier "absolute" raises serious historiographical problems, which can scarcely be dealt with by citing a single instance in which Mead used that word in a phrase where neither the noun "culture" nor the adjective "cultural" appeared (Freeman 1983b:169). It is no doubt the case that some anthropologists (notably Kroeber), in particular polemical contexts, made statements to which Freeman's phrase might seem an appropriate gloss. But its use, either directly or by implication, to characterize the Boasian school, or any individual Boasian, is to say the least extremely problematic.

15. Although portions of the present argument clearly bear on issues in the Samoan controversy, it is not intended as a systematic treatment of those issues or of that discussion. For reasons indicated in part in the text below, many of the more important issues are beyond my competence to judge, and will probably remain so; some others closer to my competence can only be touched on in the present argument. Major items in the debate so far include the "special section" of the December 1983 number of *American Anthropologist*, "Speaking in the Name of the Real: Freeman and Mead on Samoa"; the two numbers of the 1984 volume of *Canberra Anthropology*, "Fact and Context in Ethnography: The Samoa Controversy"; Rappaport 1986; Holmes 1987; S. Murray 1990. Many documents relating to the debate have been reproduced in Caton 1990. At every point along the way, Freeman has offered his own commentaries and rebuttals, as well as additional evidence supporting his critique, both in print (e.g., Freeman 1987, 1989, 1991a, 1991b) and in extensive correspondence with participants and other interested parties, including myself.

only in ritualized contests, but "in virtually all other areas of their society" (147). Rather than being one of the "most peaceful peoples in the world," Samoans were prone to aggressive behavior (163). Instead of wearing their religion lightly, they were "a highly religious people" (179). Contrary to Mead's suggestion that the Samoan child was succored by "women of all ages . . . none of whom have disciplined it," Samoans shared the biologically based "primary bond between mother and child" that was characteristic of all humans, and were subject to "quite stringent discipline" (203, 205). Far from lacking "deeply channeled emotions," they were people of "strong passions" (212, 215). Instead of condoning casual adolescent lovemaking, their sexual mores emphasized the "cult of virginity" (234); male sexuality, far from being unaggressive, was manifest in one of the world's highest incidences of rape (244). Rather than enjoying a carefree time of gradual adjustment to adult roles, Samoan adolescents had a delinquency rate ten times higher than that of England and Wales (258). In short, the Samoans were not a Polynesian version of Benedict's Apollonian Zuni; like all mankind, they were a complex mixture of Apollonian and Dionysian motives (302).

When Ethnographers Disagree . . .

Although he wrote before the critiques of Redfield's Tepoztlán and Mead's Samoa, John Bennett's 1946 account of the contrastive "interpretations of the basic dynamics of Pueblo society and culture" may nevertheless serve as a convenient reference point for more general remarks on the Apollonian ethnographies of the 1920s, "Lacking any close familiarity with Pueblo research," Bennett eschewed an assessment of the "organic" and "repressive" interpretations "from the standpoint of excellence of field work and general scientific operations." Assuming that "the workers on both sides" were "careful students of culture" and "respectable" members of the "academic fraternity" of "professional anthropologists," he did not attempt to say that one side represented "good" and the other "bad" ethnography (1946:370).

Four decades ago, when the relatively small community of professional anthropologists faced the future full of confidence that "the science of man" could meet the challenges of expanding ethnographic opportunity in the postwar world, one could perhaps take for granted that they shared a methodological consensus. But intervening history—by now precipitated in several genres of anthropological writing about the problems of fieldwork and of ethnographic representation (cf. Gravel & Ridinger 1988)—has made such consensus much more problematic. By the time of Lewis's critique of Redfield, methodology was implicitly very much at issue; and in the case of Freeman's critique of Mead, so also was the nature of the "professional fraternity" itself (Rappaport 1986).

For the positivistically inclined – and for those postpositivists who still cherish the conviction that there may be criteria for judging the relative adequacy of conflicting factual or interpretive statements about human action in a social world – the possibility must be acknowledged that "when ethnographers disagree . . . someone is wrong" (Heider 1988:75). But with the ante of ethnographic competence now trebled, and issues of method and epistemology more explicitly problematic, an historian without ethnographic experience has even more reason than Bennett had in 1946 to refrain from evaluative judgments of ethnographic adequacy. This is even more the case in view of other issues that Bennett did not discuss: whether the ethnographic "objects" subject to differing interpretations may have "actually" differed, insofar as the observers had focussed on different subcultural groups or regional variants, or as the result of cultural change over time (cf. Heider 1988); or whether the response of the people under study to the ethnographers studying them may have led them to present themselves differently to different observers.[16]

Despite these caveats, certain contrasts between the Apollonians and the critics do suggest themselves, even to an ethnographic outsider or, for that matter, to a nonethnographer. If one compares the six anthropologists involved in terms of such obvious factors as time in the field, linguistic competence, or number of informants, one may easily note differences among them, which *prima facie* incline one to regard the Apollonian ethnographies as perhaps more open to question (cf. Naroll 1962). The more so, since fieldwork was never the forte of either Benedict or Redfield; and while Mead was to become a highly productive, innovative, and methodologically self-conscious fieldworker, Samoa was her maiden effort, which she herself came later to regard as the product of a methodologically less sophisticated era (Mead 1961:xv).

But if this might lead us to believe that the anti-Apollonians were on the whole more reliable ethnographers, it does not resolve all the factual or interpretive differences at issue. The truth or falsity of any given eth-

16. On this issue, Gartrell (1979) is extremely suggestive, along lines that are surely relevant to the present discussion. Contrasting her own ethnographic experience with that of another woman ethnographer who studied the same African people during the same period, Gartrell explained the factual and interpretive differences between them in terms of differences in their expectations of fieldwork, their local sponsorship, their choice of interpreters, their perceived gender roles, etc. – all of which elicited quite differing "exclusionary maneuvers" from the people they were trying to study. Significantly, the interpretive consequences were especially marked in regard to cultural personality and ethos – the areas most at issue in the critique of Apollonian ethnography.

nographic "fact" (or even the definition of such an entity) is not so simple a matter as the more positivistically inclined critics would seem to feel; and this is even more true of ethnographic interpretations, which may relate to ethnographic facts in ways that are by no means straightforward. Simply as an instance, we may briefly consider the problem of the incidence of forcible rape in Samoa, which has been a much-debated issue in the Mead/Freeman controversy. According to Mead, rape was "completely foreign to the Samoan mind" (1928c:487), but had occurred "occasionally" since "the first contact with white civilization" (1928b:93). In contrast, Freeman was at some pains to argue that forcible rape had been frequent in Samoa at the time Mead was there, and gave as the reason for his delay of publication the fact that it was only in 1981 that he was able to get into the archives of the High Court of American Samoa, where he found documentary evidence on the issue (Freeman 1983a:xvi). In a later commentary, he noted that these records had revealed that "during the years 1920–29 twelve Samoan males (five of them in American Samoa and seven of them in Western Samoa) were tried and convicted of forcible rape or (in two cases) of attempted rape" (1983b:119). Granting that Freeman's work has succeeded in calling into question not only some of the specifics but also the general tenor of Mead's account of Samoan sexuality (cf. Romanucci-Ross 1983), the evidence on rape in the 1920s remains somewhat problematic, especially to anyone epistemologically disinclined to accept Freeman's dogmatic assertion that "even a single verified case" would refute Mead (1983b:119). Even disregarding the problem of the influence of "white civilization," or of the quality of the court records, or of the location of the two attempted rapes—not to mention that of the cross-cultural definition of such a category—we might ask whether five rapes in American Samoa during a ten-year period is merely "occasional" or a "high incidence," and wonder whether this is a matter that can be settled by comparing Samoan figures from a later date with those elsewhere in the world. If interpretation must intervene to give meaning to "facts" even in one (not so) simple quantitative case, how much more so in judging the "wrongness" or "rightness" of facts/interpretations in three different ethnographic situations. Clearly, that is not a task to be undertaken in the present essay.

On the other hand, one cannot ignore the (interpretive) fact that the contrasts Bennett found between the "organic" and "repressive" interpretations of Zuni—harmonious integration vs. covert tension, tranquility vs. hostility, cooperation vs. individualism, voluntarism vs. authority, permissive vs. coercive child-rearing—are echoed in the later Redfield/Lewis and Mead/Freeman debates. Clearly, the contrast is of more than local ethnographic significance, and in attempting to contextualize it, we must look beyond the specific cases. Although there are distinct limitations to the interpretation that can be offered here, we may take a few steps toward their more adequate historical contextualization by looking at the Apollonians and their critics with a view to contrasts of personal biography and of cultural moment.[17]

Considered first in terms of biographical commonalities among the six anthropologists, the present materials allow only limited generalization. Thus neither class nor gender nor nationality will distinguish all of the Apollonians from all of the critics. On the other hand, the fact that the Apollonians, unlike the critics, were all presidents of the American Anthropological Association, may suggest a more general contrast in terms of professional and personal marginality: whereas the Apollonians were (save Redfield on the maternal side) "Old Americans," the critics (two Jews and a New Zealander) may perhaps be thought of as cultural (as well as professional) outsiders. One might speculate that the former, insofar as they became alienated from the dominant culture, would be inclined to value cultural alterity—while simultaneously taking for granted the possibility of reform within their own culture. In contrast, the latter were more concerned with the problem of mobility within a dominant culture, and therefore emphasized commonalities of human capacity—even as they tended to view society in more conflictual terms. And the fact that the critics—younger in each case by half a generation—were people whose work in a particular ethnographic area was in some sense forestalled by a personally significant other of major professional reputation may have helped to motivate or to sustain their critiques. In Freeman's case, this motive may have been enhanced by an identification with Mead's New Zealander second husband, who was also a critic of Mead's ethnography (Fortune 1939).[18]

17. Among these limitations, the most striking is the obvious asymmetry in the contextualization of the Apollonian ethnographers and their later critics. The treatments of the former—all of them now dead—have not only been much lengthier, but have also drawn more extensively, if unsystematically, on less public sorts of source materials (including Benedict's reconstruction of her primal scene, Redfield's Rorschach, and the "outtakes" from Mead's published autobiographical writings). If, as Bennett suggested, it is up to the sociologist of knowledge (or, in this case, the historian of anthropology) "to seek out biases and stresses obviously not completely apparent to the researchers" (1946:374), a fully adequate approach to that task would require the same sort of treatment (and the same sorts of source materials) for the critics as for the authors of Apollonian ethnographic interpretations. Failing that, there is a risk of implying that Goldfrank, Lewis, and Freeman were unencumbered by unconscious bias—a proposition they might find flattering, but which the historian of anthropology must regard as questionable. I take it for granted that members of the "repressive" school are not immune to scotomization and projection (cf. Devereux 1967)—though the question of the relative strength of such tendencies in different observers remains an open (and a difficult) one.

18. Since Mead's Samoan research has been contextualized here in relation to her early biography and American cultural currents in the 1920s, interpretive symmetry might suggest a similar contextualization of Freeman's critique. Although extended consideration of this

The fact that the Apollonians were all published poets might suggest a metamethodological predisposition toward what Bennett spoke of as "logico-aesthetic integration" (1946:371). And there is perhaps other evidence to support this, including the Rorschachs of Benedict (Goldfrank 1978:126) and Redfield (Roe 1950), and the often-noted propensity of Mead for the quick apprehension of cultural totality—evidenced in a remark to Boas three weeks after arriving in Manus on her second fieldwork expedition: "The outlines of the culture are emerging more and more each day" (BP: MM/FB 1/6/29). The obverse of this atemporal integrative inclination might be a tendency to minimize the importance of disruptive historical event—be it factional struggle, revolutionary foray, or tropical hurricane. In contrast, the critics seem to have been impelled to call up against integrating cultural totalizations controverting evidence of an historical or a quantitative character. Granted that this may have been motivated by the demands of argument, and that the critics were not without totalizing agendas of their own. Granted also the avowed nomothetic goals of the early Redfield, and the strong strain of scientism present in the early Mead and recurrent throughout her career. Nevertheless, the fact that Mead relegated historical change and quantification to an appendix (and that they did not reappear in the second more "professional" monograph) suggests that a basic methodological commitment had been made. No doubt it was, as Boas' comments on the statistical and clinical methods suggest, a defensible one. But as Mead's own later comment on "the historical caprice which had selected a handful of young girls to stand forever like the lovers on Keats' Grecian urn" reminds us (1961:iii), her interpretation depended very much on the subjective apprehension of a cultural pattern frozen in a timeless moment. While it would not do to reduce the matter to a simple contrast of humanist and scientist, it does seem that some underlying metamethodological opposition was, or came to be, at issue between the Apollonians and their critics.

The two groups may also be contrasted in terms of certain theoretical and attitudinal presuppositions. As a starting point, we may note that all of the anthropologists involved were, in the early phases of their careers, identifiable as Boasian cultural determinists. For the Apollonian ethnographers, that viewpoint was certainly a part of the context of research—in Benedict's case, less perhaps in the original fieldwork than as the critical factor in subsequent ethnographic interpretation; in Redfield's, simply as a general orienting assumption; in Mead's, in the very formulation of the

---

issue would obviously depend on much fuller biographical and cultural historical information, a suggestive starting point can be found in the discussion of gender roles, sexual mores, adolescent aggression, attitudes to authority, etc., in New Zealand in Ausubel (1960).

fieldwork problem. But it is worth noting among them also the major orienting influence of a more diffuse body of evolutionary assumption that seems in retrospect quite un-Boasian (though in fact expressions of it can also be found in Boas' work). Especially in the cases of Redfield and Mead, it was the opposition of the "civilized" and the "primitive" (the "folk" being intermediate between the two), as much as any specific cultural determinism, which conditioned the interpretation of ethnographic data.

The attitudes of Apollonian ethnographers toward the contrast implicit in that opposition were more complex than the terms "primitivist" or "cultural relativist" might suggest—primitivism, like relativism, being a very relative matter. Even in what has come to be regarded as its *locus classicus* (Benedict 1934), cultural relativism was a problematic concept; a double-edged sword, it could be wielded both in the cause of cultural tolerance and in the cause of cultural criticism. When used to justify the established ways of "primitive" others to the denizens of a "civilization" threatening to eradicate them, it presented those practices in a generally favorable light. But when used to question the established ways of "this crazy civilization," the "limits of outrage" that might be "plumbed" in "scandalous" cultures became negative reference points rather than positive models (Benedict, in Mead 1959a:330–31). Benedict made a point of disavowing "any romantic return to the primitive"—"attractive as it sometimes may be" (1934:19–20). For her, as for Mead, cultural integration could be negative as well as positive, and two of her three cultural cases were presented in starkly negative terms. Thus the "paranoid," "treacherous," "Puritan" Dobu lived out "without repression man's worst nightmares of the ill-will of the universe" (172), and the "megalomaniac paranoid" Kwakiutl "recognized only one gamut of emotion, that which swings between victory and shame" (222, 215). The common denominator of comparative characterization was less the Apollonian Zuni than an implicitly critical vision of American civilization. What Benedict yearned for was not so much homogeneity as a more tolerant individuation.

In the case of Redfield, there are signs of similar ambivalence. In the study of Tepoztlán, the idealization of the folk was largely implicit in the general descriptive material, the contrastive aura of place—surfacing in such comments as the opposition between "the folk, a country people among whom culture is built up, and the urban proletariat, among whom it tends to break down" (1930a:6). At the same time, it also seems clear that Redfield identified with the process of "sophistication" by which the folk were transformed; and over time, he was to become troubled by the concept of cultural relativism.

There is a similar tension in the case of Mead. One can find in *Coming of Age* strikingly pluralistic passages, resonant more of Herder than Rousseau, including a foreshadowing of Benedict's "great arc" of culture: "each primitive people has selected one set of human gifts, one set of human values, and fashioned for themselves an art, a social organisation, a religion, which is their contribution to the history of the human spirit" (1928b:13). But many of the contrasts that Mead drew were quite conventionally evolutionary: Samoan culture was "simpler," lacking in "individualization" and "specialized feeling." What it offered was not so much a general cultural alternative as a point of critical comparison: "granting the desirability of [the] development of [a] sensitive, discriminating response to personality, as a better basis for dignified human lives than an automatic, undifferentiated response to sex attraction, we may still, in the light of Samoan solutions, count our methods exceedingly expensive" (211). In the end, Mead's purpose was to realize "the high point" that only "a heterogeneous culture" could attain (248).

Clearly, the matter is more complex than the contrast Bennett drew between the "value orientation" of the "organic" school toward the "solidified, homogeneous group life" of preliterate culture and that of the "repressive" school in favor of the "greater individuation" and heterogeneity of "urban life" (1946:366). And yet a certain romantic primitivist spirit was clearly manifest in the Apollonian ethnographies – in the very process of denial ("attractive as it may sometimes be"); in the specific descriptive material; in what Bennett called "the general linguistic atmosphere," and in the strikingly ambivalent attitude toward "the heterogeneity of modern life" (364–65). Confirmed by the response of contemporary readers, it was also evident by contrast in the response of their later critics, none of whom could be called romantic primitivists, and all of whom became critical of the doctrine of cultural relativism.

Despite their evolutionary residues and their varying receptivity to psychoanalysis, the Apollonians were disinclined to view human behavior systematically in terms of three notable "isms" of modern social theory: Darwinism, Marxism, and Freudianism – the more so, perhaps, since their own characteristic "ism," that of cultural determinism, had been advanced as an antidote to prevailing determinisms of biology, economics, and psychology (cf. Lowie 1917). In contrast, each of the three critics seems to have been strongly influenced by one or more of these eponymic "isms" at critical points in his or her intellectual development.

From this point of view, it is tempting to continue the argument in terms of cultural moment, with Marxism especially in mind. Just as the Apollonian ethnographies may be contextualized as expressions of a certain tendency within Boasian anthropology in the 1920s, when the nature of culture and its relation to civilization were particularly problematic for American intellectuals, so the critiques of those ethnographies might be seen as expressions of the 1930s. Boasian influence was by this time well established in American anthropology, and the discipline was entering a more differentiated phase; externally, the Great Depression overrode issues of American cultural identity, facilitating a view of culture that was more differentiated, more conflictual, more subject to economic and environmental determinants. In support of such an interpretation one might note the fact that Lewis and Goldfrank were both resident in the Columbia department in the factional period after Boas' retirement in 1936, and that, in differing ways, both were strongly affected by the Marxist radicalism so influential among intellectuals in the 1930s (Goldfrank 1978; Rigdon 1988; Kuznick 1988).

However, the fact that in Freeman's case the relevant eponymic "isms" are those of Freud and Darwin, and that his move away from cultural relativism and determinism came two decades later, suggests that the critique of Apollonian ethnography must be contextualized in terms of other cultural moments besides the 1930s. Although it is beyond the scope of this essay to do more than mention them, two later cultural moments seem especially worthy of brief comment: the early 1950s, when Lewis published his critique of Redfield and Holmes undertook his restudy of Ta'u; and the early 1980s, when Freeman published his critique of Mead.

In contrast to the response of Apollonian ethnographers in the earlier post–World War I decade, that of anthropologists to the experience of World War II was a movement away from cultural relativism. This time, the transvaluing impact of war was not to call into question the verities of Western civilization but rather to reassert the values of universal humanity and the controlling promise of scientific knowledge against the horror of the Holocaust and the universal terror of the atomic bomb. The turn/return was evident even in the three Apollonians. In the short period before her death in 1948, Benedict seems to have experienced a resurgence of the "faith of a scientist," and became involved in a large-scale comparativist project on "Contemporary Cultures" (Mead 1959a:431, 434). Redfield wrote a book on *The Village That Chose Progress* (1950), and also organized a large-scale comparativist project, which he viewed as part of a "great conversation" of civilizations that might contribute to the permanent establishment of a peaceful world community (GS 1980a). Mead did a restudy of the New Guinea community she had studied on her second field trip, which the war in the Pacific had catapulted from the "stone-age" into the "modern world" (1956:xi); the neo-evolutionary impulse of the 1950s was even more evident in her general work on *Continuities in Cultural Evolution* (1964). Looking backward at the postwar period, Eric Wolf noted "the repression of the romantic motive in anthropology" and the resurgence of universalistic and scientizing tendencies in the postwar period (1964:15). In this context, the problem of ethnographic reliability was handled by calls for more rigorous methods and the systematization of "restudies"; although the period was one of optimistic interdisciplinary cross-fertilization, the professional identity of cultural anthropology was never really at issue.

In contrast, Freeman's critique of Mead's ethnographic adequacy came after a decade of "crisis in anthropology" and the end of its "classical" period (cf. GS 1982b), and in the context of a resurgence of biological determinism in the human sciences (Caplan 1978). Furthermore, his critique explicitly called into question the cultural determinism which (although never "absolute") had been central to the discipline's definition during the preceding half century. From the beginning, it seemed clear that the professional identity of cultural anthropology was at issue, and the resistance to Freeman was widespread among American anthropologists, despite the ambivalence many of them felt toward Margaret Mead. From the perspective set forth at the beginning of the present essay, what was at issue was not only the basic conceptual orientation of cultural anthropology, but also its methodological values (and the mythistory that sustained them).

From another perspective, however, it might be argued that Freeman was simply reasserting other methodological values that are also very much a part of the anthropological tradition: the value placed on a comparative study of human variation; the value placed on the potential integration in a single embracive discipline of a number of approaches to the study of human variability (traditionally, the "four fields" of biological, linguistic, archeological, and cultural anthropology); the value placed on the "scientific" character and status of such an integrated comparative enterprise; and the value placed on general statements about the nature and causes of human diversity as the goal of such a scientific inquiry (cf. GS 1982b:411–12). Just as the four methodological values previously mentioned (above, p. 282) were products of the "ethnographicization" of anthropology in the early twentieth century, these four are products of the previous evolutionary period, and may be regarded as its enduring residue. Although pushed into the background during the "classical" period, they have never been erased completely from the disciplinary identity, and were in fact expressed at various points in the work of the Apollonian ethnographers. Paradoxically—in view of the vehemence of Freeman's attack—they were quite strongly evident in much of the work of Margaret Mead. And it might be argued that they have in fact been reasserted by defenders of the American discipline, who have insisted, *contra* Freeman, that it has always assumed an "interaction" of culture and biology.

All of which might lead one to argue that, just as there are limits to the easy contextualization of the Apollonians and their critics in terms of personal biography, so are there limits to easy contexualization in terms of cultural moment.[19] Just as the case of Freeman suggests that the "repressive" critiques were not all expressions of a single cultural milieu, so also the case of Goldfrank reminds us that not all 1920s Boasians can be characterized as "organicists," even to the extent that term is appropriate for the Apollonians. What has been called here "*the* ethnographic sensibility of the 1920s" might more accurately be spoken of as "*an* ethnographic sensibility"—strikingly manifest in certain individuals in a particular cultural historical moment, but not necessarily peculiar to it or invariably in them.

Shifting, thus, the axis of contextualization away from the historically specific, we may ask whether the organic orientation might be an expression of a more enduring anthropological viewpoint. Bennett seems to have been inclined to identify the "organic" orientation with the anthropological outlook itself, arguing that it must be "seen in a context of theory basic to much of anthropology," which was "an expectable outgrowth of the anthropological preoccupation with preliterate communities" (1946:364). Wolf's later comment on the subsequent "repression of the romantic motive in anthropology" (1964:15) suggests another alternative—the more so, another generation on, when a reaction against scienticizing tendencies that began in the later 1960s has become quite widespread, and the issue of relativism has been reinscribed on the agenda of anthropological discussion (Geertz 1984; Hatch 1983). Eschewing "cycles" or "pendulum swings," or any notion of recurrence that cannot be grounded in specific historical context, we may nevertheless wonder if there is not some enduring relationship between anthropology and outlooks similar to those Bennett called "organic" and "repressive."

Here we may take a clue from the opposition Franz Boas described a century ago between the methods of the physicist and of the cosmographer/historian, between a fragmenting analytic method and one based on an empathetic integrative understanding. On the one hand, the physicist studied phenomena that had an "objective unity," resolving them into their

19. On the matter of cultural moment, it may be worth commenting briefly on the failure of this essay to emphasize the racialist and hereditarian milieu of the 1920s as a factor in the formation of Apollonian ethnography (cf. Weiner 1983). While it is undoubtedly true that the emergence of Boasian cultural determinism cannot be adequately understood historically without reference to immigration restriction, the eugenics movement, and Nazism, as well as various other currents of racialist and hereditarian thought and social action in the late nineteenth and early twentieth centuries (cf. GS 1968a; above, pp. 94–113), the contextual factors emphasized in the present essay seem to me more directly relevant to an interpretation of the Apollonian ethnographies. (It should be noted also that the biological determinism Mead confronted in her Samoan ethnography was more a generically human than a racially specific one—cf. Mead 1928b.)

elements, which were investigated separately and comparatively, in the hope of establishing or verifying general laws. On the other, the cosmographer/historian insisted on the validity of a holistic study of complex phenomena that had "a merely subjective unity"—whose elements "seem to be connected only in the mind of the observer." Motivated by "the personal feeling of man towards the world" around, such study required the observer "lovingly" to "penetrate" into the secrets of the phenomenon, until its "truth" could be affectively apprehended—without concern for "the laws which it corroborates or which may be deduced from it." Boas did not propose a resolution of the epistemological and methodological issues separating the physicist and the cosmographer/historian; rather, he granted the equal validity of the two approaches, each of which originated in a fundamental tendency of the human mind (Boas 1887).

Although Boas wrote "The Study of Geography" at a point when his own transition from physics to ethnology was still in process (GS 1968a: 133–60; cf. 1974d:9–10), his remarks may tell us something about the discipline toward which he was moving, as it has developed in the century since he wrote. More obviously than in the case of many other "ologies," cultural anthropology focusses on complex phenomena whose elements seem to be connected only in the mind of the observer. Insofar as their study is necessarily motivated by the personal feeling of the observer, and conditioned by the experience of the observer in the process of observation, these highly subjective objects of study must be perceived and conceived in terms that reflect this subjectivity. It may well be that not all aspects of these phenomena are equally so conditioned (cf. Gartrell 1979); but so long as anthropologists continue to be interested in broadly contrastive characterizations of otherness, subjectivity will be both the object and the instrument of their endeavor. If methodological sophistication may to some extent bring that subjectivity under control, it seems unlikely that method can ever eliminate entirely the anxiety aroused by the subjective encounter with otherness; and, as Boas' opposition implies, it may in fact be that our understanding is in some profound sense dependent on that anxiety (cf. Devereux 1967).

If this is the case, then it seems unlikely that the tension between the "organic" and the "repressive" orientations—any more than that Boas postulated between the methods of analysis and understanding—will ever disappear from anthropology. Just as the latter opposition is long traditional in the epistemology of the human sciences, so the former is long traditional in the history of Western attitudes toward the processes of culture and civilization. And just as anthropology has traditionally been a field of epistemological contention, so has it been a field of attitudinal ambivalence. In the future, as in the past, advocates of one or the other epistemological or attitudinal position will attempt to claim the field; and in that contending process, the bounds of generally accepted knowledge of human unity and diversity will no doubt enlarge. But in the area beyond those bounds, where the reach into otherness continues to exceed the anthropologist's grasp, we can expect the tension to be manifest, within and between individual anthropologists and within and between phases in the history of the discipline. From this point of view, what has been called here the ethnographic sensibility of the 1920s may be viewed in culturally perduring as well as historically specific terms: on the one hand, as the manifestation of a particular moment, on the other as an expression of one of several dualisms inherent in the Western anthropological tradition.

8

Paradigmatic Traditions in the History of Anthropology

Since the mid-nineteenth century, anthropology has claimed the status of a science—sometimes stridently, sometimes ambivalently; at times, by an assertive self-definition, at times, by a flexible redefinition of science itself. There is of course a long tradition of internal debate about epistemological issues and about the relationships of the component subdisciplines of a somewhat problematically integrated inquiry, some of which have, historically, a closer relation to the biological and earth sciences. Among themselves, anthropologists have been inclined to savor the fact that, unusually if not uniquely among scholarly disciplines, they participate in the umbrella associations of the natural sciences, the social sciences, and the humanities, and are able to assert a claim upon the financial resources of all three. But in facing the public, they have in general insisted on their status as members of a larger scientific community, and on the whole, the world of science has given credence to that claim—though not without an undercurrent of informal patronization, and moments of more serious questioning.

In the history of science, the status of anthropology has been somewhat marginal. When the history of what were then called the "behavioral" sciences achieved a journal in the middle 1960s, the "sciences of man" constituted one short and undifferentiated entry in the annual "Critical Bibliography" number of *Isis*, the leading journal in the history of science. But as the latter-day "revolt against positivism" gained momentum, various social scientific disciplines turned toward history; during the same period, increasing numbers of intellectual historians sought new fields to plow. With the greater yield of work, the history of the behavioral/social/human sciences won a greater degree of recognition within the history of science. In 1981, psychology, sociology, economics, and cultural anthropology were each given separate recognition under "the sciences of man" (physical anthropology having already long been included under "biological sciences"); three years later, the encompassing rubric was gender-neutralized as "social sciences."

Although one of my early articles was published in *Isis* (1964), and several in the early numbers of the *Journal of the History of the Behavioral Sciences* (e.g., 1965), my ties to the historical profession began to stretch after I joined the University of Chicago Department of Anthropology in 1968. I served one term on the editorial board of *Isis*, and have been a member of the board of the *Journal of the History of the Behavioral Sciences* since its founding. But I rarely attend annual professional meetings in history or the history of science. Nevertheless, I have always thought of myself, *au fond*, as an historian, and after 1981 this historical identity was to some extent reasserted, when, as the only "available" candidate, I became Director of the Morris Fishbein Center for the History of Science and Medicine, and continued in that position until 1992. In that capacity, I was of course particularly interested in furthering the history of the inquiries which, in the aftermath of the second revolt against positivism, were increasingly to be called the "human sciences"—for a number of years, in an informal interinstitutional faculty seminar known as the Chicago Group in the History of the Social Sciences, in 1986 at the Summer Institute in the History of the Social Sciences at the Center for Advanced Study in the Behavioral Sciences, and since 1983 in the History of the Human Sciences Workshop at the University of Chicago.

Even so, my role in the more general history of science community has continued to be a marginal one. As a senior representative of what to many historians of harder sciences is still a slightly dubious one, I am called upon occasionally to review books and manuscripts. But my only substantial contribution to the history of science literature *per se* is a recent attempt, for an encyclopedic compendium, to represent the whole history of anthropology, from the Greeks to the present, in six thousand words. The editors, reflecting no doubt the pervasive influence of Thomas Kuhn in the history of science over the last several decades, originally chose "Revolutions in Anthropology" as the rubric under which to represent the field in microcosm to a more general history of science community. Having moved toward the history of anthropology as a member of the same history department in the early 1960s, I had long found Kuhn's work congenial. *The Struc-*

ture of Scientific Revolutions (1962) was for me one of those few radically innovative works that one reads with a sense of *déjà vu*—as if what one was inclined already to believe was being now finally made explicit. Construing paradigms as unstated bodies of assumption grounded more in practice than in theory, as incommensurable disciplinary "world views," Kuhn's argument seemed much in the tradition of modern American cultural anthropology. In some earlier writings, I made a fairly self-conscious effort to apply the paradigm notion, worrying whether the social sciences were "pre-paradigmatic" and to what extent they practiced "normal science" (1965, 1968a). But I always regarded Kuhn's work as heuristic rather than definitive, and have been inclined to treat the idea of paradigms as a resonant metaphor, to be applied flexibly when it seemed to facilitate the understanding of particular historical episodes. Although well aware that philosophers and historians of science have engaged in debate about the meaning of paradigm and whether Darwinism was really a "scientific revolution" (Greene 1980), I have persisted in this loose construction, albeit not without a certain rhetorical and conceptual discomfort (1987a).

Responding to ideas Dell Hymes suggested about paradigms, traditions, and "cynosures" in his introduction to the history of linguistics symposium (Hymes 1974), I have recently found it convenient to think in terms of "paradigmatic traditions." On the one hand, it seemed that certain episodes in the history of anthropology—notably, the emergence of social evolutionism around 1860 and its rejection after 1900—could fruitfully be thought of as scientific revolutions, in which the opposing points of view had something of the character of paradigms, insofar as they were held by distinct groups of inquirers with different assumptions about what the proper aims and methods of anthropological research should be. But since it was clear that the major alternatives before 1900 could be traced back to the Greeks, and that until well into the twentieth century the history of anthropology could be seen as an alternation of their cynosuric dominance, it seemed that the paradigm notion, which in Kuhn's formulation emphasizes synchronic discontinuity, needed to be modified to allow for paradigm-like bodies of assumption that perdured through long periods of time. Hence, "paradigmatic traditions"—with apologies to Tom Kuhn and all those involved in the still on-going epistemological, conceptual, and methodological debate about his work.

Attentive readers of this essay will no doubt notice that after about 1920 the idea of paradigmatic traditions fades into the background. Before that time there is an implicit correlation of paradigmatic dominance and periodization, with developmentalism/evolutionism dominant before 1800 and again after 1860, and the early-nineteenth-century ethnological tradition reemergent after 1900 (cf. 1978b, which attempted a schematic definition of six major periods in the history of anthropology). There is also a suggestion that, in the wake of the early-twentieth-century "revolution in anthropology," disciplinary discourse in what I have called the "classical period" (c. 1920–c. 1965) was unified by a synchronic and broadly "functional" paradigm—which, in terms of the previous history of anthropology, might find its traditional roots in either Montesquieu or Herder, depending on whether ethnographic integration is conceived in British functional (or structural-functional) or in American cultural terms. More recently, coming from another national tradition, "structuralism" may claim an alternatively integrative paradigmatic status, for which a "traditional" ancestry may no doubt be found (Lévi-Strauss 1962).

But by the end of the classical period, paradigms and periods—historiographical heuristics ever to be lightly held—become even more problematic. The fragmentation of anthropology, first among the "four fields" and then among the various "adjectival anthropologies" into which sociocultural anthropology has subsequently become ever more divided, makes it increasingly difficult to find a consistent reference point for the paradigm idea. A recent history of "political anthropology" identified six "paradigms" that had developed in this subfield by 1974 (the "action," "processual," "neo-evolutionary," "structural," "political economy," and "culture history" paradigms), and referred as well to the "Oxbridge," "transactional," "symbolic interactional," "game theory," "subaltern," "Marxist," and "interpretive," and an as-yet-undefined "new paradigm [of] the 1990s" (Vincent 1990:407, 418, 386, 402, 424)—thus reinstantiating the indeterminacy that historians and philosophers of science have found in the paradigm concept since its original formulation thirty years ago (cf. Kuhn 1974).

Periodization, too, seems not without its problems as one approaches the present. After devoting several seminars to anthropology before the "crisis" and since its "reinvention," I am more inclined to see World War II as perhaps a significant break within the classical period. Assuming, however, that there was a substantial unity of anthropology from its "ethnographicization" to its "crisis," the question remains how to characterize the years since then. It is an artifact of historical periodization that the last period always ends in the present moment; but whether that moment, or any other recent moment, marks a significant historical transition is another matter—about which my backward-looking historicist temperament makes me disinclined to speculate. For the present, then, here is my "big picture" of anthropology's past—painted on a very small canvas, in very tight strokes.

Defining the Domain of Anthropology

In 1904 Franz Boas defined the domain of anthropological knowledge as "the biological history of mankind in all its varieties; linguistics applied to people without written languages; the ethnology of people without historic records; and prehistoric archeology." More than any other "anthropologist," Boas may be said to exemplify the putative unity of this domain, since (virtually alone among his confrères) he made significant contributions to each of these four inquiries in the course of his long career. But despite the fact that he was perhaps the most important single figure in the institutionalization of an academic discipline called "anthropology" in university departments in the United States, Boas already felt in 1904 that there were "indications of its breaking up." The "biological, linguistic and ethnologic-archeological methods are so distinct," he believed, that the time was "rapidly drawing near" when the two former branches of anthropology would be taken over by specialists in those disciplines, and "anthropology pure and simple will deal with customs and beliefs of the less civilized peoples only . . ." (1904b:35).

Given the weight of institutional inertia and of residual commitment to the norm of disciplinary unity, it remains arguable today whether Boas' prediction is yet likely to be achieved. Nevertheless, the fact that its leading practical exemplar regarded the unity of anthropology as historically contingent rather than epistemologically determined suggests that no general historical account of that "science" may take its unity for granted. In spite of the all-embracing etymological singularity of the term *anthropology* (Greek *anthropos:* man; *logos:* discourse), the diverse discourses that may be historically subsumed by it have only in certain moments and places been fused into anything approximating a unified science of humankind. In continental Europe in Boas' time, "anthropology" referred (and often does today) to what in the Anglo-American tradition has been called "physical anthropology." As such, it was distinguishable from and historically opposed to "ethnology"—a discourse that, etymologically, was somewhat more diversitarian (Greek *ethnos:* nation).

In this context, the historical development of anthropology may be contrasted to two ideal typical views of disciplinary development. The first is a Comtean hierarchical model in which the impulse of positive knowledge is successively extended into more complex domains of natural phenomena. The second is a genealogical model in which, within each domain, disciplines may be visualized as growing from a single undifferentiated "ur"-discourse (with the biological sciences developing out of natural history, the humanities out of philology and the social sciences out of moral philosophy). As against these two fission models, "anthropology" in its inclusive Anglo-American sense is better viewed as an imperfect fusion of modes of inquiry that were quite distinct in origin and in character – deriving in fact from all three of these undifferentiated "ur"-discourses.

Insofar as a common denominator may be extracted from Boas' contingent descriptive definition of anthropology, it would seem to imply an opposition between Europeans, who have written languages and historical records, and "others," who have not. Indeed, it may be argued that the greatest retrospective unity of the discourses subsumed within the rubric "anthropology" is to be found in this substantive concern with the peoples who were long stigmatized as "savages," and who, in the nineteenth century, tended to be excluded from other human scientific disciplines by the very process of their substantive-cum-methodological definition (the economist's concern with the money economy; the historian's concern with written documents, etc.). From this point of view, to study the history of anthropology is to study the attempt to describe and to interpret or explain the "otherness" of populations encountered in the course of European overseas expansion. Although thus fundamentally (and oppositionally) diversitarian in impulse, such study has usually implied a reflexivity which reencompassed European self and alien "other" within a unitary humankind. This history of anthropology may thus be viewed as a continuing (and complex) dialectic between the universalism of "anthropos" and the diversitarianism of "ethnos" or, from the perspective of particular historical moments, between the Enlightenment and the Romantic impulse. Anthropology's "recurrent dilemma" has been how to square both generic human rationality and the biological unity of mankind with "the great natural variation of cultural forms" (Geertz 1973:22).

The Biblical, Developmental, and Polygenetic Traditions

A second unifying tendency within Boas' definition is historical, or more generally, diachronic, since history in the narrow sense seemed precluded by the lack of documents. For Boas, the "otherness" which is the subject-matter of anthropology was to be explained as the product of change of time. Although Boas in fact wrote at the verge of a revolutionary shift toward a more synchronic anthropology, the history of anthropology up until his time may be schematized in terms of the interplay of two major diachronic traditions that were, in a broad sense, paradigmatic, both of them counterpointed by a more synchronic tradition which, because of its heterodoxy, only very briefly achieved paradigmatic status. In the discussion that follows, these traditions will be designated as the "biblical" (or "ethnological"), the "developmental" (or "evolutionist"), and the "polygenetic" (or "physical anthropological").

The ultimate roots of anthropological thought are more often traced to the Greek than to the biblical tradition. However, it may be argued that during the period of European expansion the underlying paradigmatic framework for the explanation of "otherness" derived from the first ten chapters of Genesis. Many intellectual currents contributed to anthropological speculation, among them environmentalist and humoralist assumptions from the Hippocratic and Galenic traditions, hierarchical notions from the "Great Chain of Being," medieval conceptions of the monstrous, etc. (Friedman 1981; Lovejoy 1936; Slotkin 1965). But the dominant paradigmatic tradition (paradigmatic in the sense of providing a more or less coherent *a priori* framework of assumption defining both relevant problems and the data and methods for their solution) was that iconically embodied in the second of John Speed's "Genealogies of Holy Scriptures" in the King James Bible. There, growing from the roof of the Ark resting on the top of Mount Ararat in Armenia, was a genealogical tree with three major branches: the descendants of Japhet in Europe, of Sem in Asia, and of Ham in Africa, traced on out to their various representatives in the ancient world ("Phrigians," "Bactrians," "Babylonians," etc.) (Speed 1611). In this context, the fundamental anthropological problem was to establish putative historical links between every present human group and one of the branches of a biblical ethnic tree that linked all of humankind to a particular descendant of Adam and Eve. Since what had diversified humankind in the first instance was the confusion of tongues at Babel, the privileged data for reestablishing connections were similarities of language, augmented by such similarities of culture as survived the degenerative processes that were a concomitant of migration toward the earth's imagined corners. Since all humans were offspring of a single family, and ultimately of a single pair, the physical differences among them were secondary phenomena, characteristically attributable to the influence of the environments through which they had migrated during the six millennia allowed by the biblical chronology—if not to the direct intervention of God (as in "the curse of Ham").

The biblical anthropological tradition, which saw the (characteristically degenerative) differentiation of humankind in terms of movement through space within a limited and event-specific historical time, may be contrasted with a Greco-Roman paradigmatic tradition deriving from the speculations of Ionian materialists. Perhaps most influentially embodied in Lucretius's *De Rerum Natura*, this tradition saw time as an enabling rather than a limiting factor, and conceived diachronic change in progressive processual rather than degenerative historical terms. Rather than losing divinely given knowledge as they moved through space in time, human groups acquired knowledge gradually, responding to organic needs and environmental stimuli in an adaptive utilitarian manner, as they groped their way forward step by step from a state near that of the brutes to the most advanced civil society. Although human differentiation was construed in terms of status on a generalized developmental scale rather as the product of a specific sequence of historical events, the Greco-Roman paradigm was still in a broad sense diachronic (Hodgen 1964).

While the biblical and the developmental traditions represent the dominant paradigmatic alternatives in Western anthropological thought before 1900, it is useful to distinguish a third major paradigmatic tradition: the polygenetic. Foreshadowed in tribal and classical notions of autochthonous origin, it became a matter of more serious speculation in the aftermath of the discovery of the New World, the peopling of which posed a major problem for the orthodox monogenetic tradition. A few writers, most notoriously Isaac de la Peyrère in 1655, went so far as to suggest that the peoples of the New World did not descend from Adam (Popkin 1987). However, it was nearly a century before Linnaeus included mankind (American/choleric; European/sanguine; Asiatic/melancholic; African/phlegmatic) in the *System of Nature* (1735), and still a generation later before systematic comparative human anatomical data began to be collected. Even then, most of the early physical anthropologists remained, like Johann Blumenbach, staunchly monogenist. But given the growth of comparative data within the framework of a static pre-evolutionary view of biological species, a "polygenetic" approach to human differentiation became in the nineteenth century an alternative to be considered seriously. From this point of view, human "races" (often distinguished by the forms of their crania) were, like animal species, aboriginally distinct. Unaffected by the forces of environment, they had remained constant throughout the relatively short span of human historical time—as the images on the 4,000-year-old monuments discovered by Napoleon's expedition to Egypt confirmed (Slotkin 1965).

The Darwinian Revolution and the Differentiation of National Anthropological Traditions

Although Rousseau had envisioned in 1755 a unified science of man carried on by philosopher-voyagers who, shaking off "the yoke of national prejudices," would "learn to know men by their likenesses and their differences" (1755:211), it was more than a century before his dream began to be realized. For most of that time, the vast bulk of anthropological data was collected incidentally by travellers, missionaries, colonizers, and naturalists. Insofar as the activity was tied to a knowledge-tradition, it was much more likely to be that of natural history than social theory. Furthermore, the forms of "anthropology" institutionalized in the major European nations differed strikingly in their relation to the three paradigmatic traditions just described.

During the pre-Darwinian nineteenth century, the focal anthropological issue was posed by the explosion of the data of human diversity that was produced by European expansion, in the context of advances in the regnant sciences in the human and biological domains—comparative linguistics and comparative anatomy. From a classificatory and/or genetic point of view, the central question was "Is mankind one or many?" Until midcentury, comparative Indo-European (i.e., Japhetic) linguistics provided a model of inquiry which promised to provide a classification of humankind in terms of its most distinctive feature, but which would also link all human groups to a single source. Exemplified in the works of the staunchly monogenist James Cowles Prichard, this goal was institutionalized in several of the "ethnological" societies founded around 1840 (GS 1971, 1973a).

By the 1850s, however, a distinctly physical anthropological current, modelling itself on comparative anatomy and often polygenist in tendency, had begun to separate itself from the ethnological (formerly biblical) paradigm. Foreshadowed in the works of certain French investigators, and in the "American School" of Samuel G. Morton (Stanton 1960), this trend was realized institutionally in the "anthropological" societies founded by Paul Broca in Paris in 1859 and by James Hunt in London in 1863 (GS 1971). Although the term *anthropological* had in fact been previously employed as a theological/philosophical category, it was now used to affirm the need for a naturalistic study of humankind as one or more physical species in the animal world.

This newly asserted physical anthropological tendency in fact proved resistant to Darwinism, which seemed to the polygenetically-inclined simply a new and speculative form of monogenism (GS 1968a:44–68). However, the Darwinian revolution was to have a major impact on speculation in the older ethnological tradition. On the one hand, the greatly extended "antiquity of man," confirmed by the discoveries at Brixham Cave in 1858, made the gradual formation of contemporary races by modification of a single apelike progenitor seem more plausible. On the other, the revolution in time made extremely unlikely the ethnological task of establishing plausible historical connections over the whole span of human existence. Furthermore, Darwinism posed a problem for which the new "prehistoric" archeology offered extremely inadequate evidence: providing a convincing evolutionary account of the cultural development that might link modern man with an apelike ancestor. In this context, the development paradigm came again to the forefront of anthropological attention in the last third of the nineteenth century, especially in the Anglo-American tradition (GS 1987a; cf. Van Riper 1990).

During this period, sociocultural evolutionists attempted to synthesize the data of contemporary "savagery" collected by travellers and naturalists (including that now obtained by correspondence or in response to more formal questionnaires such as the *Notes and Queries in Anthropology* prepared by a committee of the British Association for the Advancement of Science in 1874). By arranging such present synchronic data on a diachronic scale, it was possible for "armchair" anthropologists to construct generalized stage-sequences of development in each area of human culture. In Britain, E. B. Tylor (1871) traced the evolution of religion from primitive "animism" through polytheism to monotheism, while John McLennan (1865) followed the evolution of marriage from primitive promiscuity through polyandry to monogamy. In the United States, Lewis Henry Morgan (1877) traced a more general development from "lower savagery" through three phases of "barbarism" up to "civilization."

These sequences depended on a generalized assumption of human "psychic unity," which enabled anthropologists to reason backward from an irrational "survival" in a higher stage to the rational utilitarian practice underlying it. However, the sequences thus reconstructed by the "comparative method" in fact assumed a polar opposition between "primitive" and "civilized" mentality. And in the mixed Darwinian/Lamarckian context of late-nineteenth-century biological thought these cultural evolutionary sequences took on a racialist character. The human brain was seen as having been gradually enlarged by the accumulative experience of the civilizing process, and the races of the world were ranked on a double scale of color and culture (as when Tylor suggested that the Australian, Tahitian, Aztec, Chinese, and Italian "races" formed a single ascending cultural sequence). While much of day-to-day anthropological inquiry reflected a continuing interest in the ethnological affinities of different groups, what is sometimes called "classical evolutionism" was both the theoretical cynosure and the dominant ideological influence in anthropology in the later nineteenth century (GS 1987a).

In general, anthropological thought in the late nineteenth century attempted to subsume the study of human phenomena within positivistic natural science. However, "anthropology" itself was by no means a transnational scientific category. In England, the post-Darwinian intellectual synthesis of ethnological and polygenist tendencies in classical evolutionism was reflected institutionally in 1871 by the unification of the Ethnological and Anthropological Societies in the Anthropological Institute. In the United States, a similarly inclusive viewpoint was evident in J. W. Powell's governmental Bureau of Ethnology (1879), which, despite its title, had as its avowed mission the organization of "anthropologic" research among American Indians (Hinsley 1981). In principle if not always in practice, "anthropology" in the Anglo-American tradition attempted to unify the four fields later specified by Franz Boas. By contrast, on the Continent, where Darwinism did not exert such a strongly unifying influence, "anthropology" continued to refer primarily to physical anthropology. Although Broca's École d'Anthropologie included chairs in sociology and ethnology, those studies had for the most part a quite separate development, largely under the aegis of Emile Durkheim and his students (Gringeri 1990; GS 1984b). And although by 1900 the fossil gap between existing primate forms and the anomalously large-brained Neanderthals had been narrowed by the discovery of "Java Man," physical anthropology continued to be heavily influenced by a static, typological approach to the classification of human "races," primarily on the basis of measurements of the human cranium, using the "cephalic index" developed by Anders Retzius in the 1840s (Erickson 1974).

The Critique of Evolutionism in American Cultural Anthropology

In this context, the critique of evolutionary assumption elaborated by Franz Boas between 1890 and 1910 contributed to a revolutionary reorientation in the history of anthropology. Born of a liberal and assimilated German-Jewish family, and trained in both physics and geography, Boas began his career from a position of cultural marginality and scientific intermediacy, somewhere between the dominant positivistic naturalism on the one hand, and the romantic and *Geisteswissenschaft* traditions on the other (an opposition classically delineated in his 1887 essay on "The Study of Geography").

After a year of ethnogeographic fieldwork among the Baffin Island Eskimo, Boas settled in the United States, carrying on general anthropological fieldwork among the Indians of the Pacific Northwest, where he worked under the auspices of both Powell's Bureau of Ethnology and a committee of the British Association for the Advancement of Science chaired by Tylor. By 1896, Boas had developed a neo-ethnological critique of "the comparative method" of classical evolutionism. Arguing on the basis of a study of the borrowing and diffusion of cultural elements among Northwest Coast Indians, he insisted that detailed historical investigations of specific culture histories must precede the attempt to derive laws of cultural development. Parallel to this, Boas criticized the evolutionary idea of "primitive mentality," arguing that human thought generally was conditioned by culturally varying bodies of traditional assumption—a viewpoint sustained also by his analyses of American-Indian grammatical categories. Similarly, his physical anthropological researches—including a study of the modification of headform in the children of European immigrants—called into question racialist arguments based on cranial typology.

Boas' anthropology was characteristically critical rather than constructive. Nevertheless, his work laid the basis for the modern anthropological conception of culture as pluralistic, relativistic, and largely freed from biological determinism. His student A. L. Kroeber, a major articulator of the cultural viewpoint, initially invoked the autonomy of the cultural in 1917, simply as a heuristic device, and since then, there has been a recurrent anthropological interest in the culture/biology interface. But the general thrust of Boasian anthropology was to mark off a domain from which biological determinism was excluded. Initially, that delimitation depended on an insistence on the essentially historical character of cultural phenomena, as exemplified in Edward Sapir's "Time Perspective in Aboriginal American Culture: A Study of Method" (1916). But if the first-generation Boasians occasionally spoke of themselves as the American Historical School, the major thrust of Boasian anthropology after 1920 was in fact away from historical reconstruction. On the one hand, the emergence of a more time-specific archeology (with the development of stratigraphic approaches after 1910, augmented after World War II by carbon 14 dating) tended to devalue historical reconstructions based on the distribution of "culture elements" over "cultural areas." On the other, the Boasian interest in the cultural basis of human psychological differences led toward a synchronic study of the integration of cultures and of the relation of "culture and personality"—tendencies archetypified in Ruth Benedict's widely influential *Patterns of Culture* (1934).

Although the "culture and personality" movement and the study of "acculturation" were being superseded by the 1950s by more sociologically oriented approaches, "culture" remained the predominant focus of anthropological inquiry in the United States. As graduate training began its explosive spread beyond the four centers founded before World War I (Harvard, Columbia, Berkeley, and Pennsylvania) and the half-dozen additions of the interwar period, it usually continued to include at least introductory training in each of the "four fields." Most practitioners, however, had long since specialized in no more than one of them; and physical anthropologists, linguists, and archeologists had, during the interwar period, founded their own professional organizations. While the American Anthropological Association (founded in 1902) continued to include specialists in all four fields, it was dominated by those who specialized in what Boas and the first generation of his students still called ethnology—which by the 1930s was in the process of being rechristened cultural anthropology.

Fieldwork, Functionalism, and British Social Anthropology

In Great Britain, the early-twentieth-century "revolution in anthropology" took a somewhat different course. As in the United States, where the Boasians carried on and elaborated the fieldwork tradition pioneered by the Bureau of Ethnology, a key factor was the development of a corps of academically trained ethnographic fieldworkers. However, what was to become the archetypical field situation for British anthropologists differed considerably from that of their early Boasian counterparts. In the United States, where transcontinental railways facilitated relatively short visits to Indian reservations, ethnographers studied the "memory culture" of elder informants, often by collecting "texts" (which Boas thought might provide for a nonliterate culture the equivalent of the documentary heritage that was the basis of humanistic study in the Western tradition). By contrast, British ethnographers, travelling weeks by sea to the darker reaches of the world's largest empire, became the archetypical practitioners of extended participant observation of the current behavior of still-functioning social groups. Foreshadowed in the work of Baldwin Spencer and Frank Gillen among the Australian Arunta in 1896, implemented among the graduates of A. C. Haddon's Torres Straits Expedition and by younger members of the "Cambridge School" in the first decade of the century, the "lone-ethnographer" model of inquiry was in fact formalized by W. H. R. Rivers in his description of the "concrete method" for the 1912 revision of *Notes and Queries.* The person most closely associated with this development, however, was Bronislaw Malinowski, who came from Poland in 1910 to study under Edward Westermarck and Charles Seligman at the London School of Economics. During World War I, Malinowski spent almost two years among the Trobriand Islanders off the northeastern coast of New Guinea, and in 1922 he gave the new methodology its mythic charter in the opening chapter of *Argonauts of the Western Pacific.*

During the 1920s, Malinowski moved briefly toward Freudian psychoanalysis by offering the matrifocal Trobriand family to suggest a modification of the universal Oedipus complex (GS 1986b). However, there was no British analogue to the American culture-and-personality movement. The latter may be regarded as offering an explanatory alternative to nineteenth-century evolutionary assertions of racial mental differences. In Britain, however, the critique of evolutionism focussed not on its biological implications, but rather on its tendency, archetypified in the *Golden Bough* of James G. Frazer, to explain human behavior in intellectualist utilitarian terms (Ackerman 1987). By 1900, attacks had already begun on Tylor's doctrine of animism, which had explained human religious belief as a premature and failed science (with the experience of dreams and death suggesting the hypothesis of a soul distinct from the human body). Echoing William James, R. R. Marett suggested a "pre-animistic" basis of religious belief in the much more affect-laden Melanesian concept of *mana* (an awe-inspiring supernatural power manifesting itself in the natural world). During the following decade, theoretical discussion centered on the mixed socioreligious phenomenon of totemism, which McLennan had defined in 1869 in terms of the linkage of animistic belief and exogamous matrilineal social organization. To this, William Robertson Smith had added the idea of the occasional communal consumption of the totem animal—an armchair conception which to Frazer seemed confirmed ethnographically by Spencer and Gillen's research among the Arunta (R. Jones 1984). In the decade before World War I, social anthropological debate swirled about the problem of totemism, with special reference to the Arunta and other Australian data, which were assumed by evolutionists to provide evidence of the most primitive human state.

It was in this context that British anthropology, which in its Tylorian and Frazerian phase gave priority to the problem of religious belief, shifted toward the study of religious ritual, and more generally, toward the study of kinship and social organization, which had been a special concern of the American evolutionist Lewis Henry Morgan during his pre-evolutionary "ethnological" phase (Trautman 1987). Building on his own pioneering ethnographic study of the Iroquois in the 1840s, Morgan had attempted to solve the problem of the peopling of America by using an ethnographic questionnaire to collect worldwide data on *Systems of Consanguinity and Affinity* (1871). Recast in developmental terms, his distinction between the "classificatory" and "descriptive" systems of kinship provided a conceptual framework for the ethnographic work of his Australian correspondents Lorimer Fison and A. W. Howitt. Augmented by the "genealogical method" developed by Rivers in the Torres Straits in 1898, Morgan's approach was eventually to provide the conceptual groundwork for modern British social anthropology, although not, however, until it had been detached from its diachronic evolutionary framework.

That process took place in two phases in the work of Rivers and his student A. R. Radcliffe-Brown. Rivers himself underwent a "conversion" from evolutionism to a diffusionary "ethnological analysis of culture" in 1911. However, his attempt to reconstruct *The History of Melanesian Society* (1914a) was still heavily dependent on the evolutionary concept of "survival," which assumed that certain existing social customs or kinship terms need not be explained in terms of their present function, but rather in terms of their correspondence with prior social organizational forms. In contrast, Radcliffe-Brown moved away from evolutionism via the more functionalist sociology of Emile Durkheim. His break with Rivers focussed specifically on the utility of "survivals" in sociological analysis, and involved a general rejection of any "conjectural" approach to diachronic problems in "social anthropology," which in 1923 he took some pains to differentiate from "ethnology" (GS 1984b).

At that time British anthropology was excited by the confrontation between the "heliolithic" diffusionism of Rivers' disciples Grafton Elliot Smith and William Perry at University College London and the psychobiological functionalism of Malinowski at the London School of Economics. Sustained by grants from the Rockefeller Foundation, Malinowskian functionalism had, by 1930, become the dominant British current. But during the next few years some of Malinowski's more important students shifted their theoretical allegiance to Radcliffe-Brown, who after two decades of academic wanderings (from Cape Town to Sydney to Chicago), finally succeeded in 1937 to the chair at Oxford. Although the Association of Social Anthropologists formed at Oxford in 1946 included representatives of several different viewpoints, it was Radcliffe-Brown's synchronic natural scientific study of "social systems'—overlaid upon the Malinowskian fieldwork tradition—that gave British social anthropology its distinctive character.

The Synchronic Revolution, the "Classical Period," and the Emergence of International Anthropology

Despite these differences of phase and focus, there were many common features in the development of British social and American cultural anthropology in the first half of the twentieth century. In both countries, anthropology in the pre-academic museum period had been oriented largely toward the collection of material objects (whether artifacts or bones) carried into the present from the past; in both cases there was a dramatic turn toward the observational study of behavior in the present. Although an interest in evolutionary or historical questions never disappeared entirely from either national tradition, anthropological inquiry was no longer primarily conceived in diachronic terms. And while Radcliffe-Brown insisted, during his Chicago period, on the differences between his viewpoint and the more dilute "functionalism" of some American cultural anthropologists, there is a looser sense in which one may speak of synchronic functionalism as a paradigm in the Anglo-American tradition. This was even more the case after World War II, when American anthropologists went overseas in large numbers for fieldwork, and began at home to feel the influence of functionalist theory in American sociology.

In both countries, one may speak of anthropology as having become "ethnographicized." Although the goal of cross-cultural comparison and scientific generalization continued to be acknowledged, the most distinctive common feature of Anglo-American anthropology in what may be called its "classical" period (c. 1925–c. 1965) was the central role of ethnographic fieldwork. Rather than providing items of information for armchair anthropological theorists, fieldwork became the certifying criterion of membership in the anthropological community and the underpinning of its central methodological values: i.e., participant observation in small-scale communities, conceived holistically and relativistically, and given a privileged role in the constitution of theory. In both countries, this ethnographically oriented study of social and cultural behavior tended to separate from and to dominate the other anthropological subdisciplines, although in the more pluralistic structure of American academic life, the ideal of a general anthropology uniting the traditional four fields continued to have a certain potency.

Elsewhere, however, the course of subdisciplinary development was rather different. On the European continent, where the inclusive four-field tradition had never taken root, physical anthropology continued to have a largely separate development on into the twentieth century, and to be relatively unaffected by the Boasian critique—especially in Germany, where during the Nazi period, the discipline was redefined as *Rassenkunde* (Proctor 1988). In Germany and in central Europe, the ethnological tradition continued to be strongly diffusionist and historical up until the mid-twentieth century, although some ethnographic fieldwork was carried on. In France a modern ethnographic tradition did not develop until after the founding in the 1920s of the Institut d'Ethnologie, in which Durkheim's nephew Marcel Mauss played a leading role (Clifford 1982; Gringeri 1990). It was not until 1982 that the French equivalents of cultural anthropologists were to take the lead in founding the Société d'Anthropologie française after the American model. This development reflected not only the intellectual interchange that had occurred between the French and the Anglo-American traditions after 1960 under the influence of the structuralism of Claude Lévi-Strauss but also the influence of a tendency that can be called international anthropology, or the internationalization of the Anglo-American tradition.

Although international congresses of "anthropologists" or "prehistorians" or "Americanists" had been held periodically since the 1860s, it is only since World War II that International Congresses of Anthropological and Ethnological Sciences have been held on a regular basis over a long period (in Philadelphia, Moscow, Tokyo, Chicago, Vancouver, Delhi, and Zagreb). Reinforced after 1960 by the international journal *Current Anthropology*, edited by Sol Tax, these congresses have been at the same time forums for diversity and media for the diffusion of a certain homogenizing tendency, in which sociocultural anthropology in the emergent Anglo-Franco-American mode has predominated, but the other major subdisciplines have continued to be represented. However, the embracive four-field conception associated with the American tradition has still had a certain inertial influence, reinforced by the overwhelming numerical predominance of American anthropologists within the world anthropological community.

The "Crisis" and "Reinvention" of Anthropology

In the very period in which an international anthropology began to be realized, however, there were dramatic changes in the world historical relationship of the peoples who had traditionally provided the scholars and the subject matter of anthropological inquiry. For more than a century, the anticipated disappearance of "savage" (or "primitive" or "tribal" or "preliterate") peoples under the impact of European expansion had been a major impetus to ethnographic research, which was carried on under an umbrella of colonial power. By the 1930s, these categories had already become problematic, and field research was beginning to be undertaken in "complex" societies. But despite the postwar interest in peasant communities and the processes of "modernization," anthropology retained its archetypically asymmetrical character, as a study of dark-skinned "others" by light-skinned Euro-Americans. With the end of colonial empires, however, the peoples that anthropologists had traditionally studied were now part of "new nations" oriented toward rapid sociocultural change, and their leaders were often unreceptive to an inquiry which, even after the critique of evolutionary racial assumption, continued to be premised on sociocultural asymmetry. Indeed, many Third World intellectuals now began to regard as ideologically retrograde (and even as racist) the characteristic modern anthropological attitude of relativistic tolerance of cultural differences. What had served in the 1930s to defend "others" against racialism seemed now to justify the perpetuation of a backwardness founded on exploitation. In the politically charged context of major episodes of postcolonial warfare, there had developed by the late 1960s what some were inclined to call the "crisis of anthropology" (GS 1982b).

The sense of malaise—which was widespread in the human sciences—manifested itself in a number of ways: substantively, ideologically, methodologically, epistemologically, theoretically, demographically, and institutionally. In the face of rapid social change and restrictions on access to field sites, it was no longer realistic, even normatively, to regard the recovery of pure, uncontaminated non-European "otherness" as the privileged substantive focus of anthropological inquiry. Nor was it possible to regard such inquiry as ethically neutral or innocent of political consequences. A new consciousness of the inherently problematic reflexivity of participant observation called into question both the methodological and epistemological assumptions of traditional ethnographic fieldwork. In the context of a general questioning of positivist assumption in the human sciences, there were signs of a shift from homeostatic theoretical orientations to more dynamic ones. And even the very growth of the field was now a problem, as the government funding of the 1950s and 1960s began to be restricted, and Ph.D.s began to overflow their accustomed academic niches, beyond which anthropology had yet to establish a viable claim to significant domestic social utility. In the face of predictions of the "end of anthropology," there were, by the early 1970s, radical calls for its "reinvention" (Hymes 1972).

The majority of anthropologists, however—reflecting either a residue of prelapsarian confidence or a sense of the weight of institutional inertia—seem to have taken for granted that the discipline would carry on indefinitely. And indeed, it seemed clear that by the mid-1980s, the crisis had been domesticated. A decade after the call for the discipline's reinvention, the major academic anthropology departments continued to carry on a kind of business as usual, despite the diffiulties of funding research and the still-constricted job market for the students they were training. Nevertheless, it seems clear that the classical period of modern anthropology had come to an end sometime after 1960, and the usual business of postclassical anthropology differed in significant respects from what had gone before.

Reflexivity, Fission, and the Dualism of the Anthropological Tradition

At the demographic center of the discipline in the United States, the centrifugal forces observed by Boas in 1904 had multiplied. It was no longer a question simply of the coherence of the four major subdisciplines, but of a multiplication of "adjectival anthropologies" (applied, cognitive, dental, economic, educational, feminist, historical, humanistic, medical, nutritional, philosophical, political, psychological, symbolic, urban, etc.)—many of them organized into their own national societies. And while it was possible to interpret this proliferation as a sign of the continued adaptive vigor (or the successful reinvention) of the disciplinary impulse, there was inevitably concern about how, in the last decade of the twentieth century, that impulse might be defined.

Once the reflexivity implied in the original anthropological impulse had been raised permanently to disciplinary consciousness, and the forces of sociocultural change had removed many of the more obvious distinctions on which an asymmetrical anthropology had been premised, it was clear that "anthropology pure and simple" would *not* "deal with the customs and beliefs of the less civilized peoples only." But it was less clear how a more anthropologically embracive study would be carried on. In many situations, both in the developing countries and the traditional centers of the discipline, the line between anthropology and applied sociology was no longer clear. At the same time, the traditional concern with exotic otherness persisted, although now once again historically and textually oriented, in the context of rapid cultural change and the reaction against positivistic natural scientific models. Not only were particular cultural groups beginning to be studied in more historical terms, but the distinctive features of otherness itself—including now the notion of the "tribe"—were beginning to be seen as contingent products of the historical interaction of European and non-European peoples in the context of world historical processes. As the manifestly observable differences between peoples diminished, culture was pursued into the crevices of encroaching homogeneity. In this context, there was an increasing sense of the problematic character of the central concept in terms of which otherness had long been interpreted by anthropologists.

For more than a century, the idea of culture had been the single most powerful cohesive force in anthropological inquiry. Although that concept was relativized and given an autonomous determinism by the Boasian critique of evolutionary racial assumption, biological and evolutionary concerns were not eliminated from anthropology. And while a systematic evolutionary viewpoint was slow to inform physical anthropology and archeology, the period after World War II saw important developments in the field of "paleoanthropology," as well as the resurgence of a submerged neo-evolutionary tendency within American cultural anthropology. During the same years, in the context of a closer association with Parsonian sociology, cultural anthropologists began to think more seriously about just what "culture" was. By the end of the 1960s, a conceptual polarization was beginning to be evident. On the one hand, there was a tendency—most strikingly evident in what came to be called symbolic anthropology—to treat cultures in humanistic idealist terms as systems of symbols and meanings, with relatively little concern for the adaptive, utilitarian aspect of cultural behavior. On the other hand, there was a materialistic countercurrent which insisted that culture must be understood scientifically in adaptive evolutionary terms, whether in the form of "techno-environmental determinism," or in the even more controversial form of "sociobiology," which seemed to many to threaten a resurgence of racialist thought in the human sciences.

Although the vast majority of American anthropologists came to the defense of Margaret Mead when a critique of her Samoan fieldwork was generalized as an attack on the notion of cultural determinism (Freeman 1983a), it is by no means clear that the ambiguities of the culture concept have been resolved. Indeed, it might be argued that beneath the recent polarization lies the paradigmatic opposition that characterized thinking about human differences before the early-twentieth-century "revolution in anthropology." In the case of Greco-Roman developmentalism, the continuity with neo-evolutionism is manifest; in the case of the biblical/ethnological paradigm, it is less clearcut. But the fact that the emergence of symbolic and interpretive anthropology is spoken of as the hermeneutic turn, and also the fact of preoccupation with linguistic phenomena, suggest a level at which it may exist. Be that as it may, the historically constituted epistemic dualism underlying modern anthropology is real enough, and seems likely to endure. From this point of view, Boas—who in other writings insisted on the independent legitimacy of both the *natur-* and the *geisteswissenchaftliche* approaches to the study of human phenomena—may perhaps serve as a guide to the future as well as to the past of the discipline.

Postscriptive Prospective Reflections

Although the essays collected in this volume were written under the backward-facing aegis of historicism, during the time I was composing the introductions I was forced at several moments to think more about the present and the future of anthropology than is my wont. As it happened, I was more involved than usual in the graduate training program of the Chicago department, first in the second half of the "Systems" course (the historical introduction to anthropological theory) and then as chair of the Committee on Graduate Studies in Sociocultural and Linguistic Anthropology and occasional participant in the Faculty-Student Liaison Committee. During the same period, there were also several discussions in the department about the prospects for "anthropology in the 1990s."

It had been a decade since I was involved in "Systems," and I was struck by certain hints of change in what might best be called the anthropological sensibility of the student group. Although they were more than willing to take on the heavy load of work we demanded, a number of them seemed somehow resistent to what I regard as an historical understanding. Presocialized to postmodern discourse, they found the past already "defamiliarized." The problem seemed to be one of *re*familiarization: how to make the anthropology of a prior period familiar to them, in the sense of being understandable in its own terms, or as part of a deeper structuring of anthropological inquiry, rather than prejudged as another form of colonial discourse. "They"—as several students pointed out—were in fact a diverse group, and might here more accurately be glossed as the handful whose comments were at the time and in retrospect most striking. But they did make some striking comments—including (in a subsequent discussion) the previously mentioned one about not wanting to do fieldwork among people in far-away places.

What I was tempted to regard as a similarly portentous interchange took place even more recently in the faculty-student committee, when an issue was raised about the large world map on the second-floor landing in Haskell Hall (in which the Department of Anthropology is housed). To gloss the matter in terms the student interlocutors might find resonant, the map apparently suggested to them that "the sun never sets on the colonial empire of Chicago anthropology." The little green, red, and yellow stickers (for fieldwork planned, in process, or being written up) locating the field sites of Chicago student and faculty ethnographers were in fact explicitly equated with flagpins marking the location of spies at the Langley headquarters of the CIA. In a similar way, the snapshots sent back over the years by students in the field and then tucked under the edges of the map's covering glass by one of the department's administrative assistants were now read as icons of hegemonic colonial domination. The actual relations of the actors involved—dark-skinned "informants" surrounding light-skinned ethnographers (some in "native" dress)—or the motives of those who took or sent the snapshots were not germane. De- (or re-?) contextualized, the assemblage was simply a text to be deconstructed. And the fact (pointed out by a student who had visited other places before choosing Chicago) that similar displays exist in many anthropology departments simply confirmed the broader discursive significance of the display.

There was no denying, however, that the map had been "defamiliarized": I doubt that any of us who actually participated in the discussion will soon see it again in quite the same taken-for-granted way we did before. We may choose to privilege the presumably innocent self-representation of a department proud of its extended ethnographic enterprise, and of members anxious to document their rapport—if not simply to send a snapshot back to friends at home. But contrapuntal to that meaning will be another, which suggests (among other things) a questioning, at a symbolic level, of the twentieth-century tradition (and the methodological values) of an ethnographic anthropology.

There are other signs of such questioning. Recently, one of my colleagues—whose own research has shifted from the field to the library—has offered a course with the resonant title "Rethinking the Field," in which the tradition of an ethnographically based anthropology is deliberately problematized. And in advising students whose interests now transcend traditional boundaries, the question has recently arisen how today to define the two "ethnographic areas" in which every "pre-field" student is by statute required to demonstrate a competence. In the past, these would normally have been the larger geographical region in which a field site was located and another such region on which there was a relevant theoretical literature—areas plottable on that controversial map. But in a complexly historical and culturally kaleidoscopic postmodern world, viewed through lenses of multiple interdisciplinarity, it is no longer so easy to define just what an "ethnographic area" might be.

The local knowledge of these portents (if such they be) may be read against the broader history which these essays episodically treat. The "methodological values" of an ethnographic anthropology imply, as a necessary methodological fiction if not an empirical reality, the existence of bounded ethnographic entities, into which the anthropologist may, after a fashion, be incorporated, and, in a manner of speaking, learn to know from the inside—without sacrificing that privileged marginality (as "stranger/friend") which presumably enables a totalizing understanding (cf. Powdermaker 1966:9) In their archetypal embodiments, these bounded entities were often literally islands, although from the beginning many ethnographic "islands" have in fact been land-locked. Even in relation to such an island, whether literal or notional, any kind of totalizing knowledge (or description) was very problematic. By defining some set of bounded issues to structure the inquiry (either before or after the fact), anthropological theory of course helped to solve the problem. So also, the selection of some standard ethnographic textual model, often itself theoretically motivated: if not *Notes and Queries* or the Malinowskian odyssey, then the life- or annual-cycle, the cosmogonic myth or the microcosmic event, the central ritual or the kinship system—all the specific forms that have yet to be systematically studied by the theorhetoricians of "ethnographies as texts" (Marcus & Cushman 1982; Clifford 1983; Clifford & Marcus 1986).

In the early days of the classical period, however, the problems of an ethnographic anthropology did not seem insurmountable. Not only were islands bounded, so was the universe of ethnographic discourse. In this context, one is struck by the retrospective ethnographic insouciance of Ian Hogbin, one of Malinowski's early students, recalling how easy it was in 1930 to control the ethnographies, not only of their ethnographic areas, but of all the British colonial world: one could literally read "all there was" of "modern fieldwork" for all of the Pacific and Africa—the rest by implication being dismissible as the pre-academic amateurism of travellers, missionaries, or colonial administrators (Beckett 1989:41–42).

At once a methodological fiction and an artifact of incipient professionalization, the boundedness of ethnographic discourse became increasingly problematic throughout the classical period. In the years following World War II, students sat amazed by the ethnographic virtuosity of figures like Fred Eggan who still taught courses in "world ethnography" (GS 1979a). But by then, as Hogbin recalled, "the great flood of ethnographies" had already started flowing, until "today it is impossible for a Melanesian expert to read all that's been published in as small an area as Melanesia" (Beckett 1989:42).

Nor is it only professional ethnographies that have risen in flood. In every anthropological generation the boundaries of relevant theoretical literature have been redefined and extended. While there is no doubt a tendency for old questions either to be put aside or simply to be discussed in a more fashionable conceptual language, there are also new questions to be answered, new concepts to be explored, new theoretical totems, both classic and modern: along with Durkheim and Weber there are now Marx, Gramsci, Bakhtin, and Foucault (Ortner 1984; Fernandez 1991; Ulin 1991). And with the concurrent rehistoricization of anthropology—the reemplacement of a synchronic ethnographic entity into both local and world historical temporal process—all that could once be dismissed as amateur (missionary and travel accounts, records of colonial administrators) becomes relevant source material (Comaroff & Comaroff 1991; Sahlins 1985). In short, the range of potentially relevant literature for any ethnographic project threatens, in principle if not in practice, to become overwhelming—even if the object of inquiry had retained its bounded island character.

But of course it has not. Parallelling this explosion of the boundaries of the relevant ethnographic discourse is an erasure of the boundaries of its ethnographic object. To some extent, this is merely the obverse of the breaking of theoretical bounds; a Native American group conceptualized as a problem in acculturation is in a significant way more loosely bounded than when conceptualized as a problem in salvage or memory ethnography. To some extent, it is a matter of shifting regional ethnographic foci; African peoples, even when dubiously conceptualized as "tribes," are less clearly bounded than Oceanic islands. To some extent, it is a matter of shifting foci of sociocultural research: already by the 1930s the newly academicized ethnographers were turning to the study of more complex groupings, whether as products of social change, or as synchronic social phenomena. The bounding of an ethnographic entity presented itself very differently to Lloyd Warner among the Murngin of Northern Australia than it later did to Warner and a staff of thirty in the *Yankee City* of Newburyport, Massachusetts (Warner & Lunt 1941).

With the end of traditional colonial regimes and the ensuing "crisis of anthropology," the problem of ethnographic boundaries was further complicated, as even the boundary between the observer and the observed began to be redefined. There had been a time when "getting it down" seemed a relatively unambiguous act, morally as well as epistemologically. Anthropologists and their informants could be seen as forming a single moral-epistemological community, dedicated to the preservation of traditional cultural forms (GS 1982b:412). Within this preservationist little community, however, the lines between observer and observed, viewed in the prevailing positivistic frame, were clearly defined, and problems of method were usually discussed in terms of bridging this gap: creating rapport (Herskovits 1954), establishing a role (Paul 1953), dealing with "lying informants" (Passin 1942), or penetrating "behind many masks" (Berreman 1962).

By the mid-1960s, however, the relations of ethnographers to the peoples they studied had become much more problematic—pragmatically, politically, ethically, and epistemologically. Just as the object of ethnographic inquiry had been destabilized, so also was the position of the observer. No longer sheltered by colonial power, ethnographers still carried the albatrosses of primitivist condescension and colonial guilt; compromised by the attempts of government to involve them in "counterinsurgency" in an era of postcolonial warfare (Horowitz 1967; Wakin 1992), they now faced radically different problems of access to the field. In some areas it was simply no longer possible; in others, it had now to be negotiated (on different terms at different levels) among peoples in "new nations" bent on "development." "Relevance"—the battle cry of young anthropological radicals at home—was to become in many areas a condition of entry into the field.

The peculiar marginality of the ethnographer (stranger/friend; outsider/insider), which had always been ambiguously experienced by both parties, was newly problematized. Aware of the traditional association of "anthropology" with the study of "primitives," once-colonized peoples were disinclined to see themselves simply as the subject/objects of disinterested empathic study. Anthropologists (sometimes now preferring to present themselves as "sociologists" or "historians") were forced to reconsider the now highly charged boundary between the observer and the observed, the self and the other. Fieldwork began to be reconceptualized in "self-reflexive" and "dialogic" terms (Scholte 1972; Dwyer 1982), and the ethics of the endeavor became a matter of serious concern (Fluehr-Lobban 1991).

Over a much longer period, the ethnographer's implicit (and scarcely ever analyzed) comparative point of reference—the particular Euro-American society from which he or she came—had also been destabilized. If nineteenth-century and early-twentieth-century anthropologists could casually take their own "civilization" and its analytic categories as interpretive points of departure and return, the intervening years had made anthropologists more systematically conscious of the problems of cultural and categorical translation. In each generation, a veil of ethnocentrism was lifted, until even the "traditional quartet" of kinship, economics, politics, and religion was attacked as an "undefined and vacuous" set of "metacultural categories embedded in European culture" which had been uncritically "incorporated into the analytic schemes" of anthropologists (Schneider 1984: 181–85).

As this compounding series of boundary problems made the traditional ethnographic enterprise (studying "people in far-away places") multiply problematic, "bringing it all back home"—a slogan of those bent upon "reinventing anthropology" (Hymes 1972)—has seemed an increasingly likely alternative. That previously mentioned model anthropologist of the *Anthropology Newsletter* (above, p. 93) in fact did her fieldwork in North America; and while the little stickers on our departmental map are quite widely dispersed, there is now a thicker concentration in the region north of the Mediterranean and west of the Urals.

The many and far-reaching ramifications of these changes have of course been matters of concern to many anthropologists—including, at a theoretical level, a querying of the very notion of culture, and of what, in the pastiching processes of the postmodern world, "a culture" might be (e.g., R. Foster 1991). But there is a practical ethnographic level at which such theoretical issues are manifest—what, with a bow to Gertrude Stein, might be called "the Oakland problem": "there is no there there." Students working on broad-ranging cultural issues in complex societies (as quite a few are now wont to do) discover that it is hard to define an ethnographic locus, or to define its relation to a larger world: twenty families on a Pacific Island, or in a Mexican village, may constitute a major portion of the presumed ethnographic entity—but what does a hard-won quasi-intimacy with twenty Parisian families tell us about the changing culture of modern France? What are the forms of totalization adequate to such an unfocussed ethnographic locus?

Such problems are of course not new, and there are "solutions" more satisfying than Margaret Mead's (pre-postmodern?) suggestion, back in 1953, that "a twenty-one-year-old boy born of Chinese-American parents in a small upstate New York town who has just graduated *summa cum laude* from Harvard and a tenth-generation Boston-born deaf mute of United Kingdom stock are equally perfect examples of American national character, *provided that their individual position and individual characteristics are taken fully into account*" (Mead 1953:648). One option, by no means new, is to find a "there" in Oakland: to define, within a "complex" society, the equivalent of a bounded-island entity in which one can seek an empathic insider's knowledge by the traditional "methodology" of participant observation—a street gang, a women's credit cooperative, a first-year medical class, a Moscow gypsy theater. One has only to consult the program or abstracts of the annual meetings of the American Anthropological Association to see how popular this option is. What many see as the vitality of contemporary anthropology (when attendance at the annual Association meetings has been breaking records) is largely dependent on its continuing viability.

But even if island analogues are still to be found, the relation of that local knowledge to global issues has still to be faced (Marcus & Fischer 1986; Ulin 1991). The time has long since passed when students could simply be urged, after "at least two years in a first field study of a primitive society"—broken half way for collation and evaluation of the materials collected—to study a second and different type of society (Evans-Pritchard 1950:76). With the exponential expansion of the range of historically implicated or theoretically constituted connections, the contextualization of an unfocussed ethnographic entity is as problematic as its totalization. Forgiven a play on words, one might say that as the locus of ethnography loses focus, the hocus-pocus of the ethnographer's magic becomes ever more implausible.

The more so, as entextualization has itself become problematic. The "genre blurring" which has been seen as an aspect of the "refiguration of social thought" (Geertz 1983) has affected ethnography as well. Whether or not one chooses to speak of a "crisis of representation" in ethnographic anthropology, it seems clear that the last decade or so has indeed been an "experimental moment" in the methodology of "writing culture" (Marcus & Fischer 1986; Clifford & Marcus 1986). But if the still largely programmatic manifestos of the mid-1980s might now more easily find published ethnographic exemplars, it is not clear that these amount to the emergence of one or more ethnographic genres that might serve the same paradigmatic function as, say, the kinship system or the life-cycle did for earlier generations of ethnographers. Indeed, for postmodern literizing anthropologists, the very notion of formal replication may be problematic in a way that it never was to an earlier scientizing generation, for whom replication had in principle a positive methodological resonance. Insofar as the idea of the experimental becomes itself paradigmatic, the apprentice (even the journeyman) ethnographer may be hard put to find an easily viable ethnographic model.

It would not be surprising if in the face of all this there were to be a general failure of ethnographic will. Reading in the fieldwork record of the last century, one is struck by variations in what might be called moral-psychological tone. In the letter-diaries of Franz Boas (Rohner 1969), that tone is very different from the diaries of Bronislaw Malinowski (1967); and while the ambivalent and ambiguous complexity of the latter should make one all the more wary of cohort generalization, I cannot help recalling my awareness, shortly after entering the Chicago department, of a number of occasions when the dominant tone of returning fieldworkers seemed to be an anxiety of guilt. Not Mead's fear that somehow she might have failed Papa Franz, but rather the fear that ethnographic activity itself had been in some sense inherently exploitative.

Two decades further on, I sometimes wonder if one unanticipated consequence of all the since-published self-reflexivity might not have been to make the ethnographic enterprise—an inherently anxious and ethically perplexing adventure which in certain regions of the world is physically dangerous as well—so problematic psychologically, morally, and politically, that given its epistemological and representational difficulties, students might understandably prefer to do their research in the library. And yet those who have made this choice are still a small minority. Many at Chicago now work in the archives, but usually to supplement a project defined primarily in terms of fieldwork in a more or less traditional mode. And though many of the faculty are past the age of active fieldwork themselves, recent discussions of the future personnel of the department suggest that the commitment to an ethnographically oriented anthropology is at least as strong among them.

Even so, I think it would be a mistake to dismiss those portents out of hand. If we lack the retrospective perspective that might enable us to mark off the last quarter century as a distinct period in the history of anthropology, there is a cumulative dynamic in the changing circumstances of anthropology that must make one wonder about its future. The fundamental progressivism of our cultural image of human knowledge does not encourage systematic speculation about the decline or death of disciplines. But from the time anthropology was first institutionalized in the form of "ethnology" around 1840, its future has been problematic in ways quite different from those of other human sciences. The very proclamations of its founding were accompanied by death knells for its subject matter (GS 1971), and these have since been sounded many times (Gruber 1970). At about the time that Boas was predicting its subdisciplinary fragmentation, others were forecasting its demise—the British historian William Maitland suggesting that "by and by, anthropology will have the choice between being history and being nothing" (1911:295). At the time of the "crisis," there were again predictions of "the end of anthropology" (Worsley 1970), and premonitions of disciplinary mortality can still occasionally be heard today.

More recently, the "blurring of genres" has raised new issues in the bounding of anthropological inquiry. What began as a promising "anthropological turn" among historians and students of literature (Cohn 1987; Manganaro 1990) can now be read as threatening the "decentering of anthropology." With the emergence of "cultural studies" (Brantlinger 1990), the conceptual and methodological orientations of anthropology have been diffused throughout the humanities; more recently, professors of English, emboldened by the "new historicism," now poach within the very *sanctum sanctorum* of anthropology, attacking the culture concept itself as mere "superstition" borrowed, in fact, from nineteenth-century literary discourse (Herbert 1991; cf. Torgovnick 1990). As one of my colleagues ironically suggested, "soon we will be of interest only as native informants."

Barring decline or death, there is of course transformation. If periods in history may in some sense be generational phenomena (Marías 1967) marked by powerful cohort-defining experiences (war, depression, civil turmoil, etc.), there might be grounds for expecting the "crisis" of anthropology to work itself out over a more extended period—for anthropology to be "reinvented" not all at once, but over several decades. Anthropologists who came of age in the late 1960s and early 1970s, experiencing the crisis and critique of anthropology and the call for its reinvention, tenured by 1980, have since become influential voices in the discipline, helping to form recent generations of undergraduates who, responding to various "postmodern" tendencies by now well established in collegiate education, come to an anthropology which is already "deconstructed." One such periodic sentence can scarcely hope to capture all the tendencies, intellectual or otherwise, that might help to define an historical period in generational terms: the emergence of an openly Marxist tendency in American and British anthropology (Bloch 1985; Vincent 1985), the rise of feminist anthropology (Di Leonardo 1991), the reflexive, textual, and postmodern turns (Sangren 1988); or, in the surrounding world, neocolonialism, late capitalism, the end of communism—to mention some of the main contenders. But the demographics of disciplinary expansion do suggest that the explosive growth of the early 1960s might be followed in the 1990s by a changing of the guard in anthropology.

What the outcome of all this may be—whether the end of anthropology, or a period-ending transition, or simply *plus ça change* . . . —will, to fall back on the obvious, be more evident in a decade. There are, of course, programmatic candidates for paradigmatic reintegration: among them, various forms of postmodernism (Stephens 1990), attempts to synthesize postmodernism and political economy (Ulin 1991), or, more recently, an anti-postmodern call to "decolonize anthropology" by synthesizing four major reinventive streams—"neo-Marxist political economy, experiments in interpretive and reflexive ethnographic analysis, a feminism which underscores the impact race and class have upon gender, and traditions of radical Black and (other) Third World scholarship"—in a more fully realized dialogical anthropology (Harrison 1991:2).

Alternatively, one may look to the past for images of the future. Although Maitland had in mind a pre-ethnographic evolutionary anthropology sustained by a triumphant colonialism, and did not envision the revolution that was shortly to transform anthropology, the historical option looks much more likely today than it did during the classical period. The last twenty years have seen the emergence of a variety of historical modes in anthropology, one of the most powerful being the historical anthropology of the colonial process itself (Asad 1991; Comaroff & Comaroff 1992). In another historical mode, one can also imagine a portion of anthropology becoming, as Boas might have predicted, an exotic analogue of classical scholarship, in which the reconstituted texts and preserved artifacts of nonliterate peoples are subjected to continuing analysis and reinterpretation. Or it might move, as it previously has in various times and places (cf. Kloos 1989), in a more sociological direction, with Euro-American anthropologists retreating to self-study, and native anthropologists elsewhere claiming the right to study themselves (Fahim 1982). While such work might still be carried on in something approximating a traditional ethnographic mode, this double movement would further blur a long traditional disciplinary boundary of subject matter, and might be expected to blur conceptual and methodological boundaries as well. Another previous tendency with obvious present relevance would be the anthropology of contemporary problems, either of the erstwhile center or the now globalized periphery. These might take the liberal form of cultural critique, the more radical form of seeking the empowerment of subject populations (Downing & Kushner 1988) or forms that echo the more conservative applied anthropology of the classical period (e.g., a symbolic anthropology of advertising, or a management-oriented study of corporate cultures [Dunkle 1992]). Finally, one can even imagine, three-quarters of a century after the critique of evolutionism and the debiologization of anthropology, a return to biological and evolutionary issues, if not as sociobiology, then in the "interactive" mode advocated by other anthropologists besides Derek Freeman (e.g., Durham 1990).

Where (or whether) among these (or other) tendencies a center may be found, and hold, is beyond the vision of this historian. At an American Anthropological Association session several years ago, "Assessing Developments in Anthropology," several speakers suggested that anthropology in the year 2000 would look very much like anthropology in 1989. One of them did so by emphasizing the enduring potency of three "well-established research projects": the Boasian or cultural, the Darwinian or evolutionary, and the Durkheimian or social structural (Kuper 1989). Another pointed to the vibrant pluralism of the meetings themselves—all those hundred of papers on topics from adaptation and AIDS to Zapotecs and zooarcheology; rather than evidence of the decentering or fragmentation of anthropology, it was the future seen and working in the present (Kottak

1989). Both, however, seemed to share a commitment to "the ethnographic record" as "the central shared heritage of anthropology" (Kuper 1989).

Despite the transformation of its traditional subjects, the blurring of its boundaries, the decentering of its discourse, it seems likely that the sheer force of institutional inertia, if nothing else, will maintain anthropology until well into the twenty-first century. If historical critique and historical process have deconstructed the radical alterities of the modern age, the postmodern era has witnessed the proliferation of a variety of reconstructed othernesses, including, most recently, the fragmenting ethnic identities of the postcommunist world. If the conditions of ethnography have been transformed, the ethnographic impulse that helped to define modern anthropology has not spent its force. A striking aspect of some recent critical tendencies is their continuing insistence on an ethnographic grounding (Marcus & Fischer 1986). Similarly, many of those who resist the postmodern literizing tendency—whether in the name of science, or of "anti-anti-scientism"—do so by reaffirming the values of an ethnographic anthropology (cf. GS 1989c).

Even so, there can be little doubt that students entering the field today face unprecedented problems of professional self-definition. In a very real sense, they must each, in becoming anthropologists, reinvent the field for themselves—rebounding it, if not rebinding it, in the process. Retaining myself a strong residual faith in its perdurance as an historically constituted entity, I hope that these essays may perhaps help them in their quest.

References Cited
Manuscript Sources
Index

References Cited

AA	*American Anthropologist*
AJPA	*American Journal of Physical Anthropology*
BAAS	British Association for the Advancement of Science
HAN	*History of Anthropology Newsletter*
HOA	*History of Anthropology*
IJAL	*International Journal of American Linguistics*
JAI	*Journal of the [Royal] Anthropological Institute*
JHBS	*Journal of the History of the Behavioral Sciences*
PAPS	*Proceedings of the American Philosophical Society*

Ackerman, R.
1987 *J. G. Frazer: His life and work.* Cambridge.

Appell, G. N., & T. N. Madan
1988 Derek Freeman: Notes toward an intellectual biography. In *Choice and morality: Anthropological essays in honor of Professor Derek Freeman,* ed. Appell & Madan, 3–26. Buffalo, N.Y.

Arensberg, C. M.
1937 *The Irish countryman: An anthropological study.* New York.

Arnold, M.
1869 *Culture and anarchy.* Cambridge (1957).

Asad, T.
1973 Ed., *Anthropology and the colonial encounter.* London.
1991 Afterword: From the history of colonial anthropology to the anthropology of western hegemony. *HOA* 7:314–24.

Austen, L.
1945 Cultural changes in Kiriwina. *Oceania* 16:14–60.

Ausubel, D. P.

1960 *The fern and the tiki: An American view of New Zealand national character, social attitudes and race relations.* North Quincy, Mass. (1971).

BAAS

1874 *Notes and queries on anthropology, for the use of travellers and residents in uncivilized lands.* London.

1884–1902 *Report[s] of the . . . 54th [and succeeding] meeting[s].* London.

1887 Third report of the Committee . . . investigating and publishing reports on the physical characters, languages, industry and social condition of the north-western tribes of the Dominion of Canada. In *Report of the 57th meeting,* 173–83. London.

1912 *Notes and queries on anthropology.* 4th ed. London.

Bade, K.-J.

1977 Colonial missions and imperialism: The background to the fiasco of the Rhenish mission in New Guinea. In *Germany in the Pacific and Far East, 1870–1914,* ed. J. A. Moses & P. M. Kennedy, 312–46. St. Lucas, Queensland.

Balandier, G.

1951 The colonial situation: A theoretical approach. In *The sociology of black Africa: Social dynamics in central Africa,* trans. D. Garman, 34–61. New York (1970).

Barkan, E.

1988 Mobilizing scientists against racism, 1933–39. *HOA* 5:180–205.

Barrett, P.

1989 The paradoxical anthropology of Leslie White. *AA* 91:986–99.

Bartlett, F. C.

1959 Myers, Charles Samuel. In *Dictionary of National Biography 1941–50.*

Basehart, H., & W. W. Hill

1965 Leslie Spier, 1893–1961. *AA* 67:1258–77.

Bashkow, I.

1991 The dynamics of rapport in a colonial situation: David Schneider's fieldwork on the islands of Yap. *HOA* 7:170–242.

Bateson, M. C.

1984 *With a daughter's eye: A memoir of Margaret Mead and Gregory Bateson.* New York.

Baudet, H.

1965 *Paradise on earth: Some thoughts on European images of non-European man.* New Haven, Conn.

BE. See under Manuscript Sources.

Beals, R. L.

1943 Anthropology during the war and after. Memorandum prepared by the Committee on War Service of Anthropologists, Division of Anthropology and Psychology, National Research Council.

Beard, C. A., & M. R. Beard

1942 *The American spirit: A study of the idea of civilization in the United States.* New York (1962).

Beckett, J.
1989 *Conversations with Ian Hogbin.* Oceania Monograph 35. Sydney.

Beloff, M.
1970 *Imperial sunset: Britain's liberal empire, 1897–1921.* New York.

Benedict, R.
1923 *The concept of the guardian spirit in North America.* New York (1964).
1928 Psychological types in the cultures of the Southwest. In Mead 1959a: 248–61.
1930 Review of Redfield 1930a. *New York Herald Tribune Books* (Nov. 2): 24.
1932 Configurations of culture in North America. *AA* 34:1–27.
1934 *Patterns of culture.* Boston.
1935 The story of my life. In Mead 1959a:97–117.
1939 Edward Sapir. *AA*:41:465–77.
1940 *Race: Science and politics.* New York.

Bennett, G.
1960 From paramountcy to partnership: J. H. Oldham and Africa. *Africa* 32: 356–60.

Bennett, J. W.
1944 The development of ethnological theory as illustrated by studies of the Plains sun dance. *AA* 46:162–81.
1946 The interpretation of Pueblo culture: A question of values. *Southwestern Journal of Anthropology* 2:361–74.

Bennett, W. C.
1947 *The Ethnogeographic Board.* Washington, D.C.

Bensaude-Vincent, B.
1983 A founder myth in the history of sciences? The Lavoisier case. In *Functions and uses of disciplinary histories,* ed. L. Graham et al., 53–78. Dordrecht.

Berreman, G.
1962 *Behind many masks: Ethnography and impression management in a Himalayan village.* Society for Applied Anthropology Monograph 4. Ithaca, N.Y.

Bidney, D.
1944 On the concept of culture and some cultural fallacies. *AA* 46:30–44.

Biskup, P., B. Jinks, & H. Nelson
1968 *A short history of New Guinea.* Sydney.

Black, R.
1957 Dr. Bellamy of Papua. *Medical Journal of Australia* 2:189–97, 232–38, 279–84.

Blanchard, D.
1979 Beyond empathy: The emergence of action anthropology in the life and career of Sol Tax. In *Currents in anthropology: Essays in honor of Sol Tax,* ed. R. Hinshaw, 419–43. The Hague.

Bloch, M.
1985 *Marxism and anthropology: The history of a relationship.* Oxford.

Boas, F.
1887 The study of geography. *Science* 9:137–41.
1889 On alternating sounds. *AA* 2:47–52.
1894 Classification of the languages of the North Pacific Coast. In *Memoirs of the International Congress of Anthropology, 1893,* ed. C. S. Wake, 339–46. Chicago.
1900 Sketch of the Kwakiutl language. *AA* 2:708–21.
1904a The vocabulary of the Chinook language. *AA* 6:118–47.
1904b The history of anthropology. In GS 1974c:23–36.
1911a *Handbook of American Indian languages.* Part I. Washington, D.C.
1911b *The mind of primitive man.* New York.
1915 Will socialism help to overcome race antagonisms? *New York Call* (April):4.
1917 Introduction. *IJAL* 1:1–8.
1919 Colonies and the peace conference. *The Nation* 108:247–49.
1920a Classification of American languages. In 1940:211–18.
1920b The methods of ethnology. In 1940:218–89.
1924 Evolution or diffusion? In 1940:190–94.
1928 *Anthropology and modern life.* New York.
1929 Classification of American Indian languages. In 1940:219–25.
1930a Some problems of methodology in the social sciences. In 1940:26–69.
1930b Anthropology. *Encyclopedia of the Social Sciences* 3:73–110.
1936 History and science in anthropology: A reply. In 1940:305–11.
1938a *The mind of primitive man.* Rev. ed. New York.
1938b Methods of research. In *General anthropology,* ed. Boas, 666–86. New York.
1940 *Race, language and culture.* New York.
1945 *Race and democratic society.* New York.
1972 *The professional correspondence of Franz Boas.* Microfilm edition. Wilmington, Del.

Boaz, N., & F. Spencer
1981 Eds., Jubilee issue, 1930–1980. *AJPA* 56(4).

Boutilier, J., et al.
1978 *Mission, church and sect in Oceania.* Ann Arbor, Mich.

BP. See under Manuscript Sources.

BPBM [Bernice P. Bishop Museum]
1926 *Report of the director.* Honolulu.

Brantlinger, P.
1990 *Crusoe's footprints: Cultural studies in Britain and America.* New York.

Breslau, D.
1988 Robert Park et l'écologie humaine. *Actes de la Recherche en sciences sociales* 74:55–63.

Brew, J.
1968 Ed., *One hundred years of anthropology.* Cambridge, Mass.

Brigard, E. de
1975 The history of ethnographic film. In *Toward a science of man,* ed. T. Thoresen, 33–63. The Hague.

Brinton, D. G.
1890 *Essays of an Americanist.* Philadelphia.
1891 *The American race: A linguistic classification.* New York.
1895 The aims of anthropology. *Science* 2:241–52.

Brooks, M.
1985 Lucjan Malinowski and Polish dialectology. *Polish Review* 30:167–70.

Brooks, V. W.
1915 *America's coming-of-age.* New York.

Brown, E. R.
1979 *Rockefeller medicine men: Medicine and capitalism in America.* Berkeley, Calif.

Brown, R.
1973 Anthropology and the colonial rule: Godfrey Wilson and the Rhodes-Livingstone Institute, Northern Nigeria. In Asad 1973:173–98.

Brown, R. L.
1967 *Wilhelm von Humboldt's conception of linguistic relativity.* The Hague.

Brunhouse, R. L.
1971 *Sylvanus G. Morley and the world of the ancient Mayas.* Norman, Okla.

Bulmer, M.
1980 The early institutional establishment of social science research: The Local Community Research Committee at the University of Chicago, 1923–1930. *Minerva* 18:51–110.

Bulmer, M., & J. Bulmer
1981 Philanthropy and social science in the 1920s: Beardsley Ruml and the Laura Spelman Rockefeller Memorial, 1922–29. *Minerva* 19:347–407.

Burton, J. W.
1988 Shadows at twilight: A note on history and the ethnographic present. *PAPS* 132:420–33.

Butinov, N. A.
1971 A nineteenth-century champion of anti-racism in New Guinea. *Unesco Courier* (November): 24–27.

Butterworth, D.
1972 Oscar Lewis, 1914–1970. *AA* 74:747–57.

Caffrey, M. M.
1989 *Ruth Benedict: Stranger in this land.* Austin, Tex.

Caplan, A. L.
1978 Ed., *The sociobiology debate: Readings on ethical and scientific issues.* New York.

Carneiro, R.
1981 Leslie White. In *Totems and teachers: Perspectives on the history of anthropology,* ed. S. Silverman, 209–54. New York.

Carter, P. A.
1968 *The twenties in America.* New York.

Caton, H.
1990 Ed., *The Samoa reader: Anthropologists take stock.* Lanham, Md.

Chamberlain, L., & E. A. Hoebel

1942 Anthropology offerings in American undergraduate colleges. *AA* 44: 527–30.

Chapman, W. R.

1981 Ethnology in the museum: A. H. L. F. Pitt Rivers (1827–1900) and the institutional foundations of British anthropology. Doct. diss., Oxford Univ.

1985 Arranging ethnology: A. H. L. F. Pitt Rivers and the typological tradition. *HOA* 3:15–48.

Chase, S.

1931 *Mexico: A study of two Americas.* New York.

1948 *The proper study of mankind.* New York.

Chauvenet, B.

1983 *Hewitt and friends: A biography of Santa Fe's vibrant era.* Santa Fe, N.M.

CIW [Carnegie Institution of Washington]

1929–40 *Yearbook.* Washington, D.C.

Clifford, J.

1982 *Person and myth: Maurice Leenhardt in the Melanesian world.* Berkeley, Calif.

1983 On ethnographic authority. *Representations* 1:118–46.

1988 On ethnographic self-fashioning: Conrad and Malinowski. In *The predicament of culture: Twentieth-century ethnography, literature and art,* ed. Clifford, 92–113. Cambridge, Mass.

Clifford, J., & G. E. Marcus

1986 Eds., *Writing culture: The poetics and politics of ethnography.* Berkeley, Calif.

Coben, S.

1976 Foundation officials and fellowships: Innovation in the patronage of science. *Minerva* 14:225–40.

Codrington, R. H.

1891 *The Melanesians. Studies in their anthropology and folklore.* Oxford (1969).

Cohn, B.

1987 *An anthropologist among the historians and other essays.* Delhi.

Cole, D.

1985 *Captured heritage: The scramble for Northwest Coast artifacts.* Seattle.

1988 Kindheit und jugend von Franz Boas: Minden in der zweiten hälfte des 19. jahrhunderts. *Mitteilungen des Mindener Geschichtsvereins* 60:11–34.

Collier, P., & D. Horowitz

1976 *The Rockefellers: An American dynasty.* New York.

Comaroff, J.

1991 Humanity, ethnicity, nationality: Conceptual and comparative perspectives on the U.S.S.R. *Theory and Society* 20:661–87.

Comaroff, J., & J. L. Comaroff

1991 *Of revelation and revolution: Christianity, Colonialism and Consciousness in South Africa.* Chicago.

1992 *Ethnography and the historical imagination.* Boulder, Col.

Conrad, J.
1902 Heart of darkness. In *Youth: A narrative and two other stories,* 49–182. Edinburgh.

Cowan, J.
1979 Linguistics at war. In Goldschmidt 1979:158–68.

Cowan, J., et al.
1986 Eds., *New perspectives in language, culture and personality: Proceedings of the Edward Sapir Centenary Conference, Ottawa, 1–3 October 1984.* Amsterdam.

Cressman, L. S.
1988 *A golden journey: Memoirs of an archaeologist.* Salt Lake City, Utah.

Czaplička, M. A.
1916 *My Siberian year.* New York.

Darnell, R.
1969 The development of American anthropology 1879–1920: From the Bureau of American Ethnology to Franz Boas. Doct. diss., Univ. Pennsylvania.
1970. The emergence of academic anthropology at the University of Pennsylvania. *JHBS* 6:80–92.
1971a The Powell classification of American Indian languages. *Papers in Linguistics* 4:71–110.
1971b The revision of the Powell classification. *Papers in Linguistics* 4:233–57.
1974 Lore and linguistics in American anthropology: alternative models of cultural process. Paper, American Anthropological Association.
1977a History of anthropology in historical perspective. *Annual Review of Anthropology* 6:399–417.
1977b Hallowell's bear ceremonialism and the emergence of Boasian anthropology. *Ethos* 5:13–30.
1986 Personality and culture: The fate of the Sapirian alternative. *HOA* 4: 156–83.
1988 *Daniel Garrison Brinton: The "fearless critic" of Philadelphia.* Philadelphia.
1990 *Edward Sapir: Linguist, anthropologist, humanist.* Berkeley, Calif.

De Laguna, F.
1960 Ed., *Selected papers from the American Anthropologist, 1888–1920.* Washington, D.C.

Devereux, G.
1967 *From anxiety to method in the behavioral sciences.* The Hague.

Di Leonardo, M.
1991 *Gender at the crossroads of knowledge: Feminist anthropology in the postmodern era.* Berkeley, Calif.

Dixon, R. B.
1928 *The building of cultures.* New York.

Docker, E. W.
1970 *The blackbirders: The recruiting of South Seas labour for Queensland, 1863–1907.* Sydney.

Dorsey, G. A.
1926 *Why we behave like human beings.* New York.
Downing, T. E., & G. Kushner
1988 Eds., *Human rights and anthropology.* Cambridge, Mass.
Drever, J.
1968 McDougall, William. In *International Encyclopedia of the Social Sciences.* New York.
Driver, H. E.
1962 *The contribution of A. L. Kroeber to culture area theory and practice.* Indiana University Publications in Anthropology and Linguistics 18. Bloomington, Ind.
Dunkle, T.
1992 A new breed of people gazers. *Insight,* Jan. 13, 10–13.
Dupree, A. H.
1972 The *Great Instauration* of 1940: The organization of scientific research for war. In *The twentieth century sciences,* ed. G. Holton, New York.
Durham, W.
1990 Advances in evolutionary culture theory. *Annual Review of Anthropology* 19:187–242.
Dwyer, K.
1982 *Moroccan dialogues: Anthropology in question.* Baltimore, Md.
Eggan, F.
1937 Historical changes in the Choctaw kinship system. *AA* 39:34–52.
1968 One hundred years of ethnology and social anthropology. In Brew 1968: 119–52.
Ellen, R. F., et al.
1988 Eds., *Malinowski between two worlds: The Polish roots of an anthropological tradition.* Cambridge.
Elliott, M.
1987 *The School of American Research: The first eighty years.* Santa Fe, N.M.
Embree, J.
1945 Applied anthropology and its relation to anthropology. *AA* 47:516–39.
1949 American military government. In *Social structure,* ed. M. Fortes, 207–25. Oxford.
Emeneau, M.
1943 Franz Boas as linguist. In *Franz Boas, 1858–1942.* Memoirs of the American Anthropological Association 61:35–38. Menasha, Wis.
Epstein, A. L.
1967 Ed., *The craft of social anthropology.* London.
Erasmus, C., & W. Smith
1967 Cultural anthropology in the United States since 1900: A quantitative analysis. *Southwestern Journal of Anthropology* 23:111–140.
Erickson, P. A.
1974 The origins of physical anthropology. Doct. diss., Univ. Connecticut.
1984–88 Ed., *History of anthropology bibliography* (with supplements 1–4). Occasional Papers in Anthropology No. 11, Department of Anthropology, Saint Mary's University. Halifax, Nova Scotia.

Evans-Pritchard, E. E.
1946 Applied anthropology. *Africa* 16:92–98.
1950 *Social anthropology*. In *Social anthropology and other essays*, 1–134. Glencoe, Ill. (1962).

Fabian, J.
1983 *Time and the other: How anthropology makes its object*. New York.

Fagette, P.
1985 Digging for dollars: The impact of the New Deal on the professionalization of American archaeology. Doct. diss., Univ. California, Riverside.

Fahim, H.
1982 Ed., *Indigenous anthropology in non-Western countries*. Durham, N.C.

Fairchild, H.
1961 *The noble savage: A study in romantic naturalism*. New York.

Fardon, R.
1990 Ed., *Localizing strategies: Regional traditions of ethnographic writing*. Edinburgh.

Fass, P.
1971 *The damned and the beautiful: American youth in the 1920s*. New York.

Feit, H. A.
1991 The construction of Algonquian hunting territories: Private property as moral lesson, policy advocacy, and ethnographic error. *HOA* 7:109–34.

Fenton, W. N.
1947 *Area studies in American universities*. Washington, D.C.

Fernandez, J.
1991 Ed., *Beyond metaphor: The theory of tropes in anthropology*. Stanford, Calif.

Firth, R. W.
1957 Ed., *Man and culture: An evaluation of the work of Bronislaw Malinowski*. New York (1964).
1963 A brief history (1913–63). In *Department of anthropology* [London School of Economics] *Programme of courses 1963–64*, 1–9.
1975 Seligman's contributions to Oceanic anthropology. *Oceania* 44:272–82.
1977 Whose frame of reference? One anthropologist's experience. In Loizos 1977:9–31.
1981 Bronislaw Malinowski. In *Totems and teachers: Perspectives on the history of anthropology*, ed. S. Silverman, 103–37. New York.
1989 Second introduction: 1988. In reprint edition of Malinowski 1967, xxi–xxxi. Stanford, Calif.

Firth, S.
1972 The New Guinea Company, 1885–1899: A case of unprofitable imperialism. *Historical Studies* 15:361–77.
1973 German firms in the Pacific Islands, 1857–1914. In *Germany in the Pacific and Far East, 1870–1914*, ed. J. A. Moses & P. M. Kennedy, 1–25. St. Lucas, Queensland.
1983 *New Guinea under the Germans*. Melbourne.

Fischer, J.
1979 Government anthropologists in the trust territory of Micronesia. In Goldschmidt 1979:238–52.

Fisher, D.
1978 The Rockefeller Foundation and the development of scientific medicine in Britain. *Minerva* 16:20–41.
1980 American philanthropy and the social sciences: The reproduction of conservative ideology. In *Philanthropy and cultural imperialism: The foundations at home and abroad,* ed. R. F. Arnove, 233–69. New York.

Fison, L., & A. W. Howitt
1880 *Kamilaroi and Kurnai: Group-marriage and relationship . . .* Osterhout N.B., Netherlands (1967).

Fitting, J. E.
1973 Ed., *The development of North American archaeology.* Garden City, N.Y.

Flannery, R.
1946 The ACLS and anthropology. *AA* 48:686–90.

Flis, A.
1988 Cracow philosophy of the beginning of the twentieth century and the rise of Malinowski's scientific ideas. In Ellen et al. 1988:105–27.

Fluehr-Lobban, C.
1991 Ed., *Ethics and the profession of anthropology: Dialogue for a new era.* Philadelphia.

Forge, A.
1967 The lonely anthropologist. *New Society* 10:221–23.

Fortes, M.
1941 Obituary of C. G. Seligman. *Man* 41:1–6.
1953 *Social anthropology at Cambridge since 1900.* Cambridge.
1969 *Kinship and the social order: The legacy of Lewis Henry Morgan.* Chicago.

Fosdick, R. F.
1952 *The story of the Rockefeller Foundation.* New York.
1956 *John D. Rockefeller, Jr.: A portrait.* New York.

Foster, G. M.
1953 What is folk culture? *AA* 55:159–73.
1969 *Applied anthropology.* Boston.
1979 The Institute of Social Anthropology. In Goldschmidt 1979:205–16.

Foster, G. M., et al.
1979 Eds., *Long-term field research in social anthropology.* New York.

Foster, R.
1991 Making national cultures in the global ecumene. *Annual Review of Anthropology* 20:235–60.

Frantz, C.
1974 Structuring and restructuring of the American Anthropological Association. Paper, American Anthropological Association.
1975 The twentieth-century development of U.S. anthropology: Universities, government, and the private sector. Paper, American Anthropological Association.

Frazer, J. G.
1887 *Questions on the customs, beliefs and languages of savages.* Privately printed pamphlet. Cambridge.
1900 *The golden bough: A study in magic and religion.* 2d ed., 3 vols. London.
1910 *Totemism and exogamy.* 4 vols. London (1968).
1931 Baldwin Spencer as anthropologist. In Marett & Penniman 1931:1–13.

FP. See under Manuscript Sources.

Freed, S. A., & R. S. Freed
1983 Clark Wissler and the development of anthropology in the United States. *AA* 85:800–825.

Freeman, D.
1962 Review of *Trance in Bali,* by Jane Belo. *Journal of the Polynesian Society* 71:270–73.
1965 Anthropology, psychiatry and the doctrine of cultural relativism. *Man* 65:65–67.
1972 *Social organization of Manu'a* (1930 and 1969), by Margaret Mead: Some errata. *Journal of the Polynesian Society* 8:70–78.
1980 Sociobiology: The "antidiscipline" of anthropology. In *Sociobiology examined,* ed. A. Montagu, 198–219. New York.
1983a *Margaret Mead and Samoa: The making and unmaking of an anthropological myth.* Cambridge, Mass.
1983b Inductivism and the test of truth: A rejoinder to Lowell D. Holmes and others. *Canberra Anthropology* 6:101–92.
1986 Some notes on the development of my anthropological interests. Unpublished manuscript.
1987 Comment on Holmes's *Quest for the real Samoa. AA* 89:903–35.
1989 *Fa'apua'a Fa'amū* and Margaret Mead. *AA* 91:1017–22.
1991a On Franz Boas and the Samoan researchers of Margaret Mead. *Current Anthropology* 32:322–30.
1991b "There's tricks i' th' world": An historical analysis of the Samoan researches of Margaret Mead. *Visual Anthropology Review* 7:103–28.

Friedman, J. B.
1981 *The monstrous races in medieval art and thought.* Cambridge, Mass.

Freire-Marreco, B.
1916 Cultivated plants. In *The ethnobotany of the Tewa Indians,* by W. W. Robbins, J. P. Harrington, and B. Friere-Marreco, 76–118. Bureau of American Ethnology Bulletin 55, Washington, D.C.

Frye, N.
1957 *The anatomy of criticism.* Princeton, N.J.

Galton, F.
1883 *Inquiries into human faculty and its development.* London.

Garrett, J.
1982 *To live among the stars: Christian origins in Oceania.* Geneva.

Gartrell, B.
1979 Is ethnography possible? A critique of *African Odyssey. Journal of Anthropological Research* 4:426–46.

Gatschet, A. S.
1890 *The Klamath Indians of southwestern Oregon.* 2 vols. Washington, D.C.

Geertz, C.
1967 Under the mosquito net. *New York Review of Books* (Sept. 14): 12–13.
1973 *The interpretation of cultures.* New York.
1983 Blurred genres: The refiguration of social thought. In *Local knowledge: Further essays in interpretive anthropology,* 19–35. New York.
1984 Anti-anti-relativism. *AA* 86:263–78.
1988 *Works and lives: The anthropologist as author.* Stanford, Calif.

Geison, G.
1978 *Michael Foster and the Cambridge School of physiology: The scientific enterprise in late Victorian society.* Princeton, N.J.

Gerould, D.
1981 *Witkacy: Stanislaw Ignacy Witkiewicz as an imaginative writer.* Seattle.

Gillen, F. J.
1896 Notes on some manners and customs of the Aborigines of the McDonnell Ranges belonging to the Arunta tribe. In *Report of the work of the Horn scientific expedition to central Australia,* ed. W. B. Spencer, Vol. 4, 162–86. London.

Givens, D. R.
1986 Alfred Vincent Kidder and the development of Americanist archaeology. Doct. diss., Washington Univ., St. Louis, Mo.

Gluckman, M.
1963 Malinowski—fieldworker and theorist. In *Order and rebellion in tribal Africa,* ed. Gluckman, 24–52. London.
1967 Introduction. In Epstein 1967:xi–xx.

Godoy, R.
1977 Franz Boas and his plans for the International School of American Archaeology and Ethnology in Mexico. *JHBS* 13:228–42.
1978 The background and context of Redfield's *Tepoztlán. Journal of the Steward Anthropological Society* 10:47–79.

Goldenweiser, A. A.
1917 The autonomy of the social. *AA* 19:447–49.
1926 *Early civilization: An introduction to anthropology.* New York.
1941 Recent trends in American anthropology. *AA* 43:151–63.

Goldfrank, E. S.
1927 *The social and ceremonial organization of Cochiti.* Memoirs of the American Anthropological Association 33. Menasha, Wis.
1943 Historic change and social character: A study of the Teton Dakota. *AA* 45:67–83.
1945a Irrigation agriculture and Navaho community leadership: Case material on environment and culture. *AA* 47:262–77.
1945b Socialization, personality and the structure of Pueblo society (with particular reference to Hopi and Zuni). *AA* 47:516–39.
1978 *Notes on an undirected life: As one anthropologist tells it.* New York.

1983 Another view: Margaret and me. *Ethnohistory* 30:1–14.
Goldschmidt, W. R.
1959 Ed., *The anthropology of Franz Boas.* San Francisco.
1979 Ed., *The uses of anthropology.* Washington, D.C.
Goldstein, M. S.
1940 Recent trends in physical anthropology. *AJPA* 26:191–209.
Gould, E.
1981 *Mythical intentions in modern literature.* Princeton, N.J.
GP. See under Manuscript Sources.
Gravel, P. B., & R. B. M. Ridinger
1988 *Anthropological fieldwork: An annotated bibliography.* New York.
Greene, J.
1980 The Kuhnian paradigm and the Darwinian revolution in natural history. In *Paradigms and revolutions: Applications and appraisals of Thomas Kuhn's philosophy of science,* ed. G. Gutting, 297–321. Notre Dame, Ind.
Greenop, F. S.
1944 *Who travels alone.* Sydney.
Griffin, J.
1959 The pursuit of archaeology in the United States. *AA* 61:379–89.
Grillo, R.
1985 Applied anthropology in the 1980s: Retrospect and prospect. In *Social anthropology and development policy,* ed. R. Grillo & A. Rew, 1–36. London.
Gringeri, R.
1990 Twilight of the sun kings: French anthropology from modernism to post-modernism, 1925–50. Doct. diss., Univ. California, Berkeley.
Grossman, D.
1982 American foundations and the support of economic research, 1923–29. *Minerva* 20:59–75.
Gruber, C. S.
1975 *Mars and Minerva: World War I and the uses of higher learning in America.* Baton Rouge, La.
Gruber, J. W.
1967 Horatio Hale and the development of American anthropology. *PAPS* 111:5–37.
1970 Ethnographic salvage and the shaping of anthropology. *AA* 72:1289–99.
GS. See under Stocking, G. W., Jr.
Guthe, C.
1967 Reflections on the founding of the Society for American Archaeology. *American Antiquity* 32:433–40.
Haddon, A. C.
1890 The ethnography of the western tribe of Torres Straits. *JAI* 19:297–440.
1895a *Evolution in art.* London.
1895b Ethnographical survey of Ireland. In BAAS, *Report of the 65th meeting, BAAS,* 509–18. London.

1901 *Head-hunters: Black, white and brown.* London.

1901–1935 Ed., *Reports of the Cambridge Anthropological Expedition to Torres Straits.* Vol. 1 (1935); Vol. 2 (part 1) (1901); Vol. 2 (part 2) (1903); Vol. 3 (1907); Vol. 4 (1912); Vol. 5 (1904); Vol. 6 (1908). Cambridge.

1903a The saving of vanishing data. *Popular Science Monthly* 62:222–29.

1903b Anthropology: Its position and needs. Presidential address. *JAI* 33:11–23.

1906 A plea for an expedition to Melanesia. *Nature* 74:187–88.

1922 Ceremonial exchange: Review of B. Malinowski's *Argonauts of the western Pacific. Nature* 110:472–74.

1939 Obituary of Sydney Ray. *Man* 57:58–61.

Hale, H.

1884 On some doubtful or intermediate articulations. *JAI* 14:233–43.

Hale, N. G.

1971 *Freud and the Americans.* New York.

Hall, G. S.

1907 *Adolescence: Its psychology and its relations.* 2 vols. New York.

Hall, R. A., & K. Koerner

1987 Eds., *Leonard Bloomfield: Essays on his life and work.* Amsterdam.

Hallowell, A. I.

1937 Cross-cousin marriage in the Lake Winnipeg area. In 1976:317–32.

1960 The beginnings of anthropology in America. In De Laguna 1960:1–90.

1965 The history of anthropology as an anthropological problem. *JHBS* 1: 24–38.

1976 *Contributions to anthropology: Selected papers of A. Irving Hallowell.* Chicago.

Halpern, S.

1989 Historical myth and institutional history. Unpublished manuscript.

Hanc, J.

1981 Influences, events, and innovations in the anthropology of Julian H. Steward: A revisionist view of multilinear evolution. Master's thesis, Univ. Chicago.

Handler, R.

1983 The dainty and the hungry man: Literature and anthropology in the work of Edward Sapir. *HOA* 1:208–31.

1986 Vigorous male and aspiring female: Poetry, personality and culture in Edward Sapir and Ruth Benedict. *HOA* 4:127–55.

1989 Anti-romantic romanticism: Edward Sapir and the critique of American individualism. *Anthropological Quarterly* 62:1–14.

Haraway, D.

1977 A political physiology of the primate family: Monkeys and apes in the twentieth-century rationalization of sex. Paper, American Academy of Arts and Sciences, Boston.

1988 Remodelling the human way of life: Sherwood Washburn and the new physical anthropology, 1950–1980. *HOA* 5:206–59.

1989 *Primate visions: Gender, race and nature in the world of modern science.* New York.

Hare, P. H.
1985 *A woman's quest for science: Portrait of anthropologist Elsie Clews Parsons.* New York.

Harris, M.
1968 *The rise of anthropological theory: A history of theories of culture.* New York.

Harrison, F. V.
1991 Ed., *Decolonizing anthropology: Moving further toward an anthropology for liberation.* Washington, D.C.

Harrington, J.
1945 Boas on the science of language. *IJAL* 11:97–99.

Hatch, E.
1973a *Theories of man and culture.* New York.
1973b The growth of economic, subsistence, and ecological studies in American anthropology. *Journal of Anthropological Research* 29:221–43.
1983 *Culture and morality: The relativity of values in anthropology.* New York.

Heider, K. G.
1988 The Rashomon effect: When ethnographers disagree. *AA* 90:73–81.

Hempenstall, P. J.
1987 *Pacific islands under German rule: A study in the meaning of colonial resistance.* Canberra.

Herbert, C.
1991 *Culture and anomie: Ethnographic imagination in the nineteenth century.* Chicago.

Herskovits, M. J.
1946 Review of Montagu, *Man's most dangerous myth. AA* 48:267.
1953 *Franz Boas: The science of man in the making.* New York.
1954 Some problems of method in ethnography. In *Method and perspective in anthropology: Papers in honor of Wilson D. Wallis,* ed. R. F. Spencer, 3–24. Minneapolis, Minn.

Hertzberg, H. W.
1971 *The search for an American Indian identity: Modern pan-Indian movements.* Syracuse, N.Y.

Hewitt de Alcantara, C.
1984 *Anthropological perspectives on rural Mexico.* London.

Hezel, F. X.
1983 *The first taint of civilization: A history of the Caroline and Marshall Islands in pre-colonial days, 1521–1885.* Honolulu.

Higham, J.
1955 *Strangers in the land: Patterns of American nativism, 1860–1925.* New Brunswick, N.J.

Hinsley, C. M.
1981 *Savages and scientists: The Smithsonian Institution and the development of American anthropology, 1846–1910.* Washington, D.C.
1985 From shell-heaps to stelae: Early anthropology at the Peabody Museum. *HOA* 3:49–74.

Hobhouse, L. T., G. C. Wheeler, & M. Ginsberg
1915 *The material culture and social institutions of the simpler peoples.* London (1930).
Hocart, A. M.
1922 The cult of the dead in Eddystone Island. *JAI* 52:71–112.
Hockett, C. F.
1954 Two models of grammatical description. *Word* 10:210–34.
Hodgen, M. T.
1964 *Early anthropology in the sixteenth and seventeenth centuries.* Philadelphia.
Hogbin, H. I.
1946 The Trobriand Islands, 1945. *Man* 46:72.
Holborn, H.
1969 *A history of modern Germany, 1830–1945.* New York.
Holland, R. F.
1985 *European decolonization, 1918–1981: An introductory survey.* New York.
Holmes, L. D.
1957a The restudy of Manu'an culture: A problem in methodology. Doct. diss., Northwestern Univ.
1957b Ta'u. Stability and change in a Samoan village. *Journal of the Polynesian Society* 66:301–38, 398–435.
1987 *Quest for the real Samoa: The Mead/Freeman controversy and beyond.* South Hadley, Mass.
Hood, D.
1964 *Davidson Black: A biography.* Toronto.
Hooton, E.
1935 Development and correlation of research in physical anthropology at Harvard University. *PAPS* 75:499–516.
HoP. See under Manuscript Sources.
Horowitz, I. L.
1967 Ed., *The rise and fall of Project Camelot: Studies in the relationship between social science and practical politics.* Cambridge.
Hose, C., & W. McDougall
1912 *The pagan tribes of Borneo.* London.
Howard, C.
1981 Rivers' genealogical method and the *Reports* of the Torres Straits Expedition. Unpublished seminar paper, Univ. Chicago.
Howard, J.
1984 *Margaret Mead: A life.* New York.
HP. See under Manuscript Sources.
Hrdlička, A.
1918 Physical anthropology: Its scope and aims; its history and present status in America. *AJPA* 1:3–23.
Hsu, F. L. K.
1979 The cultural problem of the cultural anthropologist. *AA* 81:517–32.

Huizer, G., & B. Mannheim

1979 Eds., *The politics of anthropology: From colonialism and sexism toward a view from below.* The Hague.

Humboldt, W. von

1836 *Linguistic variability and intellectual development.* Trans. G. C. Buck & F. A. Raven. Miami (1971).

Hyatt, M.

1990 *Franz Boas, social activist: The dynamics of ethnicity.* New York.

Hyman, S. E.

1959 *The tangled bank: Darwin, Marx, Frazer and Freud as imaginative writers.* New York (1966).

Hymes, D. H.

1961a On typology of cognitive styles in language. *Anthropological Linguistics* 3:22–54.

1961b Review of Goldschmidt 1959. *Journal of American Folklore* 74:87–90.

1962 On studying the history of anthropology. *Items* 16:25–27.

1964 Ed., *Language in culture and society.* New York.

1970 Linguistic method in ethnography: Its development in the United States. In *Method and theory in linguistics,* ed. P. L. Garvin, 249–311. The Hague.

1971 Foreword. In M. Swadesh, *The origin and diversification of language,* v–x. Chicago.

1972 Ed., *Reinventing anthropology.* New York.

1974 Ed., *Studies in the history of linguistics: Traditions and paradigms.* Bloomington, Ind.

1983 *Essays in the history of linguistic anthropology* Amsterdam.

Hymes, D. H., & J. Fought

1975 American structuralism. In *Historiography of Linguistics,* ed. T. A. Sebeok, 903–1176. Current Trends in Linguistics 10. The Hague.

Im Thurn, E.

1883 *Among the Indians of Guiana.* New York (1967).

Iverson, R. W.

1959 *The communists and the schools.* New York.

Jacknis, I.

1985 Franz Boas and exhibits: On the limitations of the museum method of anthropology. *HOA* 3:75–111.

Jackson, W.

1986 Melville Herskovits and the search for Afro-American culture. *HOA* 4: 95–126.

Jacobs, M.

1951a Bismarck and the annexation of New Guinea. *Historical Studies, Australia and New Zealand* 5:14–26.

1951b The Colonial Office and New Guinea, 1874–84. *Historical Studies, Australia and New Zealand* 5:106–18.

Jakobson, R.

1944 Franz Boas' approach to language. *IJAL* 10:188–95.

1959 Boas' view of grammatical meaning. In Goldschmidt 1959:139–45.

James, W.

1973 The anthropologist as reluctant imperialist. In Asad 1973:41–70.

Jarvie, I. C.

1964 *The revolution in anthropology.* London.

1966 On theories of fieldwork and the scientific character of social anthropology. *Philosophy of Science* 34:223–42.

1989 Recent work in the history of anthropology and its historiographic problems. *Philosophy of the Social Sciences* 19:345–75.

Jenness, D.

1922–23 *Life of the Copper Eskimo. Report of the Canadian Arctic Expedition.* Vol. 12, *Southern party 1913–16.* Ottawa.

Jenness, D., & A. Ballantyne

1920 *The northern D'Entrecasteaux.* Oxford.

Jerschina, J.

1988 Polish culture of modernism and Malinowski's personality. In Ellen et al. 1988:128–48.

Jones, E. M.

1988 Samoa lost: Margaret Mead, cultural relativism and the guilty imagination. *Fidelity* 7:26–37.

Jones, R. A.

1984 Robertson Smith and James Frazer on religion: Two traditions in British social anthropology. *HOA* 2:31–58.

Joos, M.

1986 *Notes on the development of the Linguistic Society of America, 1924–1950.* Foreword by C. Hockett & J. M. Cowan. Privately printed. Ithaca, N.Y.

Jorion, P.

1985 Review of GS 1983. *L'Homme* 25:159–61.

Joyce, R.

1971a Australian interests in New Guinea before 1906. In *Australia and Papua New Guinea,* ed. W. J. Hudson, 8–31. Sydney.

1971b *Sir William MacGregor.* Melbourne.

Julius, C.

1960 Malinowski's Trobriand Islands. *Journal of the Public Service* (Territory of Papua and New Guinea) 2:5–13, 57–64.

Jung, C.

1923 *Psychological types: Or, the psychology of individuation.* Trans. H. Baynes. New York.

Kaberry, P.

1957 Malinowski's contribution to field-work methods and the writing of ethnography. In R. Firth 1957:71–92.

Karl, B., & S. N. Katz

1981 The American private philanthropic foundation and the public sphere, 1890–1930. *Minerva* 19:236–70.

Karsten, R.
1923 *Blood revenge, war and victory feasts among the Jibaro Indians of eastern Ecuador.* Bureau of American Ethnology Bulletin 79. Washington, D.C
1932 *Indian tribes of the Argentine and Bolivian Chaco.* Societas Scientiarum Fennica. Helsinki.
1935 *The head-hunters of western Amazonas.* Societas Scientiarum Fennica. Helsinki.

Keen, B.
1971 *The Aztec image in western thought.* New Brunswick, N.J.

Kelly, L. P.
1980 Anthropology and anthropologists in the Indian New Deal. *JHBS* 16: 6–24.

Kenyatta, J.
1938 *Facing Mount Kenya: The tribal life of the Gikuyu.* London.

Kevles, D. J.
1985 *In the name of eugenics: Genetics and the uses of human heredity.* Berkeley, Calif.

Kidder, A. V.
1924 *An introduction to the study of southwestern archaeology.* New Haven, Conn.

Kimball, S.
1979 Land use management: The Navajo reservation. In Goldschmidt 1979: 61–78.

King, K.
1971 *Pan-Africanism and education: A study of race philanthropy and education in the southern states of America and east Africa.* Oxford.

Kirchway, F.
1924 Ed., *Our changing morality.* New York.

Kirschner, P.
1968 *Conrad: The psychologist as artist.* Edinburgh.

Kloos, P.
1975 Anthropology and non-western sociology in the Netherlands. In *Current anthropology in the Netherlands,* ed. P. Kloos and H. Claessen, 10–29. Rotterdam.
1989 The sociology of non-western societies. *The Netherlands Journal of Social Sciences* 25:40–50.

Kluckhohn, C.
1943a Covert culture and administrative problems. *AA* 45:213–227.
1943b Obituary of Malinowski. *Journal of American Folklore* 56:208–14.

Kluckhohn, C., & O. Prufer
1959 Influences during the formative years. In Goldschmidt 1959:4–28.

Koffka, K.
1925 *The growth of the mind: An introduction to child psychology.* Trans. R. M. Ogden. New York.

Kohler, R. F.
1978 A policy for the advancement of science: The Rockefeller Foundation, 1924–1929. *Minerva* 16:480–515.
1991 *Partners in science: Foundations and natural scientists, 1900–1945.* Chicago.
Kottak, C.
1989 Comments at the session on Assessing Developments in Anthropology, American Anthropological Association.
Kroeber, A. L.
1909a Noun incorporation in American languages. *Verhandlungen des XIV Internationales Amerikanisten-Kongress, Vienna,* 569–76.
1909b Classificatory systems of relationship. *JAI* 39:77–84.
1910 Noun composition in American languages. *Anthropos* 5:204–18.
1911 Incorporation as a linguistic process. *AA* 13:577–84.
1917 The superorganic. *AA* 19:163–213.
1920 Review of Lowie 1920. *AA* 22:377–81.
1923 *Anthropology.* New York.
1931 Review of Redfield 1930a. *AA* 33:286–88.
1935a History and science in anthropology. *AA* 37:539–69.
1935b Review of Benedict 1934. *AA* 37:689–90.
1936 Kinship and history. *AA* 38:338–41.
1943 Structure, function, and pattern in biology and anthropology. *Scientific Monthly* 56:105–13.
1944 *Configurations of culture growth.* Berkeley, Calif.
1946 The range of the *American Anthropologist. AA* 48:297–99.
1952 *The nature of culture.* Chicago.
1953 Ed., *Anthropology today: An encyclopedic inventory.* Chicago.
1960 Statistics, Indo-European, and taxonomy. *Language* 36:1–21.
Kroeber, A. L., & C. Kluckhohn
1952 *Culture: A critical review of concepts and definitions.* Cambridge.
Kubary, J.
1873 Die Palau-Inseln in der Südsee. *Journal des Museum Godeffroy* 1:177–238 [page numbers refer to the manuscript English translation in the Human Relations Area Files in New Haven, Conn].
1885 *Ethnographische Beiträge zur Kenntniss der Karolinischen Inselgruppe und Nachbarschaft.* Vol. 1, *Die sozialen Einrichtungen der Pelauer.* Berlin.
Kubica, G.
1988 Malinowski's years in Poland. In Ellen et al. 1988:89–104.
Kuhn, T.
1962 *The structure of scientific revolutions.* Chicago.
1974 Second thoughts on paradigms. In *The essential tension: Selected studies in scientific tradition and change,* ed. F. Suppes, 293–319. Chicago.
Kuklick, H.
1973 A "scientific revolution": Sociological theory in the United States, 1930–45. *Sociological Inquiry* 43:3–22.
1978 The sins of the fathers: British anthropology and African colonial ad-

ministration. *Research in the Sociology of Knowledge, Science and Art* 1:93–119.
1991 *The savage within: The social history of British anthropology, 1885–1945.* Cambridge.

Kuper, A.
1983 *Anthropology and anthropologists: The modern British school 1922–1972.* London.
1989 Anthropological futures. Paper, American Anthropological Association.
1991 Anthropologists and the history of anthropology. *Critique of Anthropology* 11:125–42.

Kusmer, K.
1979 The social history of cultural institutions: The upper-class connection. *Journal of Interdisciplinary History* 10:137–46.

Kuznick, P. J.
1988 *Beyond the laboratory: Scientists as political activists in 1930s America.* Chicago.

La Feber, W.
1963 *The new empire: An interpretation of American expansion, 1860–1898.* Ithaca, N.Y.

Landtman, G.
1917 *The folk-tales of the Kiwai Papauns.* Societas Scientiarum Fennica. Helsinki.
1927 *The Kiwai Papuans of British New Guinea: A nature-born instance of Rousseau's ideal community.* London.

Lang, A.
1901 *Magic and religion.* London.

Langham, I.
1981 *The building of British social anthropology: W. H. Rivers and his Cambridge disciples in the development of kinship studies, 1893–1931.* Dordrecht.

Langlois, C. V., & C. Seignobos
1898 *Introduction to the study of history.* Trans. G. G. Berry. New York (1926).

Laracy, H.
1976 Malinowski at war, 1914–1918. *Mankind* 10:264–68.

Lasch, C.
1965 *The new radicalism in America (1889–1963): The intellectual as a social type.* New York.

La Violette, F.
1961 *The struggle for survival: Indian cultures and the Protestant ethic in British Columbia.* Toronto.

Lawrence, P.
1964 *Road belong cargo: A study of the cargo movement in the southern Madang district of New Guinea.* Atlantic Highlands, N.J. (1979).

Layard, J.
1942 *Stone men of Malekula.* London.

1944 *Incarnation and instinct.* Pamphlet. London.
Leach, E.
1957 The epistemological background to Malinowski's empiricism. In R. Firth 1957:119–37.
1965 Introduction to reprint edition of Malinowski 1935:I, vii–xvii.
1966 On the "founding fathers." *Current Anthropology* 7:560–67.
1980 On reading *A diary in the strict sense of the term:* Or the self-mutilation of Professor Hsu. *RAIN* 36:2–3.
1990 Masquerade: The presentation of self in holi-day life. *Cambridge Anthropology* 13(3):47–69.
Lears, J.
1981 *No place of grace: Antimodernism and the transformation of American culture, 1880–1920.* New York.
LeClerc, G.
1972 *Anthropologie et colonialism: Essai sur l'histoire de l'africanisme.* Paris.
Legge, J.
1956 *Australian colonial policy: A survey of native administration and European development in Papua.* Sydney.
Leuchtenberg, W. E.
1958 *The perils of prosperity, 1914–1932.* Chicago.
Levenstein, H.
1963 Franz Boas as political activist. *Papers of the Kroeber Anthropological Society* 29:15–24.
Lévi-Strauss, C.
1962 Jean-Jacques Rousseau, founder of the sciences of man. In *Structural anthropology,* Vol. 2, 33–43. Harmondsworth, Eng.
Lewis, O.
1951 *Life in a Mexican village: Tepoztlán restudied.* Urbana, Ill. (1963).
1953 Controls and experiments in anthropological fieldwork. In Kroeber 1953: 452–75.
1960 Some of my best friends are peasants. *Human Organization* 19:179–80.
Li An-che
1937 Zuni: Some observations and queries. *AA* 39:62–76.
Linton, A., & C. Wagley
1971 *Ralph Linton.* New York.
Linton, R.
1936 *The study of man.* New York.
1939 Marquesan culture. In *The individual and his society: The psychodynamics of primitive social organization,* ed. A. Kardiner, 137–95. New York.
1945 Ed., *The science of man in the world crisis.* New York.
Logan, R. W.
1965 *Betrayal of the Negro: From Rutherford B. Hayes to Woodrow Wilson.* New York.
Loizos, P.
1977 Ed., [Special number on colonialism and anthropology.] *Anthropological Forum* 4(2).

London, H. I.
1970 *Non-white immigration and the "White Australia" policy.* New York.

Louis, W. R.
1967 *Great Britain and Germany's lost colonies, 1914–1919.* Oxford.

Lounsbury, F.
1968 One hundred years of anthropological linguistics. In Brew 1968:153–226.

Lovejoy, A. O.
1936 *The Great Chain of Being: A study in the history of an idea.* Cambridge.

Lovejoy, A. O., & G. Boas
1935 *Primitivism and related ideas in antiquity.* Baltimore, Md.

Lowie, R. H.
1917 *Culture and ethnology.* New York (1966).
1920 *Primitive society.* New York.
1929 Review of Mead 1928b. *AA* 31:532–34.
1937 *The history of ethnological theory.* New York.
1940 Native languages as ethnographic tools. *AA* 42:81–89.
1943 The progress of science: Franz Boas, anthropologist. *Scientific Monthly* 56:184.
1959 *Robert H. Lowie, ethnologist.* Berkeley, Calif.

Lugard, F. J. D.
1922 *The dual mandate in British tropical Africa.* London (1965).

Lynd, R. S., & H. M. Lynd
1929 *Middletown: A study in American culture.* New York.

Lynn, K. S.
1983 *The air-line to Seattle: Studies in literary and historical writing about America.* Chicago.

Lyon, E. A.
1982 New Deal archaeology in the southeast: WPA, TVA, NPS, 1934–1942. Doct. diss., Louisiana State Univ.

Lyons, G. M.
1969 *The uneasy partnership: Social science and the federal government in the twentieth century.* New York.

MacClancy, J.
1986 Unconventional character and disciplinary convention: John Layard, Jungian and anthropologist. *HOA* 4:50–71.

MacCurdy, G. G.
1919 The academic teaching of anthropology in connection with other departments. *AA* 21:49–60.

McDowell, N.
1980 The Oceanic ethnography of Margaret Mead. *AA* 82:278–302.

Mackenzie, S.
1927 *The Australians at Rabaul: The capture and administration of the German possessions in the southern Pacific.* Sydney.

McLennan, J. F.
1865 *Primitive marriage.* Edinburgh.

McLuhan, T. C.
1985 *Dream tracks: The railroad and the American Indian, 1890–1930.* New York.
McMillan, R.
1986 The study of anthropology, 1931 to 1937, at Columbia University and the University of Chicago. Doct. diss., York Univ.
McNeill, W. H.
1986 *Mythistory and other essays.* Chicago.
McNickle, D.
1979 Anthropology and the Indian Reorganization Act. In Goldschmidt 1979: 51–60.
Maine, H. S.
1858 Thirty years of improvement in India. *Saturday Review* 5 (Feb. 6): 129.
Mair, L. P.
1948 *Australia in New Guinea.* London.
Maitland, F. W.
1911 The body politic. In *Collected papers,* ed. H. A. L. Fisher, Vol. 3, 285–303. Cambridge, Eng.
Malinowski, B.
1908 O zasadzie ekonomii myslenia [On the principle of the economy of thought]. Trans. E. C. Martinek, Master's thesis, Univ. Chicago 1985.
1912 The economic aspect of the Intichiuma ceremonies. In *Festkrift tillegnad Edvard Westermarck i Anledning av hans femtidrosdag den 10 Novemer 1912,* 81–108. Helsinki.
1913a *The family among the Australian aborigines.* New York (1963).
1913b Elementary forms of religious life. In 1962:282–88.
1913c Review of *Across Australia,* by B. Spencer and F. J. Gillen. *Folk-Lore* 24:278–79.
1915a The natives of Mailu: Preliminary results of the Robert Mond research work in British New Guinea. In Young 1988:77–331.
1915b *Wierzenia pierwotne i formy ustroju spotecznego* [Primitive religion and social differentiation]. Polish Academy of Science. Cracow.
1916 Baloma: Spirits of the dead in the Trobriand Islands. In *Magic, science and religion and other essays,* 149–274. Garden City, N.Y. (1954).
1922a Ethnology and the study of society. *Economica* 2:208–19.
1922b *Argonauts of the western Pacific: An account of native enterprise and adventure in the archipelagoes of Melanesian New Guinea.* London.
1923 Science and superstition of primitive mankind. In 1962:268–75.
1926a Myth in primitive psychology. In *Magic, science and religion and other essays,* 93–148. Garden City, N.Y. (1954).
1926b Anthropology and administration. *Nature* 118:768.
1926c *Crime and custom in savage society.* Paterson, N.J. (1964).
1927 *Sex and repression in savage society.* London.
1929a *The sexual life of savages in northwestern Melanesia.* London.
1929b Practical anthropology. *Africa* 2:22–38.

1929c Review of *Report of the Commission on Closer Union of the Dependencies in Eastern and Central Africa. Africa* 2:317–20.

1929d Review of *The Kiwai Papuans of British New Guinea* by G. Landtman. *Folk-Lore* 40:109–12.

1930a The rationalization of anthropology and administration. *Africa* 3:405–29.

1930b Race and labour. *Listener* 4: supplement no. 8.

1931 A plea for an effective colour bar. *Spectator* 146:999–1001.

1934 Whither Africa? *International Review of Missions* 25:401–7.

1935 *Coral gardens and their magic.* 2 vols. Bloomington, Ind. (1965).

1936 Native education and culture contact. *International Review of Missions* 25:480–515.

1937 Introduction to J. E. Lips, *The savage hits back,* vii–ix. New Haven, Conn.

1938 Introduction to Kenyatta 1938:vii–xiii.

1938b The anthropology of changing cultures. In *Methods of study of culture contact in Africa,* Memorandum XV of the International African Institute, vii–xxxv. London (1939).

1939 Modern anthropology and European rule in Africa. *Convegno di Scienze morali e storiche, 4–11 Ottobre 1938–XVI.* Tema: L'Africa, Vol. 2, 880–901. Reale Accademia d'Italia. Rome.

1943 The Pan-African problem of culture contact *American Journal of Sociology* 48:649–65.

1944 Sir James George Frazer: A biographical introduction. In *A Scientific theory of culture and other essays,* 177–222. New York (1960).

1945 *The dynamics of culture change: An inquiry into race relations in Africa.* New Haven, Conn. (1965).

1962 *Sex, culture and myth.* New York.

1967 *A diary in the strict sense of the term.* New York.

Mandelbaum, D. G.

1982 Some shared ideas. In *Crisis in anthropology: View from Spring Hill, 1980,* ed. E. A. Hoebel et al., 35–50. New York.

Manganaro, M.

1990 Ed., *Modernist anthropology: From fieldwork to text.* Princeton, N.J.

Manson, W. C.

1986 Abram Kardiner and the neo-Freudian alternative in culture and personality. *HOA* 4:72–94.

MaP. See under Manuscript Sources.

Marcus, G. E.

1986 Contemporary problems of ethnography in the modern world system. In Clifford & Marcus 1986:165–93.

Marcus, G. E., & D. Cushman

1982 Ethnographies as texts. *Annual Review of Anthropology* 11:25–69.

Marcus, G. E., & M. Fischer

1986 *Anthropology as cultural critique: An experimental moment in the human sciences.* Chicago.

Marett, R. R.
1900 Pre-animistic religion. *Folk-Lore* 11:162–82.
1921 Obituary of Marie de Czaplicka, *Man* 60:105–6.
1941 *A Jerseyman at Oxford.* London.

Marett, R. R., & T. Penniman
1931 Eds., *Spencer's last journey: Being the journal of an expedition to Tierra del Fuego by the late Sir Walter Baldwin Spencer with a memoir.* Oxford.
1932 Eds., *Spencer's scientific correspondence with Sir J. G. Frazer and others.* Oxford.

Marías, J.
1967 *Generations: A historical method.* Trans. H. C. Raley. University, Ala.

Matthews, W.
1877 *Ethnography and philology of the Hidatsa Indians.* Washington, D.C.

Mauss, M.
1923 [Obituary of W. H. R. Rivers]. In *Ouevres.* Vol. 3, *Cohesion sociale et divisions de la sociologie,* ed. V. Karady, 465–72, Paris (1968).

May, H.
1959 *The end of American innocence: A study of the first years of our time, 1912–1917.* New York.

May, M. A.
1971 A retrospective view of the Institute of Human Relations at Yale. *Behavioral Sciences Notes* 6:141–72.

Mead, M.
1927 Group intelligence tests and linguistic disability among Italian children. *School and Society* 25:465–68.
1928a *An inquiry into the question of cultural stability in Polynesia.* New York.
1928b *Coming of age in Samoa: A psychological study of primitive youth for western civilisation.* New York.
1928c The role of the individual in Samoan culture. *JAI* 58:481–95.
1930 *The social organization of Manu'a.* Honolulu.
1932 *The changing culture of an Indian tribe.* New York.
1953 National character. In Kroeber 1953:642–67.
1954 The swaddling hypothesis: Its reception. *AA* 56:395–409.
1956 *New lives for old: Cultural transformation—Manus, 1928–1953.* New York.
1959a Ed., *An anthropologist at work: Writings of Ruth Benedict.* Boston.
1959b Apprenticeship under Boas. In Goldschmidt 1959:29–45.
1961 Preface to reprint edition of 1928b:xi–xvi.
1962 Retrospects and prospects. In *Anthropology and human behavior,* ed. T. Gladwin & W. Sturtevant, 115–49. Washington, D.C.
1964 *Continuities in cultural evolution.* New York.
1969 Introduction to the 1969 edition; Conclusion 1969: Reflections on later theoretical work on the Samoans, in reprint edition of Mead 1930:xi–xix, 219–30.
1971 Preliminary autobiographical drafts, in MeP.

1972a *Blackberry winter: My earlier years.* New York.
1972b Changing styles of anthropological work. *Annual Review of Anthropology* 2:1–26.
1977 *Letters from the field, 1925–1975.* New York.
1979 Anthropological contributions to national policies during and immediately after World War II. In Goldschmidt 1979:145–57.

Megill, A.
1989 What does the term "postmodern" mean? *Annals of Scholarship* 6:129–52.

Meier, A.
1963 *Negro thought in America, 1880–1915.* Ann Arbor, Mich.

Meggers, B.
1946 Recent trends in American ethnology. *AA* 48:176–214.

Meltzer, D. J.
1983 The antiquity of man and the development of American archaeology. *Advances in Archaeological Method and Theory* 6:1–51.

Meltzer, D. J., et al.
1986 Eds., *American archaeology, past and future: A celebration of the Society for American Archaeology, 1935–85.* Washington, D.C.

Mendelsohn, E.
1963 The emergence of science as a profession in nineteenth-century Europe. In *Management of scientists,* ed. K. Hill, 3–48. Boston.

MeP. See under Manuscript Sources.

Miklouho-Maclay, N. N.
1950–54 *Sobranie Sochineii.* 5 vols. Moscow.
See also Sentinella 1975; Tumarkin 1982b.

Miner, H.
1952 The folk-urban continuum. *American Sociological Review* 17:529–36.

Mintz, S.
1953 The folk-urban continuum and the rural proletarian community. *American Journal of Sociology* 59:136–43.

Mitchell, P.
1930 The anthropologist and the practical man: A reply and a question. *Africa* 3:217–23.

Mitchell, R. E.
1971 Kubary: The first Micronesian reporter. *Micronesian Reporter* 3:43–45.

Modell, J.
1974 The professionalization of women under Franz Boas, 1900–1930. Paper, American Anthropological Association.
1983 *Ruth Benedict: Patterns of a life.* Philadelphia.

Morawski, J.
1986 Organizing knowledge and behavior at Yale's Institute of Human Relations. *Isis* 77:219–42.

Morgan, L. H.
1871 *Systems of consanguinity and affinity of the human family.* Osterhout N.B., Netherlands (1970).

1877 *Ancient society, or researches in the lines of human progress from savagery through barbarism to civilization.* New York.

Moseley, H. N.

1879 *Notes by a naturalist on the Challenger . . .* London.

Moses, I.

1977 The extension of colonial rule in Kaiser Wilhelmsland. In *Germany in the Pacific and Far East, 1870–1914,* ed. J. A. Moses & P. M. Kennedy, 288–312. St. Lucas, Queensland.

MPL. See under Manuscript Sources.

MPY. See under Manuscript Sources.

Mulvaney, D. J.

1958 The Australian aborigines, 1606–1929. Opinion and fieldwork. In *Historical Studies: Australia and New Zealand* 8:131–51, 297–314.

1967 The anthropologist as tribal elder. *Mankind* 7:205–17.

1989 Australian anthropology and ANZAAS: "Strictly scientific and critical." In *The commonwealth of science: ANZAAS and the scientific enterprise in Australia, 1888–1988P,* ed. R. MacLeod 196–221. Melbourne.

Mulvaney, D. J., & J. H. Calaby

1985 *"So much that is new": Baldwin Spencer, 1860–1929, a biography.* Melbourne.

Murdock, G. P.

1932 The science of culture. *AA* 34:200–15.

Murphy, R. F.

1972 *Robert H. Lowie.* New York.

1976 A quarter century of American anthropology. In *Selected papers from the American Anthropologist, 1946–1970,* ed. Murphy, 1–22. Washington, D.C.

1991 Anthropology at Columbia: A reminiscence. *Dialectical Anthropology* 16:65–81.

Murray, J. H. P.

1912 *Papua or British New Guinea.* London.

Murray, S.

1988 The reception of anthropological work in sociological journals. *JHBS* 24:135–51.

1989 Recent studies in American linguistics. *Historiographia Linguistica* 16: 149–71.

1990 Problematic aspects of Freeman's account of Boasian culture. *Current Anthropology* 31:401–7.

Murray-Brown, J.

1972 *Kenyatta.* London.

NAA. See under Manuscript Sources.

Naroll, R.

1962 *Data quality control—a new research technique: Prolegomena to a cross-cultural study of cultural stress.* Glencoe, Ill.

NAS [National Academy of Sciences]

1964 *Federal support of basic research in institutions of higher learning.* Washington, D.C.

Nash, D., & R. Wintrob
1972 The emergence of self-consciousness in ethnography. *Current Anthropology* 13:527–42.

Nash, R.
1970 *The nervous generation: American thought, 1917–1930.* Chicago.

Needham, R.
1967 *A bibliography of Arthur Maurice Hocart (1883–1939).* Oxford.

Nelson, H.
1969 European attitudes in Papua, 1906–1914. In *The history of Melanesia,* 593–624. [2d Waigani Seminar]. Canberra and Port Moresby.

NRC [National Research Council]
1938 *International directory of anthropologists.* Washington, D.C.

Ogburn, W. F.
1922 *Social change, with respect to culture and original nature.* New York.

Onege, O.
1979 The counterrevolutionary tradition in African studies: The case of applied anthropology. In Huizer & Mannheim 1979:45–66.

Opler, M.
1946 A recent trend in the misrepresentation of the work of American ethnologists. *AA* 48:669–71.

Ortner, S.
1984 Theory in anthropology since the sixties. *Comparative Studies in Society and History* 26:126–66.

Ottonello, E.
1975 From particularism to cultural materialism: Progressive growth or scientific revolution? Paper, American Anthropological Association.

Paddock, J.
1961 Oscar Lewis's Mexico. *Anthropological Quarterly* 34:129–50.

Pagden, A.
1982 *The fall of natural man: The American Indian and the origins of comparative ethnology.* Cambridge.

Paluch, A. K.
1981 The Polish background of Malinowski's work. *Man* 16:276–85.

Pandey, T. N.
1972 Anthropologists at Zuni. *PAPS* 116:321–37.

Panoff, M.
1972 *Bronislaw Malinowski.* Paris.

Parmentier, R. J.
1987 *The sacred remains: Myth, history and polity in Belau.* Chicago.

Parnaby, O. W.
1964 *Britain and the labor trade in the southwest Pacific.* Durham, N.C.

Partridge, W. L., & E. M. Eddy
1978 The development of applied anthropology in America. In *Applied anthropology in America,* ed. Partridge & Eddy, 3–45. New York.

Passin, H.
1942 Tarahumara prevarication: A problem in field method. *AA* 44:235–47.

Paszkowski, L.
1969 John Stanislaw Kubary—naturalist and ethnographer of the Pacific islands. *Australian Zoologist* 16(2):43–70.
Patterson, T. C.
1986 The last sixty years: Toward a social history of archeology in the United States. *AA* 88:7–26.
Paul, B.
1953 Interview techniques and field relationships. In Kroeber 1953:430–51.
Payne, H. C.
1981 Malinowski's style. *PAPS* 125:416–40.
Payne, K. W., & S. O. Murray
1983 Historical inferences from ethnohistorical data: Boasian views. *JHBS* 19: 335–40.
Pearson, K.
1924 *Life, letters and labours of Francis Galton.* Vol. 3, *Researches of middle life.* Cambridge.
Pells, R. H.
1973 *Radical visions and American dreams: Culture and social thought in the Depression years.* New York.
Pelto, P. J.
1970 *Anthropological research: The structure of inquiry.* New York.
Perham, M. F.
1956 *Lugard: The years of adventure, 1858–1898.* London.
1960 *Lugard: The years of authority, 1898–1945.* London.
Pletsch, C.
1982 Freud's case studies and the locus of psychoanalytic knowledge. *Dynamis* 2:263–97.
Pollack, H. E.
1958 Department of Archeology. In Carnegie Institution, *Yearbook 57,* 435–55. Washington, D.C.
Popkin, R. H.
1987 *Isaac la Peyrère (1596–1676): His life, work and influence.* Leiden.
Porter, D.
1984 Anthropology tales: Unprofessional thoughts on the Mead/Freeman controversy. *Notebooks in Cultural Analysis* 1:15–37.
Porteus, S. D.
1969 *A psychologist of sorts: The autobiography and publications of the inventor of the Porteus Maze Tests.* Palo Alto, Calif.
Pound, E.
1915 E. P. Ode pour l'election de son sepulchre. In *Personae: The collected poems of Ezra Pound,* 187–91. New York (1926).
Powdermaker, H.
1966 *Stranger and friend: The way of an anthropologist.* New York.
1970 Further reflections on Lesu and Malinowski's diary. *Oceania* 40:344–47.
Powell, J. W.
1877 *Introduction to the study of Indian languages.* 1st ed. Washington, D.C.

1880 *Introduction to the study of Indian languages.* 2d ed. Washington, D.C.

Prichard, J. C.
1848 *Researches into the physical history of mankind.* Vol. 5. London.

Proctor, R.
1988 From *Anthropologie* to *Rassenkunde* in the German anthropological tradition. *HOA* 5:138–79.

Purcell, E.
1973 *The crisis of democratic theory: Scientific naturalism and the problem of value.* Lexington, Ky.

Quiggin, A. H.
1942 *Haddon the head-hunter.* Cambridge.

RA. See under Manuscript Sources.

Rabinow, P.
1977 *Reflections on fieldwork in Morocco.* Berkeley, Calif.

Radcliffe-Brown, A. R.
1922 *The Andaman islanders.* Glencoe, Ill. (1964).
1923 The methods of ethnology and social anthropology in *Method in social anthropology,* ed. M. N. Srinivas, 3–38. Chicago (1958).
1930 Applied anthropology. Australia and New Zealand Association for the Advancement of Science, *Report of the 20th meeting,* 267–80. Brisbane.
1931 The present position of anthropological studies. In *Method and theory in social anthropology,* ed. M. N. Srinivas, 41–95. Chicago (1958).

Radin, P.
1933 *Method and theory of ethnology: An essay in criticism.* New York.

Rappaport, R. A.
1986 Desecrating the holy woman: Derek Freeman's attack on Margaret Mead. *American Scholar,* 313–47.

Redfield, R.
1919 War sketches. *Poetry* 12:242–43.
1928 My adventures as a Mexican. *University of Chicago Magazine* 20:242–47.
1930a *Tepoztlán, a Mexican village: A study of folk life.* Chicago.
1930b The regional aspect of culture. In *Human nature and the study of society,* 145–51. Chicago (1962).
1934 Culture changes in Yucatan. *AA* 36:57–69.
1937 Introduction to F. Eggan, *The social organization of North American tribes.* Chicago.
1941 *The folk culture of Yucatan.* Chicago.
1950 *Chan Kom: The village that chose progress.* Chicago.
1953 *The primitive world and its transformations.* Ithaca, N.Y.
1955 *The little community.* Chicago.
1956 *Peasant society and culture.* Chicago.

Redfield, R., R. Linton, & M. J. Herskovits
1936 Memorandum for the study of acculturation. *AA* 38:149–52.

Reed, J.
1980 Clark Wissler: A forgotten influence in American anthropology. Doct. diss., Ball State Univ.

Reingold, N.
1979 National science policy in a private foundation: The Carnegie Institute of Washington. In *The organization of knowledge in modern America, 1860–1920*, ed. A. Oleson & J. Voss, 313–34. Baltimore, Md.
Resek, C.
1960 *Lewis Henry Morgan, American scholar.* Chicago.
RF [Rockefeller Foundation]
1924–37 *Annual Report.* New York.
Richards, A.
1939 The development of fieldwork methods in social anthropology. In *The Study of society*, ed. F. C. Bartlett, 272–316. London.
1944 Practical anthropology in the lifetime of the International African Institute. *Africa* 14:289–300.
1957 The concept of culture in Malinowski's work. In R. Firth 1957:15–32.
Rigdon, S. M.
1988 *The culture facade: Art, science and politics in the work of Oscar Lewis.* Urbana, Ill.
Riggs, S. R.
1893 *Dakota grammar, texts and ethnography*, ed. J. O. Dorsey. Washington, D.C.
RiP. See under Manuscript Sources.
Rivers, W. H. R.
1899 Two new departures in anthropological method. BAAS, *Report of the 69th meeting*, 879–80. London.
1900 A genealogical method of collecting social and vital statistics. *JAI* 30: 74–82.
1904 Genealogies[,] kinship. In Haddon 1904, Vol. 5, 122–52.
1906 *The Todas.* Osterhout N.B., Netherlands (1967).
1907 On the origin of the classificatory system of relationships. In *Anthropological essays presented to E. B. Tylor*, ed. N. Balfour et al., 309–23. Oxford.
1908 Genealogies[,] kinship. In Haddon 1908, Vol. 6, 62–91.
1910 The genealogical method of anthropological inquiry. *Sociological Review* 3:1–12.
1911 The ethnological analysis of culture. In *Psychology and ethnology*, ed. G. E. Smith, 120–40. London (1926).
1912 General account of method. In BAAS 1912: 108–27.
1913 Report on anthropological research outside America. In *Reports upon the present condition and future needs of the science of anthropology*, by W. H. R. Rivers et al., pp. 5–28. Washington, D.C.
1914a *The history of Melanesian society.* 2 vols. Osterhout N.B., Netherlands (1968).
1914b *Kinship and social organization.* London (1968).
1916 Sociology and psychology. In *Psychology and ethnology*, ed. G. E. Smith, 3–20. London (1926).
1922 Ed., *Essays in the depopulation of Melanesia.* Cambridge.

Roe, A.
1950 Interview with R. Redfield. (See under Manuscript Sources, RoP.)
1953a A psychological study of eminent psychologists and anthropologists, and a comparison with biological and physical scientists. *Psychological Monographs* 67:1–55.
1953b *The making of a scientist.* New York.

Rogge, A.
1976 A look at academic anthropology: Through a glass darkly. *AA* 78:829–42.

Rohner, R. P.
1969 Ed., *The ethnography of Franz Boas.* Trans. H. Parker. Chicago.

Romanucci-Ross, L.
1976 Anthropological field research: Margaret Mead, muse of the clinical field experience. *AA* 82:304–17.
1983 Apollo alone and adrift in Samoa: Early Mead reconsidered. *Reviews in Anthropology* 10:86–92.

Rooksby, R. L.
1971 W. H. R. Rivers and the Todas. *South Asia* 1:109–21.

Rossetti, C.
1985 Malinowski, the sociology of modern problems in Africa, and the colonial situation. *Cashiers d'Etudes Africaines* 25:477–503.

Rousseau, J. J.
1755 *Discourse on the origin and foundations of inequality.* In *The first and second discourses,* ed. R. D. Masters. New York (1964).

Rowley, C. D.
1958 *The Australians in German New Guinea 1914–1921.* Melbourne.
1966 *The New Guinea villager: The impact of colonial rule on primitive society and economy.* New York.

RP. See under Manuscript Sources.

Rutkoff, P. M., & W. B. Scott
1986 *New School: A history of the New School for Social Research.* New York.

Sack, P. G.
1973 *Land between two laws: Early European land acquisitions in New Guinea,* Canberra.

Sack, P. G., & D. Clark
1979 Eds., *German New Guinea: The annual reports.* Canberra.

Sahlins, M.
1985 *Islands of history.* Chicago.

Sangren, P. S.
1988 Rhetoric and the authority of ethnography: Postmodernism and the social reproduction of texts. *Current Anthropology* 29:405–36.

Sanjek, R.
1990 Ed., *Fieldnotes: The makings of anthropology.* Ithaca, N.Y.

Sapir, E.
1911 The problem of noun incorporation in American languages. *AA* 13:250–82.
1915 The Na-dene languages, a preliminary report. *AA* 17:534–58.

1916 Time perspective in aboriginal American culture: A study in method. In *Selected writings of Edward Sapir in language, culture and personality,* ed. D. G. Mandelbaum, 389–462. Berkeley, Calif. (1963).
1917a Linguistic publications of the Bureau of American Ethnology, a general review. *IJAL* 1:76–81.
1917b Do we need a superorganic? *AA* 19:441–47.
1919 Civilization and culture. *Dial* 67:233–36.
1920 The heuristic value of rhyme. In 1956:496–99.
1921 *Language.* New York.
1922a Culture, genuine and spurious. *Dalhousie Rev.* 2:358–68.
1922b The Takelma language of Southwestern Oregon. Extract from *Handbook of American Indian Languages,* Part 2, ed. Boas. Washington, D.C.
1924 Culture, genuine and spurious. In 1963:308–31.
1928 Observations on the sex problem in America. *American Journal of Psychiatry* 8:519–34.
1930 The discipline of sex. *American Mercury* 19:13–20.
1931 The concept of phonetic law as tested in primitive languages by Leonard Bloomfield. In 1963:73–82.
1936 Internal linguistic evidence suggestive of a northern origin of the Navaho. *AA* 38:224–35.
1963 *Selected writings of Edward Sapir in language, culture, and personality.* Ed. D. G. Mandelbaum. Berkeley, Calif.

Saville, W.
1912 A grammar of the Mailu language. *JAI* 42:397–436.

Scarr, D.
1969 Recruits and recruiters: A portrait of the labour trade. In *Pacific island portraits,* ed. J. Davidson & D. Scarr, 95–126. Canberra.

Schneider, D. M.
1968 Rivers and Kroeber in the study of kinship. In reprint edition of Rivers 1914b:7–16.
1984 *A critique of the study of kinship.* Ann Arbor, Mich.

Scholte, R.
1972 Toward a reflexive and critical anthropology. In Hymes 1972:430–57.

Schrempp, G.
1983 The re-education of Friedrich Max Müller: Intellectual appropriation and epistemological antinomy in mid-Victorian evolutionary thought. *Man* 18:90–110.

Seligman, C. G.
1910 *The Melanesians of British New Guinea.* Cambridge.

Seligman, C. G., & B. Z. Seligman
1911 *The Veddahs.* Cambridge.
1932 *Pagan tribes of the Nilotic Sudan.* London.

Sentinella, C.
1975 Ed., *Mikloucho-Maclay: New Guinea diaries, 1871–1883.* Madang.

Shapiro, H. L.
1959 The history and development of physical anthropology. *AA* 61:371–79.

Sherzer, J., & R. Bauman
1972 Areal studies and culture history: Language as a key to the historical study of culture contact. *Southwestern Journal of Anthropology* 28:131–52.

Shils, E.
1970 Tradition, ecology and institution in the history of sociology. *Daedalus* 99:760–825.

Singer, M.
1968 Culture. *International Encyclopedia of the Social Sciences* 3:527–43.

Slobodin, R.
1978 *W. H. R. Rivers.* New York.

Slotkin, J. S.
1965 *Readings in early anthropology.* Chicago.

Smith, A. G.
1964 The Dionysian innovation. *AA* 66:251–65.

Smith, B.
1960 *European vision and the South Pacific: A study in the history of art and ideas.* London.

Smith, E.
1973 *Some versions of the Fall: The myth of the Fall of Man in English literature.* London.

Smith, E. W.
1934 The story of the Institute: The first seven years. *Africa* 7:1–27.

Smith, M.
1959 Boas' "natural history" approach to field method. In Goldschmidt 1959: 46–60.

Solmon, L. C., et al.
1981 *Underemployed Ph.D.'s.* Lexington, Mass.

Sontag, S.
1966 The anthropologist as hero. In *Against interpretation,* 69–81. New York.

Sorenson, J.
1964 Some field notes on the power structure of the American Anthropological Association. *American Behavioral Scientist* (February):8–9.

SP. See under Manuscript Sources.

Speed, J.
1611 The genealogies of holy scriptures. In *The holy bible: A facsimile in a reduced size of the authorized version published in the year 1611.* Oxford (1911).

Spencer, F.
1981 The rise of academic physical anthropology in the United States (1880–1980): An overview. In Boaz & Spencer 1981:353–64.
1982 Ed., *A history of American physical anthropology, 1930–1980.* New York.
1990 *Piltdown: A scientific forgery.* London.

Spencer, W. B., & F. Gillen
1899 *The native tribes of central Australia.* New York (1968).

Spicer, E. H.
1979 Anthropologists and the War Relocation Authority. In Goldschmidt 1979: 217–37.

Spier, L.
1929 Some problems arising from the cultural position of the Havasupai. *AA* 31:213–22.

Spiro, M. E.
1982 *Oedipus in the Trobriands.* Chicago.

Spoehr, F. M.
1963 *White falcon: The house of Godeffroy and its commercial and scientific role in the Pacific.* Palo Alto, Calif.

SSRC [Social Science Research Council]
1926 The Hanover conference, Aug. 23–Sept. 2. 2 vols. Mimeographed. New York.

Stanton, W.
1960 *The leopard's spots: Scientific attitudes toward race in America, 1815–59.* Chicago.
1975 *The great United States exploring expedition of 1838–1842.* Berkeley, Calif.

Starn, O.
1986 Engineering internment: Anthropologists and the War Relocation Authority. *American Ethnologist* 13:700–20.

Stearns, H. E.
1922 Ed., *Civilization in the United States: An inquiry by thirty Americans.* New York.

Stephens, S.
1990 Postmodern anthropology: A question of difference. Unpublished manuscript.

Stern, G., & P. Bohannan
1970 *American Anthropologist:* The first eighty years. *Newsletter of the American Anthropological Association* 11:1, 6–12.

Steward, J. H.
1938 Review of F. Eggan, ed., *The social organization of North American tribes. AA* 40:720–22.
1950 *Area research.* New York.
1959 Review of Mead 1959a. *Science* 129:323.

Stewart, T. D.
1943 Editorial. *AJPA* 1:1–4.
1949 The development of the concept of morphological dating in connection with early man in America. *Southwestern Journal of Anthropology* 5: 1–16.
1981 Ales Hrdlička, 1869–1943. In Boaz & Spencer 1981:347–52.

Stipe, C.
1980 Anthropologists vs. missionaries: The influence of presuppositions. *Current Anthropology* 21:165–79.

Stirling, E.
1896 Anthropology. In *Report of the work of the Horn scientific expedition to central Australia*, ed. W. B. Spencer, Vol. 4, 1–161. London.

Stocking, G. W., Jr.
1960 Franz Boas and the founding of the American Anthropological Association. *AA* 62:1–17.
1964 French anthropology in 1800. *Isis* 55:134–50.
1965 On the limits of "presentism" and "historicism" in the historiography of the behavioral sciences. *JHBS* 1:211–18.
1966 The history of anthropology: Where, whence, whither? *JHBS* 2:281–90.
1967 Anthropologists and historians as historians of anthropology: Critical comments on some recently published work. *JHBS* 3:376–87.
1968a *Race, culture, and evolution: Essays in the history of anthropology.* New York.
1968b Empathy and antipathy in the heart of darkness. *JHBS* 4:189–94.
1968c Review of R. L. Brown 1967. *AA* 70:1039–40.
1971 What's in a name? The origins of the Royal Anthropological Institute: 1837–71. *Man* 6:88–104.
1973a From chronology to ethnology: James Cowles Prichard and British anthropology, 1800–1850. In reprint edition of Prichard, *Researches into the physical history of man*, ix–cx. Chicago.
1973b Review of Humboldt 1836 (1971). *Isis* 64:133–34.
1974a Benedict, Ruth Fulton. In *Dictionary of American Biography, Supplement IV, 1946–1950.* New York.
1974b Growing up to New Guinea. *Isis* 65:95–97.
1974c *The shaping of American anthropology, 1883–1911: A Franz Boas reader.* New York.
1974d The basic assumptions of Boasian anthropology. In 1974c:1–20.
1974e Some comments on history as a moral discipline: "Transcending textbook chronicles and apologetics." In Hymes 1974:511–19.
1974f Wissler, Clark. In *Dictionary of American Biography, Supplement IV, 1946–1950.* New York.
1976a Radcliffe-Brown, Lowie, and *The history of ethnological theory. HAN* 3(2):5–8.
1976b Patterns, systems, and personalities. *Times Literary Supplement* (March 12).
1976c Ed., *Selected papers from the American Anthropologist, 1921–45.* Washington, D.C.
1977a Contradicting the doctor: Billy Hancock and the problem of Baloma. *HAN* 4(1):4–7.
1977b The aims of Boasian ethnography: Creating the materials for traditional humanistic scholarship. *HAN* 4(2):4–5.
1978a The problems of translating between paradigms: The 1933 debate between Ralph Linton and Radcliffe-Brown. *HAN* 5(1):7–9.
1978b Die Geschichtlichkeit der Wilden und die Geschichte der Ethnologie, trans.

W. Lepennies. *Geschichte und Gesellschaft: Zeitschrift für Historische Sozialwissenschaft* 4:520–35.

1979a *Anthropology at Chicago: Tradition, discipline, department.* Chicago.

1979b The intensive study of limited areas—Toward an ethnographic context for the Malinowski innovation. *HAN* 6(2):9–12.

1980a Redfield, Robert. In *Dictionary of American Biography, Supplement VI, 1956–1960.* New York.

1980b Innovation in the Malinowskian mode: An essay review of *Long-term field research in social anthropology. JHBS* 16:281–86.

1982a The Santa Fe style in American anthropology: Regional interest, academic initiative, and philanthropic policy in the first two decades of the Laboratory of Anthropology, Inc. *JHBS* 18:3–19.

1982b Anthropology in crisis? A view from between the generations. In *Crisis in anthropology: View from Spring Hill, 1980,* ed. E. A. Hoebel et al., 407–19. New York.

1982c Preface to the reprint edition of 1968a.

1983a Ed., *Observers observed: Essays on ethnographic fieldwork. HOA* 1.

1983b Afterword: A view from the center. *Ethnos* 47(1–2):172–86.

1984a Ed., *Functionalism historicized: Essays on British social anthropology. HOA* 2.

1984b Radcliffe-Brown and British Social Anthropology. *HOA* 2:131–91.

1984c Qu'est ce qui est en jeu dans un nom? In *Histoires de l'anthropologie,* ed. Rupp-Eisenreich, 421–33. Paris.

1984d Academician Bromley on Soviet ethnography. *HAN* 11(2):6–10.

1985 Ed., *Objects and others: Essays on museums and material culture. HOA* 3.

1986a Ed., *Malinowski, Rivers, Benedict and others: Essays on culture and personality. HOA* 4.

1986b Anthropology and the science of the irrational: Malinowski's encounter with Freudian psychoanalysis. HOA 4:13–49.

1986c Why does a boy "sign on"?—Malinowski's first statement on practical anthropology. *HAN* 13(2):6–9.

1987a *Victorian anthropology.* New York.

1987b Margaret Mead, Franz Boas, and the Ogburns of science. *HAN* 14(2): 3–10.

1988a Before the falling out: W. H. R. Rivers on the relation between anthropology and mission work. *HAN* 15(2):3–8.

1988b Ed., *Bones, bodies, behavior: Essays on biological anthropology. HOA* 5.

1989a Ed., *Romantic motives: Essays on anthropological sensibility. HOA* 6.

1989b Los modelos de Malinowski: Kubary, Maclay y Conrad como arquetipos etnográficos, trans. F. Estévez. *Eres* 1:9–24.

1989c Back to the future III, IV, V, VI, N, . . . or Boas? Paper, American Anthropological Association.

1990 Malinowski's diary redux: Entries for an index. *HAN* 17(1):3–10.

1991a Ed., *Colonial situations: Essays on the contextualization of ethnographic knowledge. HOA* 7.

1991b Included in this classification: Notes toward an archeology of ethnographic classification. *HAN* 18(1):3–11.

1991c *Books unwritten, turning points unmarked: Notes for an anti-history of anthropology.* Bloomington, Ind.

N.d. On the influence of Robert Park on Robert Redfield. Unpublished manuscript.

Strenski, I.
1982 Malinowski: Second positivism, second romanticism, *Man* 17:266–71.

Strong, W.
1933 The Plains culture area in the light of archaeology. *AA* 35:271–87.

Suggs, R. C.
1971 Sex and personality in the Marquesas: A discussion of the Linton-Kardiner report. In *Human sexual behavior,* ed. D. S. Marshall & R. C. Suggs, 163–86. New York.

Sullivan, P. R.
1989 *Unfinished conversations: Mayas and foreigners between the two wars.* New York.

Sulloway, F.
1979 *Freud, biologist of the mind: Beyond the psychoanalytic legend.* New York.

Swadesh, M.
1951 Diffusional cumulation and archaic residue as historical explanations. In Hymes 1964:624–37.

Swayze, N.
1960 *Canadian portraits: Jenness, Barbeau, Wintemberg; the manhunters.* Toronto.

Symmons-Symonolewicz, K.
1958 Bronislaw Malinowski: An intellectual profile. *Polish Review* 3:55–76.
1959 Bronislaw Malinowski: Formative influences and theoretical evolution. *Polish Review* 4:17–45.
1960 Bronislaw Malinowski: Individuality as theorist. *Polish Review* 5:53–65.
1982 The ethnographer and his savages: An intellectual history of Malinowski's diary. *Polish Review* 27:92–98.

Tal, U.
1975 *Christians and Jews in Germany: Religion, politics, and ideology in the Second Reich, 1870–1914.* Ithaca, N.Y.

TaP. See under Manuscript Sources.

Taylor, W. W.
1948 *A study of archeology.* Memoirs of the American Anthropological Association 69. Menasha, Wis.
1954 Southwestern archeology: Its history and theory. *AA* 56:561–75.

Te Rangi Hiroa [Peter Buck]
1945 *An introduction to Polyesian anthropology.* Bishop Museum Bulletin 187. Honolulu.

Thalbitzer, W.
1904 *A phonetical study of the Eskimo language.* Copenhagen.

Thomas, W. L., Jr.
1955 Ed., *The yearbook of anthropology.* New York.
Thompson, L.
1944 Some perspectives on applied anthropology. *Applied Anthropology* 3:12.
Thoresen, T. H.
1975 Paying the piper and calling the tune: The beginnings of academic anthropology in California. *JHBS* 11:257–75.
Thornton, R. J.
1983 Narrative ethnography in Africa, 1850–1920: The creation and capture of an appropriate domain for anthropology. *Man* 18:502–20.
1985 "Imagine yourself set down . . . ": Mach, Frazer, Conrad, Malinowski and the role of imagination in ethnography. *Anthropology Today* 1(5): 7–14.
N.d. Malinowski's reading, writing, 1904–1914. Unpublished manuscript.
Tinker, H.
1974 *A new system of slavery: The export of Indian labour overseas, 1830–1920.* London.
Todorov, T.
1982 *The conquest of America: The question of the other.* New York (1984).
Tomas, D.
1991 Tools of the trade: The production of ethnographic knowledge in the Andaman Islands, 1858–1922. *HOA* 7:75–108.
Torgovnick, M.
1990 *Gone primitive: Savage intellects, modern lives.* Chicago.
TP. See under Manuscript Sources.
Trautman, T. R.
1987 *Lewis Henry Morgan and the invention of kinship.* Berkeley, Calif.
Trotter, M.
1956 Notes on the history of the AAPA. *AJPA* 14:350–64.
Trotter, R. T.
1988 An assessment of research methods training requirements in anthropology departments in the United States. Unpublished manuscript.
Tumarkin, D. D.
1982a Miklouho-Maclay: Nineteenth century Russian anthropologist and humanist. *RAIN* 51:4–7.
1982b Ed., *N. Miklouho-Maclay's Travels to New Guinea: Diaries, Letters, Documents.* Moscow.
1988 Miklouho-Maclay: A great Russian scholar and humanist. *Social Sciences* [U.S.S.R. Academy of Sciences] 19:175–89.
Tumin, M.
1945 Culture, genuine and spurious: A reevaluation. *American Sociological Review* 10:199–207.
Tylor, E. B.
1871 *Primitive culture: Researches into the development of mythology, philosophy, religion, language, art and custom.* 2 vols. London (1873).

1884 American aspects of anthropology. BAAS, *Report of the 54th meeting,* 898–924. London.

UC. See under Manuscript Sources.

UCB. See under Manuscript Sources.

Ulin, R. C.

1984 *Understanding cultures: Perspectives in anthropology and social theory.* Austin, Tex.

1991 Critical anthropology twenty years later: Modernism and postmodernism in anthropology. *Critique of Anthropology* 11:63–89.

Urry, J.

1972 *Notes and Queries in Anthropology* and the development of field methods in British anthropology, 1870–1920. *Proceedings of the Royal Anthropological Institute,* 45–57.

1984 A history of field methods. In *Ethnographic research: A guide to general conduct,* ed. R. F. Ellen, 35–61. London.

Van Keuren, D.

1982 Human science in Victorian Britain: Anthropology in institutional and disciplinary formation, 1863–1908. Doct. diss., Univ. Pennsylvania.

Van Riper, A. B.

1990 Discovering prehistory: Geological archaeology and the human antiquity problem in mid-Victorian Britain. Doct. diss., Univ. Wisconsin–Madison.

Van Willigen, J.

1980 *Anthropology in use: A bibliographic chronology of the development of applied anthropology.* Pleasantville, N.Y.

Vidich, A. J.

1974 Ideological themes in American anthropology. *Social Research* 41:719–45.

Vincent, J.

1985 Anthropology and Marxism. *American Ethnologist* 12:137–47.

1990 *Anthropology and politics: Visions, traditions, and trends.* Tucson, Ariz.

Voegelin, C. F.

1936 On being unhistorical. *AA* 38:344–50.

1952 The Boas plan for the presentation of American Indian languages. *PAPS* 96:439–51.

1954 Inductively arrived at models for cross-genetic comparisons of languages. *University of California Publications in Linguistics* 10:27–45.

1955 On developing new typologies and revising old ones. *Southwestern Journal of Anthropology* 11:355–60.

Voegelin, C. F., & Z. Harris

1952 Training in anthropological linguistics. *AA* 54:322–27.

Voegelin, C. F., & F. M. Voegelin

1963 On the history of structuralizing in 20th century America. *Anthropological Linguistics* 5(1):12–37.

Voget, F. W.

1968 *A history of ethnology.* New York.

Wagley, C., & M. Harris
1955 A typology of Latin American subcultures. *AA* 57:428–51.

Wakin, E.
1992 *Anthropology goes to war: Professional ethics and counterinsurgency in Thailand.* University of Wisconsin Center for Southeast Asian Studies Monograph 7.

Walens, S.
1981 *Feasting with cannibals: An essay on Kwakiutl cosmology.* Princeton, N.J.

Wallis, W.
1925 Diffusion as a criterion of age. *AA* 27:91–99.

Ware, C.
1935 *Greenwich village, 1920–1930: A comment on American civilization in the post-war years.* Boston.

Warman, A.
1982 Indigenist thought. In *Indigenous anthropology in non-western countries,* ed. H. Fahim, 75–96. Durham, N.C.

Warner, M.
1988 *W. Lloyd Warner: Social anthropologist.* New York.

Warner, W. L., & P. S. Lunt
1941 *The social life of a modern community.* New Haven, Conn.

Washburn, S. L.
1968 One hundred years of biological anthropology. In Brew 1968:97–118.

Washburn, W.
1975 *The Indian in America.* New York.

Wax, M.
1956 The limitations of Boas' anthropology. *AA* 58:63–74.
1972 Tenting with Malinowski. *American Sociological Review* 47:1–13.

Wayne (Malinowska), H.
1985 Bronislaw Malinowski: The influence of various women on his life and works. *American Ethnologist* 12:529–40.

Webster, E. M.
1984 *The moon man: A biography of Nikolai Miklouho-Maclay.* Berkeley, Calif.

Weiner, A. B.
1976 *Women of value, men of renown: New perspectives in Trobriand exchange.* Austin, Tex.
1983 Ethnographic determinism: Samoa and the Margaret Mead controversy. *AA* 85:909–18.

Werner, O., et al.
1987 *Systematic fieldwork.* 2 vols. Newbury Park, Calif.

West, F. J.
1968 *Hubert Murray: The Australian pro-consul.* Melbourne.
1970 Ed., *Selected letters of Hubert Murray.* Melbourne.

Westermarck, E. A.
1891 *The history of human marriage.* London.

1927 *Memories of my life.* Trans. A. Barwell. New York.

Wheeler, G. C.

1926 *Mono-Alu folklore (Bougainville Strait, Western Solomon Islands).* London.

White, I.

1981 Mrs. Bates and Mr. Brown: An examination of Rodney Needham's allegations. *Oceania* 51:193–210.

White, L.

1966 *The social organization of ethnological theory.* Rice University Studies 52. Houston, Tex.

1987 *Ethnological essays.* Ed. B. Dillingham & R. Carneiro. Albuquerque, N.M.

Whorf, B.

1935 The comparative linguistics of Uto-Aztecan. *AA* 37:600–608.

1936 A linguistic consideration of thinking in primitive communities. In Hymes 1964:129–41.

Willard, M.

1923 *History of the White Australia policy to 1920.* London (1967).

Willey, G. R.

1968 One hundred years of American archaeology. In Brew 1968:29–56.

1988 *Portraits in American Archaeology: Remembrances of some distinguished Americanists.* Albuquerque, N.M.

Willey, G. R., & J. A. Sabloff

1974 *A history of American archeology.* San Francisco.

Williams, F. E.

1939 Ed., The reminiscences of Ahuia Ova. *JAI* 69:11–44.

Williams, R.

1958 *Culture and society, 1780–1950.* New York (1960).

Willis, W.

1972 Skeletons in the anthropological closet. In Hymes 1972:121–53.

1975 Franz Boas and the study of black folklore. In *The New Ethnicity: Perspectives from ethnology,* ed. J. W. Bennett, 307–34. St. Paul, Minn.

Wilmsen, E. N.

1965 An outline of early man studies in the United States. *American Antiquity* 31:172–92.

Wilson, E. F.

1887 Report on the Blackfoot tribes. BAAS, *Report of the 57th meeting,* 183–97. London.

Winkin, Y.

1986 George W. Stocking Jr. et l'histoire de l'anthropologie. *Actes de la Recherche en sciences sociales* 64:81–84.

Wissler, C.

1922 *The American Indian.* New York.

1923 *Man and culture.* New York.

Wittfogel, K. A., & E. S. Goldfrank

1943 Some aspects of Pueblo mythology and society. *Journal of American Folklore* 56:17–30.

Wolf, E.

1955 Types of Latin American peasantry: A preliminary discussion. *AA* 57: 452–71.

1964 *Anthropology.* Englewood Cliffs, N.J.

1972 American anthropologists and American society. In Hymes 1972:251–63.

1980 They divide and subdivide, and call it anthropology. *New York Times* (Nov. 30).

1982 *Europe and the people without history.* Berkeley, Calif.

Wolf, E., & J. G. Jorgensen

1970 Anthropology on the warpath in Thailand. *New York Review of Books* (Nov. 19): 26–35.

Wolfers, E.

1972 Trusteeship without trust: A short history of interracial relations and the law in Papua and New Guinea. In *Racism: The Australian experience,* ed. F. S. Stevens. Vol. 3, *Colonialism,* 61–147. Sydney.

Woodbury, R. B.

1973 *Alfred V. Kidder.* New York.

Worsley, P.

1970 The end of anthropology. *Western Canadian Journal of Anthropology* 1:1–9.

Yans-McLaughlin, V.

1986 Science, democracy, and ethics: Mobilizing culture and personality for World War II. *HOA* 4:184–217.

Young, M. W.

1979 Ed., *The ethnography of Malinowski: The Trobriand Islands, 1915–18.* London.

1984 The intensive study of a restricted area, or, why did Malinowski go to the Trobriand Islands? *Oceania* 55:1–26.

1988 Editor's introduction. *Malinowski among the Magi. "The natives of Mailu,"* 1–76. London.

Manuscript Sources

In writing the various essays incorporated in this volume, I have drawn on researches over a thirty-year period in a variety of manuscript materials, cited herein by the abbreviations listed below. I would like again to express my appreciation to those archivists and executors who have generously assisted me at various points along the way.

BE Bureau of American Ethnology Correspondence, National Anthropological Archives, Smithsonian Institution, Washington, D.C.

BP Franz Boas Papers, American Philosophical Society Library, Philadelphia.

FP James G. Frazer Papers, Trinity College, Cambridge.

GP Francis Galton Papers, University College, London.

HoP A. M. Hocart Papers, Alexander Turnbull Library, Wellington, New Zealand (nine reels, microfilm, 1970).

HP Alfred Cort Haddon Papers, University Library, Cambridge.

MaP Elton Mayo Papers, Harvard Business School, Cambridge, Mass.

MeP Margaret Mead Papers, Library of Congress, Washington, D.C.

MPL Bronislaw Malinowski Papers, British Library of Political and Economic Science, London School of Economics.

MPY Bronislaw Malinowski Papers, Stirling Library, Yale University, New Haven, Conn.

NAA American Anthropological Association Papers, National Anthropological Archives, Smithsonian Institution, Washington, D.C.

RA Rockefeller Foundation Archives, Tarryton, N.Y.

RiP W. H. R. Rivers Papers, University Library, Cambridge.

RoP Anne Roe Papers, American Philosophical Society Library, Philadelphia.

RP Robert Redfield Papers, Department of Special Collections, Regenstein Library, University of Chicago.

SP Walter Baldwin Spencer Papers, Pitt Rivers Museum, Oxford.

TaP Sol Tax Papers, Department of Special Collections, Regenstein Library, University of Chicago.

TP Edward Burnet Tylor Papers, Pitt Rivers Museum, Oxford.

UC University of Chicago Department of Anthropology Papers, Department of Special Collections, Regenstein Library, University of Chicago.

UCB University of California, Berkeley, Department of Anthropology Papers, Bancroft Library, Berkeley, Calif.

Index